Advance Praise

Agricultural research has so far concentrated on the supply side. But while a number of research institutes contribute to the science of agricultural production, what happens to the output thereafter has been neglected. Yet, rural marketing is an extremely important area which can benefit from marketing theory and practice to reduce waste and increase efficiency of distribution of farm produce. This is the first book that talks about rural marketing not only in terms of supply of manufactured products to villages but also in terms of reforming and empowering villages through efficiency in agricultural distribution and marketing. The coverage, both in the text and in the huge number of cases, is amazing. I have no hesitation in saying that this is the best book on the subject and will be of immense use for agricultural and rural management institutes.

Vinod Mittal
Chairman, Dolphin (PG)
College of Science and Agriculture, Chandigarh

Marketers since the first decade of the liberalization of the Indian economy have realized the importance of rural markets for growth. This renewed interest on rural markets has led to a number of books on the subject. Most of them create an impression that rural consumers are waiting for the marketers to arrive and to sell them goods. Whereas, the fact is that these markets need to be carefully nurtured before they yield any success. There has always been a need for a book that would provide a holistic and realistic view of the subject and not reduce it to the marketing of 'soaps and shampoos' to them. This book takes a fresh look at the subject and provides a rounded view by incorporating the developmental aspects of rural marketing and providing cases of enlightened rural marketing.

Pratik Modi
Associate Professor of Marketing
Institute of Rural Management, Anand

Rural Marketing

Rural Marketing

Challenges and Opportunities

Dinesh Kumar

Former Associate Professor, Birla Institute of Management Technology (BIMTECH), Greater Noida

Punam Gupta

Associate Professor, Dev Samaj College for Women, Chandigarh

7/22, Ansari Road, Darya Ganj, New Delhi
Tel.: +91-11-4077 5252, 2327 3880
E-mail: orders@atlanticbooks.com
Web: www.atlanticbooks.com

Published by Atlantic Publishers & Distributors (P) Ltd 2024

Previously Published by SAGE Publications in 2017

Printed & bound in India by Atlantic Print Services

CONTENTS

DETAILED CONTENTS

LIST OF PHOTOGRAPHS

LIST OF FIGURES

LIST OF TABLES

LIST OF ABBREVIATIONS

ADVMS	Associated Distributor Vodafone Mini Stores
AGMARKNET	Agricultural Marketing Research and Information Network
AIACA	All India Artisans and Craftworkers Welfare Association
AMCUs	Automatic Milk Collection System Units
AMMA-India	Agricultural Machinery Manufacturers Association
APEDA	Agricultural and Processed Food Products Export Development Authority
API	Application Programming Interfaces
APMC	Agricultural Produce Market Committee
ARTI	Appropriate Rural Technology Institute
ATMs	Automated Teller Machines
Auto ID	Automatic Identification
B2B	Business-to-Business
BARC	Broadcast Audience Research Council
BBA	Beej Bachao Andolan
BCs	Business Correspondents
BFs	Business Facilitators
BIS	Bureau of Indian Standards
BoP	Bottom-of-the-Pyramid
BPL	Below the Poverty Line
BSC	Balanced Scorecard
Bt	*Bacillus thuringiensis*
BTL	Below-the-Line
CACP	Commission for Agricultural Costs & Prices
CAGR	Compound Annual Growth Rate
CARE	Cooperative for Assistance and Relief Everywhere
CBS	Core Banking Solutions
CCI	Cotton Corporation of India
CGIAR	Consultative Group on International Agricultural Research
CIPHET	Central Institute of Post-harvest Engineering and Technology
CPFR	Collaborative Planning, Forecasting and Replenishment
CPRI	Central Potato Research Institute
CSR	Corporate Social Responsibility
CWC	Central Warehousing Corporation
DA	Development Alternatives
DISK	Dairy Information System Kiosk
DLS	Dedicated Logistics System
DSCL	DCM Shriram Consolidated Ltd
ECA	Essential Commodities Act
EFA	Education for All
EIAS	Enterprise-wide Integrated Application System
EMIs	Equated Monthly Instalments
ERP	Enterprise Resource Planning

EU	European Union
EVF	Essilor Vision Foundation
FAO	Food and Agriculture Organization of the United Nations
FAS	Foundation for Agrarian Studies
FC	Fixed Costs
FCI	Food Corporation of India
FDI	Foreign Direct Investment
FHEL	Fresh and Healthy Enterprises Ltd
FHP	Farm Harvest Price
FICCI	Federation of Indian Chambers of Commerce & Industry
FMC	Forward Markets Commission
FMCG	Fast-moving Consumer Goods
FSSAI	Food Safety and Standards Authority of India
GCC	General Credit Card
GCMMF	Gujarat Cooperative Milk Marketing Federation
GDP	Gross Domestic Product
GDFL	Grameen Danone Food Limited
GHI	Global Hunger Index
GIAN	Gujarat Grassroots Innovation Augmentation Network
GII	Gender Inequality Index
GIS	Geographic Information System
GM	Genetically Modified
GMOs	Genetically Modified Organisms
GPS	Global Positioning System
GSK	GlaxoSmithKline consumer Healthcare
HDI	Human Development Index
HEs	Health Educators
HLFPPT	Hindustan Latex Family Planning Promotion Trust
HMSI	Honda Motorcycle & Scooter India Pvt. Ltd.
HR	Human Resources
HUL	Hindustan Unilever
HYVP	High Yielding Varieties Programme
IADP	Intensive Agricultural District Programme
IAMAI	Internet and Mobile Association of India
IAI	Irrigation Association of India
IAY	Indira Awaas Yojana
IBA	Indian Banks' Association
IBEF	India Brand Equity Foundation
ICAR	Indian Council for Agricultural Research
ICT	Information and Communications Technology
IDA	Infocomm Development Authority
IDS	Information Directed System
IDV	Individualism–Collectivism
IFC	International Finance Corporation
IFFCO	Indian Farmers Fertiliser Cooperative Limited
IMRB	Indian Market Research Bureau
IPR	Intellectual Property Rights
IRDP	Integrated Rural Development Programme

IRS	Indian Readership Survey
ISAP	Indian Society of Agribusiness Professional
ISOPOM	Integrated Scheme for Oil seeds, Pulses, Oilpalm and Maize
ITI	Industrial Training Institute
IWMP	Integrated Watershed Management Programme
JCI	Jute Corporation of India
JISL	Jain Irrigation Systems Limited
JRF	Jaipur Rugs Foundation
JRY	Jawahar Rozgar Yojana
KCC	Kisan Call Centre
KKMS	Kisan Knowledge Management System
KKT	Kan Khajura Tesan
KVIC	Khadi and Village Industries Commission
KYC	Know-Your-Customer
LFE	Light for Education
LMIS	Logistics Management Information System
LPG	Liquefied Petroleum Gas
LTO	Long-term Orientation
MAS	Masculinity–Femininity
MCI	Ministry of Communication and Information
MCX	Multi Commodity Exchange
MDA	Media Development Authority
MDG	Millennium Development Goals
MFIs	Microfinance Institutions
MGNREGA	Mahatma Gandhi National Rural Employment Guarantee Act
MGNREGS	Mahatma Gandhi National Rural Employment Guarantee Scheme
MICA	Mudra Institute of Communications Ahmedabad
MITRA	Machines Information Technology Resources Agriculture
MNCs	Multinational Companies
MoFPI	Ministry of Food Processing Industries
MoRD	Ministry of Rural Development
MoUs	Memorandums of Understanding
MPCE	Monthly Per Capita Expenditure
MRMR	MICA Rural Market Ratings
MSEs	Micro and Small Enterprises
MSP	Minimum Support Price
MSV	Mobile Service Van
NABARD	National Bank for Agriculture and Rural Development
NACOF	National Federation of Farmers' Procurement, Processing and Retailing Cooperatives of India Ltd
NAFED	National Agricultural Cooperative Marketing Federation of India Limited
NAM	National Agricultural Market
NBS	Nutrient-based Subsidy
NCAER	National Council of Applied Economic Research
NCDEX	National Commodity and Derivatives Exchange
NCRB	National Crime Records Bureau
NFBS	National Family Benefit Scheme
NFCL	Nagarjuna Fertilizers and Chemicals Ltd

NFL	National Fertilizers Limited
NFSA	National Food Security Act
NFSM	National Food Security Mission
NGOs	Non-governmental Organizations
NHM	National Horticulture Mission
NHRDF	National Horticulture Research & Development Foundation
NIC	National Informatics Centre
NIF	National Innovation Foundation
NMCE	National Multi Commodity Exchange of India Ltd
NRI	Non-resident Indian
NRLM	National Rural Livelihoods Mission
NSAP	National Social Assistance Programme
NSC	National Seeds Corporation
NSP	National Seed Project
NSSO	National Sample Survey Organisation
NTPC	National Transport Policy Committee
OPDs	Out-patient Departments
ORS	Oral Rehydration Salts
OTC	Over the Counter
P2P	Peer-to-peer
PAR	Participatory Action Research
PARI	Project on Agrarian Relations in India
PDI	Power Distance Index
PDS	Public Distribution System
PFA Act	Prevention of Food Adulteration Act
PMGSY	Pradhan Mantri Gram Sadak Yojana
PO	Participant Observation
PoS	Point-of-Sale
PPP	Public–Private Partnership
PRA	Participatory Rural Appraisal
R&D	Research and Development
RBI	Reserve Bank of India
RCF	Rashtriya Chemicals and Fertilizers
REC	Rural Electrification Corporation
RML	Reuters Market Light
RMPs	Registered Medical Practitioners
RRA	Rapid Rural Appraisal
RSP	Rural Sales Program
SA	Shakti Amma
SBSC	Sustainable Balanced Scorecard
SCVs	Small Commercial Vehicles
SECC	Socio-economic Caste Census
SELF	Solar Electric Light Fund
SEWA	Self Employed Women's Association
SFAC	Small Farmers' Agribusiness Consortium
SHGs	Self-help Groups
SKU	Stock Keeping Unit
SMBs	Small and Medium-sized Businesses

SMEs	Small and Medium Enterprises
SOVA	South Orissa Voluntary Action
SRCs	Supplier Region Companies
SRISTI	Sustainable Technologies and Institutions
SWCs	State Warehousing Corporations
TAM	Television Audience Measurement
TARA	Technology and Action for Rural Advancement
TBL	Triple Bottom Line
TDET	Technology Development, Extension and Training
TGBL	Tata Global Beverages Limited
TPDS	Targeted Public Distribution System
TRAI	Telecom Regulatory Authority of India
TRMI	Thomson Rural Market Index
TSMG	TATA Strategic Management Group
TVEs	Town and Village Enterprises
UAI	Uncertainty Avoidance Index
UIDAI	Unique Identification Authority of India
UNDP	United Nations Development Programme
UNFPA	United Nations Population Fund
UNICEF	United Nations International Children's Emergency Fund
UNIDO	United Nations Industrial Development Organization
USP	Unique Selling Proposition
VAL	Value Attitude Lifestyle
VAS	Value Added Service
VAT	Value Added Tax
VC	Variable Costs
VLEs	Village-level Entrepreneurs
VPN	Virtual Private Network
VPOs	Village Phone Operators
VPP	Village Pay Phone
VSAT	Very Small Aperture Terminal
WHO	World Health Organization
WSP	Wholesale Price
ZMET	Zaltman Metaphor Elicitation Technique

FOREWORD

A decade ago, I was introduced to the concepts of C.K. Prahalad's book, *Bottom of the Pyramid*, in an MBA course at the University of San Francisco. It was a watershed moment for me and an eye-opener to someone who was reared in the Westernized culture of Silicon Valley and the high-tech world. The ability and the imperative need to focus marketing product not just on the aspirational rich but to more than half of the world that does not have the luxuries that those in Silicon Valley enjoy was the most hard-hitting concept. It is not all about the next generation of yearly phone upgrades, the latest hundred-dollar designer jeans or the fancy schools that parents have their children compete to attend. It is more basic than these. It gets to the core of the human condition and of survival, and reflects the urgent need for change in what has become a self-absorbed Western society of consumerism, which modern advertising appeals to on a minute by minute basis.

Dr Kumar points to the fact that the principles of BoP, although ground-breaking for Fortune 500 companies, missed the mark regarding giving companies a practical guide for real rural marketing. This is because companies ignore real, ground level problems, such as distribution of products in rural markets for marketing them to consumers with limited access to resources and financial markets. It is not a replication of 'business as usual', which has focused on the wealthy and the aspirational rich. Change is needed. Rural marketing goes beyond what is typically taught in business schools. It extends beyond the traditional marketing playbooks of large corporations and pushes the envelope of what is the tried and true go-to-market marketing practice for start-ups. It starts to look at the people involved and moves beyond the cities. It focuses on individuals that businesses, governments and the media tend to ignore.

The question of ethics and sustainability comes into play in the dialogue of rural marketing. Dr Kumar highlights the need for standards by calling into attention the question of can "...the poor, whose life is a daily struggle, be seen as a source or profit?" *Rural Marketing* makes the argument that it is today an ethical imperative to rethink the very purpose of marketing and business, and shift their focus to help improve the life of the poor; it is also morally the correct way. Honest attempts to look at bringing fair and profitable business to all parties involved is a must.

The concepts discussed in *Rural Marketing* hit at the heart of what is wrong with global contemporary business culture today. The need to make a profit and maximize shareholder wealth is considered the golden standard for which others might strive for; it has created a culture of corruption, profit maximization and the exploitation of the rich, the middle-class and the poor in a never-ending culture of desire that continues to drive global business. The principles of *Rural Marketing* will impact and improve the lives of billions in the world's poorest countries. It will make a much-needed impact on the current state of the globalized business enterprise that is selfishly focused on fuelling its own desire. Change is needed, and Dr Kumar effectively points to us all in the correct direction.

Payson E. Johnston
Adjunct Professor, University of San Francisco
CEO and Co-founder, Crowdz, a California-based Start-up

PREFACE

A few years back, we visited a farmer friend in the US. He had a huge farm but, apart from a small patch on which he grew strawberries, the farm was neglected and covered with grass.

"What kind of a farmer are you," I asked. "When you don't grow anything on your land?"

His answer surprised me. He told me that usually he grew potatoes but the government had done a demand assessment and decided that no more potatoes were needed. So, they gave a subsidy to some farmers to *not* grow the crop. He was one of them.

Contrast is the situation in India. No demand assessment has ever been done, despite a plethora of government ministries and agencies. Farmers toil in their fields, poisoning their land with overuse of subsidized fertilizers and pesticides, taking loans that they cannot repay and selling out harvests to commission agents. Yet, much of the crops that they produce are simply wasted. Estimates of the International Food Policy Research Institute suggest that every year up to 67 million tonnes of crops with a value of ₹92,000 crore are wasted. This can only be described in one word: criminal.

This book is a result of analyzing why this should be so. Heavy investments go into building supply chains of cosmetics, apparels and mobile phones. Then why not so for crops and food? Why should farmers be forced to throw their produce on the roads, as it happens almost every year with some crop or the other? And finally, why should farmers be forced to commit suicide in a country that immortalizes them in the slogan: *Jai Jawan, Jai Kisan*?

Many companies treat rural marketing simply as selling goods to rural areas; many books and papers point to the immense opportunity that exists in bottom-of-the-pyramid (BoP) markets because of a large, underserved population. This is true, but it is also true that rural incomes are neither stable nor high. Then again, marketing products in a landscape in which a majority of people are poor, with little or no access to electricity, will always be a huge challenge.

This book looks at both these aspects of rural marketing—marketing to rural areas as well as empowering people so that they can participate in the market economy.

The task is not easy. And the utter failure of successive governments to correct the situation over more than 60 years leaves the task of developing rural markets to the private sector. Indeed, companies have come forward, making huge investments in infrastructure and supply chains, helping people and establishing themselves despite outdated and restrictive policies. There is much to learn from these initiatives, as this book shows.

Readers of this book will discover that marketing does not consist only of glitzy brands for the rich. After all, selling to the rich is not much of a challenge; they know brands, have enough money to buy them and are exposed to the latest media and developments. There is much greater challenge to empower a person who is not aware of the brands, does not have money and is not exposed to the media.

In the process, marketing itself goes through a transformation. Modern marketing concentrates on the rich, developing products for them to maintain their lifestyles and to show off to the not-so-rich underlings, who they are. This theory changes completely when marketing to poor customers in remote areas is done, thus giving rise to what is described as the *fourth sector*.

Managers have to change their orientation completely while operating in rural areas. Part of the problem is that people living in cities have no idea about how people live in rural India, whereas the rural people constitute two-thirds of the population. They are invisible to managers and the media. The life in rural India has been succinctly described by Dr Muhammad Yunus in his book, *Creating a World Without Poverty* (2007):

> Imagine if the global electronic communications system of the banking world suddenly collapsed and every financial institution in the world suddenly stopped functioning. Banks everywhere would shut their doors. ATM screens would go blank. Credit and debit cards would no longer work. And billions of families would be unable even to put groceries on the table. Well, this is exactly the situation that half of the world's population lives with every day—a non-stop horror story.

This book describes marketing in this horror story.

This book goes beyond describing mere efforts to sell products in villages. We feel that it is important to involve people and solve rural problems, and the market will develop itself. The book describes process involved in rural marketing and the transformation of businesses into social businesses. It is organized in three parts.

Part I gives an introduction to rural marketing with a new definition of the subject. It also includes size and structure, and segmentation of rural markets. A comparison is made between urban and rural markets. It profiles the rural consumer, while rural shopping habits and changes in consumption is described in detail. The personality of the rural consumer is analyzed from Hofstede's cultural dimensions.

Part II dwells on rural marketing strategy. It shows how rural marketing is changing the very nature of companies. The process of pricing and promotion in rural markets, use of media and rural communication mix, along with the importance of below-the-line (BTL) techniques and personal selling in rural areas is described in detail. How the principles of marketing must change in rural areas are explained. also describes how distribution channels for rural areas must be designed and used. Pricing strategies for rural markets and promotion as a component in marketing communication are also explained.

Part III describes agribusiness components and management. Marketing of agricultural inputs and agricultural produce are both discussed as part of rural marketing. The trends in agricultural marketing and the role played by the Agricultural Produce Market Committees (APMCs) are explained. Even after many decades of Independence, we find decrepit supply chains for the most important commodities—food. The supply chains can be improved through investments in information technology (IT); hence technology initiatives are also discussed. Human resource (HR) aspects of managing a rural sales force, including training, recruitment, organization and compensation, are discussed and are conceived as distinct from managing an urban sales force. Finally, the future of rural marketing has been looked at, which leads us to discover inclusive growth and a new BoP approach. New technologies such as big data promise to change the face of rural marketing.

PEDAGOGICAL FEATURES

We have incorporated a number of features in the book that will help teachers in using the book. These are as follows:

- **Opening and Closing Cases:** Each chapter starts and ends with a case study linked to the concepts described in the chapter. The opening case gives indicators about what the student can learn while the closing case applies concepts to real-life situations. Using these case studies in class will be exciting and will lead to interesting discussions.

- **Mini Case Studies:** Every chapter has a number of mini case studies ending with a question. These keep alive interests of the students and are important aids in learning. Instructors can use these cases to illustrate concepts and involve their students in the learning process.
- **Images:** The book has a number of images that help readers to visualize what is described in the text. These, we feel, are important additions and will help illustrate the actual story on the ground.
- **Chapter-end exercises:** Three types of chapter-end exercises are included—concept review questions, critical thinking questions, and projects and assignments. These can be used to involve and test students. The projects give research ideas, practical exposure and opportunities that students can take up during the course.
- **Web resources:** This book also comes with a companion website with resources for use by instructors in the classroom. Please visit https://study.sagepub.in/kumar&gupta_RM for Instructors' Manuals, chapter-wise PPT slides and much more. Wherever possible, we have given links to web resources. Instructors can use these in class while going through the chapters. A number of videos have been suggested, which can be used in class.
- **Reliable and well-researched text:** We have tried to provide a reliable and well-researched text. The facts and figures have been cross-checked from published sources which have been cited in the text.
- **Theory and practical applications:** The book is a balance of theoretical explanations and practical applications. Each chapter is illustrated with real-life examples through mini case studies which help to explain the concepts.
- **References from respected journals:** We have referred to a large number of journals, books and published sources while writing this book. These references are provided in each chapter. This will be a great help for those taking up further research. Some of these references can well be used to encourage extra reading in the classroom.

REFERENCE

Yunus, M. 2007. *Creating a World without Poverty*. New York, NY: PublicAffairs.

ACKNOWLEDGEMENTS

Writing this book took us to a number of villages. It was an eye-opener to discover that even in today's time and age, villages existed just 2–3 hours away from a large city without electricity or water connections. Their day ends when it begins to become dark. Wherever we went, we were welcomed by enthusiastic people. We asked them why they did so, considering that we had never met before. They smiled, "Because no one comes here."

We met uneducated women who had started viable businesses by sheer grit and effort. We talked with self-help groups and to village dealers and retailers. We are grateful to all such people who talked to us and let us be part of their lives, even if it was for a short time. We owe our sincere thanks to the people and those who facilitated these visits.

We would also like to thank our colleagues who have always been supportive of our work. Thanks are due to Dr Babita Dosajh, Assistant Dean, Amity Global Business School, Mohali, for her inputs during the invaluable discussions we had with her. Heartiest thanks to Dr H. Chaturvedi, Director, Birla Institute of Management Technology (BIMTECH) and N.N. Sharma, Associate Professor, Strategic Management, BIMTECH, for encouraging us to research and write. They have been a source of inspiration and guidance, always ready to extend a hand when we got stuck.

We have kept the style easily readable even as latest research has been included in the book. We hope that the many case studies in the book—the Mini Case Studies as well as the Opening and Closing Cases—form the basis of discussion in your classes. We also hope that they inspire young people to take a fresh look at the subject.

We would also like to extend our gratitude to the reviewers of the book, whose encouraging comments and valuable suggestions helped us improve the text. Our special thanks to Dr M. Karthik, Programme Head, PGDM International Business, Institute of Public Enterprise, Hyderabad and Dr Raj Kamal, Department of Business Administration, Faculty of Management, MJP Rohilkhand University, Bareilly.

We welcome your comments and suggestions on the book. Our e-mail address is: mmindchd@gmail.com and we look forward to interact with users of this book.

Dr Dinesh Kumar
Dr Punam Gupta

ABOUT THE AUTHORS

Dinesh Kumar, PhD, is Professor of Marketing at Chandigarh. He has been associated with well-known management schools such as Birla Institute of Management Technology (BIMTECH); Fore School of Management; Amity Global Business School, Mohali; University Business School, Panjab University, Chandigarh and others as visiting faculty member. After finishing his MBA from Panjab University, Dr Kumar gained a wide experience in sales, marketing and rural distribution for over 15 years. He switched to teaching in 1995 on receiving a teaching fellowship from Norway. He has taught at leading business schools and written extensively on sustainable development, environment and social marketing. In 2015, he presented a paper at Queen Mary University of London (co-authored with Punam Gupta). He is the author of *Marketing Channels* (2012), *Consumer Behaviour* (2015) and *The Connected Consumer* (2016).

Punam Gupta, PhD, is Associate Professor at Dev Samaj College for Women, Chandigarh, where she has been working since 1980. She did her PhD research in English literature. She was awarded gold medal during her BA Hons (English) and again for obtaining the first position in Panjab University in MA (English). Dr Gupta has written many research papers and participated in seminars on issues such as gender sensitization, green economics, environment studies, value education, media and society. She also participated in UGC SAM Workshop on Capacity Building for Women Managers in Higher Education. She was the co-author of the paper on *Social Marketing and Behaviour Change,* presented at Queen Mary University of London in 2015. She has also recently published a book on English grammar for Indian students.

Section I

The Rural Market

1

CHAPTER

Introduction to Rural Marketing

LEARNING OBJECTIVES

This chapter lays the foundation of rural marketing. It does not treat the subject as a sub-set of mainstream marketing but argues that rural marketing is a unique and separate discipline. After reading the chapter, you will be able to:

- Understand the various frameworks of rural marketing and what it consists of.
- Analyze what is rural market and how it is defined in the empowerment and developmental context.
- Learn about the 4A, 5D frameworks and the theory of market separations.
- Define rural marketing as an interplay of capability enhancement and social objectives.
- Understand the barriers and enablers of rural marketing and use them for better strategy.
- Learn how to make use of the rural marketing opportunity while protecting rural livelihoods, and the ethical issues relating to it.

Opening Case
Low-cost Innovation: Aravind and Narayana Hrudayalaya

One of the most challenging problems in India is that of providing health care in bottom-of-the-pyramid (BoP) markets. Increasing population increases demand for health care, but facilities and doctors are inadequate. Access to medical care is reflected in the number of hospital beds per 1,000 people, and this figure for India stands at 0.7. This huge demand cannot be met by existing methods—that of a doctor seeing one patient at a time—but would require an impossible number of doctors, writes *The Economist* (2012). A new model was therefore required. This case study describes the efforts of two pioneers, Dr Devi Shetty and Venkataswamy, or Dr V, in revolutionizing health care in India.

Narayana Hrudayalaya: Around 2.5 million people require heart surgeries in India every year but only 80,000 to 90,000 are performed by the country's hospitals. For many people, quality medical care is either inaccessible or unaffordable. Dr Devi Shetty of Narayana Hrudayalaya Institute of Cardiac Sciences, Bangalore, offers an assembly line approach to heart surgeries, without compromising on quality. Formerly personal physician to Mother Teresa, he was influenced by her work to invent quality health care that could be made widely accessible and affordable.

Dr Shetty went about reducing costs to make heart surgery affordable through 'process innovation'. This means that at Narayana Hrudayalaya, only surgeons do the most complex procedures; other trained workers do everything else. The result is surgeries that cost less than US$2,000 each, about one-fifteenth as much as a similar procedure in America. Dr Shetty applied the 'the Walmart approach' in medical care in a field as complex and costly as cardiac care. He has been able to reduce costs by redesigning processes and negotiating creative partnership deals.

Dr Shetty decided to create a chain of large 'health cities' across the country. He started a 1,400-bed cancer and multispecialty hospital in Bangalore—the largest cancer hospital in the country, which includes an orthopaedic hospital, an eye hospital, research facilities and rooms for about 50 training programmes. His plan is to build 5,000-bed 'health cities' across India, expanding to Kolkata, Hyderabad, Jaipur and Ahmedabad. The aim is to do a heart operation for US$800 from the point of admission to the point of discharge, compared to the cost of cardiac surgeries in the United States which can cost up to US$50,000 and, in India, around US$5,000–7,000. This is leading to a new health care model not only for India but also for the world. Patients come to the Bangalore facility from more than 50 countries.

At Narayana Hrudayalaya, surgeries cost less than US$3,000, irrespective of the complexity of the procedure or the length of hospitalization. Of these, about 30 per cent are covered under a micro-insurance plan for health care called Yeshasvini that reimburses part of the cost at about US$1,200 per surgery. Yeshasvini was launched in 2002 and is run by an independent trust in association with the Karnataka state government.

As volumes increase, further economies of scale were achieved. High volumes help the hospital while negotiating prices for everything from basic supplies to medical equipment. The Bangalore heart hospital performs about 30 surgeries a day—the highest number of cardiac surgeries done by any hospital in India. The hospital's mortality rate of around 2 per cent and hospital-acquired infection rate of 2.8 per 1000 ICU days are comparable to the best hospitals across the world. In an article in *Forbes India*, C.K. Prahalad wrote that the mortality rate in Narayana Hrudayalaya is "much lower than in New York State for similar kinds of heart disease."

Patients are reached in villages through a network of rural clinics and via telemedicine facilities. Narayana Hrudayalaya has a unique principle—no one is denied treatment due to a lack of funds. Dr Shetty uses a hybrid pricing model by providing private rooms at higher cost for rich patients, which offsets the losses incurred from treating the poor.

Costs are kept low. Construction costs at his hospitals are less than half of that for others. Profit and loss account is analyzed on a daily basis to work out how much concession can be given the following day. This allows the hospital to fulfil a great social need without compromising on profitability.

Apart from the surgeries, it has large out-patient facilities. Increasing volumes have helped lower costs: staff costs are spread over a large number of customers. For example, the company is able to save about 40 per cent by importing surgical gloves in container loads from

Malaysia. By using digital X-ray technology, the cost of film is saved. CT scanners, MRI and other machines are used for 14 hours a day, which reduces per unit costs.

The hospital enters into innovative partnerships. For instance, expensive equipment for blood gas analysis and catheterization laboratory equipment have been installed by companies who recover costs by selling the chemical reagents or through referrals. In this way, the hospital saves on the cost of the machines, while the supplying companies also profit. Kiran Mazumdar-Shaw of Biocon, who owns a stake in the company, credits Narayana Hrudayalaya with consistently focusing on training and development of specialized skills.

Aravind: The method of cost reduction through assembly line techniques is found in other areas of health care. India's LifeSpring hospitals slash the price of childbirth by augmenting doctors with less expensive midwives to about one-sixth of those in a private clinic. The Aravind Eye Care System offers surgery to about 400,000 patients per year. Operating rooms have two beds so that surgeons can perform two operations at the same time.

Named after Sri Aurobindo, Aravind's non-profit network includes 11 hospitals (Figure 1.1), a research institute, an intraocular lens factory, eye banks, the Aravind Medical Research Foundation and training facilities. Since its foundation in 1976, Aravind has treated 29 million

FIGURE 1.1
Distribution of Aravind eye hospitals across Tamil Nadu.

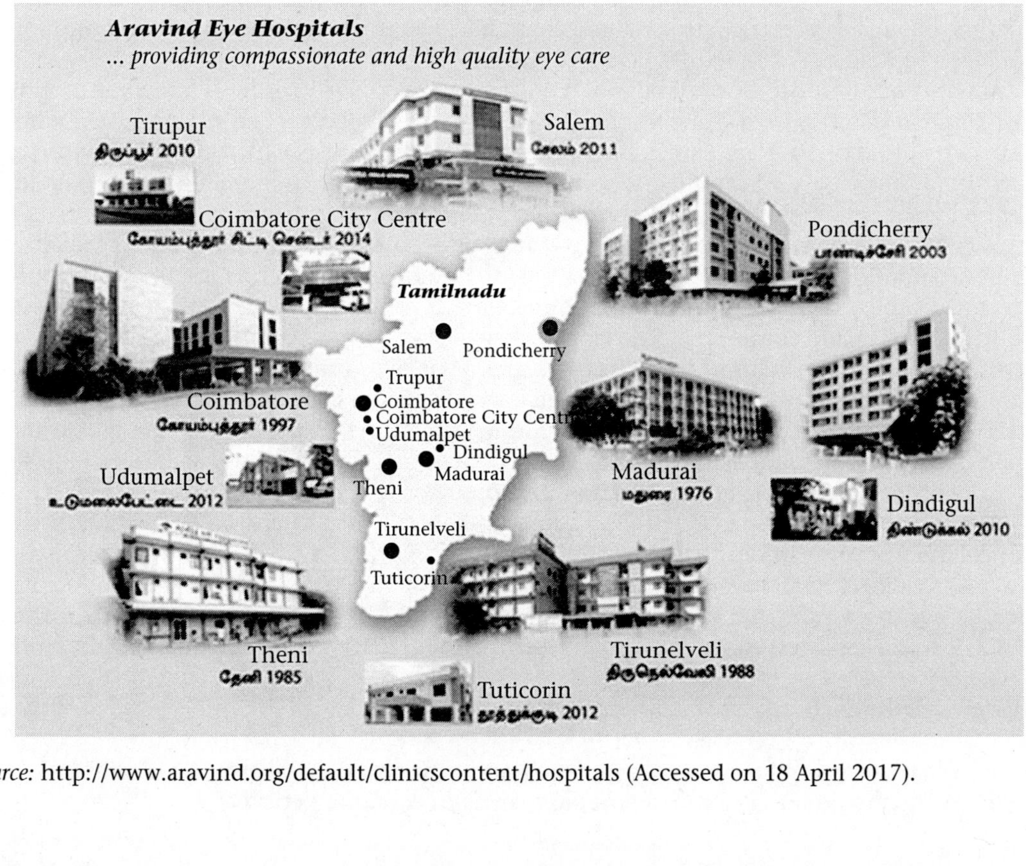

Source: http://www.aravind.org/default/clinicscontent/hospitals (Accessed on 18 April 2017).

patients and performed 3.6 million eye surgeries and laser procedures, making it the world's largest and most productive eye care service group.

It too follows an assembly line approach to eye care. India is home to a quarter of the world's blind and every year at least four million Indians develop cataracts. Aravind's doctors perform 2,000 surgeries per year versus the national average of 400. Apart from its scale, Aravind provides treatment that is either free or heavily subsidized for the poor, who mostly come from the remotest villages in the region.

By using a hybrid pricing model, it earns from rich patients to serve the poor. Cataract surgery, including a two-night stay at the hospital, medication for a month and the cost of the implanted lens; costs ₹750 compared to costs in other hospitals of around US$1,000. The quality of treatment is the same for every patient, but non-paying patients are given a basic hard lens and a room to share with other patients where they get a mat on the floor. Paying patients can choose soft lenses and higher categories of rooms. To ensure uniform quality of care, each eye doctor is rotated between the free and paying parts of the hospital.

One unique feature is Aravind's well-trained workforce of ophthalmic assistants, consisting of young village women with two years of training to take on the routine tasks in the operating room. This frees doctors to focus on diagnosis and procedures. It uses a just-in-time approach to deliver affordable, quality health services. This reduces cost because, instead of two doctors, each surgery is performed by one doctor with two assistants.

Aravind is one of the world's great models of social entrepreneurship. It also operates 30 vision centres or primary eye clinics, enabling it to reach farther into the hinterland. At these village centres, a vision technician can examine patients and also arrange consultations with doctors via videoconference, thus saving them a trip to the city. Patients who require surgery are taken to Madurai at Aravind's cost and treated for free.

Aravind was founded by Govindappa Venkataswamy, or Dr V, as he is known. An ophthalmic surgeon, Dr V started Aravind after his retirement. He persuaded his sister, G. Natchiar, and her husband, Dr Nam, both Harvard-educated eye surgeons, to join. They mortgaged their homes to raise seed capital and set up an 11-bed eye clinic in a rented house. The family devised what Dr V called a service-cum-business model.

Now it has its own training institute, which offers a two-year postgraduate specialization in ophthalmology. A big difference is that at private hospitals doctors are under pressure for revenues, but by contrast, they practise 'honest medicine' at Aravind, with a balance between clinical practice and community work.

In 1992, Aravind began to make its own lenses within a price of US$2 to US$10, replacing imported lenses that cost US$150. Today, its manufacturing unit, Aurolab, makes two million lenses every year, exporting them to 120 countries, and has 7 per cent of the global market share for intraocular lenses by volume. The product portfolio has expanded to include suture needles, microsurgical blades, lasers and eye drops.

Aravind aims to perform one million surgeries annually by the end of 2020. It has provided consultancy services to nearly 300 hospitals in India, Bangladesh, Africa and Latin America. It has also undertaken to manage other hospitals in India. It also invests in research for prevention of eye diseases. It has exported its training model to about 30 developing countries. In 2008, it won the Gates Award for Global Health and in 2010, Conrad N. Hilton Humanitarian Prize.

While reading this chapter, try to answer the following questions:

1. What are the trends in rural marketing and how will they impact the future?
2. What should be the approach of companies in rural marketing?

3. How can marketing principles be applied/modified to rural areas?
4. What are the ethical issues and how can companies make use of the rural opportunity while enhancing rural livelihoods?

Sources for this Case Study:

Web Resource

Narayana Health website: http://www.narayanahealth.org

Other Sources

Mahajan-Bansal, Neelima. 2009. "CK Prahalad: A unique combination of strategic vision and financial acumen," *Forbes*, July 7. Available at: http://www.forbesindia.com/interview/magazine-extra/ck-prahalad-a-unique-combination-of-strategic-vision-and-financial-acumen/1912/0 (Accessed on 18 April 2017).

Knowledge@Wharton. 2010. "Narayana Hrudayalaya: A Model for Accessible, Affordable Health Care?" 1 July. Available at: http://knowledge.wharton.upenn.edu/article/narayana-hrudayalaya-a-model-for-accessible-affordable-health-care/ (Accessed on 18 April 2017).

The Economist. 2012. "The Future of Medicine: Squeezing Out the Doctor," 2 June. Available at: http://www.economist.com/node/21556227 (Accessed on 18 April 2017).

INTRODUCTION

Rural marketing is generally understood as 'marketing goods and services to villages'. Or its scope is expanded by adding the term 'agricultural marketing', which takes into account the flow of produce from rural to urban areas. Many articles and papers on rural marketing start by describing the huge opportunity that rural areas represent: more than 800 million people who have little access to modern goods. Writers lament that though a large number of people live in villages, many companies have been unable to tap this big opportunity. Indeed, many writers suggest that rural marketing is an easy task: a huge opportunity to be exploited, a saviour for companies that face saturation in urban markets and a means of getting out of the recessionary cycle that urban markets are prone to.

One of the most celebrated writers, C.K. Prahalad (2005), exhorted companies to tap the fortune at the BoP, that is, to try to exploit the huge purchasing power of the large numbers of poor. His idea was to eradicate poverty through profits. Closer to home, popular literature is replete with descriptions of the wonderful opportunities offered by rural markets. Bijapurkar and Shukla (2015) strike a similar note, "When a large mass of a whopping 180 million households starts to move, even though at varying speeds, and some quite slow, it still makes for a market opportunity that is already larger than the urban market." Practitioners too have fallen into this trap. "The water's warm and the ocean's calm. Dive in; it's time to discover what lies beyond the horizon," is the advice given by Saigal (2015).

Based on such thinking, most writers have presented the view that rural marketing can be done by applying existing commercial marketing knowledge to a virgin market. Much of the rural marketing effort thus consists of trying to convince people in villages to buy products and brands offered by multinational companies (MNCs) and other big companies, who in turn look at population data and want to grab the unexplored potential of villages.

This is rather a simplistic understanding of the subject. Companies that have followed this proposition have faced insurmountable problems in terms of distribution of goods and selling them to consumers who have limited purchasing power and do not have access to financial markets. Many companies have discovered that marketing in rural areas is not as simple as tapping into a virgin market waiting to buy all those wonderful products that find ready buyers in urban areas. A report by Accenture (2013) says, "India's rural markets present opportunities that companies seeking to become high-performance businesses cannot afford to ignore. But the size and scale of those markets have been offset by concerns about the profitability of these markets and the durability of rural demand."

Our analysis in Chapter 2 shows that the rural market is not very easy to exploit. Rural marketing is not simply tapping into opportunities merely by diving in. If we look closely, we find that rural marketing cannot be thought of as simply marketing in rural areas. Since even large companies struggle to get their rural marketing approach right, there is a need for a proper understanding of the subject and to redefine strategy based on market realities. We first look at the existing frameworks of rural marketing.

FRAMEWORKS OF RURAL MARKETING

Ask anyone about marketing, and the answer will most probably be about selling, advertising or about some big brands. This is not surprising, because most marketing that is taught in business schools is urban market oriented. Our approach usually rests on the visible, urban aspects of marketing, and that is why we tend to ignore areas where a large number of people live. It is an approach described by the Pareto principle: that there is an unequal relationship between inputs and outputs. Urban issues get disproportionately high attention by governments, policy makers and the media, but the large section of the population that lives in rural areas is largely ignored (Figure 1.2).

That is why, most marketing undertaken in villages is seen as just an extension of urban advertising, distribution and promotion. This stream of thought tries to apply marketing principles to rural customers, based on segmentation variables and marketing finished goods to them. These companies target only those who can afford the products and is, therefore, limited in its scope. The second school of thought is that rural marketing consists of agriculture: it focuses on marketing of agricultural produce and of agricultural inputs, that is, it is limited to grains, cash crops and inputs such as fertilizers, pesticides, seeds and farm machinery.

However, selling to the poor has been unprofitable for many companies, but is also morally repugnant. Can and should the poor, whose life is a daily struggle, be seen as a source of profit?

FIGURE 1.2

Rural areas, home to more than two-thirds of the population, get a minimum attention of companies and policy makers; most of their attention is on urban markets, which represent just one-third of the population.

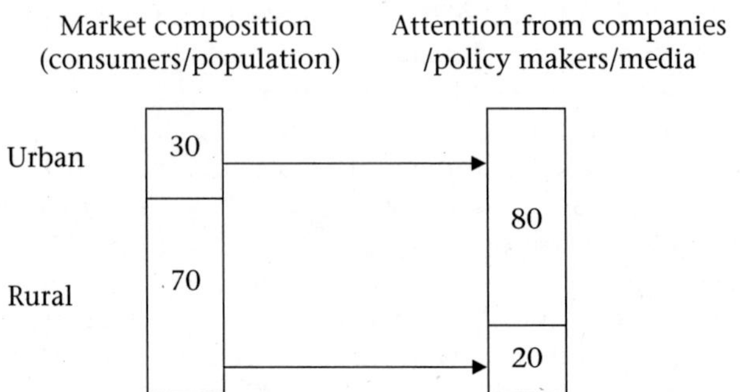

Unfortunately, much of rural marketing literature exactly does that. As we have noted earlier, it suffers from the flaw that it treats rural marketing as an extension of marketing. Jha (1988) has shown the weaknesses of the existing rural marketing literature, which are true even today:

1. **Participants:** It ignores the majority of rural population, that is, the rural poor.
2. **Products:** It concentrates on tangibles and ignores some of the basic needs such as health, education, drinking water, housing, transportation, labour, land, money and so on. Even in tangibles, the focus seems to be exclusively on economic goods.
3. **Modalities:** It is not concerned about development of market centres and supporting institutions.
4. **Norms:** It ignores norms of behaviour, liabilities of various parties and methods of operation, even with regard to conventional goods.
5. **Outcome:** Marketing literature is negligent about the expected outcomes.

This book will show that companies, which change their approach to marketing and understand markets and consumers, and try to solve local problems, are more likely to be successful than mere copycats of urban strategy. But first, we learn how our understanding of rural marketing has grown over the years.

Three frameworks of rural marketing have been suggested. These are helpful to understand rural marketing but give a somewhat limited approach to the subject. The first is defining what is rural, the second is based on flow-of-goods and the third is a historical perspective.

Defining Rural

The term 'rural' is defined in several ways.

According to the Planning Commission of India, a town with a maximum population of 15,000 is considered rural in nature.

The National Sample Survey Office (NSSO) defines 'rural' as follows:

- An area with a population density of up to 400 per sq. km.
- Villages with clear surveyed boundaries but no municipal board.
- A minimum of 75 per cent of male, working population involved in agriculture and allied activities.

The Census of India 2001 defines urban India and it is implied that rural means the areas which are not urban. Urban India is defined as:

- All statutory places with municipality, corporation, cantonment board or notified town area committee.
- Minimum population of 5,000.
- Density of population of at least 400 per sq. km. (1,000 per sq. mile).
- At least 75 per cent of male, working population engaged in non-agricultural activities.

By this definition, rural means areas with population of less than 5,000.

Reserve Bank of India (RBI) defines rural areas as those areas which have a population of less than 49,000 (Tier-3 to Tier-6 cities).

Private companies have their own way of defining rural markets. Their approach is on market potential: small towns that are far from big cities would also be treated as rural areas for marketing purposes. Similarly, all areas with a population of less than 5,000 are taken as rural; however, all towns with a population up to 2.5 lakh should also be included as a rural market as the marketing approach in such towns will be quite different from that of the metros.

Flow-of-goods Concept

This concept looks at the origin of goods and their destination (Table 1.1). If goods flow from urban to rural areas, it is seen as part of rural marketing. This is the common connotation of the term. The flow of goods from rural areas to cities, and rural to rural areas, is added to rural marketing as an afterthought. In the four flows, except the flow of goods from urban to urban, the other boxes are seen to be part of rural marketing. The kinds of goods that flow are described here.

- **Urban to rural:** Pesticides, fertilizers, fast-moving consumer goods (FMCG) products, tractors, bicycles and vehicles, and consumer durables fall in this category.
- **Rural to urban:** In this category, we have agricultural produce such as grain, fruits and vegetables, milk and related products, forest produce, spices and so on. This is the view taken by the National Commission on Agriculture, which says that central to rural marketing is a 'saleable farm commodity'.
- **Rural to rural:** This category consists of activities between two villages, such as selling tools, handicrafts, consumables and services to each other.
- **Urban to urban:** This category consists of goods and services produced and offered in urban areas, and these are not considered as part of rural marketing.

While this is rather broadly accepted, it raises some interesting questions:

- Would McDonalds and other food chains be doing rural marketing because its raw materials are grown in villages, and is therefore rural to urban?
- Would all the fashion brands such as Arrow and Tommy Hilfiger be doing rural marketing as they make much of their apparel from cotton, which is grown in rural areas?
- What is the difference between the marketing done by Amul and, say, a multinational corporation?
- If a factory is set up in a rural area to leverage lower rentals and labour costs, would it be rural marketing?

TABLE 1.1

Flow-of-goods framework of rural marketing.

From/To	Rural	Urban
Rural	Local goods and produce, services	Agricultural produce, Handicrafts
Urban	Finished goods: FMCG and white goods, Agricultural inputs	Goods and services

Source: Adapted from Jha (1988).

When we consider questions like this, we find that the flow-of-goods concept, though widely accepted, is not an accurate assessment of the term and concept of rural marketing. This is illustrated by Mini Case Study 1.1, which describes Amul's integrated approach to marketing.

Mini Case Study 1.1

Amul: An Integrated Approach in Rural Marketing

Amul is one of the most endearing brands of India. It is the largest food brand in India with an annual turnover of ₹20,735 crore for the year ended March 2015, which is equivalent to the combined revenue of the food businesses of its three closest rivals Nestlé, Hindustan Unilever Limited (HUL) and ITC Limited (based on their figures for FY14). It is owned by Gujarat Cooperative Milk Marketing Federation (GCMMF), and its cooperative revolution has made India the largest producer of milk in the world.

What sets Amul apart is its approach to marketing and sourcing of raw materials (Figure 1.3). It connects farmers and their animals with supply chains. Procedures for collecting and checking milk are simplified, and by connecting dealers through the business-to-business (B2B) network, the company is able to streamline supplies of its products with better demand forecasting.

FIGURE 1.3

The Amul model empowers producers and connects right up to the consumer.

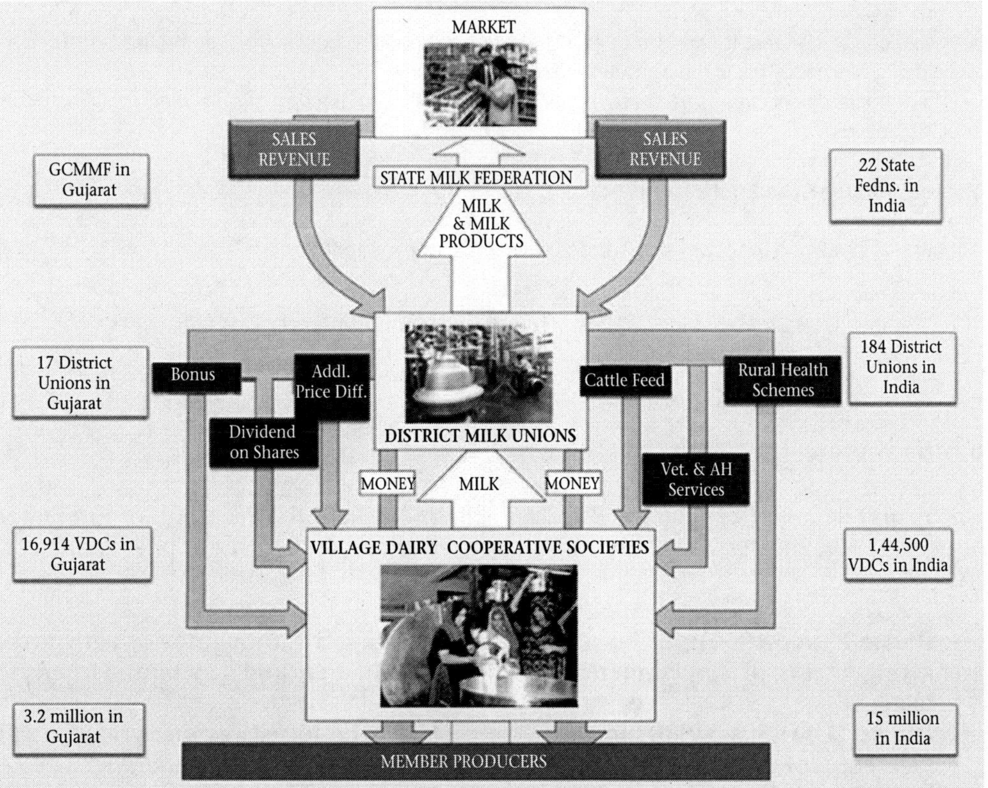

Source: Reproduced from Amul website: http://www.amul.com/m/about-us (Accessed on 18 April 2017).

The Amul model, as explained on its website, consists of:

- Establishment of a direct linkage between milk producers and consumers by eliminating middlemen.
- Milk producers (farmers) control procurement, processing and marketing.

The logistics behind the Amul operation are evident from the fact that 15 million milk producers supply milk to 144,500 dairy cooperative societies across the country. Their milk is processed in 184 district co-operative unions and marketed by 22 state marketing federations. The milk collection centres were automated and enterprise-like integration was taken up (see Chapter 10).

This enables Amul to track milk production and productivity region-wise in Gujarat. The geographic information system (GIS) is also used to monitor veterinary health and controlling outbreak of diseases. Another system has a database of cattle owned by farmers, containing their medical history, reproductive cycle and history of diseases. Farmers were given access to information related to best practices in breeding and rearing cattle. The system is used to forecast milk collection and monitor the produce of milk from individual sellers.

One can argue that connecting farmers and helping them is not strictly a part of marketing. But that is how rural marketing is different from mainstream marketing. It has to involve and empower the suppliers and customers, without which they will hardly have the purchasing power required to buy the products and brands on offer. For example, small and marginal member farmers do not have access to finance, veterinary services and support services in animal husbandry. By helping provide these services, Amul has ensured a regular supply of its raw material—milk.

This case study shows that the scope of rural marketing goes much beyond merely supplying goods and services to villages. It consists of empowering rural people, building or reinforcing institutions and developing markets. This is the approach taken by this book.

Why should companies start doing things that are beyond the scope of rural marketing? Is it part of their objectives?

Sources for this Case Study:

Web Resource

"About Us" section in Amul website: http://www.amul.com/m/about-us

Other Source

Kumar, Dinesh. 2012. *Marketing Channels*. New Delhi: Oxford University Press.

Historical View

Kashyap and Raut (2006) have listed three distinct phases in the evolution of rural marketing from the 1960s, during which the term changed its meaning. These phases are described here.

- **Phase I (pre-1960):** In this phase, rural marketing was thought of as agriculture marketing, that is, of supplying rural produce to urban areas and agricultural inputs to rural markets.
- **Phase II (1960s–1990):** In the second phase, the focus was on agricultural inputs. Marketing of non-farm rural produce was considered as rural marketing. The country had taken the road of Green Revolution, and scientific farming practices were adopted.

This led to demand of fertilizers, pesticides, high-yield variety seeds, agricultural implements such as tractors, harvesters, pump sets and so on. Companies such as Mahindra & Mahindra, Escorts, Eicher, Sriram Fertilizers and Indian Farmers Fertiliser Cooperative Limited (IFFCO) made inroads into rural areas. The government encouraged marketing of rural products and Khadi and Village Industries Commission (KVIC) along with societies and emporiums were set up. Exhibitions and craft *melas* (fairs or festivals) in urban areas helped expand the market for rural products, though in limited ways.

- **Phase III (1991–present):** In 1991, the country took steps towards liberalization resulting in focus on consumer goods. Due to saturation in cities, companies faced lack of growth in urban areas and they turned their attention to rural areas. Prahalad's (2005) book on BoP marketing and several papers by Indian commentators gave impetus to such thought, and the recessionary periods convinced companies about the potential of rural markets and the need to exploit them.

In this viewpoint, rural marketing is understood today as the kind of marketing where multinational, large companies and retail companies go to rural areas. Rural marketing is treated as a subset of marketing, and it is assumed that existing marketing theory can be applied directly to rural areas. Keeping with this trend, Dogra and Ghuman (2008) define rural marketing as "planning and implementation of marketing function for the rural areas." Based on such thinking, companies have tried to sell their products in villages by modifying distribution channels, or by offering smaller packs or cheaper variants.

But as Erik Simanis (2012) shows, the strategy of "low price, low margin, high volume" does not work for long. Many companies have had to withdraw from rural markets as they found them unprofitable. He writes that the model has not quite worked for a large number of companies who have ventured into rural areas.

Plenty of failures illustrate the difficulty.

- The Indian government's efforts at marketing a low-cost tablet computer for poor and rural students have failed miserably. The computer, called Aakash, was touted as one of the 'world's cheapest' innovations. The tender was won by Datawind, which was to sell the tablets to the Indian government for about ₹2,290 each; the government was to subsidize, so that it would cost even less to students and teachers. The government has conceded that it was a failure.
- Hewlett Packard started a project called 'e-inclusion', which sought to enable "all the world's people to access the social and economic opportunities of the digital age." It had to be closed because its objectives were not tied to the company's mission.
- Procter & Gamble invented a water purification powder called PUR for BoP markets, but it was a commercial failure. It is now being distributed by a philanthropic enterprise.
- In 2007, SC Johnson launched Community Cleaning Services, a BoP business aimed at creating employment in a slum in Nairobi, Kenya but could not make profits.
- DuPont tried to alleviate malnutrition and open new markets by selling soya-fortified snacks in a pilot programme in India, but had to drop the project.
- India's public distribution system (PDS) is a government-sponsored chain of shops for distributing basic food and non-food commodities to the needy sections of the society at very cheap prices. The system is often blamed for its inefficiency and rural–urban bias. It has not been able to fulfil the objective for which it was formed. Moreover, it has frequently been criticized for instances of corruption and black marketing, according to *The Economic Times* (2015).

Because of these and other failures, many people have questioned whether there is a mirage at the BoP. But *The Guardian* (2014) notes, "That doesn't mean that business should leave the task of fighting poverty to governments or aid organizations. Companies can bring unique value to the poor." In this book, we discover how this can be done.

The mistake made by these initiatives is that only one aspect of the marketing mix was sought to be changed—packaging, pricing or distribution. Rural marketing, however, calls for a paradigm shift in approach. Applying existing marketing theory to rural marketing does not quite work because many questions arise when we see market realities, some of which are as follows:

1. **Distribution:** How to send small packets over large distances where transportation or courier services are irregular or non-existent?
2. **Promotion:** How to promote goods in areas which are media dark, lacking regular communication channels?
3. **Pricing:** How to keep prices low when the costs of sending goods and servicing them in remote areas are extremely high?
4. **Feudal outlook:** How to promote modern products in areas which see modernization as a threat to their culture?
5. **People:** How to find educated managers willing to work in rural areas, where sending sales or service personnel regularly is uneconomical?
6. **Payments:** How to collect payments, sometimes very small, from areas where intermediaries are poor and lack access to formal financial channels?
7. **Intermediaries:** How to find warehouses and intermediaries to support the marketing activities of companies?
8. **Purchasing power:** How to sell in areas where people are desperately poor and farmers are committing suicide because of economic reasons?
9. **Sachet marketing:** How to achieve volumes and a high penetration rate to make low-priced sachet marketing profitable?
10. **Selling effort:** How to deploy, train and retain the sales force in geographically diverse areas?

These questions are enough to flummox the brightest marketing students and managers, but must be asked before a company embarks on a rural marketing adventure. They also show why existing marketing knowledge cannot be applied to rural areas, and why a new approach in rural marketing is needed.

This new approach consists of *social innovation*, or applying new ideas that work in meeting social goals (see Chapter 12). Several companies are doing that—we have covered several case studies in this book describing companies that have adopted unique and innovative approaches in rural areas. We see from the experience of these companies (Table 1.2) that mere selling of goods in rural areas is not enough, but companies have to rise to solve some local problems so as to be accepted in rural society.

As Anderson and Markides (2007) explain, it is not about creating new product features but adapting existing products to customers who have fewer resources or a different cultural background. It is less about creating new business models or competing, but about establishing basic market ingredients such as distribution channels and customer demand from the ground up. These themes are covered in this book.

TABLE 1.2

Companies that have gone beyond business objectives and incorporated social objectives in their purpose.

Company/Brand	Business	Social Objectives
Alibaba	Online portal	Organizing villages in China to become producer communities
Amul	Milk and milk products	Organizing milk Co-operatives, helping farmers with livestock and to get higher milk prices
Aravind/Narayana	Health care	Providing world class health care while reducing cost, village outreach
Bandhan Bank	Banking	Providing microcredit; organizing thrift village societies
Bata	Footwear	Providing low-cost footwear by reducing factory cost, helping village women to set up distribution business
Bolthouse Farms	Fruits and vegetables	Encouraging the habit of healthy snacks
Café Femenino	Coffee growing	Establishes high trade standards for coffee and other products. Introduces 'Fairtrade', certifying companies that pay producers a living wage and meet other social and environmental standards
Essilor	Eye care	Providing villagers eye care and spectacles at low cost
Fabindia	Apparel, furnishings, health products	Organizing artisan communities and getting better prices for their products
General Electric	Machines for medical diagnosis	Reinventing machines to make them cheaper and portable for rural areas
Google	Digital services	Internet penetration in villages, capacity building
Grameen Bank/ Bandhan Bank/ Grameenphone	Banking/telecom services	Organizing people for microfinance/cheap telecom services to villages in Bangladesh
HUL	FMCG, consumer products	Helping villagers set up distribution business, educating about hygiene and changing habits, mobile-based entertainment for remote villages
ITC	FMCG, consumer products	Providing information and trading portal through IT choupals
Jain Irrigation	Irrigation and drip irrigation equipment	Buyback of farmer produce, arranging financing and government subsidies for them
Jaipur Rugs	Carpets and rugs	Training local artisans and empowering them
Kiva/Rang De	Crowd-sourcing	Providing funding for small businesses in villages through crowd-funding
MittiCool	Refrigerator and appliances	Low-cost appliances that do not work on electricity
Novartis	Medicines	Providing health care and branded medicines to villages

(Table 1.2 Contd.)

(Table 1.2 Contd.)

Company/Brand	Business	Social Objectives
Pepsi	Potato chips and snacks	Introduced new varieties, help and educate farmers, buyback of produce at good prices
Reliance Fresh	Retail	Farm-to-fork distribution, sourcing directly from villages
SELCO	Solar lighting	Providing cheap lighting solutions to villages
Tata Tea	Branded tea	Helping villagers set up distribution business
Usha	Sewing machines	Helping women to start stitching businesses through sewing schools in villages

RURAL MARKETING DEFINED

Based on the experience of the companies mentioned in the previous section, we attempt a definition of rural marketing. The low-cost and sachet strategies that are generally quoted in this context can be easily copied and become unprofitable in the long run. These companies clearly have done something different and their guiding principles are *inclusion, efficiency and innovation*. These principles are illustrated in our opening case of Aravind and Narayana hospitals.

We need a definition of rural marketing that takes into account these three guiding principles if we are to succeed in rural areas. An alternative approach is therefore needed—one that sees rural consumers as people. Once we recognize that, we begin to see rural consumers as part of the developmental process and marketing acquires a deeper purpose, summed up by the definition of rural marketing provided by Pratik Modi (2009), "as any marketing activity whose net developmental impact on rural people is positive."

Drawing from this idea, we define rural marketing as *a process that consists of developing and empowering people in rural communities through capability enhancement and social innovation, to facilitate a two-way marketing of economic and social goods between rural and urban areas.*

This definition can be explained as having four aspects:

1. *A process that consists of developing and empowering people in rural communities:* Developing and empowering people means that rural incomes must be enhanced by making the people producers of economic goods. Help is provided to existing producers to become more efficient by removing market separations, and thereby enable them as consumers.
2. *Two-way marketing of economic and social goods between rural and urban areas:* Any definition of rural marketing must include social goods because corporations are in a position to deliver these goods, and these are not measured in economic terms but still help in bringing large parts of disadvantaged populations within the purview of marketing.
3. *Capability Enhancement:* Amartya Sen (1993) has given what is called the 'capability approach to development'. He argues that development is about the freedom of choice in all spheres: a person's capability refers to the alternative combinations of 'functionings'—referring to the various things a person may value doing or being, such as being adequately nourished, being healthy and being able to take part in the life of a community. The focus of development thus morphs into increasing a person's capability set or the freedom to lead the life she/he values.

4. *Social innovation:* Rural marketing requires a high degree of social innovation. Social innovation is defined as any new initiatives—products, services or models—that meet social needs more effectively than existing alternatives, and simultaneously create new social relationships and collaborations. INSEAD's social innovation website defines it as "the introduction and development of new business models, and market-based mechanisms that deliver sustainable economic, environmental and social prosperity." New business models are created through initiative, inventiveness and creativity. This gives rise to a different type of business with primarily a social focus rather than a profit-oriented one. Such models encourage a more participatory approach. The success of Grameen Bank and Amul shows that social innovation does, indeed, create businesses that become powerful forces for the social good. The case study about Jaipur Rugs at the end of this chapter also demonstrates both enhancing capabilities and social innovation.

If we look at the subject from this perspective, rural marketing becomes a tool that delivers both rural empowerment and marketing of goods and services, thus broad-basing its domain to cover a variety of market relationships. This enhances the role of marketing considerably. Companies will therefore have to change their approach and their organization structures, modify their missions and invest in rural empowerment. It may be argued that empowerment is not really a task of private companies, but unless purchasing power is enhanced, companies can only focus on a small part of the market, since many of India's poor live in rural areas. Some companies have succeeded by linking agriculture and rural enterprises to rural and urban markets. Our mini case study on Amul shows that this has been done quite well.

This book argues for treating rural marketing as a subject, distinct from marketing, because companies should not merely sell products to rural areas but should facilitate a better standard of living for rural consumers. This can happen if companies approach the problem with two mindsets: building capabilities and investing in social innovation. This change in approach is essential if companies are to succeed in rural markets. Since many attempts to reap the 'fortune at the bottom of the pyramid' have failed because they followed the traditional methods of marketing of making profits by supplying goods to the poor—a new approach is needed. Only when companies focus on the developmental aspect of their interventions, they can succeed in rural areas.

We describe three approaches which help us to understand rural marketing, keeping in view the ground realities in India. These are the 4A approach, the 5D framework and the theory of market separations.

The 4A Approach

Marketing students are quick to learn the concept of marketing mix consisting of the 4Ps. While the 4P framework provides a basis of understanding the subject, it needs modification to work in rural markets. The 4A approach (Figure 1.4) modifies the 4P approach and helps change the focus of companies marketing in rural areas, with acceptability, affordability, availability and awareness as its focus. The traditional approach of offering suitable products, building distribution chains, adjusting the price–value equation and using effective promotion must necessarily be modified because rural consumers are unlike urban ones. "By focusing managerial attention on creating awareness, access, affordability and availability (4As), managers can create an exciting environment for innovation," writes C.K. Prahalad (2012).

FIGURE 1.4
The 4A approach to rural marketing.

Acceptability: Understanding customers Modifying products Overcoming social, cultural, economic barriers Fulfilling local needs	**Affordability:** Offering a price-value combination Functional and sturdy products Empowering rural people, match ability to pay Offer-enabling mechanisms
Availability: Ability to fulfil small orders regularly Logistics and infrastructure creation Vast and uneven spread Developing intermediaries	**Awareness:** Fitting in the local culture Region specific, focused promotions Below-the-Line activities over vast areas Lack of media and channels

The suggested 4A framework consisting of availability, affordability, acceptability and awareness modifies the 4P framework.

The approach is described here.

Product—Acceptability

Rather than focusing on product features, companies have to modify the products to gain acceptability in rural areas. This means understanding customers and modifying products to suit their needs. It also means incorporating features that make the products more useful in rural areas. For instance, in rural areas that suffer erratic electric supply, mobile phones have been made more useful by adding the torch feature. Companies providing phones with local language displays are more popular than the ones with English displays only. This is how products are made acceptable to rural consumers.

Government data (see Chapter 2) shows that much of rural population has low incomes and seasonal jobs related to agriculture. This means that companies have to cater to millions of people who are poor and have low disposable incomes. Affordability of the product or service thus becomes of prime importance. Some companies have addressed this problem by introducing small packs and sachets (see Mini Case Study 1.2). They have helped companies penetrate rural markets. Such packs make a variety of products more affordable, encouraging trials and use. Most FMCG companies have followed this strategy to enter rural markets through small packs of soaps, shampoos, beverages, biscuits and butter to boost consumption and make products affordable. However, distribution and profitability of small packs remains in question. Companies must sell small lots of five or ten sachets to small shopkeepers who are scattered over large areas. Such shopkeepers also require regular servicing. But employing a large number of salespersons results in the operation becoming unprofitable, because volumes are difficult to build and penetration rates remain low.

Other companies have developed cheaper variants of their products. This sometimes does not quite work because consumers in rural areas are value conscious. Cheap products are in any case supplied by local manufacturers, so brands have to think of innovative strategies.

Mini Case Study 1.2

Encouraging Acceptability

LG Electronics developed a customized TV for the rural market in 1998 with the brand name Sampoorna. Low-cost ice-boxes were provided by Coca-Cola to get over the problem of lack of electricity and refrigeration in rural areas: tin boxes for new outlets and thermocol box for seasonal outlets. Insurance companies that have tailor-made products for the rural market have performed well. HDFC Standard tied up with non-governmental organizations (NGOs) and offered reasonably priced policies as group insurance covers. State Bank of India introduced Tiny Account which can be operated with just a paid volunteer equipped with a small box, with biometric measurement (for fingerprints) and a mobile that enables communication with the zonal office. Such innovations are both creative as well as helpful.

Mobile device companies tailor their products for rural consumers. Nokia introduced a basic handset with a torch and an alarm clock. In December 2008, the company launched Nokia Life Tools, which is a range of agriculture, education and entertainment services designed especially for consumers in small towns and rural areas of emerging markets. The product was meant to provide timely and relevant information customized to the user's location and personal preference directly on their mobile services. Companies are now designing products especially for rural markets.

Samsung introduced stabilizer-free direct-cool refrigerators to take care of voltage fluctuations. It added silver-nano features in semi-automatic washing machines for use in areas where the water quality is not good. Telecom companies such as Bharti Airtel and Idea Cellular provide service messages in local languages and alerts on commodity prices at the nearest wholesale market and even English language tutorials. The most popular value-added service is music, especially in local dialects. Tata Chemicals launched a water purifier, Swach, that targets the lower-income group in rural India and aims to resolve one of the crucial issues plaguing India, that is, access to clean drinking water.

How can acceptability be improved? What other methods can companies employ?

Price—Affordability

One common mistake is to assume that rural areas will buy cheap products since many people living there are poor. But one of the important keys to rural markets is affordability, that is, the ability of customers to pay for products that provide reciprocal value. Further, rural consumers do not want bells and whistles with their products, but ones that are functional and sturdy that work in the rural environment. Hence, pricing of product offerings with respect to value becomes crucial. Since affordability does not mean selling cheap and low quality products, companies have to take innovative approaches to meet customers' expectations within their ability to pay (see Mini Case Study 1.3).

Assuming that the product is made available, companies have to make their products acceptable to rural people. Products that are designed specifically for rural markets—fulfilling a felt need or delivering value—stand a better chance of getting accepted. This means that companies must understand the rural consumers and think creatively to solve their problems.

Mini Case Study 1.3

Affordability

Companies often resort to small packs to enter rural markets. This encourages trial purchase and people can try out and use a consumer product that they otherwise would not. Small packs also make the product affordable but companies face problems related to transportation and distribution. Though they work in some categories, are small packs the magic strategy to conquer rural markets?

This is because micro-packs find it difficult to achieve profitable volumes. Coca-Cola introduced its 'Chhota Coke' priced at ₹5 in 2004, making it affordable. Pepsi too followed suit. However, the company struggled to manage costs and make a profit at that price point. It found that the packaging cost for small packs was higher. For the Chhota Coke, the packaging costs worked out to 33 per cent of total cost, compared to 16 per cent for a one-litre bottle.

Both companies found that the ₹5 price point was just not feasible. They had to subsequently raise the price by ₹2, vacating the price point altogether. Since then, both firms have been cautious in their approach when targeting the BoP with low priced products.

To get over the cost of glass bottles for small packs, Coke re-entered its powdered ready-to-drink orange-flavoured drink called Fanta Fun Taste at ₹5 in sachets. Pepsi launched Lehar Gluco+, a lemon-flavoured drink in 200 ml packs in a plastic cup, under its joint venture with Tata Global Beverages. The plastic cups, similar to ice cream cups, make the cost of packaging viable. The idea was to reduce the packaging material cost per serving.

In 2004, Godrej introduced three brands of Cinthol, Fair Glow and Godrej in 50 gm packs, priced at ₹4–5, meant specifically for Madhya Pradesh, Bihar and Uttar Pradesh—the BIMARU states. HUL launched a variant of its largest selling soap brand, Lifebuoy, at ₹2 for 50 gm to target the rural market.

Parle Agro has been marketing conical tetrapacks of Frooti for ₹5. First launched in 2004, Tetra Classic Aseptic packs were initially available for ₹2.50 for 65 ml. The company later increased the quantity of the beverage to 100 ml and 200 ml packs as well. Parle Agro says that these packs do not require much refrigeration and is using distribution through tea stalls, fruit shops and other small unconventional outlets. As a result, distribution reach has significantly improved for the company.

Nestlé and GlaxoSmithKline Consumer Healthcare (GSK) too launched products for rural markets. Nestlé launched a low-priced variant of Maggi noodles developed for the rural and semi-urban markets. 'Rasile Chow' is gravy noodles at ₹4, 'Maggi Masala Magic' is a taste enhancer in single-use sachets priced at ₹2 each. GlaxoSmithKline launched 'Asha', a milk food–drink under the Horlicks brand for rural consumers in Andhra Pradesh. Asha is 40 per cent cheaper than the regular variant of Horlicks. Coca-Cola launched a fortified beverage called 'Vitigo' in 18 gm sachets at ₹2.50 each across villages in Odisha. The Company tied up with a microfinance institution, BISWA, for distribution.

HUL's 'Operation Bharat' tapped rural markets through low priced sample packets of its toothpaste, fairness cream, shampoo, cream and other products. CavinKare, which makes Nyle and Chik shampoos and Fairever Fairness Cream, marketed sachets with a price tag of ₹1 and are among the company's strongest volume drivers. Liquefied petroleum gas (LPG) companies have introduced small-sized cylinders, ensuring that price remains affordable. Bharti Airtel lowered its recharge sizes by launching a ₹10 coupon valid for 10 days for the rural markets. Idea Cellular had also introduced rural calling card that charged only 50 paisa per minute for a local call. Philips and even Eveready have brought out cheap lanterns to replace the kerosene ones, specifically targeted for the rural market.

Is lowering strategy a long-term solution? How should companies respond?

Source for this Case Study:

Business Standard. 2011. "The ₹5 Conundrum." 8 July. Available at: http://www.business-standard.com/article/management/the-rs-5-conundrum-111070800033_1.html (Accessed on 18 April 2017).

Place—Availability

Since villages are scattered over large distances, companies have to focus on availability by building distribution channels that are able to fulfil small orders on a regular basis. The task is not easy, as rural roads and transportations are not dependable. Companies are thus unable to build regular supply channels. Many depend on their dealers who send goods only when it is economically viable for them. This results in irregular supply. But building supply channels for India's more than 6 lakh villages spread over 3.2 million sq. km is more than a logistical task.

Product availability and visibility affects purchase decision and brand choice, volumes and market share. But distributors do not find it economically feasible to send stocks, and collecting payments is not an easy task. Companies have traditionally relied on distributors, hiring sub-dealers or travelling traders. These traders visit the nearby town, load their vans with an assortment of goods and sell in villages (see Chapter 6). Making use of sub-stockist or sub-dealers in rural India has been found to be successful for many product categories but deep penetration cannot be achieved.

Other companies have adopted direct selling, using company delivery vans, tying up with noncompeting companies or setting up stalls in rural melas or *haats* (markets, held on a regular basis in rural areas). A variety of vehicles, including autorickshaws, bullock carts and even boats in the backwaters of Kerala are used. Rural markets or *mandis* (wholesale agricultural markets) are used for direct sales by many companies. Bharat Petroleum Corporation Limited initiated a 'Rural Marketing Vehicle' designed for the supply of cooking gas to villages.

Some large companies have got over the problem of availability by creating a whole ecosystem from the scratch and tried to remove market separations. By helping rural people, they created supply chains as well as fulfilled their social responsibility (see Mini Case Study 1.4). Schemes, as ITC's e-choupal have provided rural infrastructure and resulted in creating supply chains to rural areas.

Mini Case Study 1.4

Tackling Availability

In rural marketing, a major challenge is to supply small quantities of goods to distant, remote villages. Dealers are hesitant to commit resources to go deep into the hinterland for small volumes. Companies have tackled these problems in different ways.

HUL has built a strong distribution system called Project Shakti by organizing village women called Shakti Ammas into self-help groups (SHGs), which helps its brands reach the interiors of the rural market (see Chapter 8). Coca-Cola has a hub-and-spoke distribution model to reach villages. The company depot supplies its large distributors twice a week. These large distributors act as hubs and they in turn appoint and supply to smaller distributors in adjoining areas.

To reach distant villages, small vehicles are used. Cycle, auto, hand-cart and camel-cart are used to transport small quantities of goods. Others share marketing resources through horizontal marketing approaches. Airtel and Samsung, for instance, tied up with IFFCO to sell their mobiles and services. Airtel has also set up rural centres called 'I serve' to provide services in rural areas. These centres help to activate, reactive and recharge mobile connections, sell SIM cards and provide value-added services.

Photo 1.1
Transporting goods to villages often means using cheap and innovative methods.

Source: Photograph by Dinesh Kumar.

Idea Cellular introduced a rural calling card and for after-sales service, it introduced 'Care Vans', which go village-to-village every month following a fixed route to cover a cluster of villages in one outing.

Hero Honda followed a hub-and-spoke model in channelizing its products in rural areas. In order to meet the sales requirements of rural areas, it has started the concept of 'services on wheels.'

Rural distribution is a major challenge in rural marketing. How can firms provide low-priced goods when costs of distribution (small packages, long distances, small vehicles) are high?

Promotion—Awareness

There are three main problems in rural promotions. First, these have to focus on creating awareness in the local idiom. Second, since the reach of the mass media is limited in rural areas, companies have to depend on below-the-line (BTL) techniques, which are difficult and costly to organize over a very large number of villages. Third, the communication has to be region specific, so the messages have to be changed for every micro-market. Companies that are tuned to using mass media through uniform national campaigns, thus have to change their entire approach towards creating awareness.

Much of the focus on spreading awareness is on the 'communication mix' that works in urban markets. In rural areas, the need is to start social movements that can accelerate diffusion of products and ideas across the population. How Dr Muhammad Yunus spread the idea of microcredit as explained in Mini Case Study 1.5, but, as Kumar (2015) writes, "If a movement is seen as a quick marketing fix, it is highly unlikely to succeed."

Though television penetration has increased, availability of electricity remains a problem. That is why, BTL campaigns using targeted, unconventional media must be used. Events, such as fairs and festivals are occasions for brand communication, since outings are rare and those are means of enjoyment and splurging. Local fairs and festivals thus hold a special place in rural marketing. Cinema vans, shop-fronts, walls are other means that have been utilized to increase brand visibility. Using traditional arts is also very effective in its awareness campaigns in rural areas. The key dilemma for companies is to reach rural areas without hurting the company's profit margins.

Mini Case Study 1.5

Spreading Awareness

Spreading awareness in areas where media reach is limited, poses a great challenge for companies. They have to rely on non-traditional, BTL techniques to reach rural consumers, even though such efforts are time consuming and involve great efforts. Even the BTL techniques have to be modified for rural areas.

When Dr Muhammad Yunus started microcredit in Bangladesh, spreading awareness was a long and arduous process because of firmly entrenched social norms. Even talking to the target consumers—the women—was prohibited. So, how was he to spread the idea of microfinance? He describes how people were made aware of the idea in his book, *Banker to the Poor* (2007):

> Because of the rules of purdah, we never dared enter women's houses...I would stand in a clearing between several houses, so that everyone could see me and observe my behaviour. I usually brought one of my female students with me. This go-between would enter the house, introduce me, and speak on my behalf. She would then bring back any questions the women might have. I would answer the questions, and back the girl would go. Sometimes she would shuttle back and forth for over an hour...often the young girl would not catch all my ideas or the women's questions would get jumbled.

Very often awareness is spread in villages through person-to-person interaction. Explaining how health care ideas spread, Gawande (2013) explains, "Though we yearn for technological solutions, people talking to people is still the way that habits change." That is to say, companies have to start a buzz and get people talking about products.

Events and mobile vans get people to experience products and start the buzz. Godrej Consumer Products uses radio to reach the local people in their language. Coca-Cola uses a combination of TV, cinema and radio to reach rural households. LG Electronics uses vans and road shows in local languages. Idea Cellular incorporated the folklore art form of Burra Katha (a travelling theatre troupe) to create brand awareness in Andhra Pradesh. HUL relies heavily on BTL campaigns to reach villages. Promotional events are organized both by the company and its stockists through mobile vans in villages. Such events are described in detail in Chapter 7.

How can companies start buzz or social movements in rural areas?

Sources for this Case Study:

Gawande, Atul. 2013. "Slow Ideas." *The New Yorker,* 29 July. Available at: http://www.newyorker.com/magazine/2013/07/29/slow-ideas (Accessed on 12 May 2017).

Yunus, Muhammad. 2007. *Banker to the Poor: Microlending and the Battle against World Poverty.* 3rd Edition; New York: Public Affairs.

The 4A approach helps in building rural marketing strategy distinct from strategies followed elsewhere and provides a framework for an understanding that would be more successful in such areas. An addition to this, there is the 5D framework, described in the next section, which has a somewhat different approach.

5D Framework

The 5D framework proposed by Bhan (2009) gives another aspect to rural marketing and stresses on the need for design, distribution, demand, development and dignity.

It looks at products from the point of view of customers—that all products or services must have an immediate value for BoP consumers. Through *design,* they should provide value to rural consumers, *distribution* should ensure easy availability, *demand* has to be created and then matched by supply, *development* improves the purchasing power of consumers and *dignity* means not talking down to consumers. The basis of this approach is that those in the lower income strata, particularly in the developing world, are not really 'consumers' but extremely careful 'money managers' who must allocate resources for betterment of their families. Expenses are often seen as investments that give the best returns.

Products meant for rural areas must satisfy some unmet needs and also enhance the livelihood or quality of life of rural consumers. All products have to, therefore, focus on benefits and keep into account the ground realities in which the product will be bought and consumed. The 5D elements are explained here.

Design

Products must be designed specifically for rural areas. Merely offering cheaper versions by lowering quality would be a bad strategy. Instead, companies have to invest in 'reverse engineering', which means starting with the price the customer can pay, then innovating to deliver products and thereby make a profit. That is why design plays an important role and offerings must be redesigned to meet customer needs. There are many examples of such redesign efforts that have delivered value to rural customers and profits to companies (see Chapter 12). Low-cost refrigerators that work on limited or no electricity supply, reusable packaging, solar charging batteries that power small lighting sources, portable medical devices and so on have been designed to meet marketing realities in rural areas. Companies often make the mistake of treating rural customers like those in the west who have to be attracted to products in the face of almost unlimited choices, but in rural markets the customer has very limited choices and must perceive value in the product.

Distribution

There is a need to strike alliances among companies to reach remote areas. Since traditional channels do not work, innovative distribution methods are used in rural areas (see Mini Case Study 1.6). Distribution in rural areas must be lean and incur low cost. Channels must acquire the ability to cater to small demand from scattered areas and somehow reach goods where they are needed in time. Chapter 6 describes some initiatives that are very effective in rural areas.

Demand

Several challenges arise in managing demand. First is to communicate with customers so that they get interested in products, second is supplying small quantities on a regular basis and third is keeping in constant touch with consumers to assess future demand. In cities, wholesalers aggregate demand and place orders in economic quantities, but in rural areas retailers are small and demand is difficult to assess.

Development

Companies have to invest in the social and economic development of communities they wish to serve commercially in order to raise the incomes of the people living in them. Initiatives to increase employment or to improve education and health will have impact on their earning power, thereby increasing the market size. It may be argued that development cannot be done by private companies and is in the purview of government agencies. But unless people get more incomes, they will hardly be able to buy the products, no matter how good they are. Collaborations with other companies, investments in technology and working with NGOs are ways of developing and serving rural markets.

Dignity

This is an important addition to the rural marketing framework that is ignored by other models. Companies often start selling lower quality goods in rural areas, which labels the consumer in a way that is demeaning to them. Rural consumers do not want to be talked down to nor they want to see themselves as being deprived. That makes rural marketing quite complex. Marketing managers trained in traditional marketing practices will have to change their mindset and develop new sets of tools keeping in mind the dignity of consumers.

Mini Case Study 1.6

Using Distribution Channels Creatively

"Coca-Cola seems to get everywhere in developing countries, yet essential medicines don't. Why?" This question is asked on the website www.colalife.org, which promises to "build unlikely alliances to save children's lives." It shows how the networks that Coca-Cola and other companies can open up their supply chains for distributing simple medicines to remote areas.

PHOTO 1.2
Colalife uses the manual distribution system to send medicines to remote areas.

Source: http://www.colalife.org/2009/08/15/colalife-mdcs-and-coca-colas-manual-distribution-system/ (Accessed on 18 April 2017). Under Creative Commons license.

Using Coca-Cola's manual distribution system, colalife sends medicines to remote areas in Africa by inserting a packet in the soft drinks crate (Photo 1.2). It has also developed Kit Yamoyo (Photo 1.3), an anti-diarrhoea kit that contains 4g/200ml sachets of Oral Rehydration Salts (ORS), Zinc, Soap and an instruction leaflet. The Kit Yamoyo packaging acts as a measuring device for the water needed to make up the ORS. It has won Product Design and Ethical Product of the Year awards for 2013. Both the product and the packaging work very well together—the packaging and the kit design fits into Coca-Cola crates.

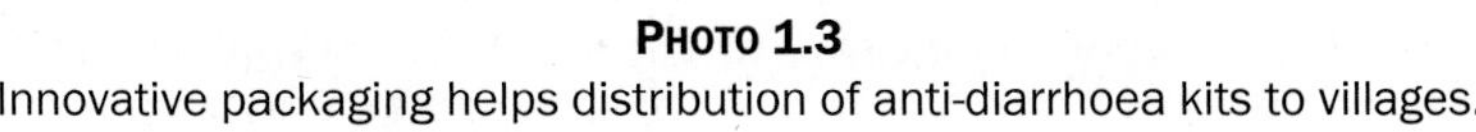

PHOTO 1.3

Innovative packaging helps distribution of anti-diarrhoea kits to villages.

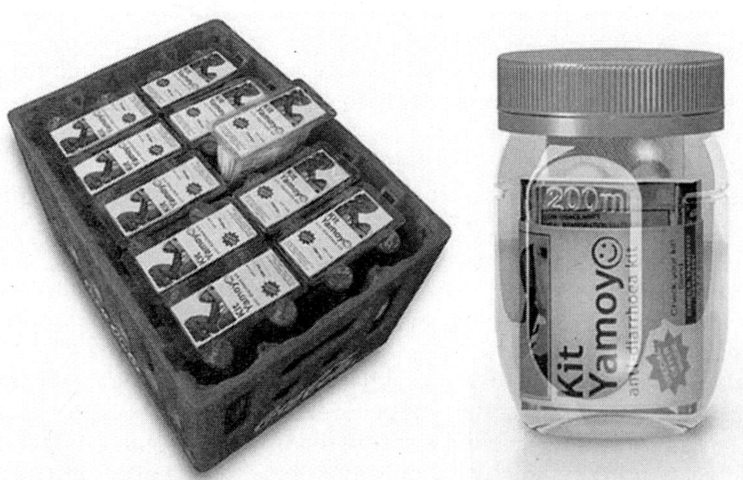

Source: http://www.colalife.org/2013/10/15/kit-yamoyo-packaging-looking-to-the-future/ (Accessed on 27 April 2017).

This is an example of innovative distribution and creative collaborations to send products to remote areas.

Can companies collaborate to create common distribution channels in villages? How?

Source for this Case Study:

Berry, S. 2009. "ColaLife, MDCs and Coca-Cola's Manual Distribution System." *Colalife*, 15 August. Available at: http://www.colalife.org/2009/08/15/colalife-mdcs-and-coca-colas-manual-distribution-system/ (Accessed on 18 April 2017).

Both the 4A and the 5D frameworks can be explained as measures in trying to remove *market separations* between companies and consumers. The theory of market separations, explained in the next section, shows how marketing can be seen as removing separations between exchange and consumption, which is quite relevant in rural areas.

Theory of Market Separations

Rural marketing cannot be understood without understanding the theory of market separations. According to this theory, producers and consumers are separate and marketing tries to remove the separations to cause consumption to occur. Seen in this light, marketing acquires quite a different meaning from the ideas perpetrated in popular literature.

Bartels (1968) has given a definition of marketing based on separations as follows: "Marketing is the process whereby society, to supply its consumption needs, evolves distributive systems composed of participants, who, interacting under constraints—technical (economic) and ethical (social)—creates the transactions or flows which resolve market separations and result in exchange and consumption."

Market separations keep rural consumers separated from producers, inhibiting them as consumers. Four kinds of market separations distinguish rural markets. These separations reduce considerably the applicability of modern marketing methods in such areas.

1. **Spatial separation:** It refers to the physical distances between producers and consumers. Rural markets are scattered and suffer from spatial separation as distances are large; many villages remain cut off from the rest of the country.
2. **Temporal separation:** It refers to the time it takes to reach rural consumers, which is usually large. It is the difference between production and consumption, or the time taken to service distant markets.
3. **Informational separation:** Media channels have a limited penetration in rural areas. Thus, rural consumers suffer from lack of information both as producers and consumers. As producers, they lack information relating to efficient production methods as well as market conditions, such as supply and demand that affect prices. As consumers, they lack information relating to products and brands, their use and availability.
4. **Financial separation:** Many rural consumers are poor. The lack of purchasing power, combined with lack of financial institutions, access to formal financial markets, credit and insurance, contribute to financial separation.

Bartels argued that one of the primary roles of marketing is to reduce or remove these separations and facilitate the process of consumption. "Whatever is done in the marketing process must contribute to the removal of these and other separations," he wrote. Rural marketing has to be understood in this context. Unless companies take into account the nature of these separations found in rural environments, their efforts at marketing are unlikely to bear fruit.

Seen in this light, the role of marketing becomes not merely to provide goods and services but to also invest in institutions that reduce market separations. This considerably enhances the role of marketing in rural areas. Companies that have been successful in rural areas understand this and involve people both as producers and consumers. How do they do this is shown in Table 1.3.

In trying to remove market separations, rural marketing has to take up roles that are not envisaged in traditional marketing. Apart from supplying of goods and services, as many believe to be the role or marketing, it also means establishing infrastructure so that rural people can participate as producers in formal markets, thereby leading to income generation. This, in turn, turns them into becoming consumers in those very markets. Initiatives that keep the developmental aspect into marketing are the way forward.

For instance, the e-choupal initiative of ITC tried to remove market separations by providing information to the rural customer. The initiative empowered farmers by providing them information as producers and at the same time with goods and services for consumption. The e-choupal information kiosk is linked to the Internet and provides information on weather, agro-inputs, cropping patterns and other farming information to farmers. The information also empowered rural people as producers by increasing farm productivity, while at the same time building a relationship with the company. The farmer who sells produce at ITC's *Choupal Sagar* fetches a better price compared to selling at mandi. At the same time, the Choupal Sagar

TABLE 1.3

Market separations and how to resolve them.

Type of Separation	Effect on Markets	Task of Companies in Rural Markets
Spatial	Large distances, making distribution difficult	Develop innovative distribution systems, develop new methods and use methods involving local people to reach rural consumers
Temporal	Time taken to service markets	Localize production, develop poor people as entrepreneurs; develop local solutions
Informational	Lack of information resulting in inefficient markets	Provide information support to rural consumers both as producers and consumers
Financial	Lack of purchasing power results in low demand, lack of access to formal financial systems	Companies have to treat rural consumers as producers also, and source goods and services from them, thereby reducing poverty and increasing purchasing power

retail stores provide products that they need for consumption: farmers can shop using the cash earned from selling their produce. This is an example of how companies can fill the market separations to develop markets and build consumers over the long term.

We have analyzed some well-known rural marketing initiatives on the basis of the market separations they removed (Table 1.4). It is seen from Table 1.4 that only when a company tries to remove all four separations, it becomes very successful in rural areas. Companies that remove one separation (such as competing on price) may succeed for a while, but will find its advantage erode away after some time.

TABLE 1.4

Status of some rural marketing initiatives.

Marketing Initiative	Impact on Market Separation	Status
Sachet marketing	Removes financial separation by making products affordable	Successful only in a few product categories or for trials; unable to achieve volumes that are profitable
Project Shakti (by HUL)	Removes spatial separation	Very successful, incremental benefits to villages not known
ITC choupal	Removes all four separations	Very successful, empowers farmers with information and buy back
Amul	Removes all four separations	Very successful, started the white revolution in India
Grameen Bank	Removes all four separations	Very successful, helped start a social movement
Hariyali stores (rural retail—organized)	Removes spatial separation	Closed. Other initiatives are struggling
Nirma	Removes financial separation, competition on price	Successful when started, market share now decreased considerably

A company that seeks to remove all four separations has many tasks ahead of it. It has to be a multi-pronged effort, right from removing problems in designing low-cost goods to communication and distribution. This constitutes the rural marketing process which is described next.

THE RURAL MARKETING PROCESS

The rural marketing process must remove all the separations mentioned in the last section. Based on these, we describe the rural marketing process as consisting of five tasks (Figure 1.5). The five steps are described here.

- **Product redesign:** Products have to be redesigned to deliver value. It calls for innovation in both design and pricing, reducing costs across production and distribution. The customer should be able to see the value in buying the product, that is, it must make life of the rural customer simpler in some way.
- **Awareness:** Companies have to develop capabilities for BTL campaigns, arranging demonstrations and encouraging trials. They must also identify opinion leaders and have a system of approaching such individuals regularly with information on new products and to maintain relationships. For example, the Kan Khajura Tesan (KKT) initiative

FIGURE 1.5
The rural marketing process.

Product redesign: Customer value proposition

Awareness: Trials, demos, BTL campaigns, Opinion leaders

Purchase: Supply chain and Payment chain re-invention

Service and after-sales experience: Infra for providing service

WOM: Community leader and aspirational use

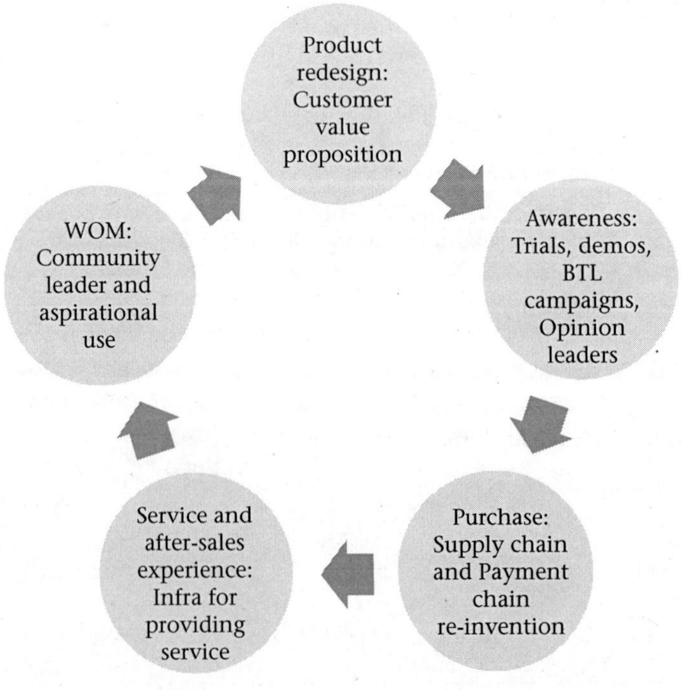

of HUL, which offers ad-based entertainment on demand, is a channel created specifically for rural areas. It is described in detail in Chapter 7.

- **Purchase:** The product offered for purchase has to be backed by supply and payment chains. These too have to be reinvented for rural areas. Supply chains must overcome the lack of transport channels and that too with regularity, while payments channels have to account for a large number of small transactions. Purchase is facilitated when both these systems are in place.
- **After-sales service:** Innovative approaches are needed to create after-sales service in rural areas. Companies have to invest in mobile units or other means to establish a presence in areas where footfalls are low, such as Honda (see Mini Case Study 1.7).
- **Word-of-mouth recommendations:** A good purchase experience followed by good service establishes positive word-of-mouth publicity for the company. When community leaders are also involved, this translates into wide publicity.

All these steps have to be done as an integrated plan. A piecemeal approach is unlikely to work in the long run. For success in rural areas, companies have to understand both the barriers and enablers to marketing, which are described in the next section.

Facilitating the Process

The reason that companies face problems in realizing the rural marketing potential is that they fail to address the problem of inadequate infrastructure, low literacy and high levels of poverty. That is why, projections of topline growth and market penetration in rural areas often go haywire and the sustainability of the rural marketing initiatives comes into question. Lack of connectivity, bad roads, railways and communication channels are big hindrances. Other problems are lack of skilled talent, fragmented demand patterns, the lack of information on rural markets and consumers, and limited access to financing options. Timely data collection on demographics and consumption patterns is difficult; data analysis is not easier. As rural customers depend on agriculture, poor crops can reduce demand projections. The rural marketing process is facilitated by removing the barriers and supporting the enablers (Table 1.5).

TABLE 1.5
Barriers and enablers of rural marketing.

Barriers in Rural Marketing	Opportunities in Rural Marketing
Inadequate infrastructure	Government investments, improved rural infrastructure in some areas
Inadequate local skills and talent	Training and skill development of local talent undertaken by agencies
Inadequate sales, distribution networks and information	Using technology to leapfrog and getting over distribution challenges
Large investments required	Improved access to financing and technology
Non-availability of proper warehouses, cold chains	Favourable government policies to build rural storage facilities

(Table 1.5 Contd.)

(Table 1.5 Contd.)

Barriers in Rural Marketing	Opportunities in Rural Marketing
Political/local resistance from local communities	Social networks, non-traditional partnerships
Inadequate communication channels	Underserved markets, reliance on word-of-mouth communications
Inadequate purchasing power of consumers	Many government and private initiatives improves standard of living
Lack of data about consumers and markets	Improved technology and data on local markets in some markets
Cultural and language barriers	Aspirational consumption increasing

In its study, Accenture (2013) found that rural markets account for a significant portion of revenues and profits for many companies that have been able to use the enablers and got over the barriers in rural marketing. What these companies have done is summarized here:

- **Reach 'the last mile':** To reach the last mile (Photo 1.4), companies depend on either traditional channels or small traders. Small traders visit towns using small vehicles such as tempos, scooters and bicycles. They buy stocks in small quantities to sell in villages. This system is irregular and is limited by the reach of the small trader. In traditional channels, the sub-dealers or sub-stockists buy from wholesalers and serve small towns and large villages. Remote villages remain unserved as it is not economical to send small quantities of goods. To reach the last mile or small villages, some companies have used the concept of village entrepreneur—individuals who sell products in their villages on a part-time basis. This 'feet-on-street' approach can help in reaching villages where sub-stockists cannot reach, but the company has to change its own marketing set-up to deal with thousands of such village entrepreneurs. Others methods tried by companies are to add levels to their distribution channels or by using e-commerce to reach interiors.
- **Micro-segmentation:** Companies use micro-segmentation techniques to locate small segments of population that are doing better than others. By targeting these prosperous customers rather than the rural market as a whole, they are able to build sizeable volumes. Technologies, such as GIS mapping help to locate such segments.
- **Channel relationships:** Another essential is that companies must build skills of channel partners and village entrepreneurs. Most operate on the small scale. Upgrading them on skills and even financial assistance to achieve scale is required. Further, companies have to build partner relationships to achieve passion and motivation. Even familial bonds have to be built with partners. Amul, for instance, went the extra mile and developed bonds with its suppliers through services for their animals.
- **Value propositions:** Many companies make the mistake of targeting rural markets without trying to understand the cultural, economic and demographic factors. But since rural consumers are not a homogeneous market, value propositions created for urban markets do not work. Creating customer value propositions in rural marketing consists of first understanding customers, their needs and how the brand fits in their lives. Since traditions and societal bonds are strong, companies also have to understand how these influence purchase decisions. These propositions must then be communicated in the local idiom.

PHOTO 1.4
Reaching the last mile and maintaining relationships are crucial in any rural marketing effort.

Source: Photograph by Dinesh Kumar.

- **Involve stakeholders:** To gain inroads into village societies, all stakeholders have to be involved. Companies have to prove that the business is beneficial for everyone. By focusing on consumers' needs rather than on profits, companies build symbiotic relationships with stakeholders, creating an ecosystem to build awareness of their brands. By integrating local populations into their value chains and creating a vested interest in the company's survival, companies align their long-term interests with development of local communities.
- **Engage influencers:** More than media, word-of-mouth communication plays a very significant role in rural marketing. Companies have to identify these influencers and recruit them for spreading awareness about their products and brands.
- **Rural customer retention:** Customers can be retained by providing reliable and consistent after-sales service. Since building service centres in distant villages is not economically feasible, low-cost service models have to be created. Developing local resources and building low-cost support infrastructure can reduce the costs of delivering service in villages. For example, Honda has developed mobile service vans that take the dealership and service right to the doorstep of the rural customer, at a very effective cost (see Mini Case Study 1.7). Such initiatives help in customer retention and generate crucial market intelligence. It also strengthens rural bonds and relationships, which increases customer loyalty and builds trust.
- **Rural investments:** Rural markets are expensive to enter, especially when companies are bound to build infrastructure. These investments yield slow returns. For example, one information kiosk containing a computer with a V-SAT connection, costs between

Mini Case Study 1.7

Honda: Taking Service to Rural Areas

Honda Motorcycle & Scooter India Pvt. Ltd. (HMSI) has launched the mobile service van (MSV) that takes the company to the doorstep of rural customers at a very effective cost. Honda's mobile 3S set-up is equipped with Sales–Service–Spares facility, according to is website. It uses a hub-and-spoke model to expand its dealership and service outlets in a mobile format into remote areas, according to its website. The company has developed its Wave 2.0 strategy for realizing the potential in hinterlands and thereby achieving an increased market penetration.

PHOTO 1.5
Honda MSV services in remote areas.

Source: Photograph by Dinesh Kumar.

The MSV is designed to display a two-wheeler, with seating arrangement for customers, a LED display for showing the products, provision for test rides and public address system to create customer awareness via regular announcements. Two service bays provide service and genuine spare parts. Another advantage of the MSV is that it is used to train local service technicians at every hamlet.

Which other companies follow such a strategy?

₹2–4 lakhs and additional expenses for maintenance. A company that wishes to provide information services in villages must be prepared to invest crores of rupees in building infrastructure and revenues will be slow to come. Cash flow will consist of indirect revenue streams that are difficult to attribute to infrastructure. The payback period of such schemes is quite long: can companies afford to make such investments?

- **Skilled local talent:** Another problem faced by companies is to find skilled people. City-bred managers do not want to work in rural areas and local talent is not available. Young people too are not willing to stay in villages.
- **Flexible approaches:** Large companies are unable to create flexible business models because their organizational structures are rigid. This becomes a key internal barrier to establishing a successful rural presence.

Ethical Issues in Rural Marketing

In this chapter, we have discussed several ways of reaching rural markets. But this carries an inherent danger: do we not risk endangering the rural way of life and rural livelihoods? Insofar as removing rural poverty is concerned, there can be no quarrel, but marketing managers must face an ethical question while selling modern goods in rural areas: should they make money from the poor?

Students of rural marketing will do well to ponder over ethical questions such as:

1. Do we have the right to introduce an economic system of consumption and show off to villages? Should we introduce waste and pollution in villages, which are necessary by-products of marketing?
2. Should we, by selling our wonderful products in villages, destroy rural cultures and traditional ways of life?
3. Is our urban thinking and economic system better than traditional knowledge?
4. Should we start marketing to villages simply because we do not see growth in urban markets?
5. Is it right to pretend to solve rural problems such as hygiene and health when we are, in fact, merely pushing our products in the guise of social causes?
6. Should companies profit from rural people, most of them being poor and destitute?

There are no easy answers to these questions. It cannot be denied, for instance, that the penetration of the modern economic system into traditional societies has proved to be disastrous to local people and their traditional livelihoods. The free market model of capitalism that dominates our approach has caused economic and social marginalization of local communities and has resulted in enormous misery for them, and they have been excluded from the development process. Indigenous people have been forced out of their ancestral lands to make way for dams and factories, while they have been left to deal with the consequences of loss of land and livelihood.

What Schumacher wrote in 1973 about the rural poor is sadly true even today:

> Their work opportunities are so restricted that they cannot work their way out of misery. They are underemployed or totally unemployed, and when they do find occasional work their productivity is exceedingly low. Some of them have land, but often too little. Many have no land and no prospect of ever getting any. They... then drift into the big

cities. But there is no work for them in the big cities either and, of course, no housing. All the same, they flock into the cities because the chances of finding some work appear to be greater there than in the villages where they are nil.

Modern development results in a systematic depreciation of village people and the sheer neglect of small towns and villages in India is a testimony of this thinking. While in marketing we must necessarily talk of selling products to and from villages, students of rural marketing must keep the ethical questions firmly in their minds. When we do this, we find that the scope of the subject increases tremendously. The approach taken by this book is to highlight those initiatives that enhance lives in rural areas but not at the cost of bulldozing them. The emphasis of case studies in this book is on inclusion, efficiency and innovation rather than imposing urban ideas on rural people.

The approach of rural marketing, therefore, must be in line with the Sustainable Livelihoods Approach of the Food and Agriculture Organization of the United Nations (FAO): increases livelihood assets and their access, empower people and increase opportunities for diversification of livelihoods.

Many of the case studies covered in this book show that companies that focus on these objectives and keep social objectives as contributing to commercial objectives, rather than the other way round, have a better chance to succeed in rural markets. As McElhaney (2008) writes, companies have to fully integrate social objectives into the governance of the company and into existing management systems. Fortunately, as this book shows, there are a large number of companies that are doing this.

SUMMARY

Rural marketing is generally understood as 'marketing goods and services to villages'. But the rural market is neither very large nor is easy to exploit. To succeed, one has to understand the framework of rural marketing. The flow-of-goods concept and the historical view give only a limited understanding, and companies using traditional marketing to rural areas often fail. Any definition of rural marketing, therefore, has to take into account the developmental aspect, which is achieved by building capabilities through social innovation. Companies such as Amul, Essilor, ITC and HUL show that this can be done, indeed, should be done.

The chapter describes three rural marketing frameworks: the 4A and 5D approach as well as the theory of market separations. Only when spatial, temporal, informational and financial separations are removed can rural marketing initiatives really succeed. This leads us to rural marketing process, which consists of five tasks: product redesign, raising awareness, managing the purchase process, providing after-sales service and building word-of-mouth communications. Companies must try to remove the barriers and use the enablers of rural marketing in order to build successful business models. In the long run, out of the box thinking is going to succeed in a difficult, scattered market.

CONCLUSION

Rural marketing is an exciting opportunity waiting to be tapped, but this cannot be done by using methods of traditional marketing. It consists of building capabilities and investing for the long term. Indeed, many companies have shown that it is only when all four market separations are removed that they can succeed. Urban-bred and educated managers will no doubt find the idea of working in villages a cumbersome task, but a socially minded person is bound to gain satisfaction in helping others.

It has to be understood that rural marketing is not about simply supplying goods to rural areas but is a much larger subject than is generally believed. It calls for creativity and innovation, not only in supply chains but in every aspect such as communication, education, campaigns, and so on. There is indeed a fortune at the bottom of the pyramid. People who wish to do something challenging would do well to serve in India's villages.

KEY TERMS

4A approach: The 4A approach modifies the 4P approach to change the focus of marketing to acceptability, affordability, availability and awareness.

5D framework: This gives another aspect to rural marketing and stresses on the need for design, distribution, demand, development and dignity.

Capability approach: The focus of development is to increase a person's capability set or the freedom to lead the life she/he values.

Reverse engineering: Starting with the price the customer can pay, then innovating to deliver products.

Rural marketing: A process of developing and empowering people in rural communities through capability enhancement and social innovation to facilitate a two-way marketing of economic and social goods between rural and urban areas.

Social innovation: The introduction and development of new business models and market-based mechanisms that deliver sustainable economic, environmental and social prosperity.

Theory of market separations: The theory of market separations says that producers and consumers are separate and marketing tries to remove the separations to cause consumption to occur. These separations are spatial, temporal, informational and financial.

CONCEPT REVIEW QUESTIONS

1. Define rural marketing. Why is it important to consider the developmental aspect in its definition?
2. How is 'rural' defined in India? For marketing purposes, what is a practical consideration of rural?
3. Describe the flow-of-goods concept in rural marketing? What is the shortcoming of this approach?
4. Describe the 4A approach to rural marketing. How does it change the orientation of the marketing approach?
5. Describe the 5D approach in rural marketing. Explain how does it work.
6. Explain the theory of market separations. How does removing separations help in marketing?
7. Describe and explain the rural marketing process.

8. What are the ways to modify the rural marketing approach in order to make use of the opportunity to serve such areas?
9. What are the barriers to rural marketing? How do they hinder marketing efforts?
10. How is rural marketing facilitated? What steps must companies take to succeed in rural marketing?

CRITICAL THINKING QUESTIONS

1. Rural marketing is thought of as increasing capabilities through social innovation. Should private companies, whose objective is to make profits, get into such activities, which are actually within the purview of government schemes and social organizations? Will it not create a conflict with the stated objectives of a firm?
2. How is the marketing of Amul or Essilor different from the marketing of McDonalds or Arrow? What are the common elements? What is the difference in approach of companies catering to urban audiences as compared to companies catering to rural audiences?
3. The chapter lists several rural marketing initiatives that have failed. What are the reasons for their failure? What mistakes did they make? How would you have ensured that they succeeded?
4. Popular literature on rural marketing is replete with descriptions of the wonderful opportunities offered by rural markets. But many companies are not able to make much headway there. Why is this so? What are the elements that popular literature ignores?

PROJECTS AND ASSIGNMENTS

1. Search the Internet for papers on rural marketing. Make a list of rural marketing approaches suggested by them. Analyze these approaches and suggest whether they are adequate to study the subject.
2. Visit some villages. Take a look at the state of rural retail there. Do you find any organized chains operating there or are the needs fulfilled by local shops? Undertake a survey to find out about the shopping habits of rural consumers.
3. Select any of the projects undertaken by large companies such as Amul, Essilor, Project Shakti and ITC Chaupal. Conduct a study to find out their socio-economic impact on the individuals as well as a village. Do you find that such a project has made a difference to the lives of people?
4. Interview the marketing manager of any company and find out what is the approach of the company towards rural marketing. Analyze the approach and suggest any changes that you can think of.

WEB RESOURCES

Amul videos. Available at: http://www.amul.com/m/video_media

A video on Eye Mitra and information. Available at: http://www.inclusivebusinesshub.org/profiles/blogs/empowering-communities-through-access-to-affordable-vision-care

Videos on global initiatives of Essilor. Available at: https://www.essilorseechange.com/website/content-type/video

A report on Essilor. Available at: http://www.essilorseechange.com/website/wp-content/uploads/2015/03/Essilor_See_Change_05_03_2015_DOUBLES.pdf

FAO Livelihood Support Programme (2001–2007). Available at: www.fao.org

Honda website: http://www.honda2wheelersindia.com/honda-launches-unique-mobile-service-van-initiative-to-tap-rural-customers-further-to-its-last-touch-point/

INSEAD Social Innovation website: http://centres.insead.edu/social-innovation/who-we-are/index.cfm

REFERENCES

Accenture. 2013. "Masters of Rural Markets: Profitably Selling to India's Rural Consumers." Report available at: https://www.accenture.com/in-en/~/media/Accenture/Conversion-Assets/LandingPage/Documents/4/Accenture-Masters-of-Rural-Markets-Selling-Profitably-Rural-Consumers.pdf (Accessed on 18 April 2017).

Anderson, Jamie, and Costas Markides. 2007. "Strategic Innovation at the Base of the Pyramid." *MIT Sloan Management Review*, 1 October fall. Available at: http://sloanreview.mit.edu/article/strategic-innovation-at-the-base-of-the-pyramid/ (Accessed on 18 April 2017).

Bartels, R. 1968. "The General Theory of Marketing." *Journal of Marketing* 32 (January): 29–33.

Bhan, Niti. 2009. "The 5D's of BoP Marketing: Touchpoints for a Holistic, Human-centered Strategy." 5 January. Available at: http://www.core77.com/posts/12233 (Accessed on 18 April 2017).

Bijapurkar, R., and Rajesh Shukla. 2015. "Marketers Must Revise Their Rural Marketing Formula Based on Hard Facts, Say Consultants." *The Economic Times Brand Equity*, 18 March.

Dogra, B., and Ghuman, K. 2008. *Rural Marketing: Concepts and Cases*. New Delhi: Tata McGraw Hill.

Jha, M. 1988. "Rural Marketing: Some Conceptual Issues." *Economic and Political Weekly* 23 (9), 27 February: M8–M16.

Kashyap, P., and Raut, S. 2006. *The Rural Marketing Book*. New Delhi: Bizantra.

Kumar, Dinesh. 2015. *Consumer Behaviour*. New Delhi: Oxford University Press.

McElhaney, Kellie. 2008. *Just Good Business: The Strategic Guide to Aligning Corporate Responsibility and Brand*. San Francisco: Berrett–Koehler Publishers.

Modi, Pratik. 2009. "Rural Marketing: Its Definition and Development Perspective." *International Journal of Rural Management* 5 (1): 91–104.

Prahalad, C.K. 2005. *The Fortune at the Bottom of the Pyramid: Eradicating Poverty through Profits*. New Delhi: Wharton School Publishing.

———. 2012. "Bottom of the Pyramid as a Source of Breakthrough Innovations." *Journal of Product Innovation Management* 29 (1): 6–12.

Press Trust of India. 2015. "Government acknowledges irregularities in targeted PDS." *The Economic Times*, 4 August. Available at: http://economictimes.indiatimes.com/news/politics-and-nation/government-acknowledges-irregularities-in-targetted-pds/articleshow/48344135.cms (Accessed on 28 April 2017).

Saigal, Rahul. 2015. "A Quick & Notsoeasy Guide to Going Rural for Marketers." *The Economic Times Brand Equity*, 18 March.

Schumacher, E.F. 1973. *Small Is Beautiful: Economics as if People Mattered*. London: Blond and Briggs.

Sen, A. 1993. "Capability and Well-being." In M. Nussbaum and A. Sen (eds.), *The Quality of Life*. Oxford: Clarendon Press.

Simanis, Erik. 2012. "Reality Check at the Bottom of the Pyramid." *Harvard Business Review*, June. Available at: https://hbr.org/2012/06/reality-check-at-the-bottom-of-the-pyramid (Accessed on 18 April 2017).

The Guardian. 2014. "The Base of the Pyramid: Will Selling to the Poor Pay off?" 22 May. Available at: https://www.theguardian.com/sustainable-business/prahalad-base-bottom-pyramid-profit-poor (Accessed on 18 April 2017).

Closing Case
Jaipur Rugs: From the Poorest Hands to the Richest Feet

This book argues that rural marketing is not just about selling goods in rural areas, as is assumed, but about social innovation and creating business models that uplift rural folk which gives them purchasing power and ultimately helps in developing markets. Rural marketing is thus a two-way street in which people are empowered as companies solve their problems, and the resultant purchasing power develops markets. Companies that do this stand a greater chance of success than those who try to sell cheap goods in an impoverished countryside. This case study describes Jaipur Rugs, whose founder improved the lot of thousands of weavers and artisans.

Jaipur Rugs is the manufacturer and exporter of carpets and rugs. What sets the organization apart is its commitment to uplift the lives of weavers with whom it works. It sources the products from village artisans, supplying them raw materials, designs and keeping a strict check on quality.

Founded by Nand Kishore Chaudhary, or NKC as he is called, the company works with nearly 41,000 skilled, home-based artisans across eight Indian states, 80 per cent of whom are women. The Jaipur Rugs Foundation (JRF) was established in 2004, which receives a percentage of the profits earned by Jaipur Rugs. A unique feature is that social development interventions such as financial inclusion, insurance linkages, health and eye check-up camps, and functional literacy workshops are organized to improve the lives of the weavers. Jaipur Rugs has an inclusive business model, which delivers value to customers while improving the living standard of the artisans and works towards their socio-economic empowerment.

NKC started the business with a borrowed ₹5000 and set up two carpet looms in 1978 in his house. He engaged unemployed weavers and learnt the process. The business picked up: in two years, 6 additional looms were acquired. The carpets were supplied to a Jaipur-based export house, which supplied the raw material and finished carpets were delivered to it. The earnings were reinvested to buy more looms.

After eight years of supplying to exporters, NKC decided to start direct exports. Gujarat was made as the main production base where the state government provided training to the tribal artisans and even equipped them with carpet weaving looms. A rapport was established with the tribals and the artisans and they were trained in weaving high quality carpets. The operation gradually scaled up. The company maintained quality control and the finished goods were sent to Jaipur for inspection and export.

Jaipur Rugs hired professional managers as it scaled up, but they came with egos and expectations and were unable to work with local artisans. The business suffered as a result. As a consequence, NKC discovered and now works with the philosophy of *finding yourself through losing yourself*, that is, giving up of one's own ego and self-importance and becoming more sensitive to other human beings. This helped in focusing on the workers.

Jaipur Rugs now has 22 branch offices and takes care of all the aspects of production—from raw material procurement to exports. To manage the distribution in the United States, Jaipur Rugs Incorporated was established. The model is illustrated in Figure 1.6.

FIGURE 1.6
The Jaipur Rugs business model.

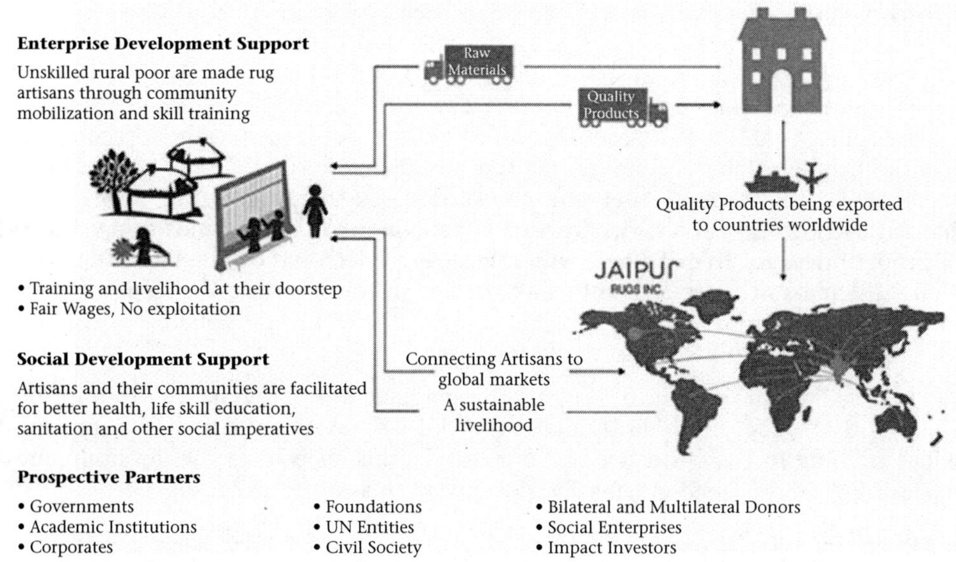

Source: Jaipur Rugs Foundation Annual Report 2013–14.

The business model and its unique features of Jaipur Rugs are described here.

Business model: The company seeks to empower village artisans by giving them a sustainable livelihood at their homes, overcoming their difficulty of travelling. Jaipur Rugs supplies raw material at their doorsteps and quality supervisors regularly travel to inspect the looms in order to ensure quality and consistent output. Payments are also made every month at their homes. The artisans are thus able to work comfortably from home and with flexibility. This way, women become financially independent and mothers with young children can work at home and get to decide their own work hours around their family schedules. Also, they lose no time in getting materials, transporting it or collecting payments. The company supports weavers in obtaining government subsidies, helps to finance cost of the looms and lends its looms to deserving weavers until they are able to purchase their own.

When completed, the rug is picked up at the doorstep of the weavers and passed on for inspection and despatch. In this way, Jaipur Rugs has created a global supply chain that connects BoP workers to produce high quality products that are accepted in international markets. It has eliminated the role of middlemen. The raw material for the carpets as well as the money earned by them is paid directly to them.

Training and literacy: Skill development trainings are organized either in the villages or in a common location. JRF installs weaving looms and trains them on the processes required to be followed. The weavers are given training to ensure that proper processes are followed. The weavers are then given the job which they do in their own localities. Since the rugs are hand-woven, they tend to have defects. The company has a mission, Zero Defect, which lays down the processes and a checklist that the weaver must follow. The concept of Quality Circles, or volunteer worker groups, has been implemented. These groups meet regularly, brainstorm and solve problems. It provides skill training, computer-aided design training and entrepreneurship development. Most of the women weavers have never attended schools and so this is an invaluable addition to their lives.

Social innovator: JRF sees itself as "a social innovator promoting the cause of artisans by providing them with decent work opportunities and thus leading them towards their socio-economic well-being," as stated in its annual report for 2013–14. It establishes bonds with the village communities and artisans. It encourages 'entrepreneurship development' together with 'social development': the first focuses on the economic well-being of the artisans and their communities through skill development and livelihood support, while the second focuses on their social well-being through interventions, awareness generation and linkages. These two complement each other. Earlier, the weavers were exploited at the hands of agents and did not get proper prices for their labour, which has been overcome by the Jaipur Rugs business model. The JRF makes the weavers into stakeholders in the business. It also gets the weavers Artisan Cards, a government initiative that allows artisans several benefits, helps them get health insurance and forms SHGs of weavers.

Health: JRF conducts a six-month-long Alternative Education Programme (AEP) for illiterate artisans and other village community members who have not completed primary education. It provides training in basic literacy and numeracy skills, as well as the development of an understanding of health, hygiene, family life, education and the environment.

Low investment: Jaipur Rugs works on very low fixed costs by decentralizing the work. Rug production is done purely on a contractual basis. The manufacturing operations such as dyeing, washing, machine carding, machine spinning and weaving looms are outsourced. This reduces capital requirement and allows for operational flexibility.

IT infrastructure: The company uses modern techniques in its business, such as enterprise resource planning (ERP) systems, connecting the production and marketing processes. This helps it connect with its geographically diverse supply chain, facilitating delivery of raw materials, regular communication with the weavers and the monitoring of the weaving work. To help in exports, a search engine optimizer ensures that the company shows up prominently in web searches, and since many buyers from different countries did not understand English, the websites were launched in other languages as well.

Questions for discussion:

1. Why should rural empowerment and development be part of rural marketing?
2. Why do you think that by solving local problems, companies are more likely to be successful than mere copycats of urban strategy in rural areas?
3. Does rural marketing consist of merely supplying goods to rural areas or does it have a larger purpose?
4. What should be the approach of companies in rural areas?

Sources for this Case Study:

Web Resource

See the pictures and videos of Jaipur Rugs. Available at: http://www.jaipurrugs.org/

Other Sources

Jaipur Rugs Foundation Annual Report 2013–14. Available at: http://www.jaipurrugs.org/annual-reports (Accessed on 18 April 2017).

Bansa, Rashmi. (2014). *Take me home: The inspiring stories of 20 entrepreneurs from small-town India with big-time dreams*. Chennai: Westland.

Mahajan-Bansal, Neelima. 2009. "The Magic Carpet." Forbes India, 27 July. Available at: http://forbesindia.com/article/beyond-business/the-magic-carpet/2312/2#ixzz43shAS77J (Accessed on 12 May 2017).

2
CHAPTER

The Rural Market

LEARNING OBJECTIVES

Companies can hope to sell in rural areas only if they know rural markets well. Merely following urban strategies or segments does not work. The objective of this chapter is to describe a 360-degree view of rural markets, its size and characteristics, emphasizing that the companies have to take a granular approach to succeed in such areas. After reading the chapter, you will be able to:

- Learn about composition, size and structure of rural market.
- Understand the features and composition of rural markets.
- Analyze the paradox in rural markets and resolve it.
- Resolve the problems in rural markets to meet their full potential.

Opening Case
Fevicol Ka Mazboot Jod

Fevicol is a brand in India which is more than 50 years old. It has become a brand name and endeared itself in urban and rural minds with clever, memorable and humorous advertising along with innovative products.

Fevicol, made by Pidilite Industries, is an industrial adhesive used in making furniture. This case study describes how it has become a household brand and a preferred name in the industry, and its rural push.

Fevicol ads, created by its ad agency O&M, have played a crucial role in the phenomenal success of the brand with an earthy humour. It has become the largest selling adhesive in Asia and is present in over 50 countries. Some of the memorable campaigns launched by the company were:

- Following the theme of 'some bonds are as unbreakable as the Fevicol bond', it started with the 'dam laga ke haisha' (put all your strength into it) in the 1980s.

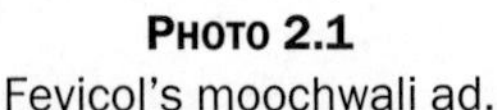

PHOTO 2.1
Fevicol's moochwali ad.

Source: http://www.pidilite.com/ad-gallery.html (Accessed on 27 April 2017).

- The 'Moochwali' (Photo 2.1) ad tells the story of a girl who has a moustache attached to her face during a school play in her childhood, which stuck to her till death.
- In Dabangg 2, the brand name was featured in a hit item number 'Mere photo ko mere photo ko seene se yaar, Chipka le saiyan Fevicol se', featuring Kareena Kapoor with Salman Khan.
- Fevicol's 'Dahi Handi' ad reinforced the brand promise of 'the strongest bond', showing a several-storey-high human pyramid built during the *Janamashtami* celebrations with the theme of getting stuck.
- Fevikwik's 'Pyaun Pyaun' multimedia marketing campaign across TV, radio and digital space was a humorous take on different scenarios from the life of a simple man, encouraging the usage of Fevikwik to common items such as footwear, mug, spectacles and toys.

The high-recall advertisements created a pull for the brand among retail consumers. Hence, instead of generating sales just from hardware stores, consumers began asking for the brand by name.

In an interview with *BusinessLine*, the Managing Director of Pidilite, M.B. Parekh, explained that the products were made available to anyone who wanted to stock them, and not just distributors, as they gained popularity. Thus, stationary stores started stocking them and their use in schools was encouraged. Carpenters were made to join its Champions Clubs, which introduce Fevicol's new variants specific to the trade. Through Fevicol Furniture Books, it shows the multiple uses of its brands.

The Creative Craft initiative expands usage through various art and crafts activities. It repackaged the brand for easy use in tubes, then glue-sticks (Fevistick), Fevicol Glue Drop and other user-friendly versions. Sub-brands such as Fevicryl (arts and crafts products) and Fevikwik (instant glue) were launched. Pidilite's Annual Report for 2015–16 describes the initiative taken by Luisa and Hervé who work with villagers to create handmade paper items in Auroville to empower locals and contribute to their well-being. The initiative produces jewellery, vases, lamps and wall art apart from paper products.

Pidilite has a strong rural focus and has set up a 'rurban' division to concentrate on the distribution in the semi-urban regions. A separate team for selling in 'rurban' markets was set up to serve the towns with a population ranging from 5,000 to 50,000. A separate dedicated distribution network was created, since in the 'rurban' market, a lot of product promotion activity is involved.

Under its social and community initiatives, it helps villages through a variety of products.

Agriculture and horticulture: The Company has made arrangements and signed memorandums of understanding (MoUs) with various institutes and organizations, for providing technical inputs to farmers. The company has collaborated with Coastal Salinity Prevention Cell for cotton, National Horticulture Research & Development Foundation (NHRDF) for onion, Junagadh Agriculture University for groundnut, coconut and other horticultural crops.

Water management: Pidilite supports activities for conservation of water and usage of water soluble fertilizers. Drip irrigation, well-water recharging, Roof Rain Water Harvesting Systems projects have been implemented.

Model village development: Kaushalya Kalsar (Bhavnagar, Gujarat) was identified for development as a model village. An initiative was started for making every villager 'Swaccha', 'Swastha', 'Saksham' and 'Sakshar' for cleanliness and skill development. The company has created a brand 'Kaushalya Kalsar' for promoting arts and crafts made by the villagers of Kalsar. Under the Digital Kalsar drive, villagers have been trained in the usage of computers. The company has launched a programme to provide e-learning facility for all the primary government schools in Mahuva Taluka.

Sanitation: The company has supported villages of Mahuva Taluka by providing financial assistance and technological interventions for construction of toilets.

Women initiatives: The company has set up 60 SHGs through collaboration with Self Employed Women's Association (SEWA). Various training sessions and awareness sessions have been organized for the Mahilas for encouraging savings, managing finances and investing in the appropriate income-generating initiatives.

Health care: Pidilite supports Hanumant Hospital, which conducts free out-patient departments (OPDs), free eye check-up camps, cataract surgeries and ENT check-up camps. Six centres for patients suffering from Parkinson's disease have been functioning in Bhavnagar, Mahuva, Surat, Baroda, Rajkot and Ahmedabad.

Education: Mobile van education in remote villages of Bhavnagar district is supported by the company. It supports Shri N.N. Mehta Memorial Education Trust in Mahuva, which provides scholarships and prizes for sports and cultural activities. The company has collaborated with FOX Broadcasting to screen documentaries of National Geographic channel in Gujarati language. These documentaries are shown in villages in Gujarat for enhancing the knowledge base of the villagers.

Skill development initiatives: A pilot project in collaboration with Government of Gujarat in Bhavnagar and Mahuva expanded Industrial Training Institute (ITI) initiatives across the state. The company has taken over three new ITIs in public–private partnership (PPP) model.

The company has collaborated with Government of Gujarat for various Kaushalya Vardhan Kendras in Bhavnagar district. Assistance is provided by the company in trainer selection, improvement in quality of skill imparted, course content and so on.

While reading this chapter, try to answer the following questions:

1. What do you learn from Fevicol's strategy about rural marketing?
2. Why was it necessary for the company to start social community and rural projects?
3. For rural marketing campaigns, which elements are essential for them to be a success?
4. How can companies locate high growth areas to start distribution in rural areas?

Sources for this Case Study:

Web Resource

Watch the Pidilite campaigns over the years at: http://www.pidilite.com/ad-gallery.html

Other Sources

Chatterjee, Purvita. 2010. "A Tale of Sticky Success." *The Hindu Business Line*, 25 February. Available at: http://www.thehindubusinessline.com/todays-paper/tp-brandline/a-tale-of-sticky-success/article1010770.ece (Accessed on 18 April 2017).

Kar, Sayantani. 2009. "How Fevicol Moved Up the Stickiness Curve." *Business Standard*, 28 December. Available at: http://www.business-standard.com/article/management/how-fevicol-moved-up-the-stickiness-curve-109122800019_1.html (Accessed on 18 April 2017).

Laghate, Gaurav. 2013. "Fevicol Benefits Most from Association with Dabangg2." *Business Standard*, 29 January. Available at: http://www.business-standard.com/article/companies/fevicol-benefits-most-from-association-with-dabangg2-113012900701_1.html (Accessed on 20 April 2017).

Pidilite Annual Report 2015–16. *Joy of Creation*. Available at: http://www.pidilite.com/company/financial_reports/pdf/annual_report_121_1.pdf (Accessed on 19 April 2017).

"The Artistry of Auroville Papers." 2015. *Auroville Today*, Issue Nos. 311–12 (June–July). Available at: http://www.auroville.org/contents/3697 (Accessed on 20 April 2017).

INTRODUCTION

Rural markets represent large numbers of underserved people. Both in terms of numbers of people and volumes, rural markets are enticing for companies that face stagnant growth in saturated urban markets. It is believed that rural markets represent the 'blue ocean' or vast unlimited opportunities for managers and are considered as virgin territories.

But the opportunity is not easy to crack. Rural markets are complex and scattered and they require huge investments and innovative approaches. A marketing manager has to operate in areas which have suffered decades of neglect and lack even the basic infrastructure, such as transport, electricity, education, purchasing power and financial institutions, which are taken for granted in urban markets. That is why, cracking rural markets is a difficult task and companies have to understand all aspects of doing business there.

We have seen in Chapter 1 that rural marketing does not mean simply selling goods in rural areas. It is much more than that; companies have to try to remove market separations so as to be successful in such areas. This chapter takes a 360-degree view of rural markets and describes its characteristics that impact rural marketing strategies. It describes the size of the rural market and its demographic and economic profile. First, we look at a BoP portrait by Hammond et al. (2007), which uses household survey data to measure the empirical size and scope of BoP markets.

A BOP PORTRAIT

The World Resources Institute report (Hammond et al. 2007) explains that a large segment of the low-income population—the 4 billion people of the BoP—is not integrated into the global market economy and do not benefit from it. It further says that BoP markets are often rural and very poorly served, dominated by the informal economy, and, therefore, relatively inefficient and uncompetitive. Yet these markets represent a substantial share of the world's population. Data from 110 countries show that the BoP makes up 72 per cent of the population, with an overwhelming majority in Africa, Asia, Eastern Europe, Latin America and the Caribbean. They also share other characteristics:

- **Significant unmet needs:** Most people in the BoP have no bank account and no access to modern financial services. Most do not own a phone. Many live in informal settlements with no formal proof of residence. And, many lack access to water and sanitation services, electricity and basic health care.
- **Dependence on informal livelihoods:** Most people in the BoP lack access to markets to sell their labour, handicrafts or crops and have no choice but to sell to local middlemen who exploit them. As small-scale farmers and fishermen, they are vulnerable to destruction of the natural resources they depend on but are powerless to protect. In effect, informality and subsistence are poverty traps.
- **Impact of a poverty tax:** Many in the BoP pay higher prices for basic goods and services than wealthier consumers. This is in the form of extra payment or effort required to obtain the goods and services. But, they often receive lower quality as well. For example, the poor often pay more for transportation to reach a distant hospital for their treatment, or have to take loans from moneylenders at very high interest rates, or buy sachets or small quantities of goods in which the per unit cost is much higher than if purchased in bulk.

Any rural marketing strategy has to reduce difficulties faced by people in remote areas. So, while companies look for potential in such markets, they must try to solve local problems. The opening case of Pidilite shows how companies must be active in rural areas and do activities much beyond the scope of marketing in order to realize its true potential.

POTENTIAL OF RURAL MARKET

The potential of rural markets in India is visible when we consider two factors: the general rise in the level of prosperity as people move away from agriculture and find alternative employments, and the large government investments and schemes for rural areas. However, such trends ignore that rural markets are also marked with deep caste, religious and economic disparities. Though recent trends have created pockets of prosperity in Indian villages, large sections of the population have been pushed to the fringes of existence.

The general rise in the level of prosperity has brought in two dominant shifts in the rural consumption patterns. First, because of lifestyle marketing, people want to use the products that are used in urban markets. There is also an element of conspicuous consumption, as people want to show their neighbours that they are modern by consuming the latest products and brands. Second, better communications and branding have caused a shift in preference for branded goods. That is the reason that rural markets are said to represent huge opportunities. The factors that have contributed to some amount of modernization of villages are:

1. **Large population:** According to the Census 2011, 833 million people, representing more than two-thirds of Indian population, lives in villages. This population is also increasing annually. Moreover, these consumers are underserved, that is, many companies simply do not have a presence in rural markets. This attracts companies who see an immense opportunity as urban markets are saturated.
2. **Market growth:** While urban markets are more or less saturated and have witnessed turmoil due to international financial crises and high inflation, rural markets have been relatively cocooned from such shocks. According to a study by India Brand Equity Foundation (IBEF, 2015), per capita gross domestic product (GDP) in India has grown at a compound annual growth rate (CAGR) of 6.2 per cent in its rural regions since 2000. Rural per capita consumption increased by 19 per cent annually in the period from 2009–10 to 2011–12. In the same period, spending in rural India touched US$69 billion. The market has been growing at 3–4 per cent per annum adding more than one million new consumers every year.
3. **Mobile, Media and IT penetration:** Television, mobile phone and information technologies have succeeded to reach rural people in areas where the government has failed miserably. These technologies are helping to bring villages into the mainstream of national life. They are helping in spreading awareness and education, besides providing much needed information about the weather, agricultural practices and prices, and providing access for public health and other developmental initiatives. They are also bringing financial services right up to the doorstep of villagers and have created channels for communication and interaction for companies to aid in their marketing efforts, increasing the potential of rural markets manifold.
4. **Impact of globalization:** Improved global information is also providing rural areas an exposure to global products and international practices. Agricultural producers can improve their productivity and earn better prices by following global practices and trends. Increase in literacy and exposure to urban lifestyles has also helped adopt sophisticated lifestyles by rural population.
5. **Increase in income and rural indebtedness:** Better agricultural practices, such as the green revolution and introduction of high yield crops, in some areas have contributed to agrarian prosperity. Moreover, dependence on agriculture is decreasing due to people finding alternative livelihoods and also because of the development and social security programmes undertaken by the government. This has resulted in an increase in income in rural areas and a consequent increase in purchasing power. However, there has also been a spurt in rural indebtedness, as is apparent in the number of farmer suicides reported from across the country.
6. **Accessibility of markets:** Improved roads and communications are changing Indian villages. They are improving access to villages to sell produce on the one hand and for providing market access to companies on the other.
7. **Improved literacy and awareness:** Due to increased literacy and education as well as greater awareness in rural markets, there has also been a change in consumer behaviour. Rural customers are no longer willing to accept inferior products and are gradually becoming discriminating buyers. This has resulted in higher demand for consumer goods and durables in rural areas (see Mini Case Study 2.1). According to an Accenture report, "Rural consumers are particularly aspirational, striving to purchase branded,

high quality products" (Accenture 2013). The report notes that rural consumers are better networked and they proactively seek information through multiple sources.

8. **Better employment opportunities:** Employment opportunities are also slowly improving in rural areas. Government schemes such as Integrated Rural Development Programme (IRDP), Jawahar Rozgar Yojana (JRY) and Training Rural Youth for Self-employment have created new employment opportunities in rural India. Cooperative and public sector banks are extending loans to rural people, thereby creating employment opportunities for them. There has been a large inflow of funds for rural development from the government, NGOs and private companies under their corporate social responsibility schemes.
9. **Government policies:** There are many government schemes for rural areas, as described in the next section. These schemes have helped improve living standards in rural areas.
10. **Better financial facilities:** Slowly and steadily, rural areas are getting access to financial services. Microfinance, loans by public sector and cooperative banks, the Kisan Credit Card—all are helping to bring rural population into the mainstream.
11. **Improved exports:** The EXIM Policy of the government has emphasized the importance of agricultural exports and announced measures like the setting up of agro-export zones, removal of procedural restrictions and marketing assistance.
12. **Remittances from abroad:** Remittances from Indians working abroad to their relatives back home have contributed sizeably to the development of villages. These have led to growing rural income and purchasing power.

Although these factors are influencing rural areas, it should be remembered that the growth is not widespread or uniform. There are pockets of prosperity. The growth in rural markets is helped by several government initiatives and schemes, while the implementation varies. Some of these are described in the next section. These schemes have resulted in huge transfer of funds to rural areas and have contributed to the development of rural markets.

Mini Case Study 2.1

Dabur: Packaged Fruit Juices

Packaged fruit juices are traditionally considered to be urban market products. Dabur found, much to its surprise, that that these products were very popular in small towns as well. The company says that growing health awareness and health consciousness has contributed to a growth for packaged juices in smaller towns. Pomegranate and cranberry juice are popular in interiors of Punjab, while plum juice has a high demand in smaller pockets of North East India. The company is witnessing the market share of packaged fruit juices grow substantially in rural areas.

As a result, Dabur has expanded its distribution of juices to cover smaller villages. In 2013, it doubled its distribution reach from 14,000 to 36,000 villages and is reaching out to villages with a population of 3,000. Earlier, 40 per cent of the overall company sales used to come from rural India, which has grown to 50 per cent within one year.

A report by Technopak says that semi-urban and rural India comprised just 10 per cent of the ₹1,000-crore branded and packaged fruit juices and nectars market in 2012, but compounded annual growth is projected to be 20–25 per cent and the market is expected to increase to ₹2,900 crore in 2017.

Packaging has become more convenient; for the semi-urban market, Dabur has a 200 ml pack priced at ₹20. It has launched flavours such as pink guava and litchi juice that are well liked by rural consumers. New variants in the form of drinking yogurts, milk shakes and a combination of fruit juices and yogurt have also been launched.

Which other product categories can see high demand in rural areas? How can packaging be modified?

Sources for this Case Study:

Bali, Shinmin. 2014. "'Awareness, Affordability, Availability': George Angelo, Dabur India." *Campaign India*, 11 August. Available at: http://www.campaignindia.in/article/389811,awareness-affordability-availability-george-angelo-dabur-india.aspx (Accessed on 20 April 2017).

Nair-Ghaswalla, Amrita. 2014. "Dabur Finds a Ripe Rural Market." *The Hindu Business Line*, 5 January. Available at: http://www.thehindubusinessline.com/companies/dabur-finds-a-ripe-rural-market/article5541963.ece (Accessed on 20 April 2017).

GOVERNMENT INITIATIVES

In every budget since Independence, the government has announced schemes and initiatives for rural areas. While there are huge leakages, some parts of the allocations have reached the village folk, improving their lot considerably.

1. **Mahatma Gandhi National Rural Employment Guarantee Act (MGNREGA):** The largest scheme of the state-sponsored employment in the world, MGNREGA guarantees a minimum 100 days of employment out of the 365 days in a year to every willing household in rural areas. MGNREGA is playing a leading role in transforming rural India. A National Council of Applied Economic Research (NCAER) study showed that the Act helped in lowering poverty by almost 32 per cent between 2004–05 and 2011–12 and prevented almost 14 million people from falling into poverty. The scale of the scheme is obvious from the budget allocation of ₹38,500 crore for it in 2016–17, making it the highest budget spend on MGNREGA. Disbursement of this amount as wage payments to rural households leads to better incomes and consequent increase in demand.
2. **National Rural Livelihoods Mission (NRLM):** The NRLM was launched by the Ministry of Rural Development (MoRD) in June 2011. Aided in part by the World Bank, the Mission aims at creating institutional platforms for the rural poor, enabling them to increase household income through sustainable livelihood enhancements and improved access to financial services. NRLM has now been renamed as Aajeevika. The objective of the NRLM is to reduce poverty by enabling the poor households to achieve self-employment and offer skilled wage employment opportunities. The main features of the Mission are to provide enhanced capital subsidy for the beneficiaries, easy access for credit from banks at low rate of interest, skill development and placement programmes. Aajeevika–NRLM is the second largest programme of MoRD in terms of allocation and coverage, designed to reach 7 crores below the poverty line (BPL) households across the country.

3. **Pradhan Mantri Gram Sadak Yojana (PMGSY):** Launched in 2000, it is a centrally sponsored scheme to assist states in providing good, all weather connectivity to unconnected habitations with a population of 500 and more. For the hill states, desert areas, tribal areas and selected tribal and backward districts, the objective is to connect habitations with a population of 250 and more. The programme envisages single all weather connectivity.
4. **Indira Awaas Yojana (IAY):** IAY is a scheme of the MoRD to provide houses to BPL families in the rural areas. It is now known as Pradhan Mantri Awaas Yojana.
5. **National Social Assistance Programme (NSAP):** Announced in the budget for 1995–96, this programme was meant to provide social assistance benefits to the aged, the BPL households in the case of death of the primary breadwinner and for maternity. The NSAP now comprise Indira Gandhi National Old Age Pension Scheme (IGNOAPS), Indira Gandhi National Widow Pension Scheme (IGNWPS), Indira Gandhi National Disability Pension Scheme (IGNDPS), National Family Benefit Scheme (NFBS) and Annapurna.
6. **Integrated Watershed Management Programme (IWMP):** The main objective of the IWMP is to restore the ecological balance by harnessing, conserving and developing degraded natural resources such as soil, vegetative cover and water. This enables multi-cropping and the introduction of diverse agro-based activities, which help in providing sustainable livelihoods to the people residing in watershed areas. In addition, the scheme of Technology Development, Extension and Training (TDET) is also being implemented to promote development of cost effective and proven technologies to support watershed management. The distinguishing characteristic of the IWMP approach is its emphasis on livelihoods, especially for families without any assets.

Apart from these schemes, a number of programmes have generated incomes to rural people and helped improve their lifestyles. Some of these are:

- Drought Prone Areas Programme
- Fisheries Development (Blue Revolution)
- High Yielding Varieties Programme (HYVP—Green Revolution)
- Hill Areas Development Programme
- Integrated Rural Development Programme (IRDP)
- Intensive Agricultural Area Programme (IAAP)
- Intensive Agricultural District Programme
- Jawahar Rozgar Yojana (JRY)
- Operation Flood I, II and III (White Revolution)
- Small Farmers Development Agency

These programmes have helped farmers in rural areas increase their incomes and enhance skills. Apart from these, there are a number of policies and programmes that are specifically designed to raise the standard of the rural people in the fields of health, education, sanitation, and so on.

Despite these schemes of the government and interventions of private organizations, rural markets as a whole are still neither developed nor accessible (see Chapter 4). While there has been a general improvement in prosperity, there has also been a huge increase in desperate poverty, inequalities and rural indebtedness. This gives rise to a paradox, that is, why are companies unable to build viable businesses in rural areas despite the existence of opportunity? The rural market paradox is described in the next section.

THE RURAL MARKET PARADOX

Almost every report on rural marketing starts with a description of the huge potential it has; more than two-thirds of the 1.2 billion people living there spending some US$69 billion annually. These reports lament the fact that companies do not serve rural markets properly, thereby losing out on a great opportunity. They are seen as great opportunities waiting to be tapped. Since urban markets are more or less saturated, companies look for top-line growth by selling in rural areas.

An Accenture report, *Masters of Rural Markets* states, "India's rural markets represent an opportunity no company can afford to ignore" (Accenture 2013). It says that rural markets are growing at rates faster than urban areas, and rural consumers are beginning to buy lifestyle products. "Between 2009 and 2012, spending in rural India reached US$69 billion, significantly higher than the US$55 billion spent by urban populations," the report states. A Deloitte (2014) report states, "Rural and semi-urban areas will be key drivers of India's economic strength in the coming years, providing markets for a wide range of products and services. The value of rural India's consumer goods market is expected to rise to US$100 billion by 2025." McKinsey's report *Bird of Gold* expects incomes to triple by 2025, and while "the new wealth and consumption will be created in urban areas, rural households will benefit too."

Dr C.K. Prahalad had shown that there is a fortune at the bottom of the pyramid. In his 2005 book, *Fortune at the Bottom of the Pyramid,* Prahalad described the BoP proposition as follows:

- There is huge purchasing power in BoP markets, which companies can tap to make significant profits by selling to the poor.
- Companies can thereby bring prosperity to the poor, and thus can help eradicate poverty.
- MNCs can lead the way in selling to the poor and reducing poverty.

The opportunity is indeed huge. Prahalad wrote that there were huge profits to be made by serving globally the 4–5 billion people who live on under US$2 a day, a market that is valued globally at US$13 trillion a year.

This reasoning has not come true. Few companies have actually been able to build profitable businesses in BoP markets. Large parts of rural areas still remain untouched by companies. Karamchandani et al. (2011) have expressed reservations about attempts to conquer BoP markets. "Despite the extent of the markets and the volume of the hype, few multinational firms have built sizable businesses serving people who survive on just a few dollars a day," they write.

It is hardly a wonder that many rural retail initiatives have either had to shut or had to scale down the operations (see Mini Case Study 2.3). The kind of purchasing power and change in consumer behaviour that was imagined by these retail companies simply did not exist.

Economic projections apart, poverty, indebtedness, and isolation persist in rural markets (see Mini Case Study 2.2). We try to unravel this market paradox by looking at the economic geography and then looking at the size and characteristics of rural markets.

Mini Case Study 2.2

Rural Opportunity or Desperation?

According to data from the National Crime Records Bureau (NCRB) reported in *The Times of India* (2017), there was a total of 12,602 agriculture related suicides in India in 2015, about 2% higher than 12,360 such suicides reported in 2014. Most farm suicides have been linked to debt, rise in input costs, water scarcity, price volatility and crop failure due to pest attacks and disease. More than 3 lakh farmers have killed themselves in India since 1995.

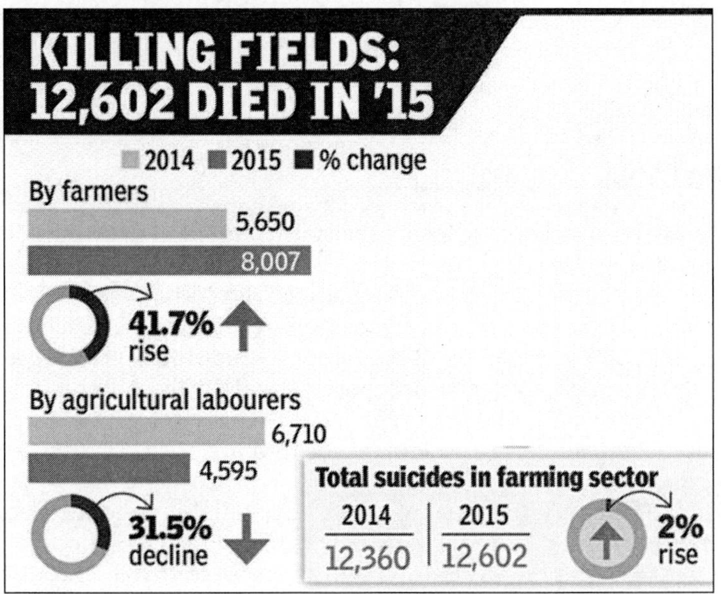

Source: Times of India (2017).

Five key states—Maharashtra, Andhra Pradesh, Chhattisgarh, Madhya Pradesh and Karnataka—still account for two-thirds of the farmer suicides in the country. But the phenomenon is spread across the country. Paradoxically, Maharashtra (3,146 suicides) India's richest state, tops the list for the 12th year in a row, accounting for 60,750 farm suicides since 1995.

The data has to be taken with a pinch of salt, shows the analysis of Sainath (2014a, 2014b). Chhattisgarh, a state that saw 14,000 farmer suicides from 2001 to 2010, suddenly has none at all after 2010. Pondicherry, has declared a zero figure in 2011–13 but in 2009, it reported 154 farmer suicides. Clearly, there is something wrong in the government figures.

Though Chhattisgarh's farmer suicide numbers are reported to be zero, its numbers of suicides in the 'Self-employed (Others)' column have risen dramatically, more than doubling in the years when there have been zero farmer suicides. This is repeated in figures of other states as well.

Do these figures point to rural desperation or opportunity? Do "India's rural markets represent an opportunity no company can afford to ignore," as the Accenture report (2013) points out, or do we go by the Deloitte report (2014), "[Will] rural and semi-urban areas [...] be key drivers of India's economic strength in the coming years, providing markets for a wide range of products and services?" Can companies that wish to market in rural areas ignore the stark reality of poverty in India's villages when they think of tapping such markets?

How would you explain the rural marketing paradox? How should companies approach rural markets?

Sources for this Case Study:

Kakodkar, Priyanka. 2017. "Farmer Suicides up 42% between 2014 & 2015" *Times of India,* 6 January. Available at: http://timesofindia.indiatimes.com/india/farmer-suicides-up-42-between-2014-2015/articleshow/56363591.cms (Accessed on 20 April 2017).

Sainath, P. 2014a. "Have India's Farm Suicides Really Declined?" *BBC News,* 14 July. Available at: http://www.bbc.com/news/world-asia-india-28205741 (Accessed on 20 April 2017).

———. 2014b. "Maharashtra Crosses 60,000 Farm Suicides." Available at: https://psainath.org/maharashtra-crosses-60000-farm-suicides/ (Accessed on 18 April 2017).

Economic Geography

Reports that talk of the untapped market opportunity in rural areas miss the fact that the opportunity is not evenly spread.

While there is opportunity in terms of population, rise in income and education levels of some groups, there is also desperate poverty marked by widespread hunger, exploitation and farmers' suicides. Sekhar and Padmaja (2013) write, "Rural India presents a baffling dichotomy of images—on the one hand persisting poverty and on the other hand corporate giants betting big on the growing potential of rural markets." That is why, one strategy for rural markets does not work; companies have to look at micro-markets in a granular way (see Closing Case of this chapter).

McKinsey and Company (2014) has worked out India's economic geography in 2025 showing the growth potential of India's districts (Ablett et al. 2014). India's growth drivers vary across different geographic units—some districts have high economic growth, others are middling performers and still others lag the overall economy. The urbanization rate of a district shows how fast its economy is growing. The report finds that per capita GDP of urban and semi-urban districts (defined as those with urbanization greater than 60 per cent and between 35 and 60 per cent, respectively) is four to five times that of rural districts (those with urbanization of less than 15%). Second, income growth varies in states and districts. Certain regions will add consuming class households faster, while in other regions, the ranks of the new aspiration related buying (but not yet consuming class) segment will rise faster. Companies have to develop their data on which districts will grow faster than others in terms of economic and income potential. The division of 640 districts in terms of GDP growth is shown in Table 2.1.

The analysis given in Table 2.1 helps in identifying high growth areas and segments. The Suzuki example in our Closing Case shows how dissecting the market into rural niches based on geography and occupation helped in identifying prosperous pockets which the company could target with tailor-made custom strategy. As a result, its rural share of revenue multiplied in an otherwise stagnant market. Such strategies followed by other companies have resulted in finding marketing opportunities in rural areas.

To understand why the rural paradox exists and why companies are not able to build profitable businesses in rural areas, it is important to understand the composition and characteristics of the rural market, which is described in the next section.

TABLE 2.1
India's economic geography.

	Rural	Transition	Semi-Urban	Urban	Total
No of districts	153	219	84	33	640
Share of GDP (2012)	12	32	25	28	100
GDP growth rate (2002–12)	6.6	6.7	8.1	9.8	7.7
Average population per district (million)	2.0	2.1	2.8	5.0	1.9
Ave per capita GDP (₹000, 2012)	33.6	60.3	94.9	149.1	71.6

Source: Ablett et al. (2014).

Mini Case Study 2.3

Rural Retail Bites Dust

Many companies have tried to serve rural markets. Efforts to serve such markets through organized retail, however, have not been too successful. The idea was to provide all needs of the rural consumer under one roof: consumer goods, agricultural products, fuel, financial services, and so on. The assumption—promoted by consultancy firms—was that villages were scaling up and there was aspiration-related buying in villages. Rural consumers, it was imagined, would love the supermarkets because people wanted convenience and all the goods that were popular in urban markets. But the volumes have been elusive. While some chains have been doing badly, others have had to shut down their shops altogether.

DCM Shriram Consolidated Ltd (DSCL) spent a decade in trying to establish a chain of Hariyali Bazaar retail stores in rural areas, selling farm products, groceries and household goods. By 2008, it had become the biggest rural retail chain in India with about 300 stores. Though revenue crossed ₹850 crore in 2011–12, it did not report profits. Its net loss touched ₹106 crore in 2011–12 (Photo 2.2).

PHOTO 2.2
A Hariyali store—rural retail has faced great problems of survival.

Source: http://www.exchange4media.com/marketing/pitch-exclusiveorganised-retail-turns-to-bharat_43191.html (Accessed on 20 April 2017).

Triveni Engineering had established 42 rural outlets, the Khushali Bazaar outlets, in Uttar Pradesh and Uttarakhand through Triveni Retail Ventures Ltd. After incurring losses for five years, it closed in 2010. The company was a major player with retail space of over 1,25,000 sq. ft.

Business Today reports that other rural retail chains, such as ITC's Choupal Saagar and Godrej-Future Group joint venture, Aadhaar, have also faced a tough time.

This is surprising when we consider the rural market opportunity widely reported in the press. It is believed that rural incomes and consumption have been rising steadily over the years. Higher support prices of wheat, paddy, sugarcane and other crops have raised the prosperity of farmers. Average wages under the National Rural Employment Guarantee Programme have risen to ₹128 in 2012/13 from ₹65 in 2006/07. The average monthly per capita spending in rural areas has jumped 36 per cent to ₹1,430 in 2011–12 from ₹1,053 in 2009–10. McKinsey also says that rural consumers are aspirational and seek all the brands that are popular in the country. It is a mystery where all the increased purchasing power went and why rural people did not take to organized retail the way it was assumed by the above companies.

So, why does organized retail face such a problem in rural areas? What are the factors that were ignored by the organized retail companies?

Sources for this Case Study:

Modi, Ajay. 2010. "Triveni Shuts Down Rural Retail Biz." *Business Standard*, 16 April. Available at: http://www.business-standard.com/article/companies/triveni-shuts-down-rural-retail-biz-110041600012_1.html (Accessed on 18 April 2017).

———. 2013. "Lost in the Outback." *Business Today*, 4 August. Available at: http://www.businesstoday.in/magazine/features/cracking-the-rural-market-organised-retail-chains/story/196804.html (Accessed on 25 April 2017).

COMPOSITION OF THE RURAL MARKET

Consumers in rural areas require a wide variety of goods and services. These consist of consumer goods for their personal use, farming implements and goods that are used in agriculture and services, which constitutes the life in rural areas. Here, the term agriculture does not mean merely growing food crops, but also allied activities such as poultry farming, fishing, animal husbandry, cottage industries, and so on. Besides these, there are health centres, schools, cooperatives, transport and other activities that require both products and services to carry on with their activity. Based on this understanding, we can describe the composition of the rural market into three main components, as shown in Table 2.2.

Rural markets, however, do not represent a unified structure and lie scattered across the country. However, they have some common features which are described in the next section.

Features of Rural Markets

In terms of number of people, the Indian rural market is almost twice as large as the entire market of the USA or that of Russia But, since the market is not developed, it poses tremendous challenges. Rural marketing is dependent on rural development; the lack of development hampers the efforts of many companies. Some large companies have undertaken

TABLE 2.2
Components of the rural market.

Consumer market (consisting of individuals and households)	**B2B Market** (consisting of farmers and others engaged in some form of production)	**Services Market** (required by both consumers and producers in rural areas)
Consumer goods: Consisting of toiletries, cosmetics, textiles, garments, footwear, food products, and so on **Durables:** Consisting of kitchen appliances, furniture, conveyance like bicycles, two-wheelers and cars, media articles like radio and TV, mobile phone, refrigerator, sewing machine, watch, washing machine and a host of durables	**Consumable products:** Rural areas require a wide range of products, such as agriculture consumables like fertilizers and pesticides, animal feed, seeds, medicines, petrol and oil **Durable products:** There is a need in rural markets for tractors and trailers, harvesters, pump sets, generators, boats and fishing nets, food processing and storing equipment	(i) Repair of machines, transport facilities (ii) Banking, credit, insurance, financial services, micro-payments and microcredit (iii) Health care, education, communication services (iv) Agricultural services and advice, rearing practices, vets and animal hospitals (v) Marketing services, dealers, storing and warehouses for agricultural produce

management of social and economic change in the rural sector which, in turn, helps in their marketing efforts. But large areas still remain isolated. Each area has its own characteristics, but some common ones have been described here.

- **Large and scattered market:** Though the rural market of India is very large in terms of number of people and area, it is a scattered market. People are spread over 6 lakh villages throughout the country.
- **Seasonal income:** Since nearly 60 per cent of the people earn their living—directly or indirectly—from agriculture, they have seasonal income. Rural prosperity is tied with agricultural prosperity and the quality of monsoons.
- **Traditional outlook:** Tradition and old customs are still alive in Indian villages. Many villages tend to be isolated from urban areas and hence maintain their own beliefs and lifestyles. Many villages still have feudal societies.
- **Diverse socio-economic lifestyles:** Rural consumers have diverse socio-economic lifestyles ranging from the very luxurious to the destitute. There are large regional variations as well. Rural markets exhibit linguistic, religious and cultural diversities and economic disparities. There are sharp and varied regional preferences, habit patterns and behavioural characteristics.
- **Lack of infrastructure:** Rural areas in India suffer from total lack of infrastructure or have very poor infrastructure. Facilities such as roads, warehouses, communications, electricity and financial institutions are woefully inadequate.
- **Large numbers of rural poor:** The market is undeveloped, as the people who constitute it still lack adequate purchasing power. There are a large number of households that have been isolated from the development process, with poor standard of living, low per capita income and socio-cultural backwardness. Incomes are highly skewed, with certain sections of society completely isolated.

- **Media dark environments:** Rural communities are media dark, in the sense that they lack newspapers, TV and other types of media exposure. Though this is changing rapidly, spreading marketing messages among rural consumers still remains a huge challenge.

The rural market potential is no doubt huge, but requires detailed knowledge to realize it. In the next section, we define the characteristics of the rural market and the rural market environment. This helps us in understanding rural markets and consumers.

MARKET SIZE

There is no definition of the term rural. We rely on census of India which describes rural as something that is not urban. According to its definition, urban means all places with a municipality, corporation, cantonment board or notified town area committee, and all other places which satisfy the following criteria (known as Census Town):

- A minimum population of 5,000
- At least 75 per cent of the male main workers engaged in non-agricultural pursuits
- A density of population of at least 400 per sq. km

By this definition, the term rural means places that have a population of less than 5,000 and density of less than 400 per sq. km, where 75 per cent of male workers are engaged in agriculture. Going by this definition, the Census 2011 estimates number of rural units or villages in India as 6.40 lakh, which is about the same as Census 2001 (Table 2.3).

The number of urban units, according to Census 2011, is 7,935. This shows that companies face the huge task of serving a number of villages or locations, which is 80 times that of towns. The rural marketing effort, thus, has to be labour-intensive since it requires a huge manpower to serve these locations.

Market size is analyzed on the basis of the following eight factors:

1. Population
2. Literacy level
3. Exclusion of women
4. Growth rates
5. Rural infrastructure
6. Skewed ownership of goods
7. Communication and media
8. Financial inclusion and credit availability

TABLE 2.3

Number of villages in India.

Census 2001	6,38,588
Census 2011	6,40,867

Source: Census of India.

Population

In terms of number of people, India's rural market is huge. The rural population of India is bigger than the total population of many countries in the world. Rural demographics show that rural and urban populations are different in terms of size, growth, sex and literacy levels in the country as well as in different states.

The Census of India 2011 figures show that a large part of India's population still resides in rural areas (Table 2.4). The figures show that the total population of India was 1,210.2 million in 2011, of which the rural population was 833.1 million and the urban population was 377.1 million. India's population is estimated to be 1342 million in 2017 (www.populationpyramid.net/india/2017). To put these figures in perspective, consider that the population of USA is put at 324 million in 2017 (US Census website: www.census.gov), which means that the rural population in India (estimated to be 872 million in 2017) is 2.69 times the population of USA.

The growth rate of population in India in 2001–11 is 17.64 per cent. The growth rate of population in rural and urban areas is 12.18 per cent and 31.80 per cent, respectively. Bihar (23.90%) exhibited the highest decadal growth rate in rural population.

The slowing down of the overall growth rate of population is due to the sharp decline in the growth rate in rural areas, while the growth rate in urban areas remains almost the same.

There is also a wide variation in the rural population figures among states. Census 2011 shows that the three biggest states in terms of rural population are Uttar Pradesh, Bihar and West Bengal. Uttar Pradesh has the largest rural population of 155.11 million (18.62% of the country's total rural population) followed by Bihar 92.07 million (11.1%) and West Bengal 62.21 million (7.5%). Sikkim, Mizoram and Goa have the smallest rural populations. Sikkim has a rural population of 0.45 million (0.1% of the country's total rural population) followed by Mizoram at 0.52 million (0.1%) and Goa at 0.55 million (0.1%).

Though the proportion of rural population declined from 72.19 per cent in 2001 to 68.84 per cent in 2011, the figures show that more than two-thirds of people live in India's villages and small towns. Himachal Pradesh has the largest proportion of rural population (89.96% of its total State population). The urban population increased from 27.81 per cent in 2001 to 31.16 per cent in 2011.

This attracts the attention of many companies and researchers who see this population as a huge market to sell their products.

However, the comparison with populations of other countries is faulty. That is because, the purchasing power of rural populations in India as compared to those in developed nations is entirely different. Much of India's rural population is poor and lacks purchasing power. There is a great inequality of income and certain segments lack access to resources. Thus, while a rural inhabitant of USA can afford a comfortable lifestyle, many people barely subsist in rural

TABLE 2.4

Distribution of India's population (in million).

	2001	2011
Indian population	1029	1210
Rural	743	833
Urban	286	377

Source: Census 2011—Provisional Population Totals.

India. At the bottom rung, there is a sizeable population consisting of the lower castes. Census 2011 figures show that there are 201.4 million people belonging to scheduled castes (Dalits) and 104 million to scheduled tribes (tribals or adivasis). This means that about 300 million of the total 833 million rural people, that is, about 36 per cent, live on the fringes. As mentioned earlier, Indian society in rural areas is still feudal and untouchability is still common. Writing about Dalits, Kumar (2014) notes:

> They were denied all the human rights and were forced to perform the filthiest occupations. They were supposed to serve the other classes of Hindu Social Order. In this sense Dalits were excluded in every walk of life... an ex-untouchable is deprived in all spheres, the social, economic, political, educational and religious spheres.

It only follows that some 36 per cent of the huge rural population that we see as constituting the rural market are excluded from it deliberately by rural society. But this is not all.

Those living below the poverty line and marginally above it also lack resources for market participation. If we exclude the poor and those barely above the poverty line in rural areas, we will have to reduce the figure of rural population still further. That is to say, the size of the rural market is considerably reduced and is not as large as it looks in census figures.

Another factor that the population figures hide is that large parts of the country are suffering from extremism. Companies will be foolhardy to send their products or salesmen in such areas. According to *The India Post* (2009), "Naxalism today holds sway in vast swathes of 10 states in the country, involving about 180 districts."

Estimates of the underserved population in rural areas, therefore, have to be reduced to a great extent, because a large part of the rural population simply cannot be serviced. Companies, thus, have to reduce the number of people in rural areas that they can serve. Their calculations have to be reduced by the BPL population, the Dalits and some tribals and the areas affected by extremism. We then find that the rural market opportunity is considerably reduced. We estimate that the number of rural consumers that companies can realistically serve is about 300 million or less than half of what is shown in census figures. In this context, many of the rural marketing textbooks and reports, including those of highly respected multinational consultancies such as Deloitte, McKinsey and Accenture, are quite off the mark. It is hardly a wonder that many companies, relying on census figures, have ventured into rural areas only to face disappointment.

Literacy Levels

Literacy levels have a direct positive impact on brand awareness; educated people understand and respond to marketing messages. The higher the education levels, the greater are the impact on lifestyles. India's literacy has been growing steadily and stands at 69 per cent as per Census 2011 (Table 2.5).

Increase in rural literacy rate provides an opportunity for companies to market their products. Rural marketing efforts are stymied if people are illiterate. Despite the increase in literacy level in rural areas, which has jumped from 58.7 per cent to 68.9 per cent over the decade, India still has the largest illiterate population of adults, 287 million, or 37 per cent of the total population of such people across the world, according to UNESCO's Education for All (EFA) Global Monitoring report. Due to increase in literacy levels and expansion of media, product

TABLE 2.5
Rural literacy.

Year	2001	2011
Literacy percentage: India, overall	64.8	74.0
Rural literacy percentage	58.7	68.9
Urban literacy percentage	79.9	85.0

Source: Census of India, 2011.

awareness is higher and companies can better communicate with their rural customers. The efforts of the government, combined with those of private organizations and NGOs, have resulted in better education and higher literacy rate in rural areas.

However, there is a wide gender disparity in the literacy rate in India: effective literacy rates—that is, the total percentage of the population of an area aged seven years or above who can read and write with understanding—in 2011 were 82.14 per cent for men and 65.46 per cent for women. The literacy rate for urban women was 79.1 per cent and for rural women it was 57.9 per cent, showing a very large difference between rural and urban areas. Though the census gives a positive indication that growth in female literacy rates (11.8%) was substantially faster than in male literacy rates (6.9%) in 2001–11, societal attitudes towards female literacy remain to be cracked.

Exclusion of Women

Another feature of rural markets is the exclusion of women. While India is seen to be modernizing at a fast rate, statistics do not support this belief. The Gender Inequality Index (GII), calculated by the United Nations Development Programme (UNDP), has actually worsened over the years. According to UNDP figures, India now ranks 127 among 147 countries on the GII in 2013, better only than Afghanistan in South Asia. According to the *Wall Street Journal* (2012), the majority of the female workforce in India is unskilled and has only basic education. They often work in very poorly paid jobs with no security or benefits, and in many cases below the minimum daily wage. An illiterate woman working in an occupation that does not require skills has an average earning of ₹85 a day; an illiterate man doing such a job averages ₹177 rupees a day.

The paper further reports that women who have progressed beyond high school level make up only about 6.5 per cent of Indian women of working age, between the ages of 15 and 59 years. It quotes NSSO data: as of 2010, India had an estimated 112 million female workers. These figures included all workers doing a job for at least 30 days in the year.

Sex ratio, representing the number of females per 1000 male population, is another indication of the market. In India, the number of females has lagged behind the number of males and has reached somewhat alarming proportions. The child sex ratio in India has dropped to 914 females against 1,000 males—the lowest since Independence—in the provisional 2011 Census report. This shows a continuing preference for boys in society and the fact that females are not valued in India. Female mortality rates are high and the share of the girl child in education is low. The 2001 Census showed a sex ratio of 946 in rural areas and only 900 in urban

TABLE 2.6
Sex ratio in India.

	2001	2011
Overall		
India	933	940
Rural	946	947
Urban	900	926
0–6 Years		
India	927	914
Rural	934	919
Urban	906	902

Source: Census 2011—Provisional Population Totals, India.

areas (Table 2.6). There has been improvement in the decade 2001–11 and the figures are 947 for rural and 926 for urban areas in 2011. However, there has been a considerable decline in the sex ratio in 0–6 age group, showing that the sex ratio will continue to be skewed in years to come. It also shows society's cultural attitudes towards females that advertisers must follow (discussed in Chapter 3).

The sex ratio tells companies about the kind of products to sell and how to target them. There are restrictions on what girls might wear and how they should behave. Singh and Bhandari (2012) point out that in the case of married women, access to money is limited as it is controlled by males, particularly in non-metropolitan households. As in other traditional societies, women are required to conform to their roles of raising children and looking after the house. Even ads showing modern women do not succeed in rural areas. The combined effect is that many women are excluded from the rural market. Empowerment of women will greatly enhance the power of rural markets.

Growth Rates

The growth rate of population in India in 2001–11 was 17.64 per cent, according to Census 2011 (Table 2.7). The population growth rate in rural areas during the period was 12.18 per cent, while in urban areas it was 31.80 per cent. This shows that though India is rapidly

TABLE 2.7
Rural and urban population growth rates (in percentage).

	1991–2001	2001–11	Difference
India	21.5	17.6	–3.9
Rural	18.1	12.2	–5.9
Urban	31.5	31.8	+0.3

Source: Census of India, 2011.

urbanizing, rural areas still have a large underserved population. The slowing down of the overall growth rate of population is due to the sharp decline in the growth rate in rural areas, while the growth rate in urban areas remains almost the same.

Rural Infrastructure

Historically, infrastructure building in rural areas has been hampered not so much by the lack of intent or finances as by issues in programme design, implementation, governance and maintenance. A combination of bad policy and corruption has kept rural infrastructure in a sorry state. This is the reason why poverty continues to exist in rural India. The Annual Report 2013–14 of the Ministry of Rural Development says that using measures of human development, such as education, health and standard of living indicators, it is evident that poverty is widespread in rural India. Despite thousands of crores of rupees that have been funnelled into the rural sector by the government and other agencies, infrastructure in all areas remain pathetic, as seen from the following indicators:

- India is among those countries in the world which have high child malnutrition. India ranks 55 among 76 emerging economies in the Global Hunger Index (GHI) 2014 and trails behind countries such as Thailand, China, Ghana, Iraq, Sri Lanka and Nepal.
- Though India has achieved nearly universal enrolment in lower primary education, school attendance gaps persist among socio-economic groups. For every 100 children who enrol in Class I, about 30 drop out before reaching Class V and more than 40 before reaching Class VIII.
- Poor hygienic conditions cause high child mortality rate. The under-5 mortality rate in rural India was 56 per 1,000 live births in 2012, which remains very high.
- Rural poverty has a regional concentration in states such as Jharkhand, Bihar, Assam, Odisha, Chhattisgarh, Madhya Pradesh and Uttar Pradesh, where the proportion of the poor far exceeds their share of population. People in these states are becoming successively poorer: in 1993–94, nearly 50 per cent of India's rural poor lived in these states. This figure rose to 63 per cent in 2009–10 and 65 per cent in 2011–12.
- With the current pace of development, India will find it difficult to achieve the crucial UN Millennium Development Goals (MDG) related to reduction in poverty, hunger and infant mortality. The poverty ratio is currently 26.7 per cent.
- Suicide rates among Indian farmers were 47 per cent higher than they were for the rest of the population in 2011. In some of the states, worst hit by the agrarian crisis, they were over 100 per cent higher.

Highly Skewed Ownership of Goods

One contradiction in rural India is that while some reports talk of increased prosperity, connectivity and spending power translated in buying of luxury goods, there is also persistent poverty. The situation is so desperate that farmer suicides have multiplied over the years across India. Clearly, the development in villages is highly skewed, so also is the ownership of goods.

Sridhar and Singh (2011) report the data from a series of village surveys conducted by the Foundation for Agrarian Studies (FAS), as part of the continuing Project on Agrarian Relations in India (PARI) that began in 2005. The data on ownership of assets across social groups show the stratified nature of the demand for these goods in rural markets. In short, the data show the utter futility of making statements about an aggregative notion of 'rural demand' without taking into account the differences across social groups. The data is based on a survey in 14 villages in six states, conducted in the period 2005–09. The states included in the survey were Andhra Pradesh, Uttar Pradesh, Maharashtra, Rajasthan, Madhya Pradesh and Karnataka. The survey covered 3,139 households.

The data reveal that the ownership of TV dominates other durables and services, with households owning a television about 50 per cent in most villages. But there is low penetration of TV in villages where access to electricity is limited. However, in Dalit villages, the ownership of TV is much lower. Ownership of radio and two-in-one and cassette recorders is generally lower than that of TV, suggesting that the TV is the primary mode of entertainment and access to information. Only three households—of the more than 3,000 surveyed over the years—possessed a computer. All three were in one village—Ananthavaram—in south costal Andhra Pradesh.

In villages where almost all the residents are Scheduled Tribes, there is a sharp contrast with other surveyed villages. Data from two villages where almost all the residents are Scheduled Tribes (Dungariya in Rajasthan and Badhar in Madhya Pradesh), show a deep societal division among the surveyed villages. The fact that not a single household in either village has an electricity connection appeared to disqualify them from accessing any service or owning any of the assets.

The differences are stark. Ownership of TV in villages surveyed shows that only 7–12 per cent of Dalit households owned one, while 86 per cent and 72 per cent, respectively, of Other Caste households did so.

The results of the surveys, thus, show the extremely skewed nature of the ownership of assets across social groups. They are a clear indication that general economic 'prosperity' is not good enough to even out extreme inequalities. They also provide a sober antidote to the euphoria that prevails in the media about the extent of access to basic goods and services in rural India.

Communication and Media

Most villages exist in 'media dark' or 'media grey' environments, that is, they either lack access to media exposure altogether or have a very limited access to media. Penetration of TV is about 50 per cent in most villages, while radio penetration is just about 12–14 per cent. However, with mobile phones with a receiver option becoming common, rural areas can now be covered by radio stations wherever such services are available.

Newspapers reach rural areas depending on their proximity to cities. They are served by 'dak' editions of large newspapers, and some local papers do exist as well. However, it is ironic that 'national' newspapers ignore rural areas, where a majority of the population lives. Rural issues are conspicuous by their absence in the national press. Limited by both reach and content, such newspapers are hardly appropriate vehicles for rural marketing. Rural areas are generally 'invisible' to the national press which lacks resources and willingness to cover two-thirds of India's population living in villages. Only one large newspaper had the position of 'rural affairs editor', which has been discontinued since. A look at large newspapers and national TV reveals that they are obsessed with politics and urban issues and have failed to penetrate rural markets and to highlight rural issues in the national media.

The limited reach of the mass media imposes limitations on communications to rural consumers. Companies are at a loss as to where and how to advertise to reach the rural population. In recent years, many newspapers have started editions from smaller towns, increasing coverage to rural areas (see Mini Case Study 2.4). However, only a few of them have respectable circulations and advertising revenue.

Mini Case Study 2.4

The Village Newspaper

At a time when newspapers are struggling in other countries, they are doing well in India because of the country's burgeoning rural, local language newspapers. India has 62,000 newspapers, with 90 per cent of them in local languages. Indian newspapers are doing well as they serve smaller towns and rural markets.

However, with most local language newspapers having a circulation of less than 10,000 copies each and selling at just a few rupees for a copy, it is a struggle for survival. Small publications, mostly published in local languages and covering local issues, are able to connect with readers because of the coverage of those local issues, unlike the English newspapers. They also publish reader-generated content. For example, *Eenadu*, a Telugu newspaper, invites readers to write about their political opinions.

Grassroots papers have also sprung up. *Khabar Lahariya*, (News Waves) is an eight-page weekly local language newspaper, brought out by a collective of rural women journalists. According to its website, the *Khabar Lahariya* team sells 6,000 copies across 600 villages in Uttar Pradesh and Bihar to a readership of 80,000 per week. *Khabar Lahariya* began as the only Bundeli newspaper in India and now has editions in Bhojpuri, Awadhi, Hindustani and Bajjika. It connects with its rural audiences with its unique local language content.

Photo 2.3
Khabar Lahariya is sold in 800 villages in Uttar Pradesh and Bihar.

Source: http://khabarlahariya.org (Accessed on 27 April 2017).

Founded in 2002 by a Delhi-based NGO, Nirantar, a Centre for Gender and Education, the paper's all-female staff has forged a reputation for investigative journalism and support of grassroots causes. *Khabar Lahariya*'s bold reporting on issues concerning lower-caste communities won the 2009 King Sejong Literacy Prize from UNESCO. The newspaper is run by trained women from marginalized communities and conducts (in conjunction with Nirantar) journalist training and writing programmes for locals.

Many local newspapers are owned by politicians. The Telugu daily, *Sakshi*, published in 23 editions by Jagati Publications, is owned by Y.S. Jaganmohan Reddy, son of the late Andhra Pradesh chief minister Y.S. Rajasekhara Reddy. Launched in 2008, the newspaper was designed by the famous newspaper designer, Mario Garcia. With an introductory price of ₹2, *Sakshi* became one of the top ten regional newspapers in India.

The Marathi daily, *Lokmat*, which was founded by Bal Gangadhar Tilak, has grown its community platform by starting a club aimed at women, youth and children, and offers free medical check-ups, passes for cultural programmes and invitations to product-sampling events for members.

There are challenges of distribution and revenue streams, but rural newspapers continue to provide variety and coverage to areas that are consistently ignored by mainstream newspapers.

How can advertisers reach rural areas, considering that many areas are media dark or media grey?

Sources for this Case Study:

Web Resources

Khabar Lahariya website: http://www.khabarlahariya.in/

Sakshi website: www.sakshi.com

Other Sources

Business Standard. 2014. "Khabar Lahariya: Making Rural Media a Force for Change." 2 March. Available at: http://www.business-standard.com/article/news-ians/khabar-lahariya-making-rural-media-a-force-for-change-media-feature-114030200350_1.html (Accessed on 18 April 2017).

Knowledge@wharton. 2010. "Medium for the Masses: How India's Local Newspapers Are Winning Rural Readers." Available at: http://knowledge.wharton.upenn.edu/article/medium-for-the-masses-how-indias-local-newspapers-are-winning-rural-readers/ (Accessed on 24 April 2017).

Financial Inclusion and Credit Availability

The lack of financial inclusion is another aspect of rural markets. This means that millions of people do not have access to banking services. Yunus (2007) describes how it impacts the poor:

> None of us like the idea of apartheid. We object when we hear about such a system in any form, anywhere.... But our financial institutions have created a worldwide system of apartheid without anyone being horrified by it. If you don't have collateral, you are not credit-worthy. To the banks, you are not acceptable on our side of the world.

Rural marketing cannot succeed without dealing with this non-stop horror story, with exclusion, which prevents savings and subsequently spending on goods. Financial inclusion is essential to bring millions of people out of poverty and participate as consumers. Financial inclusion is defined as the delivery of banking services at an affordable cost to the vast sections of disadvantaged and low income group. Yunus explains, "If the poor are to get the chance to lift themselves out of poverty, it's up to us to remove the institutional barriers we've created around them. We must remove the absurd rules and laws we have made that treat the poor as nonentities."

In India, the term financial inclusion was recognized only in 2005, when RBI, in its annual policy statement urged banks to review their existing practices to align them with the objective of financial inclusion. Since then, the country has made many efforts for financial inclusion of rural population. Several initiatives have been announced from time to time. State-owned banks have been imposed priority sector lending requirements, regional rural banks have been established, the National Bank for Agriculture and Rural Development (NABARD) and cooperative banks also operate in the area. The RBI has taken several steps to reach rural markets. It has encouraged expansion of rural bank branches, resulting in increase in branch network from around 8,000 in 1969 to 86,425 rural branches as on 31 March 2016 (*The Times of India* 2016). Some of the steps taken by RBI are described here.

1. **Opening of no-frills accounts:** Rural populations can be served if they have basic banking no-frills accounts with nil or very low minimum balance with affordable bank charges and fees.
2. **Know-your-customer (KYC) norms:** People in rural areas often lack documents required to open bank accounts. KYC requirements for opening bank accounts were relaxed for small accounts in August 2005. The Aadhaar number issued by Unique Identification Authority of India (UIDAI) has helped in this direction.
3. **Business correspondents (BCs):** Realizing that bank branches in rural areas are not economically viable, RBI permitted banks to engage business facilitators (BFs) and BCs as intermediaries for providing financial and banking services. The BC model allows banks to provide doorstep delivery of services, especially cash in–cash out transactions, thus addressing the last-mile problem. With effect from September 2010, for-profit companies have also been allowed to be engaged as BCs (see Mini Case Study 2.5).
4. **Use of information technology:** Banks are using information and communications technology (ICT) to provide doorstep banking services through the BC model. Through ICT, accounts can be operated by even illiterate customers by using biometrics.
5. **Electronic banking transactions (EBT):** Electronic transactions reduce the dependence on cash. By leveraging ICT-based banking through BCs, social benefits and those provided by the government can be electronically transferred to the bank account of the beneficiary, thus reducing dependence on cash andlowering transaction costs. Electronic payments and micro-payments also introduce safety and security for rural population.
6. **General credit card (GCC):** Banks have been asked to introduce a GCC at their rural and semi-urban branches, to provide hassle-free credit to banks' customers based on the assessment of cash flow without insistence on security, purpose or end use of the credit. This is in the nature of revolving credit, entitling the holder to withdraw up to the limit sanctioned.
7. **Simplified branch authorization:** In 2009, domestic scheduled commercial banks were permitted to freely open branches in Tier-3 to Tier-6 centres with a population of less than 50,000 under general permission. In the states of North East India, including Sikkim, domestic scheduled commercial banks can now open branches in rural, semi-urban and urban centres without taking permission from RBI in each case. Banks have been mandated to allocate at least 25 per cent of the total number of new branches during a year to unbanked rural centres. Banking services need not necessarily be extended through a physical branch, but could be provided through any of the various forms of ICT-based models.

Few of these efforts, however, have been successful. Despite these initiatives, a significant proportion of rural households still remain outside the formal banking system. It is estimated that about 40 per cent of Indians lack access even to the simplest kind of formal financial services. The government's push for cashless transactions following the demonization in 2016 may well change that.

Rural initiatives have not been able to overcome the lack of reach, higher cost of transactions and time taken in providing those services. Products designed by the banks are not tailored to suit the needs of low-income families. The existing business models do not pass the test of scalability, convenience, reliability, flexibility and continuity. About 500,000 villages are yet to be provided with banking services. With better banking and payment systems, companies will find it easier to transact with rural consumers.

Financial inclusion is essential to remove the financial separation of rural consumers. Without bringing people into the mainstream, companies tapping rural markets will always face severe hurdles of doing business there. They also have to understand influences that work in rural markets, which is described next.

Mini Case Study 2.5

Banking for the Unbanked

Marketing to rural households often means creating new business models. As noted in the chapter, rural people cannot participate as consumers if they do not have access to basic financial services. Companies must employ a multi-pronged approach: modifying products, using technology, creating infrastructure and finding new ways of reaching customers. In parts of Africa, m-pesa, a mobile SMS-based micro-payments system, has brought people into the mainstream. However, such a system does not exist in India so far. This case illustrates how this approach is helping to provide banking services to millions of unbanked rural people. Many other services can piggyback on the infrastructure being created for rural banking.

It is estimated that about 40 per cent of Indians lack access even to the simplest kind of formal financial services. Several steps have been taken by the RBI over the years to increase access to the poorer segments of society, as described in the chapter. It has encouraged expansion of bank branches in rural areas. However, despite these efforts, a significant proportion of rural households still remain outside the formal banking system.

There are several problems. First is the challenge of reaching the millions of people in rural areas and provide financial services to them. Second, small accounts and transactions must be enabled. Third, rural bank branches are often not viable, since the low volume of business does not justify opening a full-fledged branch. Fourth, products designed by the banks are not tailored for low-income families: the lower the value of the transaction, the higher is the relative transaction cost. Fifth, banks simply do not know how to deal with poor customers who cannot offer collaterals or steady incomes, or to deal with millions of small payments.

Point-of-sale (PoS) machines are helping banks to reach out to rural people as a 'micro-ATM' (Figure 2.1). Banks are using these machines to open no-frills accounts villages. The bank accounts are connected by a bank identification number (BIN) through which transactions are carried out.

BCs carry the machine with them, which includes a fingerprint reader. Once all the verification is done, an account is opened. Consumers can deposit or withdraw money using the micro-ATM. The BC carries cash to help in day-to-day banking operations while providing banking services at the doorstep of rural consumers. BCs are people who have a standing in the community, such as village headmasters or postmen. They get paid about ₹6,000 a month to do the job. Small transactions are enabled for the customers.

FIGURE 2.1
PoS machines help rural distribution of banking services.

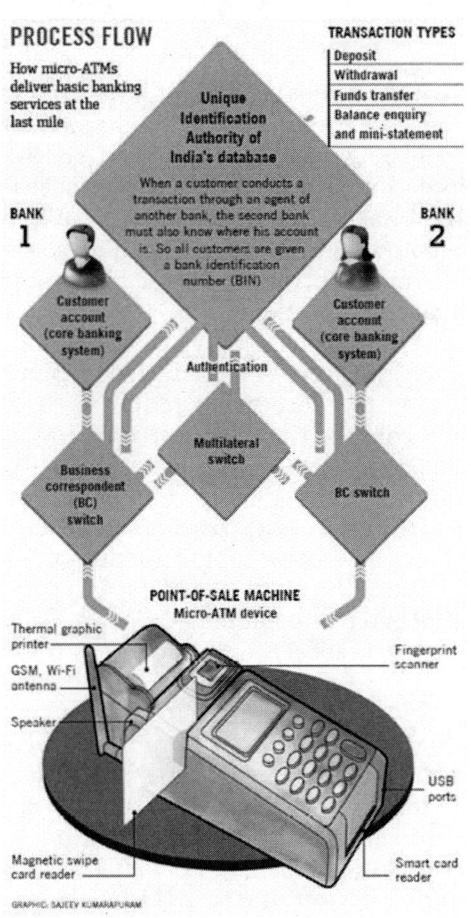

Source: Businessworld (2011).

The RBI has tied up with UIDAI and Indian Banks' Association (IBA) to make micro-ATM a pan-bank platform. Other banks have also started using this technology to help spread banking to rural areas.

It is hoped that through these methods, distribution of banking services in the country would be simplified. Apart from the distribution aspect, the initiative would go a long way to achieve financial inclusion.

Discuss the use of technology by banks in reaching rural India. Can other companies use such techniques?

Sources for this Case Study:

Chakrabarty, K.C. 2011. "Financial Inclusion: A Road India Needs to Travel" *Reserve Bank of India*, 21 September. Available at: https://rbi.org.in/scripts/BS_SpeechesView.aspx?Id=607 (Accessed 24 April 2017).

Businessworld. 2011. "Palm-top Banking." 8 October. Available at: http://businessworld.in/article/Palm-Top-Banking/08-11-2014-60927/ (Accessed on 24 April 2017).

INFLUENCES IN RURAL MARKETS

Many companies make the mistake of extending urban strategies in rural areas, but rural markets are entirely different. Malli (2009) describes the influences that operate in rural markets:

- **Intra-community influences:** Rural communities tend to be close-knit, with strong relationships within the community. That is why, rather than formal marketing efforts using mass media, companies have to depend on generating personal communications and positive word-of-mouth publicity. The influence of sources of authority is critical. These could be local leaders or celebrities, but very often it may just be the local grocer who can help brand adoption and diffusion within a rural community. Educated people, rich farmers, doctors and those holding senior government jobs, too, hold influence over rural communities.
- **Media:** The key issue in communicating to rural audiences is media access. Though penetration of TV is increasing and urban targeted communication spills over to rural consumers, there are only few exclusive rural channels of any significance in most markets. However, rural consumers are more receptive to advertising than their urban counterparts. Local media has to be used, such as publicity vans that travel to remote and scattered communities with portable communication devices and audio-visual shows. Live demos are helpful in reaching rural audiences. One such example is that of Colgate, which has created a powerful touchpoint with its Oral Health Programme. Rural consumers are offered a 'free oral check-up' and through it, the company gets a captive audience for trial and brand building.
- **Customers:** Rural consumers are slower to adopt new brands and categories than their urban counterparts. To get people to try out products, companies have to be prepared for longer lead times before their investment yields returns. But once satisfaction is gained, rural customers show high levels of loyalty and recommendation. Many brands that are no longer available in urban areas can still be found in rural India (Photo 2.4), showing longevity of brands in villages. New brands face the challenge of getting accepted, because changing rural habits is difficult.
- **Festivals and occasions:** Rural markets are marked by seasonality of demand. Rural incomes are higher during harvest months. This affects demand, which is highly seasonal and concentrated on a few months during the year. High value goods find high demand during festivals, which often coincide with harvest months. Companies thus have to understand the rural market behaviour and focus their marketing activities during times in which incomes are higher rather than distribute them over the year.
- **Entertainment:** Though TV and mobiles are increasing penetration, rural communities have limited entertainment options. This means that companies can get a ready audience if their marketing communications offer entertainment. Communications that are engaging can increase brand trials and usage. Rural consumers are more readily persuaded by marketing efforts, such as personal experience, seeing others using it or live demonstrations of the brand in action. BTL activities are, therefore, important in rural marketing.
- **Retailer:** The retailer in rural areas is just not a means to distribute goods but a powerful communication channel. This means that companies must educate retailers in rural areas and provide incentives so that they endorse and use their influence to sell a company's products.

PHOTO 2.4

Many brands that are no longer available in urban areas can still be found in rural India.

Source: Photograph by Dinesh Kumar.

- **Social platforms:** Companies must engage in social activities to build trust with the rural consumer. This also makes them more acceptable to stakeholders. For instance, HUL's clean hands campaign uses a social message of reducing disease to sell its hygiene products. Its rural marketing programme, Project Shakti, tries to make rural women independent by giving them livelihoods, distributing the company's products at the same time.

Getting favourable influence calls for much groundwork to be done. Companies would also do well to understand problems they face in rural markets, which are discussed next.

Problems in Rural Markets

Companies venturing into rural markets have to face a number of problems. Though the markets are large if we consider the population, they are unlikely to be profitable for large companies. Not only are the costs of serving rural markets very high, but villages are geographically dispersed and culturally heterogeneous, posing nightmares for distribution and marketing. Weak infrastructure adds to the woes of marketing companies as they increase the cost of doing business. The barriers to rural markets are many and are described here.

1. **Uncertain cash flow:** Consumers in rural areas live in uncertainty as their cash flows depend on agricultural conditions. "Bottom-of-the-pyramid customers aren't just poor; they live in a state of uncertainty," writes Karamchandani et al. (2011). They further state that large upfront payments are simply out of the question. In Kenya,

for example, many small farmers do not buy fertilizer because they cannot afford the large 50 kg bags.

2. **Ability to manage large numbers of low-margin, low-value transactions:** Large companies often lack the ability to manage the very large number of transactions in rural areas, each being low margin and low value. Selling small packages necessarily entail managing millions of transactions which are of very small size each. To encourage savings, some companies offer the facility of making small daily payments toward the purchase of gold as they cannot make large savings payments.
3. **Long payback periods:** Investments in rural areas involve slow returns and thus have long payback periods; many companies are simply unable to make such investments.
4. **Scattered populations:** Distribution is a major challenge while serving rural markets. Companies often face the problem of getting salesmen to travel large distances for small orders, and then sending small packets to remote areas.
5. **Informal markets and intermediaries:** Companies, which used to work in formal markets lack the ability to deal with informal markets and intermediaries.
6. **Lack of manpower:** It is not easy to find qualified managers and salespersons who are willing to work in rural areas. The severe shortage of people inhibits efforts of companies to reach villages.
7. **Lack of infrastructure:** Inconsistent electrical power, scarce infrastructure such as roads, warehouses and transport, unreliable communication systems and social norms hinder marketing efforts in rural areas. Lack of electronic payment systems makes it a cash economy, with its attendant problems.
8. **Organizational culture:** Most large corporations, run by urban educated managers, lack the culture and understanding to work in rural markets. Neither they are willing to bear the hardship of living in rural areas, nor are they able to understand the way of thinking of rural consumers.
9. **Reducing costs:** To make profits in rural markets, companies have to learn to reduce the costs of serving them. Innovative methods are needed in designing and producing new and rugged products, in sales and distribution and in financial methods. This task is often beyond managers who are used to following rigid systems in their companies. Value has to be added not by adding product features but solving customer problems.
10. **Sales and service warranties:** Even if companies are able to sell in rural areas, they face difficulties in providing service warranties. Building and maintaining service centres across rural areas calls for very high investments, which may not justify the volumes of business in small villages.
11. **Estimating demand:** Companies face the problem of estimating demand, which varies considerably. In turn, they are unable to estimate how much stock is needed to be maintained and produced.
12. **Spurious brands:** Local manufacturers supply a number of imitations of big brands. Such goods are cheaper and hence more desirable. Very often, customers cannot make out the difference between a spurious brand and the original one. Soft drinks are refilled in original bottles which give the impression of being original. Companies are unable to match the prices of imitation products and, thus, lose market share.

Despite the problems, rural markets hold promise, as many companies have shown. All it calls for is innovative ways of looking at markets. There is little doubt that rural areas hold great promise, as outlined here.

- **Emerging trends in rural markets:** Despite the problems in rural markets, it cannot be denied that a large, underserved population exists in rural areas.
- **Internet availability:** Villages have traditionally lacked information relating to a variety of uses. With the advent of Internet and affordable smartphones, they can access any information online. This opens up a channel of information, marketing and distribution of goods. Companies can have a dialogue or two-way communication through the Internet. They can empower the people by providing them crop and weather information and sell products online. By combining IT with mobile technologies, companies can reach rural customers like never before.
- **Apni mandis and kisan mandis:** Many urban areas are encouraging apni mandis or kisan mandis (farmers' markets) where agricultural producers can sell their goods directly to consumers in large towns. These help in eliminating the middleman and, thereby, the producers can earn better than what they earn by selling in the villages. At other places, farmers' cooperatives help sell village produce, providing a direct link between producers and consumers. The system helps urban consumers as well, as they get lower prices and fresh produce. For other village produce, fairs and exhibitions organized by various agencies help bring products of handicrafts and village industries to the doorstep of city dwellers.
- **Exports:** The government has been implementing several schemes to help exports of rural produce. The Agricultural and Processed Food Products Export Development Authority (APEDA) was established by Government of India in 1986, and it helps the development of industries for export by providing financial assistance and by establishing standards for exports. It helps in improving packaging and marketing outside India and reduces transaction and handling costs through a single window system to facilitate export of perishable agricultural produce (see Chapter 9). Food processing industry has also given a boost to rural areas.
- **Better farming practices:** Farmers can switch to need-based production and adopt better farming practices than they have been following in the past. Since crops are grown in particular seasons, oversupply and drastic price cuts are common in the agricultural produce. Through information on crops and demand forecasting, producers can use their farms to grow crops that are in demand, thus moving from a supply driven market to a demand driven market.
- **Food processing industry:** Food processing is being encouraged in the country. According to the Ministry of External Affairs (2016), the food processing industry is one of the largest industries in India and is ranked fifth in terms of production, consumption and export. The government encourages investments in the sector. However, a Food and Agriculture Organization (FAO) report points out that much of India's food is wasted (FAO 2013). It produces more than 110 million tonnes of fruit and vegetable and only 1.3 per cent of the output is processed by the organized sector commercially. This shows that there is immense potential for industries that process or store food produced by farmers.

As these trends become stronger and companies find ways of solving their marketing problems, rural areas may well see heightened activity in the coming years. But, at the same time, companies that devise relevant products that help make villagers' lives simple will have better chances of success.

SUMMARY

The rural market in India represents a great opportunity in terms of the presence of a large, underserved population, but few companies have been able to realize that potential to their benefit. The rural market paradox shows that even though a huge population waits to buy modern products and services, companies often fail in their efforts. Rural India presents a baffling dichotomy of images—on the one hand, there is the persisting poverty and, on the other, corporate giants are betting big on the growing potential of rural markets.

India's growth drivers vary across different geographic units—some districts have high economic growth, others are middling performers and still others lag in the overall economy. If companies can identify high growth areas and segments, they can find ways to serve them. Some companies like Suzuki have succeeded in building on this strategy of finding micro-markets and serving them profitably. The key is, thus, to understand rural markets well.

Rural markets consist of consumer markets, B2B markets and services markets. In terms of the number of people, the Indian rural market is almost twice as big as the entire market of the USA or that of the Russia. But, Indian rural areas have been suffering over the years because of bad policy, corruption in the development process and lack of infrastructure. Since the market is dependent of the general rural development process, this hampers the efforts of many companies. Rural markets are marked by large and scattered markets, seasonal income, traditional outlook and being media dark. Reaching such markets, therefore, remains a challenge.

The Census of India 2011 figures show that the total population of India was 1210.2 million in 2011, of which the rural population is 833.1 million. However, marketing calculations have to be reduced because of the BPL population, the Dalits and some tribals, and the areas affected by extremism, where markets cannot operate. We estimate that the number of rural consumers that companies can realistically serve is only about 300 million. India also has the largest illiterate population of adults, 287 million. Other features of rural markets are the exclusion of women and poor infrastructure.

Apart from the aforementioned, rural markets suffer from many other problems. Investments in rural areas involve slow returns and thus have long payback periods. Even then, there is great potential for rural markets because of the general rise in the level of prosperity and the sectional prosperity of some sub-sections in rural areas. Government schemes have also contributed to better prosperity in rural markets.

There are several emerging trends in rural markets that will help companies. Internet availability opens up channels of communication. Apni mandis and exports help in better realization for farm produce. The food processing industry is also helping rural markets in a big way.

CONCLUSION

There is little doubt that rural markets have great potential. However, simply copying urban strategies does not work; companies have to operate within the realities and culture of such markets. More than strategy, they have to change their urban mind sets. They have to learn to work with scattered and small intermediaries and reinvent their business and distribution models. There is a need to develop grassroots managers and workers who can operate in rural areas. This can be achieved if companies work closely with local communities and show their sincerity by focusing on village problems and social causes.

Companies seeking growth have to move to rural areas because their efforts in saturated urban markets will have a declining return on investment. Urban consumers can attest to the desperate efforts to sell to them through endless tele-marketing calls, SMS and e-mails. Instead, if companies concentrate on rural markets with focused offerings, their efforts will bear more fruit.

KEY TERMS

Bottom of the pyramid markets: People who live on under US$2 per day.

Financial inclusion: The delivery of banking services at an affordable cost to the vast sections of disadvantaged and low income groups.

Indira Awaas Yojana (IAY): A scheme of the Ministry of Rural Development to provide houses to the BPL families in rural areas.

Mahatma Gandhi National Rural Employment Guarantee Act (MGNREGA): The largest scheme of state-sponsored employment in the world; it guarantees wage employment in rural areas.

Media dark environments: Communities that lack newspapers, TV and other types of media exposure.

National Rural Livelihoods Mission (NRLM): This scheme provides technical assistance to states to formulate their own livelihood-based poverty reduction action plans.

Pradhan Mantri Gram Sadak Yojana (PMGSY): A centrally sponsored scheme to assist states to provide good all weather connectivity to unconnected habitations in rural areas.

Rural market paradox: Though India's rural markets represent an opportunity waiting to be tapped, few companies have been able to succeed in their rural marketing efforts.

CONCEPT REVIEW QUESTIONS

1. What is the rural marketing paradox? Why do companies make mistakes in overestimating the potential of rural markets?
2. Describe the features of rural markets.
3. Comment on India's literacy rate and how it affects marketing activities.
4. What is financial inclusion? How can it be achieved?
5. Describe the role of influences in rural areas and the types of such influences.
6. Why is it said that rural areas hold a lot of potential? List down the factors that contribute to the potential of rural markets.
7. "Rural markets remain isolated because of many problems." Describe the problems faced by companies in rural markets.
8. What are the major schemes launched by the government in rural areas? How are they helping in developing rural markets?
9. Describe the emerging trends in rural markets.
10. What is meant by media dark environments? Discuss the problems of doing business in such environments.

CRITICAL THINKING QUESTIONS

1. Review the concept of selling into micro-markets used by Suzuki in rural India. Can it work for other companies? Is it feasible for companies to undertake detailed micro-market analysis of rural markets? Are there other companies following such strategies?
2. "Most large corporations, run by urban educated managers, lack the culture and understanding to work in rural markets." Critically examine this statement and comment on the work culture of large companies that inhibit their rural market forays. How can it be overcome?
3. Though rural markets represent huge opportunity, many companies are not able to succeed there. Analyze the rural opportunity and give reasons why it is not easy to realize its potential.
4. Take a look at advertisements aimed at urban and rural markets. How are they different? How does the traditional outlook towards women affect marketing activities of large companies?

PROJECTS AND ASSIGNMENTS

1. Visit a village and tabulate the number of concrete houses and mud houses. Visit some homes and interview the householder about the brands/products that are consumed by them. Is there a difference in the consumption pattern of those living in concrete houses with those living in mud houses?
2. Prepare a presentation of the spurious brands available in rural areas. Conduct a survey of consumers to find out why they buy spurious brands and give suggestions about how companies can counter this threat.
3. Conduct a survey in your class to find out how many of your friends want to work in urban and rural areas. What do you conclude from this survey? Does it support the statement that managers and sales persons do not want to work in rural areas?
4. Visit a village and find out how many people have a bank account. How does having a bank account facilitate rural marketing? What are the problems faced by people who do not have bank accounts?

WEB RESOURCES

Indira Awaas Yojana website: http://iay.nic.in/netiay/home.aspx
Integrated Watershed Management Programme (IWMP) website: http://dolr.nic.in/iwmp_main.htm
MGNREGA website: http://www.nrega.nic.in/netnrega/home.aspx
National Rural Livelihoods Mission (NRLM) website: http://aajeevika.gov.in/
National Social Assistance Programme website: http://nsap.nic.in/
Pradhan Mantri Gram Sadak Yojana (PMGSY) website: http://pmgsy.nic.in/
UNESCO (2015): http://unesdoc.unesco.org/images/0023/002322/232205e.pdf

REFERENCES

Ablett, Jonathan, Aadarsh Baijal, Eric Beinhocker, Anupam Bose, Diana Farrell, Ulrich Gersch, Ezra Greenberg, Shishir Gupta and Sumit Gupta. 2007. "The 'Bird of Gold': The Rise of India's Consumer Market." McKinsey Global Institute. Available at: http://www.mckinsey.com/global-themes/asia-pacific/the-bird-of-gold (Accessed on 24 April 2017).

Accenture. 2013. *Masters of Rural Markets: Profitably Selling to India's Rural Consumers*. Report available at: https://www.accenture.com/in-en/~/media/Accenture/Conversion-Assets/LandingPage/Documents/4/Accenture-Masters-of-Rural-Markets-Selling-Profitably-Rural-Consumers.pdf (Accessed on 18 April 2017).

Deloitte Touche Tohmatsu Limited. 2014. "Competitiveness: Catching the Next Wave—India." Available at: https://www2.deloitte.com/global/en/pages/about-deloitte/articles/india-competitiveness-report.html (Accessed on 24 April 2017).

FAO. 2013. *Food Wastage Footprint: Impacts on Natural Resources*. Food and Agriculture Organization (FAO). Report available at: http://www.fao.org/docrep/018/i3347e/i3347e.pdf (Accessed on 24 April 2017).

Hammond, Allen, William J. Kramer, Julia Tran, Rob Katz and Courtland Walker. 2007. *The Next 4 Billion: Market Size and Business Strategy at the Base of the Pyramid*. Washington, DC: World Resources Institute (WRI). Available at: http://www.wri.org/publication/next-4-billion (Accessed on 25 April 2017).

IBEF. 2015. "Indian Rural Market." Available at the website of India Brand Equity Foundation (IBEF): http://www.ibef.org/industry/indian-rural-market.aspx (Accessed on 25 April 2017).

The India Post. 2009. "Naxal Problem Needs a Holistic Approach." July 23. Available at: http://www.theindiapost.com/articles/naxal-problem-needs-a-holistic-approach/ (Accessed on 12 May 2017).

Karamchandani, Ashish, Mike Kubzansky and Nishant Lalwani. 2011. "Is the Bottom of the Pyramid Really for You?" *Harvard Business Review*, 89 (3): 107–11.

Kumar, V. 2014. "Inequality in India: Caste and Hindu Social Order." *Transcience*, 5 (1): 36–52.

Lahiri, T. 2012. "By the Numbers: Where Indian Women Work" *The Wall Street Journal*, 14 November. Available at: http://blogs.wsj.com/indiarealtime/2012/11/14/by-the-numbers-where-indian-women-work/ (Accessed on 25 April 2017).

Malli, R. 2009. "Why the Rural Market is Different." JWT. Available at: http://www.wpp.com/wpp/marketing/marketing/why-the-rural-market-is-different/ (Accessed on 25 April 2017).

McKinsey and Company. 2014. *India's economic geography in 2025: states, clusters and cities*, October. Available at: http://www.governancenow.com/files/Indias%20economic%20geography%20in%202025%20States%20clusters%20and%20cities.pdf (Accessed on 25 April 2017).

Ministry of External Affairs. 2016. "Food Processing." Available at: http://indiainbusiness.nic.in/newdesign/index.php?param=industryservices_landing/337/1 (Accessed on 12 December 2016).

Prahalad, C.K. 2005. *The Fortune at the Bottom of the Pyramid: Eradicating Poverty through Profits*. New Delhi: Pearson Education and Wharton School Publishing.

Sekhar, S.C., and R. Padmaja. 2013. "Rural Demographics of India." *The Indian Journal of Industrial Relations*, 49 (1): 157–65.

Singh, Supriya, and Mala Bhandari. 2012. "Money Management and Control in the Indian Joint Family across Generations." *The Sociological Review*, 60(1).

Sridhar, V., and Shamsher Singh. 2011. "Rural India's Communication Divide." *The Hindu*, 26 March.

TNN. 2016. "Financial Inclusion: Banks to Open Branches in Rural Areas" *The Times of India*, 20 July. Available at: http://timesofindia.indiatimes.com/good-governance/centre/Financial-inclusion-Banks-to-open-branches-in-rural-areas/articleshow/53296912.cms (Accessed on 25 April 2017).

Yunus, M. 2007. *Creating a World without Poverty*. New York, NY: Public Affairs.

Closing Case
Suzuki: Identifying Micro-markets

Each rural market is different, and even within segments defined on the basis of economic or demographic data, there are large variations. That is why, companies have to take a granular approach of rural markets, understanding sub-groups and adopting niche marketing strategies.

The idea is described by Goyal et al. (2012) in their article, *Selling into Micromarkets*. They write that companies should look for pockets of growth within the population and identify those groups that are likely to do better than others. Companies can use the information they already have to slice and dice the geography into hundreds of micro-markets and thus concentrate on high potential segments. This strategy has been used by a number of companies to succeed in rural markets. Since rural markets are not homogenous, having a granular understanding of India's market potential helps rural marketing and segmentation efforts.

This case study describes how Suzuki increased its rural share by focusing on micro-segments in rural areas. By taking a completely different approach to markets, the country's largest car-maker has succeeded in building its rural base in the face of rising competition and sluggish market in urban areas. As a consequence, the company has been able to increase its volumes: from selling about 30,000 vehicles in rural India in 2008 to 336,463 units in rural areas in 2013–14, increasing to 415,380 units in 2014–15 has been no mean achievement for the company. At the start of FY14–15, the company targeted to sell at least one vehicle in 1.25 lakh villages, including even the small villages. More than 7 per cent of Suzuki's sales now come from villages with less than 200 households. Though there are seasonal hiccups like delayed monsoons, the company believes that the long-term growth story of rural India looks good and promising (Figure 2.2).

FIGURE 2.2

Maruti's rural growth is much higher than its urban growth rate.

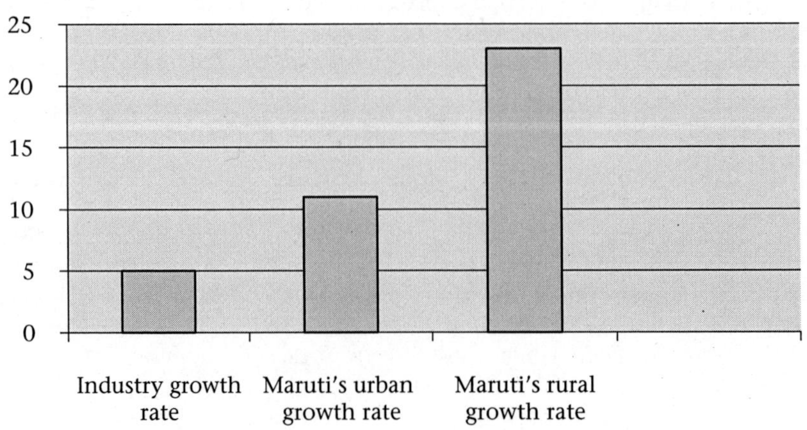

The contribution of rural sales in its total volumes has gone up from 3.5 per cent in 2008 to 31 per cent in 2013 and 34.5 per cent in 2015. The importance of the rural push is highlighted by the fact that rural sales contribute a third of the company's total sales of 1.17 million, and grew 23 per cent in 2014–15, outpacing the 11 per cent growth in urban sales. The company was able to beat industry growth rates—sales of passenger vehicles grew by 3.90 per cent in April–March 2015 over the same period in 2014, according to Society of Indian Automobile Manufacturers figures. Within the passenger vehicles segment, passenger cars and utility vehicles grew by 4.99 per cent and 5.30 per cent, respectively. The figures show that Maruti's rural success has driven the company's growth.

The company has devised a focused strategy building on the *Ghar ghar mein Maruti* campaign, betting big on its rural thrust. The company understood that rural customers were not at ease with the sophisticated showrooms and English speaking salespersons; rural customers had to be reached in a personal way and in an atmosphere that was comfortable to the target audience. Hence, the company developed its emerging market outlets and rural dealership sales executives (RDSEs). By 2014, the company had 7,800 RDSEs and a network of 680 rural outlets covering over 77,000 villages, going up to 150,000 villages by 2016.

The company has adopted a strategy to identify small clusters in rural areas to sell cars, communicating to panchayat leaders to influence potential customers. The company also focused on niche marketing having identified 372 niches, such as:

- Temple priests
- Blue pottery makers in Jaipur
- Pharmaceutical retailers
- Turmeric farmers in Tiruchengode in Tamil Nadu
- Apple growers in Himachal Pradesh
- Potato growers in West Bengal
- Painters from Madhubani

The idea was to identify numerous small segments within the economy that were doing better than others. The company created a customized strategy to target each segment. Now, these small clusters generate constant sales, many of them accounting for 3,550 vehicle sales per month and double that figure during the harvest season. Consequently, its rural share of revenue has increased almost eight times over a five-year period.

The company has introduced its 'R outlets' for rural markets. It solved the problem of providing service in remote rural areas through its MVS. The Maruti Mobile Services (MMS) had 1,031 Maruti Eeco vans by 2014 to service vehicles all over India. The company says that every month 40,000 customers use this service.

Other auto majors have also penetrated rural markets. Hyundai is also looking at rural markets. Its rural sale has risen from 12 per cent in 2011 to 20 per cent as of August 2014. It follows a hub-and-spoke model. Hyundai has set up 320 rural sales outlets, offering models such as Santro and Eon. They also provide service and repairs. Its rural presence has helped tide over the period when sales in bigger cities were stagnant and even declined. The firm plans to take up its rural sales to up to 30 per cent of its total sales.

Questions for discussion:

1. How can companies identify markets in rural areas?
2. What are the factors that impact rural demand?

3. Despite such a large, unserved market, why is it so difficult to penetrate rural markets?
4. What is the composition of the rural market and what goods are accepted there?

Sources for this Case Study:

Business Today. 2015. "Maruti Suzuki Eyes 20 Per Cent Increase in Rural Penetration." 5 April. Available at: http://businesstoday.intoday.in/story/maruti-suzuki-india-eyes-20-percent-increase-in-rural-presence/1/217746.html (Accessed on 25 April 2017).

Financial Express. 2014. "Maruti, Hyundai Rev up on Rural Market Growth." 23 September. Available at: http://indianexpress.com/article/business/companies/maruti-hyundai-rev-up-on-rural-market-growth/#sthash.KjoYFMwq.dpuf (Accessed on 25 April 2017).

Goyal, M., Maryanne Q. Hancock and Homayoun Hatami. 2012. "Selling into Micromarkets." *Harvard Business Review*, July–August. Available at: https://hbr.org/2012/07/selling-into-micromarkets (Accessed on 25 April 2017).

The Hindu. 2014. "Maruti Suzuki Targeting Double Digit Growth in FY15." 22 May. Available at: http://www.thehindu.com/business/Industry/maruti-suzuki-targeting-double-digit-growth-in-fy15/article6037316.ece (Accessed on 25 April 2017).

The Times of India. 2014. "Maruti's Rural Market Share Races from 3.5% to 31% in Five Years." 13 February. Available at: http://timesofindia.indiatimes.com/business/india-business/Marutis-rural-market-share-races-from-3-5-to-31-in-five-years/articleshow/30315161.cms (Accessed on 21 April 2017).

3 CHAPTER

The Rural Consumer

LEARNING OBJECTIVES

Understanding the rural consumer is of prime importance for any rural marketing strategy. But rural consumer behaviour varies by region, proximity to cities, education and income levels. This chapter helps understand the traditions and culture in which the rural consumer exists and profiles rural consumption on several parameters. After reading the chapter, you will be able to:

- Appreciate the importance of diverse markets and diverse behaviour in a large country like India.
- Profile the rural consumer and understand the rural society on Hofstede's cultural dimensions with their marketing implications.
- Learn about the differences between rural and urban consumers on the basis of their consumption.
- Make a profile of the rural consumer and identify rural market segments.
- Learn about rural consumer behaviour, shopping habits, changes in consumption and growing consumerism in rural areas.

Opening Case
Building Capabilities: Essilor

"Corporations that voluntarily tackle poverty and fragility, aid the disabled and the marginalized, can themselves be transformed in depth and change their purpose, mindset and culture," writes Philippe de Woot in his book, *Rethinking the Enterprise* (2014).

This case study shows how a company understood rural consumer behaviour and made products available in rural areas, thereby serving a social purpose as well.

The French company Essilor is the world's leading ophthalmic optics company. It started the '2.5 New Vision Generation', a business model in emerging countries to bring good vision to the people in need, as part of its inclusive business strategy. Its corporate mission is to enable everyone around the world to access lenses that meet his or her unique vision requirements. Some of Essilor's brands are Varilux, Crizal, Definity and Foster Grant.

Using an innovative, scalable and profitable inclusive business model, the company provides spectacles to needy people in rural areas. Many people in rural areas suffer from deteriorating vision but do not have their eyes tested because of a lack of awareness and lack of access to eye care facilities. People living in villages see the time spent travelling to see an optician in a distant town as waste of time and loss of wages. They continue to live their lives even while having problems in their vision. It is no wonder that India and China have the largest number of people with uncorrected vision: it is estimated that this will affect 3.2 billion people by 2050.

Through the 2.5 New Vision initiative, the company provides low-cost, ready-made reading glasses to people who need them. By targeting the rural poor, it achieves reach into areas where testing facilities do not exist, thus fulfilling a social cause too. Essilor overcomes high distribution and selling costs in villages tying up with micro-entrepreneurs, hospitals and NGOs, who already have their own networks of community-based workers. In this way, the company has modified its supply chain to penetrate rural markets.

Essilor has such social initiatives in many countries across the world. In India, its Eye Mitra (Friend of the Eyes) programme aims at bringing vision care to people in rural and semi-urban areas through local micro-enterprises. It brings testing facilities right up to the doorstep of the consumer through local entrepreneurs who are trained through mobile eye camps and equipped to start their own businesses, performing basic vision testing and spectacle dispensing in their outlets. The company targets equipping 7 million people by 2020.

Realizing that it could not go alone, the company started forging partnerships. Essilor Vision Foundation (EVF) was launched in India in April 2014 and has partnered with Aravind Eye Hospital to bring vision care to remote villages. Specialized mobile vans were added behind the Aravind Eye Hospital mobile van for Essilor to provide on-the-spot prescriptions for visual conditions and the sale of ready-made spectacles and stock lenses. Supported by local Rotary Clubs, trained eye-care professionals carry out eye health checks in villages providing the needy with prescription glasses, and referring others to hospital for advanced vision checks or surgery. EVF India also organizes vision awareness events in villages.

Photo 3.1

An Eye Mitra optician at work in a village (L) and an Eye Mitra village store (R).

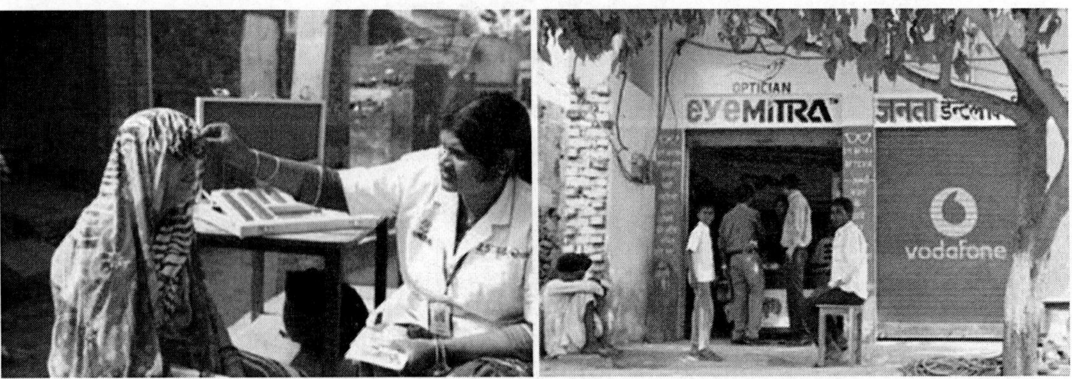

Source: Inclusive Business Action Network (2015). Reprinted with permission.

FIGURE 3.1
A pair of glasses can be of real help for villagers.

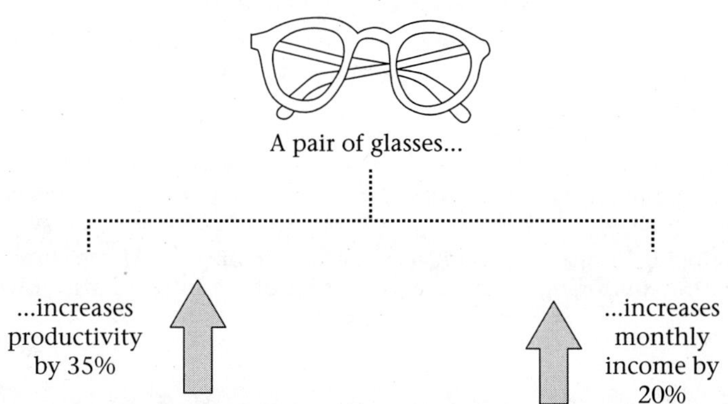

Source: https://www.warbyparker.com/buy-a-pair-give-a-pair (Accessed on 26 April 2017).

This approach has boosted Essilor's reach in villages. The company has been scaling up to reach more of the rural population in India, helping increase productivity and monthly income of the recipients (Figure 3.1).

The approach has also resulted in reverse innovation for several eyewear businesses. Online spectacles retailer Warby Parker has a business model that donates a pair of frames for every pair it sells, effectively using the revenue made from its US sales to subsidize its sales in developing markets. Since its launch, Warby Parker's growth has been phenomenal. It has received significant acknowledgement from notable investors such as Tiger Global Management and American Express.

Adlens, who manufactures variable focus eyewear, is another company that has reworked its business model through reverse innovation. It devised self-adjusting eyewear that does not require a doctor's consultation or prescription. Adlens has brought variable focus lenses into developed markets that can replace progressive lenses—a significant disruption in the industry. It also has a 'buy one give one' programme, that is, Adlens donates a pair of glasses to someone in the developing world through the buy one give one programme, says its website.

While reading this chapter, try to answer the following questions:

1. Why is it necessary for companies to study rural consumers in their environment?
2. Should a company, whose objective is to make profits, invest in solving problems of rural people? How does this impact your understanding of rural marketing?
3. How can products and services be provided to rural consumers at their doorstep? Why do they not buy even essential things like eye glasses?
4. The rural marketing opportunity can be tackled by initiatives like the ones mentioned in the case study. Do you agree? Is there an alternative method?

Sources for this Case Study:

Web Resources
Adlens website: https://www.adlens.com/social-soul/buy-one-give-one/
http://www.essilorseechange.com/

Other Sources
de Woot, Philippe. 2014. *Rethinking the Enterprise: Competitiveness, Technology and Society*. Sheffield: Grenleaf Publishing Ltd.

Essilor. 2014. "Essilor Vision Foundation Brings Vision Care to Rural Southern India." 11 December. Available at: https://www.essilor.com/en/medias/news/essilor-vision-foundation-brings-vision-care-to-rural-southern-india/ (Accessed on 21 April 2017).

Inclusive Business Action Network. 2015. "Empowering Communities through Access to Affordable Vision Care." The Practitioner Hub for Inclusive Business, 4 June. Available at: http://www.inclusivebusinesshub.org/profiles/blogs/empowering-communities-through-access-to-affordable-vision-care (Accessed on 21 April 2017).

Wu, Chloe. 2015. Bringing Vision Care to the 'Base of the Pyramid'. 13 March. Available at: http://blog.euromonitor.com/2015/03/bringing-vision-care-to-the-base-of-the-pyramid.html (Accessed on 21 April 2017).

INTRODUCTION

Marketing theory stresses the importance of studying consumer behaviour to satisfy customer needs. This is true in rural markets as well; establishing presence in rural markets requires that companies understand the rural consumer. Indeed, a report by Accenture (2015) notes that most companies base their understanding of rural Indian consumers on the traditional view that they are price-conscious, influenced by community members and not as demanding as urban consumers. Based on this belief, marketing managers attempt to market products in rural areas by tweaking distribution channels, selling low quality goods, trying to sell smaller packages like sachets and attempting to reduce prices. In many books and research articles, it is assumed that rural marketing consists of marketing to poor people and that the 'bottom of the pyramid' can yield profits if companies make small packs and improve their distribution. Many a attempts to sell to rural consumers fail because of this simplistic understanding of rural people. Attempts at segmentation, sometimes based on geographic information, too fail.

In this chapter, we go beyond this understanding of rural customers and discover rural culture and habits which lead to consumption patterns, the basis of segmenting rural markets, and the nature of the rural consumer.

Diverse Markets

It is a mistake to assume that the rural market is one homogenous market. In fact, rural markets and rural consumers vary across regions and incomes. They consist of very affluent landlords and businessmen, traders (both big and small), people providing goods and services, marginal and contract farmers, labourers and daily wage workers. Education levels too vary, but are rising: youngsters from villages seek admission in colleges and universities in nearby towns. A host of private colleges and universities offer engineering and management courses to attract youngsters from villages and small towns.

There are also variations with regard to proximity to urban areas—villages close to towns and big cities have people who are aware of and consume modern goods. Such villages tend to be well connected by roads, enabling better distribution of goods. But villages farther away from cities often have bad roads and poor connectivity. Consisting of small markets, they are difficult to be serviced by most companies. Remote villages, deep in the hinterland, tend to be isolated. Many are 'media dark', that is, they are beyond the reach of modern media. The

TABLE 3.1
The many faces of the rural consumer.

Income: Affluent landlords, businessmen, traders, marginal farmers, contractual farmers	**Location:** Proximity of villages to cities, road connectivity, leading to better product availability
Services providers: Skilled and unskilled labour, daily wagers	**Media coverage:** Good exposure to media in villages and little exposure, called 'media dark'
Education: Varying levels, new generation seeks education in nearby towns; differences across states	**Geography:** Rural consumers in different regions and states have different characteristics
Jobs: Availability of paying jobs in rural areas; state of agriculture in a region	**Economic situation:** Economic situation of rural areas varies from region to region
	Status of women: Status of women varies across region, limiting them as consumers

composition and character of consumption also varies on the basis of geographical location; villages in different states have different spending and consumption patterns.

Because of differences in rural consumers and villages, it is impossible to treat rural consumers as one homogenous group (Table 3.1). That is why, companies face problems while marketing to rural consumers.

Clearly, the rural consumer cannot be typecast. There are differences based on geographic, demographic and psychographic variables. This implies that companies must market products creatively, targeted to serve deeply felt consumer needs (see Mini Case Study 3.1). These needs can be understood by understanding the rural marketing environment.

Mini Case Study 3.1

LG Gets It Right

In 2008, electronics firms faced a double whammy of a financial slowdown and rising input costs. The depreciating rupee and the global financial crisis were pushing up costs even as consumer demand suddenly dried up. Delayed summers and early rains, especially in North India, affected air-conditioner sales. Consumer finance companies restricted lending for purchase of consumer durables. But a large untapped market potential remained—rural markets.

To tap into rural markets, LG Electronics India Pvt Ltd (LG) had to understand consumer needs, introduce innovative products, modify distribution channels, offer products at desirable price points and establish after-sales service network. This case describes the rural strategy of the Korean electronics company, LG, which decided to invest heavily on reaching consumers. The company had to strengthen its dealer network and area offices. But, more than that, it had to understand consumer needs to serve the market. It had to come up with product offerings suitable for rural consumers and to serve an economy where disposable incomes were low. LG now generates 35 per cent of its India revenues from rural sales. The company expects future growth to come from non-metro markets. It considers all cities and towns other than India's seven largest cities to be in the semi-urban/rural category.

Understanding consumers: LG set up a lifestyle research team to understand rural consumers. It discovered that the price–value trade off was crucial in rural markets, both in terms of purchase and service. It came up with region-specific branding, which was an innovative approach for an MNC. It realized that product features must be written or explained in local languages since many rural consumers have difficulty in understanding English. To achieve this, LG invested in developing on-screen display options in Hindi, Tamil and Bengali. The company also knocked off some features from its rural offerings as a means of reducing cost. These features just added to costs and were never used. For instance, the Golden Eye feature was hardly used in televisions and consumers did not need the luxury of 200 channels. For refrigerators, it used the tagline *Mujhe Kuch Nahin Ho Sakta*, which conveyed its ruggedness to rural audience.

Products: The trend in the industry has been to introduce feature-rich stylish products which are also technologically advanced. The company decided to launch a mix of energy efficient and innovative products. It introduced new products in air conditioning, frost-free refrigeration and flat-panel display TVs, following Indian insights. Realizing the diversity of rural markets, the company decided to have different channels through its 'different models, different channels' approach. It also decided to launch a new line for rural areas, called Sampoorna and Sampoorna deluxe CTVs. The company also introduced three new models of washing machines—Popular, Delight and Dreamz—in an affordable price range. The Sampoorna range with customized features and ease-of-use was a hit, reports Accenture (2010), selling more than 100,000 sets in the first year of its launch.

Communications: Since media reach in villages is limited, LG decided to be innovative in its communication strategy. It followed the concept of local advertising and using marketing activities such as mobile vans and road shows to reach out to customers.

Service: LG India introduced its customer service initiative '211' emphasizing on 'Service When You Want'. The company claims that it can respond to customers' complaints within two hours and the time for fixing complaints varies from one hour to a maximum of 24 hours. The service initiative is backed by IT infrastructure for the 211 campaign. This has resulted in significantly improved customer satisfaction and service reliability.

This strategy of understanding rural consumers, modifying products based on insight, better distribution and service infrastructure and using affordable pricing has resulted in success for LG. It now has a sizeable presence in rural markets and consumers are taking well to its products range.

What are the needs, motivations and habits of the rural consumer?

Sources for this Case Study:

Dogra, Suvi. 2009. "LG India Will Bring Relevant Products to India, and Focus on Rural Markets, After-sales Service and IT." *Business Standard,* 26 April. Available at: http://www.business-standard.com/article/companies/lg-india-will-bring-relevant-products-to-india-and-focus-on-rural-markets-after-sales-service-and-it-109042600050_1.html (Accessed on 27 April 2017).

Mishra, Richa. 2003. "LG Bets on Economy Range, Infrastructure to Tap Rural Market." *The Hindu BusinessLine*, 3 October. Available at: http://www.thehindubusinessline.com/2003/10/04/stories/2003100400470600.htm (Accessed on 27 April 2010).

Pitchonnet. 2013. "LG Revamps Marketing Strategy for 2013, Bets Big on Futuristic Products." 25 April. Available at: http://pitchonnet.com/blog/2013/04/25/lg-revamps-marketing-strategy-for-2013-bets-big-on-futuristic-products/ (Accessed on 27 April 2010).

THE RURAL MARKETING ENVIRONMENT

The rural marketing environment is marked, among other things, by lack of infrastructure, which has a profound impact on rural consumption patterns. Issues related to electrification, transport, availability of water and communications are discussed in this section with their marketing implications.

Rural Electrification

There is a great push for rural electrification by the government. It has created a company, the Rural Electrification Corporation (REC), with the mission to facilitate availability of electricity for rural and semi-urban population and to finance and promote power projects, according to its website. According to central government figures published in *The Hindu* (2017), 591,685 out of 597,464 census villages (or 99 per cent) have been electrified. The definition of 'electrification' includes only the provision of the electricity line to that point, not actual continuous access. So even if a few houses in a village receive only a couple hours of electricity a day for a few days in the year, the village is still deemed to be electrified. Such figures are therefore misleading. However, the situation on the ground is quite different: supply remains erratic in most of the small towns and villages. The Census of India 2011 shows that close to 43.2 per cent of India's rural households continue to depend on kerosene for lighting, while even today 0.5 per cent of its population or about 897,760 households do not have access to lighting at all. It further shows that villages continue to depend on kerosene and firewood for their cooking and heating: 62.5 per cent of rural households depend on firewood for cooking. As a consequence of this:

- Demand for electrical goods and appliances is low in rural India.
- Demand for processed foods that require refrigeration, chocolates and ice creams will remain low as they cannot be stored by retailers.
- There is a need for innovative products that do not depend on regular supply of electricity (see Mini Case Study 3.2).
- Demand for batteries and generators is high.

Mini Case Study 3.2

ChotuKool: A Ready Market for Relevant Innovative Products

Rural areas have unique problems that cannot be understood by the urban-bred managers. Companies cannot directly sell the products in villages, as they sell in urban areas. That is why, product innovation and pricing is the key to enter rural markets. This is illustrated by ChotuKool, a refrigerator invented by Godrej & Boyce Ltd. The refrigerator, which weighs only about 7.8 kg, does not have a compressor and runs on battery. The success of the product has led to the company adding more low-cost innovations to its 'Chotu' family, such as a low-cost washing machine ChotuWash and a low-cost water-purifier.

ChotuKool was priced at ₹3,700 at launch, which was half the price of a normal refrigerator. With this product, Godrej was able to sell white goods to the rural poor. The maintenance cost and its portability is helping it find acceptance amongst rural entrepreneurs. The product has penetrated homes and helped rural folk in growing their businesses. A *vada pav* (an Indian snack food) vendor in a Maharashtra village, for instance, started selling chilled drinking water pouches from the refrigerator on his cart. The refrigerator was charged at night and was tugged along in his cart during the day. A flower vendor in Karnataka saved herself daily trips to buy fresh flowers by buying a ChotuKool. The product has also helped small *kirana* (grocery) store owners to stock and sell products like chocolates, cold drinks and dairy products, something that was not possible earlier due to erratic power supply.

Photo 3.2
The ChotuKool refrigerator.

Source: https://www.chotukool.com (Accessed on 27 April 2017).

Another product that has been successful is a refrigerator from MittiCool, which does not require electricity at all. It works on the principle of water evaporation and is a result of frugal innovation (see Chapter 12). Similarly, water purifiers that do not require electricity have also become popular in villages. Indeed, there is a ready market for such innovations that get over the problem of erratic electric supply.

Can you think of other products that solve local problems frugally?

Sources for this Case Study:

Web Resource
MittiCool website: www.mitticool.com

Other Source
Sharma, Shailaja. 2015. "At Godrej, ChotuKool Spawns Major Business Strategy." *DNA*, 5 December. Available at: http://www.dnaindia.com/money/report-at-godrej-chotukool-spawns-major-business-strategy-1621399 (Accessed on 27 April 2017).

Rural Transport

It is estimated that about 46 per cent of the villages are connected by all-weather roads, while 54 per cent are inaccessible during rainy seasons. Public transport system is quite poor, with private operators providing whatever they can. According to the National Transport Policy Committee (NTPC), fair weather roads connected only 55 per cent of villages. Planning Commission estimates (Figure 3.2) that the percentage of connected habitats varies from 30 per cent in many states to above 90 per cent in others. The report prepared by Working Group on Rural Roads (2011) notes that there is growing empirical evidence that links transport investment to the improved well-being of the poor and, therefore, the lack of roads hurts them directly. It is also a hindrance to rural marketing. Figure 3.2 shows the variations among states and the relationship between connectivity and poverty. Low transport connectivity leads to higher poverty levels. This aspect of rural environment results in the following:

- Bicycles are very popular because of short distances and bad roads.
- Where roads are better, the ownership of motor-vehicles increases.
- There will be a shift from non-motorized vehicles to motorized ones as road connectivity increases. Rugged cars are preferred that can survive on bad roads.
- Distribution of goods has to be done through innovative ways as formal transport does not exist.
- As bad roads cause damages to vehicles, there is a need to provide repair and after-sales service to vehicle owners in rural areas.

FIGURE 3.2

Relationship between road connectivity and poverty.

Percentage of Connected Habitations (June 2005 Data)

Rural Poverty (percentage, 1999–2000 Data)

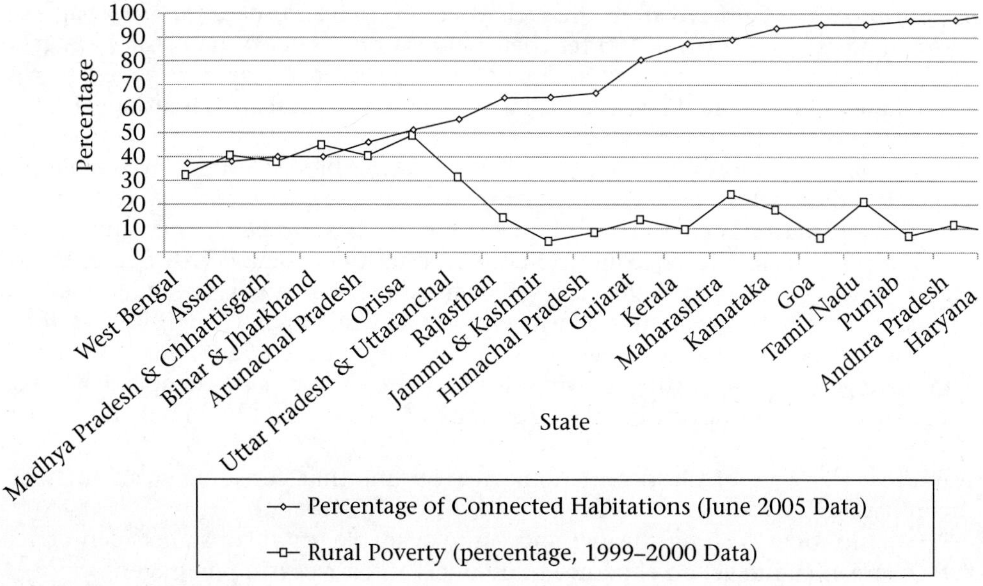

Source: Rural Road Development Plan: Vision 2025.

PHOTO 3.3

Rural roads remain neglected in India, and the situation is worse in monsoons. Note that a crane service is helpfully advertised here.

Source: Photograph by Dinesh Kumar.

Rural Communications

Villages in India have suffered from the lack of connectivity for decades. Newspapers reach certain rural areas one or two days after their publication. Though rural issues are generally ignored by newspapers, the increase in circulation of local language newspapers shows that there is a slight uptake in rural readership. TV penetration in rural areas is around 45 per cent, but is rising.

The real communication revolution in villages is being brought about by mobile phones. Landline telephones, which were earlier the monopoly of the government, were a rarity in villages. With the privatization of the sector, rural telephony has increased, especially with mobile phones. Table 3.2 shows the Telecom Regulatory Authority of India (TRAI) figures up to 28th February 2015. The table shows the stark differences in the levels of telecom penetration in urban and rural areas. The urban tele-density was 149.25 while rural tele-density was just 47.16, showing the unbalanced growth in telecoms in India since independence. But now things seem to be improving; the monthly rural growth rate of 1.11 per cent is nearly double that of 0.69 per cent in urban areas. This shows a growth opportunity for companies in rural markets, such as:

- Increased growth of phones in rural areas means that consumers can interact with companies.
- As smartphones become cheaper and easily available, rural consumers can be reached by companies and get an exposure to products and advertising messages.
- Apps for rural markets, such as for micro-payments, make it easier for people to transact.
- Apps help rural people in accessing markets, thereby leading to increase in incomes, which, in turn, will spur consumption demand.

TABLE 3.2
Telecom subscription data as on 28 February 2015.

Particulars	Wireless	Wireline	Total (Wireless + Wireline)
Total Telephone Subscribers (Million)	**960.58**	**26.72**	**987.30**
Net Addition in February, 2015 (Million)	8.24	–0.15	8.09
Monthly Growth Rate	0.86%	–0.54%	0.83%
Urban Telephone Subscribers (Million)	**557.27**	**21.48**	**578.75**
Net Addition in February, 2015 (Million)	3.82	–0.11	3.71
Monthly Growth Rate	0.69%	–0.53%	0.64%
Rural Telephone Subscribers (Million)	**403.31**	**5.24**	**408.55**
Net Addition in February, 2015 (Million)	4.42	–0.03	4.38
Monthly Growth Rate	1.11%	–0.58%	1.08
Overall Tele-density	**76.60**	**2.13**	**78.73**
Urban Tele-density	143.71	5.54	149.25
Rural Tele-density	46.56	0.60	47.16%
Share of Urban Subscribers	58.01%	80.39%	58.62%
Share of Rural Subscribers	41.99%	19.61%	41.38%
Broadband Subscribers (Million)	**81.92**	**15.45**	**97.37**

Source: TRAI (2015).

The lack of infrastructure shows that rural markets remain deprived and isolated. This is one of the reasons why they remain bound together by tradition and culture. Even Internet accessibility is a problem in many areas. Data cards do not work well. In many areas, even to load Gmail basic HTML version, it takes more than two minutes. Many areas do not get a signal at all. It is no wonder that despite advances in education and communications, the society remains deeply traditional. An understanding of the rural consumer, thus, requires an understanding of the rural society.

Mini Case Study 3.3

Getting a Mobile Signal in Rural Odisha

In Pongalapadar village in Kandhamal district, Odisha, villagers leave their huts in the afternoon and walk on a 2-km-long track over a rocky track. Avoiding snake burrows and animals like foxes or jackals, they climb a steep 100-foot-tall hillock. Arriving on a patch, they check their mobile phones for a signal. Only when they get the signal can they dial and talk to the outside world.

This walk is the highlight of their day, reports Mohanty (2015). The closest mobile tower is 3 km away, blocked by forests and the mountains that surround the village. There are no landline connections, as laying cables through the forests was not considered possible. To make a call, people have to climb one of the nearby hills to catch the signal.

Anti-Maoist operations by the police add to the fear of going for the trek, along with the fear of animals in the forests. Villagers go up once a week to make their calls.

Only two gram panchayats of the 11 in Kotgarh have mobile coverage. People of Pongalapadar must brave thick forests and snake burrows even to avail basic amenities. They have to walk three hours to Kotgarh to collect their monthly quota of subsidized rice. The nearest government hospital is 30 km away. When people fall sick, they are transported on foot in a carrier, made from a sheet tied to bamboo sticks to make a sling and carry the patient. For water, villagers depend on a mountain stream as there is no deep tube-well or handpump. Electricity, which came in the village three years ago, is erratic. Not a single house has a toilet.

Source for this Case Study:
Mohanty, D. 2015. "This Number is Not Reachable." *Indian Express*, 23 August.

Water Availability

Securing even the minimum amount of water for everyday needs is a daily struggle for many people in rural India. Public water supply is usually missing, so rural households depend on groundwater for 85 per cent of their needs. Women spend hours, or even the entire day, just fetching water for their families, according to a report by the National Commission for Women (2005) (see Mini Case Study 3.4). In other regions, water quality has deteriorated due to groundwater pollution, leading to rampant spread of water-borne diseases such as cholera, diarrhoea and typhoid. In some parts of the country, fluoride and arsenic are the other major pollutants. According to the Central Groundwater Board, the two pollutants together affect nearly 80 million people.

It is estimated that India loses 2–4 per cent of its GDP every year because of unclean water.

Mini Case Study 3.4

How Would You Sell the Promise of Bouncy Hair to These Women?

Women in Indian villages bear the brunt of water scarcity; young women drop out of school or college just to fetch water for their families. There are extreme examples, such as the village of Denganmal, 150 kilometres from Mumbai, where men marry a second—sometimes even a third—woman whose only role is to fetch water for the family by making an arduous 3-km-long trek several times in a day, reports *Mint* (2015).

A report by the National Commission for Women (2005) gives some facts about women fetching water in many rural areas:

- On an average, a rural woman walks more than 14,000 km a year to fetch water.
- Women are required to make at least three trips at 5AM, 11AM and 5PM; sometimes the number of trips is more.
- The total distance travelled per day is 9–10 km, even higher.
- The total time spent is 6–9 hours.

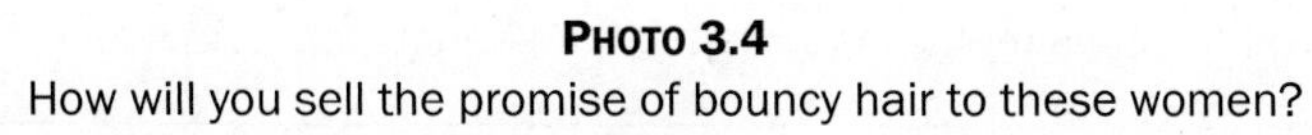

PHOTO 3.4

How will you sell the promise of bouncy hair to these women?

Source: Photograph by Dinesh Kumar.

- They carry about 30–45 litres of water per trip.
- The entire life of women in rural areas like Jaisalmer is spent on water collection and cooking. Even the girls of 8–10 years are not spared.

One Bundelkhandi saying goes something like this: "Let the husband die but the earthen pot of water should not be broken."

In such a situation, how will you sell the promise of bouncy hair to women in rural areas?

Sources for this Case Study:

Web Resource

See the video *The Long Walk to Water* at: http://www.livemint.com/Opinion/P0Z53BOwcPw4SjMRnm028L/The-long-walk-to-water.html

Other Sources

Mint. 2015. "Water Crisis: The Long Walk to Water." 29 April.

National Commission for Women. 2005. *Women and Water*. Report available at: http://ncw.nic.in/pdfreports/Women%20&%20Water.pdf (Accessed on 27 April 2017).

UNDERSTANDING RURAL SOCIETY

To understand rural consumer behaviour, it is important to understand the context in which those consumers live, that is, their society. Since individuals make buying decisions to conform to their social groups, managers must keep into consideration the society and its values while marketing products and services, otherwise they will be squarely rejected.

Rural society is a society bound by traditional values and culture. Though the younger generation is getting educated, people like to stick to their age-old beliefs and values.

TABLE 3.3

Hofstede's cultural dimensions and their marketing applications to rural India.

Cultural Dimension	Marketing Application to Rural Areas
Individualism–Collectivism	Companies should pitch for families Products must be designed for families
Power distance	Advertising that appeals to the figure of authority Rural marketing should be done through communities
Masculinity–Femininity	Big market for products for males, which help them feel macho Products that help symbolize the feminine aspirations for females Women shown in traditional roles in advertisements
Uncertainty avoidance	Brands that deliver quality and can be trusted
Long-term orientation	Belief in karma makes the society take a long-term view Consumers want reliable products

Source: Kumar (2015).

We analyze rural consumers through Hofstede's theory of cultural dimensions, which helps in understanding their consumption behaviour. Hofstede describes culture on five dimensions on which cultural values rest: individualism–collectivism (IDV), Uncertainty Avoidance Index (UAI), Power Distance Index (PDI), masculinity–femininity (MAS) and long-term orientation (LTO). Hofstede's cultural dimensions and their marketing applications are summarized in Table 3.3.

Scores assigned for these cultural dimensions for India with respect to cultural traditions in the country and are discussed next.

Individualism–Collectivism

Rural societies can be described as collectivist. Hofstede (2001) described collectivism as "societies in which people from birth onwards are integrated into strong, cohesive in-groups, which throughout people's lifetimes continue to protect them in exchange for unquestioning loyalty." India has an IDV score of 48, which shows that the society has both collectivistic and individualistic traits. The collectivist side means that people like to belong to their social framework and share the values of one's groups. That is, people are influenced by one's family and the extended family consisting of neighbours and relatives. Family, community, caste and religion form strong groups. While many individuals from rural areas live separately when they move to cities for education and employment, they maintain close ties with their families, sending money back home and visiting their families often. Even when they acquire education and jobs in cities, people exhibit strong ties to their families and traditional values. The average household size in India is 4.8, according to Census 2011 figures. The rural household size (4.9) was higher than urban household size (4.6), showing a greater preference for joint families.

The marketing implications are as follows:

1. **Large, economical packs:** Large packs of certain goods are preferred in many rural families because of two reasons. First, large packs are found suitable for large families. Second, since rural consumers cannot go very often to nearby towns for their purchases, they tend to buy large packs which also work out cheaper.

2. **Price points:** As families look for value in their purchases, goods must be provided at easy price points. Many rural consumers avoid frills and look for value in their purchases. For instance, Colgate has a range of products at different price points and also offers Colgate Cibaca at a much cheaper price.
3. **Quality and value:** Families seek quality and value. Products that deliver these have a high probability of succeeding than premium or foreign products. For instance, many companies started offering *atta* (wheat) bread and atta noodles as they were considered healthier than ordinary white bread and noodles.
4. **Importance of social groups:** Since rural society is influenced by social groups, companies must base their marketing campaigns to encourage peer influence rather than focus on the individual. Opinion leaders assume importance in marketing in rural areas.

Power Distance

Power distance is defined as the extent to which the less powerful members of the family accept the power of other members of the family. India's score is 77, and this high score indicates high inequality. People show a high degree of dependency in families, accept unequal rights, paternalistic culture and obedience to authority.

The inequality takes many forms. Older members get more respect than younger people and male members exhibit higher power than female members. Power is also held by caste, religious and community leaders. The power distance is reflected in the GII, calculated by UNDP, which has worsened over the years. According to UNDP (2017):

> India's poor performance on women's empowerment and gender equality is reflected in many indicators, particularly, the low sex ratio. The government has launched several commendable schemes to save and educate the girl child...however, in many parts of India it continues to remains low. Gender inequality is also reflected in India's low rank on UNDP's Gender Inequality Index.

Advertisements routinely publish culturally assigned roles, for example, girls in the roles of housewives and men as ogling women on the road.

The Human Development Index (HDI) is no better: India ranked 135 out of 187 countries in 2014. When inequality is factored in, it experiences a 30 per cent drop in its human development values, ranking 129 out of 146 nations.

The power distance plays itself out in several forms:

- Working women continue to get lower wages than their male counterparts.
- The majority of the female workforce in India is unskilled and has only a basic education.
- Women often work in very poorly paid jobs with no security or benefits and in many cases below the minimum daily wage.
- Female mortality rates are high and the share of the girl child in education is low.
- There are restrictions on female lifestyles and freedom, on their dress and behaviour.
- Crimes against women are on the rise across the country.
- Singh and Bhandari (2012) point out that in the case of married women, their access to money is limited as it is controlled by males, particularly in non-metropolitan households.

Companies can use the power distance in their marketing campaigns in many ways:

1. **Target products to males:** Products targeted at males will do well because males have more social and economic power. Even female-oriented products are bought by males in many societies.
2. **Cheap products for females:** Products targeted to females must be cheap and affordable. This explains why smaller packs like sachets tend to do well in product categories like shampoos and cosmetic preparations.
3. **Market through figures of authority:** Products marketed through figures of authority and opinion leaders tend to do well.

Masculinity

India scores 56 on the masculinity index, pointing to a male-dominated society. Women are discriminated against and lack many freedoms in villages. They are treated as a subordinate gender. A report in the *Indian Express* (Dogra 2015) speaks about rural attitudes as follows, "A young man in rural Haryana is entitled to the best things of life—from the extra glass of milk to the education that won't be 'wasted' on a girl." Women continue to be shown in domestic roles in advertisements for better acceptability. There is no sign that such attitudes are changing. Even young people exhibit them. Interestingly, the Global Report Card on Adolescents 2012 published by the United Nations International Children's Emergency Fund (UNICEF 2012) finds that:

- India leads in terms of under-weight adolescent girls: 47 per cent of adolescent girls aged 15–19 in India are underweight. This figure is much higher than Bangladesh (35%) and Nepal (26%).
- The largest number of anaemia cases is found in India, where more than half of girls aged 15–19 are anaemic.

The UNICEF report (2012) found that 57 per cent of adolescent boys in India think that a husband is justified in hitting or beating his wife. Over a half of the Indian adolescent girls, or around 53 per cent, think that a husband is justified in beating his wife.

This implies that while companies can cater to male egos by providing 'macho' products, products aimed at young girls are unlikely to find a mass market. The way to market feminine products in rural areas, perhaps, is to appeal to the male ego—by projecting how it will raise the status of men. The marketing messages used in urban areas showing empowered women are thus likely to be rejected by the rural consumer. For example, Rajan (2005), CMD of Anugrah Madison Advertising Pvt Ltd, mentions the case of a well-known brand of shampoo, which showed in its ad a beautiful model featuring bouncing hair. However, in the Rajasthan market, the message and the product both failed. It was found in post-research that people thought it indecent for a girl to show off her hair. Thus, men do not like the empowered women shown in urban ads, nor can ads made for urban markets be used in rural markets.

The marketing implications of this orientation can be summed up as follows:

- Companies target high-end products for males, such as motorcycles and SUVs.
- Feminine products are unlikely to do well unless targeted at the male ego.
- Much of the buying for females takes place only during their marriage, an occasion when families open their purses for dowry for the bride.
- Ads showing the empowered, liberated or the fashionable girl will be rejected.

Uncertainty Avoidance

Societies with high uncertainty avoidance scores have anxiety about the future, tend to take few risks, are concerned about security and are less open-minded. India scores 40 on this dimension and is seen to have a medium to low preference for avoiding uncertainty. This means that people like to try out new brands. They exhibit low brand loyalty and are not suspicious of new products. If there are problems with a service or product, the low uncertainty avoidance tends to overlook the defects and adjust their expectations. Companies must make sturdy products for rural markers which are dependable.

Long-term Orientation

Long-term orientation refers to the society's future-oriented perspective. India scores 51 on this dimension, which means that it has a long-term orientation. Since rural incomes depend a large part on agriculture, which is marked by uncertainty, consumers are unlikely to splurge on luxury products, but adhere to perseverance and thrift, respect of tradition and family values, honouring parents and ancestors and providing them financial support. *The Economist* (2013) reports, "High inflation has prompted households to store ever more of their savings in physical assets rather than the financial system." Savings were also held in cash. However, post the demonetization of high value currency notes in India, "household bank deposits from small towns and rural pockets exceeded expectations," reports *Business Standard* (2016).

Luxury products, thus, do not do well in rural areas where people continue to look for products that last long and deliver value. The few times that people will splurge in villages are at times of marriages, festivals and special occasions. Festivals provide motivational triggers for buying new things, when cash flows from harvests are high. White goods, clothes, upholstery and curtains are bought during festivals. For instance, in Kerala, 50–60 per cent of the sales of consumer durables of the entire year take place during Onam. A festival like Akshaya Tritiya is considered an auspicious time not just to buy gold and metal goods. New opportunities for marketing emerge: July–September is considered the non-resident Indian (NRI) season in Kerala, which almost seems like a festival in markets.

Cultural dimensions help us in understanding rural society and consumption behaviour. In the next section, we study values that impact rural buying behaviour.

VALUES OF THE RURAL CONSUMER

Traditions and cultural values explain how people behave and interact with products and brands. Social values and norms explain attitudes towards consumption. Values are the underlying beliefs of people. We discuss the values that form the basis of social thinking on several variables.

Modernity through Conformity

Indians are gradually becoming modern as result of media exposure. The trend is seen in cities, but rural areas are also tending towards modernism. Villages close to cities are more exposed to modern lifestyles. Yet, despite winds of change, Indians seek conformity. Social hierarchies are very strong and people conform to traditions and customs, even though they adopt Western clothes and language. For instance, despite increasing modernization, India registered an almost 800 per cent rise in the number of killings in the name of 'honour' reported in 2015, with 251 cases of honour killings registered by the police, according to figures presented in parliament. However, the desire to appear modern in rural areas opens up a ready market for counterfeit products: local manufacturers provide cheap goods which openly display labels of the world's best brands in clothing and consumer products.

Success and Growth

Banerjee (2008) writes that in Indian society, recognition, or social acceptability is valued more than individual achievement. This is more evident in rural areas. Success is enjoyed from the perspectives of a group than an individual. Rural folk look down upon city life, which encourages individual growth and success. This prevents them from accepting ads based on urban values and products that overtly promote individualism.

Age and Youthfulness

India has the world's largest youth population—356 million 10–24-year-olds according to the United Nations Population Fund's (UNFPA) State of the World's Population. However, millions in this group remain locked in a struggle with poverty as the country has failed to create formal jobs for them. Only 22 million belong to the urban middle class. The rest find low paying jobs such as security guards; millions of young people living in rural India have few opportunities for jobs and remain underemployed. With little purchasing power, they are unlikely to buy branded products.

Happiness and Adaptability

Indian culture stresses upon spiritual growth and materialistic gain is not considered the prime route to ensuring happiness. Though this is changing fast, such thinking is still evident in villages, where religion and rituals are followed more than in urban areas. Many people follow religious sects and godmen. However, rural society is slowly acquiring materialistic tastes and new products like cars, mobile phones, white goods and consumer goods are being bought in large numbers. With government initiatives like MGNREGA, there has been increase of incomes in rural areas which is helping rural consumption. The Emerging Consumer Survey 2014 conducted by Credit Suisse notes that the increase in rural investments "underlines a significant uplift in consumer markets geared to the lower income consumer" (Credit Suisse 2014).

Religion and Spirituality

The many religions of India add their traditions and festivities to the country. Dedicated television channels transmit religious messages round the clock. They also sell 'blessed products' to help ward off the evil eye and other ailments. Camps and ashrams are hugely popular, with holy products to match. The second is to use culture by selling medicines and nature cure products. Anything with the word 'ayurveda' and 'yoga' attached to it conjures up images of Indian culture and people are quick to adapt to them. The success of Patanjali, which sells a wide variety of products from medicines to FMCG goods, can be attributed to this factor (see Mini Case Study 3.5). Yoga, too, has become a big business in India, with several resorts offering 'yoga vacations' to Indians and foreigners. Rural tourism is a big opportunity. Also, companies can devise marketing strategies based on religious festivals when the rural consumer is most open to buying goods.

Mini Case Study 3.5

Patanjali—Cashing in on Indian Traditions

Patanjali Ayurved Limited, with its headquarters at Haridwar, Uttarakhand, was established on 13th January, 2006 with Acharya Balkrishna as its majority stakeholder as well as Managing Director. It is involved in manufacturing as well as distribution of products ranging from food, beverages to cosmetics and fabric care. The company has made rapid advances in expanding its reach across many segments and currently operates a plethora of brands. Its many products include grocery and staples, foods, beverages, personal care, health care and household products.

Patanjali sells on the unique selling proposition (USP) of tradition. Its consumer ads stress on purity while health care products are sold on the platform of ayurveda, the traditional Hindu system of medicine. Its brand ambassador is Baba Ramdev, a famous yoga guru. It advertises its products in yoga camps, word-of-mouth publicity and on TV ads.

Patanjali has reported a sales growth of 150 per cent in 2015–16 of ₹5,000 crore with a target to double this figure in 2016–17. This puts the company ahead of MNCs like Nestlé, Colgate-Palmolive and Procter & Gamble in India, reports *Business Standard* (2016).

Though there are other companies like Dabur, Hamdard and Himalaya in the same space, the association with a yoga guru has helped the company a great deal. The allusion to tradition and religion has also helped. Though the company was started in 2006, its exponential growth started only after the Bharatiya Janata party came to power.

How can companies use tradition and religion to sell their products?

Source for this Case Study:

Business Standard. 2016. "Baba Ramdev's Patanjali Aims to Double its Revenue to ₹10,000 cr in 2016–17." 27 April.

Rituals and Customs

Religions also give different sets of rituals to their followers. The challenge before companies is to understand and use the rituals practised in villages to sell products. There are, in fact, many things that are common between religion and marketing. Brands that have rituals and superstitions associated with them are much 'stickier' than those that do not.

Traditions

Companies also use traditions to position their products. The Indian tradition of offering sweets to celebrate occasions or festivals, for example, was used effectively by Cadbury Dairy Milk. The company came up with advertisements with the tagline *Kuch meetha ho jaye*

(Let's have something sweet). The tradition of using herbal remedies has resulted in many companies offering soaps, cosmetics and medicines made with traditional Indian herbs. The Indian habit of hoarding gold was used effectively by Tanishq, which showed heavily decked up ladies in its advertisements with the tagline, *Parampara ki nayi kahani* (A new story of tradition).

Languages

Mobile phone makers use local languages to expand their markets. They introduced the Hindi SMS facility because they realized that a large section of the population was not familiar with English. MNCs frequently use Indian names to connect with Indian consumers, more so when they venture into rural markets, such as LG, which introduced its Sampoorna line of products.

Companies also learn to use languages creatively. Advertising often combines local languages with English words to appeal to the masses. National Geographic launched a series of programmes called *Mission Udaan*. Godrej introduced a small refrigerator named 'ChotuKool', not only combining two languages and but also using a popular word as well for better acceptability. In rural areas, there is a greater appeal for brands using local languages. Names like Agni Tea, Mahindra's Bhoomiputra and Sarpanch series of tractors have worked well in these markets. Hollywood movies dubbed in languages have been huge hits in India.

Symbols

Marketing is done through symbols in rural marketing. Coca-Cola realized that in rural markets, brand names are not very relevant as people associate a brand more with visuals and symbols. This also helps get over the literacy hurdle. Well-known brands are recognized through elementary symbols. Coca-Cola resorted to visual branding to encourage brand recognition, connecting its brands with symbols. The *thanda matlab Coca-Cola* campaign launched in 2002 used the word that describes cold drinks, *thanda*, to appeal to the rural consumer. It featured Aamir Khan in six characters, using rural settings. Political advertising and campaigns, too, largely rely on symbols such as bicycle, elephant, scales and so for better recall.

The cultural elements, their importance and the implication for rural brand architecture is summed up in Table 3.4.

TABLE 3.4

Importance of cultural elements in rural brand architecture.

Cultural Element	Importance	Rural Brand Architecture
Language	Use of local languages in marketing communications	Specific campaigns for specific activities; dedicated local communications teams
Symbols	Understand symbols and signs used in regional cultures	Integrate symbols in brand architecture and communications
Rituals	Strong and enduring rituals, traditions and customs	Build brands around local cultural symbols, use local traditions for BTL campaigns
Family	Strong role of family	Family-oriented products and brands

(Table 3.4 Contd.)

(Table 3.4 Contd.)

Cultural Element	Importance	Rural Brand Architecture
Social cohesion	Emphasis on collectivism	Cultivate rural role models and opinion leaders
Social friction	Social divisions based on caste and other factors	Avoid segmenting markets to fall into the image trap
Gender gap	Low status of women	Big market for male-oriented products, females in traditional roles
Age	Reverence for old age	Involve senior people as opinion leaders
Religion	Strong role of religion and religious leaders	Religious occasions and symbols to build brands

Rural Opinion Leaders

Though film stars and sportspersons are used as opinion leaders in both urban and rural markets, rural markets are different. Rural market opinion is likely to be influenced by local leaders and shopkeepers, educated people, religious leaders and people with regular jobs.

Ratna and Mehra's study (2015) of demographic characteristics opinion leaders for non-life insurance products in India shows that opinion leaders in rural areas are more likely to be:

1. older in age and were mostly in the age group of 40–50 years,
2. mostly men,
3. highly educated,
4. belonging to larger families of four or more members,
5. coming from a mix of rural and urban backgrounds,
6. mostly in private employment, and
7. coming from the same social class as the others.

These characteristics match the cultural beliefs of the target audience (discussed previously) and can well be extended to other product categories. Though opinion leaders will be different in categories like, for example, cosmetics, the psychological set-up of people in rural India suggests that older, educated men will have a greater impact on local opinion.

Opinion leaders help in rural consumers opening up to brands. Slowly consumers are realizing that it is important to buy a branded product for its quality. But local brands and products still pose a formidable challenge to brands and are able to compete on price. Thus, companies must also recognize changes and learn to make tailored products and strategies that appeal to rural consumers. Merely copying urban strategies in rural areas is unlikely to work, which is explained elaborately in the next section.

OPENING UP TO BRANDS

Changes are happening slowly in Indian villages. Despite the huge differences in rural consumers, companies are failing to respond to the changing needs and behaviours despite the huge growth potential. A one-size-fits-all strategy does not work for all villages. Further, companies also must keep into account the changing socio-economic dynamics influencing the spending decisions of rural customers. This is a critical change unfolding in India's hinterlands, writes Rajan (2005). He says that huge changes are taking place that impact buying and consumption across villages, but the consumer cannot be taken for granted. An advertisement by Idea reflects this—it says that rural people cannot be taken for a ride, thanks to easy availability of the Internet (*No ullu banaying*).

However, a radical change is required. Usually the following assumptions are made about the rural consumer:

- He is conscious about getting value for money.
- He is impressed by endorsements by local leaders or icons.
- He is a value buyer and does not like to pay extra for bells and whistles.
- He understands symbols and colours better.
- He has no sense of urgency in his lifestyle.
- He has high involvement in any product purchased, especially in high-end products.
- Divisions based on caste, community and other hierarchical factors continue to exist in rural areas.
- Perceptions, traditions and values vary from state to state and, in some cases, from region to region within a state.

Many of the aforementioned assumptions about the rural consumer are being challenged because of large changes that are taking place, albeit slowly, across the countryside. An Accenture survey (2013) finds that the conventional wisdom that rural consumers care most about price and settle for substandard offerings is quite wrong. It says that rural consumers have aspiration and they strive to purchase branded, high quality products: around 71 per cent of respondents had purchased branded products and 59 per cent consider them as trustworthy. Companies make the mistake of working on assumptions of the past, but the expectations of rural Indian consumers differ markedly from those of previous generations. Rural consumers are moving away from value driven by low prices but seek quality products that reflect their aspirations, according to Sanjay Dawar, MD for Accenture's Strategy practice in India. The report points to lack of importance of ads—only 7 per cent of the respondents said that advertisements influence their final buying decisions.

The change in rural consumers in some areas is happening because of the following reasons:

- **Increase in incomes:** Incomes in rural areas have risen, leading to greater purchasing power. Investments in rural infrastructure by the government are beginning to yield results.
- **Mindset:** Rural consumers are upgrading from locally available products to branded products. This shows that rural populations are slowly moving towards better awareness and lifestyles.
- **Awareness:** Several modes of communication, both conventional and unconventional, have made their way to the hinterlands of India. Rural consumers are today exposed to a variety of entertainment sources and other stimuli because of increasing media reach. Around 35 per cent of rural India watches television, which influences consumer patterns.
- **Consuming potential:** According to the Central Statistical Organization, India is a consumption-led economy because of its high private final consumption expenditure, that is, monthly per capita expenditure (MPCE) levels of 60 per cent of its GDP.

- **Mobile phones:** Deep penetration of mobile phones has resulted in better connectivity and awareness of rural consumers. As smartphones and e-payment systems are becoming popular, further changes in consumption behaviour are expected to happen.

Credit Suisse's Emerging Consumer Survey 2014 notes that investment in rural infrastructure appears to be paying off and raising income expectations at a faster pace than their urban counterparts. A rural middle class is emerging. The survey found that confidence among rural people about the future was much higher than their urban counterparts. Rural areas are witnessing a much bigger improvement than urban areas in most categories. The survey shows there has been a sharp fall in consumers wishing to buy unbranded items. Consumption of items such as beer, spirits, meat and cigarettes as well as access to the Internet has been rising and there is scope for further improvement. However, rural consumers' confidence depends on several factors and varies with erratic monsoons and economic conditions.

In terms of spending categories, there has been growth in discretionary categories such as smartphones and cars in 2013. This trend is expected to continue to products such as watches and branded goods. There was a sharp fall in consumers wishing to buy unbranded items, as consumers are becoming more brand conscious. A study conducted by Tripathi (2014) showed that rural consumers like to buy branded products and associate the use of branded FMCG goods as a status symbol. Among the products that had high brand recall were: Babool toothpaste, Breeze soap, Godrej No.1 soap, Hamam soap, Ghadi detergent, and Nirma. The most popular biscuits brand was 'Parle-G'. Parle Kismi bar and toffees are popular among rural consumers instead of chocolates and eclairs. Another finding was that rural consumers are brand loyal: once they like a product, they keep on consuming the same product for years. They neither switch their brand nor do they try new products every now and then. The study also examined their perception regarding the quality of branded products in comparison to non-branded products. Rural consumers perceive the quality of branded products as better than non-branded products.

Yet, the findings need to be taken with a pinch of salt and cannot be taken as common for all villages. Rural buying behaviour differs on the basis of region, purchasing power and individuals. Further, the aspiration-based consumer buying is not static: a bad monsoon changes rural consumers' confidence quickly. Brand loyalty also depends on availability—since rural shops stock limited number of brands, the consumer really has no option but to buy whatever is available. Companies that use general figures of growth and duplicate urban strategies in rural areas tend to make mistakes.

The findings highlight some very important characteristics of rural customers. The differences with urban consumers are discussed next.

DIFFERENCES BETWEEN RURAL AND URBAN SHOPPERS

Many companies make the mistake of having one campaign for cities and rural areas. But not only are cities and villages different, but they also vary from region to region. The differences across regions are quite huge. A look at Table 3.5 shows that to market to rural consumers, companies need to adopt micro strategies by understanding consumers in each region.

Several research studies contrast rural and urban consumers. Jha's (2013) study of rural consumers of Bihar shows that television is a major source of information for both urban and rural consumers. For an urban consumer, newspaper is the second most important source of information. However, for a rural consumer radio is the second most important source of information, followed by newspaper. The rural consumer also gets information from various

TABLE 3.5
Differences in rural and urban consumers.

Rural Consumer	Urban Consumer
Bound by tradition, social norms and religion; consumers tend to be close minded	Modernity pulling at tradition; consumers appear outwardly modern but are traditional at heart
Many consumers in high and middle income groups buy in bulk, are brand conscious and look for convenience. Buying is mostly done from nearby towns	Though families buy on a monthly basis, trips to nearby stores and supermarkets are more common. Impulse buying and consumption of fast foods is high
Marked preference for fresh food items; foodgrains purchased in bulk	Preference for fresh vegetables, but processed foods also bought. Only large families buy in bulk
Mostly cash economy; local traders provide credit	Credit and debit cards becoming popular.
Erratic supply of electricity makes stocking of ice creams and chocolates difficult	Larger per capita consumption of ice creams and chocolates
Trips to nearby towns are a source of enjoyment, where several products are bought together	Shopping for daily items is seen as a chore.
Largely a value buyer, is turned off by gimmicks	Willing to try premium products; gets influenced by advertising
Likes direct communication in local language, rejects the modern idiom and unable to respond to bizarre humour appeals	Communication in a mix of languages, likes quirky communications and influenced by hype
Male-oriented products likely to do well as females are not given importance	Working women and higher education for girls make female-oriented products successful
Buys products that are easily available. Exhibits brand loyal behaviour; easy bait for imitation products	Mostly brand loyal but willing to experiment, discerning about brands; lower income segments buy imitation products
Purchases are highly influenced by families or opinion leaders like elders or local shopkeepers	Highly influenced by families, but individual preferences on the rise; dependent on online advice and peers
Buying power depends on good monsoons and harvests	Buying power is stable due to a social class dependent on fixed salaries

other sources like retailers, wall paintings, van operations and weekly markets. The research shows that rural consumers have become value conscious as reflected by their buying behaviour. Brands like Micromax and Karbon used this to establish themselves in rural markets—both these mobile companies targeted the rural market with their long battery backup benefit.

Patel and Prasad (2005) conducted a study on brand awareness of rural consumers and their behaviour towards various FMCG brands. The study revealed that local brands rule the market due to easy availability, awareness and influence of retailers on consumers. Prajapati and Thakor's (2012) study of rural buying behaviour of toothpaste shows that the rural consumers are more concerned about the quality and brand name of the oral care products purchased by them. Furthermore, it was also found that once the rural consumers found that certain brands are suitable to them, they do not change it easily. With regard to toothpastes, Colgate and Close Up were found to be the favourite brands. It was also found that rural consumers follow recommendations of the retailers for buying toothpastes.

Mini Case Study 3.6

Small Packs for Rural Areas

Consumers use small packs for different reasons and companies must understand these. Small packs like sachets make it easy for consumers to try out products. While categories like tea, shampoo, condiments and tobacco brands sell on the basis of convenience, telecom companies offer small recharge packs for affordability. These work for both urban and rural areas.

But there are other factors as well. Very often consumers do not want to pay for a service that they cannot use for a variety of reasons. Tata Sky discovered that rural consumers did not want to pay for the whole month when the service could not be used because of lack of electricity or other reasons. Armed with this insight, Tata Sky started offering a ₹8 recharge coupon that lets users access the DTH service for one day at a time, reports *The Economic Times* (2015). This is the smallest recharge as Dish TV has a minimum recharge of ₹10, while Airtel Digital TV offers a recharge of ₹35.

Small recharges work in another way—they bring back customers with deactivated services. Tata Sky is also hoping that TV viewers in rural areas will be converted to their services from analogue services.

Do small packs and recharges encourage new users?

Source for this Case Study:

The Economic Times. 2015. "Now Recharge DTH TV for Just ₹8, Tata Sky Launches Sachet Size Coupons." 9 April.

Urban and Rural Incomes

Regional differences and rural–urban differences are stark when we compare per capita incomes between urban and rural areas. Estimates by Dholakia, Pandya and Pateriya (2014) show that rural per capita income (₹45,798) was less than half of urban income (₹118,750) in 2011–12. The state with the highest rural per capita income was Haryana with ₹87,614, followed by Kerala with ₹75,126. The states with lowest per capita in rural areas were Bihar with ₹20,800 and Uttar Pradesh with ₹25,937. This shows great differences in incomes and purchasing power in villages. In urban areas, by comparison, per capita incomes were much higher: Haryana had an urban per capita income of ₹175,960 followed by Maharashtra with ₹168,178. The lowest per capita income in urban areas was in Bihar with ₹58,336 and Uttar Pradesh with ₹59,541 (Table 3.6).

Table 3.6 shows a great variation in per capita incomes and points to two conclusions:

- **Rural–Urban differences:** Incomes in urban areas are more than double of rural areas. While some of the difference is reduced when we consider higher cost of living in urban areas, it explains why there is an exodus from Indian villages to cities. People hope that by migrating to cities they can earn better. The differences also point to differences in buying behaviour. People in rural areas would tend to buy more basic goods while those in urban areas could afford expensive products and services. That is why, marketing strategies for urban areas do not work in rural areas.
- **Regional differences:** Differences between the lowest and highest income states once again show huge variations—per capita income in Haryana is more than four times that of Bihar. This shows that villages are not same across India. People in the poorest villages see a daily income of about US$1 a day. There is a clear lesson for companies: approach

states with different strategies. Apart from that, companies must devise income improvement plans that put money in the poor consumers' pockets. This has resulted in a host of initiatives that help both poor consumers and generate demand for companies. This book describes several such ventures that fall in the category of 'social business'.

TABLE 3.6

Comparison between urban and rural per capita incomes (selected states) for 2011–12.

	Per Capita Income (Rural)	Per Capita Income (Urban)
India	**45,798**	**118,750**
States with highest per capita incomes		
Haryana	87,614	175,960
Kerala	75,126	106,439
States with lowest per capita incomes		
Bihar	20,800	58,336
Uttar Pradesh	25,937	59,541

Source: Dholakia et al. (2014).

Urban and Rural Consumption Expenditure

We now look at consumption expenditure in urban and rural areas. The NSSO report on MPCE (2011) shows that people in urban areas spend much more in all categories than rural people (Table 3.7). This shows that people consume less in rural areas. It also shows that the level of prosperity is much higher in urban areas, adding to their tendency to splurge on non-essentials like entertainment. While this can be justified on the grounds that there is lack of spending opportunities in villages, it certainly shows the impact of lower incomes in rural areas.

Table 3.7 can be interpreted in another way—the lower consumption in rural areas shows that there is a great opportunity for companies to tailor-make products that will be accepted by rural consumers (see Mini Case Study 3.6). When we consider that rural population is double that of urban population, we see a sizeable opportunity for social business and rural marketing.

TABLE 3.7

Comparison of rural and urban MPCE.

Break-up of MPCE by 20 Broad Item Groups: All-India, 2009–10					
	Monthly per Capita Exp. (₹)			Monthly per Capita Exp. (₹)	
Item Group	Rural	Urban	Item Group	Rural	Urban
Cereals & cereal substitutes	145	162	Fuel & light	85	138
Pulses & their products*	35	49	Clothing & footwear***	65	115
Milk & milk products	81	137	Education	38	161
Edible oil	39	53	Medical	57	99

(Table 3.7 Contd.)

(Table 3.7 Contd.)

Break-up of MPCE by 20 Broad Item Groups: All-India, 2009–10					
	Monthly per Capita Exp. (₹)			Monthly per Capita Exp. (₹)	
Item Group	**Rural**	**Urban**	**Item Group**	**Rural**	**Urban**
Egg, fish & meat	50	72	Conveyance	36	112
Vegetables	87	112	Other consumer services	44	124
Fruits	26	63	Misc. goods, entertainment	53	113
Sugar, salt & spices	60	73	Rent	5	115
Beverages, refreshments & proc. food**	78	159	Taxes & cesses	2	16
Food total	**600**	**881**	Durable goods	36	81
			Non-food total	**453**	**1104**
Pan, tobacco & intoxicants	31	30	**All items**	**1054**	**1984**

* includes gram **includes purchased cooked meals *** excludes tailoring charges

Source: NSSO (2011).

Urban and Rural Lifestyles

An interesting insight into the differences between rural and urban consumers is obtained when we consider consumption by age and lifecycle stages (Table 3.8). Children in urban areas are more likely to spend their time in front of a video console than rural children. Health drinks, chocolates and branded breakfast foods are popular in urban areas. In comparison, rural children will consume locally produced candies and cereal-based breakfast. Urban teenagers are more likely to spend their time at malls, fiddling with their cell phones, while rural teenagers are more likely to be absorbed in television and movies. Young people (20–40 years)

TABLE 3.8

Products and services consumed at different stages of lifestyle in rural and urban areas.

Age	Life Cycle Stage	Urban	Rural
Below 12	Child	Video games, chocolates, beverages/health drinks	Toys, ice candy, *daliya*
13–19	Teenage	Cell phones, motorcycles, Internet	Bicycle, television, cinema
20–40	Young	Car, personal, computer, branded clothing, alcohol, stores/malls	Motorcycles, telephone, LPG, tailored/unbranded clothes, country/local (*haat bhatti*) liquor, haat
40–60	Middle age	Luxury car, credit, cards, house, health insurance, holiday trips	Tractor, kisan credit card, postal savings, mela
Above 60	Old	Clubs, theatre, parks	Choupal, playing cards, pilgrimage

Source: shodhganga.inflibnet.ac.in:8080/jspui/bitstream/.../08_chapter%203.pdf (Accessed on 21 December 2016).

in urban areas splurge on cars, computers, IMFL and branded clothes, while the preference for rural youngsters is motorcycle, country liquor and unbranded clothes. Their hang-out is malls in urban areas and the choupal or a local *dhaba* (local restaurant or tea shop) in rural areas. Young men in villages can hang around, doing nothing, but girls are expected to stay at home doing chores.

As they grow older, people in urban areas are likely to spend on a luxury car, house and holiday trips. In rural areas, people prefer to spend on a tractor and during fairs and melas. The older men can be seen in clubs, theatres and parks in urban areas, while in villages they spend time at the choupal playing cards.

The differences in rural and urban consumers show very clearly that companies cannot rely on urban strategies to work in rural areas. Each region has to be treated separately and the local values need to be incorporated in all marketing communications. Based on these differences, we can now attempt to profile the rural consumer in the next section.

PROFILING THE RURAL CONSUMER

Rural consumers are distinct from one another depending on their income and education. That is why, they cannot be thought of as one homogenous group. Some things are common among all groups, such as spending on aspiration needs, desire to get education, less exposure to brands and products and preference for fresh foods. Food items are bought locally and there is a premium on fresh products; hence, packed and frozen food products do not find their way in their shopping basket. But their buying behaviour differs in terms of what they buy and where they buy it from. Companies need to understand this to target rural areas, otherwise they will end up making mistakes. Organized retail chains, for instance, tried to bridge the distribution gap by starting stores that stocked agricultural products to consumer goods. Many of these, such as Hariyali stores, have had to shut shop, because going to a nearby town for shopping was also an enjoyable outing, during which other chores were also accomplished. People belonging to the lower income strata also had no use for such stores as they preferred to buy from the local market rather than going to a distant place to buy from the organized store. Buying from haats and melas is enjoyable for all income groups. Another common element is that, because of a marked preference for boys, male-oriented products do well than those targeted at females.

Kakati and Ahmed's (2014) study of two districts of North East India reveals clusters with distinctively different Value Attitude Lifestyles (VALs) characteristics. The study found that rural consumers can be grouped on the basis of distinctive clusters as follows:

1. Conservative, family-oriented and peace loving
2. Independent, new and variety seeking
3. Adaptable, self-sufficient and optimistic
4. Socially conscious and hard-working

Based on this, we can say that rural consumers exhibit some or all of the following traits:

- **Traditional outlook:** Rural populations, by and large, remain rigid and conservative. The society is custom bound and high emphasis is placed on traditions, rituals and customs (see Mini Case Study 3.7). As habits and beliefs are difficult to change, this makes the job of brands and new products difficult.

- **The role of the family:** The joint family remains the dominant force in rural areas. Family ties are strong. Business and agriculture are traditionally controlled by joint families.
- **Occupation:** The rural economy is largely dominated by agriculture and trading. Though the contribution of agriculture is falling over the years, it still has a major share in rural areas. In services, most jobs have been hereditary.
- **Social mobility:** Social mobility is limited—trades and services are usually carried out by families for generations. The influence of caste remains strong, which is another factor hindering mobility. Status is determined by birth.
- **Resistance to change:** Deep-rooted beliefs and customs contribute to resistance to change. Though education is bringing about a very slow churning, rural populations generally show habitual buying behaviour.
- **Deprived customers:** Due to distribution bottlenecks, many brands are not able to reach villages. Cheap products of lower quality and imitation products thus make inroads in rural areas. Many basic services are not available in villages.

Mini Case Study 3.7

Using Local Culture in Marketing

As mentioned in the text, rural societies remain traditional and tied to their culture more than urban societies. This implies that companies must use local languages and symbols to communicate brand benefits in such markets. This case study describes some companies that have used local traditions and culture effectively.

The insurance company ICICI Prudential used *sindoor* in its communications. Sindoor is commonly used by married women and is the symbol of protection and long life in Indian culture. It effectively conveyed protection and care to the target audience.

The Ministry of Tourism communicates the importance of being honest with foreign tourists through the traditional belief that a guest must be respected. It used *Atithi Devo Bhava* (Guest is God) to convey to people that tourists who come to the country should not be harassed or cheated.

The importance of clean water was linked to the fact that people pray the natural elements in religious tradition. This was used by Aquaguard water purifier, when it linked water with the custom of prayer. The ad used a song in the background that described how life revolved around water and that pure water was an important part of traditional prayer offering or making a wish. The lines used were *Yeh jal hai, amrit hai/Yeh dhan hai, jeevan ha* (This is water, it is wealth and life).

Incense sticks are part of prayer in Asian countries. ITC launched its incense stick brand Mangaldeep with fragrance-locked packaging to keep the sanctity of the incense sticks to be offered for prayers.

The mother is a symbol of care and nourishment. Many brands use the image of a caring mother to convey this. Horlicks uses a caring mother in its communication to symbolize nutritional value and care of the food consumed by children. The pain reliever brand Moov also uses a mother who ensures happiness of her family by working hard and using the product to keep her up and going. Maggi and Bournvita, too, use mothers to convey their message, as do a host of other brands.

Nutrition and good health for the family is conveyed by Nestlé when it launched Maggi Atta Noodles. The ad says that a packet is equivalent to three rotis, making it meaningful for the rural consumer.

Pillsbury launched by General Mills, uses the traditional roles of woman as mother, daughter, daughter-in-law and wife. By using the brand, women could expect acceptance and pride in their traditional roles. Spices brands too built on this theme.

Can you identify other brands that use tradition, cultures and symbols to the rural consumer?

RURAL MARKET SEGMENTATION

Rural market segmentation can be done on various variables.

Occupational Segmentation

Occupational or sociological segmentation is based on source and consistency of income. In rural markets, occupation determines income and forms a significant basis for segmentation. Though there are variations across regions, about 40 per cent of rural consumers are engaged in agriculture, followed by wage earners with 35 per cent. This shows that nearly three-fourths population of rural India has unstable income and depends on agriculture. Such incomes vary with monsoon and climatic conditions. Companies need to design offering for consumers with unstable income. Selling goods on equated monthly instalments (EMIs), which is popular with the urban salaried class, will cause difficulty for rural consumers. The occupations in rural areas (Table 3.9) are summed up as:

- **Artisans, farm labourers:** Consisting of carpenters, blacksmiths, craftsmen and labourers.
- **Small farmers:** Farmers with very small holdings or with a share in jointly held farms.
- **Tenant farmers:** Tenant farmers who work on leased or rented land to share the crops and income with owners of the land.
- **Medium level farmers:** Farmers with economically efficient size of landholdings.
- **Large farmers:** Zamindars, rich money-lenders and people with very large, ancestral land. They also tend to be local leaders and politicians, with links in urban areas, giving their land on lease to tenant farmers.

TABLE 3.9

Occupational pattern of rural population.

Occupation	Rural Population (Percentage)
Farming and agriculture	60.29
Agriculture wager	17.11
Business and craft	7.20
Non-agriculture wager	6.40
Salaried and others	10.0

Source: NSSO (2011).

Thomson Rural Market Index (TRMI)

Hindustan Thomson Associates developed a guide to rural market segmentation in 1972 and revised it in 1986. They collected data in 335 districts based on 26 variables. The TRMI is based on 10 variables having strong correlation to rural market potential.

1. Agricultural labourers
2. Gross cropped area

3. Gross irrigated area
4. Area under non-food crops
5. Pump sets.
6. Fertilizers consumption
7. Tractors
8. Rural credit
9. Rural deposits
10. Electrification

Based on these factors, the districts are classified as A, B, C, D and E, in order of high to low market potential.

MICA Rural Market Ratings (MRMR)

The MRMR is a useful marketing tool and a multimedia guide to rural India. It has been developed by the Mudra Institute of Communications Ahmedabad (MICA) in association with ML Infomap Pvt. Ltd., New Delhi. The rural market index indicates the rural market potential of all the districts of India, analyzed on 42 variables. Using digital mapping technology, it presents maps of all districts, shaded to indicate the level of market potential. Managers can thus graphically see areas with different patterns of market potential, along with related data such as bank loans, demographics, infrastructure, and so on. The tool also gives location of 'haats', or actual rural markets. By clicking on a haat, one gets to know the days of the week the market takes place. Routing can be done through the road and railway map of India, which is incorporated in the software.

Income and Savings

The 68th round survey on level and pattern of consumption expenditure was conducted between July 2011 and June 2012 by the NSSO. The household MPCE shows that the average MPCE was around ₹1,430 for rural India and about ₹2,630 for urban India. Thus, the average urban MPCE was about 84 per cent higher than the average rural MPCE for the country as a whole, although there were wide variations in this differential across states. An analysis in *Mint* (2014) shows that:

- **Low levels of consumption:** For rural India, the median MPCE was ₹1,198. Only about 10 per cent of the rural population reported household MPCE above ₹2,296 and only 5 per cent reported MPCE above ₹2,886. While average MPCE was ₹1,054, the median rural MPCE was ₹895, signifying half the rural population belonged to households with consumption expenditure below ₹30 per day. For urban India, the median MPCE was ₹2,019. Only about 10 per cent of the urban population reported household MPCE above ₹4,610 and only 5 per cent reported MPCE above ₹6,383.
- **Food accounts for half the expenditure:** For the average rural Indian, food accounted for 52.9 per cent of the value of consumption during 2011–12. This included 10.8 per cent for cereals and cereal substitutes, 8 per cent for milk and milk products, 7.9 per cent on beverages, refreshments and processed food and 6.6 per cent on vegetables. Among non-food item categories, fuel and light for household purposes accounted for 8 per cent, clothing and footwear for 7 per cent, medical expenses for 6.7 per cent,

education for 3.5 per cent, conveyance for 4.2 per cent, other consumer services for 4 per cent and consumer durables for 4.5 per cent. For the average urban Indian, 42.6 per cent of the value of household consumption was accounted for by food.

- **Inequalities have risen:** The data shows that the per capita expenditure level of the urban consumer is now 91 per cent higher than his rural counterpart, compared with 80 per cent in the earlier 61st round of the survey conducted in 2004–05.
- **Consumption expenditures are rising:** The survey shows an increase in consumption power across the country. The rural per capita consumption has grown 6 per cent in 2009–10 against 1.2 per cent in 2004–05. Similarly, urban per capita consumption has risen 6.8 per cent compared to 2.9 per cent in the earlier survey.

The study shows that average rural MPCE during 2011–12 stood at around ₹1,430 for rural India, a 35.7 per cent increase compared to the 2009–10. Of the total expenditure, rural households spent less than half on food items, suggesting rise in wages. The average urban MPCE was 84 per cent higher than rural areas. The share of expenditure on food declined substantially from 53.6 per cent to 48.6 per cent in rural areas and from 40.7 per cent to 38.5 per cent in the urban areas. The faster rise in the share of non-food expenditure in rural areas suggests a rise in wages. The rural wages went up from ₹231.59 a day in 2009–10 to ₹299 a day in 2011–12, a 29 per cent increase. *The Economic Times* (2013) reports that as MGNREGA has led to increase in wages, people in rural areas are spending more on non-food items. Within food, the share of protein-based items went up in the consumption basket. The share of milk and milk products went up from 8.6 per cent in 2009–10 to 9.1 per cent. Among non-food items, the share of durable goods in the consumption basket of rural areas went up from 4.8 per cent to 6.1 per cent.

The highest score for rural areas in India is from Kerala where monthly per capita consumer expenditure is almost one-third more than the national average. Nine out of India's 17 large states do better than the national average for rural areas. Among the northern states, he three states doing better than the national average are Haryana, Punjab and Rajasthan.

Segmentation on incomes show a wide variation in consumer behaviour as described here.

- **High income:** Those belonging to upper strata—landlords, large farmers, businessmen and traders—exhibit distinct buying and consuming patterns. Much of their buying is done from nearby towns since they have large vehicles like jeeps and tractor trolleys. A trip to the town means buying goods for the whole month; most of the buying is done in bulk. In this way, their buying behaviour is closest to consumers in developed countries, who stock goods in their basements. Only a few daily consumables are bought from the local market. The high income group is also most likely to be influenced by brands and advertising.
- **Middle income:** Large middle income families also buy many products in bulk. Food items like grains are purchased in bulk while fresh produce is bought on a daily or weekly basis. Small middle class families are likely to buy most of their needs from the local market. The middle income group is likely to be more dependent on local stores than the high income group. Rather than buying brands, people in the middle income group are likely to get their clothes stitched locally (Photo 3.5).
- **Lower income:** People in the lower income group depend on local stores and markets for all their needs. Local shopkeepers provide them credit, advice and easy delivery, which suits these consumers. Purchasing is done more often, though in lesser quantities. People in the lower income group are also likely to buy smaller packs.

PHOTO 3.5
A village shop selling local goods.

Source: Photograph by Dinesh Kumar.

Ownership of Goods

Segmentation of rural households can be made on the basis of ownership of particular goods. Such a segmentation analysis reveals categories that are growing or declining. It also shows opportunities for selling goods with little penetration in rural areas.

Data from NSSO in its report no 541 (2012) reveals interesting trends. While the ownership of households with bicycle is somewhat stable and declining for radio, the ownership for categories like motorcycle, car, television and refrigerator shows an increasing trend, showing the increasing prosperity of people over the years. Sewing machines seem to be going out of fashion but coolers and air-conditioners are being sold more (Table 3.10).

TABLE 3.10

Percentages of households having specific durable goods, from 1993–94 to 2009–10, all-India.

	Percentage of Rural/Urban Households Possessing a Specific Durable Good					
	R	U	R	U	R	U
Year	Bicycle		Motorcycle/Scooter		Motor Car/Jeep	
1993–94	32.7	37.1	2.1	11.6	0.2	1.2
1999–2000	40.5	39	4.5	18.4	0.4	2.7
2004–05	47.1	41.7	7.7	26	0.8	4.6
2009–10	54.9	41.1	13.9	33	1.4	6.5
	Radio		Television		Refrigerator	
1993–94	26.8	41.8	7	40.5	0.9	12.3
1999–2000	30.4	35.1	18.7	59.5	2.7	22.9
2004–05	26.3	33.6	25.6	66.1	4.4	31.9
2009–10	26.5*	23.3*	41.7	75.8	7.1	39
	Sewing Machine		Electric Fan		Air Cooler	
1993–94	5.6	18.4	15.9	56.6	0.5	6.4
1999–2000	7.4	20.3	26.3	68.5	1.7	10.9
2004–05	9.5	23.8	38.4	81.8	2.9	18.2
2009–10	10.9	21.7	55.2	90.6	5.0^	21.4^

*includes 2-in-1's ^includes air conditioners

Source: NSSO (2012).

FIGURE 3.3

Penetration of durables in rural and urban India.

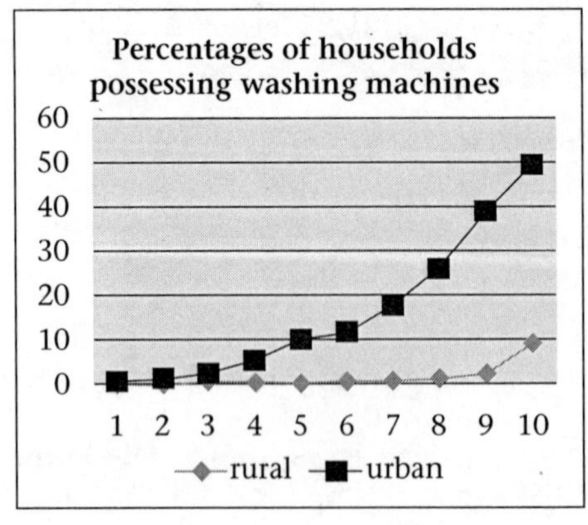

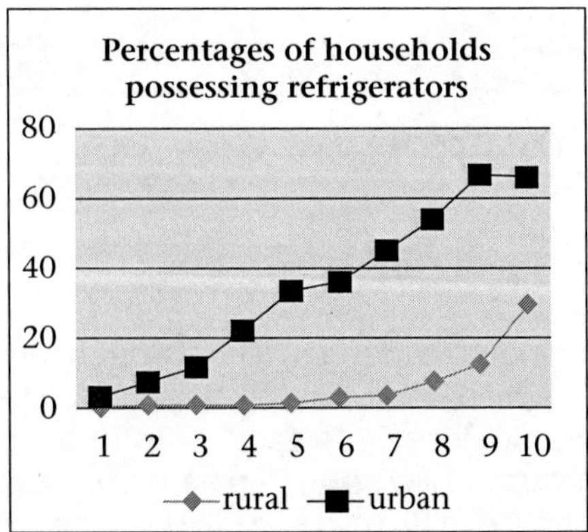

(Figure 3.3 Contd.)

(Figure 3.3 Contd.)

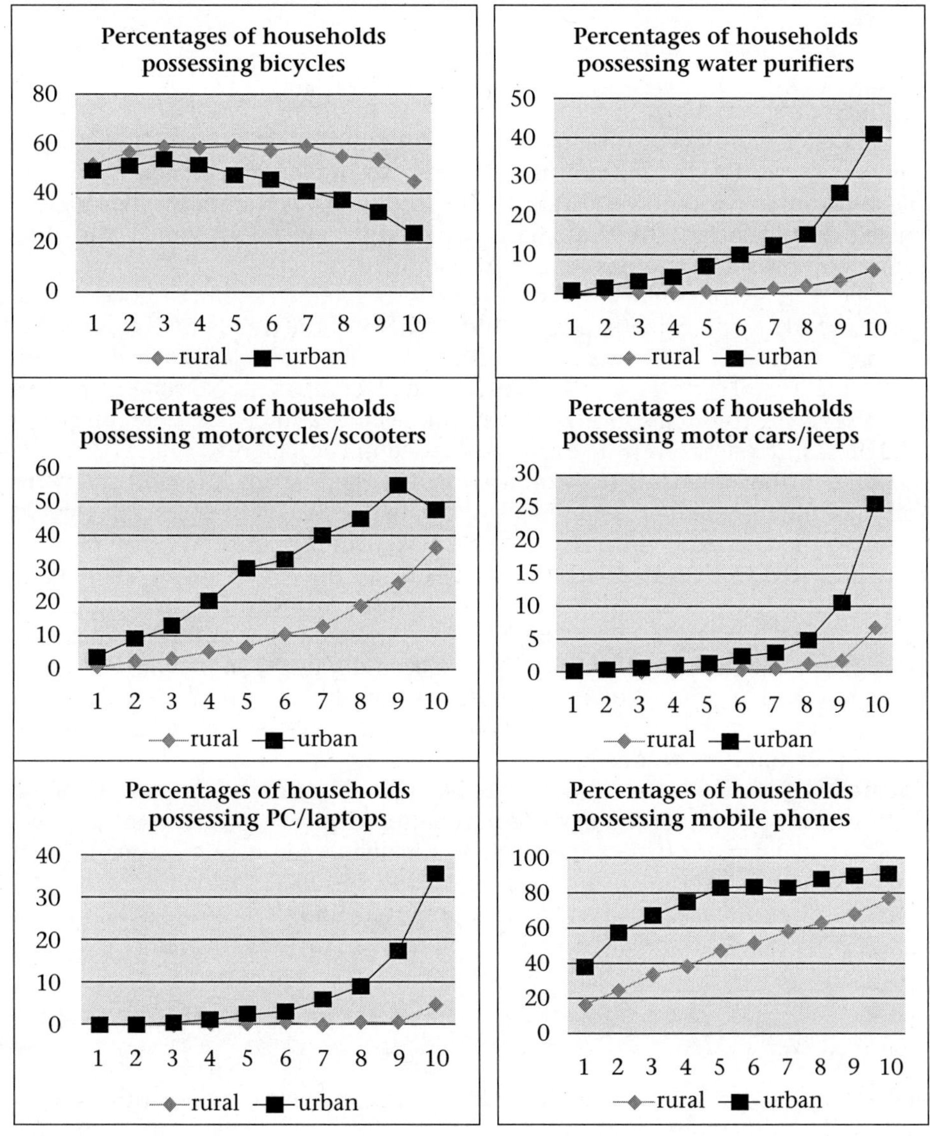

Source: NSSO, Government of India. (2012).

The growth rates and comparison with urban households is shown in Table 3.10. The ownership (Figure 3.3) shows a rising trend for all categories of durables. Mobile phones have the steepest graph, showing quick adoption, a result of falling prices and easy availability. In other categories, penetration levels are quite low, revealing a looming opportunity for companies. However, innovative marketing and financing schemes need to be offered to increase adoption of durables.

SUMMARY

Rural markets and rural consumers vary across regions and incomes. They are diverse, ranging from affluent landlords to marginal farmers and contract labourers. There are also regional variations, including variations in terms of proximity to urban areas. Despite modernization and improved education levels, rural society is still bound by traditional values and culture. When we consider Hofstede's cultural dimensions, we find that rural society is marked by high collectivism traits and power distance and medium uncertainty avoidance, and it is a highly male-oriented society. All these have marketing implications which must be considered by companies wishing to enter rural markets.

Rural society can also be understood on the basis of values. The importance of modernity, success and growth, youthfulness, adaptability, religion and rituals and customs has been discussed in this chapter. Values such as traditions, symbols and languages have immediate relevance to rural brand architecture, which are used by companies. No rural marketing initiative can be a success without a consideration of rural values and beliefs. Rural opinion leaders, having the most influence, can be identified and used in campaigns.

The chapter further discusses how rural areas are opening up to brands. Penetration of mobile phones, the Internet and cable TV as well as better road connectivity in rural India are contributing to the changing villages. Conventional wisdom that rural consumers care more about price and settle for substandard offerings is being proved wrong in many cases. Rural consumption behaviour is changing because of increase in incomes, government spending, change in mindsets, increase in awareness levels and increase in consuming potential.

Differences in rural and urban consumers have been discussed on income levels, consumption expenditure and lifestyles. Rural consumers are found to be conservative, family oriented and peace loving; independent and variety seeking; adaptable, self-sufficient and optimistic; socially conscious and hard working.

Several methods of rural segmentation have been described in the chapter. Rural marketing segmentation can be done on the basis of occupations, income and savings and ownership of goods. The NSSO data on these variables is an invaluable resource for segmenting markets. Companies also use two tools for rural segmentation: the TRMI, which is based on 10 variables having strong correlation to rural market potential; and the MRMR, which indicates the rural market potential of all the districts of India analyzed on 42 variables.

CONCLUSION

Rural markets have specific requirements, but tapping into rural areas requires the conventional wisdom of first understanding the customer. Since rural areas vary across regions in terms of purchasing power, education, loyalty to traditions and a host of other variables, a one-size-fits-all strategy does not work. Instead, each district needs to be treated as a separate marketing region. Within regions, too, proximity to urban areas plays an important part in modifying consumer response to products and brands.

Some things are common, though. Rural consumers remain value-oriented and are likely to avoid the bells and whistles that their urban counterparts do not mind paying more for. Pricing remains a crucial factor. But rural consumers do not want cheap or low quality products.

Several companies have cracked the rural marketing code. Companies need to crack the jigsaw puzzle of distribution, value-oriented products, price points and after-sales service, to succeed in scattered villages. Consumer goods companies like Dabur, HUL, Marico and Godrej are now getting a major part of their revenues from rural marketing, similar to durables producers like LG, Hero and Maruti. At the heart of these successful strategies, there is a deep understanding of rural consumers and their buying patterns. Rural marketing remains a difficult terrain but companies can succeed once they understand what rural consumers want.

KEY TERMS

Hofstede's theory of cultural dimensions: Helps in understanding rural consumption behaviour based on five dimensions of culture.

Individualism–Collectivism: Hofstede described collectivism as "societies in which people from birth onwards are integrated into strong, cohesive in-groups."

Long-term orientation: This dimension refers to the society's future-oriented perspective.

Monthly per Capita Expenditure (MPCE): Amount spent on consumption expenditure incurred per person in an economy.

Masculinity: The extent to which the society is dominated by male members.

MICA Rural Market Ratings (MRMR): A multimedia guide to rural India, developed by the Mudra Institute of Communications Ahmedabad (MICA), which indicates the rural market potential of all the districts of India analyzed on 42 variables.

Occupational segmentation: Segmentation based on occupation, source and consistency of income.

Power distance: The extent to which the less powerful members of the family accept the power of other members of the family.

Thomson Rural Market Index (TRMI): A rural index developed by Hindustan Thomson Associates based on data from 335 districts based on 26 variables.

Uncertainty avoidance: The way that a society deals with the unknown situations.

CONCEPT REVIEW QUESTIONS

1. In what ways is rural consumer behaviour different from the behaviour exhibited by urban consumers?
2. Are rural markets homogenous? In what ways are rural consumers different?
3. Describe rural society on the basis of cultural dimensions and discuss their marketing applications.
4. Explain how rural societies are more traditional than urban societies.
5. Explain how opinion leaders are influential in rural areas. Identify some real-life rural opinion leaders.
6. Describe the behavioural aspects displayed by rural consumers.
7. List down the differences in rural and urban shoppers and their buying behaviour.
8. How are the consumption habits of rural people different from those of urban consumers? Discuss the MPCE figures and describe.
9. Discuss the profile of the rural consumer based on VALs study.
10. Explain the various ways in which rural markets can be segmented?

CRITICAL THINKING QUESTIONS

1. In what ways do power distance play out in rural societies? How can managers make use of this aspect?
2. Do you think that by changing language, rural markets can be targeted effectively? Give examples of mixture of language that have worked and those that have flopped.
3. "There is a critical change unfolding in India's hinterlands." Do you agree with the statement? In what ways have India's villages changed or remained the same?
4. Small packs like sachets do well in categories that are sold on convenience or those that are targeted to women. Is this statement true?

PROJECTS AND ASSIGNMENTS

1. Collect advertisements targeted to rural consumers. Analyze these ads on the basis of Hofstede's cultural dimensions. Do you see any use of cultural elements in these ads?
2. Visit a village and enquire from people who they hold in high esteem. What can you make out from their choice of opinion leaders? Are they influenced in buying by film stars and sportsmen?
3. Conduct a survey in a village of your choice as to the brand preference of consumers with regard to different product categories. Explain which brands are more popular and why?
4. Observe the changes in a village due to investments made by the government. Conduct a study about income levels and show how they are impacting consumption behaviour.

WEB RESOURCE

Rural Electrification report as on 31 March 2015: http://www.cea.nic.in/reports/monthly/dpd_div_rep/village_electrification.pdf

REFERENCES

Accenture. 2010. "Masters of Rural Markets: The Hallmarks of High Performance." Available at: https://www.accenture.com/t20160914T044700__w__/in-en/_acnmedia/Accenture/Conversion-Assets/LandingPage/Documents/4/Accenture-Masters-Rural-Markets.pdf (Accessed on 26 April 2017).

———. 2013. "Masters of Rural Markets: Profitably Selling to India's Rural Consumers." Available at: http://www.accenture.com/in-en/Pages/insight-rural-india-markets-research-2015.aspx

———. 2015. *Rural Markets: The New Rural Consumer in a Digital World*. Accenture Business Journal for India. Available at: https://www.accenture.com/in-en/india-business-journal (Accessed on 27 April 2017).

Banerjee, Saikat. 2008. "Dimensions of Indian Culture, Core Cultural Values and Marketing Implications: An Analysis", *Cross Cultural Management: An International Journal* 15 (4): 367–78. doi:10.1108/13527600810914157

Business Standard. 2016. "Post Demonetization, Rural and Semi-urban Collections Surpass Expectations." 12 November.

Census. 2011. Office of the Registrar General & Census Commissioner, India. Available at: http://www.censusindia.gov.in/2011census/hh-series/hh01.html (Accessed on 26 April 2017).

Chandrasekhar, C.P. and Jayati Ghosh. 2017. "Are Modi Government's Power Promises Being Fulfilled?" *The Hindu*, 30 January. Available at: http://www.thehindubusinessline.com/opinion/columns/c-p-chandrasekhar/modi-government-and-rural-electrification-programme/article9509973.ece (Accessed on 27 April 2017).

Credit Suisse. 2014. "Emerging Consumer Survey 2014." Available at: http://publications.credit-suisse.com/tasks/render/file/index.cfm?fileid=E78BA562-9486-225A-8E2196F57A74B6A4 (Accessed on 27 April 2017).

Dholakia, Ravindra H., Manish B. Pandya, and Payal M. Pateriya. 2014. "Urban–Rural Income Differential in Major States: Contribution of Structural Factors." Working Paper No. 2014-02-07, Indian Institute of Management (IIM) Ahmedabad.

Dogra, Chander Suta. 2015. "Here Comes the Son: A Young Man in Rural Haryana is Entitled to the Best Things of Life." *Indian Express,* 12 April. Available at: http://indianexpress.com/article/india/india-others/here-comes-the-son-a-young-man-in-rural-haryana-is-entitled-to-the-best-things-of-life/ (Accessed on 25 April 2017).

The Economic Times. 2013. "Rural Spending Rises 35.7% during 2010–12: NSSO." 21 June.

The Economist. 2013. "India's Demographic Challenge: Wasting Time." 11 May.

Hofstede, Geert. 2001. *Culture's Consequences: Comparing Values, Behaviors, Institutions and Organizations Across Nation*. Thousand Oaks, CA: Sage Publications.

Jha, M. 2013. "A Comparative Study of the Buying Behaviour of Rural and Urban Consumers Towards Mobile Phone in Bihar." *International Journal of Advanced Research in Management and Social Sciences* 2 (4): 114–25.

Kakati, R.P., and S. Ahmed. 2014. "Rural Market Dynamics and Product Penetration." *The IUP Journal of Marketing Management* 13 (1): 59–77.

Kumar, Dinesh. 2015. *Consumer Behaviour*. New Delhi: Oxford University Press.

Ministry of Rural Development, Government of India. 2007. "Rural Road Development Plan: Vision 2025." May. Available at: http://pmgsy.nic.in/downloads/vision2025.pdf

Mint. 2014. "Rural India Tops Consumption Charts." 3 April.

National Commission for Women. 2005. "Report on Women and Water." Available at: http://ncw.nic.in/pdfreports/Women%20&%20Water.pdf

NSSO. 2011. "Level and Pattern of Consumer Expenditure, 2009–2010." NSS Report No. 538, NSS 66th Round, National Sample Survey Office. Ministry of Statistics and Programme Implementation, New Delhi. Available at: http://mospi.nic.in/sites/default/files/publication_reports/NSS_Report_538.pdf (Accessed on 27 April 2017).

———. 2012. "Household Consumption of Various Goods and Services in India." NSS Report No. 541, NSS 66th Round, National Sample Survey Office. Available at: http://mospi.nic.in/sites/default/files/publication_reports/nss_report_541.pdf (Accessed on 25 April 2017).

Patel N., and R. Prasad. 2005. "The Unique Rural Identity." *Indian Management* (October): 72–76.

Planning Commission. 2011. "Working Group on Rural Roads in the 12th Five Year Plan." *Government of India,* October. Available at: http://planningcommission.gov.in/aboutus/committee/wrkgrp12/transport/wgrep_rural.pdf (Accessed on 18 April 2017).

Prajapati, S., and Mital Thakor. 2012. "Competitive and Innovative Promotional Tools Used by Toothpaste Companies for Rural Market & Its Impact on Consumer Buying Behaviour in Gujarat." *Researcher's World* 3 (2): 82–86.

Rajan, R.V. 2005. "A Profile of the Rural Consumer." *Business Line,* 10 February. Available at: http://www.thehindubusinessline.com/todays-paper/tp-brandline/a-profile-of-the-rural-consumer/article2204116.ece (Accessed on 24 April 2017).

Ratna, P.A., and S. Mehra. 2015. "Opinion Leaders for Increasing the Market for Non-life Insurance Products in India." *International Journal of Business Innovation and Research* 9 (2): 210–28.

Singh, Supriya, and Mala Bhandari. 2012. "Money Management and Control in the Indian Joint Family across Generations." *The Sociological Review* 60 (1): 46–67.

TRAI (Telecom Regulatory Authority of India). 2015. "Press Release on Telecom Subscription Data as on 28th February." Press release available at: http://www.trai.gov.in/Content/PressReleases.aspx

Tripathi, P. 2014. "Effects of Brand Endorsements by Opinion Leaders on Rural Consumer Buying Behavior." *International Journal of Multidisciplinary Approach and Studies* 1 (4): 226–35.

UNDP. 2017. "About India: Challenges." *United Nations Development Programme*. Available at: http://www.in.undp.org/content/india/en/home/countryinfo/challenges.html (Accessed on 10 April 2017).

UNICEF. 2012. "Progress for Children: A Report Card on Adolescents." Available at: http://www.childinfo.org/files/PFC2012_A_report_card_on_adolescents.pdf (Accessed on 12 April 2017).

Closing Case
Reaching the Rural Consumer

FMCG companies need to reinvent their models to reach rural areas. This case study describes the initiatives of two companies that use innovative approaches to reach rural consumers.

Tata Tea's Gaon Chalo: In 2005, Tata Tea Limited was faced with a problem of stagnant market shares. HUL was the market leader with 22 per cent market share, while Tata Tea trailed at 16 per cent. Though the market was growing, the company was faced with unrelenting competition from local suppliers. This consisted of tea packed in polythene bags purchased at tea auctions. Not only was such unbranded tea cheaper than packaged tea, but its higher margins (up to ₹40 per kg) also served as an incentive for local shopkeepers to push the sales of unbranded tea. The margin for packaged tea was less than half this figure.

Faced with this situation, some players entered into a price war. But sales schemes do not offer a permanent solution to the challenge posed by local suppliers who tend to operate with few overheads of advertising or a large distribution infrastructure.

The company found that the coverage of the villages was inadequate. The challenge was obvious: how to reach the villages and make the distribution so effective that consumers would switch to Tata Tea. The route chosen was through NGOs in Uttar Pradesh who worked with the local people and knew their customs. The NGOs were selected with the help of Sir Ratan Tata Trust and the Dorabji Trust.

A pilot project was started in December 2005 in a village near Varanasi. The NGOs became the first level rural dealers who acted as distributors. The goods were supplied to mobile dealers who visited a fixed number of villages, kept the supply lines open for rural retailers and also collected payments. As the distribution expanded, market penetration also happened. The company improved its market share from 16.7 per cent in March 2006 to 19.2 per cent in June 2007 and 21.4 per cent in March 2008. In the same period, the nearest competitor, HUL, lost its market share from 21.2 per cent to 18.9 per cent. Today, Tata Tea boasts of 'number one position in volume terms'. However, in 2014, HUL's market share was reported at 31 per cent and Tata Tea was 25 per cent. These figures show that branded products were gaining popularity in the Indian market.

The project had two interesting impacts. First, it participated in the empowerment of rural people by increasing their incomes. Second, it was able to build an exclusive rural distribution chain at a considerably low cost. It showed that rural consumers like to buy good quality products if they are available. Thus, selling to rural areas hold the key to a company's marketing strategy. It also shows why it is important to understand rural consumers' preferences. Companies that ignore their customer base face the great risk of being taken over by local brands.

HUL's Khushiyon Ki Doli: HUL started an initiative to reach rural areas through its Khushiyon Ki Doli campaign. Its website says that the main objective of the campaign was to reach out to media-dark villages and connect with the direct users of the products to create greater preference for the company's brands.

The initiative consists of a van equipped with a LCD TV, a DVD player and a small generator—called *doli* or *palki*—that goes around villages and shows HUL's commercials on television. A doli or palki, which is a traditional symbol of happiness traditionally used to carry a newly wed bride to her new home, adds interest among villagers. In 2011, the company

Photo 3.6

HUL's Khushiyon Ki Doli is a means to reach village folk.

Source: Technospot (2010).

extended this to five states—West Bengal, Bihar, Maharashtra, Andhra Pradesh and Uttar Pradesh—thereby covering around 70,000 villages, 25 million consumers and 4 lakh retailers.

A team of promoters invite villagers to a collection point known as *mohalla*, where they are made aware of the company, its products and the importance of hygiene habits. The promoters give live demonstrations and speak in local languages. Simple quizzes and games are conducted, generating trial among consumers.

The promoters also go from home to home offering promotions to encourage trials. Another team visits all the shops in the village to ensure that they are stocking the company's brands. This BTL technique helps in connecting with the audience, generating buzz, encouraging trials and improving market coverage.

These two companies show that rural initiatives need to be innovative and interesting. Rural folk respond when companies make the effort to reach out to them.

Questions for discussion:

1. BTL campaigns are effective, but tend to be very expensive when done over scattered areas. How can they be made more effective?
2. Search for and describe other rural campaigns that have been successful.
3. Do you think that involving NGOs is a good idea for selling goods in rural areas? What are the advantages and drawbacks of this kind of an operation?
4. Compare the two approaches described here. Discuss their strengths and weaknesses. How can they be made more effective?

Sources for this Case Study:

Businessworld. 2010. "Tata Tea's Rural Marketing Project Has Changed Lives." 31 October.

HUL. 2012. "HUL Contacts 25 Million Rural Consumers through Khushiyon Ki Doli." Available at: https://www.hul.co.in/news/news-and-features/2012/hul-contacts-25-million-rural-consumers-through-khushiyon.html (Accessed on 27 April 2017).

Technospot. 2010. "HUL's 'Khushiyon Ki Doli'—A New Campaign Strategy." 30 May. Available at: http://www.technospot.in/huls-khushiyon-ki-doli/ (Accessed on 27 April 2017).

Section II

Strategies for Rural Marketing

4

CHAPTER

Rural Marketing Strategy

LEARNING OBJECTIVES

Companies have followed different strategies to serve rural markets. This chapter describes the marketing strategies that have been used by companies with great success. After reading the chapter, you will be able to:

- Learn about the approaches to rural marketing over the years.
- Understand how companies become 'rural masters'.
- Analyze different rural marketing strategies followed by companies.
- Analyze the concept of social business and how it is used to serve rural customers.
- Learn about new initiatives such as e-commerce and peer-to-peer (P2P) funding that help increase rural incomes.

Opening Case
Fabindia: Profits with Equitable Distribution

One company that combines marketing and distribution with empowering artisans at the same time is Fabindia. The company today not only has supply chains to source quality products from villages, but it also strengthens the artisan community by linking them to the market and even running a school in Bali, Rajasthan.

In 1960, John Bissell, a buyer from Macy's, came to India on the invitation of the All India Handicrafts Board to examine market opportunities for traditional handicrafts of India. He saw that while there was very rich variety of handloom fabrics in the country, the artisans and weavers were desperately poor. Bissell stayed back and set up Fabindia in New Delhi with the objective of helping the producers with a system of 'inclusive capitalism', that is, of selling the handicrafts at a profit but also ensuring "a fair, equitable, and helpful relationship with our producers, and the maintenance of quality."

Fabindia began exports of handloom home furnishings sourced from villages. In 1976, it opened a retail store in New Delhi, which became very popular, and sales began to increase. Today Fabindia links over 55,000 rural producers to modern urban markets, thereby providing marketing support for the producers while also creating sustainable rural employment and preserving India's traditional handicrafts. *The Economic Times* (2016) reports that Fabindia Overseas has crossed ₹1,000 crore sales figure to become the largest retail apparel brand in the country, significantly ahead of companies such as Zara and Levi's India.

"At Fabindia we celebrate India, and endeavour to bring all that we love about India to customers around the world," states Fabindia's vision statement. To do this, the company endeavours to make traditional products that delight customers, and to "harness the transformative power of a well-run business committed to profitable growth." However, the company takes up the two-fold task of marketing products while also strengthening its community of customers, designers, artisans, farmers, makers and entrepreneurs. Its website says that it is committed to provide products that delight them and also to protect the environment.

Fabindia provides marketing inputs to the craftsmen of India. Earlier the craftsmen had no access to markets or designs. They produced whatever they could and tried to sell directly to customers or were exploited by middlemen. Fabindia broke that chain and linked the craftsmen to designers and buyers, thereby providing a direct link with the market (Figure 4.1). As John had envisaged, the company adopted indigenous skills and designs suitable for the market, providing those inputs for production, and by regular supervision, it ensured that production commitments were met.

The company guides artisans to produce contemporary designs that find favour with urban consumers even while using their indigenous techniques. It provides inputs of design, quality control, access to raw materials and production coordination. Its business model consists of training artisans and upgrading them. It combines three business operations—buyers who can estimate demand requirements, designers who develop contemporary designs and the producer, who was earlier separated from the marketing and design process. Designers too had to be trained as they could not work with handlooms of different regions. A team of 'domain specialists' was created, who would work with designers: while the designer would be

FIGURE 4.1
The Fabindia business model combines three essential business operations.

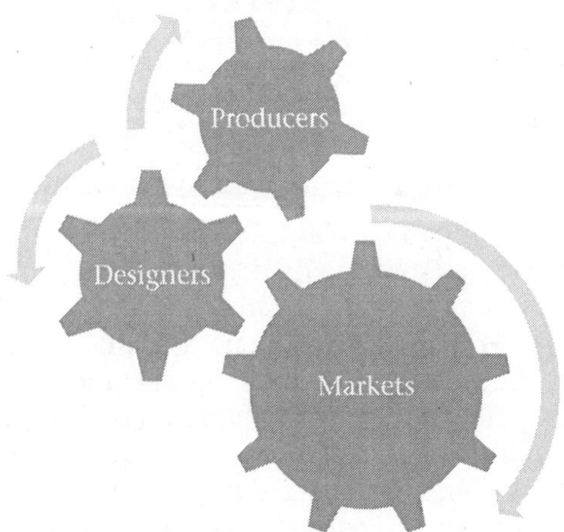

responsible for the 'look' of the product, the domain specialist would be responsible for technical aspects of production.

The company's product line consists of handwoven textiles, hand block printing, hand embroidery or handcrafting home products. However, it has slowly expanded its range. Home products were introduced in 2000, organic food products in 2004 and personal care products in 2006. Apart from ready-to-wear garments and accessories, furniture, lighting, stationery, tableware, cane baskets and a selection of handcrafted utility items are sold. Fabindia Organics carries several types of cereals, grains, pulses, spices, sugar, tea, coffee, honey, fruit preserves and herbs. Its range of authentic personal care products includes soaps, shampoos, hair oils, pure oils, moisturisers, body scrubs, face packs, hair conditioners and skin care products. The new range of products was sourced from the same communities with whom it had built up deep relationships over the years. Fabindia moved to engage not only with handloom weavers in these communities but also with farmers and woodwork artisans.

To establish recognition of handicrafts as distinctive, value-added products and to distinguish them from machine-made garments, Fabindia set up the All India Artisans and Craftw orkers Welfare Association (AIACA) in 2003. AIACA established the Craftmark, through which retailers of handmade products could seek certification and use the licensed 'Craftmark' logo to denote their product as a genuine Indian handloom product. This helped Fabindia to establish its brand. *The Economic Times* (2015) says that Fabindia is among the Indian retailers that are being courted by mall owners as their ethnic products have been posting high sales with no or little competition from global players.

The model of Fabindia can be summed up as making profits with equitable distribution. In the words of William Bissell, Managing Director of Fabindia since 1999, "In addition to making profits, our aims are constant development of new hand-woven products, a fair, equitable, and helpful relationship with our producers, and the maintenance of quality on which our reputation rests." The business model combines two opposing objectives—profitable growth and meeting social goals.

To achieve self-sufficiency and financial independence of the artisan community, Fabindia has set up Supplier Region Companies (SRCs), which are community owned enterprises, to coordinate the operations of artisans in a particular geography. The SRCs provide access to common facilities, implement standard systems, train artisans and consolidate supplies from the regional cluster that they covered. That is, all the upstream operations of the value chain were managed by SRCs while Fabindia would focus on marketing and distribution. Fabindia's product selection committee centrally determine monthly requirements and allocate orders to the appropriate SRC. The SRCs would then distribute the order among their members through a transparent bidding process; SRC members compete over individual chunks of orders and collaborate across the entire scope of the order.

To strengthen the community, Fabindia started a school in the village of Bali, Rajasthan in 1992. The idea was to empower young people in rural Rajasthan through a model school. Here, literacy rates have been traditionally low, especially among women. The school adopts creative approaches to education to bring out each child's inherent talents and includes environmental education in a local context.

Questions for discussion:

1. Comment on Fabindia's strategy. Why do you think it worked?
2. In marketing handlooms and village products, what problems did the weavers face? How were they resolved?

3. Compare the business model of Fabindia and KVIC. Why was Fabindia able to create a brand while KVIC and even the state handlooms emporia do not have that kind of equity?
4. How can marketing inputs help village industries? Can they be made into strong brands?

Sources for this Case Study:

Web Resources

Craftmark video: https://www.youtube.com/watch?v=lG_BU0kZTe0

Fabindia website: http://www.fabindia.com/

Fabindia School website: http://www.fabindiaschools.org/bali/aboutusover.html Watch TEDxDelhi - William Bissel, CEO of Fabindia: https://www.youtube.com/watch?v=MIbSNx3KALY

Watch William Bissell, Managing Director, Fabindia, talk about the story of the brand at: https://www.youtube.com/watch?v=3ChjLDbLfnU

Other Sources

Ramachandran, J., Anirvan Pant and Saroj Kumar Pani. 2012. "Building the BoP Producer Ecosystem: The Evolving Engagement of Fabindia with Indian Handloom Artisans." *Journal of Product Innovation Management* 29 (1): 33–51.

Singh, Radhika. 2010. *The Fabric of Our Lives: The Story of Fabindia.* New Delhi: Viking—Penguin Books.

The Economic Times. 2015. "Why Local Brands like FabIndia and Metro Are Being Pursued More by Shopping Malls." 27 August.

———. 2016. "Fabindia Crosses ₹1,000 Crore in Sales; Becomes Largest Retail Apparel Brand in the Country." 19 January.

INTRODUCTION

Slowly but surely, rural consumers are changing. As villages gain exposure to modern products and media, they prefer to purchase branded, high quality products. Several reports and studies have highlighted that the expectations of today's rural Indian consumers differ markedly from those of previous generations. They are moving away from purely economic concepts of value, driven by low prices, towards a broader notion of value that combines price with utility, features of products and services.

Fan et al. (2015) have shown the economic and social change that has occurred in rural China over a period of time as they are being exposed to modern lifestyles (Table 4.1). It can be observed that quite a similar process is happening among rural consumers in India.

The changes are slow and vary across regions, but signs of change are visible across the country. How can companies tweak their strategies to take part in the transformation taking place?

However, many companies have not been able to succeed in the rural India. We have seen in the earlier chapters that many BoP and rural ventures that were started with great hopes have either failed or achieved only modest success at great cost. While some companies have built sustainable models for rural markets, whose case studies are covered in this book, others have retreated from the space and prefer, instead, to simply contribute some money to NGOs to fulfil their corporate social responsibility. Success in rural markets, however, depends on what strategy the company uses, which are described in the subsequent sections.

TABLE 4.1
Economic and social changes in rural areas.

Traditional Patterns	Changing Trends
Use of limited goods	Perception of material improvement and aspiration to buy more products
Lack of innovativeness—distrust of new products	Orientation towards the market
Limited aspirations	Broader aspirations and horizons, better education, rising expectations
Limited world view	Broader world view, interest in education, and consumer goods
Purchase decisions based on economic value based on low prices	Broader notion of value that combines price with utility, features of products and services
Need-driven buying	Aspirational buying
Traditional values of thrift and savings	Materialism and consumerism

Source: Adapted for Indian conditions from Fan et al. (2015).

RURAL MARKETING STRATEGIES

Though villages are changing slowly, a majority of rural consumers constitute in part the BoP market, which represents the population of the world that primarily lives and transacts in an informal market economy. It was first articulated by C.K. Prahalad when *The Fortune at the Bottom of the Pyramid* was published in 2002. Many companies, including NGOs and other ventures have tried to cash in on this fortune. The approach has spawned new phrases such as: 'inclusive business', 'sustainable livelihoods' and 'social business'.

An explanation of the marketing strategies in BoP markets is given in the book, *Base of the Pyramid 3.0: Sustainable Development through Innovation and Entrepreneurship* (Fernando and Hart 2015), which says that companies often take an incremental approach while trying to serve such markets. It describes early efforts in rural marketing as 'BoP 1.0' and 'BoP 2.0'. BoP 1.0, which has been followed by many rural ventures, consists of adapting existing products, reducing price points and extending distribution to villages. In the preface to the book, Stuart Hart likens BoP 1.0 to a 'child with a hammer', that is, if a child is given a hammer, everything looks like a nail to him. Companies use the same strategies they have been following in the past to influence rural customers, who look like a lot of new, though smaller nails to them.

BoP 2.0 goes a step further—it stresses the importance of co-creating products and creating compelling value propositions for customers, using innovative techniques and leapfrogging to sustainable technologies. Hart shows the distinction between the two approaches as follows: "If BoP 1.0 model can be summarized as 'finding a fortune at the BoP' then BoP 2.0 can be characterized as 'creating a fortune with the BoP'."

Bop 3.0 describes the evolving approach to serve rural and BoP markets. It goes beyond co-creating products to changing the very approach of companies towards marketing. It calls for a complete change in purpose and mindsets of companies and investments in social businesses rather than commercial ventures. Strategies followed in rural markets in these three approaches are described here.

Rural Marketing Strategy—BoP 1.0

Companies are following various strategies to serve rural markets. These are described as follows:

1. Product strategies
2. Pricing strategies
3. Cost strategies
4. Distribution strategies
5. Promotion strategies

Product Strategies

This section describes some of the common product strategies that companies have used to penetrate rural markets. These range from selling small packs, innovative product design, sturdy products and giving names that are more acceptable in rural India.

1. **Small units:** Keeping affordability in view, products have been made available in small packing in rural India (Photo 4.1), which also results in low cost. Offered at a convenient price point, such packs also encourage trial purchases. However, this strategy also necessitates change in supply chains as retailers have to be serviced more often and supplied in very small lots—say, six or ten sachets at a time. This strategy has been used in

PHOTO 4.1

Companies have used the strategy of supplying small packs to reach rural areas. The strategy, however, calls for redesigning supply channels.

Source: Photograph by Dinesh Kumar.

case of shampoos and biscuits. However, in products not bought in villages, large packs are preferred as they help in reducing trips to the town to buy them. This behaviour is described in Chapter 2.

2. **Product design:** Designs need to be modified to suit rural habits and lifestyles. Electric gadgets, for example, must sustain irregular voltage and long periods of electricity cuts. The Godrej ChotuKool is an example of complete product redesign for rural areas. "Rural consumers show a distinct preference for bright colours," write Kotler et al. (2009), which is used by products such as Lifebuoy and Tiger biscuits. They give the example of Hindustan Latex Ltd, which found in a survey in Uttar Pradesh that rural households preferred bright colours. It then decided to re-launch its Rakshak condoms in bright yellow and red colours as these were considered the colours of festivity.
3. **Sturdy products:** Products need to be redesigned for ruggedness, which are more suitable for rural markets. They must not only be sturdy but also look capable of withstanding rough transportation and usage. Very often products are required to be transported in carts over bad roads so that they survive the ordeal. They must also withstand usage by several family members.
4. **Brand name:** People in rural areas now show brand name awareness. However, companies need to use a name that strike a chord with rural audiences. For example, Shaw Wallace named brands as *Shabnam*, *Josh*, *Janeman* and *Rangeela* to capture rural markets. Jha (2014) writes that portrayal of recognizable logos on the package assists in brand recognition and recall. These widely understood symbols help rural customers in making brand associations and generating recall.

Pricing Strategies

Pricing for rural areas requires innovative approaches. The price points have to be kept in mind while, at the same time, not compromising with the utility and sturdiness of the product. While it is true that rural preference for branded products is increasing, companies must avoid the tendency to introduce frills and increase the price. Very often rural consumers prefer basic products at good prices. Some of the pricing strategies that can be followed are given here.

1. **Low-unit packs:** Companies have to avoid unnecessary frills as affordable packs have a better chance of trials and gaining acceptance. Many rural consumers at the lower end of the economic lifestyle, such as small and marginal farmers and labourers, do not purchase large packs. Cavinkare's Chik shampoo (see Mini Case Study 4.1) became the trendsetter some years ago when it introduced shampoo sachets priced at ₹0.50. This helped the product succeed in rural and BOP markets. Godrej sold its Expert hair colour and Nupur henna at ₹5 and ₹10 price points. HUL introduced Pepsodent toothpaste in a sachet of ₹4, while Pepsico introduced its Kurkure brand in packs of ₹3 and ₹5. Uninor, Vodafone and Tata Docomo provide daily recharges of as little as ₹5. Such low-unit packaging is convenient for rural customers and results in high levels of trial purchase.
2. **Packaging:** Rural users reuse packaging for storage and price in the advantage gained from it. Reusable packaging is very popular as the boxes are used as containers to store goods. That is why, packaging must be rugged. Another reason for it is that products are required to be transported over long distances, over bad roads.
3. **Value engineering:** Value engineering refers to the technique in which costly raw material is substituted with the cheaper materials, without sacrificing the quality or functional efficiency of the product. Companies follow this technique to create products that serve the purpose they are meant for, but at considerably lesser costs.

Mini Case Study 4.1

CavinKare: A Pioneer in Small Packaging

CavinKare was the first to make sachet marketing a success in India. C.K. Ranganathan, chairman and managing director of CavinKare, says that the idea of sachet was of his father's who felt that liquid could be packed in sachets as well. He pioneered small packs of talcum powder in 100 gm, 50 gm and 20 gm packs when it was sold only in tin containers, and later salt sachets of as low as 5 gm were also introduced. His idea was that everyone should be able to use the products.

In 1983, Ranganathan bought a shampoo-packing machine for ₹3,000 and named it Chik Shampoo after his father. The product did not succeed immediately. When Chik entered the market, Velvette Shampoo was being marketed aggressively by Godrej. Then a scheme was introduced—customers could exchange five sachets of any shampoo for a Chik Shampoo sachet, free. This was highly successful. Later, the scheme was altered so that the company gave one free Chik Shampoo sachet in exchange of five Chik Shampoo sachets only. Soon, consumers started asking for Chik sachets only. The sales went up from ₹35,000 to ₹12 lakh a month.

After that, jasmine and rose fragrances were introduced. The company roped in actor Amala as its model, and its sales rose further to ₹1 crore a month. Market share increased steadily and in 1992, Chik dominated South India.

At that time, large companies sold products in big bottles only and that too from fancy stores. They did not consider the small kirana stores, nor did they focus on the rural market. Ranganathan writes that when Chik went to the rural areas of South India, people hardly used shampoo there. The company showed them how to use it through live demonstration on a young boy, asking those assembled to feel and smell his hair. Next, Chik Shampoo-sponsored shows of Rajniknath's films were organized, with Chik advertisements in between the movie, followed by live demonstrations. Free sachets were distributed among the audience after these shows. This worked wonders in rural Tamil Nadu and Andhra Pradesh—after every show, shampoo sales went up.

After seven years, the company ventured into Meera Herbal powder. As new products were introduced, the name of the company was changed from Beauty Cosmetics to CavinKare in 1998; with C and K spelt in capitals, being Ranganathan's father's initials. Cavin in Tamil means beauty and grace.

Later, the company introduced perfumes. Since good perfumes came at a huge price, they were beyond the means of ordinary people. The company introduced a ₹10 pack of Spinz perfume which was again successful. Fairever cream was launched in 1997 even against well-entrenched competition. The company launched its product containing saffron, which is traditionally used to get a fair complexion. Again, sales galloped. This was followed by Indica hair dye.

Ruchi pickles in sachets was launched next; the company currently sells about 5,000 tonne of pickles per annum. Today the company is a well-diversified group with brands in personal care, professional care, food, snacks, dairy products and beverages.

CavinKare has a strong distribution footprint, reaching more than 3 million outlets through more than 6,000 stockists. The company has replicated the success at home in foreign lands as well, serving consumers in more than 13 countries. It is currently marketing and distributing the Adidas and Jovan personal care range in India. It also markets Tiger Balm, which is available in all medical outlets as well as in mom and pop stores across India.

Which other products can benefit from this strategy? What are the challenges faced by companies when they sell small packs?

Sources for this Case Study:

Web Resources

CavinKare website: http://www.cavinkare.com/corporate.html

See NDTV programme, "Boss's Day Out: C K Ranganathan of CavinKare" at: http://www.ndtv.com/video/shows/boss-s-day-out/boss-s-day-out-c-k-ranganathan-of-cavinkare-aired-november-2006-307962

Other Sources

Business Standard. 2015. "CavinKare Plots a New Route." 29 June.

Rediff.com. 2007. "The Inspiring Success Story of CavinKare." 22 March. Available at: http://www.rediff.com/money/2007/mar/22bspec.htm (Accessed on 26 April 2017).

Mini Case Study 4.2

Mobile Phones in the Small Town

Rural India is taking to smartphones. A report by International Data Corporation says that Tier-2 and Tier-3 cities will fuel the growth and contribute to volumes of the Indian smartphone market in the coming years. Increased data penetration and reach of e-commerce is helping in the market growth.

However, the non-urban consumer has different needs than what appeals to the urban consumer. Brands such as Micromax, Intex, Lava International and Karbonn have been successful in smaller towns by offering features and value with affordable pricing. Intex uses digital platforms, sporting events and on-ground events to reach small towns. The company offers products with dual SIM, long-lasting battery, bigger screens and high-end processors. Its Matrabhasha phone enables communication in 21 Indian regional languages and it has a big data saver function and a women safety app called 'Sashakt'. The company has set up over 70 Intex Smart World experience stores spread over 50 cities. Festive occasions are used for a direct connect with the consumer. Intex's ownership of Gujarat Lions adds interest in the brand.

Micromax focuses on shifting consumers from feature phones to smartphones. The company realized that more upgrade opportunities exist in Tier-2 or Tier-3 towns. It used comedian Kapil Sharma and actor Rana Daggubati in its promos using local languages and broadcasting them on regional channels. This helped the brand connect with consumers in small towns.

Karbonn Mobiles has set up its distribution at the district and taluka levels, covering 90 per cent of Tier-2 and Tier-3 districts in the country. This also helps to provide servicing in remote areas. The company has extensively used radio with activities such as *Karbonn Kamaal Ka Juke Box* in Agra. The brand used canter vans in Maharashtra and Uttar Pradesh to support the launch of its multimedia devices range. Apart from providing products with local language functions, tie-ups with online marketplaces and leveraging the festive buying season has helped the company improve market penetration.

The strength of these brands is that they provide a product that is high on specifications while being affordable at the same time. Chinese phones are available with cheaper prices but Indian brands counter this with better distribution and service. They are creating point of sale visibility and thus score over foreign brands.

How did Indian brands fight off competition from Chinese brands in rural India?

Source for this Case Study:

Financial Express. 2016. "A 'Smart' Footprint." Brand Wagon News, 22 April.

Cost Strategies

Cost is a great deterrent for a rural marketing plan. Marketing managers struggle to control costs in serving rural markets—large distances, small orders, lack of economical transportation, non-availability of warehouses, excessive spoilage and damages are some of the problems that we have described in this book. Each of these adds to the cost (see Mini Case Study 4.2). It would not be wrong to compare the cost model for rural India to organizing an Indian wedding—budgets can quickly go out of control and unforeseen expenses may arise suddenly. Rural marketing also need long-term interventions and their results are difficult to measure in the short term. Managers used to serving urban markets, find it difficult to anticipate the many costs in reaching villages.

Identifying consumer clusters calls for heavy expenses as data is not available and has to be collected personally. Rural India does not have data such as Indian Readership Survey (IRS) or Broadcast Audience Research Council (BARC), which can provide some basis for a marketing manager to work with.

Apart from information cost, logistical costs are a major component of rural marketing costs. The cost of acquiring customers is also high, according to *The Economic Times* (2015). If the cost of acquiring an urban consumer is ₹100, the acquisition cost comes to ₹180–200 in a rural market, since BTL techniques must be used. This becomes uneconomical if the company is selling a low-cost stock keeping unit (SKU) since profits do not justify the cost. This is the reason that most rural marketing plans fail. Several strategies are suggested to keep costs under control in rural marketing:

1. **Target one district at a time:** Instead of rolling out an all India rural plan, companies should approach one district at a time. These initiatives require full commitment of the company. Since each district is different, it is important to focus energies on one district before adding more areas.
2. **Avoid dependence on third parties:** A company must build its own dedicated team to tackle rural marketing. A third party can be involved only when the company wants to scale up. In this way, it can create benchmarks for costs and potential benefits.
3. **Do not extend urban strategies:** The common mistake made by many companies is to replicate urban strategies in rural areas. This does not work. Rural areas require their own pitch, advertising and distribution. These must be worked out for each specific area. That is why, it is important to treat each area as distinct.
4. **Find data for each village:** A lot of factors will have to be considered to assess market potential. Some of the factors to consider in each village are: penetration of TV and mobiles, number of school-going children, state of the economy and social exclusion and connectivity to the highway. Consumer behaviour has also to be looked at closely. For instance, if the objective is to introduce cleaning products in a village, it would be important to see how many people use ash for cleaning dishes and then progress to those using counterfeit bars.
5. **Use BTL techniques:** Instead of looking for advertising media, which is difficult to find in villages, companies must demonstrate products via live skits or kiosks in fairs, haats (weekly markets) and gatherings. For example, Godrej Consumer Products monitors brand awareness levels pre and post the activity to determine whether to scale it up or not. Keeping track of the cost per contact and keeping a targeted payback period helps as well.
6. **Work with local people:** Companies should work with local people who can be helpful in providing reach and service. For example, after struggling to increase penetration in rural areas for three years, Tata Sky (see Mini Case Study 4.3) started identifying local repairmen with whom they could partner. The local repairman, usually called

Mini Case Study 4.3

Tata Sky

Tata Sky embarked on an ambitious plan, providing its products and services at every pin code and village in the country. The company admits that it is extremely difficult to penetrate these areas because of lack of dealers. To tide over this problem, the company identified repair workshop operators for fridge and other electronic goods and gave them training to later make them part of the Tata Sky dealer network. Now it has its presence in six lakh villages supported by 210,000 dealers nationwide.

The company devised a clever campaign to target the non-urban India. The message was, *Phone ghumao, Tata Sky lagao*, meaning that Tata Sky could reach anywhere if one could connect a phone call. The endearing ad film was shot in a seemingly remote area of Ladakh, which showed two young girls searching a network on their mobile phone. One girl tells the other to stop wasting time as no one will come to their remote location. The girl persists and makes a call to the Tata Sky Helpline number and says that she lives in a *kuccha* hut in Ladakh and asks if she could get Tata Sky in her house. A voice tells her: *Madam aapka phone lag gaya, toh samajho connection bhi lag gaya*. The ad further explains: *Aap India ke kisi bhi kone mein ho, bas phone ghumao, Tata Sky lagao*.

Though Dish TV is the strongest DTH player, Tata Sky attempted to establish itself as a pan-India player. The company found that 60 per cent of its new subscribers in four years were from outside India's top 20 cities.

The company has built its sales and service infrastructure in all regions of the country. Using local repairmen as its contact point, it has strengthened its distribution and after-sales service infrastructure. The local repairmen work under the supervision of the company and are provided training for the purpose. This has made the expansion easy.

At the same time, it designed better and more relevant applications for rural customers. It introduced value-added services such as Actve English, Actve Vedic-Maths and Actve Fun Learn, which became very popular in smaller towns. It also repackaged some content because rural customers want content in Hindi and local languages. The electronic programme guide or EPG is also available in Hindi. Simple gaming options such as Sudoku are offered based on the insight that rural kids do not have smartphones, iPods and computers. The company has set up call centres in nine different places with local accents, so that someone calling from a region will be greeted in the local language and accent.

Better customer service, viewing quality and value-added services are pushing DTH over cable in remote areas. Tata Sky's 'Showcase'—on which newly released movies are available in satellite quality—has been very well-received in the rural markets.

Do you think this strategy can be replicated by other products and service? How?

Sources for this Case Study:

Web Resource

Watch the Tata Sky ad at: https://www.youtube.com/watch?v=DOvjrd9PiHA

Other Sources

Bhagia, R. 2013. "Tata Sky's Rural Play." *Afaqs!* 19 December. Available at: http://www.afaqs.com/news/story/39485_Tata-Skys-rural-play (Accessed on 27 April 2017).

Tata. 2012. "Where the Sky is the Limit." March. Available at: http://www.tata.com/article/inside/53C5k8jDrw8=/TLYVr3YPkMU (Accessed on 27 April 2017).

The Economic Times. "Aim to Ensure Every Pincode & Village Have Tata Sky Dealers." 10 August.

Sonu, became the local contact for the company. The repairmen were volunteers and not permanent hires with Tata Sky, so the distribution worked on a variable cost model. The company trains the repairmen but saves on infrastructure cost, because it does not have to set up offices in villages. This is a good way of keeping costs in check.

Distribution Strategies

Distribution to villages requires new and innovative approaches. Such distribution models are covered in Chapter 6. Companies have to figure out how to reach villages—through existing wholesalers or establishing dedicated channels. In doing so, it will have to consider various options as described in the following:

1. **Direct distribution or appointing sub-dealers:** One of the major decisions a company has to take is whether to distribute through existing channels and wholesalers or establish a direct rural channel. Though extending the reach of existing dealers is much cheaper, the company is limited in terms of penetration—dealers will only supply at places where they incur minimal cost. On the other hand, direct channels will help reach the most remote regions but call for very high investments.
2. **Depots:** To ease distribution, a company must establish its depots at places from where villages can be served easily in the manner of hub-and-spoke models. Identifying such places and getting adequate space in backward areas is a difficult task. Usually warehouses are not available in rural areas.
3. **Seasonal Demand:** Annual events like melas provide buying opportunities to villagers (Photo 4.2). Accenture (2013) finds that about half of a rural household's purchasing takes place during these annual events. Supply chains have to be geared to meet such

PHOTO 4.2
Shops decked up on way to the village fair. Most purchasing takes place during fairs.

Source: Photograph by Dinesh Kumar.

seasonal demand even while the demand is minimal in the rest of the year. Annual events provide a very good platform for sales because people visit these events to make purchases. It is estimated that there are about 8,000 melas that are held in rural India every year. By making products available in these annual melas, mandis and agricultural markets, a firm can cover a large section of the rural population. An indicative list of festivals and gatherings of India is given in Chapter 7. This does not include haats and melas.

4. **Logistical challenges:** Companies venturing into rural markets face great logistical challenges such as scattered markets, poor roads and infrastructure, lack of financial intermediaries, and so on. A detailed discussion on these is available in Chapter 6.

Promotion Strategies

Communication is important in marketing. Promotion plays a major role in changing behaviour and product adoption among rural consumers. However, it is difficult to find communication channels that are favoured by rural consumers since reach of mass media is limited. Moreover, messages have to be tailor-made for each region. A number of issues like illiteracy and socio-cultural values pose challenges in developing communication strategies for the rural markets. Experience marketing and BTL techniques are more effective than media in villages but organizing such activities for lakhs of villages is an arduous and costly task. Promotion strategies are covered in Chapter 7. However, some of the strategies followed by some companies is described here.

1. **Indian models and actors:** Popular Indian models and actors attract rural audiences. Sports stars are also popular among rural audiences.
2. **Wall paintings:** Wall paintings are the advertising method where the reach of mass media is limited. Companies such as Coca-Cola, Pepsi and Tata, along with some smaller companies, advertise their products through paintings.
3. **BTL techniques:** Rural consumers are better networked and proactively seek information through multiple sources. Additionally, women and children now play a more empowered role in purchasing decisions and travel farther to buy goods and services. Providing product experience to them is best done through BTL techniques.
4. **Using local languages:** Ads in local languages have more probability of being noticed than those in English and Hindi. Salesmen trained in local language are required. Local events must be organized in villages and the community should be involved.
5. **Personal selling:** Rural marketing involves more intensive personal selling efforts as compared to urban marketing. To effectively tap the rural market, a brand must associate it with the lives of rural folk. Rural sales strategy will include hiring employees who spend time in rural areas and who are comfortable with the local language and customs.

Although the BoP 1.0 strategies have worked for companies, sustained success in rural markets is gained when they go beyond the traditional understanding of marketing and sales. Companies also do not need negative publicity that they are making profits off poor people. Hence the next approach evolved, which consists of involving consumers as co-creators.

The BoP 2.0 Approach—Co-creation

Co-creation is a business strategy in which brands and consumers work together to create better products and services. For the purpose of this book, it means involving people who are not served by traditional markets. It is an emerging strategy, aided by Internet technologies which help to connect with customers. It calls for a complete change in management thinking because the traditional approach has been 'top-down', that is, to develop products by the R&D departments that are then launched in the market. Now consumers become active partners in developing products. But the task is not easy, since companies have to go and meet BoP consumers directly due to the low Internet penetration. Involving rural customers and getting them to share their knowledge also calls for an entirely different set of skills that urban market researchers use (see Chapter 5).

Porter and Kramer (2011) write that companies must act to reconcile business and society, which can be done by 'creating shared value' so as to generate value at the same time for the company as well as meeting needs of a social nature. It involves making use of company know-how and reconfiguring relations throughout the value chain. Companies can create shared value in three different ways: (a) re-conceiving new products and markets, (b) redefining productivity in the value chain and (c) building supportive industry clusters at the company's locations.

The aim of co-creation is to develop products and consumer value by involving the customer in the process of creation. It re-shapes the way in which companies think and innovate: it calls for a restructuring and integrating R&D, marketing activities and market research.

Co-creation is a difficult process because it means involving many stakeholders and activities, which include the following:

- All stakeholders must be involved, including NGOs, social entrepreneurs, financial partners and potential consumers.
- Deep relationships and partnerships must be established by companies in villages.
- Attempts must be made to use the experience and understanding of local people and organizations that provide linkage with rural people.
- Companies must first learn rural skills and impart its own knowledge through training of the villagers so that they can actively participate in the process.
- Companies have to work on open systems and have no way to protect their intellectual property.
- A completely different set of market research skills are required to involve the villagers in the process.

Co-creation involves BoP consumers to play active roles in the company's value chain by becoming co-producers, suppliers or distributors (Figure 4.2). It empowers consumers as it creates employment and builds skills. Companies benefit by creating products that are more relevant to consumers and get local people to work for them. The company understands customer needs, local conditions and culture and uses these insights to develop new products and enter new business opportunities.

The Bop 3.0 Approach—Social Business

"We are in a new era," writes Sabeti (2011), continuing that a new business model is emerging, driven by social aims. This new sector, or social business, has potential to change the face of capitalism. A social business has two characteristics: a commitment to social purpose and

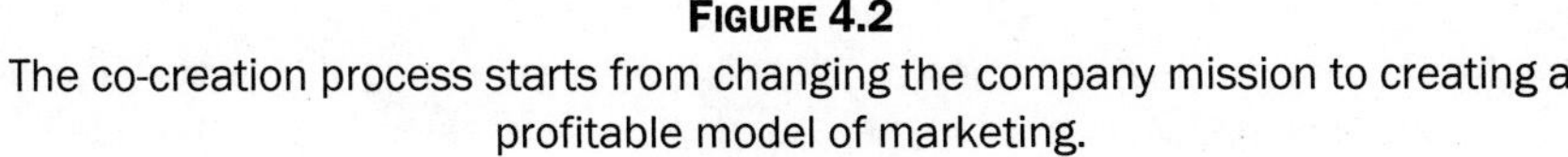

FIGURE 4.2
The co-creation process starts from changing the company mission to creating a profitable model of marketing.

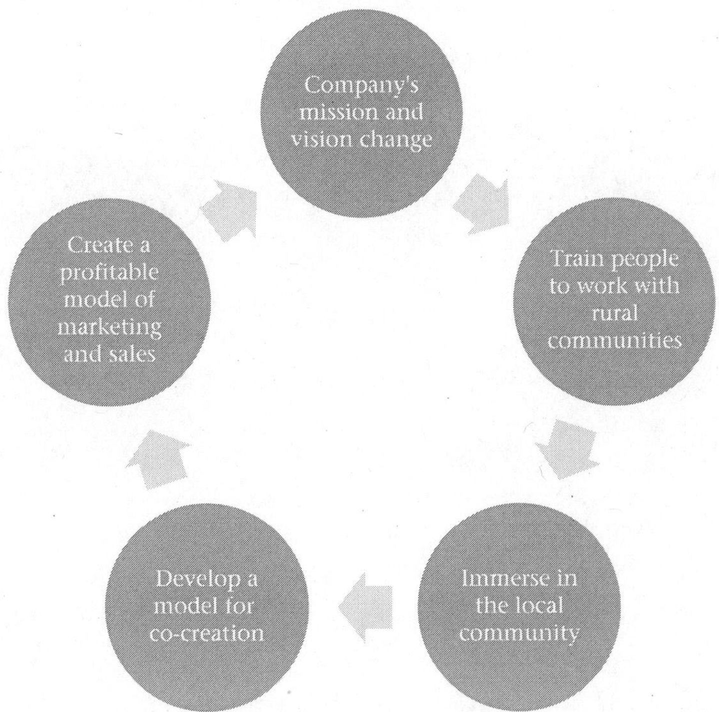

reliance on earned profits. This is the BoP 3.0 approach, which implies that companies have to change their very approach to business. Instead of profit-making as their main objective, companies must keep social objectives in focus and become social businesses.

Some companies indeed develop techniques and approaches that help rural people in the long run, which in turn increases their purchasing power and help them become loyal customers (Figure 4.3). It becomes a positive cycle in which the company solves a problem of rural customers, which helps increase their income or the proceeds from their produce. This then results in higher purchasing power that facilitates buying goods and services and availing better education, resulting in people having better lifestyles and awareness, leading to still better incomes.

The aforementioned cycle can only be started if companies go beyond their traditional role of mere selling and try to add value to the lives of rural customers in some way. Indeed, some companies do so and become 'rural masters', as described by Accenture (2013). What these companies do differently is described in the next section.

Santos et al. (2015) write that increasingly the business of business may now have to be *more than business*, since companies are being asked to address many societal expectations. The approach is gaining ground as companies cannot tap poor rural consumers without solving their problems and increasing their purchasing power. Not only are markets limited if people are poor, but selling to them also attracts the charge that companies are profiting from the poor.

FIGURE 4.3

A positive rural marketing strategy. Companies help villages in improving village output, which in turn results in more purchasing power in their hands to buy improved and better products.

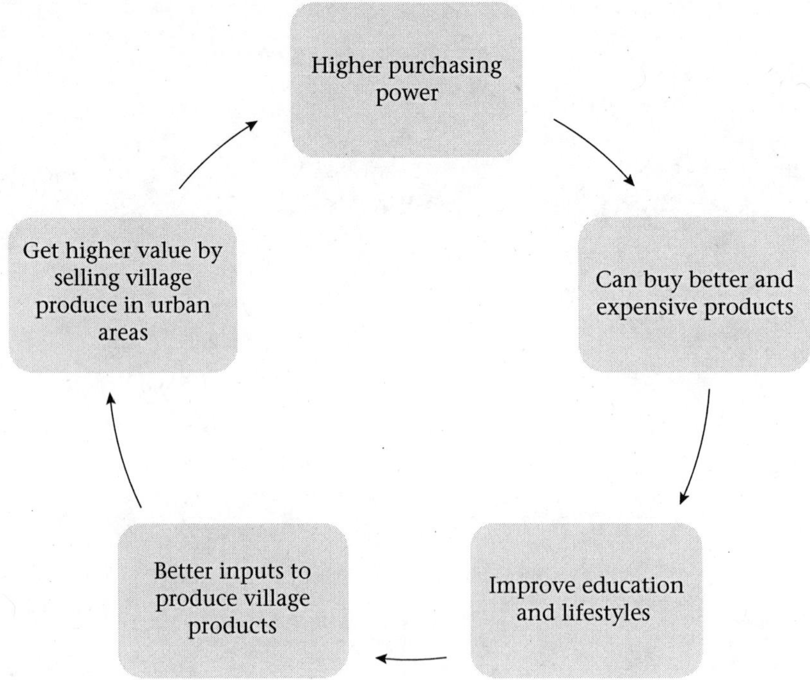

A social business is one which is run like a normal business in the sense that it seeks profits, but is different in the sense that the profits are reinvested in development of society in some way or in the business itself.

Yunus et al. (2010) explain that social business is one in which all the costs are recovered and surpluses generated are reinvested in the business. This is distinguished from other forms of business, as shown in Figure 4.4. Profit-making businesses attempt to maximize their profit and recover their investment and costs in order to build a self-sustaining and profitable operation. The non-profit organizations and NGOs work for social profit but have to depend on funding as they do not recover their costs and are in that sense unsustainable. Social business combines both financial *and* social profit maximization so that they have sustaining, profitable operations, but the promoters do not make profits, which are reinvested in the business to serve society. This means, social business is like a regular business which markets products and services but does not pay dividends to promoters.

They further describe that social business lies between the profit maximizing companies and non-profit organizations. It is, thus, a means of using managerial skills creatively so as to solve social problems. It therefore has three objectives:

- First, it seeks to alleviate social problems, including poverty.
- Second, it must be run sustainably, that is, it should recover its costs.
- Third, profits are reinvested in the business rather than paid to shareholders.

FIGURE 4.4
Nature of social business.

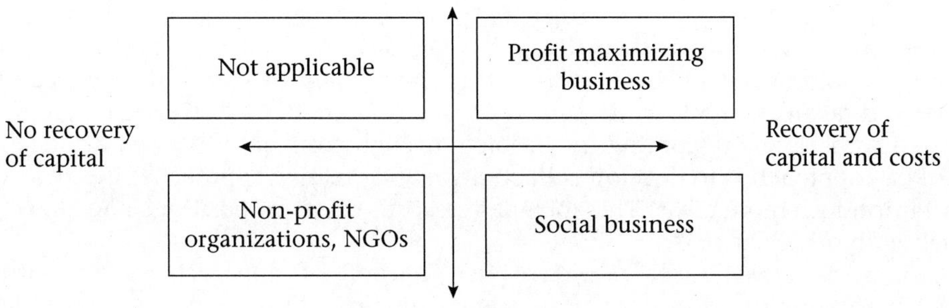

Source: Yunus et al. (2010).

Social businesses have a *value proposition,* that is, a way of serving customers and offering them value, and *a value constellation,* consisting of building an internal value chain and also an external one with suppliers and partners. Finally, it must generate profits through conventional ways of doing business.

Various companies have built social businesses (see Mini Case Study 4.4). Essilor, for instance, has succeeded in making reading glasses to poor populations in villages who lack the resources to pay for an eye test or spectacles (see Chapter 1). Fabindia (see Opening Case) has helped rural weavers and artisans supply market-friendly products and thus provides an outlet for them. Renault Mobiliz has set up 'solidarity garages' which repairs cars of poor customers at a nominal cost. Its website says that people on low incomes can buy a car or have their car repaired at a Renault Socially Responsible Garage. It also has an investment firm, Mobiliz Invest which provides financing for businesses that offer innovative mobility solutions to improve the quality of life for socio-economically disadvantaged people. Café Femenino (see Chapter 9) provides help to women coffee growers and gets them a fair price for their produce. Jain Irrigation (see Chapter 9) helps farmers increase their income and offers a buy-back for their produce. There are endless examples of such interventions.

Unlike a profit-maximizing business, the prime aim of a social business is not to maximize profits, although it generates profits. Yunus and Weber (2010) explain that the objective of entrepreneurs and companies must change from a single orientation of profit maximization to "maximization of profit and doing good to people and the world." Furthermore, business owners do not receive any dividend out of the business profits. The following are the characteristics of a social business:

- **Purpose and mindset:** The company must have social objectives as its core purpose and ambition. It cannot be treated as just another marketing or distribution problem.
- **Open innovation:** In BoP 2.0, companies co-create solutions in partnership with the poor, rather than simply market low-cost products in rural areas. Companies have to move to open innovation, that is, drawing on the 'wisdom of the crowd' to develop completely new solutions. Participatory grassroots innovations may take BoP business to a whole new level in the years ahead, opines Hart (2015).

- **Innovation ecosystem:** While BoP 2.0 recognized the importance of engagement with the community, it still tended to view the business as driven by the venture's strategy, price point, business model or value proposition. It is becoming increasingly clear that BoP ventures will need to be embedded in a larger innovation ecosystem, including technology providers, funders, capacity builders, partners and supply chain players.
- **Innovation for the last mile:** Many BoP ventures failed because they could not produce volumes or returns in distributing small quantities of goods over sparsely populated rural areas. While earlier approaches to rural marketing stressed on gaining effective distribution, overcoming the problem of high costs has remained a challenge. The BoP 3.0 approach is to develop collaborative and creative approaches in the area of distribution in remote areas. This includes creating value propositions and sharing channels with other partners.
- **Cross sector partnership networks:** The BoP 2.0 approach was to partner with NGOs and other players in villages. Some companies have 'outsourced' their customer facing functions to NGO partners. The next approach is to have more complex partnerships with not only NGOs but with governments, customers and academic partners.
- **Sustainable development:** The BoP 3.0 approach is to integrate both environmental sustainability and an integrated triple bottom line perspective into the objectives of the company, as opposed to the earlier approach of private companies trying to build models to serve the poor, create livelihoods and alleviate poverty in remote areas.

Mini Case Study 4.4

Social Entrepreneurs across the World

Bornstein (2007) in his book, *How to Change the World*, describes social entrepreneurs as "transformative forces: people with new ideas to address major problems who are relentless in the pursuit of their visions, people who simply will not take 'no' for an answer, who will not give up until they have spread their ideas as far as they possibly can." He is the founder of Ashoka, the largest network of social entrepreneurs worldwide, with nearly 3,000 Ashoka Fellows in 70 countries putting their ideas into practice on a global scale. Ashoka has provided start-up financing, professional support services and connections to a global network to social businesses. Ashoka launched the field of social entrepreneurship and has multi-sector partners who contribute to solving social problems.

Ashoka's mission is to enable people to become 'everyone a changemaker'. It therefore helps in training people with the skills and a purpose so that they can contribute ideas and solve problems for the community. It brings people, resources and ecosystems together to bring about a social revolution. It has a network of private, philanthropic and citizens and hopes to achieve large-scale social innovation through entrepreneurial experience.

Bornstein tells the stories of leading social entrepreneurs in Asia, Africa, Latin America and the United States. He writes that "social entrepreneurs are uniquely suited to make headway on problems that have resisted considerable money and intelligence. Where governments and traditional organizations look at problems from the outside, social entrepreneurs come to understand them intimately, from within." Some large organizations helping social businesses are given here.

Google.org: Tech entrepreneurs are using innovation to tackle some of the world's biggest challenges. It invests in teams with bold ideas that create lasting global impact. (www.google.org)

Omidyar Network: A philanthropic investment firm started by the eBay founder. It supports people to improve their lives by investing in market-based efforts that catalyze economic and social change. The network works in the areas of education, financial inclusion, governance and property rights (Available at: https://www.omidyar.com/initiatives).

The Acumen Fund: Acumen invests in companies and leaders who serve the poor in genuine, empowering ways, to solve the problems of poverty. Its website says that it believes access to critical goods and services is a key to unlocking the poverty trap. Providing access to critical goods and services can result in improved capabilities and a significant increase in productivity (Available at: http://acumen.org/sectors/).

Ashoka: Ashoka is a network of social entrepreneurs worldwide. Founded by Bill Drayton in 1980, Ashoka pioneered the field of social entrepreneurship and looks for entrepreneurial talent and new ideas to solve social problems (http://india.ashoka.org/about).

The Skoll Foundation: Jeff Skoll, a former eBay executive, started his foundation to drive large-scale change by investing in, connecting and celebrating social entrepreneurs and innovators who help them solve the world's most pressing problems (Available at: http://skoll.org/about/about-skoll/).

Do you know of any social businesses in your area?

Source for this Case Study:

Bornstein, David. 2007. *How to Change the World: Social Entrepreneurs and the Power of New Ideas*. New York, NY: Oxford University Press.

The Challenges of Viability, Legitimacy and Competitiveness

Though social enterprises have a major role to play in BoP marketing, they find it hard to earn profits. Foster and Bradach (2005) found that such ventures have unrealistic expectations and therefore are not able to generate revenue.

Peter Drucker had pointed out that businesses need a 'functioning society' to be able to make profits. But, emerging countries have weak government institutions and markets. Millions of poor are kept out of the developmental process as these countries pursue policies mainly for the rich. Jäger and Sathe (2014) write that companies must learn to find solutions to basic everyday challenges such as erratic electricity, bad roads, low education, unstable political environments, poverty, criminality and much more. Their study of strategy and competitiveness in Latin American markets illustrates that the construction of a community road may not be a matter of corporate social responsibility as much as it is a 'business necessity' since business cannot operate without it. Such investments may be essential for the company to be able to operate at all.

Often, social enterprises fail to see the challenges of viability, legitimacy and competitiveness in emerging markets. In less developed markets with poor infrastructure, investments to improve social and environmental performance are necessary to ensure the firm's viability and legitimacy. The challenges are described as follows:

- **Viability:** Companies must be able to function despite informal markets, weak institutions and poor infrastructure, such as bridges, roads and security systems. Sometimes investments may be required in these before the business can be viable.

- **Legitimacy:** Their second challenge is to find legitimacy within the local communities and societies in which the company operates. In less developed countries like India, where a large percentage of the village population lives in poverty, a company must not be seen as profiting from the poor.
- **Competitiveness:** A company's competitiveness is its ability to provide products and services that create greater value for customers than those of the competition. Further, if the company works on open systems for co-creation, the ideas can quickly be copied. Competitiveness is developed by creating some system or investment that the competitor finds hard to replicate.

PHOTO 4.3

Unhygienic conditions at an agricultural market in India. Should companies invest in social goods in order to gain legitimacy?

Source: Photograph by Dinesh Kumar.

The Rural Masters

Using the strategies described here, some companies have achieved high market shares and profitability in rural markets. Such companies with a high rural innovativeness and performance are dubbed as 'rural masters' in a report by Accenture (2013). Such companies achieve rural market share by "focusing on execution excellence, implementing novel strategies to serve rural consumers and drawing on a deep understanding of consumers' cultures and needs."

The challenges experienced by companies can be classified into three major categories—reaching, acquiring and retaining India's rural customers.

Rural Customer Reach

As we have mentioned earlier, rural markets have huge obstacles in terms of poor distribution networks, partners with limited capabilities, long payment cycles and weak marketing channels. This makes the 'high cost to serve the rural markets' unsustainable. Higher costs are driven by higher logistics costs in rural areas. Recruiting and selecting channel partners is an additional critical challenge they face in reaching rural customers. This can be overcome by:

1. **Reaching 'the last mile':** Companies have to use a multi-pronged approach to reach rural consumers for deeper penetration (see Mini Case Study 4.5). They find channel partners who can help them. Hybrid models of distribution are used rather than extending conventional urban models to rural areas. Some companies have adopted the village entrepreneur ('feet-on-street') model. Others have added layers to their distribution to reach dispersed rural customers. Still others are leveraging e-commerce and alternate channel partners. These and other models of distribution are described in Chapter 6.
2. **Market expansion:** Using detailed market scanning and segmentation, GIS mapping and other technologies, companies build a comprehensive, multidimensional picture of target segments. Adopting a variable cost model gives them the flexibility to change course if they are not getting desired results.
3. **Channel relationships:** Rural areas require that companies train and upgrade channel partner skills to implement their sales strategies. They create sustainable channel partner relationships and ensure that their partners remain motivated. In many instances, they also build familial bonds with their partners to strengthen trust.

Mini Case Study 4.5

Emami's Rural Push

Emami Ltd is a FMCG major with sales of ₹2,217 crore in 2015. It has a strong rural presence and generates more than 40 per cent of its revenue from rural sales. This case study describes how the company follows a unique strategy to serve rural markets.

Realizing that rural consumers wanted the products that were used by their urban counterparts but at cheaper price points, the company focused on introducing small packs. It launched Zandu balm and Navratna oil in ₹2 and ₹1 packs, respectively, and also Navratna talcum powder pouches priced at ₹1. The company also improved sales of categories such as skin cream and health supplements, which have low penetration, through this approach in rural areas.

Photo 4.4
Emami uses brand ambassadors to promote brands in local languages.

Source: Emami Annual Report, 2014–15.

Rural consumers are engaged through various means, including regular participation in haats, melas, *jatra* (a folk-theatre form of Bengali theatre) and festivals. Thus, the company has a strong presence in melas such as the Sonepur mela, Sawan mela, Kanlinga yatra and the Kumbh mela. The BTL activities undertaken at these melas and haats helped create a strong brand presence, improving rural penetration and awareness. The company wooed the modern trade channels through trade meets to enhance engagements with trade partners and implemented IT initiatives at the dealer level, improving secondary sales visibility. This helped it consolidate its urban and rural reach and ensured direct access to consumers.

To advertise, the company uses wall painting and retailer dealer boards to build visibility of its brands in rural markets and advertising in movie theatres in rural areas. District newspapers are also used for advertising as well as innovative BTL activities especially developed for rural India. The company runs sales vans in some districts to reach the last mile consumers.

Emami also uses brand ambassadors effectively. The celebrity appeal creates aspirational values and widens the intended target audience group for niche products. Though it does not have different ambassadors for urban and rural areas, it selects them based on their appeal and popularity since its brands have mass appeal. Amitabh Bachchan, Hrithik Roshan, Kangana Ranaut, Kareena Kapoor, Shah Rukh Khan and others have endorsed the company's products at the national level, while southern superstar NTR Jr endorses the Navratna brand in the South. This has made it a market leader in niche products. Shah Rukh Khan helped a lot: it helped Emami penetrate the rural market because of his star power. In 2006–07, sales from Fair and Handsome cream were ₹25–27 crore, which nearly quadrupled to ₹100 crore in 2008–09.

The company was started in the 1970s, when the Indian FMCG market was dominated by foreign products. Strong innovation helped their first products—talcum powder, vanishing face cream and cold cream—gain a foothold in the market. For instance, when most of such products were packaged in tin containers, it introduced plastic containers with labels printed on imported paper, making it look like a foreign product.

In 2004, Emami introduced Fair and Handsome and became the first-mover advantage in men's fairness cream and stayed ahead of competitors such as HUL and L'Oreal. Today, the product enjoys a market share of 59.1 per cent, way ahead of HUL's Fair and Lovely Max Fairness for men, which has a 25 per cent market share.

Emami operates in the niche category. Four of its key brands—Navratna oil, Boro Plus, Fair and Handsome and Zandu—together contribute about 70 per cent of Emami's topline. Navratna oil had a market share of 67.4 per cent in the cool oil category and Boro Plus accounted for 76.3 per cent of all antiseptic creams sold in India in 2015. Emami's pain relief portfolio—Mentho Plus balm, Fast Relief and Zandu balm—garnered a 60.9 per cent market share in 2014–15.

The synergy between innovation, marketing and distribution has translated into enviable growth for the company. In five years ending 2015, Emami has grown at a CAGR of 17 per cent, compared to the Indian FMCG sector's 12 to 15 per cent growth in the same period. The company's market capitalization has grown more than 20 times: from ₹948 crore on 31 March 2005 to ₹22,820 crore as of 31 March 2015.

Emami has launched several product extensions to build on this growth, with brands such as Zandu Vigorex, Emami 7 Oils in One, Boroplus Face Wash and Fair and Handsome Face Wash for men.

Project Swadesh is also an important feedback mechanism. Insights gathered from visits to rural markets led to developing a cooling talcum powder. For villagers, fragrance was not the only attribute required. They expressed a need for something which could keep their body cool in extreme summers. This insight resulted in developing Navratna Cool Talc.

Sources for this Case Study:

Web Resource

See the "Founder's Message" on Emami Ltd website: http://www.emamiltd.in/about-us/4/founders-message.php#sthash.d289moS7.dpuf

Other Sources

"Emami Limited Annual Report, 2014–15: The Next Orbit." Available at: http://www.emamiltd.in/images/annualreportpdf/20150710052510small181.pdf (Accessed on 27 April 2017).

Forbes India Magazine. 2015. "Emami Ltd: Mover and Shaker." 24 July.

Mint. 2013. "Emami Pushes Direct Distribution in Rural Market." 23 July.

Outlook Business. 2015. "Down the Country Road." 23 January.

Rural Marketing. 2014. "40–45% Revenue Comes from Rural India." 13 August. Available at: http://www.ruralmarketing.in/interview/advertising-and-marketing/40-45-revenue-comes-from-rural-india

Rural Customer Acquisition

To acquire rural customers, businesses must understand the cultural, economic and demographic dimensions, which:

1. **Define a unique value:** Successful companies continuously attempt to know rural customers and delivering experiences tailored to their needs, values and preferences. They invest in developing capabilities such as customer analytics to gain insights into rural consumers and their needs.
2. **Engage influencers:** Word-of-mouth plays a strong role in acquiring rural customers than it does in urban markets. Companies engage individuals with high standing in rural communities as 'influencers'. Key stakeholders are ranked according to their influence and support. Influencers shape rural customers' perceptions of their business and offerings, boost brand image and customer satisfaction while reducing customer acquisition costs.

Rural Customer Retention

Because of the high cost of customer acquisition in rural areas, customer retention is important to succeed. Building trust and providing after-sales service with local communities can result in better customer retention. This can be done by:

1. **Developing low-cost models for after-sales support:** Companies must try and build a dedicated low-cost after-sales infrastructure using local resources who provide 'no-frills service' (see Mini Case Study 4.3) or leverage technology to decrease the costs of delivering that service. After-sales support provides customer feedback, generates market intelligence and strengthens a company's rural bonds, which increases customer loyalty.
2. **Build trust:** Companies often make the mistake of treating rural consumers as those in urban areas, and offer them the same value proposition they offer to urban markets. These value propositions pay little attention to how the product meets the unique needs and wants of specific rural customer segments. The emphasis is on selling products to new areas. This does not work in the long run, so companies have to integrate into the strong rural social fabric in rural areas by:

   a. **Engaging with stakeholders to create trust:** Companies build symbiotic relationships with a large set of stakeholders that focus on consumers' needs. In the process, they build an ecosystem of stakeholders.
   b. **Investing in community development:** Companies align their long-term interests with development of local communities to build synergistic relationships. Strong relations are built by integrating local populations into their value chains as partners with a vested interest in the company's survival.

It becomes clear that rural masters go beyond merely supplying goods to rural areas but try to do things differently. Their attempt is to solve some problem faced by rural people, and by addressing problems they gain their trust. The case of Jain Irrigation (see Chapter 9) shows how companies expand the definition of textbook marketing to penetrate rural markets.

FIGURE 4.5
Rural distribution is not merely about supplying goods, but in offering solutions to remote customers.

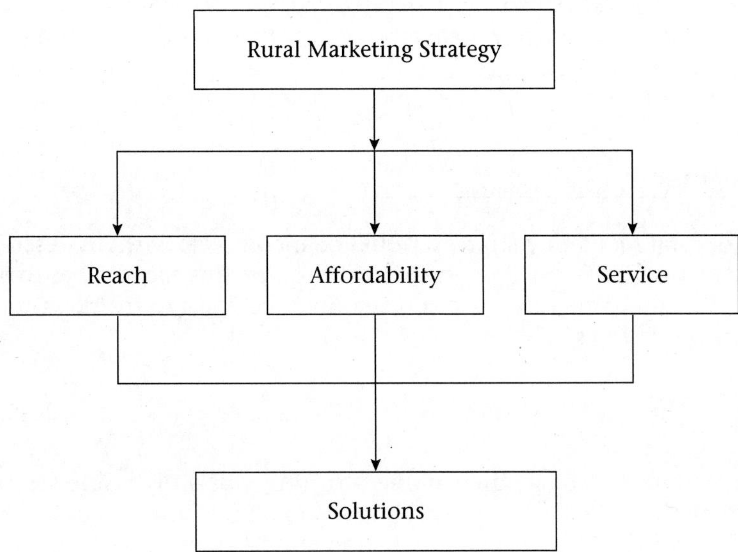

Problems of rural customers can be solved if companies tackle one or all three aspects of marketing. We have summarized the approach in Figure 4.5—a rural marketing strategy can succeed if it addresses some need of the consumer, in terms of reach, affordability or service. All these are geared towards one objective: providing solutions to rural consumers. If the consumer realizes that his life is made simpler by the company, a trust and a long-term relationship will result.

- **Reach:** Reach means placing products in proximity to consumers in the right package, at a right location and at the right time. Companies have to focus on developing strong relationships with their customers to know the 'right' products that should be kept in stock. Reach is achieved by developing an effective distribution network consisting of depots that can serve surrounding villages. But innovative approaches are needed as well. For instance, HUL hiring female entrepreneurs in villages and Tata Sky working with village repairmen are innovative ways in which these companies have improved their reach.
- **Affordability:** Issues of affordability are addressed by re-engineering products so that prices are reduced without sacrificing functionality. Companies resolve affordability issues by making available premium quality products in packages at affordable price points. Developing products specifically for rural markets, such as Godrej ChotuKool, not only helps make the product affordable but also solves a problem for rural consumers. Affordability also gives rise to activities enhancing farmers' incomes and has fostered a whole new industry of microfinance.
- **Service:** The third aspect is providing service in remote areas, which is another daunting task. Very often machines lie useless in rural areas because service is not available. Unrepaired refrigerators are good only for storage, for instance. Providing service

at the doorstep helps solve a major problem for rural consumers. Banking services through BCs also solve a problem while achieving rural penetration at the same time.

Once we understand that all rural marketing must have problem solving at its heart, we realize that rural marketing must go beyond a narrow understanding of business that only seeks profit maximization, but instead become a kind of social business.

Latest Developments

Our discussion of rural marketing strategy would be incomplete without describing new tools and developments that have emerged in recent times. In this section, we explain how concepts such as P2P funding, microfinance and e-commerce point to the potential of transforming rural marketing strategies.

P2P Funding

P2P funding is the practice of lending money to individuals or businesses through online services that connects lenders directly with borrowers. P2P lending websites, through online services, connects borrowers and lenders of money and have become popular in mobilizing funds for lending to poor people in developing and developed countries. Through P2P borrowing, or crowdfunding, poor people can take a loan to start a small business, which increases their income and help them upgrade their living standards.

This is how P2P funding works: the website lists the loan requirements of the individuals giving details of how the money will be used. Lenders select the lender or the project that they wish to fund and pay the website through their credit card. Funding is done in parts, so that lenders may give as little as they wish, sometimes as low as US$10. In India, on a P2P site, Rang De, one can make a social investment of as less than ₹100. Once the total amount required is collected, it is given to a local partner, such as an NGO, who disburses the loan to the borrower who starts repaying the site as soon as it is possible. The money is thus returned to the lender, sometimes with a nominal interest, who may then choose to re-invest it or withdraw (Figure 4.6).

A number of sites have started such funding: Babyloan, Kiva, MicroPlace, Lendbox, and so on. In India, Rang De claims to have raised ₹434 million as social investment with 99.83 repayment rate. It has 9,421 social investors and disbursed about 48,000 loans, of which 93 per cent were women. *Mint* (2016) reports that in 2015 alone, around 20 new online P2P lending companies were launched in India and some 30 start-ups in the P2P lending business are operating in India. The RBI has proposed to define the rules for this emerging business. Johnson et al (2010) however, opine that P2P sites do not result in reducing transaction costs as envisaged and suffer from verifiability of information provided: solving these issues will decide whether peer-to-peer lending ever becomes a reality.

Microfinance

Affordability of rural consumers can be improved by providing small loans by which they can start businesses and thereby earn a living for themselves. These micro-loans, called 'microcredit' (providing small loans) or 'microfinance' (providing financial services) were pioneered by Muhammad Yunus, who turned conventional banking on its head by giving

FIGURE 4.6
How a P2P site, Rang De works.

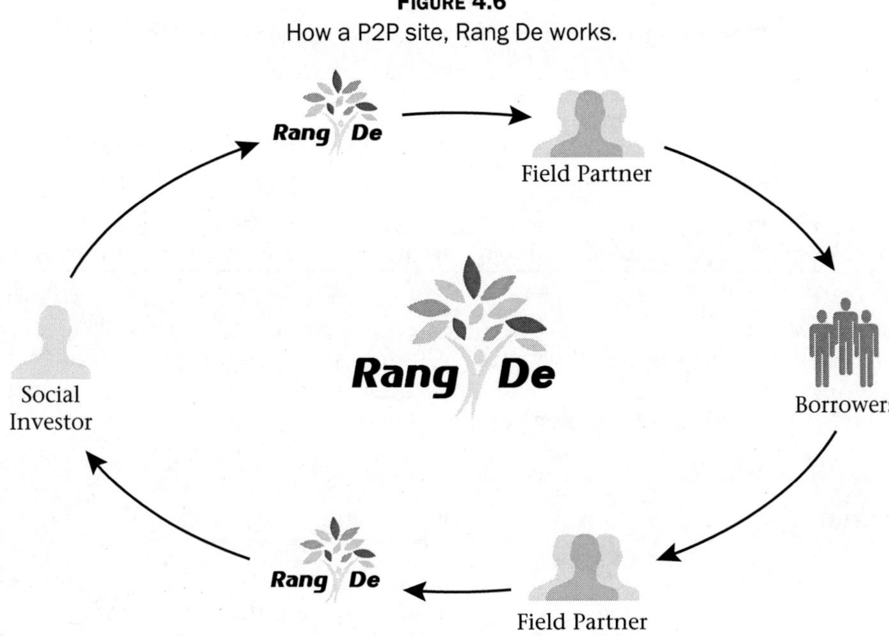

Source: https://www.rangde.org/how-rang-de-works (Accessed on 28 April 2017).

loans to people who are too poor to access traditional banking channels. Micro-loans, sometimes as low as US$27, are given to people living in extreme poverty, who do not have access to formal sources of finance, and have nothing to offer as collateral required by traditional banks (see Chapter 12). Yunus and the Grameen Bank he had founded were jointly awarded the Nobel Peace Prize in 2006 for their efforts. In 2011, Yunus co-founded Yunus Social Business–Global Initiatives to empower social businesses to address and solve social problems around the world.

This thinking, described by Yunus and Jolis (2007) in *Banker to the Poor*, resulted into an innovation in banking which changed the lives of millions of poor across the world. Microloans are given by the Grameen Bank to extremely poor people to buy, say, a sewing machine or a cow, with which they could start a small business. No collateral was required and a banking system was created, which is based on mutual trust, supervision, accountability, participation and creativity.

Microcredit addresses the issue of affordability for rural consumers. It helps them become producers by starting small businesses and the resultant increase in income leads to consumption of branded goods. It also leads to better living. Khandekar and Zaman (2011) report that microfinance is a big instrument in poverty reduction—it reduces by 1.6 per cent per year among borrowers. Moreover, microfinance programmes have spillover effects on the non-borrowers—their poverty level goes down by 0.3 per cent a year, they conclude. Each borrower, for instance, has to commit to 16 'decisions' including educating children, hygiene, planting seedlings and stopping the practice of dowry. Many microcredit institutions also spawn SHGs leading to better individual and social decisions.

The idea has spread worldwide. Loans are provided to women in groups of five, signing for each other's loans, so that they could support one another. Table 4.2 shows the difference between microfinance and conventional banking.

TABLE 4.2

Difference between microfinance and conventional banking.

Microfinance	Conventional Banking
Small loans, poor borrowers	Large loans, rich borrowers
Lending based on trust or social capital	Loans only on collateral
Rural and BoP customers	Mostly urban customers
Microfinance institutions go to customers through agents	Customers go to the bank

Micro-payments, or making small payments through smartphone apps, can further help in rural marketing initiatives. Customers and small traders can make payments by using these apps, even if formal banking channels do not exist.

E-commerce

E-commerce is another strategy that promises to transform rural marketing. As Internet access improves in villages due to various government and private initiatives, e-commerce can play a great role in both (a) supplying goods to villages and (b) encouraging villagers to become producers and supply their production to the rest of the country. Already, e-commerce companies have invested in logistics to fulfil orders from small towns and villages. But the success of e-commerce depends on increasing purchasing power in rural areas. This can be done by providing help to start specialized manufacturing in village clusters, as has been done in China. The portal Alibaba has helped develop village manufacturing clusters, called Taobao villages, which produce goods and supply on the Alibaba platform (see Chapter 10). This has transformed poor, remote villages into prosperous producer villages.

It is time that companies harness the power of Internet to empower villages. This can indeed be done. In India, companies such as Fabindia (see Chapter 6) and Jaipur Rugs have helped villages make products to international standards that find an easy market in India and abroad. The government helps market village produce through KVIC and state crafts emporia. NGOs have also helped in the marketing of food processing articles and other produce in cities. E-commerce companies also list some village products in their portfolio of goods offered. But a wide transformation of villages, which can be brought about by linking villages to the national and international marketplace, has been missing so far. Established companies have also not invested in supply chains that originate from villages due to a variety of reasons.

SUMMARY

Rural consumers constitute in part the BoP market, which represents the population of the world that lives and transacts in an informal market economy. While some companies have built sustainable models for BoP markets, others have retreated from the space. Success in rural markets depends on what strategy the company uses. The initial approach, called BoP 1.0, consists of adapting existing products, reducing price points and extending distribution to villages. BoP 2.0 goes a step further; it stresses on the importance of co-creating products and creating compelling value propositions for customers. Increasingly, the BoP 3.0 approach is gaining ground, which calls for a complete change in purpose and mindsets of companies, that is, to invest in social businesses rather than in commercial ventures.

In the earlier approaches, products were tweaked for rural markets through selling small packs and sturdy products at lower price points. Companies also had to deal with high costs of serving rural markets and rework distribution strategies to overcome seasonal demand and logistical challenges. Similarly, promotion strategies also had to be changed.

This strategy evolved into BoP 2.0, which stressed on the importance of co-creation in which brands and consumers work together to create better products and services. Co-creation involves BoP consumers to play active roles in the company's value chain by becoming co-producers, suppliers or distributors.

BoP 3.0 goes a step further, showing that companies have to change their very approach to business. Instead of profit making as their main objective, companies must keep social objectives in focus and become social businesses. A social business lies between the profit maximizing companies and non-profit organizations. It is a means of using managerial skills creatively so as to solve social problems. Social businesses, however, have to meet the challenges of viability, legitimacy and competitiveness in emerging markets.

Companies with a high rural innovativeness and performance that have achieved high market shares and profitability in rural markets are dubbed as 'rural masters'. These companies have learnt to reaching, acquiring and retaining rural customers through a variety of strategies. A rural marketing strategy can only succeed if it addresses some need of the consumer, in terms of reach, affordability or service. All these are geared towards one objective: providing solutions to rural consumers.

Some more developments have been described, which help in devising rural marketing strategies. P2P funding is the practice of lending money to individuals or businesses through online services that connects lenders directly with borrowers. Through P2P borrowing, or crowdfunding, poor people can take a loan to start a small business, which increases their income and help them upgrade their living standards. E-commerce is another strategy that promises to transform rural marketing. As Internet access improves in villages, e-commerce can play a great role in both (a) supplying goods to villages and (b) encouraging villagers to become producers and supply their production to the rest of the country.

CONCLUSION

Developing a marketing strategy for rural markets is not an easy task and calls for a complete change in the mindset of companies and managers, as this chapter shows. The task is not merely to supply goods to villages, but to help local communities improve their purchasing power, too. The corporate sector thus sees doing business in rural areas as blurring the line between legitimate business and meeting their corporate responsibility. However, this is necessary as incomes in rural markets have not matched those of urban areas. Trying to sell in villages will thus be difficult as people would not be able to afford goods and companies will also be looked down upon as profiteering from the poor.

India lives in her villages, wrote Gandhiji, adding that "we have to concentrate on the village being self-contained, manufacturing mainly for use." It is ironic that today we are talking of a rural marketing strategy that does the same—involving villagers in co-creation and starting social enterprises. Gandhiji's wisdom holds to this day.

KEY TERMS

BoP 1.0: A rural marketing approach that consists of adapting existing products, reducing price points and extending distribution to villages.

BoP 2.0: A rural marketing approach that stresses on the importance of co-creating products and creating compelling value propositions for customers, using innovative techniques, and leapfrogging to sustainable technologies.

BoP 3.0: An approach in which companies have to change their very approach to business: instead of profit making as their main objective, companies must keep social objectives in focus and become social businesses.

Bottom-of-the-pyramid (BoP): A term used to represent the population of the world that primarily lives and transacts in an informal market economy.

Co-creation: A business strategy in which brands and consumers work together to create better products and services.

Microfinance: Providing small loans to poor people who are not served by traditional banking channels by which they can start businesses and thereby earn a living for themselves.

Peer-to-peer (P2P): P2P funding is the practice of lending money to individuals or businesses through online services that connects lenders directly with borrowers.

Rural Masters: Companies with a high rural innovativeness and performance that have achieved high market shares and profitability in rural markets.

Social business: A social business is one which is run like a normal business, as it seeks profits, but is different in the sense that the profits are reinvested in the development of society in some way or in the business itself.

CONCEPT REVIEW QUESTIONS

1. What are the economic and social changes taking place in villages and how do they impact consumption?
2. Explain the BoP 1.0 and 2.0 approaches. How are they different?
3. What are the strategies that companies have pursued in the BoP 1.0 mode?
4. How does the study of consumer behaviour help in rural marketing? What aspects need to be studied?
5. What are the advantages and challenges of implementing a co-creation strategy?
6. What is a social business? Describe its characteristics. How can it help in rural marketing?
7. Who is a rural master? How do rural masters succeed in reaching, acquiring and retaining India's rural customers?
8. Describe some of the latest developments that are impacting rural marketing strategies and how they affect plans of companies.
9. Why does major rural purchasing take place during fairs and festivals? Name some major fairs in your region.

10. How can microfinance and P2P funding help rural marketing initiatives? Is it advisable for companies to get into these?

CRITICAL THINKING QUESTIONS

1. Do you agree with the statement that the model of social business will usher in a new era and change the way we do business in future? Or is it a passing phase? Give reasons for your answer.
2. Companies that venture into rural marketing often end up making investments for social improvement, even though it is not their job. Why do they do this? Is it right, considering that development activities are part of the government domain?
3. "There is one and only one social responsibility of business—to use its resources and engage in activities designed to increase its profits..." (Milton Friedman). Do you agree? In the light of this chapter making a case for social business, how would you reconcile the traditional objectives of business to social ones? Should they be reconciled at all?
4. "Rural marketing is a blend of BoP approaches." Taking the case of a company actively engaged in rural areas, describe its strategies. Critically examine them and show how they can be improved.

PROJECTS AND ASSIGNMENTS

1. Take a look at some rural marketing initiatives. Classify them as BoP 1.0, 2.0 or 3.0 initiatives. Comment on their success or failure. How could they have handled the situation better?
2. Study some of the social organizations described in this chapter. How are they fulfilling their twin objectives of making profits and meeting social objectives? How do they reconcile these two conflicting objectives?
3. Read the books, *How to Change the World* and *A World Without Poverty*. Summarize them and discuss them with your friends. How far do you think they are revolutionary?
4. Conduct a survey with some companies to find out how they view rural marketing. Find out what strategies they follow. Comment on your findings.

WEB RESOURCES

Watch "C.K. Prahalad on Development Through Enterprise": https://www.youtube.com/watch?v=hspszh4YtsE

Watch "Muhammad Yunus: Ending Poverty with Microfinance and Other Social Businesses": https://www.youtube.com/watch?v=M3tZwzYrDiE

Watch "IFC Microfinance: Helping Small Businesses Grow in Colombia" : https://www.youtube.com/watch?v=KMg0VvznEZQ

Watch "Story of Annapurna Pariwar microfinance to empowerment: Medha Samant at TEDxIIMRanchi": https://www.youtube.com/watch?v=LtslFAMvZEU

International Finance Corporation (IFC) website: http://www.ifc.org/wps/wcm/connect/Industry_EXT_Content/IFC_External_Corporate_Site/Industries/Financial+Markets/MSME+Finance/Microfinance/

Renault Mobiliz website: https://group.renault.com/en/commitments/mobility-2/renault-mobiliz-program/

REFERENCES

Accenture. 2013. "Masters of Rural Markets: Profitably Selling to India's Rural Consumers." Available at: http://www.accenture.com/in-en/Pages/insight-rural-india-markets-research-2015.aspx

Fan, Jie, Thomas Heberer and Wolfgang Taubmann. 2015. *Rural China: Economic and Social Change in the Late Twentieth Century*. New York: Routledge.

Foster, W., and Jeffrey L. Bradach. 2005. "Should Nonprofits Seek Profits." *Harvard Business Review*, February. Available at: https://hbr.org/2005/02/should-nonprofits-seek-profits (Accessed on 27 April 2017).

Hart, Stuart L. 2015. "Prologue: Defining the Path Towards BoP 3.0." In *Base of the Pyramid 3.0: Sustainable Development Through Innovation and Entrepreneurship,* edited by Casado Cañeque, and Stuart L. Hart. Sheffield: Greenleaf Publishing.

Jäger, Urs P. and Vijay Sathe (eds). 2014. *Strategy and Competitiveness in Latin American Markets: The Sustainability Frontier*. Cheltenham Glos, UK: Edward Elgar Publishing.

Jha, M. 2014. "Issues & Perspective of Marketing Strategy for Delivering Value to the Rural Consumer." *Asia Pacific Journal of Marketing & Management Review* 3 (1): 88–98.

Johnson, S., Arvind Ashta and Djamchid Assadi, 2010. "Online or Offline? The Rise of 'Peer-to-Peer' Lending in Microfinance." *Journal of Electronic Commerce in Organisations* 8(3), 26–37.

Khandker S., and Hassan Zaman. 2011. "The Impact of Microfinance." *The Daily Star*, 13 March. Available at: http://www.thedailystar.net/news-detail-177457 (Accessed on 27 April 2017).

Kotler, Philip, Abraham Koshy, Mithileswar Jha and Kevin Lane Keller. 2009. *Marketing Management: A South Asian Perspective*, 13th Ed. New Delhi: Pearson Education.

Porter, Michael E., and Mark R. Kramer. 2011. "Creating Shared Value." *Harvard Business Review*, January–February. Available at: https://ncg.org/sites/default/files/resources/HarvardBusinessReview_Creating_Shared_Value.pdf (Accessed on 27 April 2017).

Mint. 2016. "RBI Proposes P2P Lending Regulations." 29 April.

Prahalad, C.K., and Stuart L. Hart. 2002. "The Fortune at the Bottom of the Pyramid." *Strategy+Business* 26 (First Quarter): 1–14. Available at: https://www.strategy-business.com/article/11518?gko=9a4ba (Accessed on 27 April 2017).

Sabeti, Heerad. 2011. "The For Benefit Enterprise." *Harvard Business Review*, November. Available at: https://hbr.org/2011/11/the-for-benefit-enterprise (Accessed on 25 April 2017).

Santos, Filipe, Anne-Claire Pache and Christoph Birkholz. 2015. "Making Hybrids Work: Aligning Business Models and Organizational Design for Social Enterprises." *California Management Review* 57 (3; Spring). Available at: http://journals.sagepub.com/doi/pdf/10.1525/cmr.2015.57.3.36

The Economic Times. 2015. "Why Cost Is the Ultimate Deterrent for a Sound Rural Marketing Plan and How Brands Combat It." 18 March. Available at: http://economictimes.indiatimes.com/magazines/brand-equity/why-cost-is-the-ultimate-deterrent-for-a-sound-rural-marketing-plan-and-how-brands-combat-it/articleshow/46594319.cms (Accessed on 27 April 2017).

Yunus, Muhammad, and Alan Jolis. 2007. *Banker to the Poor: Micro-lending and the Battle Against World Poverty*. 3rd Edition; New York, NY: Public Affairs.

Yunus, Muhammad, and Karl Weber. 2010. *Building Social Business: The New Kind of Capitalism That Serves Humanity's Most Pressing Needs*. New York, NY: Public Affairs.

Yunus, Muhammad, Bertrand Moingeon and Laurence, Lehmann-Ortega. 2010. "Building Social Business Models: Lessons from the Grameen Experience." *Long Range Planning* 43, 308–325.

Yunus, Muhammad, Frédéric Dalsace, David Ménascé and Bénédicte Faivre-Tavignot. 2015. "Reaching the Rich World's Poorest Consumers." *Harvard Business Review*, March. Available at: https://hbr.org/2015/03/reaching-the-rich-worlds-poorest-consumers (Accessed on 25 April 2017).

Closing Case
Bandhan: A Bank with a Difference

Across the world, social businesses are changing the way business is done. In India, the Bandhan Bank started as a social business and was later transformed into a bank. This case study describes the journey of Bandhan, which began as a not-for-profit microfinance enterprise in 2001 with the idea of making a significant contribution towards alleviation of poverty by empowering women. It became a non-banking finance company in 2006. It is the first instance in India of a microfinance entity transforming into a universal bank. It received approval from the RBI to start a banking company on 17 June 2015. Its investors include International Finance Corporation (IFC), Small Industries Development Bank of India and Caladium Investment Pte Ltd, a company managed by GIC Special Investments Pvt Ltd.

Photo 4.5
Bandhan managing director Chandra Shekhar Ghosh with Bandhan customers.

Source: Mint (2014).

Initially, it had 501 branches with a ₹10,500 crore loan book and 19,500 employees. The bank plans to have 71 per cent of the branches in rural India, with at least 35 per cent in unbanked rural pockets. Its area of operation is West Bengal with the maximum number of branches, followed by Bihar, Assam, Maharashtra, Uttar Pradesh, Tripura and Jharkhand. The company has its headquarters in Kolkata and has two divisions—micro-banking and general banking.

Bandhan works at the village level using unique approaches. For example, *Mint* (2015) reports that when it was announced that it would be awarded a licence to become a bank, it handed piggy banks to all its borrowers—around 6.7 million in number. They were encouraged to start saving in them so that when the banking license was obtained, every borrower would have saved at least ₹1,000 to open a savings account. Chandra Shekhar Ghosh, Founder, Managing Director and CEO of Bandhan Bank says, "My commitment to the poor remains. They continue to be my focus and the bank would offer more services to them."

Bandhan, meaning bond or togetherness, refers to the bond with the credit-deprived poor in Eastern India's villages. For many existing banks, financial inclusion is an obligation forced by RBI. But for Ghosh, serving the unbanked segments of the society has been the mission of his life. Ghosh, who has a degree in from Dhaka University in statistics, has worked with Building Resources Across Communities (BRAC), where he got training in one of the most poverty-stricken areas of Bangladesh and which introduced him to microfinance. In 2001, he borrowed ₹1.75 lakh from a moneylender at an interest rate of 7.5 per cent per month, and another ₹25,000 from his sister and brother-in-law, to start a microfinance company with only two staff members. The group started to give small loans—as small as ₹1,000—to poor borrowers in Konnagar and nearby Bagnan areas in Kolkata suburbs, at an interest rate of 15 per cent. Operating through doorstep service centres, it gives loans without collateral.

Ghosh is not a conventional private banker. He focuses on BoP banking. Bandhan Bank hopes to subsidize financial inclusion with profits from high-margin businesses and to keep banking costs low. Unlike private sector banks, it avoids aggressive marketing but instead looks for 'strategic expansion'. When it was small, loans would be disbursed in cash through instant approvals at group meetings. Most of the village branches are concrete structures furnished with a few chairs, a table and a bed for the staff. Cash is physically carried by Bandhan's staff to rural households. Bank staff develops a deep emotional connect with its customers and has maintained a repayment rate of 99 per cent.

It remains to be seen whether this model could work in a formal bank. Bandhan will need to invest in technology, like hand-held devices, to make doorstep banking foolproof.

Bandhan plans to continue its microfinance operations, but as a bank. "Mircofinance and our reach in rural areas are our biggest strengths," says Ghosh. Nearly 70 per cent of Bandhan's operations will be concentrated in rural areas. It follows the Grameen model of banking (see Chapter 12). Under this model, credit decisions are taken at the branch level, which facilitates quick disbursal of loan in about a day's time. As the borrowers do not have income statements or credit records, branch level verification process is done.

Questions for Discussion:

1. The case study shows a very high level of commitment of Bandhan employees. Is such a level of commitment really possible in commercial organizations? If no, how can institutions like Bandhan be built?
2. Comment on the strategy adopted by Mr Ghosh in building Bandhan Bank. Can it be replicated?

3. Managing a not-for-profit microfinance enterprise is one thing, managing a bank is quite another. How can Bandhan recover costs of managing high-cost urban branches and still hope to keep serving the poor? Has its objective been diluted?
4. "Institutions like Bandhan depend on the vision, risks and commitment of one man." Comment on this statement. How can such development be institutionalized?

Sources for this Case Study:

Web Resource

Watch: Khas Mulaqaat with CS Ghosh of Bandhan Bank: CNBC Awaaz. https://www.youtube.com/watch?v=6c8dWQZqVZI

Other Sources

Business Standard. 2014. "Bandhan, India's Newest Bank, Takes Shape." 14 August.

Bornstein, David. 2007. *How to Change the World: Social Entrepreneurs and the Power of New Ideas.* Updated Kindle Edition; Oxford University Press.

Firstpost. 2015. "Bandhan Bank is Born: Chandra Shekhar Ghosh's Incredible Journey from a Sweet Shop to Owning a Bank." 23 August. Available at: http://www.firstpost.com/business/bandhan-bank-is-born-chandra-shekhar-ghoshs-incredible-journey-from-a-sweet-shop-to-owning-a-bank-2301082.html (Accessed on 27 April 2017).

Mint. 2014. "Bandhan Building up Capital Base Ahead of Banking Licence Issue." 25 February. Available at: http://www.livemint.com/Companies/X6M0Yt8LU26CwmW62NnvyN/Bandhan-building-up-capital-base-ahead-of-banking-licence-is.html (Accessed on 27 April 2017).

———. 2015. "Bandhan Bank Faces Many Challenges and Opportunities." 20 September.

The Hindu. 2015. "Bandhan Joins Indian Banking League with 501 Branches." 24 August.

5
CHAPTER

Marketing Approach and Rural Research

LEARNING OBJECTIVES

Companies usually use existing marketing approaches and strategies, or modify them to serve rural markets. This chapter describes the marketing principles that have been used by companies and shows how they can be modified. It also describes market research methods that are successful in rural markets. After reading the chapter, you will be able to:

- Learn about the marketing principles and how they are modified for rural marketing.
- Understand the new tools for rural marketing.
- Analyze different methods of rural market research.
- Learn about participatory approaches in understanding rural customers.
- Learn about ethnographic research and projective techniques of market research.

Opening Case
How the Hand-washing Habit was Encouraged Using a Marketing Approach

The legitimate aim of marketing is to sell products and services to make a profit. Can marketing principles be used to solve problems in rural and cut-off areas? Indeed, many organizations have a lot to learn from marketing to bring about lasting changes that they seek in BoP markets.

Diarrhoea is a common cause of morbidity and a leading cause of death among children aged less than five years, particularly in low- and middle-income countries, as stated in *Hand washing for Preventing Diarrhoea Review* (Ejemot et al. 2009). Hand-washing interrupts the transmission of diarrhoea-causing pathogens. Though it is an easy way to prevent diseases, and despite its low cost and proven benefits, rates of hand-washing with soap are very low throughout the developing world (The World Bank, 2005). Both knowledge of the practice and availability of water and soap are the basic requirements. Mere washing with water is not enough; soap helps in removing pathogens and also chemically kills contaminating and colonizing flora making hand-washing more effective.

Success in building the hand-washing habit is, however, limited. Studies by the World Bank on hand-washing habits in Peru and Vietnam show that campaigns relying on mass media and limited community intervention often fail. A study of a large-scale hand-washing campaign in Vietnam in 2010 (Chase and Quy-Toan 2012) shows that there was no difference between the treatment and control groups, with no impact on health or productivity.

Most campaigns to encourage hand-washing place emphasis on the threat of disease to get people to change their behaviour and educating people about transmission of disease. The failure of many of these campaigns suggests that focusing on disease prevention is not a very effective way to change behaviour. The need is to change the habits and motivations of the target audience.

The Marketing Approach

The *Global Hand-washing Handbook* describes a marketing approach and says that the only way to change long-held habits related to hand-washing is to understand the factors that drive and facilitate hand-washing among the target consumers. The marketing approach focuses on the needs of the target audience and determines the nature and scope of the promotional activities based on the perspective of the target audience.

- **Lowering environmental and cultural barriers:** Barriers in the environment include access to water, the high cost of soap, lack of hand-washing facilities and strong cultural practices in parts of Africa and Asia. These barriers need to be addressed while changing habits.
- **Transforming old habits:** The aim of hand-washing promotion is not to achieve a single event but to instil a new habit that is followed automatically after every contaminating event. Essentially, new habits must be instilled replacing old ones.
- **Finding motives and drivers:** Drivers motivate particular behaviours. They come in the form of emotions and the feelings. Discovering drivers and motivators is key to successfully promoting the hand-washing habit.

The problem is not one of social marketing alone, as the Chief Marketing and Communication Officer of Unilever, Keith Weed (2012), explains. He writes that Unilever engages directly with consumers through its brands. The Lifebuoy soap brand spearheads the company's efforts to reduce childhood mortality through the simple act of hand-washing regularly. The brand campaigned at the Kumbh Mela in India, to raise awareness about good hand-washing habits, partnering with more than 100 restaurants and cafés at the festival. The Kumbh Mela is one of the largest gathering of people on the banks of the Ganges, and so it was the ideal place to propagate a social message. For every food order placed, the first *roti* carried the branded message *Lifebuoy se haath dhoye kya?* (Did you wash your hands with Lifebuoy?). The words were heat stamped onto the baked roti to draw attention at the time when hand-washing is critical. More than 2.5 million branded rotis were consumed during the month-long campaign. Lifebuoy also placed soap in the toilets of each of the eateries to enable people to wash their hands with soap before eating.

The company uses its 'Five Levers for Change', a set of principles that can change motivations among children to learn the habit of washing hands.

1. **Make it understood:** The message should be clear.
2. **Make it easy:** Improve access so that the habit is easy to implement.
3. **Make it desirable:** Lifebuoy also taps into the desire of new mothers to be good mums, so that others can emulate them.

Photo 5.1

The Lifebuoy roti campaign.

Source: HUL (2015).

4. **Make it rewarding:** People start following practices if they expect a reward.
5. **Make it a practice:** Lifebuoy campaigns run for a minimum of 21 days and include quizzes, posters and songs to encourage habit formation.

A similar approach was used in another effort near Chandigarh. It used these principles, and also elements of marketing, to identify the target population, communicate to them, get them involved and thereby inculcate the habit of washing hands after toilet or before eating meals, apart from general hygiene. Though many social workers from government organizations and NGOs came to the colony and talked about the importance of education, hygiene, and so on, there was no follow up and, as a result, there was scepticism about efforts to teach people. The efforts of do-gooders had resulted in people turning away from their efforts. People also did not want to be lectured on their lifestyles.

Five principles of social campaigns were used, that is, of making it understood, easy, desirable, rewarding and, finally, building it into a habit. The following marketing principles were used:

Target market: The target market was identified as poor people, without having access to or the ability to send their children to schools. To ensure that parents accompanied their children, Sundays were chosen for the activity.

PHOTO 5.2

A magician shows tricks to children in a locality. The hand-washing theme was built into the magic show.

Source: Photograph by Dinesh Kumar.

Message: The event was marketed as a fun and excitement-filled magic show in which people could win prizes, too (Photo 5.2). No social message was sought to be imparted and there was no hint of hand-washing in the advertising message. This was one of the chief reasons that a large crowd gathered on the day of the event.

Communication: Instead of using media or printed posters, a person went around the locality on a bicycle announcing the message through a loud speaker, so that it reached each and every home. Small leaflets showing a magician's picture were also distributed. At the same time, the message had to be devised that appealed directly to children and their parents.

Tangibility: Tangibility was achieved by offering prizes to participants. Children who participated in the event would get a free soap if they promised that they would wash hands with it before meals and after toilet. The promise of a freebie associated with the event generated anticipation and excitement around the event. Another tangible element was added by volunteers who cut the overgrown nails of children, showing the dirt trapped in them that was likely to be ingested.

The events were conducted in a local school. On the appointed day, a magician enthralled the audience with magic tricks. After every few tricks, he would invite children from the audience who thought they had clean hands. Then he would show the real 'magic'—their hands under ultraviolet light and magnifying glass, which showed up that the hands were not clean as they thought. "All this will go in your stomach when you eat," he would say, drawing sighs from the audience. Washing of hands with plain water was not enough, he showed, and emphasized that adding the soap was needed. He would then distribute soaps to them and ask them to wash their hands. Volunteers helped the children wash their hands and

Photo 5.3

A volunteer cuts the nails of children, adding to tangibility of the message.

Source: Photograph by Dinesh Kumar.

demonstrated how the hands and nails could be cleaned. After the washing, the magician again showed their hands in ultra violet light, which were clean.

The integrated approach helped in affecting long-term changes in the target audience. The message was formulated that not only generated excitement but also fulfilled the need of the audience to get entertained. It was executed in a manner that was at once acceptable to the people, without sermonizing or teaching. Mothers were also involved, who would serve to remind their children to wash hands. Therefore, the chances of succeeding in habit formation were quite high.

A medical camp was organized as a follow up of the activity in which people could get free consultation from doctors. This too generated a lot of interest because people living in low-income areas often lack medical facilities. Free medicines were also distributed.

While reading this chapter, try and answer the following questions:

1. How can principles of marketing be modified and used in rural marketing?
2. Can rural habits be changed? How?
3. What are the effective ways of doing market research in villages?
4. How can markets be identified and segmented?

Sources for this Case Study:

Web Resources

Unilever website: http://www.unilever.com/sustainable-living/healthandhygiene/handwashing (Accessed on 12 June 2014).

Watch the hand washing ad at: https://www.youtube.com/watch?v=izujd5D5NiI

Watch the roti stamping campaign: http://www.youtube.com/watch?v=e_2tQekUDy8

Other Sources

Chase, Claire, and Quy-Toan, Do. 2012. "Handwashing Behavior Change at Scale: Evidence from a Randomized Evaluation in Vietnam." The World Bank Policy Research Working Paper 6207.

Ejemot, R.I., Ehiri J.E., Meremikwu, M.M. and Critchley, J.A. 2009. "Hand Washing for Preventing Diarrhoea (Review)." The Cochrane Collaboration; published by JohnWiley & Sons, Ltd. Available at: http://onlinelibrary.wiley.com/doi/10.1002/14651858.CD004265.pub2/pdf (Accessed on 27 April 2017).

Galiani, Sebastian, Paul Gertler and Alexandra Orsola-Vidal. 2012. "Promoting Handwashing Behavior in Peru: The Effect of Large-Scale Mass-media and Community Level Interventions." The World Bank Policy Research Working Paper 6257.

Gupta, Punam, and Dinesh Kumar. 2015. "Hand-washing—Using Marketing Techniques for Handwashing Habit Formation among Children." In workshop on Social Marketing and Behaviour Change, organized by British Academy of Management and MARCOMMS Event *Social Marketing and Behaviour Change* 24 April. Queen Mary University of London.

HUL. 2015. "Lifebuoy Creates Innovative ROTI reminder." 25 February. Available at: https://www.unilever.com/brands/brand-stories/lifebuoy-creates-innovative-roti-reminder.html (Accessed on 25 April 2017).

The Global Public Private Partnership for Hand-washing. *The Handwashing Handbook*. Available at: http://documents.worldbank.org/curated/en/681501468141299225/pdf/323020Handwashing1handbook02005.pdf (Accessed on 11 April 2017).

Weed, Keith. 2012. "Change Consumer Behavior with These Five Levers." HBR Blog Network, 6 November. Available at: http://blogs.hbr.org/cs/2012/11/change_consumer_behavior_with.html (Accessed on 27 April 2017).

INTRODUCTION

Drucker (1985) had written, "...the purpose of business is to create a customer, the business enterprise has two—and only two—basic functions: marketing and innovation." True for all businesses, it really sums up the very purpose of rural marketing. Companies need to find new ways to serve customers who are often poor and live in far-flung areas, and the way to do this is through innovation not only in products but also in the very way that marketing is done.

This has been done in various ways in the past. The most common approach is to apply marketing principles to rural marketing, an approach that has worked for some companies though many others have burnt their hands in the process. In research papers published in India and in many company approaches, the narrative of rural marketing has been as follows:

- India has a large rural market consisting of more than 800 million consumers.
- These consumers are underserved.
- Therefore, a huge opportunity exists to make money by selling to villages.

This makes the task of rural marketing look simple: just send some products to rural areas or open stores there and people will buy them happily. This, however, may work in the short run only. For long-term presence in rural markets, companies have to understand the environment, rural consumers and their behaviour. This is not an easy task. A way to do this is through the marketing approach—using marketing tools and principles—and through market research. In both, it is required that urban approaches are modified or are completely changed. This chapter describes how marketing tools and principles have been modified for BoP marketing. It also deals with methods of rural market research.

MARKETING PRINCIPLES IN RURAL AREAS

Marketing thought has progressed over the years and companies have modified their approaches to rural marketing as they have moved along. Earlier they were just content with supplying goods to rural areas, but as this book shows, many of these companies have adopted innovative approaches of solving problems and have thus endeared themselves to rural customers, establishing long-term relationships.

Seybold (2001) writes that relationships with customers do not just exist in a vacuum. Companies need to examine broader customer scenarios, which include customers' unique needs, wants and expectations and individual uses for products/services. They need to study the customer scenario—the broad context in which customers select, buy and use products and services. This is true in rural areas because little is known about the consumer. The need and motivation of using products is also quite different for rural customers than for urban customers. The application of marketing principles to rural marketing precludes that companies know their customers. In both marketing approaches and market research, this is an important element for rural success.

Marketing Approaches

Marketing has evolved over a period of time. The first approach, used widely in rural marketing, has been summed up by what is known as the *production concept*: sell whatever a company is able to produce. There is no modification of products and the same strategies that the company uses in urban markets is replicated in rural areas. If this did not work, the thinking moved to the *sales concept*, which called for aggressive sales effort and pushy salespersons, because companies had built excess capacities and wanted to get rid of their stocks. This is unlikely to work in rural areas and is, in any case, a short-term strategy. Customers turned away from such an approach, so the *marketing concept* was born, which focused on satisfying customers' needs rather than pushing products that companies could produce. This led to the study of consumer behaviour and needs. As people became more aware, they questioned the role of marketing and the tremendous waste it produced, aptly described by Packard in his book, *The Waste Makers* (1960). Could marketing be used for changing society and create a better world? Thus was born the *societal marketing concept*, which means using the tools of marketing in changing habits or attitudes.

This evolution can be seen in the approach to rural marketing as well. Initially, some companies tweaked products and distribution to reach villages. Much effort was expended on building products for rural markets. Some were stripped down versions of products sold in urban areas (to reduce the cost), while others got packed in small units. These strategies worked to some extent. Other companies, however, tried to understand and solve problems in rural areas. By using the societal concept, they have established themselves and succeeded in villages. Such cases are discussed throughout the book and in this chapter as well.

Marketing Mix

Marketing consists of actions undertaken to elicit desired responses from a target audience. The commonly used framework is that of *marketing mix* consisting of 4Ps—product, price, place and promotion. This is also understood as 4Cs—customer solutions, customer cost, convenience and communication. Companies work out a combination of the 4Ps or the 4Cs to make products that will be acceptable by the target audience. They have modified products, channels, promotional techniques and offered products at convenient price points to make rural folk buy their products. But this approach has not been found to be sufficient in rural markets. The 4Ps have thus been modified to 4As in the case of rural marketing—availability, affordability, acceptability and awareness (see Chapter 3).

- **Product–acceptability:** Farmer consumers are more interested to know the technical details or the performance of agricultural inputs. There is higher importance of product knowledge and advisory services provided by a company. Rural farmers generally show their liking for simple and easy to use products. Acceptability is increased if the packaging of a product has pictorial demonstration, is convenient and it is easy to use. Additional packaging increases the cost but gives advantage. The product literature on the cover packaging and in the user manuals should be expressed in simple and local language, providing clear benefits. The products should meet the expected needs of rural farmers and provide them value.
- **Price–affordability:** Agricultural inputs and industrial products share similar response patterns from users. Buyers of agricultural inputs are more quality conscious than price conscious, but in India they rely on word-of-mouth recommendations. The important factor is pricing, which has to be in accordance with their expectation. Subsidies are provided for agricultural inputs, which tend to skew usage patterns.
- **Place–availability:** The levels of channel and the network intensity required for agricultural inputs are higher than that required for industrial products. The channel plays the role of both pull as well as push function. It is supported by demonstrations, personal contacts and other extension means. Direct contact with retailers must be established. Cooperative societies, PDS, village weekly markets, fairs and festivals are utilized to ensure adequate distribution of agro-inputs.
- **Promotion–awareness:** As the number of prospects is large, diverse and spread across different regions, the product requires innovative promotion. Promotional activities are required to be undertaken through local media. Positive word-of-mouth publicity through local reference groups and opinion leaders is considered as the key to success in the rural markets. Traditional art forms such as puppet shows and street plays or creating awareness through village *panchayat* members can prove to be fruitful. Other methods such as distribution of pamphlets, use of mobile vans for publicity and advertising through wall posters can also assist in establishing a relationship with the consumers.

Segmentation

At the centre of all rural marketing, there is the rural customer. Companies realize that none of their attempts would succeed without understanding the rural consumer. They follow techniques such as *market segmentation*, the process of profiling and identifying distinct groups in the population who would be interested in a product. Some of the differences on which market segments are identified are:

- **Geographic:** Based on physical location of the customer.
- **Demographic:** Finding differences on the basis of population statistics.

- **Psychographic:** Identifying different lifestyles based on activities, interests and opinions.
- **Socio-cultural:** Based on social classes and cultural life.
- **Personality:** Finding about the consumers' personality, perception, learning and attitudes.
- **VALs:** The Value Attitude Lifestyle framework is a technique for psychographic segmentation. It helps discover lifestyles of customers.

However, segmentation depends on data, which is scarce in rural markets. For example, agricultural income is not taxed in the country. Both small and large farmers include income from other sources as agricultural income. The economy is largely cash-based, hence accurate data on rural incomes is not available. Moreover, the character and nature of villages, the lifestyle of the people and their consumption patterns vary within the same district. For instance, villages close to a highway will show a different pattern than a village located, say, 10 km away in the interior. That is why, the usual segmentation techniques hardly work in rural areas. They will at best aggregate the many diversities that one finds in villages and reliance on such data will lead to faulty conclusions.

Companies can only broadly use segmentation techniques to understand customers. What they require is granular information, for instance, data on communities doing well within a poor and underserved landscape (see Closing Case of Chapter 2 on Maruti). In the absence of data, companies have to depend on another technique—observation. But this calls for deep insight, which is often lacking. Marketing managers also have to give up their comfort zones and travel deep into rural areas.

Similarly, differentiating markets on the basis of demographic, psychographic or other basis will depend on physical observation by an astute marketing person rather than data. This calls for entirely different market research methods that are discussed later in this chapter.

Relationship Marketing

What works in rural areas is what is known as *relationship marketing*, which is the process of building long-term economic, technical and social relationships with customers, suppliers and distributors. Company men trained in selling often lack relationship building skills. Nowhere is this more evident than in rural markets, where the influence of word-of-mouth recommendations is far more important than any promotion technique. Rural folk depend on opinion leaders—respected people in the community—for product recommendations. The role of local shopkeepers is also very important, as people tend to buy what is pushed by the retailer. Failure to build relationships with these ground level soldiers has cost many large companies dearly, because dealers only send products to village stores on which they get good margins. As a consequence, local brands are bought more frequently than reputed urban brands.

Marketing Channels

There are three types of channels that companies build to reach their market segments. The first is a *communication channel* that effectively communicates to the target segment. For this, a combination of media and BTL methods are used. Second, *distribution channels* deliver and display the goods and services to customers where they want them. Delivery of after-sales service must also be built into distribution channels. Finally, *selling channels* are required to affect transactions and interact with customers. Sales persons push the products along these channels. Companies must figure out the kind of salespersons they should have and the level of their interaction. Banks and insurance companies are required to facilitate transactions, but their presence in village areas is still limited.

Since rural marketing requires deeper interactions with customers than urban markets, communication channels are crucial. The lack of suitable media makes the task of building them quite difficult. Further, a dialogue can usually be established through physical presence. Village shopkeepers do not have proper displays and dealers with adequate warehouses, transportation vehicles and sales persons are simply not available. Companies thus face design problems in building their rural marketing channels. Very often dealers and infrastructure have to be developed in order to do business in such areas (Photo 5.4).

PHOTO 5.4

A soft drink storage in a village: the dealer simply stacks up the crates outside his door.

Source: Photograph by Dinesh Kumar.

Supply Chains

A supply chain is a longer channel than a marketing channel. The marketing channel connects companies with consumers, but the supply chain is a longer channel that starts from raw materials and goes all the way up to final buyers. The objective of the supply chain is to deliver value.

Rural markets defy the logic of supply chains. To supply in large towns, companies can use economic methods of transport, like full truckloads. To supply to villages, managers often face the problem of sending small quantities of goods over large distances on a regular basis. Innovative methods have to be used, as described in Chapter 6. Since purchasing power in villages is limited, companies often have to build supply chains that source raw materials from villages, helping villagers to become producers and thus increase their incomes. This enhanced income helps them to become consumers as well.

Competition

Another aspect of marketing is competition, which includes current and potential products that rival companies offer. In rural areas, the competition is likely to come from unbranded goods, local brands and fake brands. These are priced cheaper, as they use local materials to make and have shorter channels (see Mini Case Study 5.4). Big brands have higher costs and must be sent over large distances, pushing up their prices. Even if companies tackle problems of distribution and selling, they must find ways to fight these nimble local players (Photo 5.5).

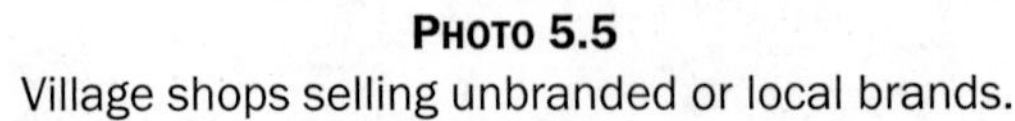

PHOTO 5.5
Village shops selling unbranded or local brands.

Source: Photograph by Dinesh Kumar.

Brand Management

Branding involves creating a unique name and image for a product in the consumers' mind. Branding aims to establish a significant and differentiated presence in the market that attracts and retains loyal customers. Rather than advertising, branding activities consist of personal communication in rural areas. A study by Anand and Krishna (2008) shows that branding in rural areas depends on quality, value for money and belongingness. Brands are often not able to bring all three things on the table. In the white goods and agro-input category, only value for money works, and not quality or product parameters. The challenge then is to encourage product trials for adoption in rural markets.

Consumer Behaviour

The study of consumer behaviour helps us to know why, how and from where consumers like to buy products. It studies motives and personality. We have covered characteristics of rural consumers in Chapter 3.

New Product Development

To serve rural markets, companies have to come up with products, services or solutions based on new and untested ideas. They must have the courage to pursue bold initiatives. The more an idea deviates from the status quo, the greater is the market opportunity and larger is the risk. New product development follows the steps of generating ideas, idea screening, concept testing, market analysis, test marketing and, finally, commercial launch. In rural marketing, however, this does not work. Usually the company has to identify a problem to solve and then use innovative techniques to solve that problem. There are no antecedents and the only help that can be accesses is the experience of rural folk. This can be unearthed by market research.

New Marketing Tools

Applying marketing principles described earlier calls for new tools. Marketing concepts cannot be used blindly, hoping that consumers will respond to stimuli. For rural marketing, innovation is required at every step. The following tools must supplement the marketing effort:

- **Re-engineering:** Hammer and Champy (1993) define re-engineering as the fundamental rethinking and radical redesign of business processes to achieve dramatic improvements in critical measures of performance, such as cost, quality, service and speed. In rural markets, this has meant cost saving in operations, reduction in pack sizes and deletion of frills from the core product, but this reduction in price should not be at the cost of quality and service. The development of ChotuKool refrigerator by Godrej (see Chapter 3) and Tata Swach are examples of successful re-engineering of existing products.
- **Innovation:** Thanks to Internet technologies, firms are realizing the importance of collaboration for creating and sustaining competitive advantage. In rural marketing, they collaborate with customers to co-create value through product innovation.

Innovation in products and processes is sought for reaching customers and reducing costs of distribution.

- **E-commerce:** E-commerce has a great potential not only to supply goods to rural areas but also to help villagers become producers. Some initiatives have already been taken. As Internet services and logistics improve (see Chapter 10) e-commerce will have a more important role to play in rural marketing. As Prahalad and Hammond (2002) had written, "E-commerce systems that run over the phone or the Internet are enormously important in BoP markets because they eliminate the need for layers of intermediaries." The initiative by Amazon (see Mini Case Study 5.1) illustrates how e-commerce helps rural products find large markets.

Mini Case Study 5.1

Amazon's 'Crafted in India'

E-commerce is an important tool in rural marketing, as shown by this mini case study on Amazon, which has started selling Indian handicrafts. Amazon launched its 'Crafted in India' store in 2015 to sell handcraft items, especially garments, jewellery and footwear. The online store features more than 4,000 products from 11 different regions and offers over 50 distinct regional crafts. On National Handloom Day on 7 August 2016, Amazon launched its new selection and expanded its Crafted in India store.

The Crafted in India store offers regional products sourced directly from handloom clusters under a partnership with Development Commissioner of Handloom. Large brands such as Jaypore, Fabindia, Indusdiva and Unnati Silks, state corporations such as Tantuja (West Bengal), Andhra Pradesh State Handloom Weavers' Cooperative society Ltd (popularly known as APCO; now Telangana) are included. The partnership has enabled cooperatives and master weavers across Kota in Rajasthan, Nadia in West Bengal and Bargarh in Odisha to launch over 1,000 selections in the store. The products carry certifications such as 'India Handloom Brand' and 'Handloom Mark'. The initiative brings digital opportunity to thousands of skilled weavers and artisans in rural India, giving them direct access to customers in India and abroad. Customers can now buy merchandise that includes Venkatgiri, Chirala, Mangalgiri, Upadda and Pochampally from Andhra Pradesh; Madurai cotton and Salem silk, Kanjeevaram silk, Chettinad sarees and Coimbatore Sico sarees from Tamil Nadu; Mysore silk, ilkal sarees and Bangalore silk from Karnataka, amongst others.

The company's website says that it wants to revive the authentic Indian handicrafts market and offers Indian crafts and designs that are both contemporary and traditional. It wants to revive the Indian handicrafts market and make every region's craft available to customers. Amazon forayed into fashion in September 2013 with the launch of the Fashion Jewellery and Watches selection. Since then, the store has added selections to grow its portfolio.

Amazon India will also train cooperatives and weavers to directly sell their products on its website. It will engage with weavers and help them sell on its platform. It may help to transform the lives of weavers and artisans to a great extent. The company has started organizing workshops in villages for this same purpose and runs an education and skilling programme for small and medium-sized businesses (SMBs) called Seller University. It helps sellers in a variety of ways:

- Fulfilment by Amazon, in which Amazon packs, ships and delivers products to customers, manages returns and does customer service on behalf of the sellers
- Easy Ship, a shipping service that makes it easy for sellers to ship products across India

- Amazon Tatkal, a studio-on-wheels to help SMBs get online within 60 minutes
- Sellers Ecosystem, providing a means to the sellers community to overcome problems of fragmentation and reach

Though NGOs and other organizations are doing similar activities, they face problems of scale and lack the marketing muscle. The entry of big players like Amazon in the handloom space provides a platform for rural artisans to sell their products to a large audience.

Can such initiatives help in rural marketing? Can you think of other such ventures?

Sources for this Case Study:

Deccan Herald. 2015. "Amazon Launches Crafted in India Store." 3 November. Available at: http://www.deccanherald.com/content/509782/amazon-launches-crafted-india-store.html (Accessed on 11 April 2017).

Business Standard. 2016. "Amazon Fashion, DC Handloom Tie-up to Expand Its 'Crafted in India' Selection." 6 August.

Gupta, Hita. 2016. "Amazon Gives Handloom Portal Crafted India a Boost, here's How." *Financial Express*, 4 August. Available at: http://www.financialexpress.com/industry/amazon-gives-handloom-portal-crafted-india-a-boost-heres-how/337695/ (Accessed on 11 April 2017).

- **Partners:** Companies have to work with local partners to penetrate rural areas. They have to move from a perspective of total control of marketing activities to developing partners whom they can trust. This means they have to learn to make deep relationships with dealers, NGOs, small entrepreneurs and customers, requiring a great shift in thinking: for a large company giving up control is often not easy.
- **Decentralization:** Managing marketing in more than six lakh villages from a single head office is an impossible task. A decentralized marketing operation is required, which is difficult for most large companies. Further, as consumption patterns differ from region to region, each district must have a unique approach. Companies have to move from being managed top-down to encouraging more initiative at the local level. In the process, they have to learn to find new methods of control.
- **Social approach:** Moving away from commercial objectives, companies need to have an approach that encourages social thinking and must have social objectives integrated in its approach. Indeed, many companies covered in this book have put social objectives above commercial objectives and have gained huge traction in rural markets.

RURAL MARKET RESEARCH

Market research helps companies know their customers. They need to find out which products consumers want and the quantity that is required to be produced, how and where to deliver and how best to reach the customers. All these are tasks of marketing research. Usually researchers go out armed with questionnaires and talk to potential consumers trying to figure out what is in their minds, how many people will actually pay the prices fixed for the products. The traditional market research steps and methods are explained here.

Steps in Traditional Marketing Research

The marketing technique that can be used can only be understood once we make a research plan. The following eight steps help to chalk out a rural research plan:

1. **Define the research problem and objectives:** This stage, also called problem definition, involves defining what is to be studied. Research objectives could involve studying rural markets, distribution methods or rural consumer behaviour. Each of these objectives will have different methods for data collection. At this stage, the firm must establish clarity about the research and what is to be achieved by it.
2. **Develop a district-wise research plan:** Since rural consumers are not homogenous, a district-wise research plan must be developed. The firm identifies what kind of research must be undertaken, works out the kind of questions that must be asked and to whom to ask those questions, along with methods of analyzing the data obtained. At this stage, hypotheses that are to be tested are devised, steps to draw a representative sample are listed and the methodology is determined to collect data from the sample. Usually qualitative research is done as villages would not have large number of respondents.
3. **Search for secondary data:** Secondary data consists of published data available with government departments such as data on census, transport, schools, public health, and so on. Rural secondary data is patchy, but the researcher can tap trade associations such as Federation of Indian Chambers of Commerce & Industry (FICCI), Confederation of Indian Industry (CII) and industry associations, consultancies and rural journals. Professional research companies such as Nielsen, Accenture, Indian Market Research Bureau (IMRB), McKinsey, Ernst and Young and others undertake research and publish reports on rural markets, but these and other secondary data give a macro view of villages.
4. **Design a primary research study:** Primary research is often needed because rural secondary data is just not sufficient. The method of collecting primary data is decided: survey, interview, observation or online data. Questionnaires are designed and translated into local languages and the methodology to conduct a primary study is chalked out.
5. **Sample selection:** Sample selection must be unbiased and as representative of the total population. This means all socio-economic groups in a village must be covered through cluster or stratified sampling. Though random sampling is preferred in urban areas, this is often not possible in villages. In villages, convenience sampling has to be done. At best, the researcher can ensure that all religious, caste and income groups are covered.
6. **Collect primary data:** Primary data collection poses a big problem for field workers—not only are large distances needed to be covered, but rural people are also suspicious of urban folk armed with questionnaires. One-to-one interviews are almost impossible as villagers usually gather around the researcher. Female researchers are needed to talk to females. People are also not aware of brands, so comparison is also difficult. Respondents often give the answer that they think is expected of them rather than their real feelings, which also is a problem that the reșearcher face. Interviews are conducted by asking participants questions in small group setting. However, the researcher must have skills to interview villagers in local languages, explaining and getting information at the same time. Sometimes, insights about rural life are obtained not by asking questions but through merely observing markets and consumers.

7. **Analyze the data:** Statistical tests are applied to check the reliability and validity of data. However, methods such as correlation, regression, discriminant analysis and factor analysis can only be used if the size of the data is large. But this is unlikely to happen in villages. Cluster analysis, to find out commonalities in elements, may be one technique that can be used in rural market research. If the research is qualitative, removing researcher bias would be a major task.
8. **Use the findings to make marketing decisions:** The last step is to make sense out of the data analysis and come to actionable points for the marketing strategy.

Sampling Methods

Sampling is necessary because it is not possible to talk to or survey every consumer or non-consumer. In sampling, we select some people and question them and hope that the findings will be applicable to all the population. Selecting the few people to interview out of the total population is called sampling. The sample has to fulfil two basic criteria: it should be unbiased and representative of the total population.

Theoretically, in an unbiased sample, each member of the population should have an equal chance of being chosen. However, this is not possible in rural areas. Certain segments of the population are socially excluded, such as women or people of certain castes. Thus, non-probability techniques are used and usually convenience sampling is done. In probability methods, stratified sampling would be important in villages, so that the respondent chooses people from each strata. Cluster sampling would also be used if clusters are easily identifiable. These are explained here.

- **Stratified sampling:** Stratification is the process of dividing members of the village into homogeneous sub-groups. Then simple random sampling or systematic sampling is applied within each sub-group. For example, a researcher may choose a sample from each of the three strata, that is, the upper, the middle and the lower class, to find out consumer behaviour across the entire population.
- **Cluster sampling:** The total population is divided into clusters and then random samples from the groups are selected. For example, we may divide the population in a village on the basis of profession and then take random samples from each of the clusters chosen.

Non-probability sampling occurs when researchers select samples based on their subjective judgement. It is often done for practical reasons such as lack of time or resources to conduct full-fledged surveys. In villages, researchers need to do surveys based on samples they can access conveniently. There are three common methods in non-probability sampling—convenience, quota and judgemental.

- **Convenience sampling:** Convenience sampling is a non-probability sampling technique in which subjects are selected because of their convenient accessibility. In villages, it means interviewing people who are present at a given time. The method, though quick, may not give reliable results.
- **Quota sampling:** In quota sampling, the population is segmented into mutually exclusive sub-groups and then entities are selected from each segment based on a specified proportion. For example, a company may wish to survey 30 people in each village, which is a quota that must be achieved.

- **Judgemental sampling:** When a researcher uses his/her judgement in selecting the entities from the population, it is called judgement sampling. For instance, a researcher may decide to interview the *sarpanch* or opinion leaders in a village, or ask them for referrals in the hope of getting quality answers. This is called judgemental sampling.

Rural Market Research

Rural market research is neither easy nor it is a series of steps, because customers are spread over large distances and are sometimes not exposed to brands and products. Secondary data on village consumption habits is patchy.

Traditional methods of market research thus have their limitations in rural areas. Since companies do not have accurate information about village buying habits, many companies have burnt their fingers trying to build supply chains to rural areas. Most companies simply look at the population data—about 850 million underserved people—and conclude about the huge opportunity it represents. But unless they know the people and what they buy, efforts at rural marketing are destined to fail.

Consumer research helps in all aspects of marketing strategy. It is needed to answer questions and help in marketing strategy. Research helps companies to:

- **Identify potential customers and segments:** Identifying rural customers and finding prosperous segments within the rural population is a major task of rural market research. This calls for gathering granular data.
- **Finding motivation to use products:** An important question to be answered is: why do people buy certain products? For example, a washing machine may be purchased for washing clothes in urban areas but may well be used to churn milk in villages. Such insights can help companies modify their products.
- **Understand existing customers:** Companies need to understand customers as to what makes them buy and what they value. They can discover who influences buying decisions and what role models are popular among the rural folk. Further, companies find out which products are purchased for functionality and which ones for aspiration in villages.
- **Identifying purchase habits:** Purchase habits or from where people like to buy, in what quantities and at what times are some of the important parameters. It results in designing specific distribution channels to serve rural areas. While some goods are purchased from the village shop, others are bought from a nearby town (see Chapter 2).
- **Develop marketing strategy:** Decisions such as product design, pricing, packaging, distribution and making communication strategies are guided by market research. Research also gives information about competitors so that companies can develop their counter offers.

Types of Consumer Research

What kind of research should be taken up in rural areas? As a first step, rural managers need to decide what research can be taken up. They need to decide which type of research is best suited for a given situation. The different types of research that can be taken up are:

1. Market Research and Consumer Behaviour Research
2. Collection of Primary or Secondary Data
3. Qualitative and Quantitative Research

TABLE 5.1
Difference in marketing and consumer research.

	Rural Marketing Research	Rural Consumer Research
Focus	The village/town, markets, competition, and environment	Decision making process of rural customers, what, how, where and why they buy.
What is researched	Products, opportunities, risks, local partners, facilities	Purchase process, motives, desires and drivers or rural folk, frequency of purchase, pack sizes
Final result	Market potential, supply and payment channels	Buying and consumption behaviour

Market Research and Consumer Behaviour Research

Companies need to know about both markets and consumers. The former is done through *market research* and the latter through *consumer behaviour research.*

Market research is defined as a systematic collection, analysis and interpretation of data related to the market and the surrounding environment. In rural marketing research, it means delving into the rural marketplace, competition analysis, channels and marketing institutions.

Consumer behaviour research is the study of preferences, motivations and buying behaviour of customers. This is done through direct observation, mail surveys, telephone or face to face interviews. The researcher attempts to understand consumers and their decision-making, influence and processes and their buying and consumption behaviour. Through consumer research, a company can find out how to respond to what people think.

The difference between market research and consumer research is summed up in Table 5.1.

Primary Research and Secondary Research

Primary research is the research where data is collected first-hand for a specific purpose. When a company takes up a study to find out the market potential of a product in a particular village, it is primary research.

Secondary research consists of data that is already available, which has already been gathered and recorded by someone else for purposes other than the current project. Secondary data consists of published sources, internal records of the company, database or journals. Unfortunately, secondary data on rural markets is inadequate. Villages do not even exist for mainstream media, unless there are accidents, suicides or fires. Most research papers published in journals on India's rural areas repeat the same homilies about the opportunity that exists in villages. International consultancies also point to this opportunity, looking at demographic data. But managers rarely have accurate data on Indian villages. Usually they rely on Census figures, which is at best a broad indicator.

Qualitative and Quantitative Research in Villages

Companies can take up quantitative or qualitative research in towns and villages. When variables can be measured or quantified, it is called quantitative research. It involves getting data from a large number of respondents or situations. This is usually difficult because rural research is extremely time consuming.

Quantitative research depends on gathering data from a large number of respondents. That is why, it is quite unsuitable in rural areas: the sheer effort to talk to rural folk is enormous—no market research agency has the huge number of researchers on its rolls to conduct surveys or focus group studies in villages. If they do, it will be a costly affair. Eliciting accurate answers is also a time-consuming process, as villagers will be suspicious of outsiders. Cultural norms will forbid the researcher from talking to women directly. Most answers will be given by males, even when the product concerns women. Further, villages within the same district may have completely different profiles, and quantitative data hides such differences.

Qualitative research focuses on information that is not measurable, such as feelings, characteristics and attitudes. It tries to find out how rural people feel about products and services, what they like or what they do not, what they want from a new product, their cultural beliefs and attitudes, influencers and hurdles to purchase. The differences between these two types of research are summed up in Table 5.2. In qualitative research, a small number of people is interviewed in-depth or a focus group is formed. The researcher probes and finds out about people's perceptions, opinions and feelings. Such research works well if we consider that companies are looking for co-creation and involving villagers in social businesses. That is why, completely different tools of rural research are needed. These are described in participatory approaches (see the next section).

TABLE 5.2

Difference between quantitative and qualitative research.

	Qualitative Research	Quantitative Research
Purpose and objectives	To find out about beliefs, attitudes, opinions, feelings, experiences and behavior of rural customers. To study underlying reasons and motivations Generating ideas about products To understand culture and value system	To measure market potential To study a sample and induce results for the rural population To quantify segments Studying characteristics of markets and consumers
Sample size	Small number of non-representative cases. Non-probability sampling methods	Large sample representing the population. Probability sampling. Results are generalized to the entire population
Question format	Open ended	Closed ended
Data format	Descriptive	Numerical
Research methods	Observation, individual depth interviews, group interaction. Participatory approaches; subjective	Questionnaires, surveys, experimentation, interviews; objective
Data collection	Unstructured or semi-structured Open ended questions Probing by researcher and disguised questions	Close-ended questions with given response choices Direct questions that require no probing
Data analysis	Descriptive, analysis of verbal responses Based on behavioral science	Statistical data analysis using on standardized methods.

Participatory Approaches

It is increasingly being realized that market research cannot be conducted in rural areas as it is conducted in cities. The rural approach has to be entirely different from urban research approaches. Companies realize that they must adopt participatory approaches, that is, the researcher must participate in the lives of village people to learn about their rituals, values, culture and lives. Chambers (1992) explains that participatory approaches enable local people to share, enhance and analyze their knowledge of life and conditions. Four methods are suggested:

- Participant Observation (PO)
- Rapid Rural Appraisal (RRA)
- Participatory Rural Appraisal (PRA)
- Participatory Action Research (PAR)

These methods are explained here.

Participant Observation (PO)

It is a type of data collection method used in qualitative research, with the aim to gain close and intimate familiarity with a given group of individuals and their practices through involvement with people in their cultural environment. The observer uses informal interviews, direct observation, participation in the life of the group, discussions, self-analysis, activities and life-histories.

In his study of a two blue collar families living in Washington, DC, Howell (1972) says that PO is like non-judgemental observation and acceptance, "an opportunity to accept people as people." He describes four stages that PO involves: (a) establishing rapport or getting to know the people, (b) immersing oneself in the field, (c) recording data and observations and (d) consolidating the information.

In the first step, the researcher gets to know the members and becomes familiar with the area. It is important to become friends, or at least be accepted in the community. In the second step, the researcher tries to get assimilated with the locals and he/she must follow the language, culture and lifestyle being followed to get accepted as a member of the community. The researcher maintains field notes and reflexivity journals to record observations, interviews and data. Personal thoughts and feelings are also recorded, though biases and subjectivities are to be avoided. A supervisor helps in avoiding these through a method called *triangulation*, which involves multiple team members gathering data about the same event. By cross-checking and comparison, biases are weeded out. Finally, the data must be analyzed. Two methods are used in data analysis. The first is *thematic analysis*, that is, arranging data according to recurrent themes found in interviews and observations, and *narrative analysis*, that is, categorizing the information and constructing coherent stories gathered from different narratives.

Rapid Rural Appraisal

RRA consists of a set of guidelines which help people to work in a structured but flexible way in rural communities and a set of tools to aid interaction with those communities.

RRA is activity carried out by a group of people from different professional fields or disciplines, which aims to learn about a particular topic, area, situation or group of people.

It is a method to collect information by talking directly to people 'on the ground', and it uses a set of guidelines on how to approach the collection of information, learning from it and the involvement of local people in its interpretation and presentation.

RRA uses a set of tools: exercises and techniques for collecting information, means of organizing that information, techniques for stimulating interaction with community members and methods for analyzing and reporting findings. RRA is described as a systematic but semi-structured field activity by a multi-disciplinary team and is designed to obtain new information and formulate new hypotheses about rural life. Research is carried out by a team of appropriate disciplines and not by individuals. Team members with technical backgrounds, social science skills and marketing research skills are included. In this way, RRA is able to get a balanced picture. The techniques of RRA include:

- Semi-structured interviews and question design.
- Cross-checking information from different sources (triangulation).
- Group interview techniques, including focus group interviewing.
- Direct observation.
- Focus group discussions.
- Preference ranking.
- Mapping and modelling.
- Seasonal and historical diagramming.

Participatory Rural Appraisal (PRA)

PRA is an approach and method for learning about rural life and conditions from, with and by rural people. It describes methods to enable local people to share, enhance and analyze their knowledge of life and conditions, to plan and to act. It draws from RRA: in RRA information is more elicited and extracted by outsiders; in PRA, it is more shared and owned by the local people. Participatory methods include mapping and modelling, transect walks, matrix scoring, seasonal calendars, trend and change analysis, well-being and wealth ranking and grouping and analytical diagramming. PRA uses group animation and exercises to facilitate information sharing, analysis and action among stakeholders. An example of using PRA has been illustrated in Mini Case Study 5.2.

Although originally developed for use in rural areas, PRA has been employed successfully in urban settings as well. The differences between PRA and RRA are summarized in Table 5.3.

The key principles of PRA are:

- **Participation:** PRA relies heavily on participation by the communities to enable local people to be involved, not only as sources of information, but as partners with the PRA team in gathering and analyzing the information.
- **Teamwork:** PRA is conducted by a local team, speaking in the local language, with a few outsiders. PRA relies on informal interaction and brainstorming among people. This is best done by a team of local people who know the area's conditions, traditions and social structure, with others having a mix of disciplinary backgrounds and experience. A well-balanced team will bring in fresh perspectives and new ideas.

TABLE 5.3
Differences between RRA and PRA.

RRA	PRA
Learning rapidly and directly from villagers: The researcher learns about rural areas by interacting with local people	Learning with villagers: The researcher learns about rural areas with and by rural people
Emphasis on efficient use of time and achievement of objectives	Emphasis on flexibility to adapt to time frame of community
Team of outsiders analyze conditions and understand local people	Local people analyze their own conditions and communicate with outsiders
Focus decided by outsiders	Focus decided by communities
Involves outside agencies and institutions to be more 'participatory'	Enables communities to make demands on outside agencies

Mini Case Study 5.2

Using the PRA Approach

Participatory approaches are used in social research but companies can benefit by following these approaches, as they help in understanding the problems of people. By making a resource map, companies can come to know what villages have and, more importantly, what they lack. Companies and entrepreneurs can use this information to provide solutions that will be easily accepted by the residents.

Mahra et al. (2016) describe the use of PRA in Salakhedi, a village in Ujjain, Madhya Pradesh. By undertaking a transect walk and during a village seminar, problems of farmers were discussed. Eight problems were identified which are listed in column 1 of Table 5.4. Clearly, residents would welcome solutions to these. We have suggested solutions to these in column 2. It is easy to see that these solutions show up business opportunities for seed, pesticide and fertilizer companies, which would otherwise not be obvious to a visitor.

TABLE 5.4
Problems identified through PRA in Salakhedi and solutions suggested.

Problem Identified	Solutions Suggested
Girdle beetle infestation in Soybean crop	Hybrid seed varieties Pesticide and chemical intervention
Termite and rodent attack in wheat crop	Short stature and resistant varieties of seed Optimum fertilizer and seed rate Pesticide and chemical intervention
Low milk production	Gradual improvement in livestock Prevention of livestock disease Better feed and other inputs

Problem Identified	Solutions Suggested
Fusarium wilt in chickpea crop	Introduction of crop rotation and new varieties Optimum fertilizer and irrigation Timely sowing Pesticide and chemical intervention
Lodging of Wheat crop	Better sowing and irrigation practices Use of hybrid seeds
Yellow rust in wheat crop	Introduction of crop rotation and new varieties Optimum fertilizer and irrigation Pesticide and chemical intervention
Foot and Mouth disease in cattle	Better rearing practices Veterinary care and availability of medicines
Pod borer infestation in chickpea crop	Introduction of crop rotation and new varieties Pesticide and chemical intervention

However, it may be noted that PRA is a technique to 'help people to help themselves'. It is a very effective tool to identify grass root problems of villages and then finding sustainable solutions. Blatant use of the technique for commercial purposes will result in farmers turning away or not opening up about their problems. Only when a trust is established will the technique be useful.

The idea is to increase the confidence of the poor, their faith in themselves, their self-reliance and not to make them use their knowledge but imposing ideas of a company or organization. By increasing awareness of their own capabilities and common interests and using this knowledge to analyze their needs, companies will find it easier to achieve cooperation. Participation of communities in their own development is important.

How can companies use the PRA approach to develop products that solve rural problems?

Source for this Case Study:

Mahra, G.S., P. Kumar, C. Solanki, D.S. Tomar, S.K. Kaushik, R. Tewari and V.K.J. Rao. 2016. "Identifying Grass Root Problems and Generating Sustainable Solutions through Participatory Rural Appraisal." *Indian Research Journal of Extension Education* 15 (4), 198–208.

- **Flexibility:** PRA does not provide blueprints but is flexible in approach. The techniques used in a particular development context are determined by variables such as skill mix of the team, the time and resources available and the topic and location of the work.
- **Optimal ignorance:** PRA work intends to gather just enough information to make the necessary recommendations and decisions.
- **Triangulation:** Working with qualitative data, PRA teams follow the thumb rule that at least three sources must be consulted or techniques must be used to investigate the same topics to ensure that the information is valid and reliable.

Participatory Action Research (PAR)

PAR is an approach to conduct research in communities that emphasizes participation and action. It seeks to understand the world by trying to change it. PAR assumes that people can solve their own problems and emphasizes collective inquiry grounded in experience and social history. It has three elements: participation (life in society and democracy), action (engagement with experience and history) and research (soundness in thought and the growth of knowledge). The process of PAR should be empowering and lead to people having increased control over their lives.

Finding about rural customers by means of questionnaires is extremely time consuming and involves great expense. Participatory research helps discover the motivations and feelings linked to a product or brand. Such methods will also prove useful, for instance, to find out how a company should deal with local products that are cheaper and very popular in rural areas as compared to branded products. When people participate in any of these methods, they feel empowered and brand loyalty may result since they feel close to the decision-making process. These methods would also be useful when participation of the local people is sought in distribution or in brand building exercises.

More Methods of Qualitative Research

Qualitative research gives us several other interesting methods of understanding rural behaviour, which can be used in participatory approaches or as part of interview techniques. Sometimes these methods are also used as standalone exercises. As we have mentioned earlier, rural consumers must be understood in the context of their behaviour, beliefs, opinions, emotions, culture and relationships. These are very difficult to uncover with the help of only traditional, urban-based market research techniques.

Qualitative methods help in identifying intangible factors, such as social norms, socio-economic status, gender roles, ethnicity and religion, and community roles, which play a very important role in rural areas. These methods, thus, are especially effective in obtaining culturally specific information about the values, opinions, behaviours and social contexts of rural people.

Such techniques include narratology, storytelling, classical ethnography, projective techniques and metaphor analysis, described later in this chapter. The basic advantage of these methods is that they study consumer behaviour as it occurs naturally and villagers in their own settings. No attempt is made to manipulate the situation. They help in getting a holistic perspective, rather than looking at a set of variables and help to discover underlying causes. Companies looking to develop new products or modify products for rural areas will find such techniques especially useful. Such techniques also help in discovering hidden needs which lead to making products that can be successful in rural markets.

Hidden Need Analysis

Goffin, Lemke and Koners (2011), in their book *Identifying Hidden Needs,* describe methods to find out about consumer needs that may not be stated or described. The authors write that companies using traditional market research often end up developing incremental, me-too products. This, however, does not work in rural areas. Companies therefore have to use sophisticated methods from psychology and anthropology to uncover customers' hidden needs, needs that they are unable to articulate or have not even recognized themselves.

To achieve this, direct questions are not adequate to interview villagers. This is because, when direct questions are asked, they speak within their own area of experience and are unable to relate to new products. For instance, while motivating rural children for washing hands, Gupta and Kumar (2015) describe that people thought that merely washing hands with water or mud was enough and there was no need for using soap (see Opening Case). An approach of fighting disease was more suitable to inculcate better hygiene habits among them. Thus, it is important to use alternative methods to discover hidden needs rather than use traditional market research methods and direct questions.

The methods used in hidden needs analysis are repertory grid analysis and lead user groups. Together with participatory research, these techniques are very effective at uncovering customers' hidden needs. However, organizational barriers need to be overcome if new methods of market research are to be adopted, because managers are mostly trained in traditional research methods and are reluctant to adopt hidden needs approaches.

Repertory Grid Analysis

Repertory grid analysis is an instrument that helps to describe how people give meaning to their experiences. It helps to decipher mental maps that people form of themselves with respect to their surroundings and experiences. It is in this personal construct that an individual lives and makes sense of one's existence. The repertory grid explores these personal constructs and attempts to see other peoples' world as they see it. Based on George Kelly's Personal Construct Theory, it consists of making a grid or matrix regarding people's perceptions. The method is particularly useful in rural marketing, as it helps find out the beliefs and attitudes of the rural consumer.

The repertory grid method consists of a semi–structured interview in which the respondent is given a triad of elements and is then asked to specify an important way in which two of the elements are alike and different from the third, which are called constructs. Often surprising results are obtained, that is, something that the researcher did not expect, which is the point of the exercise. On discovering the constructs, the participant names its polar opposites and is asked to rate them on a scale. Then, the interviewer moves on to the next triad of options. Typically, these steps are repeated until the respondent mentions no new constructs anymore.

The key is to elicit as many constructs as possible, without any suggestions from the researcher.

The method uses indirect questions and stimulates users to compare and contrast their experiences of existing products. This technique is ideal for developing new product ideas or for modifying products for rural areas.

Lead Users

Lead users are large users whose present strong needs become general in a marketplace in the future. Such customers use products under demanding conditions, such as rural areas without stable electric power. Lead users can serve as a need-forecasting laboratory for marketing research. For example, by studying needs of lead users for medical machines, General Electric invented portable machines for rural areas with a battery that could sustain long hours without recharge (see Mini Case Study 5.3).

The lead user process can be used through a four-step process:

1. Identify an important market or technical trend.
2. Identify lead users who lead that trend in terms of experience or usage.
3. Analyze lead user need data.
4. Project lead user data onto the general market.

Mini Case Study 5.3

GE: Developing New Products through Need Analysis

General Electric (GE) is one of the largest companies in the world. It faced two problems in India: its medical machines were too expensive for the Indian market where medical aid to villages is abysmal. People had to take trips to city hospitals for medical aid, as no facility existed with the technology required for tests. Medical machines could not work in rural India where electricity supply was erratic. There was a compelling need for cheaper machines that were sturdy and could be operated on batteries. Moreover, since usage in villages was low, a portable machine was needed.

To fulfil the unmet medical needs in rural areas, it set about solving these problems in its research and design facility in Bangalore, where many of the products originally designed in the West were being re-engineered for new uses in the India market.

The research resulted in developing a lightweight ECG machine for villages. It fits and can be carried in the backpack of a travelling doctor. It can take 500 readings on a single battery charge and costs only a tenth that of a standard ECG machine.

Immelt, Govindarajan and Trimble (2009) explain that it used the process of *reverse innovation*, which is opposite of 'glocalization', in which companies develop products in their home countries and distribute them worldwide. The company realized that it needed to do this before local entrepreneurs developed their own low-cost solutions to the pressing problems faced in developing countries. GE has spent close to US$3 billion since 2009 to make products that were cheaper, had better access but still had good quality. The lightweight hand-held ECG machine cost around US$1,000 as compared to the cost of US$10,000 of larger ECG machines. The company also developed a PC-based ultrasound machine.

Photo 5.6
An Embrace infant warmer.

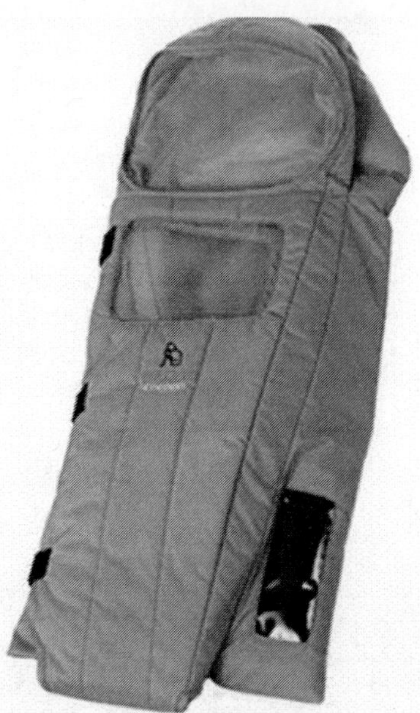

Source: http://www.embraceinnovations.com/ (Accessed on 26 April 2017).

Another problem that GE noticed was India's high infant mortality, which can be solved partly if hospitals and nursing homes have incubators for premature infants. This was another unmet need discovered while interacting with lead users, who were medical care personnel in this case. The company reinvented their incubator and reduced the cost to about US$2,000, which was still too high. The company then decided to partner with Embrace Innovations, a social enterprise, which had developed easy-to-use, portable infant warmers that do not need continuous power supply. The warmer cost only US$200 and can be used in hospitals, ambulances and wards. It can keep a baby warm for up to six hours by combining a sleeping bag with pads that could be heated in water. Embrace calls itself 'Health Tech with a heart' and has reduced the cost of incubators considerably.

A similar problem uncovered by need analysis was regarding cancer diagnosis. To sell its PET-CT cancer diagnosis machines, the company had to develop a national network to make available across states the isotopes necessary for the procedure. It had to lobby the government for permission to make isotopes in their cyclotron machines. Then, it got airlines and hospitals on board to create an efficient distribution method to transport the isotopes—which have a limited shelf life—all over India. It paid off. GE Healthcare has sold 45 PET-CT scanners, each costing about US$1.5 million, and nine cyclotrons at US$2.5 million each and expects the market for nuclear medicine procedures in India to grow at a rate of 15–20 per cent a year.

Can you think of other products developed for rural areas uncovered by lead user analysis?

Sources for this Case Study:

Web Resource

Embrace Innovations website: http://www.embraceinnovations.com/

Other Sources

Immelt, Jeffrey R., Vijay Govindarajan and Chris Trimble. 2009. "How GE Is Disrupting Itself." *Harvard Business Review,* October. Available at: https://hbr.org/2009/10/how-ge-is-disrupting-itself (Accessed on 27 April 2017).

Reuters. 2011. "Companies Forge Lean Business Models to Tap Rural India." 16 September. Available at: http://in.reuters.com/article/idINIndia-59379420110916 (Accessed on 25 April 2017).

Observational or Ethnographic Research

Ethnographic research, that is, of observing rural people in their own environment, offers insights as to how rural people use products. Anderson (2009) writes that ethnographic research is "central to gaining a full understanding of your customers and the business itself." It consists of simply watching people as they go about their lives, their response to or advertisements, using products, and so on. It is based on the assumption: "You can observe a lot just by watching."

Defined as "systematic market research observing customers in their own environment using products and services," it gives valuable insights about how people regard products. Anderson explains (2009):

> Unlike traditional market researchers, who ask specific, highly practical questions, anthropological researchers visit consumers in their homes or offices to observe and listen in a non-directed way... while this observational method may appear inefficient, it enlightens us about the context in which customers would use a new product and the meaning that product might hold in their lives.

Ethnographic research is very useful in villages, where an insight into people's lives will show what kind of products they need. For instance, many villages do not have piped water supply and villagers depend on hand-pumps or fetch it over large distances from a water source. Such water may not be clean and this gives the opportunity to develop a low-cost water purifier that does not need either piped supply or electricity. Products such as Tata Swach and HUL's Pureit fill an important need in villages. CavinKare (see Chapter 4) was also able to develop breakthrough packaging by observing that rural customers wanted small amounts of products such as shampoo and powder and do not like to invest in a big pack.

It follows a 'fly on the wall' approach. Through observation, companies learn about the problems faced by rural people and the context in which customers use products. It thus helps to spot opportunities for breakthrough innovations. Systematic observation allows market researchers to understand the role products play in people's lives. It is a non-intrusive method that does not depend on judgement of the consumers, and is therefore unbiased.

The key methods of ethnographic market research are:

1. **Visits to villages:** The researcher visits customers in their homes and collects qualitative data, such as videos of product usage and contextual interviews. Some prepared and some spontaneous questions may be asked. The researcher looks for contradictions in buyer behaviour, identifies the cultural characteristics of the customer and observes customers as they use products, which helps in discovering customer problems and needs.
2. **Audio/visual recordings:** The researcher can use recordings, if allowed by the village community. For instance, if consumers keep good care of a product or display it prominently in their home, it means that companies can associate a status with it.
3. **Product and consumer photos:** Sometimes the researcher can take photographs discreetly, for example, having a camera during a demo organized in a village. Photographs can show whether consumers are stimulated. For example, close-up pictures of consumers' eyes show the size of their iris, which expands involuntarily when stimulated.
4. **Product demos:** The effect of product demos and BTL techniques on consumers can be seen in videos and photographs, which can also show whether the consumer was stimulated or bored.

Ethnographic research is fast gaining popularity in consumer research. However, although it is the only technique that really allows companies to really know their customers, it is labour-intensive and expensive. Another problem is that if the researcher is not experienced, certain important cultural behaviours can be overlooked. Furthermore, it involves getting the trust of the villagers, otherwise they will hesitate to let anyone take pictures.

Some other qualitative research methods are described here.

Depth Interviews

An open-ended, detailed conversation with an individual conducted by a trained researcher is called a depth interview. The idea is to deeply explore the respondent's point of view, feelings, attitudes or perspectives. Such interviews are wide ranging, probing issues in detail. They are semi-structured as they do not have a set of predetermined questions. Instead, people are encouraged to speak and express their views about products at length. Depth interviews help to understand individual motivations about products and brands. However, they are time consuming and responses can sometimes be difficult to interpret. Further, it requires skilled researchers as interviewer bias may creep in.

Laddering

Laddering is an interview technique in which the interviewer probes step by step or 'peels the layers' of the participant's experience by asking probing questions to discover people's core values and beliefs. It is used in marketing to describe the link between customers' values and their purchasing behaviour. The laddering process uncovers the hierarchy of consumer perceptions and product knowledge from attributes (A), consumption consequences (C), to personal values (V):

- **Attributes:** Individuals recognize the attributes of a product easily. For example, a consumer may say, "I like this tractor, because it has a powerful engine."
- **Consequences:** Each attribute has consequences for the individual. In our tractor example, it may make its driver feel strong and powerful. There may be several consequences for each attribute.
- **Values:** Each consequence is linked to a core value of the person's life. For example, the powerful tractor makes that driver feel attractive.

These three form a chain, or ladder, that connects a product attribute to a core value. Ladders result in forming a Hierarchical Value Map that illustrates all the linkages between customers' values and their purchasing behaviour. Product attributes are means through which consumers achieve their ultimate values. We see that products are not chosen and purchased for themselves or their characteristics, but rather for the meaning they form in the minds of people.

Focus Groups

Focus groups are very useful in rural marketing research. In this, a group of about 8–12 people is formed and are asked by a moderator about their perceptions, opinions, beliefs and attitudes towards a product. The interview is conducted in an informal manner where respondents are free to give views from any aspect. Focus groups are used in trying out products and getting feedback on them and also to develop, package, name, promote or test market a new product. 'Whiteboard' exercises and using visual stimuli are helpful in focus groups.

Projective Techniques

Quite often, indirect methods are required to be used. A set of methods useful in rural marketing are projective techniques, which help in discovering the rural mind. Projective techniques are unstructured and indirect methods that encourage participants to project their feelings, thoughts, beliefs and attitudes to situations, product or brand. By projecting their feelings on something else, they reveal their own prejudices and beliefs. The situations may be vague and ambiguous, which makes the respondents project their emotions, revealing the working of their minds. Projective techniques use a disguised approach and direct questions are not asked, as in other types of research. Such techniques are especially useful because it is hard for consumers to express their deep feelings and views regarding brand images and allow participants to express their feelings without requiring them to put them into words. To get over language barriers, respondents can express themselves through stories, photographs, drawings and collages, through which all relevant brand associations are captured. Second, participants can express their opinions intuitively. For example, when respondents assign photographs or metaphors to brands, they need not explain their meanings of motivations. Such techniques are very useful in rural marketing research when respondents cannot express themselves. Projective research is used in the following ways:

- **Associative techniques:** This is a method to discover what a person associates a brand, product or company with in his/her mind. The researcher captures the thoughts immediately brought to the respondent's mind by the stimulus and this helps to decipher consumer imagery and spontaneous emotions. It shows what consumers actually think of brands or products and thus is ideal for finding out consumers' perceptions of products and their loyalty. Associative methods have been used to find out brand positioning and imagery in respondents' minds with respect to brands.

  Examples of associative techniques are asking questions such as:

  1. Which celebrity comes to your mind when you think of X brand?
     (It helps to answer the status of the brand or which celebrity should be used in promotions.)
  2. If Maruti was a person, which one would it be (show pictures of different people)?
     (It helps to discover brand personification.)

- **Word association:** This method consists of showing respondents a list of words, one by one, and asking them to respond by the first thing that comes to the mind on seeing a word. This exercise reveals a person's subconscious mind as it shows the things he/she associates with. Alternatively, a list of words is prepared in advance and shown to consumers, who say whether that attribute matches or not with the brand. Another variation is that the words and brands are written separately and respondents are asked to match the words with the brands. The words written or selected by the respondent shows the 'consumer vocabulary' associated with brands or products. Word association test is used to find out whether proper words are used in a brand's promotion. Other methods used in association tests are imagery, brand personification and brand obituary. An example of the word association technique is given here.

  Word association: Which words would you associate with Maggi?

  Easy Difficult Tasty Not tasty Nutritious Useless Snack Meal

- **Narration and storytelling:** Rural consumers love stories. A number of people can be engaged at a given time and they will love it if the story is humorous or otherwise engages them. Cayla and Arnould (2013) write, "ethnographic stories give executives a unique means of understanding market realities." They further explain about the explanatory power of ethnography and write, "ethnographic stories help firms organize ambiguous or complex human behavior into actionable fields." Researchers can understand consumers by listening to their stories about brands and their market experiences.

  Example of storytelling:
  Amul has very effectively used brand stories to reach out to people—the story of the cooperative movement founded by Dr Verghese Kurien is at once inspiring and generates interest in the brand. It resulted in a film, *Manthan*, which shows how the movement was built and the difficulties were overcome.

- **Brand mapping:** Brand mapping is a technique for visualizing the relationships between brands. Respondents are asked to group together brands according to a given characteristic and identify the key factors that differentiate one brand from another. Such an analysis helps in identifying opportunities to introduce and position products in rural areas. It also shows what attributes a company should introduce in brands to be successful in villages and how to tackle the competition. For instance, a company can elicit from consumers what a local brand means to them. Respondents are asked to illustrate the local brand in the centre of a circle. Then, consumers map what they associate with the brand and show how they are connected to one another. They are then given a few minutes during which they, working from the centre, create branches of thoughts and feelings. When completed, the respondents circle the branch most significant to them. Participants then share and discuss their mind maps with the group, making additional connections and associations. Finally, researchers aggregate these individual brand maps and their associated data to produce a consensus brand map. The completed mind maps show satisfaction, frustrations, pain points and unmet wants and needs with regard to the local brand. Core brand associations are differentiated from non-core associations. This exercise helps discover what attributes a brand should highlight or place its selling proposition on. It will also help in identifying fake brands (see Mini Case Study 5.4).

There are several other associative methods that are used in rural research:

- *Pictorial methods* are helpful to discover what cannot be expressed in words. This method helps uncover the imagery in consumers' minds about a particular brand.
- *Mood-board* approach consists of asking participants to make a collage to represent a brand from pictures or clips that they have collected. When they use pictures of people, it helps to understand brand personification.
- *Job-sorting* requires that participants connect jobs to different brands.
- *Construction* is a technique in which the respondents are asked to construct a story or a picture from a given starting point. For example, two persons are depicted in an ambiguous situation and participants are asked to tell what each of them is thinking, saying and doing. When a story is built around a picture, it shows the perception and attitude of a person.
- *Speech bubbles* is a technique where respondents are required to fill in the bubbles of the characters in cartoons or pictures describing what they are thinking or doing.
- *Completion* is a technique where respondents are given an incomplete sentence, story, argument or conversation and are asked to finish it.

Metaphor Analysis

Anyone who has worked in rural areas knows that people like to talk in metaphors. Metaphor analysis helps in discovering which metaphors are used in describing products. Metaphors such as *resham si twacha* (smooth as silk complexion) impart linguistic, visual and symbolic meaning to the brand. Visual or symbolic metaphors are extremely helpful, for example, showing a mother in the ad of child care products, a film star in an ad for brand imagery or a tiger in a motorcycle ad. Metaphors help in gaining consumers' attention and recall, evoking imagery and provoking comparisons, explaining complex products through easy-to-understand unrelated image. The technique used in this analysis is the Zaltman metaphor elicitation technique (ZMET).

Mini Case Study 5.4

Fake Brands in Rural India

Brands face a huge competition in rural India—that of fake brands. As most of the fake brands are made by small operators who are difficult to locate, companies find it difficult to fight them. It is up to managers to discover these brands and compete against them.

Some of the brands that can be found in villages are 'Daily Milk', 'Lifebody' soap and 'Fair & Lonely'. They look and sound familiar to big brands, imitate the packaging and are much cheaper than the original brands.

There are two types of fake goods:

- **Counterfeit products:** These are products bearing similar names and copying the product right up to packaging and colour schemes. Sometimes they even carry the name and address of the genuine manufacturer! The look and feel is quite similar to the real brands and it would take a discerning eye to see the difference. Discarded liquor and cold drink bottles are filled locally to sell counterfeit products.
- **Pass-off products:** These products have similar sounding names or similar spellings with just one or two letters changed. One can easily mistake 'Coigate' for 'Colgate', for instance. Such copycat brands are sold openly in villages.

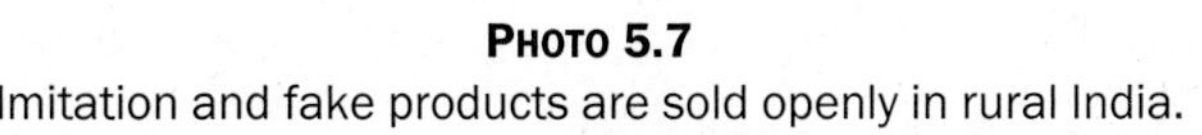

PHOTO 5.7
Imitation and fake products are sold openly in rural India.

Source: http://mig.me/discover/migworld?path=/2015/07/31/mcdonalds-fcdonalds-10-fake-brands-india-aud365/ (Accessed on 26 April 2017).

Fake brands exist in rural areas as markets are inaccessible and brands have a difficulty in reaching such areas. Illiteracy and poverty compounds the problem. Advertising on TV by the original brands actually helps the counterfeit products.

The share of fake products in the FMCG market is huge. *The Economic Times* (2016) reports that FICCI Committee Against Smuggling and Counterfeiting Activities Destroying the Economy (CASCADE) estimates that the government lost nearly ₹6,000 crore to the grey market of FMCG personal goods. The report also mentioned that 31.6 per cent of FMCG personal goods space is several shades of grey, and similarly for 21.7 per cent of the packaged foods industry. Such brands pose a serious threats to health and safety, apart from bleeding big brands.

On the whole, the brands not only suffer in terms of revenue but they also have to compromise on the brand image which, in no case, is tolerable. Therefore, various brands have come up with unique strategies to overcome their shortcomings in the rural markets and curb the growth of fake brands in rural areas.

Some companies fight back initiating legal action or changing their packaging periodically. Introducing packs that the small manufacturers cannot copy is another strategy. For instance, 'Axe' tamper-proof nozzles which cannot be detached from the body makes it difficult for counterfeits to refill the packs.

How can companies counter the threat of fake products in rural areas?

Sources for this Case Study:

The Economic Times. 2016. "Why Make in India When You Can Fake in India." *Brand Equity*, 4 May.

Indian Express. 2016. "India 5th in Fake Goods Trade; China on top." 1 May.

Comparative Scales

Comparative scales are used when there is direct comparison between objects or stimuli. *Paired comparison* is done when the consumers are required to choose between two products at the same time according to their preferences. For example, two objects are presented at the same time (Colgate, Pepsodent) and the consumer selects one. Assuming the respondent selects the first one, the selected object is paired with another brand (Colgate, Close-Up), and so on, till the final preference is arrived at.

In a *Rank Order Scale* the respondent is given a set of items and is asked to put the items in order of preference. It is a technique in which several objects or brands are given to consumers to rank according to their preference. An example of rank order scale is given in Figure 5.1. It is a quick and easy method. Analysis is done by adding the ranks of each brand from several respondents. The brand with the least aggregate score will be the most preferred brand of the sample.

Non-comparative Scaling

Comparative scaling is a technique by which feelings of rural consumers can be identified. Respondents are asked to directly compare products with respect to adjectives provided by the researcher. In non-comparative scaling, each item is scaled independently of the others by respondents on a continuous rating scale. They place a mark on a line which shows two extreme responses, such as best and worst at each end. Sometimes numbers are used to scale attributes (Figure 5.1). In rural areas, graphical aids such as smileys are used, which makes it easy for respondents to answer the question.

FIGURE 5.1
Examples of continuous rating scales.

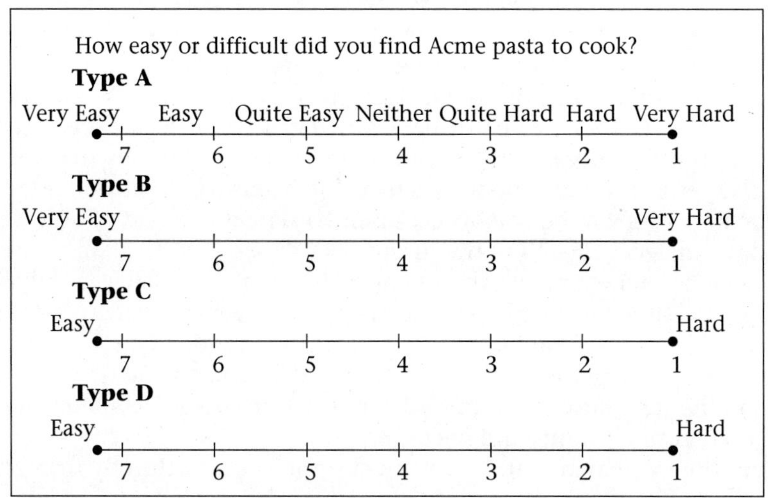

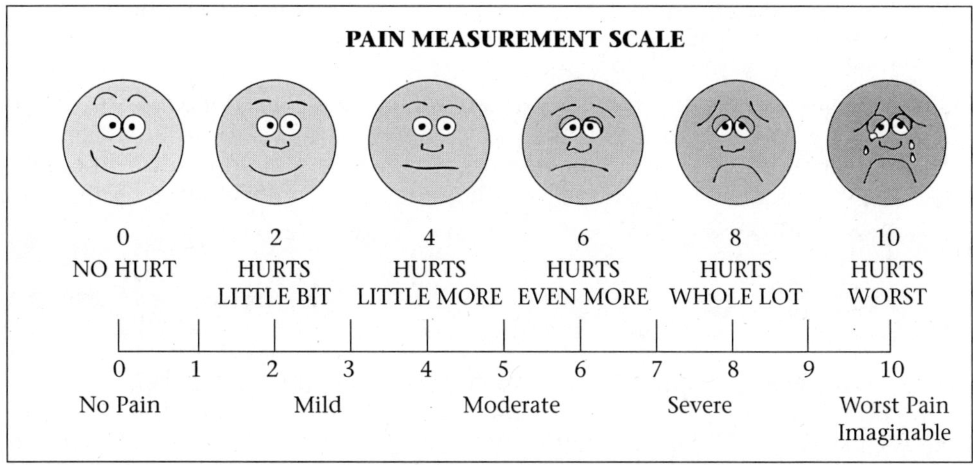

Rating scales are used to measure consumer attitudes such as perceptions, product preferences, purchase intentions and service satisfaction. They are also used to rate products and promotions, packages and attributes.

Data Analytics

As smartphones gain penetration in rural areas and Internet access becomes easier, rural market research of the future will be done through data analytics.

Data analytics refer to analysis of data from various sources about a person's behaviour. By tracking Internet usage, social media, browsing history and data from the physical world, companies can make very accurate profiles of people. Data analytics goes through terabytes of data and hundreds of variables in real time. Barton and Court (2012) write that data analytics give companies "the ability to see what was previously invisible [and] improves operations, customer experiences, and strategy." For instance, a bank can improve the efficiency of its customer service through a 360-degree view by combining information from banking touch-points such as ATM transactions, online queries, customer complaints, and so on. However, this is not all. If we add the streams of data flowing in from other sources, such as local demographics to weather forecasts, we can develop predictive systems that can significantly improve customer service and experience. As rural India gets online and smartphones become more popular, companies will be able to get granular data about the rural folk. That is why, data analysis is the market research of the future.

Smartphones are also encouraging the use of social media in villages. Analyzing such data yields information about consumer behaviour and preferences. Social media analytics help to:

- Capture consumer data from social media to understand attitudes, opinions, trends and manage online reputation—the candid conversations on social media are key to useful insights on consumer wants and needs, brand and product perceptions.
- Predict customer behaviour and improve customer satisfaction by recommending next best actions.
- Create customized campaigns and promotions that resonate with social media participants.
- Interact with participants and measure their reactions.

Traditional market research methods rely on surveys and questionnaires to understand their target market. With social media analysis tools, researchers can get to know everything about their target audience—from demographics to consumer opinions and sentiments. One advantage is that it is a real-time analysis; one does not have to wait for the results of market surveys to know the market trends.

SUMMARY

Companies have been applying marketing principles to rural marketing. For long-term presence in rural markets, companies have to understand the environment, rural consumers and their behaviour. As the thinking of marketing has evolved, companies moved to the societal concept, understanding and solving problems in rural areas, and thus have established themselves and succeeded in villages.

Concepts like 4Ps have evolved to 4As. Segmentation is not easy as rural data is not available and so companies have to depend on observation to learn about consumers. Rural sales consist of building relationships and marketing channels also have to be redesigned to reach scattered villages. Companies have to learn to fight local competition, which is likely to come from unbranded goods, local brands and fake brands. Branding in rural areas is also different as it depends on quality, value for money and belongingness. For redesigning marketing for rural areas, new tools are required, such as re-engineering, innovation, e-commerce, making relationships and working with local partners, decentralized marketing and using a social approach.

Rural market research also required different tools, because customers are spread over large distances and are sometimes not exposed to brands and products. Traditional methods of market research have their limitations in rural areas. Hence, companies must adopt participatory approaches, consisting of PO, RRA, PRA and PAR. Other qualitative methods include narratology, storytelling, classical ethnography, hidden need analysis projective techniques and metaphor analysis. Repertory grid analysis is an instrument that helps to describe how people give meaning to their experiences. It also helps to decipher mental maps. Lead users serve as a need-forecasting laboratory for marketing research.

Ethnographic research, that is, of observing rural people in their own environment, offers insights as to how rural people use products. It is fast gaining popularity in consumer research. However, although it is the only technique that really allows companies to know their customers, it is labour-intensive and expensive.

Depth interviews, or semi structured, detailed conversations, explore deeply the respondent's point of view, feelings, attitudes or perspectives, helping to understand individual motivations about products and brands. Another technique is laddering, an interview technique, in which the interviewer probes step by step or 'peels the layers' of the participant's experience by asking probing questions to discover people's core values and beliefs. Focus groups are very useful in rural marketing research.

Quite often, indirect methods are required to be used. Projective techniques use a disguised approach and direct questions are not asked, like in other types of research. Respondents can express themselves through stories, photographs, drawings and collages, and through these, all relevant brand associations are captured. Such techniques consist of associative techniques, word associations, narration and storytelling, metaphor analysis and brand mapping. Comparative scales are used when there is direct comparison between objects or stimuli. Finally, as smartphones have started gaining penetration in rural areas and Internet access is becoming easier, rural market research of the future will be done through data analytics.

CONCLUSION

Applying marketing principles to rural areas can work only when they are modified. Sometimes a complete new set of skills are required. Managers trained in urban marketing warfare are unlikely to find long-term success in rural areas. Completely different skills are required both for marketing and marketing research in villages. In fact, the very purpose of marketing is set to change. Porter and Kramer (2011) writes, "The capitalist system is under siege," adding that businesses are increasingly blamed for making profits at the expense of society and for society's failures. They ignore society's long-term interests. As a consequence, writes Sabeti (2011), business has a new purpose and a new sector of the economy is emerging, consisting of the for-benefit corporation. In rural areas, such approaches have met with great success and created long-term presence.

Since a copy of urban approaches in rural areas does not necessarily work, new methods of marketing and marketing research are required. But these are not all. It is up to the creativity of the manager to figure out newer and better ways of reaching rural areas. It is perhaps to time to rewrite the rules of marketing to include consumers in BoP markets across the globe.

KEY TERMS

Consumer behaviour research: The study of preferences, motivations, and buying behaviour of customers.

Customer scenario: The broad context in which customers select, buy and use products and services.

Data analytics: Analysis of data from various sources—such as Internet usage, social media, browsing history and data from the physical world—to make consumer profiles and learn about a person's behaviour.

Depth interview: An open-ended, detailed conversation with an individual, conducted by a trained researcher, to explore deeply the respondent's point of view, feelings, attitudes or perspectives.

Ethnographic research: Ethnographic research consists of systematically observing rural people in their own environment and is used to find out insights on how they use products.

Focus groups: A group of about 8–12 people is formed and they are asked by a moderator through informal interviews about their perceptions, opinions, beliefs and attitudes towards a product.

Laddering: Laddering is an interview technique in which the interviewer probes step by step or 'peels the layers' of the participant's experience by asking probing questions to discover people's core values and beliefs.

Lead users: Lead users are large users with specific needs whose present strong needs become general in a marketplace in the future.

Market research: The systematic collection, analysis and interpretation of data related to the market and the surrounding environment.

Market segmentation: The process of profiling and identifying distinct groups in the population to discover a target market.

Marketing channels: Channels to reach their market segments, consisting of *communication channel, distribution channels* and *selling channels*.

Marketing mix: Actions undertaken by a company to elicit desired responses from a target audience. It consists of 4Ps—product, price, place and promotion.

Participant observation (PO): A type of data collection method used in qualitative research with the aim to gain close and intimate familiarity with a given group of individuals and their practices through involvement in their cultural environment.

Participatory action research (PAR): PAR emphasizes participation and action and works on the principle that people can solve their own problems through collective inquiry. It has three elements: participation (life in society and democracy), action (engagement with experience and history) and research (soundness in thought and the growth of knowledge).

Participatory rural appraisal (PRA): PRA is an approach and methods for learning about rural life and conditions from, with and by rural people. It describes methods to enable local people to share, enhance and analyze their knowledge of life and conditions, to plan and to act.

Primary research: Research that is collected first-hand for a specific purpose.

Projective techniques: Projective techniques are unstructured and are indirect methods that encourage participants to project their feelings, thoughts, beliefs and attitudes to situations, product or brand.

Qualitative research: Consists of gathering information that is not measurable, such as feelings, characteristics and attitudes.

Quantitative research: When variables can be measured or quantified, it is called quantitative research.

Rapid rural appraisal (RRA): RRA consists of a set of guidelines to help people work in a structured but flexible way in rural communities and a set of tools to aid interaction with those communities.

Re-engineering: The fundamental rethinking and radical redesign of business processes to achieve dramatic improvements in critical measures of performance, such as cost, quality, service and speed.

Relationship marketing: The process of building long-term economic, technical and social relationships with customers, suppliers and distributors.

Repertory grid analysis: A process of semi-structured interview in which the respondents compare and contrast their experiences of existing products, thus revealing their hidden needs.

Secondary research: Consists of published and other data that is already available, which has already been gathered and recorded by someone else for purposes other than the current project.

CONCEPT REVIEW QUESTIONS

1. What is meant by customer scenarios? Why is it important to study customer scenarios in rural marketing?
2. Which marketing approach is likely to work in villages and why?
3. What are the various methods of segmentation? Which methods are likely to work in rural areas?
4. Why is it said that relationship marketing works in villages? What are the ways of building relationships there?
5. Explain some of the new tools that are used in rural marketing, citing examples for each.
6. Why do traditional methods of marketing research not work in rural areas? What kinds of methods are needed?
7. What are participatory methods of rural research?
8. Describe the methods of hidden need analysis. Why is it important to use this method in rural market research?
9. What is ethnographic research? Comment on its utility in rural market research.
10. What are the steps you will use in conducting rural market research? Describe them in detail.

CRITICAL THINKING QUESTIONS

1. Comment on the statement, "The way to do rural marketing is through innovation not only in products but the very way that marketing is done." Why is a complete innovation in marketing required for rural areas? How have companies responded to this challenge?
2. What is the difference between qualitative, quantitative and participatory research? Which type of research is suitable for rural areas and why? Which methods would you prefer?

3. Can ethnographic research, a time consuming method, be really used in villages? What are its advantages and limitations?
4. Data analytics involve analyzing data from various sources, including online activities of people. Can it be used for rural consumer research? Will rural consumers take to smartphones in a big way and share their personal information like their urban counterparts?

PROJECTS AND ASSIGNMENTS

1. Visit a village and collect brands being sold there. How many are local brands and how many are fake? Find out about their success. If you were representing a national brand, how would you fight local and fake brands?
2. Undertake a visit to a village with your friends. Go around the village taking notes of what you see. Ask questions if necessary. Compare your notes with your friends and see what problems you have uncovered and suggest solutions for them.
3. Study published literature to understand how marketing principles have been used in rural marketing. In what way were the principles modified by the companies that used them? Prepare a presentation on your findings.
4. Prepare a questionnaire to study rural consumer needs when they buy a washing machine. Find out: What were the motivations in buying the machine? What were the problems faced by rural customers?

WEB RESOURCES

See a video series on India Innovates at: http://www.thebetterindia.com/india-innovates/

See a video on participatory research at: https://media.pdx.edu/media/Participatory+Action+Research+with+Dignity+Village,+Part+1/0_6ie8snlc/29662772

"Participatory Rural Approach." Available at World Bank—Social Analysis: http://web.worldbank.org/WBSITE/EXTERNAL/TOPICS/EXTSOCIALDEV/0,,contentMDK:21233809~menuPK:3291499~pagePK:64168445~piPK:64168309~theSitePK:3177395~isCURL:Y~isCURL:Y,00.html

REFERENCES

Anand, S., and R. Krishna. 2008. "Marketing to Rural Consumers: Understanding and Tapping the Rural Market Potential." Rural brand preference determinants in India. Marketing to Rural Consumers, IIM-K, April.

Anderson, Ken. 2009. "Ethnographic Research: A Key to Strategy." *Harvard Business Review*, March. Available at: https://hbr.org/2009/03/ethnographic-research-a-key-to-strategy (Accessed on 26 April 2017).

Barton, Dominic, and David Court. 2012. "Making Advanced Analytics Work for You." *Harvard Business Review* (October). Available at: https://hbr.org/2012/10/making-advanced-analytics-work-for-you?cm_mmc=SocialHub-_-3271-_--_-4620118455841424536&goback=.gde_67086_member_172121820 (Accessed on 27 April 2017).

Cayla, Julien, and Eric Arnould. 2013 "Ethnographic Stories for Market Learning." *Journal of Marketing* 77 (July): 1–16.

Chambers, R. 1992. *Rural Appraisal: Rapid, Relaxed, and Participatory*. Institute of Development Studies Discussion Paper 311. Sussex: HELP.

Drucker, Peter F. 1985. *Management*. New York, NY: Harper Colophon.

Goffin, Keith, Fred Lemke and Ursula Koners. 2011. *Identifying Hidden Needs: Creating Breakthrough Products*. Basingstoke, UK: Palgrave.

Gupta, P., and D. Kumar. 2015. "Hand-washing—Motivating for New-habit-formation." Paper presented at Seminar on 'Social Marketing and Behavior Change', 24 April, Queen Mary University of London.

Hammer, M., and Champy, J. 1993. *Reengineering the Corporation: A Manifesto for Business Revolution*. New York: Harper Business.

Howell, Joseph T. 1972. *Hard Living on Clay Street: Portraits of Blue Collar Families*. Illinois: Waveland Press.

Mahra, G.S., P. Kumar, C. Solanki, D.S. Tomar, S.K. Kaushik, R. Tewari and V.K.J. Rao. Identifying Grass Root Problems and Generating Sustainable Solutions through Participatory Rural Appraisal. *Indian Research Journal of Extension Education*, Vol. 15 No. 4 (2016).

Packard, Vance. 1960. *The Waste Makers*. New York, NY: David McKay Company, Inc.

Porter, Michael E., and Mark R. Kramer. 2011. "Creating Shared Value." *Harvard Business Review*, January–February. Available at: https://ncg.org/sites/default/files/resources/HarvardBusinessReview_Creating_Shared_Value.pdf (Accessed on 25 April 2017).

Prahalad, C.K., and Allen Hammond. 2002. "Serving the World's Poor, Profitably." *Harvard Business Review*, September. Available at: https://hbr.org/2002/09/serving-the-worlds-poor-profitably (Accessed on 27 April 2017).

Sabeti, H. 2011. "The For-Benefit Enterprise." *Harvard Business Review*, November. Available at: https://hbr.org/2011/11/the-for-benefit-enterprise (Accessed on 27 April 2017).

Seybold, Patricia B. 2001. Get Inside the Lives of Your Customer. *Harvard Business Review*, May. Available at: https://hbr.org/2001/05/get-inside-the-lives-of-your-customers (Accessed on 27 April 2017).

The World Bank. 2005. "The Handwashing Handbook." Available at: http://documents.worldbank.org/curated/en/681501468141299225/pdf/323020Handwashing1handbook02005.pdf (Accessed on 27 April 2017).

Closing Case
Bolthouse: Selling Carrots as Junk Food

Can carrots use marketing principles and be sold like junk food?

Jeffrey Dunn, CEO of Bolthouse Farms in the US, wanted to make carrots as the preferred snack of youngsters. "Like most agricultural businesses, the company had been preoccupied for much of its 93-year history with supply: getting its products—primarily carrots but also juices and dressings—from the field and the factory to the family dinner table," he says.

Carrots were sold as they always were—in supermarket shelves or in packs. Consumers bought them and stored them in the vegetable tray of their refrigerators, where they stayed. How could the company make carrots occupy the same space that potato chips and salted snacks enjoyed in the minds of customers? On the face of it, it was an impossible task: selling them on the platform of health snacks and highlighting the beneficial qualities of carrots might appear to mothers but not to youngsters.

PHOTO 5.8
Positioning carrots as a snack food helped make it a big brand.

Source: www.babycarrorts.com (Accessed on 27 April 2017).

The company had come up with a breakthrough product in the 1990s. Supermarkets bought carrots of a particular size, shape and colour. Large and unseemly carrots had to be sold for juice or animal feed, or just thrown away. A local grower, Yurosek, processed the carrots, peeled them, cut them into pieces and sold them in bags. The 1-inch peeled round bites were called 'bunny balls', while the peeled and cut 2-inches-long carrot pieces were sold as baby carrots.

Baby carrots were a big hit. They transformed the whole industry. Yields and profits climbed. Moreover, they changed food habits: Americans loved them and carrots came to be accepted as snacks. Carrot consumption in the United States increased as a result of this invention.

Now carrots needed another push. The obvious marketing message was to stress on the healthful benefits of the product. But Dunn knew that a health campaign, talking about beta carotene or cutting calories, would not work. He knew that the approach should be similar to that of a soft drink or snack company: emotional, funny and something that appealed to impulse rather than responsibility.

Using ethnographic research and focus groups, the company tried to discover how carrots were used and how snack food companies influenced consumers. It found that while carrots went into the vegetable drawer, baby carrots were visible since they were stored on a shelf. The challenge was to get baby carrots into the category of junk foods.

Bolthouse's traditional packaging worked in the vegetable category; the 2-pound bag of baby carrots sold by it was too much work for consumers. They would unzip the bag to take out a baby carrot or two, and then close the zip. To make people eat more carrots, it knew it wanted a completely different approach. Baby carrots had to be sold as individual snack packs like potato chips bags, with bold, graphics that placed it at par with junk food. The idea was to change eating habits so that people could buy a pack of baby carrots and eat them as a convenience food.

The solution was to use marketing principles and tools to market carrots as a snack. In his interview to *Harvard Business Review*, Dunn (2015) explains how he wanted to turn Bolthouse Farms from a family farm business into an innovative, professionally managed and branded organization. First, Dunn applied a simple principle, which he had learnt during his stint at Coca-Cola, that soft drinks are sold one drink at a time. Bolthouse changed its juice packaging from large packs to single-serve bottles with an aggressive price promotion. Within nine months, it became the top-selling juice maker in the US. Then it started tweaking pricing and packaging strategies for its juices. In 2010, it decided to launch carrot snack packs, with ranch and chili lime flavours, with an expensive marketing campaign—'Eat 'Em Like Junk Food'. The campaign used TV, print and digital ads to sell baby carrots as potato chips and other snacks. It was an instant hit.

At the same time, the company expanded its distribution. The products were sold on vending machines and large retailers such as 7-Eleven and Walmart. It started using Sesame Street characters on its packaging. The product line was expanded to 27 varieties of juices and smoothies. Using smart packaging, vegetable and fruit purees were put in squeezable tubes. The company started distributing its products in grocery store chains and with big retailers such as Walmart and Costco. The Bolthouse products were placed in the "snack" sections along with products that were its direct and indirect competitors. The goal was to give parents a destination in stores where they could find fresh and healthful food for their kids. It also started selling online. In doing so, Bolthouse changed the image of vegetables in the consumer mind. The goal was to give parents a destination in stores where they could reliably find fresh and healthy food for their kids. It also started of selling online through delivery services. In doing so, Bolthouse changed the image of vegetables in the consumer mind.

TV ads were supplemented with other activities. A Twitter feed @babycarrots poked fun at popular junk food brands. Bolthouse vending machines were installed at two high schools, where it competed with chips and soda. But the investment in marketing paid off. It launched an initiative #urwhatupost, designed to encourage healthful eating through the sharing of 'food porn' images via social media. It started using Sesame Street cartoon characters in its advertising, just like FMCG companies.

Bolthouse also maintained price points like other companies. Most cold drinks and snacks in the US were sold for less than a dollar. The company priced its Fruit Tubes at 40 cents each and Veggie Snackers at 79 cents.

Since parents want more healthy snacks, Bolthouse had a new mission: 'inspire the fresh revolution' to create a healthier society. Instead of harping on the health benefits of vegetables, the company makes carrots seem cool, making them more likable and desirable. Apart from ads, it supplements the marketing effort with top-notch customer research and innovative product development. Veggie Snackers were introduced with flavours, just like other snacks.

In 2012, the company was acquired by Campbell, which has enabled Bolthouse to retain its business and control operations, sales and marketing, while it gets R&D support from Campbell. Distribution with big retailers is easier as part of a large company.

The success of 'Eat 'Em Like Junk Food' gave the company the courage to compete with the world's prominent food companies. Bolthouse Farms now sells nearly a billion pounds of carrots a year under a number of different brand names and supermarket labels. Together with Grimmway Farms, it controls more than 80 per cent of the carrot market in the US.

Questions for Discussion:

1. Comment upon the strategy of using Coca-Cola marketing techniques to a healthy snack. Can they work for other products?
2. What are the insights used by Bolthouse from consumer marketing?
3. What other categories can use such an approach? Can it be used for other food processing industries? How?
4. Develop a marketing strategy for encouraging kids to eat green vegetables, by taking insights from the case study.

Sources for this Case Study:

Web Resources

Bolthouse Farms website: http://www.babycarrots.com/

#urwhatupost initiative by Bolthouse Farms. Available at: http://www.urwhatupost.com/

Other Sources

Dunn, Jeffrey. 2015. "The CEO of Bolthouse Farms on Making Carrots Cool." *Harvard Business Review*, October. Available at: https://hbr.org/2015/10/the-ceo-of-bolthouse-farms-on-making-carrots-cool (Accessed on 27 April 2017).

Mcgray, Douglas. 2011. "How Carrots Became the New Junk Food." *Fast Company*, April. Available at: https://hbr.org/2015/10/the-ceo-of-bolthouse-farms-on-making-carrots-cool (Accessed on 27 April 2017).

6

CHAPTER

Distribution Channels for Rural Areas

LEARNING OBJECTIVES

One of the crucial jobs in rural marketing is distribution, or making goods available in the 640,867 villages across the country, many of them in remote regions. Building channels is a challenge, as modes of transport, storage and payments are limited. After reading this chapter, you will be able to:

- Analyze rural buying habits and design distribution channels.
- Learn about models of rural distribution including PDS and non-PDS models.
- Analyze the challenges faced in building channels to rural areas.
- Understand the distribution of agricultural produce and the shortcomings therein.
- Learn about innovative ways that goods are distributed to villages.

Opening Case
Taking Solar Lights to Remote Areas

Providing electricity in rural India is a big challenge. As per Twelfth Five Year Plan estimates, per capita consumption in rural households is only 8 units per month, which is just one-third of the consumption in urban households. According to Census 2011, India has 75 million households without access to electricity, and even those with access suffer from erratic supply. In its report, Idam Infrastructure Advisory (2013) writes that in spite of a large number of programmes and schemes for rural electrification, India has one of the lowest levels of access to modern energy. Even when villages are electrified, shortage of electricity causes long hours of black-outs. Lack of electric power implies that villagers have nothing to do by 6:30 in the evening.

Solar lighting allows rural families to extend their workdays. It helps increase economic activity levels in villages, as it allows businesses to operate during the evening. It also helps promote local enterprises by replacing kerosene lamps, which also pose serious health problems

PHOTO 6.1
A student beside her solar powered light.

Source: Sloan (2012).

in poorly ventilated rural homes—the World Bank estimates that 780 million women and children breathing kerosene fumes inhale the equivalent of smoke from two packs of cigarettes a day. Solar lanterns help resolve this serious health hazard. However, reaching out to the rural households and then motivating them to invest in solar lighting is a difficult task.

This case study shows how penetration of solar lighting was achieved in remote villages by innovative approaches (Photo 6.1). It shows that companies are more likely to succeed if they offer solutions rather than products. In doing so, three aspects of distribution were covered: reaching remote villages, tackling affordability and getting partners on board.

SELCO: Solar Electric Light Company (SELCO), India was established in 1995 as a social enterprise to provide sustainable energy solutions to villages. It dispels the belief of many city dwellers that villagers cannot afford or maintain sustainable technologies. SELCO works by tackling several issues:

1. Customizing products to suit rural areas based on end user needs.
2. Providing installation and after-sales service through regional energy service centres.
3. Creating channels for users to afford solar systems and providing financing packages based on their cash flow.

SELCO was co-founded by Harish Hande, an IIT alumnus, and Mr Neville Williams, founder of Solar Electric Light Fund (SELF). Hande was awarded with the Ramon Magsaysay Award for 2011 for "his pragmatic efforts to put solar power technology in the hands of the poor, through his social enterprise SELCO India." According to its website, SELCO has sold, serviced and financed over 200,000 solar systems, thus reaching a population of 1.2 million.

SELCO started its Light for Education (LFE) project to provide solar lamps to rural school children, promote education and save children from the fumes of kerosene lamps. The project is supported by schools, government, rural banks, donors and Technology Alumni Association of IIT. It started as a small experiment involving 30 students in a school in Sulliya, Dakshina Kannada district, Karnataka, and has evolved into a programme with substantial funding, reaching out to over 2,000 students across 20 districts of Karnataka. The aim of this programme is to improve the academic performance of school children by providing a reliable light source to those residing in rural areas.

LFE programme consists of the three parts: a centralized solar charging station at the school, a study light that is given to students and a pocket size battery pack which is charged in the school for use in the evening. This creates an incentive for children to attend school and for parents to send them, so that their lighting works at home. Once schooling is completed, students return the study lamps and batteries to the school, which are then redistributed to the next batch of students. This creates a sustainable model for lighting the homes of students. The replacement of kerosene brings added health benefits to households in the long run. The lights are financed through nominal user fees, which a student pays, and donor funding.

SELCO links four crucial components while distributing its services: end users, technology, financing institutions and energy services. It uses doorstep service and doorstep financing.

In an interview with *Forbes*, Harish Hande (2012) explains the bottom line in reaching rural markets, "To ensure long-term sustainability of the business and loyalty amongst users, the ecosystem required by the market—financing, technology, skilled human resources—must be adequately developed. The end-users' satisfaction with the value of the service provided is also equally important in ensuring this loyalty."

Frontier Markets: Frontier Markets was started by Ajaita Shah to provide clean-energy products to rural BoP villagers in India. She found that villagers were reluctant to purchase clean energy solutions because of the costs involved and the lack of trust in solar energy because of inferior products purchased in the past.

To get over these problems, the company opted to set up kiosks to display products, rent stalls at large fairs and exhibitions and a branded van with a dark room to show potential customers just how bright solar lights are compared to candles and lanterns. The kiosk provides free mobile phone charging via solar technology and shows the financial and other advantages of solar. Demos of various solar products are also conducted under the brand name SaralJeevan (simple life) and the kiosk becomes a tool to engage rural households.

Frontier Markets works with local people to educate and demonstrate solar energy. Products are sold and serviced through retail and service centres. The company uses a hub-and-spoke model for distribution, with branch offices serving as spokes to the central office hub. The branch office serves as its own hub, connecting to village-level entrepreneurs (VLEs). The VLEs, called *sahyogis*, are well-known people in the villages consisting of owners of retail stores and agricultural supply points and serve as a crucial link between the company and the customer. VLEs are supported with product training and earn commissions on goods sold. The company has sold more than 85,000 solar products and set up 225 retail outlets by 2015.

Simpa Networks: Simpa Networks was founded in 2010 by Paul Needham, an InfoTech entrepreneur. The company sells energy based on a 'progressive purchase' basis, that is, consumers prepay for their energy service on a pay-as-you-go system. Customers make a small initial payment to have the solar home system installed and subsequently pay per day to use the system by purchasing a 'recharge'. After using this for a period of 18 months, the user gets its ownership. The system provides free electricity.

The company employs VLEs to market its products. Credit officers review customer applications, verify their identification documents and approve their applications. Then, solar technicians install solar home systems at rural customer's homes or micro-enterprises. Simpa Networks reaches out to 9,000 customers, generates over 100 MW of clean energy and is useful to over 45,000 beneficiaries (April 2015 data).

Simpa's most popular line of products is 'Turbo', launched in September 2014, which makes up more than 90 per cent of their sales. The solar home system contains a 40 W panel, three lights, one fan and two mobile charge points. The system runtime is 12 hours and it uses 110 Wh.

While reading this chapter, try to answer the following questions:

1. How can companies achieve deep penetration in villages?
2. Why is distribution important?
3. How can rural channels be built? What are the challenges?
4. What fresh approaches can be used in rural distribution?

Sources for this Case Study:

Web Resources

"Light for Education." Available at Selco website: http://www.selcofoundation.org/wp-content/uploads/2013/10/lfe-report_2012.pdf

"The Last Mile: Selco Stories." Available at: http://thelastmileselco.in/

Video made by National Geographic on Frontier Markets: http://video.nationalgeographic.com/video/151022-gec-frontier-markets-india-solar?source=relatedvideo

Other Sources

Business Standard. 2014. "7.5 cr Indian Households without Access to Electricity: Report." 27 January.

Harish Hande. 2012. "India Can Show the Right Way to Do Business." *Forbes*, 19 May. Available at: http://forbesindia.com/article/third-anniversary-special/harish-hande-india-can-show-the-right-way-to-do-business/32936/1#ixzz48Jorywqq (Accessed on 27 April 2017).

Idam Infrastructure Advisory. 2013. "Re-energising India: Policy, Regulatory and Financial Initiatives to Augment Renewable Energy Deployment in India." Available at: http://www.indiaenvironmentportal.org.in/files/file/REPORT%20-%20REENERGISING%20INDIA.pdf (Accessed on 27 April 2017).

Koch, Wendy. 2015. "How One Woman Helped Light Rural India with Solar Lamps." *National Geographic*, 20 July. Available at: http://news.nationalgeographic.com/energy/2015/07/150720-woman-lights-rural-india-solar-lamps/ (Accessed on 27 April 2017).

Sloan, Will. 2012. "From Energy Startup to Practiced Mentor: SELCO Incubation Centre." 17 August. Available at: http://yourstory.com/2012/08/from-energy-startup-to-practiced-mentor-selco-incubation-centre (Accessed on 27 April 2017).

The Economic Times. 2012. "Simpa Networks Offers Innovative Clean Energy Solution." 21 July.

INTRODUCTION

Distribution to rural areas poses a challenge to the best of companies. Even the greatest of products fail in rural areas as companies are unable to build supply chains that can provide small quantities of goods over large distances. Distribution remains a crucial element in any marketing strategy designed to serve rural markets. In an article, Prahalad and Hammond (2002) had written, "The critical barrier to doing business in rural regions is distribution access, not lack of buying power."

PHOTO 6.2

The last mile of village distribution is usually a small shop like this. Companies face the challenge of building supply chains to reach such shops.

Source: Photograph by Dinesh Kumar.

Kapur, Dawar and Ahuja (2014) found in their research that companies that had done well in rural markets had realized that "establishing cost-effective ways to get goods to India's rural dwellers is the critical first step in penetrating these markets. Smart companies have found that they need to focus on distribution even before making the seemingly common sense moves of identifying and approaching target customers."

However, the task has been riddled with problems. Karamchandani, Kubzansky and Lalwani (2011) recognize this and write, "Despite the immensity of the markets and the volume of the hype, few multinational firms have built sizable businesses serving consumers or producers who survive on just a few dollars a day."

Several companies have tried to solve this puzzle in different ways. Initiatives like ITC's e-choupal, HUL's Project Shakti, Maruti's *Ghar Ghar Mein Maruti*, Tata Tea's *Gaon Chalo*, Honda's Go Rural, Jain Irrigation and other companies—which have been covered in this book—have succeeded in establishing sustainable rural distribution models. However, many other large chains like Hariyali stores, Godrej Aadhaar and Kisan Seva Kendras, Triveni's rural push, Six Ten and Suvidha stores have either scaled down or shut down completely. Even ITC's Choupal Sagar and Reliance Fresh had to withdraw from some cities.

This chapter describes rural distribution models as well as the problems experienced and solutions found by companies. Vachani and Smith (2008) write that distribution channels in villages should be bi-directional, that is, the feasibility of distribution can be improved by creating two-way flow of products and services. Distribution in rural areas does not mean simply to send goods to villages; it also means helping people solve some problems of isolated people. Since both aspects are tied, distribution of products to rural areas and distribution of rural produce to cities are covered in two main sections in the chapter.

DISTRIBUTION TO VILLAGES

While creating distribution channels for over six lakh villages in the country, it is important to understand rural buyer behaviour, the kind of goods bought and the preferred place to buy. Companies building supply channels to villages must also grapple with the lack of infrastructure which inhibits regular supply chains. It is also important to understand the difficulties and challenges that are faced by managers in creating such channels. These are covered in this section.

Catering to the Rural Customer

The first step in building distribution channels for rural areas is to understand the buying behaviour of the rural customer, writes Kumar (2012). For the purpose of designing distribution channels, we consider three factors in rural buyers' behaviour—socio-economic factors, type of goods sold and place of purchase.

Socio-economic Factors

Consumers belonging to different socio-economic segments exhibit distinct behaviours. High income families consisting of large farmers, landowners and traders tend to be educated and exposed to modern lifestyles. They usually have their own vehicles, such as a pickup truck or a jeep, which are used for regular trips to a nearby town for business or recreation. Most of the purchasing is done during these trips. In this respect, the purchasing behaviour of these consumers resembles that of consumers in the developed world—they visit the supermarket (in this case the nearby town) on a weekly or bi-weekly basis and stock goods for consumption over a one or two-week period (Photo 6.3). High income families also buy products for their farm or domestic use in bulk from dealers in the town and transport the goods themselves in their tractor trolleys or pick-up vans.

Middle and low income families do not have this luxury. For middle income families, a trip to the nearby town is more of an outing for fun and recreation. The kind of purchases made on these trips is of branded clothes and other products meeting their aspirations. Routine and low value purchases are done from local retailers. Such consumers do not buy in bulk but prefer to buy in small lots from local retailers.

Low-income families do not travel to nearby towns except on special occasions and tend to buy small quantities on a daily basis from local retailers. Small packs and sachets are popular with this segment. The village fair is an opportunity for a family outing and to buy high value and non-routine items such as clothes and appliances. The village fair becomes an important means of reaching a large number of rural consumers at one go. Companies, indeed, report

PHOTO 6.3

Rural folk on their shopping trip to the nearby town.

Source: Photograph by Dinesh Kumar.

that a bulk of their sales are achieved during these fairs and gatherings. Companies have to build channels to cater to these different types of consumers. A one-size-fits-all strategy will probably not work as many rural retail chains have discovered in the past to their cost. The socio-economic segments and their preferred places of purchases are summarized in Table 6.1.

TABLE 6.1

Socio-economic factors and buying behaviour of rural consumers.

Socio Economic Status	Description	Place of Purchase
High income families	Exposed to urban lifestyles, have their own vehicles	Most of the purchasing is done in bulk from nearby towns during weekly or monthly trips to the town; some products are bought locally
Middle income families	Somewhat exposed to urban lifestyles, have aspirations	Most of the purchasing is done from the village during occasional trips to the nearby town for purchase of branded clothes and high value items
Low income families	Less exposed to urban lifestyles, limited means	Buy in small quantities and sachets from local retailers; non-routine goods are purchased at village fairs

Type of Goods Sold

Consumers in villages wait for special occasions like festivals and fairs, usually held around the harvest time for big ticket purchases. Marriages are other opportunities of rural splurges. These are the times when a large portion of a company's annual sales is accomplished. Supply chains have to be built accordingly to cater to high seasonal demand and very little demand for the rest of the year. Even then, the access to dependable electricity supply will limit sales of electrical appliances. Shortage of water in many areas means that washing machines and detergent powders cannot be sold. Companies trying to reach rural consumers must look for solutions to these problems and operate as social enterprises.

Places of Purchase

As explained, low value items, food items and routine products are purchased from local retailers, but the rural consumer takes an occasional trip to the nearby town or city to buy products of a non-routine nature. It is also important to remember that people in rural areas treat the trip to the nearby town as a fun outing and it becomes a ritual to buy some products that are not available with the rural retailer. That is why, the hub-and-spoke model is used in rural distribution: the town serves as a hub that serves various villages. There is plenty of opportunity for companies to build rural distribution chains that bring goods and services to a hub that is accessible to some villages. Companies must have dealers who supply to these villages or maintain their own depots for the purpose in such towns. The types of products and the favoured areas for purchase are summed up in Table 6.2.

TABLE 6.2
Types of goods and places of purchase in rural areas.

Item	Place of Purchase
Daily items, toiletries, personal care products	Rural retail store, village fairs and nearby towns
Clothing, apparel, footwear	Village fairs, visits to nearby towns or rural retail store, travelling traders
Food items, grains, pulses	Village shops
Household items like utensils, electricals, fans	Visits to nearby towns
Agricultural inputs like fertilizers, seeds and pesticides	Dealer located in nearby town
Electronics, consumer durables	Dealer located in nearby town, village fairs
Higher Education	Nearby towns and cities
Specialized Medical services	Nearby cities
Banks	Moneylenders, post office, rural and Cooperative banks, banking correspondents
Vehicles purchase and servicing	Dealers in nearby towns
Entertainment	Village fairs, nearby towns and cities

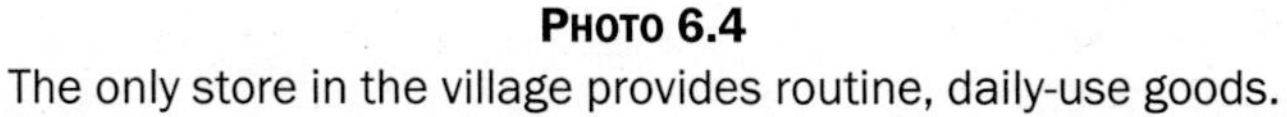

PHOTO 6.4

The only store in the village provides routine, daily-use goods.

Source: Photograph by Dinesh Kumar.

Distribution channels must be designed to cater to these buying habits. Many products are services and are best left to town and city dealers, because people like to buy them on outings with their families. Companies have to identify such towns and create their hubs there. It would only pay to develop deep supply chains either for regularly consumed goods or for goods and services that actually solve problems of rural people (see Mini Case Study 6.1). When supply chains are sought to be built for occasionally purchased goods, many of them end in failure because of poor offtake and high costs.

Small traders often fill in the gap and supply goods to villages. In many villages people depend on travelling merchants who supply goods, then on the village fair or similar gatherings and finally on a trip to nearby towns. Rural markets also consist of the less well-off who buy their daily requirements from local traders in small quantities. Travelling salesmen and merchants bring non-routine goods to their doorstep. Much of this distribution is aimed at helping consumers avoid trips to nearby towns for their requirements.

Retail hubs in towns aggregate supplies from several manufacturers. Even though these rural supermarkets supposedly bring convenience, they do not work well because rural consumers do not buy everything from a single location. Agricultural inputs are provided by dealers in towns. A few companies have taken up initiatives to involve the local people and help bring goods and services to the doorstep of the consumer. Companies have evolved their own models of distribution to cater to rural markets. These are described in the next section.

Mini Case Study 6.1

Emami Project Swadesh

Emami Ltd, the makers of Navaratna oil, Zandu Balm and Boro Plus, reaches villages through a combination of direct and indirect distribution channels.

Mohan Goenka, the director of Emami, looked at rural retailers stores offering a mix of products with equally enthusiastic shopkeepers. Goenka realized that rural areas had more potential for sales opportunities than most big cities and convinced Emami's senior management about venturing deep into the hinterland. Thus was born *Project Swadesh*, an initiative with the intention of improving the company's existing coverage of rural markets. In 2010, at the time of the launch of the programme, the contribution of rural markets to overall sales volumes was approximately 17 per cent. This figure has now risen to almost 45–50 per cent. In its first year, the project was rolled out in Uttar Pradesh, Andhra Pradesh, Madhya Pradesh, Bihar, Maharashtra, Rajasthan and West Bengal. Later, the project was extended to Tamil Nadu, Odisha, Haryana, Punjab and Gujarat.

The company realized that rural consumers were demanding products available in urban markets, though at lower price points. Under Project Swadesh, it has covered villages across 15 states and is trying for more. It now has a distribution network which comprises more than 2,800 distributors and 6.5 lakh retailers (Figure 6.1). Emami has 2,000 direct distributors and about 7,000 indirect distributors to tap the rural markets. Direct distribution, that is, stocking products with retailers without going through

FIGURE 6.1

Emami distributes its products through multiple channels.

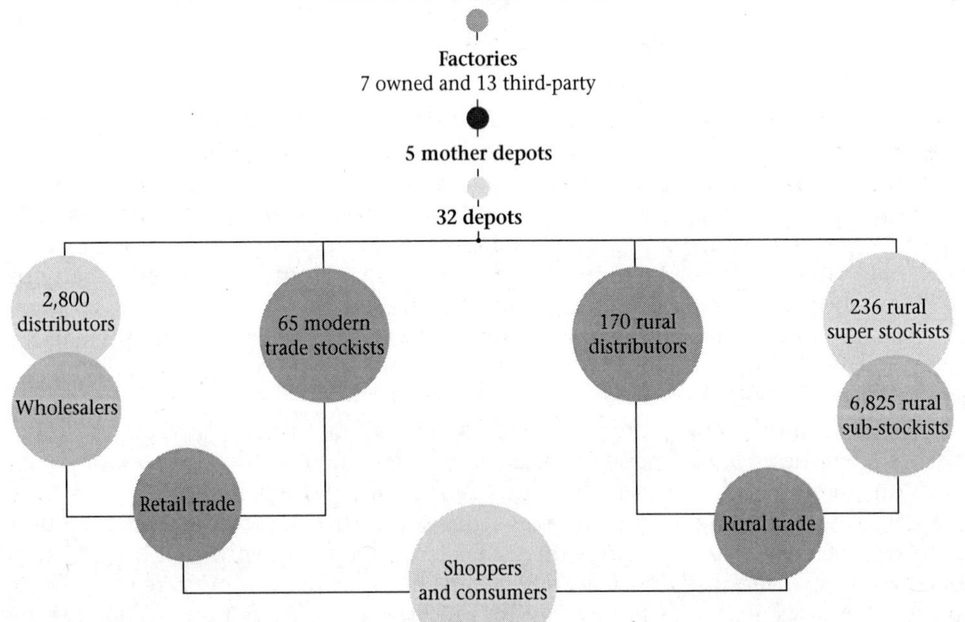

Source: Emami Annual Report 2014–15.

the wholesaler route, was used since wholesalers tend to push products with better margins. Direct distribution helps in pushing products across more geographies, thereby increasing penetration. This translates into almost 4 million retail counters, selling nearly 112 units every second.

The company has different approaches for different markets. It has a hub-and-spoke model, in which it appoints super-stockists in district headquarters or big towns who then appoint sub-stockists in the interior markets, who in turn cater to retail outlets in villages. It also runs vans from bigger towns to villages on a regular basis in some districts. It also has wholesalers who cater to the retailers coming to the big city and buy stocks. This is a strong channel facilitating indirect distribution.

The company has ramped up its IT infrastructure as well. It has set up its own warehouses in five strategic locations, instead of third-party warehouses. The company has invested considerably in manpower both at the direct and the indirect levels. In the consumer care division alone, direct manpower deployment has increased by more than 10 per cent and the increase in indirect manpower was projected to grow by more than 25 per cent by 2014–15. An exclusive rural sales team, featuring everyone from managers to front line sales people, has also been deployed to ensure exclusive focus on rural distribution.

Besides these measures, there has also been an increased emphasis on improving visibility and ensuring focused execution, resulting in increased direct outlet coverage by 64,000 outlets in 2014. The company has created a strong network of distributors and highly motivated sales teams, using modern trade as a growth engine to project its product range and information systems and technology to drive efficiency.

Source for this Case Study:

Emami Ltd. "The Next Orbit: Emami Limited Annual Report, 2014–15." Available at: http://www.emamiltd.in/images/annualreportpdf/20150710052510small181.pdf (Accessed on 27 April 2017).

Models of Rural Distribution

While companies develop their own models for rural distribution, we cannot ignore the biggest distribution initiative of the government—the PDS. Much of the food grain distribution space is taken up by the government through this programme. Government provides foodgrains at subsidized prices to vulnerable sections of society through the PDS, which is described here. The private sector operates in the non-government space and supplies to villages at market prices. Since PDS supplies only some items, the private sector fills in the gap and provides essential and other items to villages and develops its own supply chains. Companies have to figure out the best ways of reaching customers, given the high regulation in agricultural marketing.

Public Distribution System

The PDS was started in India before independence with the objective of providing food security to the poor. Under the system, foodgrains were sold from fair price shops at lower prices than the market rate. It was the first structured public distribution of cereals in India through the rationing of rice or wheat to ration card holder families. This was followed by successive governments over the years. In 1997, it was changed to Targeted Public Distribution System (TPDS) so that cheap rations could be delivered to BPL people, identified through a BPL survey.

In 2013, the National Food Security Act (NFSA) came into force, under which a rights-based approach was adopted instead of the earlier welfare approach. Under this Act, eligible beneficiaries—identified through Socio-economic Caste Census (SECC) 2011 data—are entitled to receive 5 kg of food grain at subsidized prices. Some states have already adopted the NFSA while the rest of India still follows the TPDS system.

TPDS operates through a system in which the Central government procures foodgrains from farmers at a minimum support price (MSP), allocates grains to each state, and transports them to the central depots in each state. State governments identify eligible households to which the grains are to be delivered from these depots to each ration shop. The ration shop is the last point of the distribution channel from where grains are sold to consumers.

Though the system is supposed to help poor and marginal populations, studies have revealed that is has not been very effective in its objective. For example, FAO's 'The State of Food Insecurity in the World, 2015' report points out that 194.6 million people are undernourished in India, that is, India is home to a quarter of the undernourished population in the world (FAO 2015). It also says that 51 per cent of women between 15 to 59 years of age are anaemic and 44 per cent of children under 5 are underweight. The Global Hunger Index 2014 ranks India at 55 out of 76 countries, pointing to the weaknesses of government distribution system.

Studies have also shown shortcomings in implementation. Problems have been reported pertaining to inaccurate identification of households and a leaking delivery system. Studies show that PDS suffers from nearly 61 per cent error of exclusion and 25 per cent inclusion of beneficiaries. Regarding leakage, an ICRIER study (Gulati and Saini 2015) found that at an all-India level, 46.7 per cent or 25.9 MMTs of the grain did not reach the intended PDS beneficiaries in 2011–12. Leakage was seen to be higher in the poor states: Uttar Pradesh, Bihar, Madhya Pradesh, Maharashtra and West Bengal.

An NCAER study (NCAER 2015) found that there was inappropriate identification of BPL families and that the inefficiencies in the supply chain contribute to the high cost of delivery in most states. The study also found that the supply chain of the PDS is riddled with malpractices at distribution and administrative levels. It was found that in some states, people had paid ₹14–118 for getting a new ration card even though the government charges a token fee of just ₹1.

The PDS, thus, is in need of an overhaul. A case has been made for direct cash transfers through Jan Dhan Yojana and the UID generated by the Aadhaar scheme instead of providing subsidized foodgrains, which is easily diverted. PDS is also not cost effective as its operations are too costly and the ratio between procurement and transportation is too high. Storage losses are also very high.

Saini and Kozicka (2014) write that there is a case for reducing the role of the government in food management systems of the country since the country no longer faces acute food scarcity of the 1960s. Today, the country is self-dependent and it exports a number of agricultural products. This is the right time, they write, to move from controlling price through high subsidies to income policy support that includes cash transfers to the poor. If India can make this switch, it can reap huge economic gains. Cash transfers would help in better targeting and reduce the huge costs associated with government intervention in the grain market.

Clearly, the PDS is not enough to serve the growing population of India. Private individuals and companies step in and build distribution channels to reach markets across India. They do this in various ways, working through their dealers or creating new models. These models are described here.

TABLE 6.3
Rural distribution models.

Model	Operation
1. Distribution through wholesalers	Wholesalers in a city or town take up the task of sending goods to nearby villages. They have small vehicles through which goods are sent to retailers in villages and payments collected.
2. Distribution through sub-dealers	Wholesalers appoint sub-dealers in rural areas. These sub-dealers visit the wholesalers regularly to collect goods which are transported to villages in small vehicles.
3. Distribution through local dealers/partners (hub-and-spoke model)	Company bypasses the city wholesalers and either appoints a dealer or partner in a town to serve several villages from a depot in a central town, called hub or through its own office.
4. Sales through rural sales force (direct channel)	Company has its own dedicated sales force to cover villages. Goods are supplied to the villages from the wholesaler or the depot in the nearby town. Sometimes wholesalers will appoint their own rural sales people.
5. Company outreach programmes	Using BTL techniques, companies use mobile vans to display products and to educate people how to use products. Vans are equipped with multimedia devices and villagers engaged through demos.
6. Village Entrepreneurs	Company develops entrepreneurs in villages who stock goods and popularize them among fellow villagers.
7. Local Influencers	Company works with known people in villages who can influence others. Teachers, doctors, panchayat leaders are roped in to arrange public meetings and popularize products.
8. Rural Retail Chains	Company opens retail shops in rural areas or ties up with local shopkeepers to stock goods.
9. NGO and other networks	Company uses existing networks of NGOs, microfinance, SHGs or others to sell products.
10. Rural Value Chains	Along with retail, company provides value through information and advice on agricultural practices. Company may also have buyback arrangements with farmers and thus help farmers in marketing their produce.

Models of Distribution (Non-PDS)

Villages can be served in various ways and these have been summarized in Table 6.3. The models of distribution have been developed by companies over the years and have their advantages and disadvantages, which are described in this section.

Distribution through wholesalers: This is the most common method of reaching rural areas. It entails no extra cost for the company since existing channels are used. Wholesalers load the goods in a small vehicle and send them to nearby villages (Photo 6.5). The driver delivers goods to village retailers and collects payments. Alternately, village dealers make

PHOTO 6.5

A village-trader collects goods from various wholesalers in a nearby town and takes it to villages at his own expense.

Source: Photograph by Dinesh Kumar.

weekly trips to the town and collect goods from different wholesalers, piling them up in their pick-ups, and collect goods from various sources for selling back home. The village dealers add a mark-up and cost of transportation to their cost of purchase to arrive at the selling price. There are some disadvantages in the model. First, all villages cannot be covered through this method. Second, goods become quite expensive by the time they reach the customer. Village retailers thus have to charge more than the printed MRP to cover their costs and customers are not very happy about this. A third disadvantage is that sales are dependent on the wholesaler.

Distribution through sub-dealers: In this model, the wholesaler or the company appoints sub-dealers in villages. Wholesaler commission is shared with these sub-dealers, who take up the task of supplying to rural retailers through their own salesmen. Sub-dealers are convenient because the wholesaler is assured of regular business and payment collections.

Distribution through local dealers/partners (hub-and-spoke model): In this case, the company bypasses the town wholesaler and directly appoints local dealers or partners

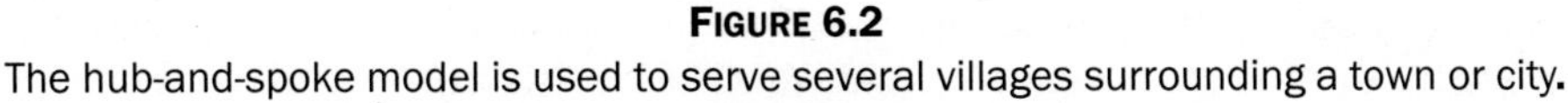

FIGURE 6.2
The hub-and-spoke model is used to serve several villages surrounding a town or city.

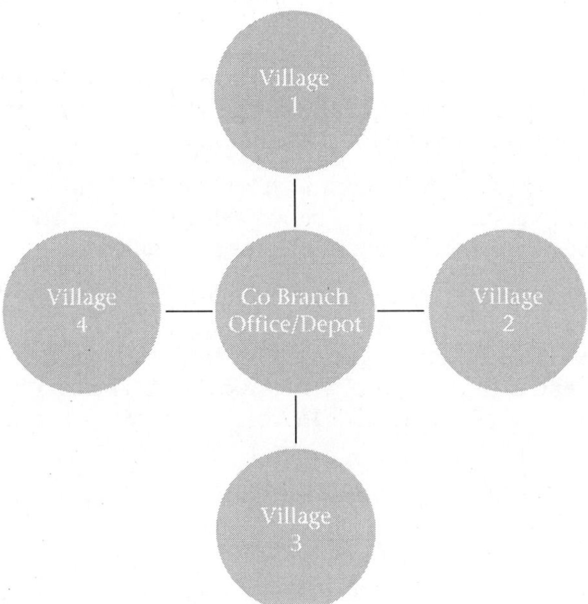

who are served through company depots in a nearby town. This resembles the hub-and-spoke model, where the company depot serves as a hub serving surrounding villages (Figure 6.2). Either the company builds its own logistics to supply goods or it requires the dealers to collect goods from the depot. This model is more expensive than working through wholesalers as the company has to maintain many depots in towns. However, the company gains full control of its rural marketing and distribution and is not dependent on dealers.

Sales through rural sales force (direct channel): Some companies appoint rural sales force to visit dealers and retailers in villages. Goods are then supplied through the company depot in the town. Small companies follow this route and are able to achieve deep penetration in their areas of operation. Wholesaler commissions are avoided but the company bears the cost of distribution. This is an expensive option since the company has to add a large number of sales people on its payroll. The advantage is that the company can serve the areas it wants to cover and is not dependent on the wholesaler or the sub-dealer. The company is also able to establish direct relationship with the rural customers.

Company outreach programmes: Outreach programmes are an effective way to reach villages, especially when demos or consumer education are required. The company uses BTL techniques to involve communities in their brands. Excitement is built by multimedia devices and direct customer experience. Consumers can experience products directly through this method, and brand loyalty can be achieved.

Village entrepreneurs ('feet on the ground'): This approach is called 'feet on the ground' approach, in which the company trains and develops entrepreneurs in villages who act as distributors and brand ambassadors. Case studies of Essilor and Project Shakti, covered in this book, are examples of this approach. The advantage of this model is that the company can reach the remotest of the villages. The village entrepreneur creates customers for the company and works for mutual benefit.

Local influencers: In this case, the company works through people who can influence others. Well-known or respected people in the village arrange community meetings and product demos to influence consumers and inculcate brand loyalty.

Rural retail chains: Companies can work with retail chains established to serve rural areas. Chains such as Hariyali, Aadhaar and Choupal, or tying up with petrol pumps, are easy ways to reach villages. However, many of these initiatives have failed.

NGOs and other networks: Another way of reaching villages is to piggyback on existing networks of NGOs, microcredit groups or SHGs. Companies work with these groups to tap their existing members. This initiative was used by Tata Tea, which started its 'Gaon Chalo' initiative with NGOs and SHGs (see Mini Case Study 6.2). This is a beneficial model as the company gets access to a set of people who are connected by a common cause. Building trust becomes much easier.

Rural value chains: Supply chains are created not only to provide goods to villages but farmers can sell their produce through the same channel. Such chains help solve farmers' problems and help them increase their income, which, in turn, is used to buy products from the supply chain. The approach, however, calls for huge investments to cover villages. ITC's e-choupal and Jain Irrigation (both covered in this book) show that rural distribution is facilitated by helping deliver value to farmers, while at the same time solving a problem for village folk.

Mini Case Study 6.2

Tata Tea—*Gaon Chalo*

Tata Tea faced problems in reaching rural areas. Unbranded tea, which was cheaper than branded ones, was preferred by consumers. It was also pushed by retailers, who got high margins from it. The company chose a unique route; it chose to work through NGOs since they knew the local people, customs and the terrain. NGOs were selected with the help of Sir Ratan Tata Trust and the Dorabji Trust. A pilot project was conducted in December 2005 in a village near Varanasi. The NGOs became the first level rural dealers and acted as distributors. They would supply the goods to mobile dealers—the second level dealers—who were entrusted with the task of visiting a fixed number of villages. There they would deal with the third level of distributors, the rural retailers, and also collect payments.

The company saw success in its pilot project. Now, the company is increasing its efforts to build stronger ties with SHGs for deeper penetration and for achieving social empowerment. This helped in creating a cost-effective brand building platform and the flexibility to address the complexities of local markets.

Today, *Gaon Chalo* is present in 18 states with direct reach in 70,000 villages, according to the company's website. It enables a platform for generating rural employment for rural youth, women and the underprivileged and even works with SHGs catering to the differently abled.

PHOTO 6.6

An agent takes Tata Tea products to his village.

Source: Tata Global Beverages website.

One such SHG is the BETI Foundation. It motivates rural people to generate additional livelihoods through the marketing of TATA tea. BETI focuses on marginalized families, single women headed households and small shopkeepers, tea shop owners, physically challenged individuals, unemployed youth, widows, retired persons and other disadvantaged people to undertake this activity. These project affiliates are then provided TATA tea at the rates that give them attractive margins on the MRP. The supplementary income is vital for families and adds value to the quality of their lives. In 2012, the 'BETI Foundation Rubaroo' was registered under the Companies Act for transactions related to the Tata Global Beverages Limited (TGBL) Gaon Chalo Abhiyan and other livelihood interventions. This intervention shows that distribution channels to rural areas can be built by involving NGOs and SHGs.

What are the advantages and disadvantages of supplying through networks? How can other companies follow this model?

Sources for this Case Study:

Web Resources

Tata Global Beverages website: http://www.tataglobalbeverages.com/company/innovations/innovation-in-communication

The BETI foundation website: http://www.betifoundation.in/gaon-chalo-abhiyan

Watch the Tata Tea Gaon Chalo short film at: https://www.youtube.com/watch?v=SC-iLCzO90M

The aforementioned ten models of distribution serve rural markets in different ways but, in each case, they have to overcome severe difficulties that arise because rural areas have traditionally been neglected in public policy. Though the government has many rural development schemes, its approach has been to throw money at villages. But, it is estimated that only 10% of government spending reaches the beneficiaries. The development route followed in India since Independence has been city-centric.

The problems in rural distribution can be described as lack of infrastructure and logistical challenges. Villages lack basic infrastructure like roads, access to education, dependable electricity, Internet and public health investments. This eerie state of neglect, which has created a different India in villages than the one in cities, is described in the next section.

STATE OF NEGLECT

Compounding the problem of rural distribution is the fact that infrastructure in villages and small towns is in shambles. A visit to villages across the country entails journeys through awful roads and power not being available for long stretches of time, while transportation of goods is yet another problem.

That is why, completely different models of distribution have to be designed. Engineers trained in supply chain logistics either fail or are unable to understand the complexities of rural distribution.

Though the market size is large, rural markets pose great challenges that are almost insurmountable in many cases. Companies face problems of reaching populations that are scattered over large areas, have difficult terrains and are connected by dirt roads. There is no reliable transport service—in any case the order sizes are too small to send by commercial transport. It is also not economical to hire people to serve these markets and managers are often unwilling to live in villages. Companies selling expensive products like white goods face challenges not only in setting up distribution channels but also in establishing service centres. Getting payments poses further challenges.

PHOTO 6.7

Merchants in a town place goods in a bus that goes to villages, where they are collected by rural retailers. There is only one bus service in a day.

Source: Photographs by Dinesh Kumar.

Due to these severe shortcomings, rural distribution can prove be a nightmare. In urban areas, distribution can be efficient. Companies can achieve economies of scale in transportation, storage and dealer management by aggregating demand. Large volumes make it economical for salesmen to cover markets and for wholesalers to invest in their fleet of vehicles. The problems of distributing to villages are summed up in the next section.

Logistical Challenges

Apart from infrastructural shortcomings described in the previous section, rural distribution remains a grim challenge. Kumar (2012) shows that there are several problems that the logistics manager faces. Markets are scattered and their small size makes it difficult to send goods in economic quantities. It is also not economic to employ salesmen as they can visit only one or two villages a day. In states where distances are less, the salesmen have to tour the countryside on foot (Photo 6.8).

Companies also face another problem in rural markets, that of poverty and low purchasing power. Many rural areas consist of few moneyed land owners and a large number of contract labourers, who by definition are poor. Small farmers are poor and often indebted because of fragmented land holdings. There are a few non-agricultural jobs but these are not well paying. The result is that a large percentage of population is poor or middle class.

Photo 6.8

A salesman visits villages on foot with samples to collect orders.

Source: Photograph by Dinesh Kumar.

Small-scale industries and local manufacturers fill in where companies cannot reach. Rural economy in India is dominated by unbranded, cheap goods made by small manufacturers. The main challenges in rural distribution are as follows:

1. Scattered markets
2. Low purchasing power
3. Low volumes per market
4. Lack of infrastructure
5. Cheap, unbranded products
6. Government control and bureaucracy

Scattered Markets

Rural markets are scattered over large areas. In some states, villages are close to one another but in others they are separated by large distances. The population density figures show how the population is scattered over large distances.

Rural demographics show why a uniform rural marketing strategy does not work. The Census 2011 figures show that the population of 1.2 billion is spread over 3,287,240 sq. km in 35 states/union territories, 640 districts, 5,924 sub-districts, 7,935 towns, and 640,867 villages. The rural population of 834 million represents 68.8 per cent of the total population. The break-up of rural population is given in Table 6.4.

However, this population is spread across a wide area with huge variations in density. Density of population, which is defined as number of persons per sq. km, is 382 persons in Census 2011 as compared to 325 persons in Census 2001. The density varies from as high as 11,297 persons in NCT Delhi to as low as 17 persons in Arunachal Pradesh. Table 6.5 shows the population densities across states. Of the 640,867 villages (Census 2011), 236,004 have a population of fewer than 500, while 3,976 have a population of 10,000 or more. Such wide variations explain why a uniform distribution strategy for the country does not quite work. Companies have to devise strategies specific to geographical areas.

Reaching these scattered villages would be one thing, but the difficult terrain also poses difficulties in building supply chains. In the hill states, roads to villages are narrow dirt tracks, while in Rajasthan, rural folk have to travel long distances over sand tracks to reach the villages. Villages in these states are poorly connected by transport services. Even in developed states like Delhi, Chandigarh or Gujarat, some villages remain poorly connected, even though they are not far from the capital cities. Over two lakh villages with population of less than 500 people do not have a retail shop.

TABLE 6.4
Rural population.

Year	Total Population (mn)	Males (mn)	Females (mn)
2001	742	381	361
2011	834	428	406

Source: Census of India, 2001 and 2011.

TABLE 6.5
Population density across states.

Density (No of People/sq. km)	No of States/UTs	Name of States
>3000	2	Delhi (11,297) and Chandigarh (9,252)
1001–2000	3	Puducherry, Daman and Diu, Lakshadweep
1000–1999	2	Bihar, West Bengal
500–999	6	Uttar Pradesh, Tamil Nadu, Kerala, Punjab, Haryana, Dadra and Nagar Haveli
200–499	12	Maharashtra, Madhya Pradesh, Rajasthan, Karnataka, Gujarat, Andhra Pradesh, Orissa, Telangana, Jharkhand, Assam, Tripura, Goa
100–199	7	Chhattisgarh, Jammu & Kashmir, Uttarakhand, Himachal Pradesh, Meghalaya, Nagaland, Andaman and Nicobar Islands
<100	3	Arunachal Pradesh, Mizoram, Sikkim

Source: Census of India (2011).

Low Purchasing Power

Even where density is higher, limited purchasing power in the majority of the population make the size of the market for many goods much smaller than it looks. The gap is filled by small traders and salesmen by supplying low quality, unbranded goods or counterfeit products. Branded goods, which are higher priced than local goods, find it difficult in areas where purchasing power is limited.

The poverty line shows the percentage of people who are poor. The RBI estimated that 21.9 per cent of India's population was below the official poverty limit in 2012. In 2013, the Planning Commission estimated that 25.7 per cent of people in rural areas and 13.7 per cent of people in urban areas were BPL. These estimates were based on the level prescribed by the Suresh Tendulkar committee, which was pegged at ₹22.42 per person per day in rural areas and ₹28.65 in urban areas. However, it was felt that this was too low a figure to measure poverty.

Using the purchasing power parity as a basis for measuring poverty, the World Bank (2014) estimated that as of 2014, 58 per cent of the total population were living on less than US$3.10 per day. This indicates that there is a large number of people living just above the line of deprivation as mentioned by the World Bank or the Planning Commission. Taking the World Bank figures, we can assume that more than half of the population is either below the poverty line or are barely surviving at low incomes. With such low levels of purchasing power, companies selling in rural markets have the task of finding purchasing power and of generating volumes in the goods they sell. With such a low customer base, venturing into rural areas is unprofitable for many companies.

Low Volumes Per Market

Since demand from villages is low, companies can neither have economical modes of transport nor is it feasible for them to assign salesmen to cover these areas. Economies of scale are thus ruled out. Even if supply chains are created, they are not economical because demand is

PHOTO 6.9

Village distribution is done through small vehicles like the motorcycle seen in this picture. The salesman supplies small quantities of goods and collects payments from retailers regularly.

Source: Photograph by Dinesh Kumar.

seasonal as most buying happens during the harvest season. Seasonal variations like weather, droughts and floods too affect demand.

According to Census 2011 data, there were a total of 640,867 villages. Table 6.5 shows that 30 of the 35 states/union territories have a population density of less than 1999 people per sq. km. It is estimated that 46 per cent of the population resides in villages with population of less than 1,999 people. That is, almost three lakh villages offer a very limited market size of a small population cluster.

The scattered population is a logistical nightmare for companies. Sending goods over long distances, in small lots, and then collecting payments, adds to huge costs. Sales efforts are also limited by low population of a village. It is also not economical to establish service centres in thinly populated rural areas. The population mostly depends on rural retailers like the one shown in Photo 6.9. Such retailers keep items required by villagers including gas cylinders and mobile recharges, apart from other goods of daily use. They are serviced by salesmen carrying products in small quantities. Other companies employ local entrepreneurs, which helps them overcome the high costs of distribution (see Mini Case Study 6.3).

Transportation

Villages lack regular transport services. In many areas, only small vehicles can ply, and sometimes not even those. Lack of regular services means that supply of goods to rural areas will remain limited. In villages connected only by one bus service, traders pay the bus conductor to send the goods to villages, where it is delivered to the retailer (Photo 6.7). Lack of roads,

Mini Case Study 6.3

Tata Motors and Vodafone: Rural Inroads

Tata Motors' rural initiative, Project Neev, was launched in three states in the year 2010. After the success of the pilot programme, the company is now rolling it out nationally and expecting to sell an additional 70,000 vehicles in rural markets annually. The company hires local people as Tata Gramin Mitras, third-party outlets called Tata Kisan Mitra and an informal network of important local influencers. It has been quite successful, selling nearly 80,000 vehicles, according to the company.

Most of the Tata Gram Mitras are freelancers that includes teachers, youth from villages, doctors, mechanics and people from panchayats. The company tries to 'promote self-empowerment' via vehicle ownership. The Gram Mitras get a regular stipend and incentives on sales. Neev markets generate enquiries with varying conversion rates. This has helped increase sales of Tata Motors' small commercial vehicles (SCVs) by 20 per cent. In states like Bihar and Madhya Pradesh, 35 to 36 per cent of total sales happen in the small markets. The company expects the total sales from the Neev markets in all 11 states to reach to 35 per cent.

The company has partnered with Indian Oil Corporation's Kisan Seva Kendras in remote regions to showcases vehicles, organize workshops and functions, loan fairs and educational programmes.

Vodafone India uses the village entrepreneur model to set up a network of Associated Distributor Vodafone Mini Stores (ADVMS) known as *laal dukaan*, or 'red stores', matching the colour of Vodafone's logo. The shops are run by locals who have invested ₹35,000 to ₹50,000 to open them. They are designed to meet all the telecom needs of customers within an 18–32 km radius, from sales to connectivity to technical support. The network serves 94 million rural subscribers through 5,500 red stores. The laal dukaans are touchpoints managed generally by a resident of the area. Vodafone uses satellite maps, superimposed over census data, to allocate sites for ADVMS. It also has an association with ICICI Bank for m-pesa, which is also helping it make inroads into the rural sector.

Can such low cost interventions work for large companies? What are the pros and the cons?

Sources for this Case Study:

Business Today. 2014. "Guns and Roses." 11 May.

Tata Motors. 2015. "India's Popular Last Mile Public Transport Brand—Tata Magic Crosses Three Lakh Sales Mark." 22 September. Available at: http://www.tatamotors.com/press/indias-popular-last-mile-public-transport-brand-tata-magic-crosses-three-lakh-sales-mark/ (Accessed on 27 April 2017).

The Economic Times. 2015. "Vodafone Invests ₹150 Crore to Ramp of Network Distribution in Andhra Pradesh & Telangana." 8 April.

sporadic supply of electricity and lack of storage facilities pose great difficulties for managers. The absence of investment in infrastructure, lack of planning and developmental norms, and the poor status of structures of governance in villages are hindrances in building distribution channels. Vehicles can barely move at 10 km/hr or less while supplying goods to villages.

Credit

Since, the presence of banks and financial intermediaries in rural areas are limited—collecting payments, getting insurance for goods and warehouses also pose challenges. According to RBI figures, 41 per cent of the population in India is unbanked, and 61 per cent is unbanked in rural areas. Only 9.5 per cent in rural areas has bank accounts. Of the rural population,

64 per cent to 97 per cent was estimated to be in the clutches of informal channels like local moneylenders. Though the government has asked banks to open bank accounts under its scheme, the Jan Dhan Yojana, people in rural areas lack access to institutional credit and insurance, and fall prey to exploitative interest rates offered by agents and moneylenders. Farmers' suicides across the country have brought such issues to the fore.

Electricity

Despite an ambitious rural electrification programme, rural India suffers from lack of regular electricity supply. While 80 per cent of Indian villages have at least an electricity line, just 52.5 per cent of rural households have access to electricity. The overall electrification rate in India is 64.5 per cent while 35.5 per cent of the population still lives without access to electricity. Erratic electricity supply means that deep freezers and refrigerators cannot work. For dealers of perishable food items and ice creams, it means that goods cannot be stored for long, or additional cost will have to be incurred to install generators. Farmers are also unable to process their produce and store it, which means that they have to sell the produce as soon as it is harvested. Building of cold chains entails huge investments in generators and facilities. In small towns and villages, power supply is erratic and unreliable. During harvest season, almost all electricity supply is diverted to farms. Products requiring stable temperatures to store get destroyed because of power cuts.

Roads

Village roads are actually just dirt tracks. This means that companies have to budget for longer lead times and damages during transit. There are disruptions in supplies due to accidents and delays at various octroi checking points. Damages during transit are common. Bad roads thus add to cost which has to be passed on to the consumer. But when customers are asked to pay more than the price printed on the product, there is less acceptability.

In villages across the country, roads are dusty, pothole-ridden tracks. Vehicles often cannot go faster than 10 km/h on these roads. Villages are sparsely populated and populations in rural areas are scattered over large areas. Travel times are sometimes very large. Breakdowns of vehicles due to bad roads delay deliveries and add to costs. It is stated in a report by Ernst & Young and Retailers Association of India (2013) that the average truck speed in India is 20–40 km/hr compared to the speed of 60–80 km/hr in developed countries. Another study (TCI–IIMC 2009) revealed that the average speed of trucks on Indian roads is about 20 km/hr, including all stoppages. The Planning Commission puts the National Highway network at 71,772 km, which comprises only 1.7 per cent of the total length of roads, implying that majority of the roads are in poor shape. Reaching rural areas is a daunting task as the terrain is very difficult. Many villages remain cut off due to lack of roads and bridges. Goods have to be transported in cycles and carts, and sometimes through ropeways (Photo 6.10) as vehicles cannot ply on such roads.

Warehousing

Another problem in rural distribution is the lack of storage facilities. Usually goods have to be stored in homes. It is difficult for companies to find dealers who have warehousing facilities. Goods are stored that are not adequately protected from weather and pests. Spoilage rates

PHOTO 6.10
Roads in many villages resemble dirt tracks, prone to landslides. In Himachal Pradesh, goods have to be sent across to remote villages in trolleys like this.

Source: Photograph by Dinesh Kumar.

are therefore high. Stores in villages cannot invest in modern display and inventory systems. Stocks are often subject to damage because of inadequate storage. Dealers complain that companies should take back damaged stocks which companies are often reluctant to do.

Bureaucracy

A transporter has to get over numerable hurdles created by the bureaucracy. An army of traffic policemen and inspectors hinder movement of goods across the country. Goods are often held up because of restrictions of inter-state transportation, sales tax, central and state taxes, octroi, vehicle documents, road permits, and so on. These problems are often sorted out with bribes, the cost of which is passed on to the consumer. The Planning Commission recognizes this and writes, "The system in vogue hinders rather than facilitates smooth flow of freight and passenger movement across the country and has thwarted the formation of single common market."

Managerial Unwillingness

City bred and educated managers and salesmen do not wish to live in villages and develop markets there. The lack of managerial talent means that rural markets remain neglected, even though there is large potential in such areas.

Communications

The lack of Internet and broadband facilities in many parts of the country means that companies are unable to keep track of agents, salesmen and consumers. They are also unable to connect village distribution to their ERP systems.

These problems hinder supply of goods to rural markets and hence companies are unable to build supply chains. The problems work both ways—they also hinder supply of goods from rural areas. As a consequence, they are unable to get good prices for their produce, which in turn results in low demand for consumer products. In order to succeed, a company creating demand has to look at distribution from both sides. The next section describes distribution of goods from villages.

DISTRIBUTION OF RURAL PRODUCTS

The shortcomings described in the previous section are a great hindrance for farmers to sell goods to markets. Apart from agricultural goods, handicrafts and industries located in rural areas must also overcome problems in distribution. Losses in transit are high. Farmers are thus unable to get good prices for their produce.

Distribution of agricultural produce is also stymied by government intervention, as explained in Chapter 9. The result is that despite huge subsidies, distribution of agricultural produce is marked by wastage, loopholes and in efficiencies.

In the absence of investments by the government or the private sector, distribution of agricultural goods is done by agents and traders. The system is marked by inefficiencies at all levels. The consumer ends up paying high prices for farm produce while the farmer is unable to get good prices. Some companies build rural outlets to get over these problems and helps farmers with raw materials and buy their produce as well (see Mini Case Study 6.4).

Mini Case Study 6.4

Mahindra Samriddhi Centres

Tractor producer Mahindra and Mahindra has stared Samriddhi Centers to drive rural prosperity by educating Indian farmers about technological inputs and solutions to farming issues. According to its website, Samriddhi organizes and delivers a comprehensive range of agriculture-related information, equipment and services. The company has 155 Samriddhi Centers throughout India, which provide insurance products, sell and maintain tractors and implements and run productivity demo farms and soil and irrigation water testing facilities. The centres also deliver knowledge updates on weather, crops, eradication of pests and diseases and mandi (agricultural markets) locations and prices.

PHOTO 6.11
A Mahindra Samriddhi store in Himachal Pradesh.

Source: Photograph by Dinesh Kumar.

The Mahindra Kisan Mitra online has information to improve farming practices and plan crop cycles, weather conditions and soil testing. It also covers commodity prices, agricultural loan schemes, insurance plans and government policies. Farmers can locate cold storage and warehouse facilities, follow global agricultural events and read other farmers' success stories.

Mahindra ShubhLabh Services were started in the year 2000 to serve farm equipment to customers. ShubhLabh provides farmers with a single source channel to access all the products, services and knowledge they need to run productive farms. Farmers are provided with a high-quality seeds including cereals, oil seeds, fruits, vegetables and seed potato, thereby enhancing the potential for improved farm productivity in several regions of India. Crop protection inputs including insecticides, fungicides, herbicides, nutrients, biologicals and plant growth promoters are also sold through Samriddhi centres. Distribution services for fresh produce, both domestically and abroad, are provided, helping exports to retailers in Europe, the UK, the Middle East, China and Southeast Asia and import foreign fruit to India.

Seed distribution was started in 2006 to supply farmers with high quality seeds of field crop and vegetable seeds, including hybrid corn, sunflower, rice, millet and fodder sorghum as well as open-pollinated mustard, fodder maize, rice and wheat. Vegetable assortment consists of hybrid tomato, hot pepper, capsicum, okra, melons, gourds, radish and cucumber and open-pollinated varieties of spinach, coriander, okra, radish and beans.

The company supplies seeds directly to more than 250 distributors who individually sell them to 20 to 50 retailers. Sales representatives work with farmers to determine the right crop varieties and provide technical support to optimize each farm's productivity, spreading awareness about new seed varieties. Seed potatoes are supplied by a processing facility in Palampur, Himachal Pradesh.

The company has emerged as the largest exporter of grapes from India, writes *Business Standard* (2015). It employs a technology called 'farm tech prosperity' to partner with farmers. Grape exports had been initiated on a small scale around 2005 by Mahindra Shubhlabh Services, which convinces local growers to turn to export-variety grapes. The company also launched grapes and apples under the brand Saboro for exports.

The company does not operate like a trader who buys when the produce is ready. Instead, it partners with farmers from the start of the season. The initiative was named *Khet se Khalihan Tak*, under which farmers are identified and then helped by a step-by-step guidance through a combination of technology and on-field help. The model is unique in that it currently allows farmers a choice when it comes to buying inputs and selling produce—there is no compulsion to deal exclusively with Mahindra & Mahindra, but the company says most of them prefer to work with it anyway. For this, a service fee is deducted from the price realized by the farmer. Farmers say that yield per acre has risen to 10 tonnes against the 6–7 tonnes earlier.

The company's intervention helps farmers get over problems like delayed payment and not getting the promised prices from traders. Those who independently wanted to export faced rejections because they could not meet standards of European Union regulations.

Volumes have increased. From six containers in 2005, the volume rose to 668 containers in 2014. In Mahindra & Mahindra's view, the organized fruit market appears to be an underexploited opportunity. The fruits industry in India is around ₹3 lakh crore and is growing at a compounded annual rate of 7–8 per cent, of which only 5 per cent falls in the organized and branded market. Companies like Bharti's FieldFresh Foods and start-ups like INI Farms that sell branded pomegranates and bananas work with farmers on contract.

Have other companies created such distribution facilities in villages? What are their advantages and disadvantages?

Sources for this Case Study:

Web Resources

Mahindra website: http://www.mahindra.com/What-We-Do/Agribusiness/Companies/Mahindra-ShubhLabh-Services

Mahindra Kisan Mitra website: http://www.mahindrakisanmitra.com/

Samriddhi website: http://www.mahindraagri.com/Home.aspx

Watch "Samriddhi By Mahindra delivering Farm Tech Prosperity" at: https://www.youtube.com/watch?v=nQeymGnQnag

Other Source

Business Standard. 2015. "Tractors, SUVs and grapes." 31 January.

Existing Marketing Systems

Farmers having surplus produce can sell it in the ways shown in Figure 6.3. However, a farmer does not have much choice since only one or two channels are available at any given area.

- Directly to the consumer at a highway near the farm or in a market near the village (farm gate sales).

FIGURE 6.3
Distribution arrangement of agricultural produce.

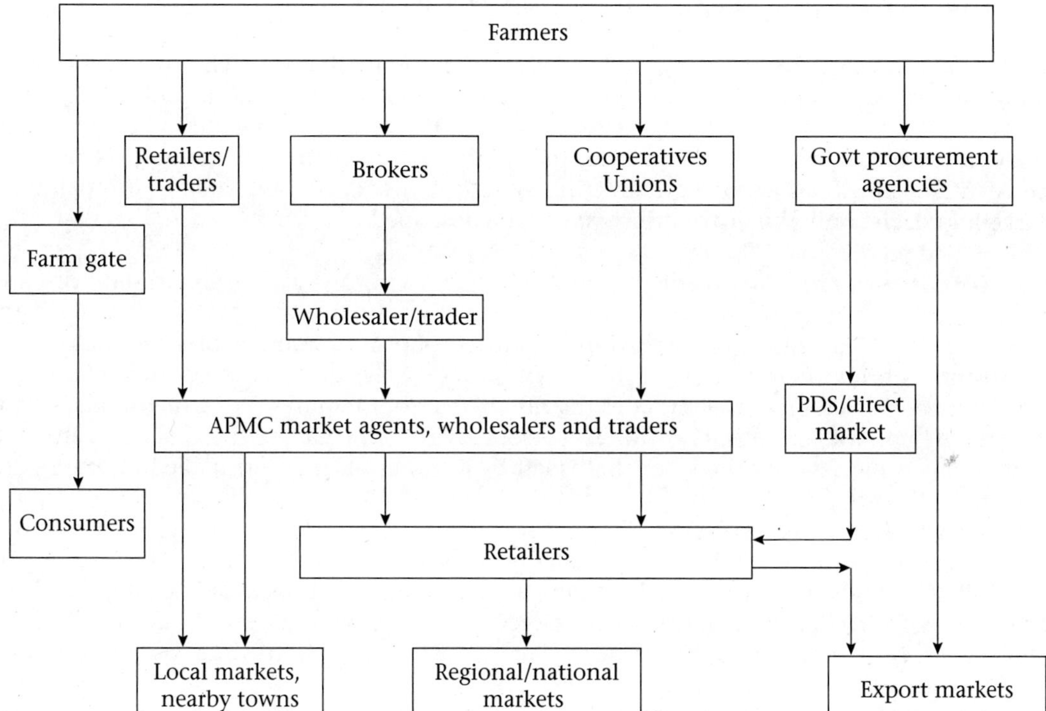

- To retailers and traders at the village who transport and sell it in nearby towns.
- At agricultural produce market committee (APMC) designated mandis.
- To brokers who facilitate trade with city-based wholesalers.
- To a cooperative organization or union of farmers.
- To government procurement agencies.
- To food processing factories situated near the farm.

Some of these choices are not practical, as growers lack marketing infrastructure to store or transport the goods. The task for farmers who have harvested their crops is just one—how to get the stock to an APMC designated market and sell quickly. APMC is a statutory market committee constituted by a state government for trade in notified agricultural, horticultural or livestock products under the Agricultural Produce Market Committee Act issued by that state government. APMCs are intended to be responsible for:

- Ensuring transparency in pricing system and transactions taking place in market area.
- Providing market-led extension services to farmers.
- Ensuring payment for agricultural produce sold by farmers on the same day.
- Promoting agricultural processing including activities for value addition in agricultural produce.

- Publicizing data on arrivals and rates of agricultural produce brought into the market area for sale.
- Setting up and promoting PPP in the management of agricultural markets.

The amenities available in or around the APMCs are: auction halls, weigh bridges, godowns, shops for retailers, canteens, roads, lights, drinking water, police station, post office, bore-wells, warehouse, farmers' amenity centre, tanks, water treatment plant, soil-testing laboratory, toilet blocks and so on. However, many of these amenities are missing in many of the APMCs. The APMC enforced marketing system is discussed in Chapter 9 (Agricultural Marketing). Here, only the distribution aspects are described.

- **Directly to the consumer:** Farmers living near a highway often set up stalls displaying their produce for passing motorists. They can also sell at a market near the farm or in the village. In some places, the APMC sets up Apni Mandis for direct marketing. Farmers bring their produce to the town on fixed days and sell to consumers at these mandis. Such a process eliminates the middleman but requires the farmer to be present at the site for long hours or hire a person, thereby increasing the cost. This method involves high-cost as the stock that is left by evening—if it is perishable in nature—has to be thrown away.
- **To retailers and traders:** To get over the problems in direct selling, farmers prefer to sell the entire stock to a local retailer or trader, who in turn transports it to a nearby APMC mandi. The farmer gets a lump sum in hand and thus avoids wastage and the costs of direct selling, but is at the mercy of traders who generally offer exploitative prices. In such a system, the trader makes a hefty commission while the producer gets low prices.
- **At APMC designated mandis:** Farmers can transport the goods to APMC designated mandis where they have to sell to authorized agents, who again exploit the farmers, squeezing them. Hefty commissions are charged by them: agents take a commission of 6–14 per cent merely to trade, as against the international norm of 0.5 per cent. In their study of peas marketing in Punjab, Sidhu et al. (2011) show that most of the produce of farmers (89%) was sold by growers in the wholesale market, while sale for local markets was just about 6 per cent. Due to problems in APMC designated Apni Mandis, the majority of growers preferred to sell green peas in the wholesale market. The study further reveals that the net price received by the farmer was about 67 per cent of the price paid by the consumer. The problems identified in Apni Mandis were:
    - Requirement to stay in the mandis for long hours.
    - Non-availability of drinking water, toilets or shelter.
    - Unhygienic conditions in the market, which become more severe in the rainy seasons.
    - Inadequate market infrastructure.
    - Frequent changes in the site of farmers.
    - Dominance of traditional retailers and traders.

It is clear that the system is exploitative and, though heavy commissions are charged, no money is ploughed into the markets to provide better facilities for farmers.

- **To brokers:** Large traders or factories appoint brokers who buy from farmers, adding to another level in the marketing channel. Such large traders supply to markets or food processors, since processors and factories located elsewhere are prohibited under APMC

Act from buying from the farmers directly. The brokers buy on behalf of their employers at the mandis. The advantage for the farmer is that all the stock is sold. The disadvantage is that they have to add brokerage cost, too.

- **To a cooperative organization or union of farmers:** Farmers' cooperatives are probably the best option as they keep the interest of farmers at heart. Some cooperatives help to market the produce or engage in processing the produce, adding value. National Federation of Farmers' Procurement, Processing and Retailing Cooperatives of India Ltd (NACOF) has been set up to organize and develop cooperative societies. However, such societies or unions do not exist in all areas, leaving the farmers to fend for themselves. Though there have been spectacular successes in areas like milk marketing, most cooperative societies suffer from political intervention and have been unable either to organize farmers or to set up processing facilities that can help them.
- **To government procurement agencies:** The government is a major buyer of agricultural produce. Organizations like Food Corporation of India (FCI) buy in bulk with the objective of stabilizing prices, distribution and maintaining buffer stocks. Farmers, however, have to deal with corruption and delayed payments. The committee that studied the working of the FCI says that it has been a total failure in achieving its objectives, reports *Indian Express* (2015). The report says that FCI did not provide effective price support to the farmers, as only 6 per cent of them received the MSP. The leakage of foodgrains supplied to the PDS was as high as 48 per cent. The buffer stocks it maintains are often very high leading to huge costs on maintenance, not to mention rotting of grains as it is usually stored in the open.
- **To food processing factories:** Sometimes, farmers also sell their produce to food-processing, sugar and oil factories situated near their farms. Through contract farming, they are assured of regular supplies from farmers. By entering into contracts with such companies, they get support like agricultural knowhow from the companies and are assured of good prices for their produce. However, such factories are few, as the food processing sector is not well-developed in India. Moreover, the APMC places restrictions on sale of goods to distant factories.

It would be clear from the list that the farmer is not actually free to sell to any channel. The APMC exercises a monopoly that often works to the disadvantage to the farmer.

An Exploitative Marketing System

The existing system for selling agricultural produce, described here, shows several shortcomings that add to the inefficiencies and also shows the exploitation caused to the farmers. These are summarized in Table 6.6 and explained in detail thereafter.

- **Bringing goods to mandis:** Once the crop is harvested, it must be brought to the nearest mandi or marketplace. The farmer piles it on trolleys, which are pulled by tractors or animals. Many farmers have to come a day prior to the auction, especially if the distance is large or when they have to avoid traffic jams due to the peak harvesting season. This adds to cost. Lodging facilities are usually not available. So, farmers have to spend the night sleeping on the trolley. If it rains, the crop is spoiled and loses value.
- **Mandis:** The mandis are designated by the APMC, which places restrictions on sale and movement of goods and monopolizes this activity (see next section). The agents or the

TABLE 6.6
Leakages in the agricultural distribution system in India.

Marketing Activity	Description and Source of Leakage
Bringing goods to mandis	Transportation costs, bulky items Lack of storage and transportation facilities
Mandis	Designated by APMC, hold monopoly position Dominated by commission agents
Display and sale	Open display, produce dumped on the ground Sight inspection No scientific grading
Auction	Open and oral auction Loss of dignity of farmer No bargaining about prices
Bagging and weighing	Cost borne by the farmer Spillage and wastage Under-weighing by staff of mandis
Payment	Piecemeal payments Multiple trips to agents No interest on delayed payments
Outbound Logistics	Multiple handling Octroi and taxes
Consumers	High prices due to multiple agents and handling Produce is often not fresh

arhatiyas come from close-knit communities and set the rules of trade to their advantage. They also know that farmers are in a hurry to sell the crop and return to their villages. This places the farmers at a disadvantage in getting good prices.

- **Display and sale:** Once at the mandi, the crop is dumped on the ground, usually in the open. Some mandis have a few sheds, but these are inadequate during the harvesting season. Agents inspect the crops visually. Grading is not done scientifically; for example, while measuring the oil content of seeds. Farmers are not able to get better prices for better produce and, so, there is little incentive to improve the quality of crops.
- **Auction:** Auction is done orally. Farmers are in no position to hold on to stocks or bargain for better prices and have to accept whatever is offered. Auctions also lead to loss of dignity of the farmers, as the inspection and price setting of their months-long labour and toil is done only within a few seconds.
- **Bagging and weighing:** Crops must be weighed and bagged for outbound transportation. The cost is borne by farmers. The mandi staff does this work, and since the spillage is considered as part payment for the work, the workers make sure that some amount of crop is always spilled, leading to loss to the farmer. There are also complaints of under-weighing by the mandi workers.
- **Payment:** Brokers exploit farmers in another way: by not paying the full amount that is due. Payments are made in instalments. Multiple trips to collect payments mean extra expenses. No interest is paid for delayed payments. Contracts are usually vocal and payment terms are to the advantage of the trader.

- **Outbound logistics:** Once it leaves the mandis, the produce is sent to retail markets or food processors by the agents. Multiple points of handling, spoilage, octroi and taxes add to the cost of the produce. In the case of fruits and vegetables, spoilage is also very high.
- **Consumers:** By the time consumers get the goods, cost has been added at various points. Costs at each stage of transactions are also added to the final price. Retailers buy their stocks from traders in towns and cities to sell in their shops. Very often the goods are not fresh by the time they reach urban markets.

This marketing system has been in existence for years and few reforms have taken place over the years. It also points to a severe lack of agricultural infrastructure in the country.

High Costs

Verma et al. (2013) studied the costs incurred in supply chains for cumin produce from Rajasthan. Cumin producers follow two channels for the marketing of cumin:

- Channel-I: Farmer → Village trader → Wholesaler → Retailer
- Channel-II: Farmer → Wholesaler (Mandi) → Retailer.

The study shows that the village trader received 5.94 per cent, wholesaler received 9.92 per cent and retailer got 15.47 per cent of the sale price. The margin of retailers was higher due to the sale of cumin in small lots to consumers. The producer's share in consumer's rupee in the regulated market of Mandor was 68.2 per cent as compared to 62.1 per cent in sale at the village level.

In another study done by Gangwar et al. (2007) of kinnow farming in Punjab, it was found that farmers commonly sold to pre-harvest contractors/traders in the area. There was no cooperative marketing society in the area. Thus, farmers get swayed by the price offered by the traders during the harvesting season.

Kinnows are marketed locally in plastic crates, gunny bags or loose. For distant markets, cardboard boxes of 10-kg capacity or wooden boxes of 20-kg capacity are used by the traders. Kinnow producers followed several marketing channels for selling their produce:

- Channel-I: Producer – Pre-harvest contractor – Wholesaler at local fruit mandi – Retailer – Local consumer
- Channel-II: Producer – Wholesaler – Local retailer – Local consumer
- Channel-III: Producer – Local retailer – Consumer
- Channel-IV: Producer – Local consumer
- Channel-V: Producer – Pre-harvest contractor – Wholesaler at distant market – Distant market retailer – Consumer
- Channel-VI: Producer – Wholesaler (distant market) – Retailer (distant market) – Consumer

This study found that aggregate post-harvest loss from orchards to consumers of kinnow in two different markets ranged from 14.87 per cent (in Delhi) to 21.91 per cent (in Bangalore). The marketing cost was found to be ₹1.94 per kg in the local Abohar market, ₹9.05 per kg in the Delhi market and ₹14.34 per kg in the Bangalore market. The cost of boxes, truck freight, commission and marketing fee are the major components of marketing cost. The producer's share in consumer's price was found to be higher in the local market sale channel. The net profit to marketing functionaries was estimated to be 49.1 per cent, 43.0 per cent and 33.2 per cent, respectively, in the local, medium-distant and long-distant markets.

The figures show that farmers suffer because of lack of kinnow-processing industries. Development of value-added quality ready-to-serve products minimize post-harvest losses and provide remunerative price to the producers. Efforts should also be made to adopt improved packaging techniques and cold storage facilities at the retailers' level.

SUMMARY

Rural distribution has two aspects: providing goods to villages and finding markets for village produce. Better prices for village produce means more purchasing power in the hands of rural producers, leading to more demand for consumer goods.

The first step in creating rural distribution channels is to understand consumer behaviour. Socio-economic factors, type of goods sold and the place of purchase give us an idea about the preferences of rural consumers. There are several models of rural distribution, the largest of which is the government-run PDS system. Companies try to reach villages by using existing wholesalers, a network of sub-dealers or local partners, direct selling and outreach programmes, village entrepreneurs (feet on the ground), piggybacking on rural retail chains or local networks or, finally, creating rural value chains. These are some of the models of rural distribution used by companies.

However, distribution is stymied by years of neglect of rural areas. Lack of infrastructure poses a great challenge for companies venturing into rural areas. Lack or roads, electricity, transportation and warehousing means that transportation of goods is a huge problem resulting in added costs of increased spoilages, losses in transit and uneconomic transportation. Apart from infrastructural shortcomings, rural distribution faces many logistical challenges including scattered markets, low purchasing power, low volumes per market, availability of cheap, unbranded products, lack of financial channels and credit sources, bad roads and so on.

These shortcomings create a great hindrance not only in terms of supplying goods to villages but also for farmers to sell their produce in markets. Losses in transit are high. Farmers are thus unable to get good prices for their produce. Farmers can sell through the following channels, wherever available: (a) directly to the consumer at the farm gate, (b) to retailers and traders at the village who transport and sell it in nearby towns, (c) at the APMC designated mandis, (d) through brokers who facilitate trade with city-based wholesalers, (e) to a cooperative organization, (f) to government procurement agencies or (g) to food processing factories. The system of agricultural marketing is highly exploitative, with farmers at the receiving end in almost all operations including transportation, display and sale, bagging and weighing and payments. Studies of costs reveal that producers are able to get only 60–65 per cent of the sales proceeds.

CONCLUSION

Distribution is the backbone of any marketing activity and rural distribution remains a challenge.

Companies have tried to tackle this aspect in many ways, from reaching villages through existing retailers to establishing a two-way distribution process that helps farmers sell their produce. But years of neglect has led to almost insurmountable problems of access, infrastructure and people. Public policy is unfortunately biased towards cities, leaving the villages caught in a time warp.

It is doubtful that things will change in a hurry in rural India. That is why, companies have to try and develop their own models of rural distribution. Indeed, some companies have tried to solve this jigsaw puzzle in their own ways, with varying degrees of success. Innovative thinking is the key to success. Companies that solve some problems of rural people are likely do well in reaching villages.

KEY TERMS

APMC: The APMC is a statutory market committee constituted by a state government for trade in notified agricultural, horticultural or livestock products under the Agricultural Produce Market Committee Act issued by that state government.

Direct channel: When a company has its own dedicated sales force to cover villages, it is called a direct channel of distribution.

Feet on the ground: The approach in which the company trains and develops entrepreneurs in villages, who act as distributors and brand ambassadors.

Hub-and-spoke model: Company appoints a local dealer or partner to serve several villages from a depot in a central town, called hub, or through its own office.

PDS: Under the PDS, foodgrains are sold from fair price shops at lower prices than the market rate, with the objective of providing food security to the poor.

CONCEPT REVIEW QUESTIONS

1. Describe the place of purchase preference for different types of consumer goods in rural areas. What impact does the place of purchase have on designing distribution channels?
2. What are the difficulties and challenges that are faced by managers in creating distribution channels for rural areas?
3. Comment on the buying behaviour of rural consumers in terms of goods purchased and the preferred place of purchase. How do socio-economic factors impact the buying behaviour of rural consumers?
4. Describe the public distribution system (PDS) of Government of India. How effective is it?
5. What are the models of distribution followed by companies when targeting rural populations? Name the companies following these models.
6. What are the challenges that companies are likely to face in rural distribution?
7. How does a scattered population pose a problem to marketing managers?
8. Describe the distribution systems of agricultural produce. How effective are they?
9. How is agricultural produce distributed in India? Comment on the advantages and disadvantages of the system.
10. Describe the APMC market system. Also describe its advantages and drawbacks.

THINKING QUESTIONS

1. Companies are taking different routes to serve rural markets, as described in the chapter. Critically examine these methods with regard to efficiency and effectiveness. Identify which industries should use which models, and why?
2. The problem of low purchasing power and seasonal incomes impact on the effectiveness of rural marketing campaigns. How can companies overcome these limitations? Does it make sense that companies take up social programmes that help improve livelihoods?
3. Many companies have tied up with NGOs or SHGs for rural distribution. How far do you think such initiatives are effective, given that the NGOs and SHGs have their own objectives to meet? Will consumers see them with trust once they know that the groups are taking up commercial activities?
4. Critically examine the system of agriculture produce distribution in the country. Is it helpful to the farmers and consumers? What improvements would you like made in it?

PROJECTS AND ASSIGNMENTS

1. Take a look at (a) FMCG, (b) fertilizer and (c) white goods availability in villages. How are the companies distributing its products in rural areas?
2. Study the APMC system of distribution of agricultural produce. Visit an APMC designated mandi and find out how effective it is. Comment on its facilities. Talk to the farmers to discover its advantages and disadvantages.
3. Visit a distributor in a town. Ask him how he distributes to surrounding villages. Ask the sub-dealers how they supply to village shops. Would it pay for companies to have their own channels to villages?
4. Study the public distribution system (PDS) by visiting a PDS shop in your city. Find out about its activities. How effective is it in distributing grain to the poor?

WEB RESOURCE

"Planning Commission Report of the Working Group on Central Roads Sector 12th Five Year Plan (2012–17)." Available at: http://planningcommission.gov.in/aboutus/committee/wrkgrp12/transport/report/wg_cen_roads.pdf

REFERENCES

Ernst & Young, and Retailers Association of India. 2013. "Movement of Goods in India." December. Available at: http://rasci.in/downloads/2013/Movement_Goods_India.pdf (Accessed on 13 April 2017).

FAO. 2015. "The State of Food Insecurity in the World." A report by Food and Agricultural Organization of the United Nations. Available at: http://www.fao.org/3/a-i4646e.pdf (Accessed on 27 April 2017).

FE Bureau. 2015. "FCI a Complete Failure, Needs Overhaul: Panel." *Financial Express*, 22 January.

Gangwar, L.S., Dinesh Singh and D.B. Singh. 2007. "Estimation of Post-harvest Losses in Kinnow Mandarin in Punjab Using a Modified Formula." *Agricultural Economics Research Review* 20 (July–December): 315–31.

Gulati, Ashok and Shweta Saini. 2015. "Leakages from Public Distribution System (PDS) and the Way Forward." ICRIER Working Paper No 294, January.

Kapur, Mamta, Sanjay Dawar and Vineet R. Ahuja. 2014. "Unlocking the Wealth in Rural Markets." *Harvard Business Review*, June. Available at: https://hbr.org/2014/06/unlocking-the-wealth-in-rural-markets (Accessed on 27 April 2017).

Karamchandani Ashish, Mike Kubzansky and Nishant Lalwani. 2011. "The Globe: Is the Bottom of the Pyramid Really for you?" *Harvard Business Review,* March. Available at: https://hbr.org/2011/03/the-globe-is-the-bottom-of-the-pyramid-really-for-you (Accessed on 13 April 2017).

Kumar, Dinesh. 2012. *Marketing Channels*. New Delhi: Oxford University Press.

National Council of Applied Economic Research. 2015. "Evaluation Study of Targeted Public Distribution System in Selected States." National Council of Applied Economic Research, New Delhi, September. Available at: http://dfpd.nic.in/writereaddata/images/TPDS-140316.pdf (Accessed on 27 April 2017).

Prahalad, C.K., and Allen Hammond. 2002. "Serving the World's Poor, Profitably." *Harvard Business Review*, September. Available at: https://hbr.org/2002/09/serving-the-worlds-poor-profitably (Accessed on 27 April 2017).

Saini, Shweta and Marta Kozicka. 2014. "Evolution and Critique of Buffer Stocking Policy of India." ICRIER Working Paper No 283, September.

TCI–IIMC. 2009. "Operational Efficiency of National Highways for Freight Transportation in India." A report by Transport Corporation of India (TCI) and IIM Calcutta. Available at: http://www.tcil.com/tcil/pdf/TCI%20&%20IIM%20Study%20Report.pdf (Accessed on 27 April 2017).

The World Bank. 2014. "Poverty and Equity." Available at: http://povertydata.worldbank.org/poverty/country/IND (Accessed on 27 April 2017).

Vachani, S., and N. Craig Smith. 2008. "Overcoming Rural Distribution Challenges at the Bottom of the Pyramid." *California Management Review* 50 (2) Winter: 52–84. DOI:10.2307/41166435

Verma, Vinod Kumar, Vishnu Shanker Meena, Pradeep Kumar, and R.C. Kumawat. 2013. "Production and Marketing of Cumin in Jodhpur District of Rajasthan: An Economic Analysis." *Agricultural Economics Research Review* 26 (2): 287–92.

Closing Case
HUL's Project Shakti: Revolution in Distribution

HUL is India's largest FMCG company. With over 35 brands in 20 categories, the company is a behemoth offering soaps, detergents, shampoos, skin care products, toothpastes, deodorants, cosmetics, tea, coffee, packaged foods, ice creams and water purifiers. As part of its rural marketing push, it faced a familiar problem—that of distribution.

HUL decided to work through local women, starting a unique project that helped it gain market penetration, while also helping poor people to increase their incomes, and thus created a unique model of rural distribution. In doing so, it had to overcome many hurdles usually faced by FMCG companies. Though rural India represents a large, untapped market, poor infrastructure, dispersed settlements, lack of education and poor roads poses great nightmares for managers. Government measures like waiver of loans, Mahatma Gandhi National

Rural Employment Guarantee Scheme (MGNREGS), and increasing MSP have resulted in an increase in disposable income in rural India. But such initiatives have made it much more difficult to get workers for distribution.

HUL had to overcome all these problems. Through a combination of microcredit, training in management and SHGs, women were encouraged to become direct-to-home distributors of a range of HUL products. This helped the company gain a foothold in unexplored rural hinterlands while also helping build sustainable livelihoods.

The initiative was called Project Shakti which started in 2001. The project combined social goals with business goals.

The process starts with the recruitment of a woman in a village willing to become a distributor. Called Shakti Amma (SA), this woman is trained and is asked to put up ₹20,000 as investment. This amount is used to buy company products for selling to others in the village, usually door-to-door or through a petty shop in one's home. Each SA usually services 6–10 villages in the population strata of 1,000–2,000 people with four or five major brands: Lifebuoy, Wheel, Pepsodent, Annapurna Salt and Clinic Plus and other brands like Lux, Ponds, Nihar and 3 Roses Tea. SAs are given HUL products on a 'cash-and-carry' basis. The company helps SAs get initial finance through microcredit, working through SHGs.

The project started in Andhra Pradesh in 2001 as the state had the most number and established SHGs. The SA takes an initial loan of ₹10,000 from her SHG to start the enterprise. In course of time, she is able to achieve a turnover of ₹10,000–25,000 every month and earn a profit of ₹750–2,000, with an average return of 8 per cent. Besides, she may also sell other products like staples, sugar, edible oil and household items to increase her income.

The Shakti programme helps HUL to have more feet on the ground or more people working for it in rural markets. SAs are able to reach far-flung areas, which were economically unviable for the company earlier. The SAs are also the brand ambassadors for the company and become users of the company products besides selling them.

To overcome the problems that women SAs were more inclined to stay at home rather than going from door to door or sell to men, the company started hosting Shakti Days, when an artificial marketplace was created with music and promotion where SAs were able to sell their products.

HUL provides training on basic accounting, selling skills, health and hygiene and relevant IT skills to Shakti entrepreneurs and equips them with smartphones, which have been enabled with a mini enterprise resource package that helps them to run their business efficiently and further augment their income. HUL has trained thousands of SAs across villages in a bid to develop an entrepreneurial mindset and make them financially independent and more empowered.

In 2010, the Shakti programme was extended to include 'Shaktimaans' who are typically the husbands or brothers of the SAs. Shaktimaans complement the SAs. They sell products on bicycles in surrounding villages, covering a larger area than SAs can cover on foot.

Project Shakti has been a remarkable success. By 2008, the company had appointed 45,000 SAs covering more than 100,000 villages in 15 states. The company aims to cover 500,000 villages and reach 600 million people.

The project has several productive offshoots. The Shakti Vani programme is a health education programme, in which trained communicators provide messages on sanitation, good hygiene practices and women's empowerment. This rural communication helps awareness and increase in SA's sales. Another initiative called i-Shakti has placed over 200 computer kiosks in rural communities. It has a range of services, including computer education and spoken English tutorials, which are otherwise not available in villages.

The company has started similar projects in some South Asian countries as well. It started Joyeeta in Bangladesh. Spin-off projects include a joint venture with CARE Bangladesh and a distribution agreement with Bata Shoes. Saubhagya in Sri Lanka was a similar project which helped Saubhagya entrepreneurs with housing renovation grants and scholarships for children, as well as broader community development investments such as clean water, wells and libraries.

These projects have increased HUL's reach to rural consumers in South Asia while significantly enhancing the income and social standing of underprivileged women. Start-ups are financed by small loans from NGOs, while the company provides the women with training and support in commercial skills. The result is a fast-growing network of thriving direct-to-consumer distribution businesses.

Shakti, Joyeeta and Saubhagya now combine to make perhaps the largest sustained rural home-to-home sales operation in the world.

Women who earlier had little or no income sources have doubled their household incomes, giving their families better education, health care and housing. These businesses are tiny but numerous. Coupled with HUL-funded schemes such as Shakti Vani or the Saubhagya scholarship scheme, they are making a community-wide impact on the quality of life.

The company combines social responsibility, sustainability and business strategy in one go.

Today, Project Shakti provides livelihood-enhancing opportunities to nearly 70,000 Shakti entrepreneurs who distribute products in more than 162,000 villages and reach over 4 million rural households, according to the HUL website. There are 48,000 Shaktimaans across India.

The majority of SAs are earning more than ₹1,000 a month. Through the Shaktimaan initiative, men in the SA families distribute HUL products to villages adjoining the respective Shakti village. Through the Geographical Information System (GIS), villages around the 'Shakti' families are tracked and, based on this, they are allotted five to six villages. They go to these villages and sell HUL products. The Shaktimaans have also been given bicycles to ensure smooth travelling between villages. The revenue earned by the Shaktimaans further augments the household income of the 'Shakti' families.

Through Project Shakti and Shaktimaan, HUL reaches over 100,000 villages across 15 states in India and over 3 million households every month. HUL works closely with various NGOs, banks and state and local government departments. On an average, a Shakti entrepreneur earns ₹700–1,000 a month, and since most of them live below the poverty line, this earning is significant, often doubling the household income.

Questions for Discussions:

1. Do you think that such a model for distribution can be replicated by other companies? How?
2. What are the advantages or drawbacks of distributing directly through village folk as opposed to supplies from distributors in nearby towns? Which would work out cheaper for the company?
3. What would be the logistical challenges of building a distribution channel involving local people?
4. This initiative combines business interests with social betterment. Can you think of other companies who have succeeded in doing this? Do they work?

Sources for this Case Study:

Web Resources

"Enhancing livelihoods through Project Shakti." Available at HUL website: https://www.hul.co.in/sustainable-living/case-studies/enhancing-livelihoods-through-project-shakti.html

"Unilever Sustainable Living Plan—India Progress 2015." Available at: https://www.hul.co.in/Images/unilever-sustainable-living-plan-india-2015-progress-report_tcm1255-483536_en.pdf

Watch "Brand Equity—A greater Lever-age in Rural Distribution—HUL" by ET Now at: https://www.youtube.com/watch?v=keTOZ4rfF6I&list=PLTxPoCf_1OHQ3_50NL88qX0tZUuAfZgSQ&index=1

Other Sources

Loman, Bart. 2006. "Unilever's Shakti Project: Empowering Rural Indian Women." In *Bottom of the Pyramid in Practice*. Nijmegen: Lambert Academic Publishing.

"Project Shakti Business Model Overview." *Equitymaster*, 10 August 2009.

"Project Shakti: It's All About Empowerment." *Indian Management*, February 2012.

Raghav Narsalay, Ryan T. Coffey and Aarohi Sen. 2012. "Hindustan Unilever: Scaling a Cost-efficient Distribution and Sales Network in Remote Markets." A Case Study by Accenture. Available at: https://www.accenture.com/_acnmedia/Accenture/Conversion-Assets/DotCom/Documents/Global/PDF/Dualpub_23/Accenture-Unilever-Case-Study.pdf (Accessed on 17 April 2017).

Sidhu, R.S., M.S. Sidhu, and J.M. Singh. 2011. "Marketing Efficiency of Green Peas under Different Supply Chains in Punjab." *Agricultural Economics Research Review* 24 (July–December): 267–73.

7

CHAPTER

Pricing and Marketing Communication in Rural Markets

LEARNING OBJECTIVES

Pricing and communications are important tools of marketing strategy. However, using these tools in rural areas requires deep understanding of the markets and consumers. Many of the pricing and communications strategies are bound to fail if affordability of consumers and local means of communicating are ignored. After reading this chapter, you will be able to:

- Learn about pricing policies and learn how to apply them in rural markets.
- Analyze the challenges of communicating to rural areas.
- Understand how to make rural communications strategy.
- Learn about the rural communications mix and how to use it effectively.
- Understand the need and importance of local media and using melas and fairs to reach rural customers.

Opening Case
HUL's Kan Khajura Tesan (KKT)

Communication is the means of getting messages across to potential consumers. In mass marketing, people are 'sprayed' with advertising and they turn up in large numbers to buy the goods that they see on TV or newspapers. But what if TV and newspapers were only available in limited numbers and areas? This is the difficulty that managers and companies face when they wish to serve rural markets. In the absence of mass media, local media must be used. More than that, innovative ideas and campaigns have to be devised.

This case study shows how a company developed its own communication channel through a completely out-of-the-box thinking. HUL, the country's largest consumer goods maker, has introduced a unique concept in reaching out to rural customers. It runs KKT, a free radio-on-demand service to reach out to villagers in remote areas. The KKT, translated as 'ear centipede', is already the largest radio station in Bihar in terms of subscribers. It is an amazing innovation in rural communication.

KKT is India's first free and on-demand entertainment mobile radio channel. It is one of the fastest growing media channels in India. It was launched in October 2013 in Bihar and Jharkhand and the service was expanded in August 2014 across Uttar Pradesh, Uttarakhand, Madhya Pradesh, Chhattisgarh, Himachal Pradesh, Haryana, Punjab, Rajasthan, Gujarat and Maharashtra.

The tagline of the station is: *Missed call lagao, muft manoranjan pao.* It is an entertainment channel on the mobile platform: a mobile phone user gives a missed call to the number 180030000123 to immediately get a return call that plays KKT for 15 minutes (Figure 7.1). Besides entertainment programmes, the channel plays advertisements of HUL brands.

The Economic Times (2014) reports that in villages of Bihar, people regularly listen to movie songs, dialogues, radio jockey talk, jokes and *shayari* on their mobile phones. There is no FM station covering many of these villages. The company says that there is a lot of demand for content or entertainment in media-dark villages and mobile phones have become their only route to that world.

Through KKT, the company knows who is listening to the programmes, unlike radio. Since mobile phones yield data about consumer habits, it has also been collecting a vast amount of data on rural consumers—data that does not exist or is hard to access. It gathers data and develops rich profiles of its listeners and plans to use them to prepare customized

FIGURE 7.1
The ad for Kan Khajura Tesan.

Source: http://www.kankhajuratesan.com/ (Accessed on 26 April 2017).

strategies for its brands. HUL has stopped advertising on radio in Bihar, because its own channel reaches more people than any radio stations. The company has printed the phone number for the channel on some of its product packs and has put up banners outside stores to increase its reach.

KKT has acquired more than 35 million subscribers across the country since its launch. The company is able to interact with about one lakh consumers every day, which means about 25,000 hours of engagement daily with consumers in Bihar. After its success in Bihar, HUL launched this service in other states.

KKT was piloted in Bihar in 2013. It was developed from a 'missed call' campaign that HUL conducted for Wheel in 2012, in which through an advertisement on All India Radio in Uttar Pradesh and Bihar it was asked to the listeners to give a missed call from their mobile phones to a particular number. When they did so, they promptly got a call back with a recording of actor Salman Khan's dialogues from his blockbuster film *Ek Tha Tiger* and his endorsement of Wheel. HUL got 16 million missed calls in four months and, by the end of the campaign, brand awareness scores for Wheel had increased by 25 per cent and its sales jumped three times in the region.

HUL has roped in several third-party firms to generate content and services for the channel, which it had initially named 'Mobile Vani' before opting for a more colloquial name.

HUL monitors usage of KKT on a 'live dashboard' that highlights the districts from where traffic is coming. It can identify the areas and the times of maximum traffic. The company is also able to access other useful information such as the frequency of the calls, the time of day the calls come in, the numbers from which repeat calls are made and, perhaps most importantly, the exact point when the caller decides to hang up. The dashboard also shows the number of ad impressions for different brands.

While reading this chapter, try to answer the following questions:

1. How can companies get over the lack of channels and devise innovative communication programmes to reach villages?
2. What channels of communication are available and what are their advantages?
3. How can pricing and communication strategies help brands achieve acceptability in villages?
4. What is the importance of local melas and media in rural marketing?

Sources for this Case Study:

Web Resource

Kan Khajura Tesan website: http://www.kankhajuratesan.com/

Watch the Kan Khajura film by Lowe Lintas at: https://www.youtube.com/watch?v=mdzFwDbk3ig

Other Sources

The Economic Times. 2014. "Hindustan Unilever Runs Bihar's Most Popular Radio on Mobile Phones." 4 March.

Gangal, A. 2014. "Kan Khajura Tesan: The Full Story." *afaqs!* 30 June. Available at: http://www.afaqs.com/news/story/41226_Kan-Khajura-Tesan-The-Full-Story (Accessed on 27 April 2017).

HUL. 2014. "Kan Khajura Tesan sets world record." 26 August. Available at: https://www.hul.co.in/news/news-and-features/2014/kan-khajura-tesan-sets-world-record.html (Accessed on 27 April 2017).

The Economic Times. 2015. "HUL Plans to Let Other Firms Use Its Mobile Marketing Channel Kan Khajura Tesan." 26 June.

INTRODUCTION

Pricing and communication are two major tools in marketing warfare. They have been used by companies to reach and influence consumers. Many brands have been built by effective use of the mass media and price variations. But when it comes to rural areas, these strategies have to be reworked because of two reasons. First, because rural markets and consumers are so diverse that many strategies that have worked in urban markets fail there. Holding price points in villages becomes impossible for companies when cost of distribution is added. Second, since communication channels do not exist or are patchy, there can be no one strategy that companies can follow in all villages across the country.

Pricing has to take into account affordability and ethical considerations (see Mini Case Study 7.1). If companies use market skimming policies and charge high prices, they attract the charge of exploiting the poor to make profits. At the same time, to meet sustainable businesses, they must meet social objectives in rural communities, as described in earlier chapters. The pricing policies must reflect these realities, while also meeting the needs of the segments buying on aspirations by selling them premium products. It is a tough act and very often textbook strategies do not work.

Similarly, communications mix for villages is also entirely different. Using participatory approaches requires direct communications in rural markets. Use of media is limited and companies have to devise entirely new communications mix to reach the rural audience. Completely new solutions, such as the one described in the opening case study on KKT, have to be developed.

This chapter describes the commonly used approaches in pricing and communications and modifies them in the light of rural realities.

Mini Case Study 7.1

Godrej Consumer Products

Godrej Consumer Products is a major player in rural markets. It captures markets by creating specific products and pricing to cater to this market. The company has witnessed rural growth at 16 per cent, which is much higher than its urban growth at 10 per cent in some years. It plans to introduce more affordable products and pricing created for the rural markets, including more stock keeping units (SKUs) specific to villages.

Godrej has increased distribution to reach out to rural markets with the addition of 1,500 sub-stockists. It has introduced new affordable products such as coconut hair cream and fast card. It has introduced its range of products including soaps, hair colours and household insecticides and thus has bucked the trend of sluggish growth. The household insecticide category, in which Godrej has presence with brands such as GoodKnight and Hit, there is 20 per cent penetration, which leaves a large untapped market. The company has a strong focus in southern markets, which has helped its household insecticide portfolio grow.

How did Godrej expand its footprint in rural areas and what should be its future strategy?

Sources for this Case Study:

Web Resource

Godrej Consumer Products website: http://www.godrejcp.com/

Other Source

The Hindu BusinessLine. 2015. "Godrej Targets Rural Markets with New Products and Pricing." 3 August.

PRICING POLICY AND STRATEGY

Much of pricing policy exists for perfect markets; it assumes that consumers have full information, are spoilt for choice, have easy access to goods, and that producers have flexible resources to increase supply and demand at will. It also assumes that people will buy some quantities of goods no matter at what price they are offered. These assumptions unfortunately do not work in rural markets; neither do consumers have full information nor do producers have flexible supply chains.

Pricing strategies come from economics. Students of economics learn about the demand curve—more goods can be sold if prices are low—and managers devise pricing policies based on costs, value, demand and competition. Pricing strategy can help a company use pricing to achieve its goals, such as achieving penetration, market share or profits. However, much of the pricing theory fails in rural marketing. This is because companies have to work around low purchasing power, availability of local brands that are priced cheaply and price points that are convenient for customers. That is why, prices for rural markets must fit market conditions and satisfy the need for affordability. In addition, the pricing must cover costs, which are quite high in rural markets.

We first describe popular pricing methods and then discuss rural pricing in detail in the subsequent sections. Some of these methods are cost-based pricing, value-based pricing, demand-based pricing and competition-based pricing.

Cost-based Pricing

Cost-based pricing policy rests on the principle of recovering all costs in manufacturing and selling a product. It is a pricing method in which a fixed sum or a percentage is added to the total cost of producing and selling a product to arrive at its selling price. The company thus recovers the costs incurred and achieves a profit as well. This method is simple and is based on internal information from financial and accounting records to give a figure of fixed costs (FC) and variable costs (VC). Cost-based pricing can be represented as a simple equation:

$$\text{Selling price} = (\text{FC} + \text{VC}) + \text{Mark-up}$$

In rural markets, apart from FC and VC, the cost of selling and distribution must be added. These are often hidden and difficult to calculate. They are also very high, because economic modes of transport do not exist. As a result, cost-based pricing method does not work in modern market conditions. It may lead to high prices in weak, scattered markets, making the effort of selling difficult. Moreover, in rural markets the challenge for companies and brands is to establish themselves. A purely cost-based pricing may lead to high prices that turn away rural consumers. By bearing in mind the prices they can charge and the costs they can pay, companies have to determine whether their costs will enable them to compete in low-cost markets where customers are concerned primarily with price, or find richer customers in the premium-price market in which they are primarily concerned with quality and features.

Value-based Pricing

Value-based pricing is a method in which price is set on the basis of the value perceived by the customer in buying and using a product. The perceived value of a product is the sum of attributes and psychological value. Consumers derive value from a product or service from their needs, preferences, expectations and desires. The job of a manager is to find out from customers and research the market to determine how value is placed on a product or service. Value-based pricing is a psychological pricing strategy. Value in the minds of the consumer is achieved by creating desire by product attributes, advertising or adding status to products. Value has to be communicated and this is not so easy in rural markets. As we have shown in earlier chapters, much of communication and consumer engagement has to be done directly by companies in the absence of mass media. Except for high-end brands, rural consumers are more likely to be swayed by functional benefits than by features that merely enhance aesthetics.

Demand-based Pricing

Demand-based pricing follows the classic demand curve taught in basic economics classes; it simply means that if prices are low, demand will be high and vice versa. Demand-based pricing focuses on the level of demand for a product or service, not on the cost of materials or of making it. According to this policy, companies try to assess demand at different prices, or the amount of products or services they can sell at different prices. Some companies, selling luxury or aspiration goods, limit supplies in order to sell their products at high prices. Others, dealing with mass production goods, use pricing policy to sell goods at low prices and hope to achieve volumes because of that. Production and sales are based on these calculations. However, it is quite difficult to estimate demand of any product based on different price levels, more so in villages. Estimating demand in rural areas is even more difficult than in urban areas, because a host of factors are at play, many of which are simply not apparent, as explained in earlier chapters.

Competition-based Pricing

Competition-based pricing is relatively simple, because the company sets its prices by looking at prices of similar products offered by competitors. Prices of competing products are used as a benchmark for setting prices. Once prices of competitors are known, the company may decide any of the following three strategies:

- **Pricing at par with the competition:** The company chooses to price its products exactly at the same price as competitors. For instance, if a cold drink is being sold at ₹25 per bottle in a market, a competing manufacture will also price its product at ₹25 per bottle.
- **Pricing above the competition:** The company sets a price higher than its competitor by highlighting the superiority of its products over those of others, hoping that customers would like to buy their superior or longer lasting product.
- **Pricing below the competition:** The company prices its products lower than those offered by competitors hoping that customers might like a cheaper product than other, more expensive but similar products.

In competition-based pricing, the company does not consider its costs of manufacturing and selling or the demand of the product, but only prices of similar products.

Each of the mentioned strategies has advantages and disadvantages. For instance, while pricing at par, the company must have a similar cost structure as that or the competitor. If the costs are higher, competition-based pricing will lead it to ruin. This method is fraught with another danger—if a company prices its products at par with local brands, it will impact consumer perception: consumers will perceive its products being of the same inferior quality as the local brands.

While pricing above the competition, the company runs the risk that customers may turn away from expensive products. Pricing below the competition carries the risk of a price war—if the competitor also reduces prices, the company is forced to reduce prices even further, which could lead to losses. In rural markets, competitors are usually low-cost local brands. Pricing at par or below the competition is almost impossible for big brands, which have higher costs. Such brands have to compete on communicating value rather than price. Innovative strategies have to be thought of rather than competing on price.

However, competition-based pricing policy is easy since competitor prices are easy to find, allowing companies to set prices quickly and with little effort.

The pricing strategies are summed up in Table 7.1.

New and Established Products

Product pricing strategies frequently depend on the stage a product or service is in its lifecycle; that is, new products often require different pricing strategies than established products or mature products. For rural pricing, most products will have to be treated as new products.

If the price is too high, volumes will not be achieved, whereas if the price is too low, it becomes difficult to recover costs of selling and distribution in remote areas. This means that

TABLE 7.1

Comparison of pricing strategies.

	Cost-based Pricing	Value-based Pricing	Demand-based Pricing	Competition-based Pricing
Definition	A pricing method in which a fixed sum or a percentage is added to the total cost of producing and selling a product to arrive at its selling price	A pricing method in which price is set on the basis of the value perceived by the customer in buying and using a product	A pricing method based on demand of a product at different levels of price	A pricing method in which the seller uses prices of similar and competing products as a benchmark of setting prices
Method	Cost-plus pricing, mark-up pricing	Advertising and psychological value assigned to product attributes by customers	Price sensitivity, price demand analysis	Competitor prices of similar products
Advantage	Easy availability of data	Can contribute to high profits	Caters to variable prices	Very easy to implement
Disadvantage	Does not vary with demand or volume	Very difficult to assess psychological value	Demand cannot be easily assessed	May lead to price wars

rural pricing should enable companies to recover their costs while, at the same time, keep their margins low through creative pricing policies. While product cycles in urban markets are shortening and companies have to recover their investments quickly, in rural markets product cycles are relatively longer and afford companies a chance to develop the markets. Companies such as Jain Irrigation, ITC, Fabindia and many others have invested for the long run and gained traction over the years.

When a company launches a new product, it follows one of two policies. One is *market skimming*, meaning that prices are kept deliberately high as there are no competitors, thus making the customers pay high price. In this case, the company tries to make maximum profit in the initial phase. Many technology-related products, for instance, follow the market skimming policy, initially pricing their products highly but decreasing them later. The opposite is *market penetration*, in which prices are initially kept low to attract customers to get them hooked on to the product. Prices are increased once the desired mass of customers has been achieved. A case in point is that of SMS in India. When introduced, it was a free service, but the prices were increased once people got used to it.

Pricing in Rural Markets

Companies devise their own price policies depending on their objectives. Dealers are usually unwilling to stock low-price goods as they earn lower commissions from them. In any case, most goods are sold at prices higher than MRP printed prices to cover the cost of reaching remote areas. Hence, customers have to really see value in the brands to pay those high prices. Rural pricing has to keep the following factors in focus:

- **Low purchasing power:** A major problem in rural areas is the lack of purchasing power. The SECC 2011 data for rural India shows that more than half of rural households depend on manual labour for livelihood and 75 per cent of the rural population, or 133.5 million families, earn less than ₹5,000 per month. This means that for majority of the population, low prices are important.
- **High selling and distribution cost:** Activities such as salesmen travelling over long distances, sending small quantities of goods and collecting small payments add to high sales and distribution costs. Companies have to figure out how these costs can be recovered.
- **Gaining consumer acceptance:** Prices have to be set keeping in view consumer acceptance. Usually the problem is in trying to sell high priced brands when similar unbranded products are available at cheaper prices.
- **Difficulty of communicating value:** High prices imply that the company is able to communicate value to the customers. This is often a difficult task in villages and it depends on direct selling.
- **Local brands are cheaper:** While in urban areas brands can use competition-based pricing, competition in villages comes from unbranded or local brands, which offer reasonably good quality. These products also have substantial loyalty. Companies have to figure out ways to fight these products that are priced much cheaper than bigger brands (see Photo 7.1).

Innovative strategies have to be devised to keep prices at low level despite the high costs of serving rural markets. Such strategies as that of Tata Tea, which partnered with local people

PHOTO 7.1

Local manufacturers are able to supply goods reasonable quality goods at much cheaper prices than national brands.

Source: Photograph by Dinesh Kumar.

instead of going through dealers, or that of Grameen Bank in Bangladesh, which was able to reduce call rates for rural customers by buying air time in bulk from Grameen phone, have been covered in this book.

Because of the aforementioned reasons, marketing in rural areas can only succeed if prices are made affordable. Many pricing methods like market skimming will fail and innovative techniques will have to be devised to reach such customers.

A Complicated Market

Prices for different market segments are devised on the assumption that all customers do not have the same needs, expectations and financial resources. Segmentation is successful when a company knows the factors that motivate particular segments to buy products. For rural markets, a company has to find out customers who are mainly motivated by price or by functionality and utility. Another important task is to find segments that are motivated by aspirations. As we have pointed out in earlier chapters, many rural customers aspire to

Mini Case Study 7.2

Rural India Scales Up

There are two distinct markets in rural India. While for a large part, cheaper products at low price points are sold, another part of the market seems to be trading up. There are signs of change in categories such as automobiles, chocolates and biscuits.

India's auto industry has long realized that they have two different markets to serve. In big cities, buyers want compact models with a large number of features such as automatic transmission, extra luggage space and daring colours. In rural areas, however, customers favour frill-free vehicles with simple maintenance and reliability.

So, while expensive vehicles with bells and whistles are being sold in cities, car companies cannot afford to neglect the traditional rural market for basic vehicles, which can sell for roughly half the price of a high-end compact vehicle, according to *Mint* (2015).

There are signs of change in another category of products. Rural consumers have started adding chocolates and cream biscuits to their monthly purchase baskets which shows that a large segment is moving from being 'deprivers' to 'aspirers', reports *The Economic Times* (2013). When consumers move from glucose biscuits to the more expensive kinds, it means that they are buying more aspiration-related products. The factors could be many, from increased incomes to more education.

The inclusion of women has also helped expand the market. In recent years, there has been an increase in girl students in secondary schools due to free education and mid-day meal schemes, which has led to an increased awareness among women about brands. Cadbury India is expanding into villages with 5,000–10,000 population in nine states and plans to cover 75–80 per cent of the rural potential. Rural India contributes about one-sixth of the total ₹5,500-crore chocolate market, while villages with a population of 5,000–10,000 contribute about 5 per cent. The nearly ₹300 crore rural market for chocolates is attractive as it is growing at 19 per cent CAGR. The company believes that rural India holds significant potential and it could be the single biggest driver of its sales in future. Many rural consumers also do not buy only small price packs of ₹2, but favour the ₹5 and ₹10 price points, showing increased purchasing power.

Ferrero India, which is concentrating on its urban network, has also witnessed demand of some of its premier brands in rural areas—Kinder Joy and Tic Tac—which are being supplied through wholesalers. Britannia Industries also reports that its variety biscuits consisting of creams and cookies were growing significantly faster than glucose in rural markets.

How can companies find prosperous segments in a landscape of poverty?

Sources for this Case Study:

Mint. 2015. "Tale of Two Indias: City Auto Buyers Go Upscale, No-frills Minis Rule Villages." 19 May.

The Economic Times. 2013. "India Inc Eyes Villagers' Growing Appetite for Sweet." 15 October.

be like urban dwellers and are willing to spend for achieving that (see Mini Case Study 7.2). Though people in rural areas are willing to spend on aspiration-motivated goods, the lack of formal banking channels and tougher availability of loans means that spending power remains limited.

Rural pricing decisions are not easy because markets are imperfect. Many of the pricing strategies do not work because of the unique nature of rural markets. Innovative approaches are more likely to succeed than time-tested methods used in urban markets.

RURAL COMMUNICATIONS

Companies have to communicate with rural consumers to gain acceptability. In the previous section we saw that companies can charge high prices in rural areas if they are able to communicate value.

In urban markets, managers are familiar with using advertising and BTL methods in areas with high footfalls, such as malls and railway stations. Such crowded places do not exist in villages. Both BTL techniques and high powered advertising pose problems in villages because people have to be collected. Advertising does not work because channels are not available, while BTL methods require going to thousands of villages. This calls for a large workforce which can spread out and contact villages directly. To devise a strategy for rural communications, companies have to understand the challenges that they face in rural markets.

Challenges of Communication in Rural Markets

Urban methods of communications, or those used in developed countries, consist of spraying consumers with advertising and beautiful images in the manner of using insect sprays, and then waiting for customers to turn up to buy products. The sprays have to be changed periodically as consumers become immune to advertising. In rural markets, it is quite a different ball game. Companies are likely to face the following challenges while communicating with rural audiences:

- **Low literacy levels:** Rural areas suffer from low literacy. Customs and traditions rule, which makes adoption of new products and practices difficult. There is also a limited penetration of print media in rural markets. Companies, therefore, face difficulties in developing their communication mix.
- **Media reach and exposure:** Though media reach is improving over the years, it is still poor in many villages. In many media-dark villages, there is limited access to television, radio and print, and hence people have limited exposure. Suitable media vehicles just do not exist.
- **Diverse audiences:** Villages in India show diverse cultures, languages, varied customs and traditions and lifestyles. This makes one-size-fits-all strategy irrelevant. Companies, used to urban-oriented mass campaigns, find it difficult to tailor-make campaigns for every region.
- **A dearth of information:** There is a shortage of information in rural areas. Lack of good local content and reliable information providers add to the dearth of relevant information that villagers can use.
- **Scattered audiences:** Mass media finds it difficult to penetrate rural areas because audiences are scattered over large distances.
- **Lack of well-developed ICT infrastructure:** Internet penetration is limited because of lack of ICT infrastructure. This is changing as there is increasing use of mobile phones in rural markets.

Any rural communications strategy will work only if the listed problems are addressed. Rural communications strategy is described in the next section.

Rural Communication Strategy

Conventional advertising and communications work partially in villages because reaching customers is difficult. A rural communication strategy can only work if two conditions are fulfilled:

1. The rural customer will choose a channel only if it solves a problem for him or adds value in some way.
2. Campaigns must be supplemented by trials and direct experience, thus BTL methods are not only effective but add excitement around a brand in rural areas.

Rural communications thus has to be seen as a two-way dialogue. Thanks to technology, this is possible today, but calls for heavy investments.

Successful companies have created a 'demand-driven' model of communication so that users get important relevant information through the channel, which is also used to send brand messages. For instance, farmers use the channel to access agricultural research and extension services offered by government departments and companies. Companies also provide similar services and advertising piggybacks on such channels. Such a strategy must include the following:

1. Overcome illiteracy barriers by conveying ideas in an audio and visual form, that is, companies must develop and execute an interface between modern and traditional communication methods.
2. Illustrate new ideas and techniques, using multimedia or personal visits and BTL techniques.
3. Create audio-visual materials that are easily understood, communicated personally through mobile vans.
4. Develop and train a cadre of village communicators who can connect with rural customers.
5. Develop localized content resonant with local cultural norms and ethos.

The media mix has to cater to the needs for content, localization, gender and culture. For example, ads targeted to females often fail, as shown in Chapter 2. In rural areas, the decision maker is likely to be male even for things used by females. Targeting females in a male-dominated society may cause a backlash for a company.

Usually, companies use the same advertisements that they have designed for urban markets and use them for rural markets by changing the language. However, if local culture and sensitivities of rural consumers are not kept in mind, such ads may create a negative impact. The effectiveness of such ads will therefore be limited.

BTL campaigns introduce the 'touch and feel' element to products, and also two-way communication where people can understand what the product is capable of doing and clarify their doubts. A product demonstration is very effective to convince rural customers. Using local and popular form of entertainment such as *puppetry, nautanki, ragini, bhangra, pala, daskathia, danda nacha, quawalli* and dance shows increases brand awareness. Many companies like LG, Samsung, Philips, Bajaj, Usha and Crompton Greaves used some of the platforms and received positive response.

Advertisements touching emotions of rural folk could drive a quantum jump in sales if they are simple, direct and more social than of aspiration or individualistic. *Hyundai Ne Bana*

Di Jodi, for example, was a wedding themed offer for the marriage season which built on social occasions.

In this section, we describe the various channels available for rural areas and also redefine the rural communications mix in the light of methods available on the ground.

The Marketing Communications Mix

The basis of modern marketing is communication and companies use a mix of methods and channels to reach their target audience. This specific blend is known as the marketing communications mix. The components of the communications mix modified for rural areas are:

- **Advertising:** Advertising is defined as any paid form of non-personal presentation and promotion of ideas, goods, or services by an identified sponsor. Most advertising is done on mass media such as print, broadcast and outdoor, but since the reach of mass media in villages is limited, rural advertising is more effective if done through wall paintings, posters (see Photo 7.2) or a mobile announcer with a loudspeaker.

PHOTO 7.2
Rural advertising is done through wall posters.

Source: Photograph by Dinesh Kumar.

- **Personal selling:** Personal selling consists of a presentation by a company's sales force to make sales and build customer relationships. Personal selling includes sales presentations, mobile shows and incentive programmes. In rural areas where media reach is limited, personal selling becomes an effective tool of influencing customers. That is why, travelling salesmen and merchants are popular in these areas. Companies too have to organize sales melas through mobile vans and offer incentives for product trials and to reach out to rural customers.
- **Sales promotion:** Sales promotion is defined as short-term incentives to encourage the purchase or sale of a product or service. People in villages are more likely to respond to such schemes than urban consumers, since they have spare time. For a company venturing into a village for the first time, or to increase trials and sales, a sales promotion offering a discount, coupon or a savings scheme is an effective way to engage them. Point-of-purchase displays, premiums, discounts, coupons and demonstrations are popular in villages.
- **Public relations:** Public relations consist of obtaining favourable publicity, building up a good 'corporate image' and handling unfavourable rumours. In urban areas, it includes building good relations with the press, but in rural areas, it means cultivating local communities and opinion leaders who speak well of the company and its products. This is helpful in dealing with negative stories and rumours as well.
- **Direct marketing:** Direct marketing refers to communications with targeted individuals directly to obtain an immediate response. The use of mail, telephone, fax, e-mail, SMS and other tools help reach specific consumers. As smartphones and Internet spread in villages, these methods can now be used more frequently than in the past. Companies venturing into rural areas have to do direct marketing and make their presence felt at village melas and fairs.
- **Apps:** Another tool of communication that has emerged is through apps. If rural consumers can be persuaded to download and use apps on their smartphones, the company can capture data of the user and make targeted offers on them. However, the app must solve a specific problem of the rural consumer in order to be useful.
- **Social media:** Smartphones enable rural consumers to make profiles on social media sites and interact with others. This becomes an important tool for brands to communicate with them. Rural customers too will get on to social media as Internet availability improves in villages. These new channels such as apps and social media have encouraged more companies to move from mass media to targeted communication and one-on-one dialogue. Rural reach demands that companies use focused marketing programmes to build close relationships with customers. Villages can be seen as narrowly defined micro-markets, and the only way to reach them is through new technology.

Today, ICT helps companies not only to keep close track of customer needs and communicate with them (see Chapter 10), but also have information about consumers at the individual and household levels. The new technologies provide new avenues for reaching smaller villages with specific and tailored messages.

Based on what works in rural areas, we can define the rural communications mix as a combination of 10 components (Figure 7.2):

- Community Radio/AIR local channels
- Village newspapers/local editions of large newspapers

- TV/Regional language channels
- Rural sales force
- Wall paintings
- BTL techniques, vans and demonstrations
- Local theatre and performing arts
- Melas and fairs
- Mobile
- Internet

Some of the important components of the marketing mix are explained here.

FIGURE 7.2
The rural communications mix.

Community Radio/AIR local channels
Village newspaper/local editions
Internet
Mobile
Rural communications mix
TV-Language channels
Wall paintings
Rural Sales Force
Local performing arts
Vans

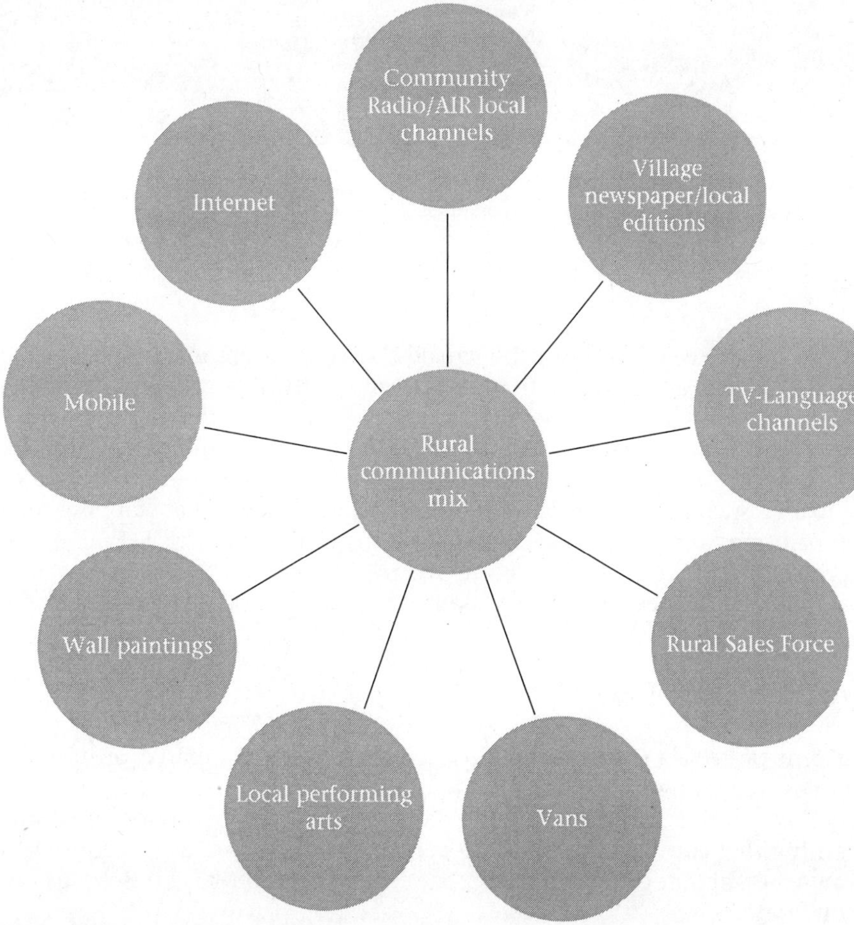

PHOTO 7.3
Wall paintings are a preferred way of rural advertising. Smaller advertisers simply write their message on a wall.

Source: Photograph by Dinesh Kumar.
Note: See the message on the wall on the left-hand side of the picture.

Wall Paintings

Wall paintings (Photo 7.3) reach even the smallest villages where mass media has not made inroads. These are cheap and serve as fixtures on walls with high visibility. Local painters do the job and villagers welcome these messages as the paint helps to protect walls. For consumer durables, direct marketing campaigns are effective. A dealer push combined with wall paintings and attractive schemes and exchange offers can give a lot of mileage in rural markets. Many durables companies such as Bajaj Auto, Hero Motocorp, LG and so on are tapping rural markets through wall paintings and have made significant inroads in rural market. Wall painting is the most widespread form of advertising and well accepted among rural consumers, and so are an effective promotional tool, because they constantly remind rural people about names and logos.

TV/Regional Language Channels

Over 75 per cent of India's urban households own a TV set, compared to just one-third of rural households, according to 2011 Census figures. The census also reveals that only 9.4 per cent of households in the country have either a laptop or a computer and only 3 per cent of them have an Internet connection. While 20 per cent of urban and 5 per cent of rural households now own a computer or laptop, just 1 per cent of rural Indian households own a computer with Internet.

However, measuring the audiences or identifying who was watching which channel has so far been a huge challenge. The problem is more acute in rural areas, where people receive

Mini Case Study 7.3

Ad Agencies and Rural India

While advertising in urban areas is done through advertising agencies, it is difficult for ads to reach villages, because agencies simply do not have the reach or understanding of rural markets. Rural agencies should have the capability to execute traditional media, such as wall paintings, and publicity through vans, rural melas and weekly haats. These are popular media of rural advertising used by the many media planners, but often difficult to execute because no agency has the number of people or facilities to execute large rural campaigns. Some advertising agencies try to overcome this by having their rural verticals to fulfil the requirements of companies but these are often not successful.

That is the reason that though rural India is stated to be the next big frontier, ad agencies are wary of serving the market.

The Economic Times (2013) reports that SMG's Xpanse unit has closed down and others such as Linterland and Anugrah Madison have seen downsizing. Ad agencies find it difficult to find traction in rural areas because of the cost. Returns are hard to come by, given the size and scale a good rural operation requires.

In 2013, OgilvyAction came up with a highly successful rural campaign—the Lifebuoy Roti reminder, which was a stencilled message about hand-washing that was imprinted on rotis sold at the Kumbh Mela. Shortly thereafter, OgilvyAction was merged with Geometry Global.

Geometry Global has 13 offices with 100 employees, 300 supervisors and 5,000 field operatives. To reach tens of thousands of villages, the agency needs satellite offices in small towns, technology for monitoring, vendor connections and the ability to manage thousands of feet-on-street. Ad agencies hardly have that kind of resources. Even if investments are made, there are few clients willing to pay the high cost of reach. A two plus reach, meaning that a consumer is connected twice a year, costs about ₹18–20 crores. There is also the problem of knowing how to run rural campaigns, which has entirely different rules and dynamics. The ones who are successful in rural communications are the local specialists with backward integration, that is, who have tie-ups with van owners, warehouses and local people.

Dialogue Factory is another exception. It is the experiential marketing division of GroupM South Asia. It won the highest number of awards at the 'Rural Marketing Forum 2014'. Dialogue Factory is known for some memorable campaigns:

- Most effective use of direct marketing—Colgate Kumbh Mela campaign
- Most effective use of direct marketing—Safe Water Network
- Social development campaign of the year—Google
- Social development campaign of the year—Safe Water Network
- Agriculture initiative of the year—GroupM Dialogue Factory

How can advertising agencies expand their reach to rural areas? How can they turn economically viable?

Sources for this Case Study:

Balakrishnan, R., and Amit Bapna. 2013. "Ad Agencies Running Away from Rural India." *The Economic Times,* 23 October.

EventFAQs. 2014. "GroupM Dialogue Factory bags at the World Brand Congress-Rural Marketing Forum 2014." 15 February. Available at: http://www.eventfaqs.com/news/ef-06637/groupm-rural-forum-1394609491078 (Accessed on 27 April 2017).

TV signals from antennas, cable or dish. Earlier, TV audience data was provided by Television Audience Measurement (TAM), a joint venture between Nielsen and Kantar Media. It enjoyed a monopoly for years, but its data was inadequate. It captured data through TAM 'people-meters', which were installed in selected homes. But the people meters—about 9,000 were installed—were not only inadequate but they were not installed in rural areas. Charges of corruption were also being levelled against the agency.

Since 2016, TV audiences are being tracked by Broadcast Audience Research Council (BARC), which is now the world's largest television audience measurement service. It is a joint venture with TAM and is now the only TV ratings body in India. BARC measures viewership habits of India's 153.5 million TV-owning households. Of these, 77.5 million are in urban India and 76 million are in rural India. Starting operations with 20,000 people-metres, the company hopes to expand it to 50,000 homes gradually.

Over 3,000 BARC Media Workstations are deployed in the industry, providing data and giving insights to subscribers. It covers 460 channels accounting for over 97 per cent of Indian TV viewership.

TV channels embed audio watermarks in their content prior to broadcast. These watermarks are not audible to the human ear, but can easily be detected and decoded using dedicated equipment, giving information about who has viewed it. The advantage of BARC is that it includes rural households in sample: in the first round, about 30 per cent of the sample comprises rural households, at an all-India level. Viewership of every individual channel can be reliably tracked, even if a programme is broadcast simultaneously on more than one channel.

A report by Tata Strategic Management Group Team published in *Business Standard* (2013) shows that more than 90 per cent of the districts in rural India have experienced positive growth in TV penetration. However, there has been significant variation observed in the growth pattern, with select districts contributing a disproportionate share to this growth. Based on their growth trend in the 2007 to 2010 period, we can classify rural India into four groups:

- **Diamonds:** High growth rate districts from FY07 to FY10. There are 79 diamond districts in India, which have seen high growth. These districts have contributed close to 28 per cent of India's rural growth and constitute 25 per cent of rural population.
- **Resilient:** Moderate to high growth every year between FY07 to FY10. There are 119 resilient districts, together contributing to 31 per cent of rural growth and 22 per cent of rural demand. The diamond and the resilient groups comprise 198 districts with 35 per cent of the rural population. More than 90 per cent of the growth in demand is accounted for by the diamond and resilient districts put together.
- **Emerging:** Districts that have picked up growth from FY08 onwards, showing growth rates of 12 per cent per annum. There were 173 emerging districts which generate 31 per cent of the demand, but contributed only to 20 per cent of rural growth. These districts demonstrated low growth in FY08 but picked up speed in subsequent years.
- **Laggards:** Districts which are growing at a low rate of less than 5 per cent per annum since 2008. There are 201 laggard districts which comprise one-third of the rural population, contribute to around 30 per cent of the demand but capture only 20 per cent of rural growth.

These districts do not follow the generally accepted wisdom of rich states and poor states. Most of the 198 diamond and resilient districts are seen to be clustered in multiple regions forming growth pockets. For example, northern Odisha accounts for a large part of the resilient rural growth in the country. Other such prominent clusters are found in the states of Andhra Pradesh, Madhya Pradesh and Rajasthan. Uttar Pradesh and Bihar do not seem to show consistent high growth and account for only nine such districts.

Mapping districts across various stages of income growth offers a powerful tool for predicting demand growth as incomes rise. Analysis of rural India indicates that companies cannot look at it as one homogenous market. Varied growth patterns suggest the need to have a tailored micro-market approach in order to address these districts.

BTL Techniques, Vans and Demonstrations

Mobile van campaign is one of the most effective communication channels for rural consumers, since it involves interpersonal communication with direct experience, creating greater visibility and deep reach. Van campaigns in rural areas pull crowds. Vehicles carrying advertisements always grab attention, thus helping better brand building, creating visibility and also encouraging trials. Rural service camps and creation of local brand ambassadors also serve as means of effective communication. Some companies put stalls at prominent locations in villages. Such stalls are not only cost effective but can also target high potential consumers, especially during festive seasons. Other crowd pullers in rural areas are rural games and tournaments. These are very popular; companies put stalls or banners at such avenues and sponsor the events. In many instances, they offer their products as prizes. Service camps are another effective brand building activity. Since word-of-mouth recommendations are very popular in rural areas, and people in the villages consult their friends, relatives or neighbours before buying any durable product, keeping the existing customers happy through service camps leads to more referrals and sales.

Village Newspaper or Local Editions of Large Newspapers

A look at mass circulated newspapers shows that villages are largely invisible to mainstream media. Apart from news of a farmer suicide or an accident, villages find very little coverage on nationally circulated newspapers. Some regional language newspapers or regional editions of larger newspapers are popular in towns but have very little reach in villages.

Among the exceptions is *Eenadu*, published in Telugu. It regularly carries tips on agriculture and animal husbandry and encourages reader participation by publishing their political opinions and grievances. Local editions of *Rajasthan Patrika* and *Dainik Bhaskar* cover local concerns.

There are also grassroots papers written and published by and for locals (see Chapter 2). A prominent example is *Khabar Lahariya*, or News Waves, a weekly newspaper based in Chitrakoot, one of the poorest districts in central India. Written in Bundeli, the local language, the paper's all-female staff has forged a reputation for investigative journalism. It has a deep support from villagers. The paper was founded in 2002 by Nirantar, a voluntary non-profit organization. Village newspapers such as *Khabar Lahariya* and *Sakshi* try to fill the rural communication gap.

An article in Knowledge@Wharton (2010) says that local papers are a hit with readers in India because of their connection to local issues. The village newspaper typically has a circulation of less than 10,000 copies and is sold at ₹1–3 per copy. Advertising is also limited. This poses great challenges of survival. If other problems such as low literacy rate and poor infrastructure are added, selling and delivering a village newspaper is not an easy task. These newspapers does not represent viable advertising options for rural marketing companies either.

Community Radio or AIR Local Channels

Community radio is a type of radio service that caters to the interests of a certain area, broadcasting content that is popular to a local audience which is often overlooked by commercial or mass media broadcasters. Globally, community radios have proliferated and provide people living in remote or isolated areas access to information. In India, the government restricts its spread.

In other parts of the world, modern-day community radio stations serve listeners by offering a variety of content that is not provided by larger commercial radio stations. Such stations carry local area news and information programmes, particularly useful for farming communities that are poorly served by other media channels. Community radio stations provide specialized content that is immediately relevant to villagers. In India, community village radio could not develop properly as government guidelines permit only NGOs and civil society organizations to own and operate community radio stations. Most community stations in India are thus run by NGOs or educational institutions and have little presence in rural areas.

India Today (2007) reports about how low-power community radio stations can help spread awareness about self-help projects, building toilets near homes, using cow dung instead of wood for cooking purposes and the perils of child marriages. In 2003, village Budhikote, 100 km from Bangalore, was facing a drought. Despite protests by people and promises from the authorities, nothing happened. Finally, Nagaraj, a reporter for *Namma Dhwani*, a community radio, broadcast the grievances of the people, which helped resolve the problem. There are several examples where village radio has helped solve local problems:

- At Bhanaj village, near Rishikesh, community radio helped in exposing the corruption in local governance.
- In Gujarat's Kutch, it addressed gender issues and empowered women who were victims of domestic violence.
- In Budhikote near Bangalore, it helped fix broken pipes and restore water supply in drought-hit areas.
- In Nizamabad district of Andhra Pradesh, it helped bridge the caste divide between Dalits and non-Dalits.
- In Palamau district of Jharkhand, it has helped stop pilferage in mid-day meals for children.

Elementary, low-cost radio stations with limited coverage could ideally serve village interests well. Village radio is a forum on which ordinary people can discuss issues concerning their lives, such as health and civic matters, share farming tips and income generation ideas and improve education (see Mini Case Study 7.4).

Pavarala and Malik (2007) write that though village radio has the potential to give voice to rural areas and can help in imparting information and empowering them, they have not been allowed to develop in India. Government policy restricts issue of community radio licenses. In December 2002, the Government of India approved a policy for the grant of licenses for setting up of community radio stations. The policy states that individuals cannot set up

Mini Case Study 7.4

Village Radio Initiatives in India

Though village community radio is an effective tool for rural marketing, government policy has so far prevented such stations to come up. The stories of some of these radio initiatives are described in this exhibit.

Hewal Vani station in Bihar: A small station was set up by Raghav Mahto in his electronics repair shop at Mansoorpur in Vaishali district of Bihar in 2001. He started broadcasting audio by fixing a transmitter on a pole with an investment of about ₹50, playing Bollywood and Bhojpuri songs and other chatter. One day, a child went missing in the village and Mahto broadcast it on his radio and helped find the child. Mahto's Radio Raghav FM Mansoorpur1, showed what an ordinary citizen with an idea and dedication could do for the community. However, it was shut down by the authorities in 2006, since individuals are not eligible for licence under the new policy.

Heval Vani station in Uttarakhand: Hewal Vani Samudayik Radio has been started in the hills of Chamba, Uttarakhand, by a group of youngsters. The programmes usually deal with local problems such as health, superstition, education and civic issues and creating transparency in local governance. Local people from in and around the village visit the station every day to be a part of some interactive programme or the other. Reporters are drawn from villages and broadcast in the local dialect.

Sangham Radio in Andhra Pradesh: Sangham Radio is a unique community radio experiment run by two Dalit women in Medak district of Andhra Pradesh. It educates villagers on biodiversity, crop patterns, nutrition, health, culture, and so on. Run by Deccan Development Society (DDS), an NGO, it aims to help village communities and give the marginalized people a voice and disseminating knowledge about issues affecting them. Villagers tune in to this radio station to hear their voices, concerns, songs and solutions to everyday problems. The primary audience is rural women from the marginalized groups and other rural people. It broadcasts daily between 8 PM to 9.30 PM

Dhimsa FM radio in Odisha: Established by a local NGO, South Orissa Voluntary Action (SOVA), in Chhapar village in Koraput district, Dhimsa Radio focuses on rural development issues while offering a platform to the villagers to voice their concerns. The station with one studio and a 50-watt FM transmitter covers a radius of 12 km and broadcasts programmes on a range of social issues. The station covers problems such as women's health issues, practice of child marriage and sanitation among others, reports *Asian Age* (2016).

Chala Ho Gaon Mein, Jharkhand: Community radio programme 'Chala Ho Gaon Mein' was initiated by an NGO, Alternative for India Development, in the regions of Palamau, Garhwa and Latehar districts of Jharkhand. The programme was first aired on 5 August 2001 from AIR Daltonganj and had completed 500 episodes by 2007. It encourages participation of grassroots communities and gives voice to local governance and social issues. Nearly 48,000 people have registered through various field programmes and nearly 32,000 local artists have participated in it. The programme provides a wide outreach of more than 7 million populations across the three districts, Palamau, Garhwa and Latehar, of Jharkhand and its neighbouring states of Uttar Pradesh, Bihar and Chhattisgarh.

Namma Dhwani in Karnataka: Namma Dhwani, which means Our Voices, India's first cable community radio station, started operating from 2002 in Budikote, Karnataka. It is today a Community Multimedia Centre, with radio, video and satellite facilities. Its signature programme is *Pathra Prabhanda*, in which it answers letters from the listeners, gives an insight into people's lives and day to day issues. An impact study of the radio station by Singh et al. (2010) found that dimensions such as leadership, family system, savings, education, health and sanitation have brought about significant changes in the life of the people in Budikote. They write that community radio can therefore play a catalytic role in changing the life of rural people.

Kumaon Vani: Kumaon Vani was launched by TERI in 2010. It promotes sustainable development among the local farming community. The radio station is attached to TERI's knowledge centre TRISHA (TERI's Research Initiative in Supi for Himalayan Advancement) that works with the local farming community to improve their livelihoods through sustainable agricultural practices. Located at an altitude of more than 2,286 m, Kumaon Vani reaches out to nearly 500 villages in Nainital, Bhimtal, Almora, Ranikhet, Kausani, Champawat, Devidhura, Pithoragarh, Betalghat, Sheetlakhet, Kausani, Gwaldham and Bagheshwar.

How can village radio serve local communities in India?

Sources for this Case Study:

Web Resources

Chala Ho Gaon Mein website: http://aidindia.com/radio/jhar_chala_ho.php

"Kumaon Vani—Community Radio Station." Available at TERI website: http://www.teriin.org/index.php?option=com_ongoing&task=about_project&pcode=2005FT01

"Sangam Radio." Available at: http://ddsindia.com/dds_news/SanghamRadio.htm

See the page on Hevalvani Samudayik Radio at: http://www.communityvoices.in/directory/community-media-profile/1411/

South Orissa Voluntary Action (SOVA) website: http://www.sovakoraput.org/

Other Sources

Asian Age. 2016. "In Orissa, FM Radio Changes Life of Tribals in Maoist-hit Pocket." 11 July.

India Together. 2010. "Sangham Radio Making Waves." 16 May. Available at: http://indiatogether.org/sangham-media (Accessed on 27 April 2017).

Singh, B.K., Rakesh Kumar, V.P. Yadav, Dan Singh and H.L. Singh. 2010. "Social Impact of Community Radio in Karnataka." *Indian Research Journal of Extension Education* 10 (2), May: 10–14.

community stations and only community-based organizations and educational institutes can be given such licenses. As a result, only educational institutes and NGOs have been able to set up community radios. Only a few of them reach rural areas. Another restriction is that such stations cannot broadcast news, so village radio cannot broadcast information on local happenings. These and other restrictions have succeeded in strangling village community radio in India. Though NGOs are running such stations in some villages, it cannot be denied that they would be pushing their own interests through such initiatives. Similarly, educational institutes are running their radio stations as a means of their advertising. Nor are these existing community radios in India as vibrant and informative as one would expect them to be.

Melas and Fairs

Instead of media campaigns, rural markets are more influenced by BTL techniques at the village level and at events such as Kumbh Mela, Onam, Rathyatra, Baliyatra and Dhanuyatra. Bloomberg (2013) reports that outdoor marketing campaigns at events like the Kumbh are becoming very popular with a large number of companies. Fairs and melas represent rural marketing opportunities for companies. People come to these gatherings in huge numbers. The biggest such gathering is the Kumbh Mela, described as the world's largest gathering. The Maha Kumbh in 2013 drew some 100 million people to Ganges in Allahabad. It was a once-in-a-decade chance for companies to reach consumers who are otherwise hard to reach. Reaching all of 100 million people from rural areas in one place was a dream for advertisers. The 2013 Maha Kumbh saw companies such as Colgate, Vodafone, Dabur and HUL participating and reaching the mass of the consumers directly.

The Kumbh is a huge draw and is an opportunity for brands, but smaller melas held all over the country, which gather some 10,000 to 20,000 people per day, are useful for experiential marketing and are therefore more marketing friendly.

Melas are important in rural marketing because they offer access to a mass of rural people who are otherwise diverse and hard to reach. Mass media does not reach many villages and is an expensive option in rural marketing. Companies find it much more cost-effective to participate in 200 melas rather than reach 50,000 villages individually (Table 7.2). Melas happen mostly at the end of the harvest season, when farmers are free and have money in their pockets. On these occasions, farmers are inclined to indulge and buy new things.

TABLE 7.2
Indicative list of fairs and festivals of India.

January	February	March
Bikaner Festival, Rajasthan	**Khajuraho Dance Festival,** Bundelkhand, Madhya Pradesh	**Chapchar Kut,** Mizoram
Guru Gobind Singh's Birthday	**Deccan Festival,** Hyderabad, Andhra Pradesh	**Elephant Festival,** Jaipur, Rajasthan
Float Festival, Madurai, Tamil Nadu	**Desert Festival,** Jaisalmer, Rajasthan	**Gudi Padwa or Ugadi,** Maharashtra, Andhra Pradesh & Karnataka
Kerala Village Fair, Kovalam, Kerala	**Eid-Milad-ul-Nabi**	**Holi**
Lohri, Punjab and Delhi	**Elephanta Festival,** Mumbai	**Hoysala Mahotsava,** Belur-Halebid, Karnataka
Makar Sankranti, Maharashtra, Karnataka, Bihar, West Bengal and Andhra Pradesh	**Goa Carnival,** Goa	**International Flower Festival,** Sikkim
Mamallapuram Dance Festival, Mamallapuram, Tamil Nadu	**Mahashivratri**	**Mewar Festival,** Udaipur, Rajasthan
Modhera Dance Festival, Sun Temple Modhera, Gujarat	**Nishagandhi Dance Festival,** Thiruvananthapuram, Kerala	**Natyanjali Festival,** Chidambaram, Tamil Nadu
Nagaur Cattle Fair, Rajasthan	**Rose Festival,** Chandigarh	**Ellora Festival,** Maharashtra
National Kite Festival, Ahmedabad, Gujarat	**Surajkund Crafts Mela,** Haryana	
Pattadakkal Dance Festival, Karnataka	**Taj Mahotsav,** Agra, Uttar Pradesh	
Pongal, Tamil Nadu, Andhra Pradesh	**Thai Pusam,** Tamil Nadu	

(Table 7.2 Contd.)

(Table 7.2 Contd.)

January	February	March
Republic Day	**Garden Festival,** Delhi	
Vasant Panchami/ Saraswati Puja, North India and West Bengal	**International Yoga Week,** Rishikesh, Uttarakhand	
April	**May**	**June**
Baisakhi, Punjab	**Ganga Dussehra,** North India	**Hemis Festival,** Ladakh, Jammu & Kashmir
Bihu, Assam		**Rath Yatra,** Odisha
Good Friday & Easter		**Sindhu Darshan Festival,** Leh, Ladakh, Jammu & Kashmir
MahavirJayanthi		**Urs,** Ajmer, Rajasthan
Ramnavami		
Vishu, Kerala		
Budh Purnima		
Pooram, Thrissur, Kerala		
July	**August**	**September**
Ashadi Ekadashi, Pandharpur	**Id-ul-Fittr**	**Ganesh Chaturthi,** Maharashtra, Tamil Nadu, Andhra Pradesh, Kerala
International Mango Festival, Delhi	**Independence Day**	**Tarnetar Mela,** Saurasthra, Gujarat
Champakkulam Boat Race, Kerala	**Janamashtami**	**Pune Festival,** Maharashtra
Guru Purnima	**Nehru Trophy Boat Race,** Kerala	
Nag Panchami, West Bengal, Maharashtra and South India	**Onam,** Kerala	
	Raksha Bandhan, North India	
	Teej, Rajasthan, Haryana and Punjab	
October	**November**	**December**
Durga Puja, West Bengal	**Hampi Festival,** Karnataka	**Kartik Ekadashi**
Dussehra	**Ka Pomblang Nongkrem,** Shillong, Meghalaya	**Konark Dance Festival,** Odisha
Diwali	**Lucknow Festival,** Uttar Pradesh	**Chennai Dance & Music Festival,** Tamil Nadu
Id-ul-Zuha (Bakr-Id)	**Muharram**	**Christmas**

(Table 7.2 Contd.)

(Table 7.2 Contd.)

October	November	December
Marwar Festival, Jodhpur, Rajasthan	**Pushkar Fair,** Rajasthan	**Kurushetra Festival,** Haryana
Navaratri	**Sonepur Mela,** Bihar	**Island Tourism Festival** in Port Blair, Andaman & Nicobar Islands
Rajgir Dance Festival, Bihar	**Gurpurab,** Punjab	**Poush Mela** in Shantiniketan, Bengal
		Gangasagar Mela, Bengal
		Vishnupur Mela, Bengal

The Economic Times (2015) reports that some melas, like the Kumbh, have religious objectives, but once the *darshan* (visiting and paying respect to the holy deity) or the *snaan* (holy bath) is done, people indulge in shopping. For rural families, melas are annual or six-monthly outings. Even women participate in large numbers; during melas and fairs, the usual social sanctions that keep women cloistered do not apply strictly. Thus, companies have the rare opportunity to reach out to women. An innovative way of tapping into mela crowds is through bus stands with audio content, as described in Mini Case Study 7.5.

Mini Case Study 7.5

AudioWala Bus Stations in Maharashtra

Vritti I-Media has developed a unique idea for rural communications—audio ads at bus stations between announcements. Along with BTL techniques, it enables to reach thousands of bus travellers who have to listen to the ads as they wait for bus announcements. It has tied up with the Maharashtra State Road Transport Corporation for audio advertisements at various district bus terminals. The audio advertisements are played along with the bus arrival/departure announcements at State Transport bus stations. Its website says that it has covered 80 bus stations across Maharashtra.

Called AudioWala Station, the ads are run through the announcement speakers at the bus stations at intervals between the arrival/departure announcements. The radio helps to inform and entertain the waiting people at the bus station, creating awareness about products and brands in rural areas. Bus stations, being the most frequented points in rural areas, have many people waiting for buses as services are poor. Since the waiting travellers are usually interested in bus arrival or departure announcements, the advertisements get an assured audience. Advertisements are aired for 16 hours every day, from 6 AM to night 10 PM daily. The frequency of advertisement broadcast can be set from an interval of 5 minutes to 60 minutes. Some of the campaigns conducted on AudioWala bus stations are:

Pidilite: Pidilite ran a campaign to tap the potential rural markets to promote its two brands—Fevi kwik and m-seal. The objective was to position both products as household essentials and increase recognition. It wanted to educate rural consumers about the easy and quick use of these products. The rural activation campaign was executed in Kolhapur, Sangli and Aurangabad areas. The products were displayed and sold at bus stations.

Parle: During the Ganesh festival season, Parle used the bus stations to tap travellers and promote a special campaign of free tea on purchase of Parle Marie biscuits. The travellers were targeted via jingles and teasers released through the announcement system, informing them about the free tea offer by visiting the nearest canteen.

Honda: Honda used the Diwali time for running a campaign for its 2-wheelers—Honda Dream Neo and Honda Dream Yuga—which were displayed at bus stations of Karnataka. The products were displayed and test rides were provided through a rural hub at bus stations. Audio messages were played between the announcements at 31 state bus stations through its computerized PA system, which encouraged people to see and engage with the brand.

Good Knight: Good Knight ran a campaign during the 'Pandharpur Aashadi Eakadasi', the biggest *yatra* of Maharashtra. It was conducted in July, the mosquito breeding season. Some 15–20 lakhs devotees visited the festival. Devotees travelling to Pandharpur were guided about the bus schedules from over 30 bus stations across the state. They were welcomed at Pandharpur through public announcement systems accompanied by jingles about Good Knight Fast Card. This audio campaign started 20 days before the main Ashadi Ekadashi to build momentum. Temporary hoarding and boards with information showing important locations and their directions, along with the Good Knight Fast Card branding, were erected around the town. All the boards, booklets, volunteer caps, t-shirts, water-cups and LED TVs were branded with Good Knight Fast Card and their tag line *Phatak se Furr*.

Can such methods catch on in villages? What innovative methods can you think of?

Sources for this Case Study:

Web Resources

See the video on Audiowala Bus Stop-Success Story-Parle: https://www.youtube.com/watch?v=U1DOeuFjW_Y

See the video on Fastcard activation Godrej Padharpur: https://www.youtube.com/watch?v=mcgdERJEVuQ

See JK Cement in Khatushaym: https://www.youtube.com/watch?v=i4lnmlYlPhQ

See the video on Audio Wala Bus Stop Campaign for Goodknight (by Vritti Media). Available at http://www.vrittiimedia.com/audio-network/ (Accessed on 27 April 2017).

To be successful at direct marketing at melas, companies have to use the following strategies:

- **Be local:** Brands use melas to provide demos and to gain visibility. It is experiential marketing at its best. For example, a company offers cooling hair oil on a customer's hand to smell it and feel its effect on the scalp. Such demos very often result in direct sales. The biggest successes at melas are local brands such as Rahat Rooh, Paanch Bhai soap or Himgange, who use local traders to gain popularity with consumers.
- **Be big:** The company presence has to appear ubiquitous. For instance, at the Kumbh Mela in 2001, Lifebuoy had 50 handwash stations, while Fair & Lovely was being sold by 500 salesmen in the style of vendors at railway stations. The idea is that stalls are not put up as an obligatory participation for mere presence, but brands have to think big and make their presence felt.
- **Be inventive:** An important need is to be innovative because old ideas do not work. Outdated technology like videos will be spurned by the consumer. For instance, at the Maha Pushkaram, a huge fair held at Rajahmundry in Andhra Pradesh, HUL distributed

3,000 special cups across 250 tea stalls to promote its tea brand, 3 Roses. The brand logo and message appeared on the cup when it was filled with hot beverage, which was a novelty for the rural audience. The brand message was thus conveyed during the moment of truth of consumption of the beverage, transforming an ordinary moment into a magical one. The company claimed a steep rise in sales for 3 Roses after the festival. Similarly, Vodafone helped visitors fight off cold at the Maha Kumbh by supplying them with branded headphones that served as ear muffs. Visitors could listen to pre-recorded *bhajans* (devotional songs) and commercial messaging while protecting their ears. Such innovative ideas are likely to be a hit with rural consumers. Colgate tied up with Airtel, using location-based targeting to give the network's subscribers an automated call from instantly identifiable radio personality, Amin Sayani (see Mini Case Study 7.6). The more inventive a brand, the more will it find resonance with visitors.

- **Be useful:** Merely selling or branding does not get consumer attention; a brand has to be useful to the people. For example, in 2003, at the Maha Pushkaram, Brooke Bond worked with the organizers to provide information at railway stations and bus stops to help visitors. People were greeted with welcome notices and pamphlets with maps of the area together with emergency contact numbers. The promotion extended to the bathing ghats where hot cups of tea were provided immediately after the holy bath. At the Maha Kumbh 2013, Dabur distributed Odomos in sachets to encourage trials. Similarly, at the Kumbh Mela in Nashik, the company gave away samples of Hajmola

Mini Case Study 7.6

Effective Use of Mobiles: Colgate at the Kumbh Mela

Colgate wanted to increase toothpaste penetration in rural India by educating consumers about oral hygiene and the benefits of using toothpaste regularly. It reached out to consumers at the Maha Kumbh Mela, using mobile and location-based technologies.

Since most of the pilgrims were from areas with low literary rates, it used voice-based communications via a mobile phone. The method was to use location-based targeting. A virtual circle around the pilgrimage site was created by tagging three nearby cellular towers. Colgate partnered with Airtel: a call was made to the cell phone the moment a visitor entered within 3–5 km radius of Maha Kumbh Mela area. This way, any local Airtel subscriber or those roaming on Airtel, were targeted the moment they entered this virtual circle around Maha Kumbh Mela. When pilgrims entered this circle, their phones received a call from Amin Sayani, a legendary Indian radio personality, telling them to visit the Colgate booth for free samples, a chance to win prizes and entertainment. It was the first campaign of its kind in India. It is reported that foot traffic to the Colgate booth increased by over 300 per cent as compared to the pre-promotion period, attracting over 700,000 visitors.

How can such similar campaigns help penetration in rural markets?

Sources for this Case Study:

Web Resources

"How Colgate Turned the Maha Kumbh Mela into the Maha Tech Mela." Available at: http://www.mma-global.com/case-study-hub/case_studies/view/27198

Mobile Marketing Association (MMA) website: http://www.mmaglobal.com/case-study-hub/case_studies/view/27198

at large eateries. Sometimes branding fails—an attempt to release branded *diyas* (an oil lamp made of clay) was met with protests and worked against the brand. But as long as the promotion is useful to consumers, it works.

Internet and Mobiles

The use of the Internet and mobiles is slowly but surely increasing in rural areas. The spread of cheap smartphones has also given a boost to rural mobile Internet users, which grew by 93 per cent between December 2014–December 2015, according to Internet and Mobile Association of India (IAMAI) figures (Figure 7.3). However, only 9 per cent of the hinterland has access to the technology, according to the report released jointly by IAMAI and IMRB.

In comparison, 53 per cent of urban areas had mobile Internet connectivity and grew at 71 per cent during the same period, thereby highlighting the urban–rural divide in the country. But IAMAI data shows that rural India is growing fast. Mobile Internet users in rural India grew from 68 million in June 2015 to 109 million in June 2016, signifying a 60 per cent growth in users.

Among rural users, on the other hand, 52 per cent said their primary reason for accessing the Internet was entertainment. Communication and social networking stood at 37 per cent and 39 per cent, respectively.

Companies can use this growing medium effectively to reach rural consumers. The opening case of KKT shows how phones are used not only to reach consumers but also to gather data about them. Colgate tied up with Airtel in a similar way; this innovative use of phones in rural melas is described in Mini Case Study 7.6.

FIGURE 7.3

Mobile Internet users in rural areas are steadily increasing.

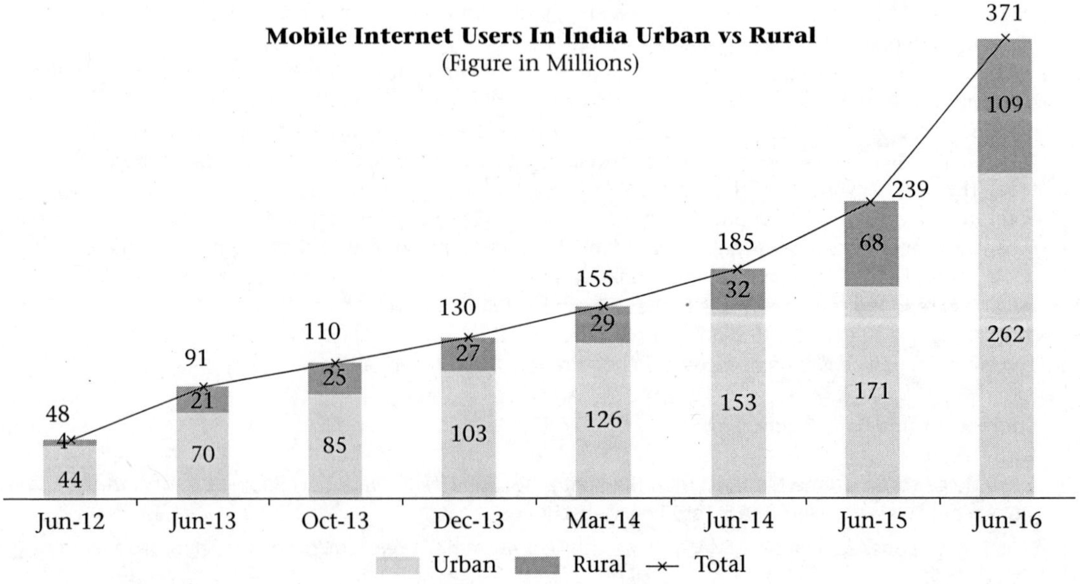

Source: IAMAI (2016).

Rural Communication Strategy

By understanding the rural reach of various media, companies can develop their communications mix. Media provides a spillover effect, but has to be used judiciously by identifying newspapers and radio stations that actually reach rural areas. Mass media is used for branding as some consumers do get to see TV ads or read newspapers. More importantly, companies have to invest in a range of BTL activities. That is why, direct demonstration and participation in melas becomes necessary. A number of companies have successfully used BTL activities in rural areas.

Village newspapers and community radios help in propagating advertising messages. Large newspapers usually have their local editions targeting small towns but find difficulty in reaching villages. Experiential marketing through vans encourage trials among rural consumers.

As the reach of TV is increasing, companies use the medium for brand building and quick reach. A range of local channels ensure that messages can reach interiors. Data from BARC will facilitate targeting in rural areas. With the increase in mobiles and Internet, companies are increasingly using newer technologies and apps.

SUMMARY

Pricing and communications are important tools of marketing strategy. This chapter discusses how they are used in rural marketing.

The economic models of price, based on costs, value, demand and competition, often fails in rural marketing because companies have to work around low purchasing power, availability of local brands that are priced cheaply and price points that are convenient for customers. Some of the pricing methods commonly used are: cost-based pricing, value-based pricing, demand-based pricing and competition-based pricing. However, rural markets are complicated. While there is a large landscape of poverty, there are segments that are prosperous. That is why, innovative approaches are more likely to succeed than time-tested methods used in urban markets.

Communication in rural markets is also fraught with problems. Among the many challenges faced by companies are low literacy levels, limited media reach and exposure, diverse and scattered audiences and lack of information and ICT infrastructure. Successful companies have created a 'demand-driven' model of communication so that users get important relevant information through the channel, which is also used to send brand messages. Traditional communications mix consists of using advertising, personal selling, sales promotion and public relations. Rural communications mix consists of community radio/AIR local channels, village newspapers/local editions of large newspapers, regional language TV channels, rural sales force, wall paintings, vans and demonstrations, BTL techniques, local theatre and performing arts, melas and fairs, mobiles and Internet.

One-third of the rural homes owns a TV, according to 2011 Census figures. More than 90 per cent of the districts in rural India have experienced positive growth in TV penetration, but only certain districts contribute a major share to this growth. Mobile van campaign is one of the most effective communication channels for rural consumers, since it involves interpersonal communication with direct experience. Local editions of large newspapers and some regional language newspapers are popular in urban areas but have very little reach in villages. Community radio can be very useful in rural areas. These have proliferated in developed countries to provide cut-off people access to information. In India, the government has restricted its spread. By understanding the rural reach of various media, companies can develop their communications mix.

CONCLUSION

Pricing and communications are two powerful tools in the marketing arsenal. For rural markets, both have to be used innovatively as the usual urban-oriented strategies do not work. The more innovative the approach, the more will be the response from rural consumers. This chapter describes some innovative methods used by companies that have worked well. What the chapter stresses is that business-as-usual approach hardly works in markets where the challenges are quite different than the ones in villages.

To be successful, specific strategies have to be worked out for specific products and specific markets. It is important to understand the rural mind to discover what would work and what would not.

KEY TERMS

Community radio: A radio service that caters to the interests of a certain area, broadcasting content that is popular to a local audience which may often be overlooked by commercial or mass media broadcasters.

Competition-based pricing: A pricing method in which the seller uses prices of similar and competing products as a benchmark of setting prices.

Cost-based pricing: A pricing method in which a fixed sum or a percentage is added to the total cost of producing and selling a product to arrive at its selling price.

Demand-based pricing: Demand-based pricing considers supply and demand curves and says that if prices are low, demand will be high and vice versa.

Value-based pricing: A pricing method in which price is set on the basis of the value perceived by the customer in buying and using a product.

Market skimming: A new product pricing strategy in which prices are kept deliberately high as there are no competitors, for which customers have to pay the high price.

Market penetration: A new product pricing strategy in which prices are deliberately kept low initially to attract customers to encourage trials and forming habits.

CONCEPT REVIEW QUESTIONS

1. What are the various pricing methods that are used by firms? Explain them.
2. Compare pricing strategies and show their advantages and disadvantages.
3. Why is it said that rural markets are imperfect and therefore traditional pricing methods cannot be applied there?
4. What is competition-based pricing? How should a company venturing into a village for the first time price its products with respect to the competition? Why?
5. What are the challenges that are faced by companies when they market in rural areas? How can they be overcome these challenges?
6. What elements will there be in the rural communications mix? Explain each element.

7. Discuss the strategy of using melas and fairs for marketing activities. Why are they used in rural marketing?
8. Since the competition faced by brands in rural areas is from fake or local brands, how can a communication plan educate village folk about them?
9. Comment upon ways of advertising used in villages. How effective are they?
10. How can social media be used for rural marketing? How can rural folk be engaged by brands through this medium?

CRITICAL THINKING QUESTIONS

1. Why is it necessary that companies venturing in rural markets should think of innovative methods of pricing and communications? Why can't traditional strategies be used in rural areas?
2. Why is it said that "for rural pricing, most products will have to be treated as new products?" What pricing policies should companies follow when placing products in rural markets? What should be the main consideration in rural pricing?
3. While there are some reports that say that rural India is scaling up, the socio-economic census points to the fact that most households are living in or are on the verge of poverty. How can companies reconcile these two opposing facts? How should they approach the task of rural pricing?
4. Community radio has not been allowed to function and grow in villages. Do you think that community radio helps rural areas and consequently rural marketing? Why do you think the government restricts it? How can these problems be overcome?

PROJECTS AND ASSIGNMENTS

1. Take a company and study its rural communications mix. Which elements are used more commonly by them? Which ones are more effective than others?
2. Visit a local mela or fair in your area. Document the marketing activities being done there. Critically assess whether these activities are useful or not. What suggestions can you give?
3. Take a look at the local edition of a large newspaper or a rural newspaper. Do they address local issues, and how? Are they able to attract enough advertising or not? Do you think that local newspapers have a role to play in rural marketing?
4. Visit some villages and click pictures of local ways of advertising and BTL methods. Explain each of them and comment how effective it is. Make a presentation and show it to the class.

WEB RESOURCES

Aspen Institute website: http://www.aspeninstitute.org/policy-work/communications-society/programs-topic/communications-policy/india/cs-joint-roundtable-co

IAMAI (2016). Available at: http://www.tele.net.in/news/item/18695-mobile-internet-user-base-to-reach-371-million-by-june-2016-says-iamai?format=pdf (Accessed on 13 April 2017).

REFERENCES

Bloomberg. 2013. "Coke, Unilever, Colgate-Palmolive Seize India's Biggest Marketing Opportunity." 8 March. Available at: http://www.bloomberg.com/news/articles/2013-03-07/coke-unilever-colgate-palmolive-seize-indias-biggest-marketing-opportunity (Accessed on 27 April 2017).

Business Standard. 2013. "Growth Markets in Rural India, Tata Strategic Management Group Team." 4 February.

Kohli-Khandekar, Vanita. 2016. "BARC Measures Habits of 153.5 mn TV Households but It's Not a Census: Partho Dasgupta." *Business Standard*, 22 April. *India Today*. 2007. "Message of the Medium." 5 March. Available at: http://indiatoday.intoday.in/story/community-radio-is-proving-out-to-be-the-boon-for-the-villagers/1/156079.html (Accessed on 25 April 2017).

Knowledge@Wharton. 2010. "Medium for the Masses: How India's Local Newspapers Are Winning Rural Readers." 14 January. Available at: http://knowledge.wharton.upenn.edu/article/medium-for-the-masses-how-indias-local-newspapers-are-winning-rural-readers/ (Accessed on 27 April 2017).

Pavarala, Vinod, and Kanchan K. Malik. 2007. *Other Voices: The Struggle for Community Radio in India*. New Delhi: SAGE Publications.

The Economic Times. 2015. "Here's How Marketers are Putting a Method to the 'Mela' Madness." *Brand Equity*, 26 August.

Closing Case
Pricing and Promotion of Telecom Services in Villages

Telecom service providers realize that rural markets hold the potential for growth as urban markets are reaching saturation points. This case study studies pricing and promotion strategies followed by them in rural markets.

The telecom industry has a unique opportunity in rural areas. It is just not the means to provide data and connectivity but much more. A study of villagers' problems by the authors shows that telecom services can help in many ways:

- **Education:** Rural schools typically lack teachers and facilities. Mobiles can fulfil education needs through lessons and educational multimedia.
- **Entertainment:** Young people use mobiles to access entertainment, which can also be used for peer-to-peer distribution.
- **Farm and agriculture:** Villagers need agricultural and weather information which affects their livelihoods, and this is provided by telecom services.
- **Health care services:** Remote villages have few or no medical services. Mobiles can bridge the gap and bring medical advice from qualified doctors to villagers.
- **Micro-payments:** Micro-payments help mobile ordering and help isolated small-scale entrepreneurs from villages.
- **Rural governance:** Mobile apps will allow access to the rural population to access government services and citizen data.

PHOTO 7.4

A village version of radio cab: On dirt tracks where no buses ply, auto owners write their numbers so that villagers can call them when required.

Source: Photograph by Dinesh Kumar.

- **Transportation:** Finding transport is a major problem in villages. Mobiles can help people find and order vehicles on demand (see Photo 7.4).

Helping solve these basic rural needs is possible for the telecom industry, which needs to communicate these benefits in their rural campaigns. Indirectly, initiatives in development activities help in developing rural markets.

In terms of promotion efforts, mass media campaigns continue to hold importance as TV and newspaper penetration in villages is rising. Last mile strategies like direct contact and participating in local fairs are needed to reach out to the sparsely distributed rural population.

Advertising campaigns have to be reworked for rural areas. Premium lifestyle images would not work, but rural issues have to be highlighted. Idea Cellular used Abhishek Bachchan for two successful campaigns. The campaign, *What an Idea Sirji!* expressed social concerns. It showed the government using mobile service to gather public opinion and support, while taking decisions impacting people's lives, a world without caste, removing disability to communicate and education for all.

Rural telecom operators have to appeal to the actualities of rural lifestyles to be successful, while not losing their urban focus. Airtel's *Har Ek Friend Zaroori Hota Hai* focused on the youth, and while it had an urban focus, the message was relevant to rural youth as well. Reliance Jio used Prime Minister Modi's picture in its ads, which was immediately recognizable for both urban and rural consumers.

Services in local dialects are important to tap rural markets. In Vietnam, the Viettel Tomato Village Plan has been present in 40 cities and provinces. It has been a runaway success. The Tomato Village plan operates in nine ethnic languages for 20 groups of ethnic minority. It enables customers to connect with a switchboard to get the services of agricultural knowledge, message sending, storytelling and online songs in ethnic languages. The switchboard also has the Q&A service in the ethnic languages from 7AM to 10 PM. Its regular prepaid brand is called Tomato and it does not come with data.

Mass media campaigns help achieve awareness, but in rural markets, they have to be supplemented by innovative last mile marketing strategies. Companies have used local theatre groups by organizing 'Dangdut' in Indonesia and 'Jatras' in India and Bangladesh. They have also relied on opinion leaders. Organizing monthly lucky draws in village markets and involving local SHGs add up to achieve rural marketing success.

Companies also participate in rural lifecycle events such as fairs and weddings. Involvement in village panchayats helps build long-term relationships. Local sports activities and other events are sponsored to gain acceptance. It is important for companies to find out about mass congregation events as well as use rural market days regularly for marketing and establishing presence.

Pricing: The usage of telecom services by rural consumers and the acceptable different price points is quite different from urban users. Communication needs and levels of affordability vary widely. A telecom service bundle for rural consumers must contain apps and data that are relevant to them, such as market information, access to banks and payments and agricultural data. To understand rural price points, consumer needs and price limits have to be understood for each consumer group and innovative offerings need to be devised segment-wise. Telecom companies use urban benchmarks for rural markets, which prevent large-scale penetration and usage. Both service charges and removing initial barriers to entry are required. Since many rural consumers live on a day-to-day basis, a more relevant pricing for rural areas would consist of a bundle that includes cost of handsets, SIM charges and usage charges. For instance, Viettel in Vietnam started the 6 seconds + 1 price in which users pay for the first 6 seconds as default after which they are charged on per second basis. This helps reduce usage charges.

Rural usage is increased by price reductions including innovative service bundling. Lowering the initial entry costs will help companies acquire rural subscribers with the hope that lower profit margins will be compensated by greater volumes. Service segmentation, that is, identifying high, medium and low users of services, can lead to innovative and profitable bundling for profitability. This can help telecom players penetrate rural areas faster.

In 2016, Reliance Jio introduced its services at considerably cheaper rates than were offered by rival companies. It modified its pricing to not only suit individual preferences but also to dominate the telecom market. Pricing of Jio's 4G services resulted in other companies reducing their rates, too. Reliance's free voice calls, cheap data packages and the elimination of roaming charges reduced the total cost of owning a phone and using telecom services, which was an instant hit with customers. The company's data packages start from ₹19, which is the telecom equivalent of sachets marketing suitable for rural India.

Grameenphone's Village Pay Phone (VPP) programme, an initiative of the Grameen Bank in Bangladesh, also innovatively reduced entry level costs for rural users. Grameen Bank provided small loans, without collateral, to the villagers—primarily women who are members of the Bank's microcredit programme—to purchase cell phones. These 'operators', popularly known as 'phone ladies' then provide telephone service to villagers, thereby earning enough revenue to repay the loan. Grameen Telecom buys airtime in bulk from a sister company, Grameenphone, so that it can charge the operator a discounted rate (see Closing Case in Chapter 10). A World Bank case study notes, "It is remarkable that, in 1997, when the cell phone was still a technological novelty the world over, Grameen Telecom successfully initiated the use of this tool for empowering the rural poor."

Questions for Discussion:

1. How can telecom companies bundle their offerings to reduce costs for rural users?
2. Suggest ways through which telecom companies can solve problems of villagers through innovative offerings, to make themselves relevant to rural users.
3. Should advertising campaigns of telecom companies use celebrities and lifestyles for advertising? Would they not alienate the villagers?
4. Does it make sense to reduce prices for rural consumers, considering that this would impact profits and sustainability in the long run? How can companies reconcile the two opposing objectives?

Sources for this Case Study:

Web Resources

"Grameen Telecom: The Village Phone Program." The World Bank. Available at: http://siteresources.worldbank.org/INTEMPOWERMENT/Resources/14648_Grameen-web.pdf (Accessed on 13 April 2017).

Reliance Jio website: https://www.jio.com/

Viettel website: http://viettel.vn/

Other Source

CKS Consulting Pvt. Ltd. 2008. "Rural Marketing Practices for Telecom Services." Available at: http://cks.in/wp-content/uploads/2012/10/RuralMarketingPractices.pdf (Accessed on 20 April 2017).

Section III

Marketing for Rural Areas

8

CHAPTER

Agribusiness

LEARNING OBJECTIVES

Agribusiness includes all activities related to agriculture, from marketing and supply of agricultural inputs to sales of agricultural produce. It forms the backbone of agricultural production. After reading this chapter you will be able to:

- Understand why agriculture should be treated like any other business.
- Learn about farm-to-fork agricultural value chains and understand how value is added at various stages as the product moves from farm to the consumer.
- Understand the five sub-sectors of agribusiness: agro-chemicals, agricultural machinery and implements, agro-inputs, agro-processing and diversified farming.
- Learn about modern additions in agribusiness that include floriculture, meat and poultry products and cold chains.
- Analyze the pros and cons of genetically modified (GM) crops, which have the potential to revolutionize Indian agriculture.

Opening Case: ITC's E-choupal: Transforming Rural India

Agribusiness has traditionally been conducted by agents and traders. This case study describes an initiative to modernize it on a very large scale.

Faced with restrictive laws that govern agricultural trading in the country, in which commissions and auctions are manipulated by agents, ITC Ltd wanted to improve its procurement to make it transparent. Lack of quality produce, grading facilities and price discovery are some of the problems companies face because they have to depend on agents. The company looked for ways to get over these. However, it was not easy, given the piecemeal approach in rural areas. For instance, several agencies have tried to solve problems of credit, procurement or food processing, depending on their focus area, but so far an integrated approach to agribusiness had been missing. This is what ITC set out to do. Through its e-choupal project, it has succeeded in changing the approach to agribusiness on a very large scale.

Stigler (1961) has shown that information is critical for the efficient functioning of markets and that a costly search lowers competition and creates inefficiencies in markets. ITC started out to remove information barriers that cause inefficiencies in rural markets, strangling farmers. The company created the e-choupal as an Internet kiosk, which also serves as a village gathering place as well as an e-commerce hub. The kiosks are run by a farmer appointed by ITC, called the *sanchalak*, who helps other farmers get information through a computer terminal. These terminals helped remove the following bottlenecks:

Price discovery: In the earlier system, the company had no interaction with farmers and depended on agents for procurement. The company would give a price band to the agent in which to procure. The agent would buy during the day and if the average price was higher than the company's band, he would not supply, saying that crops were not available at that price. He would wait for the next day when the company announced higher prices and then supply the goods. Similarly, if the average price was too low, he would supply at the higher price fixed by the company. ITC found it was paying more for its procurement and was unable to capitalize on intraday price shifts.

Quality: Agents procured goods from farmers which varied in quality and price. This was mixed for supply to the company, to reduce the agent's average procurement cost. The company was, thus, not able to get the quality that it wanted. The farmer also did not have any incentive to improve the quality of his crop.

Price inflation: The company demanded high quality, which pushed up prices in the mandi. Though only a small quantity got sold at this price, it became a benchmark for procurement.

Faced with these problems, ITC did some out-of-the-box thinking. It took a rather bold decision to provide a complete solution to farmers in the form of a platform for information, an online portal and a means to buy inputs for agriculture. The approach was based on harnessing the power of IT.

It was a daunting task, requiring huge investments in equipment and training, but the company has succeeded in providing a platform for agribusiness. For its part, ITC gets better quality of agricultural product inputs that it wants for its processing factories.

E-choupal, which started in 2000, has now become the largest Internet-based intervention in rural India. According to ITC's annual report for 2015, e-choupal has empowered more than four million farmers in 40,000 villages covering a range of crops through a network of 6,500 Internet kiosks spread across 11 states. The initiative has created large-scale societal value by making agricultural markets more efficient. It facilitates a two-way flow of goods and services in villages. It is today the world's largest rural digital infrastructure and helps in empowering the farmers by providing timely information.

Indian farmers have traditionally been trapped in a vicious cycle of low incomes > low investment > low productivity > weak market orientation > low value addition > low margin > low risk taking ability and low investment. This has limited gains in productivity in agriculture. This cycle has been broken by ITC through a market-led model, helping in growth in rural incomes. E-choupal uses IT to connect farmers in the value chain, making use of logistics, aggregation, risk and bridge financing. Village Internet kiosks help farmers access real-time information in their local language on the weather, market prices, knowledge on scientific farm practices and risk management.

PHOTO 8.1
An e-choupal centre showing a sanchalak and farmers.

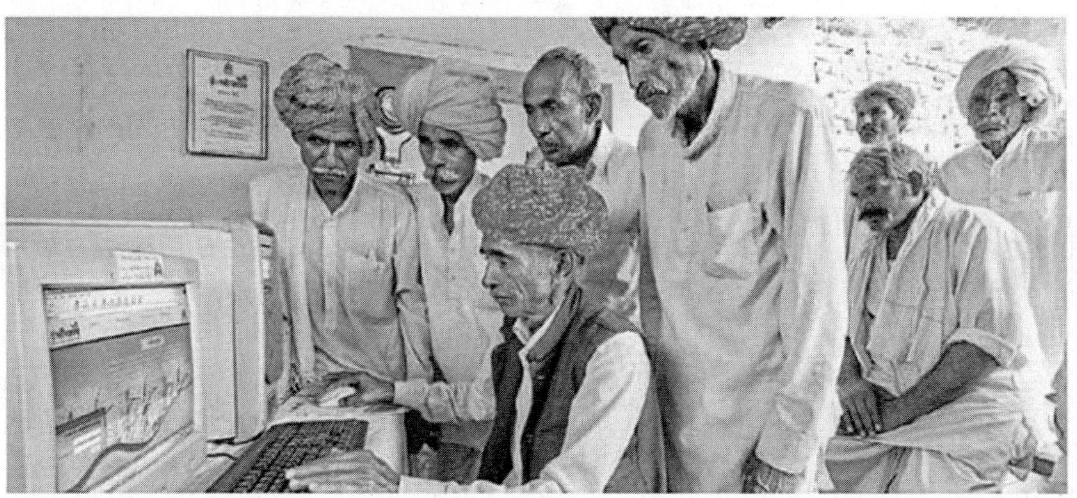

Source: ITC Limited, 2015.

Ovasdi (2006) writes that e-choupal provides five invaluable inputs.

- **Information:** Consisting of daily weather forecasts, price information and e-mail facility. All these services are provided free to the farmers.
- **Knowledge:** Farming methods, area specific knowledge, soil conditions and testing, farming methods and agricultural best practices.
- **Purchase:** Farmers can buy seeds, fertilizers, cycles and tractors and insurance policies.
- **Sale:** Price information and platform to sell crops to ITC centres and factories.
- **Development work:** Water harvesting, health and sanitation through Swasthya Choupal and SHGs.

The project has a number of social spinoffs. The 'Choupal Haat' platform provides financial services, pharmaceuticals, commercial vehicles and white goods. Choupal Saagars are integrated rural services hubs. The company has, through these, established deep rural linkages and agro-commodity sourcing expertise. The 'Choupal Pradarshan Khet' promotes field demonstrations of seed varieties and production practices for improved yield and quality in a range of agricultural and horticultural crops in more than 1,200 villages covering more than 60,000 farmers with focus on sustainable farm practices.

In creating the portal, the company built upon existing relationships. ITC has maintained a role for the traditional commission brokers, who are now called *samayojaks* ('coordinators'). The samayojaks manage physical flows in the supply chain, and they collect pricing data from local auctions and maintain records. The e-choupal venture benefits ITC by reducing procurement costs, improving quality of produce procured and creating a lucrative information franchise. For farmers, it reduces transaction costs, gets them better prices and empowers them with information.

Real-time information and customized knowledge helps in enhancing the ability of farmers to improve productivity and get better prices for their produce. They get access to branded inputs at fair prices. It also provides a direct marketing channel, virtually linking the farmer to the mandi system, which eliminates middlemen and multiple handling. Transaction costs for the farmer are therefore reduced. ITC supplies its own knowhow and has also formed partnerships with other leading companies to provide farm products and services through its platform.

The e-choupal is beneficial to both the farmers and the company. While the farmers benefit from enhanced farm productivity and through the realization of higher prices, ITC benefits from the lower cost of procurement. Costs in the supply chain that do not add value are eliminated.

Creating Internet kiosks was not easy. The company had to overcome problems of lack of infrastructure, power supply, telecom connectivity and bandwidth, apart from the challenge of imparting skills to the first-time Internet users in remote areas of rural India. The company used several alternative and innovative solutions such as solar back-up through batteries, installation of VSAT equipment, mobile choupals and local caching of static content.

Since farmers were involved right from the initial stage, the e-choupal initiative created a sense of ownership in the project. The enthusiastic response from farmers has encouraged ITC to extend the initiative to 15 states across India. The company channelizes other services related to microcredit, health and education through the e-choupal infrastructure. The kiosk provides access to loans and financial services partnering with financial institutions. Based on sanchalak recommendation, loans for farm inputs, insurance and risk management services are provided.

E-choupal has been a boon to the farmer, who was earlier dependent on the agents for all information. Costs have been reduced by eliminating intermediaries and multiple handling. New storage and handling system help build 'farm gate to dinner plate' supply chains. Farmers are encouraged to raise their quality standards and attract higher price. E-choupal is one of the few ICT projects in India that has effectively utilized e-commerce transactions for poverty alleviation, while reducing the number of middlemen.

The impact of the project has been great. Goyal (2010) has examined how the introduction of Internet kiosks providing price information affected the market for soya beans in Madhya Pradesh. Using historical data from mandis, she found that the presence of kiosks in a district was associated with an instant and persistent increase of 1.7 per cent in the average price paid at mandis in that district. The availability of price information increased the level of competition between traders, raising prices and reducing the variation in prices. The ITC intervention has resulted in farmers increasing their profits by 33 per cent. Cultivation of soya beans in districts with kiosks increased by 19 per cent on average. ITC too reduced its procurement costs by buying direct.

While reading this chapter, try to answer the following questions:

1. What is agribusiness? What are its components?
2. What ails the agribusiness sector in India? Why are there so many inefficiencies in it?
3. How can the sector be improved?

Sources for this Case Study:

Goyal, Aparajita. 2010. "Information, Direct Access to Farmers, and Rural Market Performance in Central India." *American Economic Journal: Applied Economics* 2 (3): 22–45.

ITC Limited. 2015. "Report and Accounts, 2015." Available at: http://www.itcportal.com/about-itc/shareholder-value/annual-reports/itc-annual-report-2015/pdf/report-accounts-2015.pdf (Accessed on 27 April 2017).

Ovasdi, J.M. 2006. *Management of Non-governmental Organisations: Towards a Developed Civil Society*. New Delhi: Macmillan India Ltd.

Sawhney, M. 2002. "Fields of Online Dream." *CIO Magazine*, 15 October.

Stigler, G. 1961. "The Economics of Information." *Journal of Political Economy* 69 (3): 213–25.

INTRODUCTION

Agriculture is the mainstay of much of India's population. The toil of India's 119 million farmers has made India self-reliant in food production. Growing food is a noble profession, matching with the country's defence, as illustrated in the slogan: *Jai Jawan, Jai Kissan*. This results in the mindset that farming is somehow not a business but a service to the nation. Such thinking has prevented investments of the kind that are made in businesses. Since it is seen as an essential service, the state intervenes in practically all aspects of agriculture from production to distribution—with disastrous consequences. Private investments and modernization in supply chains and technology are severely thwarted.

Damodaran (2016) raises an interesting question: "Is farming really a business?" As there are so many differences between business and farming, it would certainly appear otherwise. For instance, the government actively looks for foreign investors for its industry, yet in agriculture, it blocks farm-to-fork ventures and restricts FDI in back-end retail that can really help modernize supply chains. Further, while the government neither has any qualms about allowing medicine obtained from GM yeast cells nor does it think twice of GM mosquitoes to fight dengue, it lets itself be persuaded by NGOs and social scientists of all hues who fight tooth and nail against GM crops.

Even so, a farmer who produces a tomato is no different from an industrialist who produces shoes or steel. Both sell their products to make a living. That is why, agribusiness should be treated as such—as a business. The failure to see agribusiness like any other business has led to disastrous consequences in agriculture today. Farmers are exploited in every possible way since they are not businessmen, and restrictions are placed since agriculture is seen as a 'service' to the nation. This chapter looks at the business that is related to agriculture. The marketing of agricultural goods is the subject matter of Chapter 9. Both chapters describe all aspects of agribusiness in detail.

AGRIBUSINESS

The term 'agribusiness' was coined in 1957 by Goldberg and Davis. It includes all activities related to agriculture, including agro-chemicals, breeding, crop production (farming and contract farming), distribution, farm machinery, processing, and seed supply, as well as marketing and retail sales.

According to FAO, agribusiness denotes the collective business activities that are performed from farm-to-fork. It covers the supply of agricultural inputs, the production and transformation of agricultural products and their distribution to final consumers. Agribusiness is one of the main generators of employment and income worldwide.

As a business, agriculture gets raw materials in the form of seeds, fertilizers and pesticides. Its output is mostly perishable. Globally, traditional production and distribution methods are being replaced by well-oiled supply chains that link farmers with retailers, supermarkets and food processors. Only when farm output finds ready markets can agribusiness develop.

However, India still is stuck in outdated practices and thinking. The government approach has been somewhat contradictory:

- It wants to increase farmer incomes and thus keeps enhancing MSP of agricultural products and provides massive agricultural subsidies.

- At the same time, it is also concerned that inflation be kept under check and wants cheaper products on the shelves of markets.
- As a result, neither does the farmer get the MSP for most crops, nor do consumers get cheap products because of monopolies and long supply chains.

The results are chaotic. Subsidies distort supplies; while there is huge output of some crops, others see regular shortages and excesses and resultant price fluctuations. The MSP distorts pricing and very often farmers cannot get these prices in markets. Food processors, such as sugar mills, become defaulters in payments as they cannot pay the MSP, causing distress to the already burdened farmers. It is a strange way to conduct any business and the tragedy is that these policies affect millions of farmers in the country. It is hardly surprising that this over-regulated business does not attract the kind of investments required to modernize Indian agriculture.

Farm-to-fork

Treated as a business, farming and agribusiness has the potential to create employment and increase income levels. Small farmers must get the status of entrepreneurs since they do what other start-ups do.

One concept that is used widely in business is that of value chain, which was first described by Michael Porter (1985). In Porter's model, firms add value in various ways, such as inbound logistics, operations, outbound logistics, marketing, sales and service, which are categorized as primary activities. Secondary activities include procurement, human resource management, technological development and infrastructure. Firms add value through all these activities, which results in a cumulative value that other firms find difficult to replicate.

The term 'farm-to-fork' implies a value chain in which value is added at various stages as the product moves from the farm to the consumer. Farmers, middlemen, government agencies, food processors and retailers form a set of links in a chain of production, processing and distribution as products from farms to the consumer (Figure 8.1). Secondary activities are not shown in this figure. Globally, this value chain is increasingly being modernized. Investments are being made to control and organize the flows of inputs and products. In some countries, large corporations control parts of this value chain.

FIGURE 8.1
An agricultural value chain.

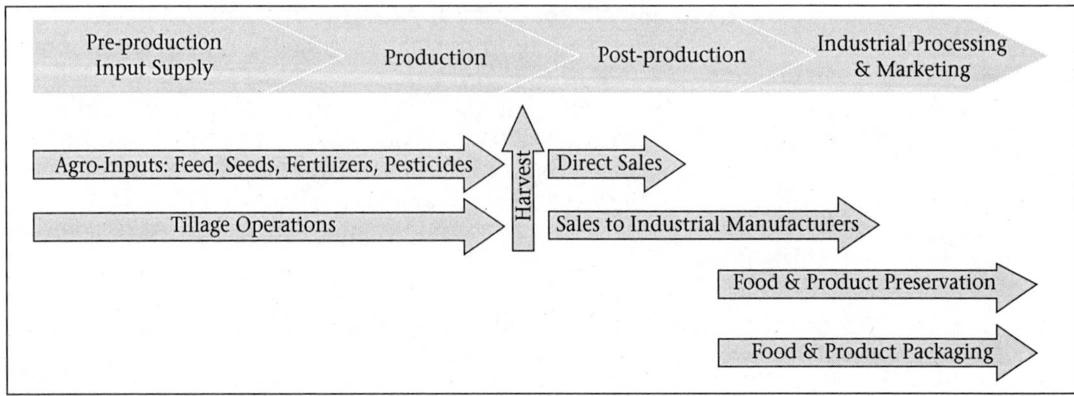

TABLE 8.1
Differences between a business and agribusiness.

Business	Agribusiness
Factors of production are under control of the manufacturer except natural calamities	Factors and risks of production change almost daily
Produce/buy in wholesale and sell in retail	Buy inputs in retail and sell in wholesale
Mergers, growth and increase in size/volume	Fragmentation of holdings and downsizing farms
Modernization and introduction of new technology	Modernization is resisted, new technologies end up in controversies
Pricing under the control of manufacturer	Pricing not under the control of producer, wild fluctuations in prices
Loans and insurance for produce	Ignored by banking channels, farms are not insured, loans obtained from moneylenders
Production and profits are taxed	Production is subsidized, profits are not taxed
Modern supply chains, modern practices and foreign investments encouraged	Primitive supply chains, FDI in modern retail blocked

Value chain analysis can help in enhancing the performance of agriculture in the country. The analysis helps identify weaknesses and provides clues to policy makers for growth in different areas. It creates a shared vision among parties in the chain, leading to collaborative relationships. It also leads to development of enterprises, food quality and safety standards, producing crops as per expected demand, quality improvement and coordinated linkages among producers, processors and retailers. Above all, it will lead to an understanding that the farmer is entitled to a profit like normal business. Secondary activities enhance agricultural productivity over the long run.

An understanding of agriculture as a business points to several shortcomings in the present system. The differences between a traditional business and agribusiness are summed up in Table 8.1. It shows how agribusiness suffers since it is not accepted as a business. It also shows how the private sector can add value at different stages of the value chain.

A comparison with the developed world, where the value chains are fully integrated, shows how investments can revolutionize agriculture. United Nations Industrial Development Organization (UNIDO) data (Table 8.2) shows how developing countries lag behind the developed world in terms of agricultural products processed and value-added. Worse, developing countries lose a huge proportion of their produce in post-harvest losses, even while they have a sizeable proportion of their population that goes hungry. That is why, agribusiness needs to be freed of government control and investments are encouraged in this crucial area.

TABLE 8.2
Comparative data on agricultural value chain.

	Industrialized Countries	Developing Countries
Agricultural products processed (%)	98	38
Value added of agricultural products processed (US$/tonne)	185	40
Post harvest losses (%)	Min	40

Source: UNIDO (2009).

It is seen from the table that investments in agricultural value chains will help solve three major problems:

- Increase farm productivity.
- Reduce the enormous waste in food production.
- Introduce modern methods of storage and transportation.

It is clear that modernization of agribusiness can help agriculture a great deal. It is, therefore, important to understand its components and their business.

Components of Agribusiness

Based on this understanding, we can discover the components of the agribusiness sector. It has five distinct sub-sectors: (a) agro-chemicals, (b) agricultural machinery and implements, (c) agro-inputs, (d) agro-processing and (e) diversified farming. We have not included agricultural marketing here, as it is covered in Chapter 9. The components of agribusiness are shown in Figure 8.2.

It is seen from the figure that agribusiness is a huge business with important links to the value chain. Several factors have influenced the growth in agro-inputs marketing, which are:

1. **Better awareness:** With better education, farmers want to invest in better and modern ways of agriculture. Many have diversified into innovative crops and adopted modern farming practices and equipment.
2. **Shortage of labour:** There is shortage of labour, especially during the sowing and harvesting season. Farmers are, therefore, becoming more dependent on farm mechanization and machines.
3. **Government programmes:** Development programmes carried out by the government with respect to income enhancement and agricultural extension services have made farmers more open to new techniques.

FIGURE 8.2
Components of agribusiness in India.

Agribusiness

- Agro-chemicals
  - Fertilizers, pesticides
- Agricultural machinery and implements
  - Tractors, irrigation equipment, tillers, motors and pumps combines
- Agro-inputs
  - Consumables, seeds cold chains
- Agro-processing
  - Food processors, meat, poultry
- Diversified farming
  - Meat and poultry, milk, floriculture GM crops

4. **Enhanced private sector and NGOs:** Multinational and Indian private sector companies, together with NGOs, have succeeded in building networks of farm education and sourcing. These have resulted in better agricultural practices in states where they are operating.
5. **Credit availability:** The spread of microfinance as well as credit availability through banks and cooperative system has made easier for the farmers to obtain funding to modernize farming.

Agribusiness plays an important role in Indian agriculture. It helps in introducing new technologies for modernization of farms and helps achieve economies of scale in agricultural production. Tools and implements help in increasing productivity of farms, fertilizers help in increasing production while pesticides save harvest and post-harvest losses due to insects, weevils and rodents. Seeds too help in modernization when high-yield varieties and bioengineered crops are introduced. The development of agro-processing industry helps add value to the produce and helps farmers save from price fluctuations. Agribusiness and its components are explained in the next section.

AGRO-CHEMICALS

Agro-chemicals refer to a class of products used in farming, such as fertilizers, pesticides, liming and acidifying agents, soil conditioners and chemicals used in animal husbandry.

Fertilizers

Chemical fertilizers have played a great role in India achieving self-sufficiency in food production. The success of India's green revolution owes much to fertilizers. India is the third largest producer of chemical fertilizer in the world, after China and USA. The consumption of fertilizers is expected to increase in the future because of food security needs. Over the years, production of nitrogen (N) and phosphorus (P) fertilizers has increased, but since there are no viable sources of potash (K) in the country, it is entirely imported.

Fertilizer is produced continuously throughout the year, but its use is seasonal. In India, it is used in high quantities during the two main cropping seasons: (a) *kharif* (April–September); and (b) *rabi* (October–March). Farmers usually buy before the season and store their requirements. Marketing of fertilizers, therefore, requires storage and supply chains to cater to the demand during these two seasons. Photo 8.2 shows how a farmer buys fertilizers on his trip to the nearby town; he buys in bulk and stores it for use during the season.

Unfortunately the marketing of fertilizers is stymied by tight government control. A plethora of rules and laws are imposed on the industry. Subsequent governments have flip-flopped several times and changed fertilizer marketing policy through many orders and laws. Fertilizer marketing and supply in the country is subsidized by the government, even after the reforms of 1991. This has led to many imbalances in demand and supply. An article in *Mint* (2015) describes the fertilizer policy as a "mess created by successive governments."

The problems that have plagued fertilizer marketing due to government policy have been:

1. Restrictions on supply by manufacturers.
2. Limited investments in the industry because of government interference, leading to over-dependence on imports.
3. Imbalanced use of fertilizer by farmers.

Photo 8.2

A farmer buys his requirements of seeds and fertilizers from the local dealers.

Source: Photograph by Dinesh Kumar.

4. Over-use of subsidized fertilizers, leading to environmental damage.
5. Price fluctuations in fertilizers.
6. Lack of knowledge of farmers about appropriate use of fertilizer.

Controls on prices and distribution were introduced through the Fertilizer Movement Control Order, 1973. Under the order, exports and inter-state movement of fertilizers were prohibited except if authorized, and search and seizure powers were enforced by the government. The supply and distribution of fertilizers were brought under the Essential Commodities Act (ECA) and manufacturers could only sell quantities allocated to them in different states during the two cropping seasons, kharif and rabi.

In 1977, the Retention Price cum Subsidy Scheme was implemented, which encouraged investment in the sector by assuring a 12 per cent post-tax return over net worth to the fertilizer producers. The Fertilizer (Control) Order, 1985 further restricted fertilizer marketing, under which the government introduced price controls, and it retained powers of telling manufactures in which states to sell the fertilizers.

After the economic reforms of 1991, the government decontrolled prices, distribution and movement for phosphatic and potassic fertilizers in 1992. But urea, the main nitrogenous fertilizer continued to remain under government control. The New Pricing Scheme was introduced in 2003 and phased decontrol of urea was undertaken. This resulted in imbalanced use of fertilizers. To correct this, the government introduced nutrient-based pricing in 2008 and nutrient-based subsidy (NBS) scheme in 2010. The idea was to control fertilizer subsidy, which was ₹26,222 crore in 2006–07, and had increased by around three times to ₹76,603 crore in 2008–09. The NBS deregulated subsidy on non-urea fertilizers. While the NBS certainly did not lead to any decline in subsidy on fertilizer, it did lead to worsening of soil nutrient quality, along with shortages and price increases. The subsidy on fertilizer, which was ₹61,264 crore in 2009–10 before the introduction of NBS, subsequently ballooned to ₹72,969 crore in 2015–16.

The sharp rise in fertilizer prices resulted in a decline in the use of phosphoric and potassic fertilizer mix, with increase in urea consumption. Although urea prices remained administered, it started selling in the black market at twice the administered prices. There was also severe shortage of urea in the market.

The net result has been an overall increase in fertilizer prices, with neither the government benefiting due to subsidy reduction nor the farmer benefiting. An unintended consequence of the price fluctuations has been a change in fertilizer mix, which in turn led to severe environmental damage.

Government controls have also resulted in low investment in the industry, which has created high dependence on imports. Under the present fertilizer policy, government spends a huge amount of money for fertilizer subsidy and this burden is increasing every year. It is further leading to inefficient use of fertilizers at the farm level.

The major players in the urea industry are IFFCO, National Fertilizers Limited (NFL), Chambal Fertilizers and Chemical Ltd., Krishak Bharati Cooperative and Rashtriya Chemicals and Fertilizers (RCF), accounting for nearly two-thirds of total urea production in the country (Table 8.3). In the top five producers, Chambal Fertilizers and Chemicals Limited is the only private sector player.

TABLE 8.3

An overview of the fertilizer industry in India, showing major players.

Public Sector	Private Sector
National Fertilizers Limited	Chambal Fertilizers & Chemicals Limited
Fertilizers & Chemicals Travancore Limited	Ajay Farm-Chem Private Limited
Rashtriya Chemicals & Fertilizers Limited	Balaji Fertilizers Private Limited
Madras Fertilizers Limited	Deepak Fertilizer and Petrochemicals Corporation Limited
Paradeep Phosphates Limited	Bharat Fertilizer Industries Limited
Pyrites, Phosphates & Chemicals Limited	Coromandal Fertilizers Limited
Hindustan Fertilizer Corporation Limited	Gujarat Narmada Valley Fertilizer Co. Limited
	Meerut Agro Chemicals Private Limited
	Duncans Industries Limited
	Karnataka Agro Chemicals
	Godavari Fertilizers & Chemical Limited
	Shri Amba Fertilizers (I) Private Limited
	Tuticorin Alkali Chemi & Fertilizer Limited
	Gujarat State Fertilizers & Chemicals Limited
	Indo-Gulf Fertilizers & Chemicals Corporation Limited
	Southern PetroChemical Industries Corporation Limited
	Maharashtra Agro Industrial Development Corporation
	Zuari Industries Limited- Fertilizer Limited
	Mangalore Chemicals & Fertilizers Limited

FIGURE 8.3
Marketing of fertilizers in India.

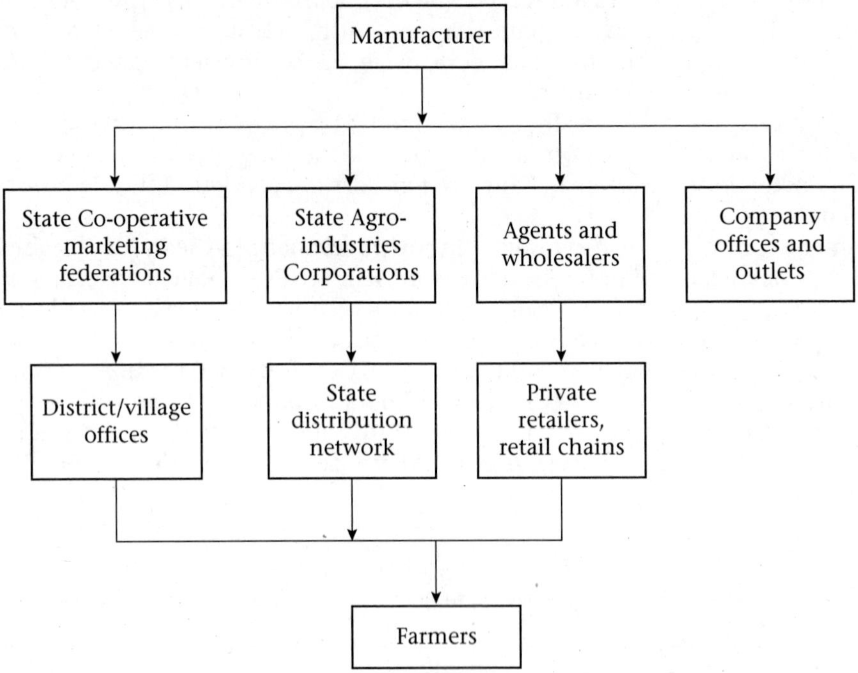

Manufacturer

State Co-operative marketing federations
State Agro-industries Corporations
Agents and wholesalers
Company offices and outlets

District/village offices
State distribution network
Private retailers, retail chains

Farmers

The marketing arrangement of fertilizers is shown in Figure 8.3. In the case of controlled fertilizers, the manufacturer cannot sell directly. Fertilizer is distributed through state cooperative marketing federations and state agro-industries corporations, who in turn either sell directly or through agents and wholesalers. In the case of decontrolled fertilizers, the company sells through wholesalers and retailers or choose to distribute directly through its own offices and outlets.

Today, large volumes of fertilizer are distributed through a network, which includes cooperatives, who supply almost 35 per cent, and private channels, which distribute the balance fertilizers. There are about 2,060 central and state warehouses with a capacity of 30.1 million tonnes. In addition, the FCI has a storage capacity of 23.95 million tonnes. The cooperatives have about 65,970 godowns with a capacity of about 14.12 million tonnes. These godowns are used for storage of foodgrains, fertilizer and other commodities.

Marketing of Agro-chemicals

The Indian crop protection industry is estimated to be ₹27,000 crore in 2013–14, growing at a CAGR of 12 per cent. Insecticides are the largest sub-segment of agro-chemicals with 60 per cent market share, whereas herbicides with 16 per cent market share are the fastest growing segment in India, according to a report published by FICCI (2012).

FIGURE 8.4
Components of the agro-chemicals industry.

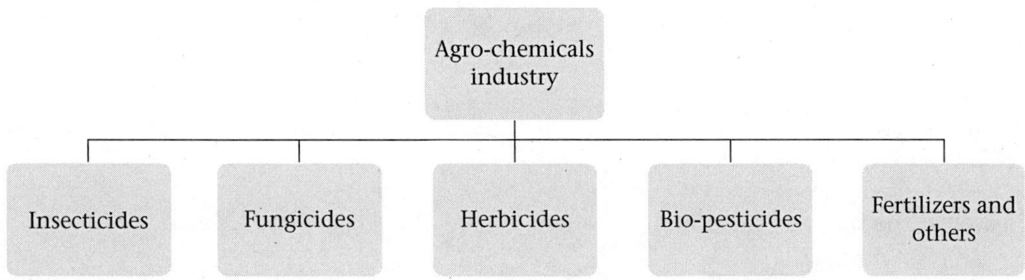

The Indian agro-chemicals market is growing over the years. India's agro-chemicals consumption is one of the lowest in the world with per hectare consumption of 0.58 kg compared to US (4.5 kg/ha) and Japan (11 kg/ha). In India, paddy accounts for the maximum share of pesticide consumption, around 28 per cent, followed by cotton (20%). The low consumption represents an opportunity for further growth of the industry.

The agro-chemicals industry consists of various types of chemicals used for crop protection as shown in Figure 8.4. The main segments in this category are:

- **Insecticides:** Insecticides are used for various crops prevent insect attacks. They are an essential part of farming.
- **Fungicides:** Many crops are vulnerable to diseases caused by fungi. Such diseases are controlled by fungicides. Fruit plants are also susceptible to fungi diseases. The market share of fungicides has increased over the years.
- **Herbicides:** Every farmer needs to fight weeds, which sap the nutrients from the soil. Either the weeds are pulled out manually by employing labour or fought with herbicides. This is the fastest growing segment of agro-chemicals and sales are seasonal, since weeds do not grow in cold weather.
- **Bio-pesticides:** Since chemical pesticides are not completely washed out and are harmful when ingested, and even leach into the groundwater, a market for bio-pesticides has opened up. Bio-pesticides are made from natural substances found in nature and are made from plants, animals or bacteria. Though it is a small segment, the bio-pesticides market is expected to grow in the future, since a segment of consumers prefer organically produced food which does not use harmful chemicals.
- **Others:** Plant growth regulators such as nematocides, rodenticides and fumigants form this category. Rodenticides and plant growth regulators are the stars of this segment.

The key market participants in the industry, which include MNCs as well as Indian companies, are as follows:

BASF India
Bayer Crop science Ltd.
Dhanuka Agritech Limited
Dow AgroSciences India Pvt. Ltd.

DuPont
Excel Crop Care Limited
Gharda Chemicals Ltd.
Meghmani Organics Limited
Monsanto India Ltd.
Rallis India
Syngenta India
United Phosphorous Limited

However, the industry faces many challenges, which are described here.

1. First is the overuse of chemicals to fight pests. The farmer panics when pests attack and uses heavy doses of chemicals to contain them.
2. Second, safety measures for workers are seldom imposed; usually they tie a cloth over their nose and mouth and spray the pesticides.
3. Third, pesticides are a health hazard not only for farm workers but consumers as well.
4. Fourth, they end up destroying the environment.
5. Fifth, India faces a high problem of fake pesticides being sold to farmers. Reuters (2015) reports that counterfeits account for up to 30 per cent of the US$4 billion pesticide market and they are continuously gaining market share in India.

Overuse of chemicals has hit Indian exports as well. *Gulf News* (2014) reports that Saudi Arabia banned the import of Indian chili due to the presence of high pesticide residues in it. The European Union (EU) also temporarily banned the import of Alphonso mangoes and four vegetables from India after it allegedly found that 207 consignments of fruits and vegetables imported from India in 2013 contained excessive pesticide residues.

The industry faces a dilemma; while crop protection measures help in killing pests and saving crops, their use destroys the environment. The FICCI report shows that the number of pests attacking crops has increased manifold since 1940 to present, as shown in Table 8.4.

The industry has to find a safe way to use agro-chemicals while also educating farmers about the type of pesticide to be used and how they must be used. At the same time, government efforts to control fake products must also be increased (see Mini Case Study 8.1).

TABLE 8.4
Growth of crop-wise pests in India.

Crop	No. of Pests in 1940	No. of Pests Now
Rice	35	240
Wheat	20	100
Sugarcane	28	240
Groundnut	10	100
Mustard	10	38
Pulses	35	250

Source: FICCI (2012).

Mini Case Study 8.1

Fakes in the Agricultural Market

It is a double whammy when a farmer spends a huge amount of money on pesticides but sees the pests having a party on his crop. That is what happens to millions of farmers in India when they are supplied fake agro-chemicals. And, this is growing; India's fake pesticide industry is expanding at 20 per cent per year while the overall market is growing at 12 per cent.

Though the government has increased inspections, corrupt officials and politicians work hand-in-glove with the counterfeiters to supply fake products. Laws are neither strict nor enforced properly, as government departments are understaffed and offenders usually get free after serving short sentences. Many pesticides that are banned abroad are also freely available in the country. A consequence of this is that companies suffer and face loss of reputation when fake brands with the same labelling are sold.

Consider the following examples of marketing of fake pesticides:

- In 2015, whiteflies attacked Punjab's cotton fields, destroying about 30 per cent of the crop. Police arrested Punjab agriculture director, MS Sandhu, for allegedly aiding the sale of fake pesticides to cotton growers (*Hindustan Times* 2015).
- In Fatehabad, Haryana, a trader was caught trying to sell ink diluted in water as Dimecron, a cotton pesticide (*India Today* 2013).
- Raids were conducted in Gulbarga, Karnataka, and fake pesticides were seized that infringed on DuPont's trademark, Coragen (*The Hindu Business Line* 2015).

It is estimated that India loses about 4 million tonnes of food every year due to fake pesticides. It is a contributor to farmer suicides, and if not checked, it may hit food security of the country.

How can the problem of fakes be tackled in the Indian market?

How can farmers be safeguarded against unscrupulous activities of traders and manufacturers?

Sources for this Case Study:

Hindustan Times. 2015. "Bad Risks, Fake Pesticides Stoke Punjab's Worst Farm Crisis in Years." 7 October.

India Today. 2013. "Pesticides: Spurious Spray." 29 July.

The Hindu Business Line. 2015. "Fake DuPont Pesticides Seized in Gulbarga." 6 November.

AGRICULTURAL MACHINERY AND IMPLEMENTS

Agriculture machinery is an important part of agribusiness. It consists of hand tools, animal drawn implements and power-operated equipment. Farm machinery helps reduce drudgery and improves efficiency and saves on inputs. Tractors, irrigation equipment, power tillers, combine harvesters, fodder cutters, sprinkler systems and tractor-driven implements form part of machines that farmers use. Singh (2009) makes a distinction between machinery that requires power and that are operated by humans. Energy intensive operations such as land preparation, tilling, milling, grinding and transport require power-operated machines. Seeding and harvesting come next, which are done manually but machines are also available

PHOTO 8.3
A farmer prepares his field with a tractor.

Source: Photograph by Dinesh Kumar.

for these tasks. Weeding, transplanting, cotton and fruit harvesting are examples of mostly human labour and is mechanized the least.

Agricultural machinery is used for harvesting, transport, seeding and planting, fertilizer application and plant protection and horticulture machinery. Since much of the machinery is made by small-scale manufacturers, testing and standardization is an important component.

Tractors and Combines

Tractors are used for a variety of purposes in the agricultural sector. Over the years, the tractor industry in India has made significant progress in production, capacity addition and technology indigenization. Both MNCs and home-grown companies provide products with varying horsepower to meet farm requirements. Tractor sales depend on size of landholding of the farmers, credit availability and income/savings, which depend on a large part on the monsoons. Though the penetration of tractors has been low, low crop yields, rising labour costs, planting of high yield varieties, modernization and increased mechanization is expected to push the growth in this segment in the next decade.

A report by Kotak Institutional Securities (2013) estimates that only 5 per cent of agricultural households own a tractor, and so sales will continue to grow in the coming years. The report expects a CAGR of tractors to be 7–8 per cent. However, fragmented landholdings prevent deep penetration. It is estimated that a farmer owning 6 acres can afford a tractor, but 82 per cent of landholdings in India are 5 acre or less. Alternate uses, such as haulage and construction may help boost demand.

Fragmented Holdings

According to the Agriculture Census 2010–11, total number of operational holdings was estimated at 138.35 million, while the total operated area was 159.59 million hectare. The average size of holdings thus comes to 1.15 ha, which is less than half of the figure in 1970–71, when the figure was 2.28 ha. The trend of average size of holdings shows a steady decline over various agriculture censuses since 1970–71.

Landholdings in the marginal category (less than 1 ha) constitute 67 per cent of the holdings in India, according to the census. The share of marginal holdings has more than doubled to 22 per cent in 2010–11 from 9 per cent in 1970–71. The share of small farm holdings, consisting of land size 1–2 ha increased from 12 per cent to 22 per cent during the same period (Figure 8.5). We see that small and marginal holdings constitute 85 per cent of the landholdings with 44 per cent of the operated area in the country.

This trend is only increasing. According to NABARD, quoted in *The Economic Times* (2013), while the country's acreage has remained stable at 140 million hectares, the number of farmers has increased from 7 crore to 14 crore, with 1 crore farmers added every five years. The landholding size will therefore continue to decrease. This will have a direct impact on farmers' capacity to invest. Without any government action on land reforms, the situation is expected to exacerbate. That is why, companies in India are looking at only modest growth in tractors and farm mechanization equipment. The decrease in landholdings will also make it difficult to maintain agriculture as a feasible profession. With farm distress expected to grow in the coming years because of fragmented holdings, agricultural machinery companies expecting high rural growth rates are bound to be disappointed.

Region-specific Growth

Tractor sales show that their demand is region specific and correlates with the size of landholding (Figure 8.6). Punjab, Haryana and western Uttar Pradesh constitute the major tractor market with about 55 per cent share of total all-India sales. Sales in Gujarat, Madhya Pradesh and Rajasthan have been witnessing good growth, with around 30 per cent share. Tractor sales in Maharashtra, Tamil Nadu, Karnataka and Andhra Pradesh show consistent growth, with about 25 per cent share. Eastern states, namely Bihar, Odisha, West Bengal and Assam have been laggards, showing just 3–5 per cent growth.

FIGURE 8.5

The pattern of landholdings shows fragmentation, which impacts farmers' ability to invest.

Category-wise average size of holding—All India (in ha)									
Category of Farmers	1970–71	1976–77	1980–81	1985–86	1990–91	1995–96	2001–02	2005–06	2010–11
Marginal (less than 1 ha)	0.41	0.39	0.39	0.39	0.4	0.4	0.4	0.38	0.38
Small (1.0 to 2.0 ha)	1.44	1.42	1.44	1.43	1.44	1.42	1.42	1.38	1.42
Semi-medium (2.0 to 4.0 ha)	2.81	2.78	2.78	2.77	2.76	2.73	2.72	2.68	2.71
Medium (4.0 to 10.0 ha)	6.08	6.05	6.01	5.95	5.9	5.84	5.81	5.74	5.76
Large (10.0 ha and above)	18.07	17.57	17.38	17.19	17.3	17.21	17.12	17.08	17.38
All Groups	2.28	2.00	1.84	1.69	1.57	1.41	1.33	1.23	1.61

Source: Calculated from Agricultural Census, various rounds, GoI#: 2010–11 over 1970–71.

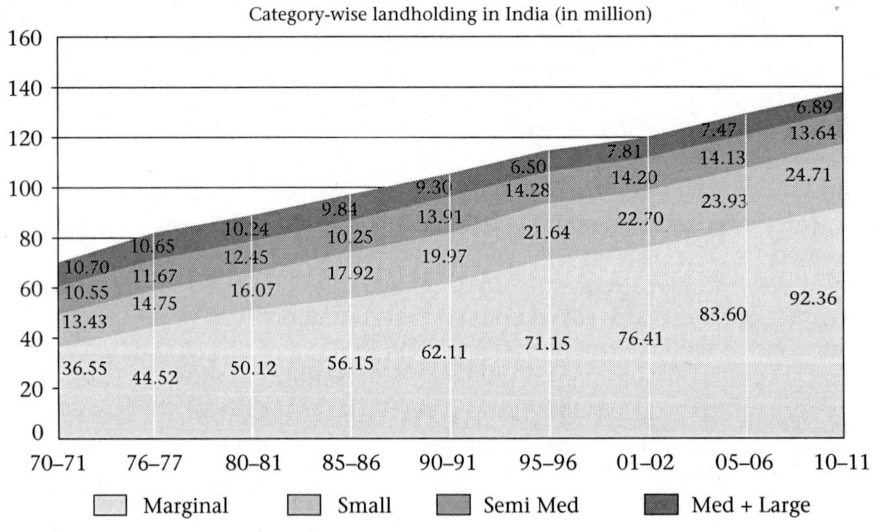

Category-wise landholding in India (in million)

Source: Agricultural Census, various rounds, GoI.

Source: https://www.nabard.org/Publication/Rural_Pulse_final142014.pdf (Accessed on 10 January 2017).

Cost and Credit Considerations

Kotak has estimated that the cost of ownership of a 15 hp tractor is lower than owning two bullocks with a cart. Given the fact that tractors work faster as well, tractors are slowly replacing bullocks in the countryside. Smaller farmers can rent a tractor, which works out cheaper,

FIGURE 8.6
State-wise average size of landholdings.

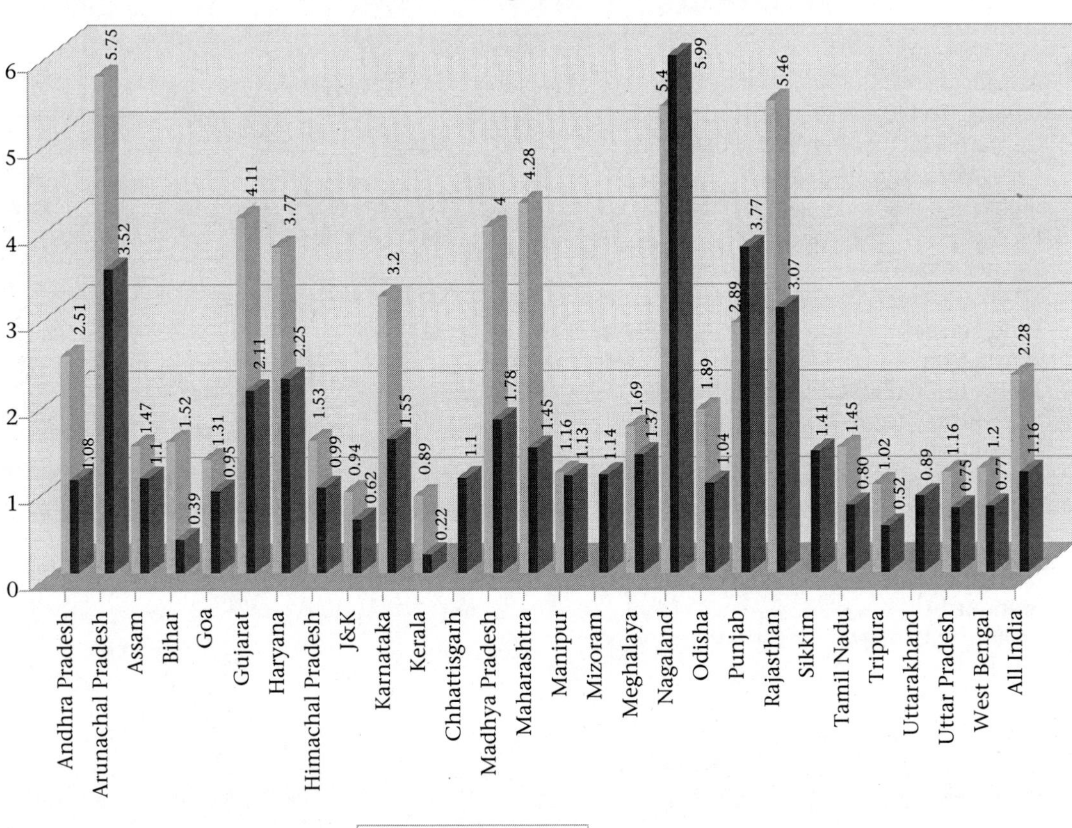

Source: Calculated from Agricultural Census, various rounds, GoI#: 2010–11, over 1970–71.

but availability during the season is limited. Hence, it is better for farmers to buy one. That is why, purchase of tractors is rising among farmers across size of holdings. However, the limited availability of bank credit facilities in rural areas affects demand of tractors. Though institutional credit has increased significantly over the years, disparities still exist in the flow of credit among states, districts, villages and even within the village. Patel (2014) points to the difficulties experienced by small, marginal and tenant farmers, households residing in remote hilly, tribal, desert or drought prone areas. This has limited the spread of tractors in the country.

Tractors are available in five categories of horsepower: less than 20 hp, 21–30 hp, 31–40 hp, 41–50 hp and above 51 hp. The maximum sales are of the 31–40 hp tractors. However, over time, the preference for higher horsepower tractors is seen to be increasing.

The major players in the tractor industry are Mahindra and Mahindra, TAFE, Escorts, Sonalika, John Deere, New Holland and HMT. In 2012, Mahindra and Mahindra held a 34 per cent market share, TAFE 18 per cent, Escorts 17 per cent and Sonalika 10 per cent. The top five companies held 80 per cent market share of the tractor market. The major manufacturers of tractors in India are as follows.

ACE Tractors
Angad Tractors
Balwan Tractors, Force Motors Ltd
Captain Tractors Pvt. Ltd
Crossword Agro Industries
Eicher
Escorts
Farmer Tractor
HMT Tractors
Indo Farm
John Deere
Mahindra Gujarat Tractor Limited
Mahindra Tractors
Mars Group
New Holland Fiat India
Preet Tractors
SAME Deutz-Fahr (India) Private Ltd.
Sonalika
Standard
Swaraj Tractors
TAFE
VST Tillers

Combines

Combines are very popular in developed countries. Harvesting with combine harvesters is becoming common where workforce is scarce or farms are very large, for example, at the time of wheat harvesting in Punjab, Haryana and Uttar Pradesh. More than 48 local manufacturers mainly in Punjab have developed combines, which are self-propelled or tractor operated. Combines are also used for harvesting paddy, soybean and gram. Entrepreneurs from Rajasthan and Punjab provide combine harvesters to farmers in Maharashtra, Gujarat, Madhya Pradesh, Andhra Pradesh and Tamil Nadu. Two known combines are the Claas Crop Tiger and Kartar K3500, which have been tested by Farm Machinery Training and Testing Institute. Institutes have been set up by the government in Haryana, Madhya Pradesh, Assam and Andhra Pradesh. They test farm equipment and also conduct training courses in operation, maintenance and repair of farm machinery and equipment. The institutes provide official testing of combine harvesters, farm implements and machinery, irrigation pumps, stationery power engines and plant protection equipment.

Irrigation Equipment

Agricultural irrigation equipment is a huge market as farmers modernize. It has helped in increasing agricultural production and revolutionized the cultivation of crops. The category includes sprinklers, pumps, irrigation pipes, paddy seeders, weeders, sprayer systems and inline drippers.

Micro-irrigation Equipment

Micro-irrigation systems supply water directly to the root of plants through a network of plastic pipes. Low discharge emitters supply water at slow and regular intervals to plants. Micro-irrigation components consist of pipes, tubes, water-emitting devices, flow control equipment, fittings and accessories. Such systems help in saving water by transporting it to the roots as compared to the traditional way in which the whole field is flooded. It also results in fewer weeds and thus improves crop yields.

Micro-irrigation technology is becoming popular with farmers all across the world. It is widely used in the USA, Israel, Australia, parts of Europe and in Asian countries. It is already being used in India and China, and due to a rising population and growing water scarcity, it will be adopted by many more farmers in times to come. Minor irrigation equipment includes micro-irrigation systems, pumps, agriculture pipes, valves and mechanized irrigation systems. Sprinklers such as spray, mist, drippers, micro-jets, fan jets, micro-sprayers and foggers are also used.

A report by Ken Research (2014), 'India Micro Irrigation System Market Outlook to 2018', says that penetration of micro-irrigation techniques by farmers is very low, though it is growing at a fast pace. The micro-irrigation system market in India has grown at a CAGR of 27.3 per cent during the period 2008–13 and is growing at a CAGR of 18.3 per cent for the period 2014–19. There is strong demand in states such as Gujarat, Rajasthan, Madhya Pradesh, Maharashtra, Karnataka, Andhra Pradesh, Tamil Nadu, Rajasthan and Haryana. Some state governments provide support for micro-irrigation projects.

The Indian micro-irrigation system industry has grown significantly over the years, but it is highly fragmented with nearly 200 companies. The Irrigation Association of India (IAI) has been set up to coordinate with the government for subsidies and policy interventions. A large number of companies in the organized and unorganized sector manufacture and install micro-irrigation system in the industry. Of these, Jain Irrigation Systems Limited (JISL) is the largest and a listed company at the stock exchange (see Closing Case in Chapter 9). JISL offers a wide range of products including drip and sprinkler irrigation system equipment, PVC and PE piping systems, photovoltaic appliances and solar pumps.

Power Tillers

Power tillers are mini-tractors with two wheels and rotary tillers and are useful in small farms. They replace animal power. Sud (2015) writes that these are very popular in paddy cultivation in Japan, but not so in India, where tractors are preferred. Tractors sell about 600,000 units per year in India, while power tillers sell less than one-tenth of that, with most of the sales happening in the southern and north-eastern states.

A power tiller is cheaper than a small tractor and has lower diesel consumption though it takes longer to complete the same job. Besides, the maintenance cost of power tillers is also far lower than that of tractors. Power tillers are more economical even for other uses, such as for running water pumps and grain threshers. It is especially useful in undulated and hilly terrains. There has been a steady growth in the sales of power tillers in the country (Figure 8.7).

However, power tillers have not been very popular with Indian farmers. One reason is that while operating, a person has to walk behind it to guide it, which not only increases drudgery but can also be hazardous. A remote control system is probably the answer, and one has been developed by Mangalore Robautonics but is yet to catch on. Second, farmers like the status attached to a bigger machine and thus prefer to buy a tractor instead.

FIGURE 8.7
Power tiller sales in India.

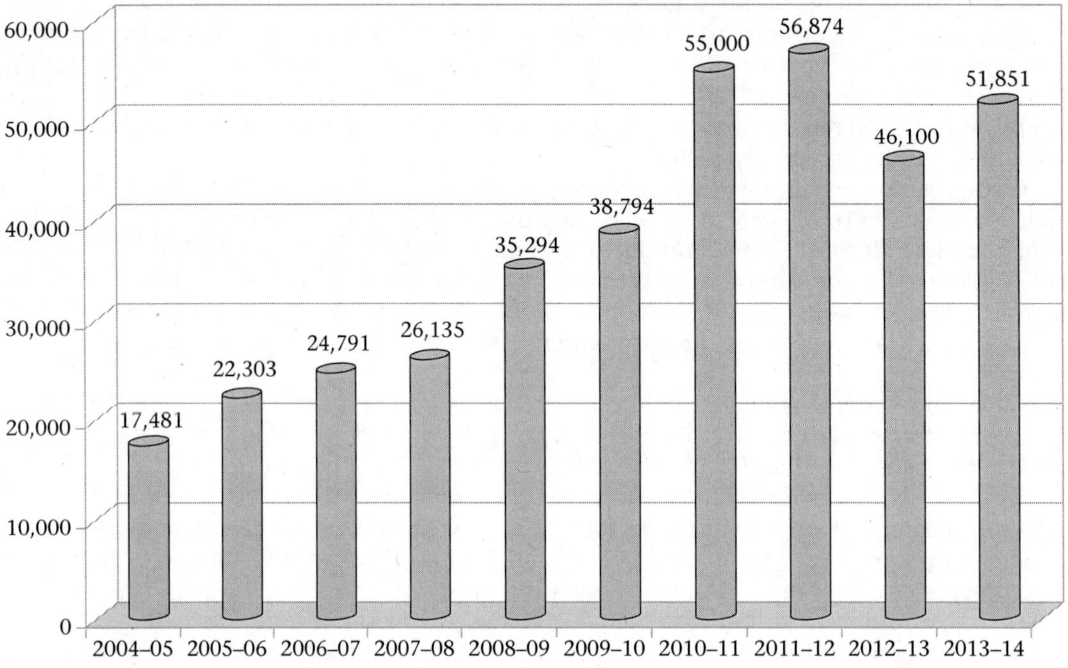

2004–05	2005–06	2006–07	2007–08	2008–09	2009–10	2010–11	2011–12	2012–13	2013–14
17,481	22,303	24,791	26,135	35,294	38,794	55,000	56,874	46,100	51,851

Source: AMMA-India.

Electric Pumps and Motors

Electric motors and diesel engines are used in agriculture and are the primary sources of stationary power for irrigation, threshing and various post-harvest agro-processing operations. Indian pumps are made according to the specifications of the Bureau of Indian Standards (BIS). Agricultural pump industries are situated in Coimbatore, Ahmedabad, Baroda, Kolkata and Dewas. Rajkot, Agra and Kolhapur are famous for oil engines.

The most popular pumps are single phase monoblock pumpsets from 0.5 hp to 2 hp range, selling about two million sets a year, followed by three-phase monoblock pumpsets 2 hp to 30 hp range and submersible pumpsets 3 hp to 30 hp range, selling 600,000 sets each per year. Bigger pumps consisting of diesel engines up to 10 hp and above 10 hp are also popular. As water tables go down in the country, larger pumps and motors will be required in the future.

Tools

Agricultural tools are used for various operations. Most of the tools are fabricated by small-scale units in towns and sold there (see Photo 8.4). The Agricultural Machinery Manufacturers Association (AMMA-India) lists more than 500 manufacturers of such tools,

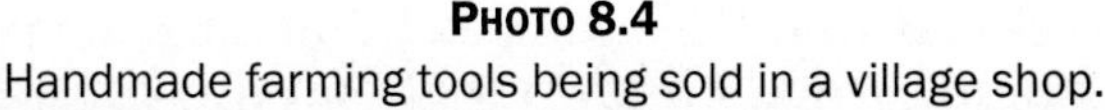

PHOTO 8.4
Handmade farming tools being sold in a village shop.

Source: Photograph by Dinesh Kumar.

but there are countless small operators who fabricate tools as required by a farmer at a particular point in time.

- **Seed bed preparation:** Various cultivators, disc harrow, mould board plough, puddler, disc harrow-cum-puddler, peg tooth harrow, spring tine harrow, rotavator and patela harrow operated by animal and tractor are the improved implements which have been adopted by farmers. Different sizes of cultivators and disc harrows are used.
- **Sowing and planting equipment:** Line-sowing helps in regulated application of fertilizers near the root zone. Mechanical weeders are used to control weeds. Mechanically metered seed drills and seed-cum-fertilizer drills operated by animals and tractors have been developed.
- **Plant protection equipment:** Weed control in irrigated and rain-fed agriculture during the kharif season is required and various equipment are available for it. Khurpis, long handle wheel hoe and peg type weeders, bullock-operated weeder and cultivator are also used for control of weeds. Low-cost hand-operated sprayers and dusters are also available.

- **Harvesting and threshing:** Harvesting and threshing equipment is used to reduce costs of production and reduction in harvest/post-harvest losses, non-availability of labour during the harvesting period. They are also used to reduce drudgery in operations. Harvesting is done in several ways—manually with sickle, with animal or stationary power threshers operated by diesel engines, electric motors or tractor power.

AGRO-INPUTS

Marketing of Seeds

The Planning Commission, in its mid-term appraisal of the 10th Five Year Plan (2002–07), said that despite a huge institutional framework for seed production both in the public and private sector, availability of good quality seeds continues to be a problem. It emphasized the need to rejuvenate the seeds sector through revamping the public sector seed companies, including the State Seed Corporations. Farmers rely on seeds saved from their earlier crop and seed replacement rate continues to about 2–10 per cent in certain states for certain crops, which is much below the desired level of 20 per cent for most crops.

The supply of seeds is also governed by several laws and orders of the government, such as the Seeds Act, 1966; the Seeds (Amendment) Act, 1972; the Seeds Rules, 1968; the Seeds (Amendment) Rules, 1973 and 1974; the Seeds (Control) Order, 1983; National Seeds Policy, 2002; Seed Control Order (Amendment) 2006; Essential Commodities Act, 1955 and the Seeds Bill, 2004.

Government has set up the National Seeds Corporation (NSC) in 1963 under the Ministry of Agriculture. Its objective is to undertake production of foundation and certified seeds. Its website states that, at present, certified seeds of nearly 600 varieties of 60 crops are being supplied through its 8,000 registered seed growers all over the country. It supplies high quality oil seeds, pulses and hybrids including vegetables to farmers. The corporation has established five quality control laboratories for seed testing and to monitor the quality of seeds. NSC is also involved in the production of tissue culture plants like banana and supplies seedlings/saplings of fruits crops through procurement from the MOU partners.

However, one reason that Indian agriculture has remained backward is because of the dominance of the public sector and interference by the government. At least in seeds production and marketing, the seed policy aims to reduce the direct involvement of government and to actively encourage the private sector to research and develop new varieties. As a result, a number of private sector firms are now supplying seeds to farmers (see Mini Case Studies 8.2 and 8.3).

Seed marketing is carried out through three channels:

1. Sale through dealers/distributors.
2. Sale through Central or state governments.
3. Sale through NSC-owned sale counter.

The corporation has about 2,500 dealers who account for more than 69 per cent of the sales. It has regional offices and area offices all over the country.

The National Seed Project (NSP) was established in 1974 and NSC was assigned the lead role to develop the seed industry in the country. It has helped in establishing various state seed corporations. It also implements schemes of the government such as the Integrated Scheme

Mini Case Study 8.2

Seed Banks: Saving Traditional Seeds

A seed bank is a type of gene bank where seeds of different crops and rare plant species are stored for future use. Since seeds can be stored for a long time without destroying their genetic qualities, seed banks ensure that seeds are available to the farmers at the time of natural calamities. They maintain stocks of foundation and certified seeds of different crops and varieties which can be used when required.

Globally, such projects have been undertaken to save seed varieties. The Svalbard Global Seed Vault, operated by the Global Crop Diversity Trust, stores seeds in Spitsbergen, Norway and is designed to survive catastrophes such as nuclear war and world war. Seeds are kept below the freezing point of water and are protected by walls of steel-reinforced concrete. The Millennium Seed Bank in West Sussex, near London, is the largest seed bank in the world which stores billions of seed samples in a nuclear bomb-proof multi-story underground vault. The former NSW Seedbank is an integral part of The Australian Botanic Gardens and has since been replaced as the Australian PlantBank.

In India, state agricultural universities and the Indian Council for Agricultural Research (ICAR) are involved in seed production and distribution. Apart from these, private and voluntary organizations have also set up seed banks across the country, some of which are described here.

Beej Bachao Andolan: The Beej Bachao Andolan (BBA) was begun in Uttaranchal by Vijay Jardhari in village Jardhargaon of district Tehri to conserve traditional seeds and also promote agricultural biodiversity, sustainable agriculture and local traditions. It is a people's campaign and works without any financial assistance from the government. After the success of the Green Revolution of the 1960s and its subsequent decline when yields began to decline, villagers realized that dependence on pesticides and fertilizers, monocultures and soil degradation was not good. The BBA started as an awareness campaign in 1989 to promote indigenous practices like the 'Baranaja' (meaning twelve grains), a traditional system of mixed farming and intercropping of 12 species. Vijay Jardhari and his friends travelled to villages to collect traditional seeds. Overcoming initial resistance, they started to set up seed banks in villages. The BBA received ₹1.5 lakh from Booker Prize winner Arundhati Roy in 2002. *The Hindu* (2014) reports that Jardhari has saved many varieties of paddy, wheat, barley, *rajma* (beans), cowpea and *navrangi dal* seeds. Some of these are resistant to droughts, floods and pests. His approach is opposite to that of the modern agricultural cartel, which promotes mono crops.

Navdanya: Navdanya is an NGO that has a large network of seed keepers and organic producers. Its website says its network is spread across 18 states in India and has helped set up 122 community seed banks across the country. Navdanya trains farmers in seed sovereignty, food sovereignty and sustainable agriculture, and provides a direct marketing, fair trade organic network as well. It has also set up a learning centre, *Bija Vidyapeeth* (School of the Seed/Earth University), on its biodiversity conservation and organic farm in Uttarakhand. Navdanya is a women-centred movement and is led by Vandana Shiva.

Annadana Seed and Soil Savers: Annadana Seed Bank attempts to create low-cost, user-friendly seed banks in unused farm-sheds at the village or panchayat level. It lays emphasis on low-cost design and use of locally available materials. In 2007, it helped setting up of the seed bank at Bio-Centre, a horticulture state farm at Hulimavu in Bangalore. The seed bank conserves and distributes varieties of organic open-pollinated vegetable seeds and is led by Sangita Sharma.

Green Foundation: The Green Foundation enables the setting up of community seed banks and networks, which act as seed repositories and provides farmers free access to indigenous seeds. Its website says that it conserves seeds ex-situ in a gene bank. It works with around 40 farmers' groups, called Krishi SHGs, covering 30 villages with focus on women and indigenous peoples. The community managed seed banks cultivate 328 varieties of indigenous seed.

Deccan Development Society: The Deccan Development Society, an NGO, works in about 75 villages in Medak District of Andhra Pradesh. The 5,000 women members work in voluntary village level associations called *sanghams*. Most of them are poor and belong to the Dalit community. Over 1,500 women farmers of DDS sanghams have established village-level community gene funds in 60 villages and have retrieved over 80 land races, which had been obliterated by modern agricultural practices.

Sahaja Samrudha: An organic farmers' collective, it has created a seed savers group in Karnataka, which has done some remarkable work in identifying rare varieties of paddy, millets, lentils and vegetables. It has started the Desi Seed Producers Company Limited, a collective of organic seed producers and seed savers, to conserve and promote seeds. The seeds are marketed under the brand name 'Sahaja Seeds'.

Given the monocultures promoted by seed companies, do these initiatives really help meaningfully?

Sources for this Case Study:

Web Resources

Annadana Seed and Soil Savers website: http://annadana-india.org/

Beej Bachao Andolan website: http://www.uttaranchal.org.uk/bba.php

Deccan Development Society website: http://ddsindia.com/

Green Foundation website: http://www.greenfoundation.in/

Navdanya website: http://www.navdanya.org/

Sahaja Samrudha website: http://www.sahajasamrudha.org/

Other Source

The Hindu. 2014. "Uttarakhand Farmer's Seed Saving Movement Holds Promise." 19 March.

Mini Case Study 8.3

Seeds Supply by Private Companies

Many private companies are producing seeds as well as marketing them. Seed production is quite different from producing other products because seeds cannot be produced overnight. Demand must be anticipated and production must be planned even three seasons in advance in some cases. The window available for offering the right seeds to farmers is only 15 to 20 days. Seeds have to be produced, packed, graded and supplied in time for the season.

Nuziveedu Seeds: Nuziveedu Seeds Ltd is India's largest hybrid seed company. The company has its presence in 19 states and markets about 200 varieties of seed products to more than 5.5 million farmers across the country.

It was started by Mandava Venkatramaiah in 1973 in Nuziveedu, Andhra Pradesh, with a vision to make hybrid cotton seed available to cotton cultivators. The seeds business was created out of a hobby and was later taken over by his son M Prabhakar Rao. Today, the company is widely recognized for its contribution to the cotton revolution of the country. Currently Nuziveedu Seeds is also supplying seeds for crops such as paddy, corn, sorghum, pearl millet, sunflower and vegetables.

The company not only provides seeds but also guides farmers through promotional campaigns and extension services. It provides educational programmes under the project titled 'Subeej Krishi Vigyan' through which farmers are educated on latest developments in crop production technologies, crop agronomy, pest and diseases management, weed management, post-harvest management and market dynamics.

Kaveri Seeds: Started in 1976 in Karimnagar, Telangana, by G.V. Bhaskar Rao, the company invested in hybrid seeds to raise corn productivity in the region. The demand for hybrid seeds picked up in 1986. Initially, Rao used to produce and distribute hybrids available from the government agencies, but later he started collecting germplasms and started investing in-house to develop new hybrids. In 1997, his company launched its first major hybrid maize called Kaveri 517.

Kaveri Seeds produces and markets 50 of its own hybrids in corn, sunflower, paddy, cotton, jawar and bajra, and in vegetables such as tomato and chilli. The company invests 7 per cent of its profit in research and development (R&D). It also has a 600-acre farm for R&D and a biotechnology lab. The focus now is on drought tolerant varieties and marker-assisted selection programme.

The company has a distribution network consisting of dealers and distributors, producing seeds over 75,000 acres of land across the country. In 2013, Kaveri Seeds was the second largest producer of hybrid cotton seeds in the country, after Nuziveedu Seeds.

Besides these, there are a large number of seed companies in the private sector in India. As the country still has to catch up with the rest of the world in terms of yields, there are enough growth opportunities in this area.

What is the scope of seed industry in India? What are the challenges?

Sources for this Case Study:

Web Resources

Nuziveedu Seeds website: http://www.nuziveeduseeds.com/about-us/company-overview/

Kaveri Seeds website: http://www.kaveriseeds.in/

Other Source

Business Today. 2014. "Seeds of Progress." 21 December.

for Oil seeds, Pulses, Oilpalm and Maize (ISOPOM), National Food Security Mission (NFSM) and National Horticulture Mission (NHM), which provide technical support to seed producing agencies. It also imparts training, creates infrastructure facilities for processing plants and storage in states, and helps in exports of seeds.

AGRO-PROCESSING

Agro-processing is a set of techno-economic activities for conservation and handling of agricultural produce and to make it usable for later use. It includes all operations from harvest till the material reaches the end users in the desired form, packaging, quantity, quality and price.

Agro-processing offers a way to use the harvested agricultural products for long-term consumption. Since India has only limited processing facilities, losses in farm produce have been estimated at ₹75,000–100,000 crore per annum. A portion of these can be contained if agricultural produce is processed for future use.

FIGURE 8.8
Diagram showing scope of food processing industry.

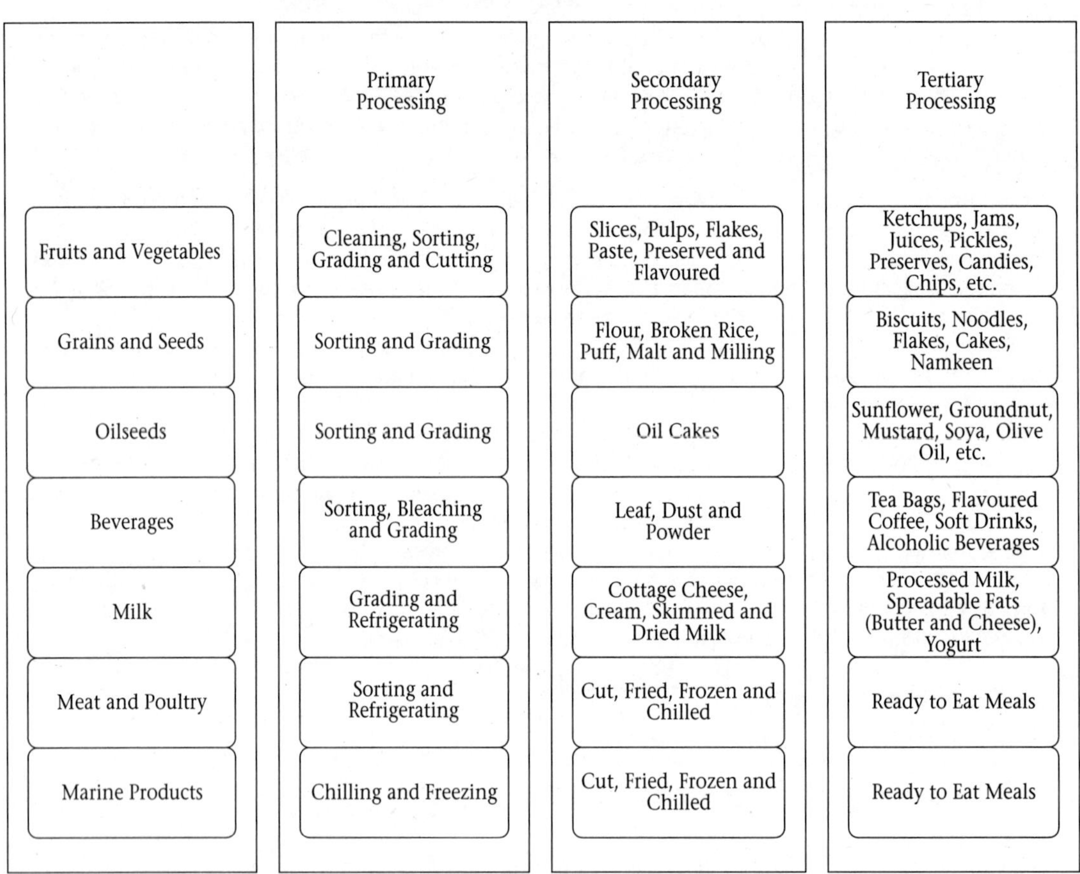

Source: Onicra Credit Rating Agency of India.

Agro-processing can be divided into three categories: primary, secondary and tertiary, as explained in Figure 8.8. Primary processing consists of sorting, grading and storage. Secondary processing means re-shaping of food for ease of consumption, while tertiary processing includes value-added food such as ready-to-eat items, juices, jams, and so on. This holds around 38 per cent share in the total processed food market (see Mini Case Study 8.4).

All agricultural produce requires some kind of processing to make it suitable for consumption. A large number of people depend on it for their livelihood. The class of produce and its derivatives are shown in Table 8.5.

Much of the processing is done in the unorganized sector: retailers do some processing and grading to sell food items, while restaurants and sweet shops process and serve ready to eat products. A large number of small and medium enterprises (SMEs) are also engaged in food processing. The sector has gained the attention of a large number of companies, both Indian and foreign. Companies such as Pepsi, Britannia, ITC, General Mills, Haldiram's, Patanjali, CavinKare, Mohun's, Kellogg's and many others buy a variety of agricultural products and

TABLE 8.5
Agricultural produce and their processed products.

Crops/Class	Processed Products
Rice	Modern rice mills, partially cooked/quick cooking rice, breakfast cereals and value-added products
Wheat	Flour mills, whole wheat/wheat bran flour, fortified wheat flour, methi atta, seven-grains atta, baked products
Maize, cereals	Corn flour, corn flakes and flavoured products, ready-to-eat snacks, starch material, corn oil, cattle feed, baby corn, breakfast foods and extruded fortified products
Floriculture	Bulbs, tubers, tuberous roots, plant for tissue culture, flowering plants, cactus, etc.
Pulses, oilseeds	Snack foods and other value-added products, packaged oil
Soya bean	Soya flour/enzyme active soya flour for bakery and fortified foods, ready-to-eat snacks
Fruits and vegetables	Snacks, pickles, jams, juices, concentrates, pulps, slices, frozen and dehydrated products, wine
Fisheries	Processed fish, packaged products, frozen goods, derivatives such as fish oil
Meat and poultry	Eggs and broilers, frozen products
Milk and dairy	Packaged milk, milk powder, condensed milk, cottage and processed cheeses, *dahi*, yogurt, ice creams, desserts, butter, ghee

convert them into snacks, drinks and breakfast cereals. Milk is processed and sold as packaged milk or derived products by Amul, Mother Dairy, Parag, Nestlé, Cadbury's, CavinKare, and so on. Pickles, jams, juices and allied products are provided by ITC, Pepsi, Coca-Cola, Mother's Recipe, Tops, HUL, and many others. Fish processing is done by cooperatives, while meat and poultry products have players such as Venky's and Godrej. Processed food products are exported by these companies as well. Pharma companies such as Dabur and Himalaya source raw materials from agricultural producers and convert them into organic medicines and products. Food chains such as McDonald's, KFC, Shree Ratnam, Dunkin Donuts, Burger King and Domino's process huge quantities of agricultural products daily.

While these companies provide packaged products for further processing or direct consumption, the Indian food processing industry accounts for 32 per cent of the country's total food market, according to the website of Ministry of External Affairs. It is one of the largest industries in India and is ranked fifth in terms of production, consumption, export and expected growth.

Government Initiatives

The government provides various incentives for the growth of food processing industries in the country. Its Vision Document 2015, prepared by the Ministry of Food Processing Industries (MoFPI), lays the plan to increase the level of processing of perishables from 6 per cent to 20 per cent and aims at trebling the size of investment in the processed food sector.

Mini Case Study 8.4

Fruit Bageecha: Processing Apples in Himachal Pradesh

Himachal Pradesh is India's second largest producer of apples, after Jammu and Kashmir. It produces three varieties—Royal Delicious, Golden Delicious and their best-selling Red Delicious—and the state's economy depends heavily on the fruit through apple-grading houses, processing plants and tourism.

The glory of the Himachal apple began in Kotgarh. In 1916, Samuel Evan Stokes, who had come to Shimla, saw that locals were quite poor. He brought seeds of Red Delicious apples from Philadelphia and distributed them free of cost to people in Thanedar, in Kotgarh. He became known as Satyanand Stokes and became a leading activist of the freedom movement.

Apples have to be transported to markets in the plains. Cold storages help in preserving the fruit to be sold in the off-season. Apple processing is done by the H.P. Horticultural Produce Marketing and Processing Corporation Ltd, a government undertaking, and other private players.

Kotgarh Fruit Bageecha Pvt. Ltd was founded by Kartik and Anuradha Budhiraja. They were media professionals based in Singapore before relocating to Kotgarh to set up their dream project, a small-scale boutique modern food processing unit. They quit their media jobs to start Fruit Bageecha in collaboration with the Mahila Mandal, bringing marketing and branding expertise to the brand. After moving to Kotgarh, they crafted unique recipes with various fruits of the region with participation and help of the farmers. Fruit Bageecha makes green apple and ginger chutney, plum, apricot and kiwi preserves and sells them in gift packs. The products are available in shops and hotels in Himachal Pradesh, and are also sold on Amazon. It has branded counters on NH22, tie-ups with the Oberoi's in Himachal and branded retail shelves in the state, apart from exporting some products as well.

PHOTO 8.5

Fruit Bageecha offers processed chutneys and preserves from Himachal Pradesh.

Source: Fruit Bageecha (reprinted with permission).

PHOTO 8.6
Processing in progress by a Mahila Mandal.

Source: Fruit Bageecha (reprinted with permission).

Their vision is to bring premium quality and healthy fruit products from Himachal to consumers in India and for export. Fruit Bageecha procures local produce and engages local SHGs to make the products, imparting skills and capital in the local economy and using fruits that would be usually discarded or wasted.

The company employs 18 people from local communities. The women from the SHGs gain financial independence, learn proper techniques of production and participate in marketing fairs and activities. Underemployed marginal farmers are engaged on part time basis for packaging and labelling, which gives them additional sources of income. As it expands, it hopes to employ more people. At 100 per cent capacity Fruit Bageecha will require 45 tonnes of fruit, expanding procurement to 370 farmers and impacting 1,850 individuals directly, according to the Anuradha Budhiraja.

The fruits are bought from local marginal farmers. They are crated at the farm, saving farmers packaging, transport and middlemen fees. The company pays 10–20 per cent higher than government support prices and payments are made immediately. B-grade fruits, consisting of small sized, discoloured or hail impacted, which cannot be sold as table fruits, are bought. Such produce usually goes to waste. In this way, the company helps generate additional income for farmers. Fruit Bageecha is the only processor in the area.

Initiatives such as Fruit Bageecha help in various ways. They provide employment and better incomes for farmers. In years of glut, when prices fall and fruit is left to rot, farmers find it a boon to sell to a processor.

Can such initiatives achieve the success and scale of big brands? How?

Sources for this Case Study:

Web Resources

Fruit Bageecha website: http://fruitbageecha.com/

HPMC website: http://hpmc.gov.in/

Other Source

DNA. 2015. "Go on an Apple Trail in Himachal, the Land of the Forbidden Fruit." 3 November.

Some of the recent major initiatives taken by the government to improve the food processing sector in India are as follows:

- Union Budget 2016–17 has opened the way for 100 per cent foreign direct investment (FDI) through Foreign Investment Promotion Board for marketing of food products from India.
- Two Indian dairy companies, Parag Milk Foods and Schreiber Dynamix Dairies, have been given permission to export milk products to Russia.
- A mega international food park was inaugurated at Dabwala Kalan, Punjab.
- The Food Safety and Standards Authority of India (FSSAI) has issued new rules for importing products and simplified the process by relaxing labelling guidelines.
- The MoFPI announced a scheme for creation of infrastructure facilities for degree/diploma courses in food processing sector, a programme for entrepreneurship development and establishing Food Processing Training Centres.
- The Spices Board is selling 30 spices and value-added products globally under the brand names 'Spices India' and 'Flavourit'.
- The government is setting up of five Mega Food Parks in the states of Bihar, Maharashtra, Himachal Pradesh and Chhattisgarh and plans to set up 42 such mega food parks across the country.
- A corpus of ₹2,000 crore was created under NABARD in the Budget 2015–16, to provide cheaper credit to food processing industry and reduction of excise duty.

Besides this, the government has set up R&D organizations for agro-processing across the country. Leading among these are the ICAR, CSIR and state agricultural universities. Many other R&D institutes also exist, some of which are:

- BCKV, Kalyani
- CFTRI, Mysore
- CIAE, Bhopal
- CIPHET Ludhiana
- CIRCOT, Mumbai
- DFRL, Mysore
- GAU, Anand

- GPBUA&T, Pantnagar
- HBTI, Kanpur
- IARI, New Delhi
- IGFRI, Jhansi
- IGMRI, Hapur
- IISR, Lucknow
- IIT, Kharagpur
- ILRI, Ranchi
- IVRI, Izatnagar
- KVIC Mumbai
- MERADO, Ludhiana
- MPKV, Rahuri
- NDRI, Karnal
- NIRJAFT, Kolkata
- OTRI, Anantapur
- PAU, Ludhiana
- PHT Institute, Pune
- PPRC, Thanjavur
- RAU, Udaipur
- TNAU, Coimbatore

However, whether food processing industry has many takers is seriously in doubt, given the fact that many of these industries remain small and fail to achieve critical mass. Only large companies with marketing muscle have established themselves in this market. Village processing initiatives have remained just that; unless they tie up with marketing companies such as Unilever, ITC, Pepsi, Nestlé and others. One of the reasons is that Indian consumers still prefer fresh produce and do not really care for processed articles (see Mini Case Study 8.5).

Mini Case Study 8.5

Food Processing: No Takers

One way to deal with extreme price fluctuations in agricultural markets is to process agricultural produce so that it can be consumed in the off-season. Farmers would gain if their excess harvested produce is made into less perishable products and this would contribute to price stability. But, while technologies for storing and preservation are available, marketing it is a major challenge. This case study describes efforts to process onions and potatoes and market them.

Onions and potatoes can be processed as dried flakes, paste or even powder. The reasoning is that raw onions or potatoes can be bought cheap during harvest time, converted into dehydrated products having longer shelf life and then sold to consumers for the rest of the year.

The season for potato harvest is from mid-December to April. Since they have a water content of 80 per cent, these rot quickly unless kept in cold storage, which again adds to cost. In any case, cold storage capacity is just not available.

Technology for dehydration of potatoes has been developed by the Central Potato Research Institute, Jalandhar. It increases shelf life by up to eight months. A mechanical unit peels, chops and dries potatoes automatically which are then packed in polythene bags for storage or for sale for cooking. The dehydrated potatoes are fully rehydrated at the time of cooking without losing their original flavour and taste.

Similar technology for drying of fresh onions and converting into flakes, paste and powder has been developed by the Central Institute of Post-harvest Engineering and Technology (CIPHET), Ludhiana. It offers a special training course for processing of onions, which includes licensing its technology. One hundred kg of onions are converted into 14–16 kg of dried flakes with a shelf life of more than nine months. They can be rehydrated before consumption to get onions and used in cooking.

However, there are few takers for these technologies. The onion dehydration plants are concentrated around Bhavnagar in Gujarat and Nashik in Maharashtra. These units export the bulk of their dehydrated onion production, while selling small quantities domestically to institutional buyers such as hotels and restaurants.

One reason for slow off-take is that Indian consumers prefer fresh vegetables and are not used to dried flakes or powder. Consumers who have tried these products say that they are as good as fresh potatoes or onions and start using them when prices rise, but go back to buying fresh produce once the prices come down. This discourages entrepreneurs, who look for steady demand.

One example is that of Mandip Singh, who set up Satnam Agri Products Ltd in 2007 for producing dehydrated potato flakes and frozen French fries at a cost ₹52.50 crore. The plant has the capacity to process 36,000 tonnes of potatoes annually, but operates at 25 per cent of its capacity, selling quantities to McCain and Haldiram's. Consumers have not been persuaded to use these products regularly.

That is perhaps a reason why food processing industry does not do too well in the country. At present, less than 10 per cent of the 45 million tonnes of potatoes and 19 million tonnes of onions produced annually in India get processed.

How can Indian consumers be persuaded to use processed food in their daily cooking? Does the food processing industry have a future in India?

Source for this Case Study:

Indian Express. 2015. "Food Processing: Paste and Powder Solution for High Veggie Prices Has No Takers." 17 September.

Despite all the measures taken by different agencies, agro-foods have been slow to pick up in the country (see Mini Case Study 8.5). Only the large companies have succeeded to establish their brands. SMEs do succeed in producing viable products but lack the marketing muscle to distribute goods across the nation or the ability to establish brands. Getting consumers to change their preference for fresh produce has also been difficult. Challenges in the agro-processing industry are described in the next section.

Challenges in Agro-processing

Many government reports and reports by international consultancies suggest that there are many opportunities in the agro-processing industry in India. They appear to be off the mark. For one, it is not easy to make a success of food processing in India yet, as described in the previous section. There are many challenges to the industry; even if the technology to process crops is available, marketing the goods or convincing customers is not an easy task. As we have mentioned, Indian customers prefer fresh agricultural products and are slow to take on processed foods. Only large companies can afford the huge marketing expenditure required to build brands. Small manufacturers struggle with quality, distribution and sales issues.

There are many other constraints as well. A FICCI survey 'Bottlenecks in Indian Food Processing Industry, 2010' (FICCI 2010) has identified top five challenges which need immediate action to stimulate the growth of the sector:

1. **Inadequate infrastructure:** More than 30 per cent of the produce from farm gate is lost due to inadequate cold chain infrastructure and inadequate logistics, estimates Kapoor (2011). Inadequate support infrastructure is considered to be the biggest bottleneck in expanding the food processing sector. Long and fragmented supply chains, inadequate cold storage and warehousing facilities, lack of transport infrastructure, lack of modern logistics and last mile connectivity are some of the problems that exist in India.
2. **Regulatory environment:** Numerous laws, under the jurisdiction of different ministries and departments, govern food safety and packaging. The multiplicity of legislation leads to contradictions of various kinds. Manufacturers of packaged food products are obligated to comply with quality standards and label declarations prescribed under multiple legislations and statues. India needs a national food processing policy with a number of legislative, administrative and promotional measures, evolved through discussions between all the stakeholders.
3. **Multiple authorities:** The multiplicity of ministries and administering authorities at both at the Central and state level has resulted in a complex regulatory system that burdens the industry.
4. **Inadequate manpower:** There is a shortage of skilled and semi-skilled workers which is a hindrance to the growth of the sector. There are strong deficiencies in technical knowhow and support and employees are unable to use modern tools and equipment.
5. **Other factors:** Constraints in raw material procurement, taxation, access to credit, lack of applied research are other major challenges for the growth of food processing sector.

It is hoped that things may change as consumer tastes change, but so far small manufacturers in food processing have remained small.

Floriculture

Floriculture consists of cut flowers, pot plants, cut foliage, seeds, bulbs, tubers, rooted cuttings and dried flowers or leaves. The important floriculture crops for cut flowers are rose, carnation, chrysanthemum, gerbera, gladiolus, gypsophila, *liatris*, nerine, orchids, *achillea*, *anthurium*, tulip and lilies. Floriculture crops such as gerberas and carnation are grown in green houses.

Chrysanthemum, roses, gaillardia, lily, marigold and other flowers are grown in the open. There has been a steady increase in demand of flowers and this has motivated many farmers to diversify. It has today become an important component of agribusiness. *DNA India* (2016) reports that floriculture has attracted farmers in states such as Tamil Nadu, Karnataka, West Bengal, Madhya Pradesh and Maharashtra. The north-eastern states, especially Mizoram, are also cultivating flowers.

The government has identified floriculture as a sunrise industry and accorded it 100 per cent export-oriented status. Flowers require great care and some have to be grown under controlled conditions, but it is a lucrative business. Much of the production is exported. After liberalization, cut flowers can be exported while seeds of international varieties can be imported. The APEDA is responsible for export promotion and development of floriculture in India. The

FIGURE 8.9
Growth of floriculture in India.

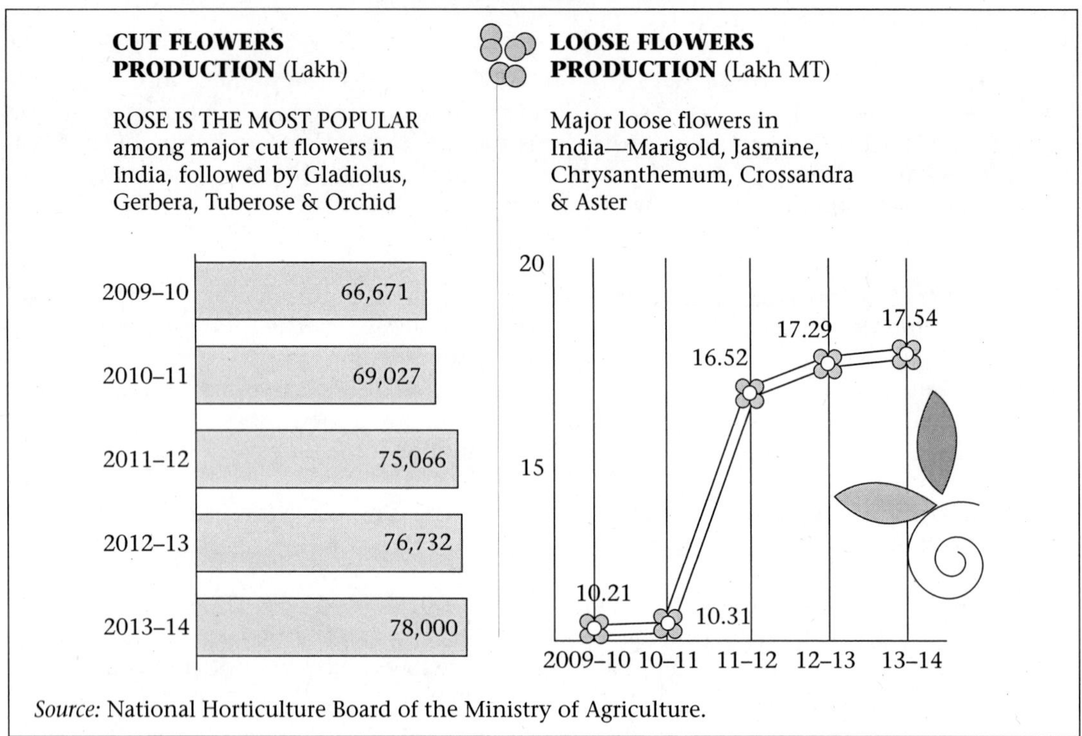

Source: Times of India (2016).

country has exported 22,947.23 million tonnes of floriculture products to the world worth ₹460.75 crore in 2014–15. The growth of the industry is shown in Figure 8.9.

The major export destinations are: United States, United Kingdom, Germany, Netherland and United Arab Emirates. Floriculture flourishes in Maharashtra, Karnataka, Andhra Pradesh, Haryana, Tamil Nadu, Rajasthan and West Bengal. However, though the country had exported floriculture products worth over ₹460 crore in 2014–15, its share is miniscule in world trade of nearly US$ 40 billion or nearly ₹272,000 crore.

Meat and Poultry Products

Next to crops, livestock has been the major occupation of the rural population. There has been an increase in demand for meat in the country as well as for exports. India has the world's largest population of livestock and is world's 5th largest producer of meat.

The total processing capacity in India is over 1 million tonnes per annum, of which 40–50 per cent is utilized, according to the MoFPI website. Traditional agricultural exports are now competing with new sectors such as buffalo meat exports. At least 70 per cent of the buffalo meat is exported. The major areas for buffalo meat production are Uttar Pradesh, Andhra Pradesh, Maharashtra and Punjab, with Uttar Pradesh being the top buffalo meat producing state producing 0.3 million tonnes in 2011.

Meat production has grown from 2.3 million tonnes at the end of Tenth Five Year Plan (2006–07) to 5.5 million tonnes at the end of the Eleventh Five Year Plan (2011–12). The annual growth rate for meat production in 2011–12 was about 13 per cent.

Indian buffalo meat is witnessing strong demand in international markets. Goat and lamb meat are relatively small segments. Rajasthan, Jammu and Kashmir, Uttar Pradesh, Gujarat, hilly regions of North and Eastern Himalayas are the Indian regions with maximum livestock population. The production levels in these two categories have been almost constant at 0.95 million tonnes with annual exports of less than 10,000 tonnes.

The industry is suffering now since the growth of vigilantes under the garb of 'cow protectors'. The government has been unable to control them. Transportation of livestock and processing has been targeted, causing harm to the industry.

Poultry is one of the fastest growing segments of the agricultural sector in India today: the growth rate of eggs and broilers has been 8 to 10 per cent per annum. India is now the world's fifth largest egg producer and the eighteenth largest producer of broilers. Poultry demand is driven by rising incomes and change in eating preferences of the population. The industry consists of small poultry farms to integrated production units producing chilled and frozen products. These plants produce dressed chicken, chicken cut parts and other chicken products and also manufacture egg powder and frozen egg yolk for export.

The maximum egg production takes place in Tamil Nadu, whereas Hyderabad has the maximum poultry and hatcheries. Besides Andhra Pradesh, Karnataka, Tamil Nadu, Maharashtra, Gujarat, Madhya Pradesh, Odisha and north eastern states are the major egg contributors.

COLD CHAINS

A cold chain is a logistics system that provides a series of warehouses and transport facilities for maintaining ideal storage conditions for perishables from the point of origin to the point of consumption in the food supply chain. It is a temperature-controlled supply chain, consisting of storage and transportation, and maintains products within an ambient range of temperature. A cold chain is essential for the transport of perishable goods, which would get destroyed if exposed to room temperature even for a short time. That is why, unbroken cold chains are required, which consist of uninterrupted series of refrigerated trucks and warehouses where products are stored within a given temperature range till they reach the customer.

Cold chains are of great value for agricultural produce and are especially useful in transporting food items, which would perish otherwise at the farm. They help in storing goods, extending their shelf life and increasing their markets. They are especially useful in agriculture, enabling goods to be stored at the time of harvest (when prices are low) and used throughout the year at places where they are required. The development of cold chains helps in reducing wastages of perishable commodities and thus providing remunerative prices.

India has a paucity of cold chains. Singh (2015) writes in *Forbes*, "Because the cold chain in India is patchy, US$13 billion of fresh food goes waste every year." Bad roads from villages, lack of proper transport, several stages in the distribution chain—all add up to produce from farmers reaching consumers after a long time, and by that time some of the produce have been destroyed. The country has 32 million tonnes of cold store capacity, but much more is required, which calls for huge investments in the cold chain. Apart from increasing the capacity in cold storage, thousands of refrigerated vehicles and improvement of roads is required.

FIGURE 8.10
Growth of cold chain industry in India.

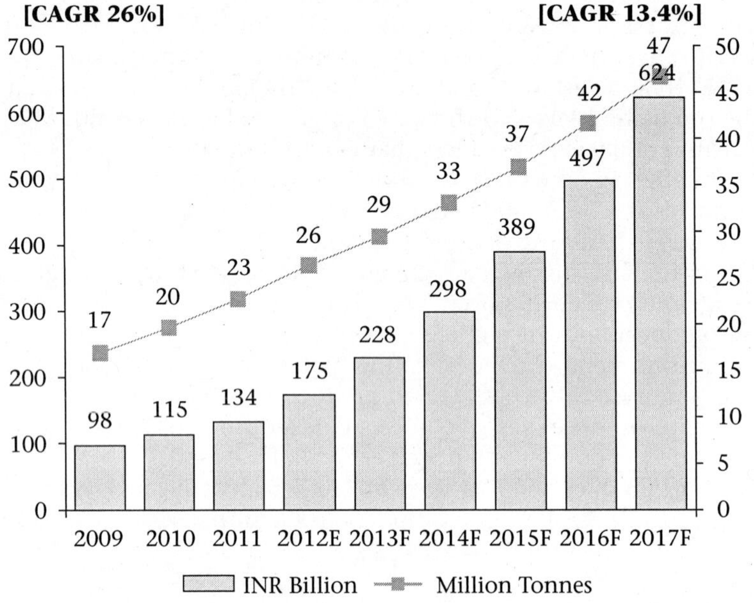

Source: Cargo Talk (2015).

India's cold chain sector has been growing at a CAGR of 13.4 per cent in 2013–16 (Figure 8.10). The cold chain market in India is ₹624 billion in 2017, according to a report by Onicra Credit Rating Agency (2014). India has 6,300 cold storage facilities with an installed capacity of about 32 million metric tonnes, mostly used for storing potatoes. Uttar Pradesh and West Bengal have more than half of the cold storage facilities in India, while other states still have to develop the infrastructure. Government policy has been restrictive; several initiatives taken by private and foreign retailers to start 'farm-to-fork' chains were nipped in the bud because of restrictions on FDI in retail.

Much of the cold stores and trucks are owned by the unorganized sector, with organized players contributing to about 10 per cent of the cold chain industry market. Cold storage warehouses of public sector undertakings such as Central Warehousing Corporation (CWC), the FCI and State Warehousing Corporations (SWCs) have about 70 per cent capacity in cold storage.

The National Centre for Cold Chain Development has been established as an autonomous centre for excellence to promote and develop integrated cold chains in India. The main objectives of the centre are to recommend standards for cold chain infrastructure and to recommend policy framework for development of cold chains. The government has also opened investment in cold chains under the automatic route for 100 per cent FDI participation.

The major organized sector players in the industry are GATI-Kausar, Gateway Distriparks Ltd., Transport Corporation of India, Container Corporation of India Ltd, Fresh and Healthy Enterprises Ltd. (FHEL), Kelvin Cold Chain Logistics Pvt. Ltd., Crystal Logistic Cool Chain Ltd., ColdEX Logistics Pvt. Ltd., and many others. A cold chain developed by Dev Bhoomi Foods for storing apples is shown in Photo 8.7.

PHOTO 8.7

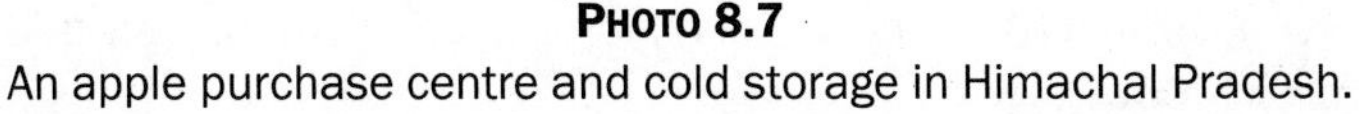

An apple purchase centre and cold storage in Himachal Pradesh.

Source: Photograph by Dinesh Kumar.

However, the industry faces many challenges, which are summarized here:

1. **High in investment:** Cold chains call for heavy investment in fixed assets such as plant and machinery, building and insulation panels. This deters many private players.
2. **Low returns:** Cold chains call for high investments but offer low returns. It is a capital-intensive industry and hence returns are low. Private companies raise funds through debt, which adds heavy interest burden on them.
3. **High energy costs:** Cold chains have high energy requirements and this results in high operating costs. Energy expenses make up about 30 per cent of the total expenses.
4. **Very high real estate costs:** The country has very high real estate costs, which increases investments.
5. **Pollution:** Refrigerated trucks burn excessive diesel, resulting in high pollution levels. With awareness about pollution rising, the industry will have to look for a trade-off between transportation and reduction in pollution levels.

GENETICALLY MODIFIED CROPS

GM crops are also part of agribusiness. GM crops are defined as plants in which the genetic material or DNA has been altered in a way that does not occur in nature. Scientists are able to use gene technology or genetic engineering to modify or transfer genes one organism into another, or between nonrelated species. Foods produced from or using GM organisms are often referred to as GM food.

GM technology is able to modify crops so that they can be kept for longer time, or become resistant to pests, or even have greater nutritional value. GM crops have increased farm outputs in countries where they have been introduced. According to the World Health Organization (WHO) website, resistance against insects is achieved by incorporating into the food plant the gene for toxin production from the bacterium *Bacillus thuringiensis* (Bt).

However, there is controversy with regard to the introduction of GM crops in India. One view is that GM crops are needed to feed a growing population. It is argued that by opposing this technology, India is poised to miss the GM technology revolution just as it had missed the industrial revolution earlier and could not reap the benefits of rapid industrialization. Already, the US Food and Drug Administration, WHO and European Commission have concluded that genetically modified organisms (GMOs) are safe to eat. The contrary view, supported by NGOs and activists, is that GM crops encourage monocultures, are unsuited to our environment and will make us dependent on foreign companies who provide a package of seeds, fertilizers and pesticides every year to make huge profits. Fears about long-term human and environment safety, market monopolies in seeds and food sovereignty, have also been expressed. The arguments for and against GM technology have been summarized in Table 8.6.

Bt cotton was the first GM crop approved for cultivation in India in 2002. It caught on, and at present, 97 per cent of India cotton cultivation area is under Bt cotton. Gulati (2016) estimates the benefits of Bt introduction in the country. He writes that India gained roughly US$55 billion over the period from 2002 to 2015 from exports of raw cotton, additional yarn

TABLE 8.6

Arguments for and against GM technology.

For	Against
Necessary to meet food requirements of a growing population	They are environmentally harmful
Helps grow more food	Reduces India's food security, increases monocultures
Require less pesticides and fertilizers	Makes us dependent on foreign companies
Increased yields, crops tweaked to have greater shelf life, also for better taste and flavour	Not good to tamper with nature
Genes can be mixed from various sources for sturdy crops	Mixing of genes is harmful, will increase allergies
No harmful effects reported from countries where GM technologies have been introduced	Pests will become immune, will make crops vulnerable to attacks from sturdy pests
Have helped farmers earn better incomes	Will result in wiping out traditional crops and farm knowledge
Green revolution has outlived its utility and new technologies are required	'Terminator' technologies means farmers cannot save seeds, will have to buy new seeds every time
Genetic modification is nothing new, people have manipulated foods and food crops for years	Much of the research done by foreign companies, intellectual property rights slow research, government research missing
Studies indicate no harm from GM crops	Studies are paid for by MNCs

Mini Case Study 8.6

Monsanto's Dilemma

The Indian GM crops saga is a convoluted one, writes *Mint* (2016). It has the world's fourth largest GM crop acreage under Bt cotton, the only GM crop allowed in the country. But the introduction of Bt cotton has courted controversy, with pricing and intellectual property rights (IPR) issues followed by government price interventions and litigation.

GM varieties of rice, wheat and okra, have been genetically modified to resist bugs and weed-killing sprays. In India, Maharashtra Hybrid Seeds Co (Mahyco) has a joint venture with Monsanto to develop biotech crops. Already, GMOs grow in 97 per cent of India's cotton fields, which has increased production tremendously.

But, reports Bunge and Mukherji (2016), after a decade of Monsanto's efforts with Mahyco to get government approval, it has not been successful, facing opposition from motley environmentalists, nationalists and government inaction. The country has conducted biotech-food-crop trials but has approved none for commercial cultivation. Litigation is also pending in the Supreme Court.

Monsanto has faced other problems too, causing it to threaten to withdraw from the country. Government price controls around seed genetics and a probe into pricing practices have thwarted the company's efforts. India is not alone. There is a push-back in GM technology in countries in the European Union, Russia and China. This has slowed global sales growth of GM seeds.

What, in your opinion, should be done about GM crops in India?

Sources for this Case Study:

Bunge, Jacob, and Biman Mukherji. 2016. "Why Monsanto's Biotech-Food Business Isn't Growing in India." *The Wall Street Journal*, 13 March.

Mint. 2016. "Genetically Modified Crops: The Way Forward." 8 February.

shipments, and savings in potential imports as a direct result of introduction of Bt cotton in the country. Farmers have seen a 3.5-fold increase in profits alone and that is the reason that more than 95 per cent of India's cotton area is under Bt, representing the fastest spread of the technology anywhere in the world. Seed costs for farmers, which were 6.14 per cent of farmers' total revenues in 2001–02, came down to 4.78 per cent in 2012–13.

Though cotton yields have more than doubled in the first decade since its introduction in 2002, it was also shadowed by controversy. Issues of pricing and IPR issues, protests by social activists and government price interventions as well as subsequent litigation have restricted growth of GM crops in the country (see Mini Case Study 8.6).

For example, Bt brinjal was cleared for commercialization in India by the Genetic Engineering Appraisal Committee in 2009 after studying the biosafety data and field trials by two expert committees. But, following protests by social activists, the government withheld the permission.

Studies have shown that GM foods do not have any human or ecological ill effects and are beneficial to farmers as they result in increased yields and resistance to pests, reports *Mint* (2016). A wide-ranging study conducted in Germany in 2014 had found that use of GM technology increased crop yields by 22 per cent, reduced chemical pesticides by 37 per cent and increased farmer profits by 68 per cent, with better results in developing countries than in developed ones.

But these studies have been questioned by opponents of GM crops, who say that the studies, regulatory bodies and scientific publications are working in tandem with multinationals providing GM technology.

Successive governments have failed to provide direction to the controversy. They have tried to regulate GM crops and their prices, but this has not helped. The government has to be more transparent, introduce the Biotechnology Regulatory Authority of India Bill and resolve contentious IPR issues that and resolve contentious IPR issues. It has kept biosafety data out about GM mustard a secret.

GM crops with increased drought resistance and reduced pesticide dependence can be developed by working with Indian and foreign research institutions. But increasingly this technology will come from foreign MNCs. As pointed out by Gulati and Sarkar (2016), the entire ICAR budget for the country was around ₹4,840 crore (US$0.8 bn) in 2014–15. But Monsanto alone had spent US$1.7 billion in R&D in 2014.

RURAL RETAIL

Despite the large size of rural markets and expectations of rural growth, the final link in rural marketing—rural agricultural retail—has not worked well, both to rural and urban customers. It was felt that rural folk had evolved enough to start buying from large superstores and hypermarkets. Even the Haryana government invested more than ₹200 crores in building agro-malls in the state (see Mini Case Study 8.7). However, most ventures had to bite the dust. Some of the rural retail ventures that either closed down or downsized operations were: Godrej Aadhaar, Choupal Sagar, DSCL Haryali Stores, Mahindra & Mahindra Shubh Labh stores, Escorts rural stores, Tata Kisan Sansar, Indianoil and Warna Bazaar in Maharashtra, among others.

Organized retail ventured into food retailing hoping to source directly from villages and established supply chains up to urban consumers. Companies such as ITC, Godrej, Walmart and Reliance made inroads into food and vegetable retail. Food chains such as McDonalds and Pepsi sourced agricultural products from rural areas, which were processed at their factories or their partners' factories to be supplied to end consumers. Food processing and packaged goods companies such as Nestlé, HUL and others also sourced produce from farmers or entered into contracts with farmers, providing them with technical help and support, including high-yield variety seeds. While some players have been successful in setting up supply chains, others have failed, most notably, Subhiksha, Six Ten and Spencer's. Foreign chains such as Walmart and Tesco were prevented from setting up their supply chains because of FDI restrictions; such retailers attracted much political protests and some exited the country. Even large players such as Reliance Retail and Big Bazaar have faced problems. Reliance Retail shut more than 60 loss-making Reliance Fresh stores in the country in 2016 as they were making losses, according to *Financial Express* (2017). It has tried various formats, spending over US$1 billion in trial-and-error to find a formula that works for India.

Recent Developments

Despite the failures, rural retail has seen a number of growing trends. It is seen as a growth industry by many consultancies. Some of the trends described in research reports are given here:

- **Huge size:** Rural and semi-urban India represents a vast, underserved market.
- **Growing fast:** Due to several government and other interventions, the market is growing fast. Many consumers show increased spending power.

Mini Case Study 8.7

Agro-malls: Non-starters

FIGURE 8.11
An auction notice for space in an agro-mall in Haryana.

Source: http://www.hsamb.gov.in/panipat%2031.pdf (Accessed on 28 April 2017).

In a case of mindless copying of urban trends, the Haryana government decided to build agro-malls in the state, so that farmers could buy their needs from a modern mall. It was proposed that the ground floor of the malls would have shops to sell agricultural goods and equipment to farmers, while the top floor would have multiplexes. They would also have food courts. These malls were launched at four places: Panchkula, Karnal, Panipat and Rohtak. Announced in 2008, the buildings were completed in 2013–14 at a cost of over ₹200 crore and auction notices were placed in ads (Figure 8.11) but found no takers.

The project was neither practical nor sensible. It ignored the fact that farmers preferred to buy from nearby towns and would see the trip to the city as an additional cost; organized retail stores for agricultural goods had already closed or scaled down (see Chapter 2). Agricultural products, in any case, were hardly the type of goods that one would go to a mall for. The urban crowd too would avoid the agro-malls even to see a movie.

In 2016, after the huge expenditure of public money, it was decided that the concept of agro-malls was not practical. For one thing, agricultural goods are not consumer goods; they are more like industrial goods. The purchase behaviour of farmers is similar to that of a company buying industrial materials; they do not look for display or variety, but go by product performance and word-of-mouth recommendations. Thus, the agro-malls were doomed to fail right from the start.

PHOTO 8.8

A faded board greets visitors at the agro-mall, Panipat.

Source: Photograph by Dinesh Kumar.

The Haryana government now has another hare-brained idea: to convert the agro-malls into general malls so that these can be utilized. However, how it plans to run the malls, considering that many malls have failed to take off. And, how the government justifies spending funds meant for farmers to run malls, remains a mystery.

How can agricultural retail be organized and modernized in the country?

Sources for this Case Study:

Web Resource

Haryana State Agricultural Marketing Board website. Available at: http://www.hsamb.gov.in/panipat%2031.pdf

Other Source

Business Today. 2015. "After Spending ₹200 Crore, Haryana to Do away with Agro-malls." 2 December.

- **Increased education and awareness:** With increased education and awareness, there is improvement in lifestyles and rural people are demanding the same goods that are sold in urban markets.
- **Change in purchase habits:** Rural consumer behaviour is also changing due to the aforementioned factors.
- **E-commerce venturing into villages:** E-commerce firms have made inroads in rural markets making people buy modern products.
- **Smartphones use is increasing in villages:** As smartphones spread in villages, companies will have more tools to engage rural customers. They will soon have big data to analyze rural consumers.

How these trends shape up in the future remain to be seen. Though they have potential, many trends do not translate into big gains because some aspects of rural consumer behaviour are ignored. For example, e-commerce companies could have been the answer to achieving rural penetration, but they discovered that sending goods to remote villages was not all that simple. The packets reached a town but sending a single packet or two to a remote village was not economically feasible for courier companies. Many of these companies started their own logistics branches, but the fact remains that sending goods to remote areas is an expensive proposition.

Though income, education and awareness are improving fast, rural markets remain difficult to be serviced. Companies have to either find prosperous segments or devise innovative approaches for sales and distribution. If a magic formula of servicing rural markets while keeping costs under control is found, their efforts will nevertheless succeed.

Agribusiness suffers from various limitations. First and foremost among them is government intervention, which often achieves the opposite objectives than the intended ones. Second, since agro-inputs are entirely different across regions, companies have to offer different products, communications and strategy in different areas. Third, the demand for agro-inputs is uneven. Agro-inputs are required only during certain times of the year. Since they are not required all the year round, companies find it difficult to invest in sales offices and channels. Fourth, there are problems of lack of storage, grading facilities and transportation. The CWC and SWCs do not extend their services to the rural areas. Private warehouses are just not enough. Finally, agribusiness requires large marketing organization and staff, which adds to the cost, which is sometimes not possible to recover. Educated youngsters who are willing to work in villages are not available.

It is hoped that the sector gets over its problems gradually and evolves into a sector that helps the farmer in the long run.

SUMMARY

The chapter describes how agriculture is treated as a service to the nation, but in fact should be treated as any other business. Agribusiness includes all activities related to agriculture, including inputs, raw materials and marketing of outputs. Agricultural value chains are described as 'farm-to-fork', which implies that value is added at various stages as the product moves from farm to the consumer. Developing countries lag behind the developed world in terms of agricultural products processed and value-added. Much of the food produced is wasted because of undeveloped value chains.

Agribusiness has five distinct sub-sectors: agro-chemicals, agricultural machinery and implements, agro-inputs, agro-processing and diversified farming. Agro-chemicals include fertilizers, pesticides, liming and acidifying agents, soil conditioners and chemicals used in animal husbandry. The agro-chemicals industry consists of various types of chemicals used for crop protection, such as insecticides, fungicides, herbicides and bio-pesticides. Agriculture machinery is an important part of agribusiness and consists of hand tools, animal-drawn implements and power-operated equipment. Agricultural tools are used for various operations. Most of the tools are fabricated by small-scale units in towns and sold there. Agro-inputs include seeds and other inputs, while agro-processing is involved in conservation and handling of agricultural produce and to make it usable for later use.

Other additions in agribusiness include floriculture and meat and poultry products. Cold chains are important in establishing storage and distribution of agricultural products. The latest addition to agriculture is the introduction of GM crops, which have the potential to revolutionize Indian agriculture. However, there is controversy regarding introduction of GM crops in India. Agribusiness, in terms of organized retail in villages, has been a failure.

CONCLUSION

To revitalize Indian agriculture, a paradigm shift in thought is required: 'agriculture' must be viewed as 'agribusiness'. The definition of agriculture merely as a system of growing food has to be viewed as "the science and practice of activities relating to production, processing, marketing, distribution and trade of food, feed and fibre," as described by Acharya (2006). That is to say, "agricultural development strategy must address not only farmers but also those in marketing, trade, processing, and agri business. In this context, efficient marketing and rural credit systems assume added importance," he writes.

Such a shift will ensure that the focus should now shift from 'only production' to 'production plus all other associated activities' that constitute agribusiness. Second, it implies innovation, so that new solutions are found for age-old problems. It is only if there is a shift in thinking of agriculture as a business when investments will be encouraged and modernization can take place.

Indian agriculture cries for modernization. It is time that government withdrew its many laws and constraints and liberalized it, just the way that industry was liberalized several years ago.

KEY TERMS

Agribusiness: Agribusiness is a term that was coined in 1957 by Goldberg and Davis. It includes all activities related to agriculture, including agro-chemicals, breeding, crop production (farming and contract farming), distribution, farm machinery, processing and seed supply, as well as marketing and retail sales.

Agriculture machinery: It is an important part of agribusiness. It consists of hand tools, animal-drawn implements and power-operated equipment.

Agro-chemicals: Refers to a class of products used in farming, such as fertilizers, pesticides, liming and acidifying agents, soil conditioners and chemicals used in animal husbandry.

Agro-processing: A set of techno-economic activities for conservation and handling of agricultural produce and to make it usable for later use.

Cold chain: A logistics system that provides a series of warehouses and transport facilities for maintaining ideal storage conditions for perishables from the point of origin to the point of consumption in the food supply chain.

Farm-to-fork: A value chain in which value is added at various stages as the product moves from farm to the consumer.

Floriculture: Consists of cut flowers, pot plants, cut foliage, seeds bulbs, tubers, rooted cuttings and dried flowers or leaves.

Genetically modified (GM) crops: Plants in which the genetic material or DNA has been altered in a way that does not occur in nature.

Micro-irrigation equipment: Micro-irrigation systems supply water directly to the root of plants through a network of plastic pipes.

Seed Banks: A seed bank is a type of gene bank where seeds of different crops and rare plant species are stored for future use.

Value chain: First described by Michael Porter (1985, Chapter 1, 11–15), it shows how firms add value in various ways, such as inbound logistics, operations, outbound logistics, marketing and sales and service (primary activities) and procurement, human resource management, technological development and infrastructure (secondary activities).

CONCEPT REVIEW QUESTIONS

1. Describe an agricultural value chain. How can it help farmers and consumers?
2. What are the components of agribusiness? What new components have been added to it over time?
3. Describe fertilizer marketing in the country. What are the drawbacks in the system?
4. What are agro-chemicals? What do they include and what are the problems in their marketing?
5. Discuss the adoption of tractors by farmers in the country over the years. What are the factors that prevent or help in their marketing?
6. How are seeds marketed? Which are the major players?
7. What is agro-processing? What does it consist of? How can crops be processed for greater value addition?
8. Describe the floriculture industry. What does it consist of and how are flowers marketed?
9. What is a cold chain? Discuss the growth of cold chains in India.
10. What are GM crops? Discuss their advantages and disadvantages.

CRITICAL THINKING QUESTIONS

1. Why should agribusiness be treated as a business like any other? What are the harms that arise if agriculture is treated as a service? Do you agree that Indian agriculture will benefit if agricultural farmers are treated as businessmen?
2. Comment on the movements that conserve traditional seeds. What purpose do they serve? Should such movements be encouraged or should the country go for modernization of seed industry?
3. Food processing is often touted as a panacea for ills in Indian agriculture and government is also setting up agro-processing parks. But, given the Indian preference for fresh products (which are also cheaper), can food processing really succeed? How can processed foods be brought into the shopping list of Indian consumers?
4. Discuss the growth of GM crops in the country. Whereas one camp says they are very harmful and traditional varieties should be encouraged, the other camp maintains that GM crops are essential for increasing food production. Which side are you on? Why?

PROJECTS AND ASSIGNMENTS

1. Visit a food processing industry in your area. Discuss its operations and problems. Find out how the products are marketed. How can you help make it into a national brand?
2. Interview a farmer and find out his perceptions about companies trying to build supply chains to his village. What are his expectations? How does he perceive the actions of the companies?
3. Take up a project to study farm mechanization in a village near your area. What is the level of modernization there? Identify the factors encouraging or hindering farm modernization.
4. Study a value chain for any agricultural product. See how value is added at different stages. Give your analysis about the efficiency of this chain.

WEB RESOURCES

"Agricultural Census of India 2010–11." Available at: http://agcensus.nic.in/document/agcensus2010/agcen2010rep.htm

Agricultural Machinery Manufacturers Association (AMMA-India) website: http://www.ammaindia.in/

AMMA-India. "Power tiller sales in India." Available at: http://un-csam.org/ppta/201411TC10/IN2.pdf

Annadana India website: http://annadana-india.org/our-work-new/

Annual Reports of Animal Husbandry Department: http://dahd.nic.in/documents/reports

APEDA website: http://apeda.gov.in/apedawebsite/SubHead_Products/Floriculture.htm

Deccan Development Society website: http://ddsindia.com/

Food and Agriculture Organization of the United Nations (FAO) website: http://www.fao.org/home/en/Ministry of External Affairs website: http://indiainbusiness.nic.in/newdesign/index.php?param=industryservices_landing/337/1

Ministry of Food Processing Industries website: http://www.mofpi.nic.in/

National Seeds Corporation website: http://www.indiaseeds.com/index.html

Navdanya website: http://www.navdanya.org/WHO website—Frequently asked questions on genetically modified foods: http://www.who.int/foodsafety/areas_work/food-technology/faq-genetically-modified-food/en/

REFERENCES

Acharya, S.S. 2006. "Agricultural Marketing and Rural Credit for Strengthening Indian Agriculture." INRM Policy Brief No. 3, Asian Development Bank, New Delhi.

Cargo Talk. 2015. "Indian Cold Chain Industry: Challenges & Impact." August. Available at: http://www.aisats.in/uploads/media_pdf/_2015-08-10_10_36_02..pdf (Accessed on 14 April 2017).

Damodaran, Harish. 2016. "Is Agriculture a Business?" *Indian Express*, 1 April.

Davis, John H., and Ray A. Goldberg. 1957. A Concept of Agribusiness. Boston, MA: Harvard University.

DNA India. 2016. "Flower Fascination: India Set to be Floriculture Trade Leader." 14 February.

The Economic Times. 2013. "Decreasing Land Holdings Biggest Challenge for Indian Agriculture: NABARD." 24 August.

FICCI. 2010. "Bottlenecks In Indian Food Processing Industry." A Survey report. Available at: http://ficci.in/sedocument/20073/Food-Processing-bottlenecks-study.pdf (Accessed on 27 April 2017).

———. 2012. "Ushering in the 2nd Green Revolution—Role of Crop Protection Chemicals." A Report on Indian Agrochemical Industry, Federation of Indian Chambers of Commerce & Industry (FICCI) and TATA Strategic Management Group (TSMG).

Gulati, Ashok, and Shreya Sarkar. 2016. "Heading Backwards." *Indian Express*, 14 March.

Gulf News. 2014. "Saudi Arabia bans import of Indian chili peppers." 9 May. Available at: http://gulfnews.com/news/gulf/saudi-arabia/saudi-arabia-bans-import-of-indian-chili-peppers-1.1330334 (Accessed on 21 April 2017).

Kapoor, Rana. 2011. "Food Processing: Key Challenges and Deliverables for Success." *The Hindu BusinessLine,* 2 October. Available at: http://www.thehindubusinessline.com/economy/agri-business/food-processing-key-challenges-and-deliverables-for-success/article2506269.ece (Accessed on 17 April 2017).

Ken Research. 2014. "India Micro Irrigation System Market Outlook to 2018." Available at: http://www.news.kenresearch.com/post/92721005228/india-micro-irrigation-system-market-potential (Accessed on 27 April 2017).

Kotak Institutional Equities. 2013. "Automobiles: Sixth Gear." 1 January. Available at: http://www.team-bhp.com/forum/commercial-vehicles/130919-kotaks-report-tractor-segment-india.html (Accessed on 27 April 2017).

Mazumdar J. 2017. "Reliance Industries Arm Reliance Retail Shuts 60 Stores as Losses Mount." *Financial Express*, 17 February.

Mint. 2015. "India's Flawed Fertilizer Policy." 1 April.

———. 2016. "Genetically Modified Crops: The Way Forward." 8 February.

Onicra Credit Rating Agency. 2014. "Indian Cold Chain Industry: Modernization of the Cold Storage Infrastructure." Available at: http://www.onicra.com/images/pdf/publications/coldchainindustryreportjune2014.pdf (Accessed on 27 April 2017).

Onicra Credit Rating Agency of India. "Food Processing Industry in India." Available at: http://www.onicra.com/images/pdf/publications/foodprocessingindustry31may.pdf (Accessed on 27 April 2017).

Patel, A. 2014. "Issues Facing Agricultural Credit in India." *India Microfinance*, 28 July. Available at: http://indiamicrofinance.com/issues-of-agricultural-credit-in-india.html (Accessed on 27 April 2017).

Porter, Michael E. 1985. *Competitive Advantage*. New York, NY: The Free Press.

Reuters. 2015. "Fake Pesticides Endanger Crops and Human Health in India." 19 November. Available at: http://www.reuters.com/article/us-india-pesticides-idUSKCN0T830J20151120 (Accessed on 25 April 2017).

Singh, G. 2009. "Agricultural Mechanisation Development in India.", in *Agricultural Mechanization and Automation* 1, edited by Paul McNulty and Patrick M. Grace. Oxford, UK: EOLSS Publishers and UNESCO.

Singh, R. 2015. "Effective Cold Chains Help Productivity." *Forbes*, 16 July. Available at: http://www.forbes.com/sites/ranisingh/2015/07/16/indias-cold-chain-needs-to-get-moving/#453f8c472e12 (Accessed on 25 April 2017).

Sud, S. 2015. "Power Tillers are Back in Business." *Business Standard*, 15 June.

Times of India. 2016. "Flower Fascination: India Set to Be Floriculture Trade Leader." 14 February. Available at: http://timesofindia.indiatimes.com/india/Flower-fascination-India-set-to-be-floriculture-trade-leader/articleshow/50979808.cms (Accessed on 10 January 2017).

UNIDO. 2009. "Agro-value Chain Analysis and Development: The UNIDO Approach." A Staff Working Paper. Vienna: United Nations Industrial Development Organization.

Closing Case
Reliance Fresh

Reliance Retail is consumer facing business of Reliance Industries Ltd. Started in 2006, it serves over 2.5 million customers every week and sources from thousands of farmers and vendors. Its loyalty programme, Reliance One, has more than 6.75 million customers. It has a nationwide network of retail outlets backed by state-of-the-art technology and supply chain infrastructure.

Reliance Retail has a multi-format strategy and operates through convenience stores, supermarkets, hypermarkets, wholesale cash-and-carry stores and specialty stores. It is the country's largest retailer with revenue of ₹20,000 crore and has a CAGR of 29 per cent in 2011–16. In 2015–16, Reliance Retail added 624 new stores, taking the total number of stores to 3,245 stores, spread over 12.8 million sq. ft.

It was not easy for the company. When it was launched, some political outfits protested and indulged in vandalism at their stores in Uttar Pradesh, West Bengal and Odisha, saying that it was anti-farmer and anti-small shops. However, the company retails farm produce in the other states.

Reliance Fresh buys vegetables and fruits from local farmers through collection centres. This reduces procurement wastage. From the collection point, the goods are transported to processing point or the retail outlets. The difference between the traditional channel and Reliance farm-to-fork is illustrated in Figures 8.12 and 8.13. It is easy to see that the company has to make huge investments in collection and processing centres, logistics and establishing stores. The end result is that the consumer gets the farm produce fresh; it is transported from the farm to store within 24 hours. By reducing the number of intermediaries, the company delivers fresh produce at cheaper rates to the consumer.

The farmer supplies the produce to Reliance's collection centres, where it is weighed and checked for visual quality. Sometimes the processing is done at the collection centre itself or it is sent to the processing centre. The products are sorted and crated for transportation, all the while stored in cool temperature to reduce spoilage. Payments to the farmers are arranged. The crated goods are transported to Reliance Fresh stores where they are displayed and stored. The whole cycle takes about 24 hours: farmers start coming in by 11AM at the collection centres. After sorting and cleaning, trucks begin loading for different stores by 4PM. After processing and crating, the trucks reach the stores early morning, by 6AM, where they are unloaded and displayed. The store opens at 7AM.

By procuring directly, Reliance Fresh is able to save on middleman commissions, costs of loading and unloading, employ economical transportation and reduce wastage. Perishable products are transported from collection centres while non-perishable products, which have longer shelf life, are procured directly from manufacturers.

Value is added at several activities in the chain:

- **Infrastructure:** Centralized centres and large stores, administrative tasks.
- **Farmers:** Quick and fair payments, ready market for produce, no exploitation.
- **HRM:** Fair remuneration, training, incentives.

FIGURE 8.12
A traditional supply chain for agricultural products.

Farmer
↓
Agent
↓
Agriculture market (APMC)
↓
Wholesaler
↓
Agent/City wholesaler
↓
Retailer
↓
Consumer

FIGURE 8.13
Reliance Farm-to-fork model.

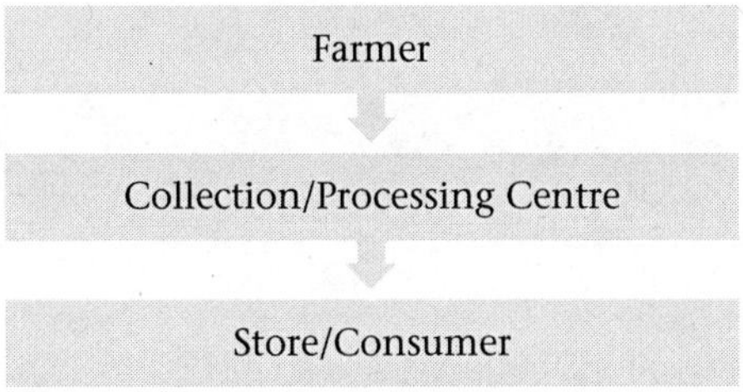

Farmer
↓
Collection/Processing Centre
↓
Store/Consumer

- **Technology:** Easy inventory control and management, customer databases and loyalty programme. The company uses modern software: SAP, RETALIX, R CONNECT PORTAL.
- **Procurement:** Good quality materials, direct buying, economical.
- **Logistics:** Economical logistics, reduction in handling and damage, vegetables and fruits are stored in foldable open crates with proper temperature.
- **Store:** Refrigeration and cooling, trained staff, hygiene and maintenance.
- **Consumer:** Targeted schemes, better service, accurate weighing, loyalty programme.

Reliance has succeeded in building an entire value chain from farmers to consumers in some states. It pays procurement price, labour and transportation charges, plus vendor and APMC charge.

The company is now in the process of creating a differentiated 'omni-commerce' model for its retail business, by integrating infrastructure built by its telecom venture Jio and Reliance

Retail. The two will augment reach to customers via online–offline product assortment across channels, through a seamless interface. As part of Reliance Retail 2.0, the company is developing platforms and building distribution ecosystems.

Questions for Discussion:

1. Comment on the value chain of Reliance Fresh. In what other ways can it add value for its customers?
2. Despite a viable business model, many Reliance Fresh stores have been closed down or downsized. Why?
3. What can be done to improve the viability of agriculture retail in the country?
4. Argue for and against organized retail in agribusiness. What is your opinion?

Sources for this Case Study:

Web Resource

Reliance Retail website: http://www.relianceretail.com/milestone.html

Other Sources

Business Standard. 2016. "Reliance to Create 'Omni-commerce'." 5 August.

The Economic Times. 2016. "Reliance Retail Reports Highest Ever Quarterly Turnover of ₹6,042 Crore in Q3." 19 January.

9

CHAPTER

Marketing of Agricultural Produce

LEARNING OBJECTIVES

Agricultural marketing is crucial not only for the country but also for millions of farmers who depend on it. But it is quite different from conventional marketing of consumer goods. After reading this chapter, you will be able to:

- Appreciate the importance of agricultural marketing for the economy and its role.
- Understand agricultural value chains and how value is added at each stage.
- Analyze existing agricultural marketing systems.
- Evaluate the state of agricultural marketing and the working of the APMCs and the National Agricultural Market (NAM).
- Understand the limitations and undertake steps for improvement of agricultural marketing.

Opening Case
Pepsi's Supply Chain

The traditional market channel for agricultural produce in India consists of several agents: Farmer » Buying Agent » Wholesaler » Selling agent » Retailer. Usually, there is no premium for quality produce, as explained in this chapter. However, as big brands have moved into food processing industries, there is increasing emphasis on quality products, suitable for processing and export.

PepsiCo was one of the first companies to build a supply chain using contract farming for potatoes in India to manufacture its Lays brand. It is the largest crop under contract farming today. Apart from potato chips, the company manufactures Cheetos and Kurkure extruded snacks, Uncle Chipps, Lehar brand of traditional snacks, Quaker Oats and Lehar Lites. The company is now procuring potatoes and other crops from several states to meet its processing requirements. Their supply chains include contract farming in *basmati* rice, tomato, chili, peanut, oranges and sea weed for its various brands.

PepsiCo entered India in 1989 with a collaboration with Punjab Agro Industries Corporation and Punjab Agriculture University. The collaboration focuses on helping Punjab farmers produce quality crops, just like farmers in developed countries. Its website says that PepsiCo India has established partnerships with over 24,000 farmers across nine states. More than 45 per cent of these are small and marginal farmers.

PepsiCo provides support to farmers through quality seeds, extension services, knowledge of modern farming practices, disease control, bank loans, weather insurance and the latest technology. It also assures buyback of their produce at agreed prices. Incomes of small and marginal farmers and their social standing have increased as a result of Pepsico intervention. Currently, about 26 per cent of Pepsi's export turnover comes from processed agricultural products.

PHOTO 9.1

Behind every packet of potato chips is a formidable supply chain that extends right up to the farm.

The company has a Farmer Connect Programme which includes:

- Guaranteed buyback of produce at predetermined prices, protecting farmers from price variations and uncertainty in selling of their produce.
- High quality inputs are provided to the farmers, including proprietary advanced seed varieties.
- Financing through tie-ups with banks.
- Crop/weather risk insurance to safeguard farm incomes.
- Plant protection and technical knowhow in association with Bayer, BASF and DuPont.
- Educating and imparting of modern farm practices, including company's R&D.

PepsiCo has three potato processing plants in India located in Punjab, West Bengal and Maharashtra. Potatoes sourced under contract farming account roughly 60 per cent of PepsiCo's total requirement.

The supply chain of potato production and supply consists of several factors:

Quality: Farmers are given inputs to produce good quality potatoes suitable for processing. Indian potatoes normally have high sugar content, but Pepsi requires potatoes with no sugar content. Its round chips come from a variety called Lady Rosetta, since they have blush pink peels. Stringent quality control at every stage—research and development, farming, storing, processing and packaging—is maintained.

R&D: The major factors affecting sugar content are crop maturity, temperature during growth, mineral nutrition and irrigation. Post-harvest factors such as mechanical stresses and storage conditions also affect sugar content. Before introducing the varieties to the farmers, extensive trials were undertaken. The company's R&D provides farmers with a package of agronomic practices suitable to the local conditions, including specific fertilizer requirements and a spraying schedule, which has been developed in collaboration with the Central Potato Research Institute (CPRI), Shimla.

Inputs: The company ensures the availability of inputs to farmers and advises on the use of these inputs. Seed potatoes of specific varieties for processing are provided by the company.

Insurance: Another important role has been to provide crop insurance by the Agricultural Insurance Company and weather insurance from ICICI Lombard. Pepsico was able to get special rates from insurance companies, because transaction costs of dealing through a company are much lower than dealing with individual farmers. It has provided institutional support with CPRI and Du Pont.

Production: Pepsico employs a team of agricultural graduates who work with the farmers to provide technical inputs and to monitor production. This makes the use of chemicals and fertilizers more timely and effective. Better production practices help to increase yield, reduce greening of potatoes and reduces the share of undersized potatoes which cannot be used.

Harvesting and packaging: Support is provided at harvesting stage also. The company's message is, 'handle potatoes like eggs, not like stones'. Packaging has also been improved so that post-harvest losses are minimized.

Grading and sorting: The potatoes are mechanically graded. They are tested for sugar content and solid content. Potatoes that do not meet the requirements are rejected.

Storage: Storage is also critical, with several factors having crucial importance: field curing, temperature and humidity control, storage and sprouting inhibition. Potatoes are stored at 12°C to control conversion of starch into sugar.

Processing: Washing, peeling, metal detection and inspection for physical damages and discolouration is done at the processing stage. The potatoes are sliced and fried, and then spices are added before packing.

Pepsico intervention is an illustration of how farmers were upgraded to produce crops with international quality requirements and thus were able to get better prices for their produce. The farmers, working as contract growers, benefit on several fronts: through extensive training and education of farmers for proper timing and method of sowing, harvesting and other field operations. Farmers' overall management capabilities are enhanced by meetings and visits by agricultural experts. Not only do they earn more, but they also get assured prices. Risks from crop infestation and weather changes are minimized as the company's extension agents are constantly working with the farmers to give timely input on these issues. Finally, weather insurance is also available, which further minimizes risks.

The advantage for the company is that it gets an assured quantity and quality of potatoes. Direct involvement with farmers enables good communication to ensure availability of produce which meets the specific quality requirements for processing.

Through its description of the Pepsi supply chain, this case illustrates the broad purview of agribusiness, which is described in this chapter. Clearly, long-term rural marketing initiatives succeed when companies solve a local problem or two.

While reading this chapter, answer the following questions:

1. What is agribusiness? What does it consist of?
2. What do farmers look for when companies start rural marketing initiatives?
3. Can an integrated approach to rural marketing help? How can it be developed?
4. What mistakes do companies commit when they try to penetrate rural areas?

Sources for this Case Study:

Web Resource

Pepsico website: http://www.pepsicoindia.co.in/Company/about-Pepsico.html

Other Source

Punjabi, M. 2015. "The Potato Supply Chain to PepsiCo's Frito Lay India." *FAO Publications*.

INTRODUCTION

For an activity that employs a majority of India's population and contributes a sizeable chunk in India's GDP, it is surprising that agriculture marketing has remained neglected over decades. Producing food and its marketing is the backbone of our country, but does not attract major investments or professional management. Instead of professionalizing these functions, populist schemes by successive governments have resulted in widespread farm distress. There is "no public debate about how to improve India's dreadfully backward agriculture," writes *The Economist* (2015). "Gangs of local commissioning agents squeeze farmers like ripe mangoes," it says. The APMCs, through which agricultural produce is sold, have established their monopolies in the name of agricultural marketing.

Farmers and consumers suffer on all inks in the supply chain. In terms of production, India has one of the lowest farm productivity in the world. In terms of marketing, it grapples with outdated and exploitative rules, and it is the small farmer who bears brunt of bad policy, bad weather and bad infrastructure. The sector cries for reforms, but while some steps were taken in 1991 to free the industry, farming has remained untouched over the decades.

This chapter shows why traditional approaches of applying marketing principles to agricultural produce do not work. The 4P marketing approach is meaningless in a sector that is strangled by governmental control. Despite the plethora of government agencies, agricultural marketing remains backward, primitive and dysfunctional.

AGRICULTURAL MARKETING

Agricultural marketing has the potential to lift the entire economy of the country and to bring it out of poverty. If we look at the agricultural value chain, we see that it has several roles:

1. Supplying agricultural produce to consumers.
2. Establishing an agricultural marketing infrastructure consisting of supply chains, warehouses and transportation.
3. Doing a demand assessment and advising farmers what to produce so that wild price fluctuations are avoided.
4. Providing incentives and agricultural knowhow to improve productivity.
5. Moving farmers up the value chain.
6. Improving the economic situation of farmers and consumers alike.

However, when we look at the progress on the ground since Independence, we find that except for the first objective—which is a necessity—none of the other objectives have been met with any degree of success, except in small pockets. Agricultural marketing has been left to the means and devices of individual farmers and some private companies in the business of food processing. These inadequacies are becoming more acute with changes taking place in global supply channels of food in domestic and overseas markets. It is hardly a wonder that instead of being an engine of growth, the agriculture sector is marked by farmers' suicides across the country.

In order to understand agricultural marketing, we first analyze the steps through which value is added in the marketing value chain.

AGRICULTURAL MARKETING VALUE CHAIN

An agricultural 'value chain' (see Chapter 8) defines the set of activities that bring a basic agricultural product from production in the field to final consumption, where value is added to the product at each stage. Here, we break up this chain further and see that value can be added to agricultural products in a number of ways (Figure 9.1). Each stage is analyzed to understand how farmers and consumers can benefit from the process.

1. **Production:** Agricultural productivity in India continues to be low. Raghavan (2014) writes that India's yield rates for rice and wheat measured in tonnes produced per hectare, are drastically lower than even BRICS counterparts. "If India's yield rates for the two crops were at China's levels, we could almost double our yields or halve the land used for the purpose," he writes. For example, in 2013, the productivity of rice was 2.4 tonnes per hectare, compared to China and Brazil who have yield rates of 4.7 and 3.6 tonnes per hectare, respectively.
2. **Harvesting and cleaning:** Crops can be harvested through manual or mechanized means. The latter is faster and leads to fewer crop losses, but it is also expensive. Many farmers cannot afford the high rentals of harvesting and threshing machines. Manual harvesting depends on availability of labour, which is in short supply during the season. Delayed harvesting adds to crop losses.
3. **Transport:** Farmers have to transport their produce to the nearest market or mandi. Tempos and tractor trollies are hired to take goods to the market over muddy village roads. The operation has to match with government buying schedule or the demand in

FIGURE 9.1
Agricultural value chain.

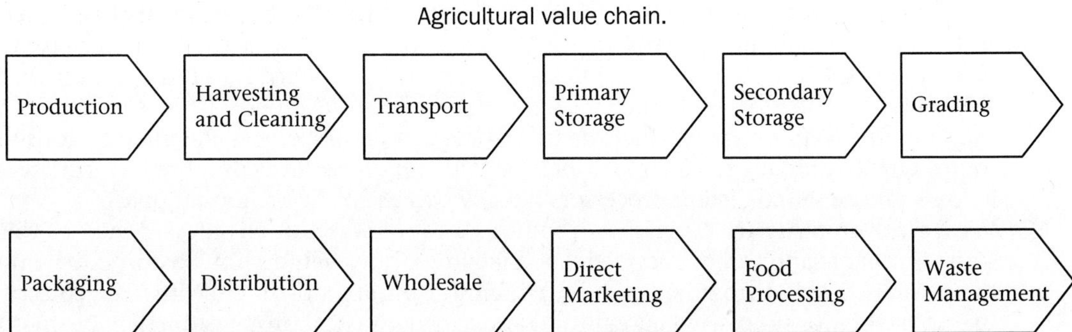

mandis. Unsold stock has to be sold at distress prices as farmers cannot store it or transport it back to their farms.

4. **Primary processing and storage:** Primary storage refers to storage of minimally processed produce. As the crop is harvested, it must be cleaned, graded and stored in a safe place protected from rodents and weather till it is transported. Cold storage facilities are required for vegetables and animal products. Usually farmers in India lack primary storage facilities.
5. **Secondary processing and storage:** When the produce goes through some more processing or is graded or cleaned, it is called secondary processing and storage. Cold chains and processing facilities close to the farm are needed for these stages. Farmers are mostly unable to add value at this stage also as they lack such processing and storage facilities.
6. **Grading:** One important value addition activity is grading, in which the produce is separated on the basis of size or quality. Grade A, referring to the best quality, is able to fetch the best prices. Through grading, farmers are able to get better prices for their produce as compared to selling ungraded produce. However, farmers have to spend time and effort to grade and must have storage facilities to be able to take advantage of this step. In the case of ungraded produce, the value addition activities are passed on to traders, who do this job instead.
7. **Distribution:** Distribution refers to sending the farmed produce where it is needed. Farmers can achieve economies of scale and logistical efficiencies at this stage, besides getting better prices. However, it needs good transport and storage facilities, the ability to hold on to their stock and knowledge of markets and prices. Many farmers fail on all fronts, and that is the reason that they depend on agents to lift their entire stocks at whatever prices they can get.
8. **Packaging:** Consumer goods manufacturers know the value of attractive packaging and labelling. Consumers are willing to pay higher prices for goods that are packed attractively and certified for their quality. Absence of grading and packing makes this step quite difficult at farm stage.
9. **Wholesale:** Usually farmers sell at wholesale prices (WSP) to agents. This saves them from spending long hours at mandis, which are usually without facilities. But this also means that they are unable to take advantage of price changes or value addition. At the mandis, farmers are under pressure to sell, as the longer they hold on to stock, the more is the deterioration of their produce.
10. **Direct marketing:** Agricultural produce is sometimes sold at farm gate or at nearby markets directly to consumers. This depends on the location of the farm. Though better prices can be obtained, it poses several problems for farmers (see section on direct marketing). Some farmers do direct selling at mandis in nearby towns. Foreign retail chains cannot invest in modern supply chains because of limitations on FDI. Indian retail chains such as Reliance Fresh and Big Bazaar source a limited amount of produce to sell in their stores.
11. **Food processing:** One way to add value to agricultural produce is to process it for later consumption. Though very limited village level processing facilities exist in some pockets, they are the exception rather than the rule. Some companies have made interventions to source quality produce for their factories (see Opening Case on Pepsi), but in most areas farmers cannot sell to distant processors directly because of APMC limitations.
12. **Waste management:** Agriculture produces a lot of waste at all stages. Much of this waste is organic and can be recycled. Such facilities, however, do not exist in India, and the waste is simply thrown in mandis, which in turn are a picture of dirt. The country has no facility for processing agricultural and animal wastes. Crop residues are burnt on the fields, causing health problems to nearby residents.

PHOTO 9.2
Direct marketing: Farmers and traders bring their produce to nearby towns and try to sell them on the roadside.

Source: Photograph by Dinesh Kumar.

It is seen from the discussion that agricultural value chains are skewed against farmers and consumers. While farmers get low prices, consumers get expensive products. The produce is also adulterated at the multiple points where they are handled. Farmers prefer to sell out to pre-harvest contractors, giving up their opportunity for value addition. A series of legal and infrastructural problems prevent them from adding value on their own. On a macro level, the country struggles to become more efficient and add value to be able to capture new global market opportunities. Modernization of value chains can help solve these problems (see Mini Case Study 9.1) but, since independence, a suspicion of agricultural modernization has stymied efforts to do so.

Mini Case Study 9.1

Café Femenino: Behind the Morning Brew

Coffee drinking is fast becoming popular in many countries, including India. It is one of the most profitable and most traded commodities in the world. It is grown mostly by small holders in South America, Africa and parts of India, but when we look at its supply chains, we discover that much of the value is appropriated by traders and companies. An estimated 60 per cent of the value is gained by MNCs who are primarily involved in curing, roasting, packaging and branding. It is estimated that conventional coffee growers typically get only 3 cents from a US$1.50 cup of coffee sold in North America.

Value is added to coffee at broadly four stages:

- **Producers:** Farmers, mostly small growers in coffee growing countries.
- **Local traders:** Engaged in procuring coffee from small growers, they mostly work for curing houses and exporters.
- **Curing works and exporters:** Aggregators of the produce and exporters.
- **Roasters:** Companies engaged in roasting, packaging, branding and selling the finished product in global markets, both wholesale and retail.

It was long felt that the coffee trade should enforce ethical production processes and empower small producers, mostly women. This can only be done if they could be moved up the value chain.

This led to the fair trade and organic coffee movements which have helped benchmark standards for coffee that is produced through sustainable environmental processes. These marketing initiatives have resulted in making fair trade coffee as a brand that fetches price premium (Figure 9.2).

Though it originated in Peru, the Café Femenino project has expanded to eight countries to include over 700 women-owned coffee farms. Now over 60 coffee roasting companies in Canada, the US and Australia buy and distribute Café Femenino coffee.

Café Femenino Foundation was founded in 2004 by Garth and Gay Smith, named in honour of 464 Peruvian women who made a decision to try to improve their own lives though their work in coffee production. The objective was to help women and their families in coffee communities, who had no voice or say in family decisions, had no control of the family resources and essentially had no rights even though they did most of the farming and processing of coffee beans. They were poor, uneducated and lived in isolation. The Foundation, a non-profit organization, provides grants to programmes and projects that enhance the lives of women and their families in coffee-producing communities.

The system works as follows. The Fairtrade system certifies products that have met trading standards that ensure that minimum prices are paid to farmers to cover their costs of sustainable production. Its website says that it acts as a safety net for farmers at times when world markets fall below a sustainable level and addresses the imbalance of power in trading relationships, unstable markets and the injustices of conventional trade. The Fairtrade label on the Café Femenino coffee signifies that the coffee has been bought at a fair, non-exploitative price from the women farmers.

The Café Femenino brand helps Peruvian women coffee producers move up the value chain as follows. Roasting companies in Canada, the US, and Australia agree to pay organic and fair trade prices for the women's coffee above the conventional coffee market price plus an additional value per pound. In addition, the roasting companies willingly pay an extra 2 cents per pound over the fair-trade price to the Peruvian farmers and the Café Femenino Foundation, which focuses on social and economic development.

FIGURE 9.2
The Café Femenino cycle.

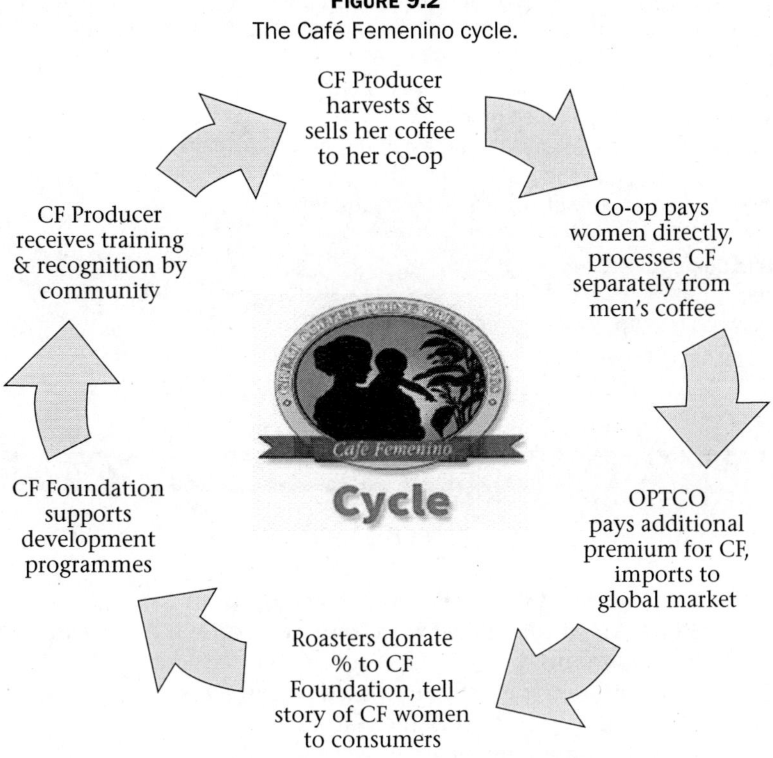

Source: http://www.optco.com/cafe_femenino.htm (Accessed on 26 April 2017).

The roasting company also donates an additional 2 per cent of its gross sales to a women's project or crisis centre in its home country. Roasters ensure that some of their own staff in important decision-making positions in their own companies are women.

Café Femenino helps women to participate in the selling process and to earn value that was earlier being passed on to traders. Today, the name symbolizes the empowerment and increased social standing of rural women farmers of coffee. By earning higher prices through fair-trade premiums received for their brand, women coffee farmers have seen great improvements in their lives and communities. Women coffee farmers are integrated into social, political and occupational organizations by using grants that enhance their status within the community. In doing so, the foundation is able to help improve the overall quality of life for the entire community and support a sustainable economic system.

Today the Café Femenino Foundation receives grant requests from numerous coffee groups and communities. The organic and fair trade premiums have helped in the improvement in local economies in many varied ways. It has funded all types of projects, such as community gardens, animal breeding programmes, health programmes, sanitation programmes, water projects, income diversification and nutrition trainings. In this way, it is making a huge difference not only in the level of poverty, but also in elevating the value of women in these remote communities.

There are now over 1,000 women coffee farmers involved with the Café Femenino Coffee Project in Peru. The women farmers participate in all farm activities: preparing the terrain, nurseries and the compost to fertilize the soil; preparing bio-fertilizers; and harvesting, de-pulping, fermenting and drying the coffee. Sales contracts for Café Femenino must be signed and committed to by a woman and a woman must participate in the sales and marketing of this coffee. An extra 2 cents per pound above the fair-trade price for green coffee is paid by the US importer of Café Femenino and these funds provide income that goes directly to the women producers.

This case study shows how producers can move up the value chain and in doing so how it helped women and coffee producing communities in remote parts of Peru and other countries.

Can India also implement something like a fair-trade? How?

Sources for this Case Study:
Web Resources
Café Femenino website: http://www.coffeecan.org/
Fairtrade website: http://www.fairtrade.net/

EXISTING MARKETING SYSTEMS

Farmers having surplus produce can sell it in the following ways, as shown in Figure 9.3:

- Directly to the consumer at a highway near the farm or in a market near the village.
- To retailers and traders at the village who transport and sell it in nearby towns.
- At APMC designated mandis.
- To brokers who facilitate trade with city-based wholesalers.
- To a cooperative organization or union of farmers.
- To government procurement agencies.
- To food processing factories situated near the farm.

The grower can, however, use these channels only if facilities exist in the area. While some farmers do have access to a highway, nearby mandis or cooperative organizations mostly do not. As they lack marketing infrastructure to store or transport goods, they are under pressure to sell the moment the crop is harvested. The task for farmers who have harvested their crops is just one: how to sell to an agent or to get the stock to an APMC designated market and sell quickly. This will be evident from a discussion of the methods described here.

- **Directly to the consumer:** Farmers living near a highway often set up stalls displaying their produce for passing motorists. They could also sell at a market near the farm or in the village. Such a process eliminates the middleman but requires the farmer to be present at the site for long hours or add to cost by hiring a person to do so. This method is high-cost as the remaining stock—if the stock is perishable in nature—has to be thrown away. Only a very small percentage of agricultural produce in the country is sold directly.
- **To retailers and traders:** To get over the problems in direct selling, farmers prefer to sell the entire stock to a local retailer or trader who, in turn, transports it to a nearby APMC mandi. The farmer gets a lump sum in hand and avoids wastage and the costs of direct selling, but is at the mercy of traders who generally offer exploitative prices. In such a system, the trader makes a hefty commission while the producer gets low prices.

FIGURE 9.3
Marketing arrangement of agricultural produce.

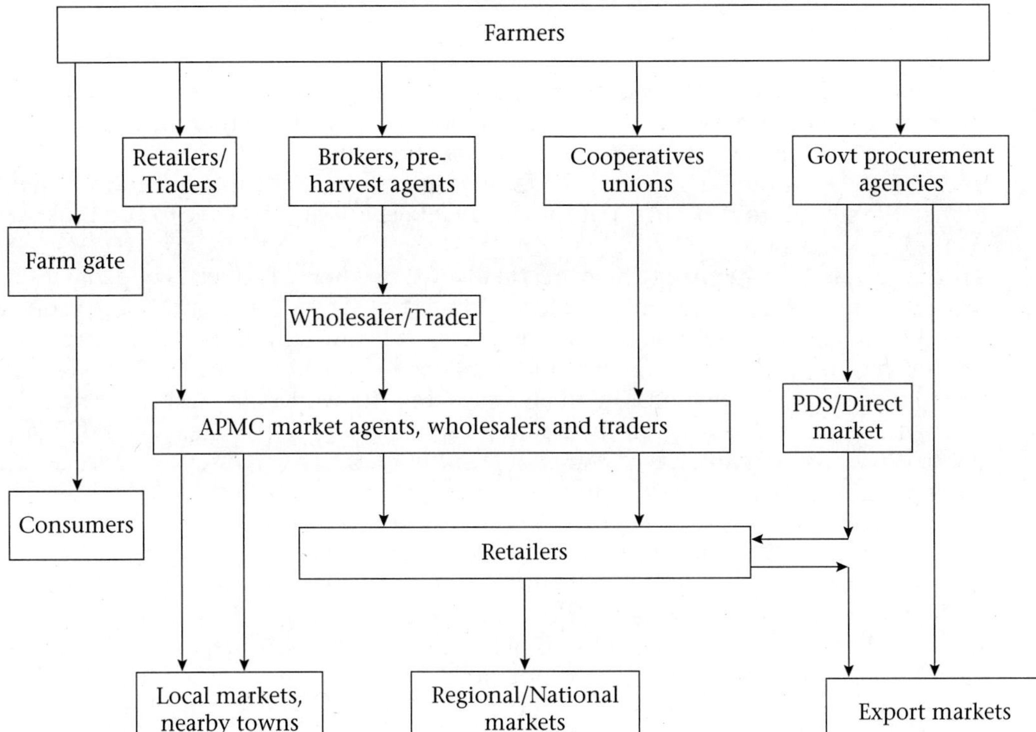

- **At APMC designated mandis:** Farmers can transport the goods to APMC designated mandis, where they have to sell to authorized agents who again exploit the farmers, squeezing them. Hefty commissions are charged by them: agents take a commission of 6–14 per cent merely to trade, as against the international norm of 0.5 per cent. In their study of peas marketing in Punjab, Sidhu et al. (2011) show that most of the produce of farmers (89%) was sold by growers in the wholesale market, while sale for local markets was just about 6 per cent. Due to problems in APMC designated Apni Mandis, the majority of growers preferred to sell green peas in the wholesale market. The study further reveals that that the net price received by the farmer was about 67 per cent of the price paid by the consumer. The problems identified in Apni Mandis were:
  - Requirement to stay there for long hours.
  - Non-availability of drinking water or shelter.
  - Unhygienic conditions in the market, which become more severe in the rainy seasons.
  - Inadequate market infrastructure.
  - Frequent changes in the site of farmers.
  - Dominance of traditional retailers and traders.

It is clear that the system is exploitative and though heavy commissions are charged, no money is ploughed into the markets to provide better facilities for farmers. It has long been felt that APMC Act should be abolished; *NDTV Profit* (2014) writes that a new line of supply chain can be created which will ensure quicker supply of these products to consumers.

- **To brokers:** Large traders appoint brokers and pre-harvest agents who buy from farmers, adding to another level in the marketing channel. Such large traders supply to markets or food processors, since processors and factories located elsewhere are prohibited under APMC Act from buying from the farmers directly. The advantage for the farmer is that all the stock is sold at once, but the disadvantage is that they have to add brokerage cost, too.
- **To a cooperative organization or union of farmers:** Farmers' cooperatives are probably the best option as they keep the interest of farmers at heart. Some cooperatives help in market the produce or engage in processing the produce, adding value. NACOF has been set up to organize and develop cooperative societies. However, such societies or unions do not exist in all areas, leaving the farmers to fend for themselves. Though there have been spectacular successes, most cooperative societies suffer from political intervention and have been unable either to organize farmers or to set up processing facilities that can help them.
- **To government procurement agencies:** The government is a major buyer of agricultural produce. Organizations like FCI buy in bulk with the objective of stabilizing prices, distribution and maintaining buffer stocks. Farmers, however, have to deal with corruption and delayed payments. The committee that studied the working of the FCI says that it has been a total failure in achieving its objectives, reports *Indian Express* (2015). The report says that FCI did not provide effective price support to the farmers, as only 6 per cent of them received the MSP. The leakage of foodgrains supplied to the PDS was as high as 48 per cent. The buffer stocks it maintains are often very high leading to huge costs on maintenance, not to mention rotting of grains as it is usually stored in the open (see Photo 9.3).
- **To food processing factories:** Farmers also sell their produce to food-processing factories situated near their farms. Many farmers enter into contracts with such companies, through which they get support from the companies and are assured of good prices for their produce. However, such factories are few, as the food-processing sector is not well-developed in India. Moreover, the APMC places restrictions on sale of goods to distant factories.

It is clear that the farmer is not actually free to sell to any channel. Though theoretically he has a number of options, the APMC exercises a monopoly that often works to the disadvantage of the farmer.

An Exploitative Marketing System

The existing system for selling agricultural produce, described here, shows several shortcomings that add to the inefficiencies and also shows the exploitation of the farmers. These are summarized in Table 6.6 and explained in detail.

- **Bringing goods to mandis:** Once the crop is harvested, it must be brought to the nearest mandi or marketplace. The farmer piles it on trolleys, which are pulled by tractors

PHOTO 9.3
An FCI godown in Haryana.

Source: Photograph by Dinesh Kumar.
Note: While some silos have been constructed, most of the grain is stored in the open, covered simply by tarpaulins, exposed to rodents and other harmful elements.

or animals. Many farmers have to come a day prior to the auction, especially if the distance is large or to avoid traffic jams of the peak harvesting season. This adds to the cost. Facilities for staying are usually not available and so the farmer spends the night sleeping on the trolley. If it rains, the crop is spoiled and loses value (see Photo 9.4).

- **Mandis:** The mandis are designated by the APMC, which places restrictions on selling and movement of goods and act as monopolies (see next section). The agents or the *arhatiyas* come from close knit communities and set the rules of trade to their advantage. They also know that the farmer is in a hurry to sell the crop and return to his village. This places the farmer at a disadvantage in getting good prices. Scenes of grain being dried near a mandi in Punjab (Photo 9.4) illustrate the many perils of agricultural marketing in the country.
- **Display and sale:** Once at the mandi, the crop is dumped usually in the open ground (Photo 9.4), exposed to the weather, rodents and other risks. If it gets wet, the farmer has no option but to spread it on an unused road. Some mandis have a few sheds, but these are inadequate during the harvesting season. Agents inspect the crops visually. Grading is not done scientifically, for example, like measuring the oil content of seeds. Farmers are not able to get better prices for better produce and so there is little incentive to improve the quality of crops.
- **Auction:** The auction is done orally. The farmer is in no position to hold on to stocks or bargain for better prices and has to accept whatever is offered. Auctions also lead to loss of dignity by the farmer as the inspection and price-setting of his produce, after months of long labour and toil, is done within a few seconds.

- **Bagging and weighing:** Crops must be weighed and bagged for outbound transportation. The cost is borne by the farmer. The mandi staff does this work, and since the spillage is considered part payment for the work, the workers make sure that some amount of crop is always spilled, leading to loss to the farmer. There are also complaints of under-weighing by the mandi workers.
- **Payment:** Brokers exploit farmers in another way: by not paying the full amount due. Payments are made in instalments. Multiple trips to collect payments mean extra expenses. No interest is paid for delayed payments. Contracts are usually vocal and payment terms are to the advantage of the trader.
- **Outbound logistics:** Once it leaves the mandis, the produce is sent to retail markets or food processors by the agents. Multiple points of handling, spoilage, octroi and taxes add to the cost of the produce. In the case of fruits and vegetables, spoilage is very high.

PHOTO 9.4

This is how we store our food 70 years after independence: A scene near a mandi in Punjab shows how the wheat crop is being dried on the roads.

Source: Photographs by Dinesh Kumar.

- **Consumers:** By the time consumers get the goods, costs have been added at various points. Cost at each stage of transactions is also added to the final price. Retailers buy their stocks from traders in towns and cities to sell in their shops. Very often the goods are not fresh by the time they reach urban markets.

It is criminal that supply chains are so primitive in our country, even though the country attained Independence in 1947, showing the complete apathy of successive governments. This marketing system has been in existence for years and few reforms have taken place over the years. Hence, farmers continue to suffer. It also points to a severe lack of agricultural marketing infrastructure in the country.

AGRICULTURAL MARKETING INFRASTRUCTURE

Agricultural marketing infrastructure has been the victim of monopoly, politics and lethargy. That is why agricultural markets are primitive; there is no common auction platform in more than one-third of regulated markets in the country. Anybody who has bought vegetables in a local mandi would have done so amid shouting hawkers, dirty mandis and piles of vegetable waste, without even having basic amenities such as drinking water or toilets. Cold storage facilities required for perishables such as fruits and vegetables do not exist in mandis. The Planning Commission (2007) has noted that facilities for storage and processing are very inadequate. The Working Group on Agriculture Marketing of the Planning Commission for the Twelfth Plan highlighted the following gaps in the marketing infrastructure.

- There was no progress in setting up wholesale markets, except in Kerala.
- There are only 1,637 grading units at the primary level in the whole country.
- Grading units are found in less than 20 per cent of the market yards/sub-yards in the 7,246 regulated markets in India; only around 7 per cent of the quantity sold by farmers is graded before sale.
- Modern storage capacity is only 30 per cent of what is required.
- Cold storage facilities are available for only 10 per cent of fruits and vegetables.
- Simple facilities such as benches to sit on and drinking water taps or toilets are not available in more than 70 per cent of the markets.
- Price information was not displayed in most markets.

These statistics show why farmers depend on arhatiyas and traders in primary markets. The lack of facilities and amenities in markets forces producers to look for agents and traders, who then squeeze the farmers like ripe mangoes. This does a long-term harm, as little investment goes to modernize the farm or marketing of agricultural produce.

The main reasons for poor market infrastructure are:

1. Market committees do not plough back the market fee collected into developing infrastructure.
2. The private sector has been prevented from developing marketing infrastructure due to government monopoly and restrictive laws.

This increases transaction costs of farmers. Woldie and Nuppenau (2011) have analyzed the marketing behaviour of Ethiopia's banana producers by employing a transaction cost economics approach. Transaction costs that affect farmers are information costs, negotiation costs, access to credit and enforcement costs.

- Information cost refers to the opportunity cost of searching for price information, the difficulty of obtaining it and reliability of the information.
- Negotiation cost is the opportunity cost of time spent and power of negotiation with agents and wholesalers.
- Monitoring and enforcement costs relate to enforcement of contracts.
- Access to credit and interest cost is an important institutional constraint in marketing and reduces transaction costs.

The farmer has no power over any factor and, as a result, his transaction costs are extremely high. The choice of where and how to sell depends on where transaction costs are minimized for farmers. Transaction costs can be reduced by creating the following facilities:

- **Storage facilities:** Whether the farmer has storage facilities to hold on to the stock.
- **Direct Sales:** Whether the farmer has enough time or manpower to sell directly to the consumer and depends on location as well.
- **Transportation:** Whether the farmer can transport the produce to the nearby town on city.
- **Access to finance:** Whether the farmer is rich enough to be able to hold on to stock.
- **Price Information:** Whether the farmer has price information in nearby markets.
- **Food processing facilities:** Whether there is a factory or a cooperative union close by that buys the produce.

Mostly, small farmers have access to neither of these and government efforts in this direction have been lacking. As a consequence, they are under pressure to sell the crop when it is harvested. They are often in deep debt by the time the crop is ready, having spent their resources in buying seeds, pesticides, irrigation and crop protection. At harvest time, they have to spend more for paying for the labour or for hiring harvesters. They cannot hold the crop since they lack storage facilities. That is why, once the crop is ready, farmers have to sell quickly. Some are approached by pre-harvest contractors or agents of APMC registered large buyers who provide advance payments to the farmers during the time of harvest. In this approach, farmers are able to cover the risk of post-harvest losses but get lower prices. The pre-harvest contractor adds another link to the marketing channel, which is shown here.

Farmer → Pre-harvest contractor → Commission agent → Wholesaler → Retailer → Consumer

Further, agricultural markets are distorted by government intervention at every stage. Direct intervention in price setting, control of markets, having almost monopoly power in procurement, restrictions on storage and subsidies distort supply at every stage of the marketing process.

GOVERNMENT INTERVENTION

Agricultural marketing is dominated by the government. The objective of this has presumably been to supply foodgrains at cheap prices to the poor and to prevent dishonest practices such as overcharging and hoarding. While this may have served a food-scarce economy, today this policy is serving to strangulate the sector; modernization and private investment shies away from investments in the marketing of agriculture. Today, though the production has increased manifold, agricultural supply chains remain primitive.

The government exercises powers through a plethora of agencies and corporations it has set up and control is exercised on practically every aspect of agricultural marketing. There are a number of farmers' cooperative agencies too, but in many of these politicians have taken over, limiting their efficiency and exercising control over them through the back door.

There are also several laws that govern agricultural and food marketing in the country, which are described later in the chapter. Apart from the laws, the procurement of agricultural products is largely done through government agencies. Large quantities of foodgrains have accumulated in the godowns of the FCI and state agencies, but much of it gets spoilt because of poor storage. There is high incidence of malnutrition and starvation across the country despite a large PDS and food subsidy. This shows the criminal neglect of food supply chains in the country (Photo 9.5).

Marketing of agricultural products is under the purview of APMC Act. But as mentioned in the previous section, licensing of traders has led to monopoly and provides little help to farmers in direct and free marketing. The APMC Act, which was enacted to protect farmers' interests and increase market efficiency and transparency, is now being used to deny

PHOTO 9.5

Food stored in godowns of the FCI.

Source: www.livemint.com

them opportunities to get better prices, to prevent competition and to guard the interests of middlemen.

A serious consequence of selling at APMC designated yards or mandis is that once agricultural produce has been brought to it, farmers can seldom take it back in the event of any unfair deal. The costs already incurred in bringing the produce to the market and in cleaning and unloading it prevent this. This robs the producer of whatever little bargaining power she/he has in price determination. Small producers with less to sell are left in a highly disadvantageous position.

APMC Monopoly

Agricultural Marketing is covered under State List in Article 245 of Constitution of India. The State Agriculture Produce Marketing (Regulation and Development) Act promoted by state governments regulates agriculture marketing within a state.

The Act requires that agricultural produce be bought and sold only in a regulated market or mandi. The marketing of agricultural products is controlled by APMCs, which are supposed to regulate agricultural markets in a notified area. The mandi collects fees for its services and taxes that go to the state government, but it has not invested the proceeds in providing better facilities and infrastructure. Farmers cannot sell their produce outside the state, which gives the mandi boards monopoly. Political interference and revenue considerations have prevented both the mandi boards and state governments to reform the system. That is one of the reasons that agricultural marketing has not kept pace with the changing times and is highly fragmented. Because of the system, a common national market for agricultural commodities has not been able to develop. It would not be wrong to say that both the government and mandi boards are earning revenue at the expense of poor farmers.

A research paper by Agricultural Economics Research Centre, University of Delhi (Tuteja and Chandra 2012) says that the State Agriculture Produce Marketing Act has been the biggest hindrance in providing a modern marketing system to farmers. It treats agricultural marketing as a localized subject confined to a specific notified area and regulates the sale of agricultural produce grown in that area between farmers and registered traders. It creates a monopoly by prohibiting traders and processors located in other states from buying in an area without a license from the APMC.

The problems with the APMC Act are summarized as follows:

1. **Monopoly:** The monopoly power of the Act deprives farmers from markets and they have to sell through designated agents.
2. **Cartelization:** Agents deliberately offer low prices to the detriment of the farmer. Farmers often have to sell below the MSP.
3. **High fees:** License fee and rents in the designated markets are very high. Farmers have to pay commission, marketing fee, APMC cess and Value Added Tax (VAT), which pushes up prices. Very often agents charge commission both from sellers and buyers. The commission rate is usually 6 per cent for perishable items and 2 per cent for non-perishables, which is very high as per global standards. Due to several layers of agents, the producer gets 20–25 per cent of the retail price and the total mark-up is as high as 75 per cent.
4. **Controlled by politicians:** The chairman of the state APMC is nominated by the government, who is in most cases a politician. The politicians milk the boards for their

own benefit, doing nothing for the farmers. For instance, *The Tribune* (2015) reports that the Punjab Mandi Board chairman, Ajmer Singh Lakhowal, has cost the Board more than ₹2 crore. The Board pays for his security cover which costs ₹1.15 crore as salary to gunmen. Lakhowal was been given a cabinet rank by the Punjab government; seven cars have been purchased for him and his escort for ₹78.12 lakh, out of funds meant for markets and farmers. Similar stories about misuse of mandi funds are reported from other states as well.

5. **Conflicting roles:** The APMC serves both as regulator and marketing agent. Thus, the regulator is undermined by revenue earning opportunities. Inefficiencies have been encouraged as a result.
6. **Delayed payments:** Agents often block a part of payment to farmers for fictitious reasons. Many transactions are done verbally and farmers are refused payment slips.
7. **No value addition:** While agents charge high fees, they add no value and have no facilities for grading, sorting or storing. Commissions are added for no value addition. The APMCs neither do demand assessment to advise farmers as to what to produce, nor do they provide any technical inputs.
8. **Opaque pricing:** Price discovery is not transparent. Usually farmers have to accept whatever prices are offered by agents. During peak harvest season, prices drop so drastically that farmers have to dump their produce on the roads. It is a regular feature of the agricultural economy that every year farmers somewhere in the country resort to distress sales of some product or the other and dump their produce, as prices drop to less than even the transportation cost.

The farmer is therefore severely limited and does not have many choices to sell his produce. Besides the APMC monopoly, the farmer has several limitations of resources. At the time of harvest, most farmers are hard-pressed for cash. They have invested in seeds, pesticides and irrigation—often by taking loans—and now look for quick recovery of their investment. It is this urgency to sell that is exploited by agents.

Next, we look at the various laws and controls that govern agricultural marketing and food supply in India and their working.

Laws Impacting Agricultural Marketing

In this section, we look at some of the laws that impact agricultural marketing and food supply in the country. Agricultural and food marketing is governed by a plethora of laws, as follows:

- Consumer Protection Act, 1986
- Edible Oils Packaging (Regulation) Order, 1998
- Environment (Protection) Act, 1986
- Essential Commodities Act (ECA), 1955
- Food Safety and Standards Act (FSSA), 2006
- Fruit Products Order, 1955
- Meat Food Products Order, 1973
- Milk and Milk Product Order, 1992
- Prevention of Food Adulteration Act & Rules (PFA Act), 1954
- Solvent Extracted Oil, De-oiled Meal and Edible Flour (Control) Order, 1967

- Standards of Weights and Measures Act, 1976
- Sugar (control) Order, 1996
- The Essential Commodities Act, 1955
- The Export (Quality Control and Inspection) Act, 1963
- The Insecticides Act, 1968
- Vanaspati (Control) Order, 1975
- Vegetables Oil Products (Control) Order, 1998

In addition, there are various food laws and standards which apply to finished products, which can be followed by food processors. Labels such as the Agmark Standards (AGMARK), Codex Alimentarius Standards and BIS Standards and Specifications help to maintain the quality of finished products. Standards also help in marketing of processed agricultural materials as consumers can depend on these labels for quality. How do some of these laws and standards work are described in this section.

Essential Commodities Act

The ECA, 1955, was enacted to prevent hoarding of essential commodities. Almost all agricultural commodities, such as cereals, pulses, edible oilseeds, oilcakes, edible oils, raw cotton, sugar, *gur* and jute are included in the list of essential commodities. A large number of orders have been put into force by the Central government and state governments under the ECA.

The Act controls virtually every aspect of agricultural marketing and supply chains. It provides for instruments such as licences, permits, regulations and orders for (a) price control, (b) storage, (c) stocking limits, (d) movement of produce, (e) distribution, (f) disposal, (g) sale and (h) compulsory purchase by the government. The measures that can be taken under the provision of the Act include licensing, distribution and setting stock limits. The government also has the power to fix price limits and prohibits selling above that limit. Black marketing of essential commodities was a major problem in the past and this has now been controlled to a large extent. However, as pointed out by Jha et al. (2010), the Act now makes it impossible to build large warehouses and modern supply chains. It prevents businesses from building centralized storage units and also makes it impossible for the private sector to play a larger role in agricultural marketing. Excessive control and intervention by the government have hampered the participation of private trade in agricultural marketing.

Some changes in the controls have been made. The dairy sector was liberalized through various amendments to the Milk and Milk Product Order, beginning in 1992. The main purpose of these changes was to allow increased participation by the private sector in marketing agricultural commodities. In response, private sector investments in the dairy sector have increased and resulted in healthy competition between cooperatives and the private sector.

Some steps towards reforms were also taken. The government removed licensing requirements and restrictions on buying, stocking and transporting specified commodities, including wheat, rice, oilseeds and sugar in 2002. This change in the ECA attracted big domestic and multinational players such as ITC, Cargil, Britannia, Agricore, Delhi Floor Mills and Adani Enterprises to the grain trade. However, the government quickly flip-flopped over the policy. There was a shortage of wheat in 2006–07, coinciding with a period of high global prices, which led to the global food crisis of 2007–08. India had to import more than 6 million tonnes of wheat. The government then reversed the decision on the ECA, hence the organized private companies had to withdraw from the grain market.

Commission for Agricultural Costs & Prices

Commission for Agricultural Costs and Prices (CACP) came into existence in 1965. It was earlier named as Agricultural Prices Commission and was set up to advise on the price policy of various crops including foodgrains, pulses, oilseeds, sugarcane, groundnut, cotton, jute tobacco, and so on, to achieve a balanced and integrated price structure in the economy. It is supposed to set prices taking into account demand and supply, cost of production, price trends in the market, inter-crop price parity, terms of trade and implications of MSP on consumers.

The failure to stabilize agricultural prices over the years shows that the CACP is ineffective in its mandate. Himanshu (2015) writes that the failure is as much institutional as it is political. Prices of essential food items, including fruits and vegetables, continue to fluctuate wildly every season showing a complete lack of any price stabilization mechanism in the country. The CACP prices have not led to farmers benefiting out of these except in the case of rice and wheat. The distorted price policy has resulted in farmers producing excessive rice and wheat at the cost of neglecting other crops, particularly pulses, oilseeds and cash crops. Food grain stocks are in excess of demand and they rot in government warehouses. The MSP is thus neither helping the farmer or the consumer but occasionally contributes to price inflation.

The CACP needs to be revamped since price fluctuations threaten the livelihood of farmers. India needs not only a sound price policy but also institutional mechanisms to deal with providing fair price to farmers and consumers.

AGMARK

The AGMARK facility is supposed to promote grades and standards of agricultural products. It has not become very popular and consumers seldom check this mark while buying products. The total quantity of produce graded at the producers' level is very low. Due to lack of awareness and low brand value, AGMARK certified output has been about 1.5 per cent of the total value of crop produce in the country. In 2010–11, exports worth only ₹180 crore were certified, which was 0.16 per cent of the total value of agricultural exports from India. Poor implementation of quality standards or laws results in widespread adulteration of food in the country.

Food Safety and Standards Authority of India

Food Safety and Standards Authority of India (FSSAI) has been established under Food Safety and Standards Act, 2006 which consolidates various acts and orders that were in force earlier. FSSAI has been created for laying down standards for food articles and to regulate their manufacture, storage, distribution, sale and import to ensure availability of safe and wholesome food for human consumption, according to its website. The lack of proper testing laboratories and outdated rules—some rules go back to 1954—have resulted in major criticisms against FSSAI (see Mini Case Study 9.2).

National Agricultural Cooperative Marketing Federation of India Limited

National Agricultural Cooperative Marketing Federation of India Ltd. (NAFED) was set up to promote and develop marketing, processing and storage of agricultural, horticultural and forest produce in the country. It also distributes agricultural machinery, implements and other

Mini Case Study 9.2

FSSAI: A Fine Mess

Adulteration of food products is common in India. The National Survey on Milk Adulteration 2011, a snapshot survey conducted by FSSAI found that 70 per cent of milk samples failed to conform to standards. FSSAI also has found contamination to be quite common among spices and other food items across the country. It found that adulteration rates vary from 20 to 40 per cent in different states in India. While Indians continue to eat adulterated food, the country penalizes big brands on flimsy grounds. Many companies have borne the brunt of arbitrary rules.

Maggi Noodles: In 2015, FSSAI said that Nestlé's noodle brand, Maggi, had excessive levels of lead and monosodium glutamate. The company had to recall the product and more than 17,000 tonnes of noodles were destroyed in furnaces of Ambuja Cement. However, many states in India had found the noodles safe. It was even found safe in Singapore and Hong Kong, and was allowed to be imported from India. Britain's Food Standards Agency too found that the noodles imported from India were safe and well within European Union limits on lead content. "The most regrettable thing about the affair, especially in a country where so many people go hungry, is that in all likelihood a lot of food has been destroyed unnecessarily," wrote *The Economist* (2015).

Lindt chocolate: Swiss chocolate Lindt decided to pull out of the Indian market after six years, as it suffered a harrowing time in the country. The FSSAI asked for detailed labelling under the Food Safety and Standards Act, 2011 and in August 2013, three containers holding goods worth about ₹750 crore were held back. All ingredients were required to be listed in descending order of composition by weight or volume. The company complied. But in January 2014, another lot was held at the ports because of a modified regulation that banned imported chocolates with vegetable oil or fat.

Starbucks: Starbucks faced a similar problem in April 2014 when two containers of its flavoured syrup were held back at the Mumbai port. The reason: FSSAI said that the product did not meet their basic requirements, even though it met the requirements of over 64 countries for almost 40 years, according to the company. It was only after the company went to the court that FSSAI had to release the shipment. The court pointed out that FSSAI had acted in an 'arbitrary and capricious manner'.

Canola oil: Large shipments of canola oil were held back for incorrect labelling, as the rules require that products must use their 'scientific name' and not their 'trade name'. Canola oil is the trade name while the scientific name is 'Rapeseed Oil'. This puts a question mark on foreign brands: Must they sell products in India with their scientific names only?

Olives: A shipment of pasteurized olives was held back as it was found to have excess salt content. The rules require minimum salt content in pasteurized olives to be between 1 to 1.5 per cent but were found to have 5 per cent. The shipment was released only after FSSAI was informed that the salt content in pasteurized olives applied to international standards and was being tested against the wrong product.

While food importers seem to be going through a world of trouble, so are restaurant owners. Chef Manu Chandra, Executive Chef and Partner at Monkey Bar, said "Cured meats, ham, cheese and other products have disappeared from the market. We're being forced to look at alternatives which might mean we'll have to compromise on the taste, flavour and quality we've been offering so far. For many, this is a deal breaker."

Current rules and regulations seem to be crippling the food industry instead of helping them deliver safe products.

What can be done to improve food marketing in the country?

Sources for this Case Study:

NDTV. 2014. "25,000 Crores Worth of Food Lying Wasted." 30 September. Available at: http://food.ndtv.com/food-drinks/25-000-crores-worth-of-food-lying-wasted-696147 (Accessed on 27 April 2017).

The Economist. 2015. "Nestlé in India: Instant Karma." 4 July.

The Hindu BusinessLine. 2014. "Food Labelling Norms Put Importers, Retailers in a Fix." 18 August.

Times of India. 2015. "70% of Milk in Delhi, Country is Adulterated." 10 January.

inputs, undertakes import and export of agricultural goods and provides technical advice in agricultural production to its members and cooperative societies. It has been recognized as a 'Star Export House' by Government of India. However, despite being a nodal agency for procurement of oilseeds and pulses, its reported turnover including exports shows that it is not very successful in meeting its objectives.

Apart from NAFED, every state has its own agricultural marketing federation.

DEFICIENCIES IN THE SYSTEM

The discussion in the previous section shows that despite a very large number of laws and restrictions imposed by the government, the problems in agricultural marketing are many. As noted earlier, government control and laws have worked as a detractor to modernize marketing. Foreign investment in supply chains and retail attracts the ire of politicians. When the price of a commodity goes up, state governments quickly ban their movement to other states and for export. Large storage facilities and cold chains have not come up because the government has made 'hoarding' illegal. Government agencies sometimes delay procurement and payments to farmers leading to distress sales. Since agricultural markets are fragmented and inefficient, farmers are often at the receiving end of agents.

The various problems in the agricultural marketing system were summarized by the Twelfth Plan Working Group on Agricultural Marketing set up by the Planning Commission (2011) as follows:

- **Too many agents:** Agricultural markets in the country are crowded with traders who operate on a small-scale in a limited market segment. For instance, in Punjab, there are as many as 22,000 commission agents; one for every 50 farmers. Then there are a host of other middlemen such as wholesalers, transporters, labour contractors and brokers in each market. As the size of their business is small, they seek large margins. Thus, the channels for marketing of agricultural produce remain long and fragmented and lack economies of scale. On an average, four to six transactions take place before the produce reaches consumers from the farmer. Each stage adds to the cost paid by the consumer, without any real value addition. These middlemen render no real service; they simply earn rent.
- **Low productivity:** India has one of the lowest farm productivity in the world, behind China and Brazil. It has a yield rate of 2.4 tonnes per hectare, placing India at 27th place out of 47 countries, reports Raghavan (2014).
- **Volatile prices:** There are wild price swings in agricultural products. Much of the produce is perishable and lack of storage facilities means that farmers have to resort to distress sale.
- **Primitive supply chains:** Supply chains can assist in moving and supplying goods where they are needed. Yet, modern storage facilities like silos are few and not seen

even in the developed states. Cold chains are inadequate. There is inadequate infrastructure for storage, sorting, grading or post-harvest management.

- **Bad policies:** Farmers are held back by bad policies and laws. An anti-hoarding law that prohibits large storage of commodities has prevented investments in storage facilities. Trade in fruit and vegetables has been restricted. Private companies that wanted to invest in 'farm-to-fork' technologies have been prevented from doing business in India. As a result, the private sector is unwilling to invest in logistics or infrastructure under the prevailing conditions.
- **Distorted markets:** Agricultural marketing is done through state APMCs which distort markets by giving undue power to commission agents. Market information is not easily accessible and price-setting mechanism is not transparent.
- **Lack of finance:** As small farmers lack access to finance and crop insurance, they have to resort to distress sales, apart from adding debt from moneylenders and the like.
- **Tremendous waste:** In India, the value of food wastage is estimated at around ₹92,000 crore per annum, according to a report in *The Hindu BusinessLine* (2016). Lack of post-harvesting facilities, warehouses and cold storage cause this massive wastage.
- **No demand management:** Factories normally produce only as much as they expect to sell. In agriculture, there is no centralized demand management, so that the farmer sows crops that are traditionally sown and are not linked to their expected demand. Price setting mechanism is not transparent; usually the farmer has to sell at prevailing mandi rates once the crop is brought to the market. Market information is not easily accessible.
- **Exploiting farmers:** The system is geared to the advantage of agents and to the detriment of farmers. As a consequence, the consumers often pay high prices but the producers get low realizations. ECA impedes free movement, storage and transport of produce.

Apart from infrastructural and other deficiencies, there are government interventions in price policy too. These are described in the next section.

PRICE POLICY

The government price policy was started to check the exploitation of farmers and consumers by traders and to stabilize prices in a food scarce economy. To meet these ends, the government controls agricultural prices through direct and indirect methods, such as:

1. Regulatory measures.
2. Market infrastructure and institutions.
3. Agricultural price policy.

The government procures grain from the farmers at an MSP, which is decided by the Central government on the recommendations of the CACP. The CACP advises the government on the price policy of food crops and other commodities, on which the government fixes the MSP of various agricultural crops, which are supplied to consumers through the PDS at controlled prices and at market prices in the open market. Traders meet the unmet demand of ration cardholders as well as the total demand of non-ration cardholders.

The CACP recommends the minimum support prices for 23 crops. The FCI and state agencies undertake procurement operations in the case of major crops such as wheat, rice and sugarcane. The NAFED provides price support for oilseeds and pulses, the Cotton Corporation of India (CCI) for cotton and the Jute Corporation of India (JCI) for jute, whenever the need arises. In reality, even for paddy and wheat, market prices often go below MSPs in several markets because of weak procurement machinery.

Controlled price policy has achieved some ends but has created many distortions as well. On the positive side, it ensures availability of food across the country and prices have remained relatively stable without many sharp price spikes. The policy has been successful in achieving the following:

1. Some producers have been able to get assured prices through the administered MSPs.
2. Price stability has been maintained in some crops.
3. Foodgrains have been made available at reasonable prices through PDS and open market operations.
4. Buffer stocks have been maintained to achieve food security.

However, the price policy has mainly benefited only a limited number of crops and farmers. In foodgrains, it has helped wheat and rice farmers and, among other crops, it has helped sugarcane and cotton crop growers. As a consequence, there has been a shift of land and resources away from pulses, oilseeds and coarse grains to wheat and paddy, which has created serious imbalances in the demand and supply of these commodities. Grave environmental problems, such as depletion of groundwater, have resulted in many parts of the country. At the same time, there have been large shortages of pulses and edible oils and the country has to resort to imports for these commodities.

The price policy has failed to address supply side imbalances and ignored the demand side. This has created distortions in the supply of food crops. On the one hand, the government is running out of storage capacity for wheat and rice, while, on the other hand, the production of pulses and oilseeds has been limited, creating a crisis like situation in 2015 (see Mini Case Study 9.3). The per capita availability of pulses in India in 2010 was 31.6 gram per day, compared to 65.5 gram per day in 1960, showing a 52 per cent decline over five decades (*Financial Express*, 2011). As a result, the country's imports of pulses and oilseeds have been rising even as wheat stocks rot in government godowns.

Mini Case Study 9.3

Wild Price Fluctuations in Agricultural Products

Prices of agricultural output fluctuate widely in the absence of any management of demand or supply. The government claims to control food inflation, but lack of supply management means that prices of agricultural products will continue to fluctuate widely in the future as well. While farmers resort to distress sales of some commodities, prices shoot up for other crops due to shortages.

These are regular features of the Indian agricultural market.

In 2015, retail prices of all major pulses crossed ₹100/kg mark. In case of *tur/arhar*, it crossed ₹200/kg in several places. In a knee-jerk reaction, the government used the tools used by centralized economies to control prices; it constituted a committee, invoked the Essential Commodities Act on traders and stockists, banned exports and imposed stocking limits on mills and large retailers. It also had to import 7,000 tonnes of tur.

Gulati and Saini (2015) write that such ineffective policy measures “only point at the rather sloppy conceptual framework the policymakers follow.” For instance, no responsibility was fixed for the alarming increase in prices. Though it was evident by early September that production of pulses was falling, government officials were complacent, which led to the very high increase. The consumer reeled under exorbitant prices of what was a staple diet for many Indians.

Since crops come in once a year while consumption is spread over the entire year, the government should have created adequate storage for the crops. But with stocking limits, legitimate traders become ‘hoarders’ and stocks are not kept for constant supply. The strategy discourages further investments in warehouses/cold storages by private parties. In absence of storage space, market prices after the harvest would collapse, while high prices would be seen for the rest of the year. Low harvest prices, in turn, discourage farmers from planting for the next season.

Second, the government suspended futures and forward markets, which give advance signals about future prices. By banning futures trading, the government was left with no data about existing stocks or likely prices to rule in coming months.

Third, the government’s decision to import 7,000 tur dal to tame its prices, shows a complete naiveté about demand and supply, since consumption of tur is between 3.3–4 million tonnes.

The Indian economy is marked by wild price fluctuations of crops every season. The prices of onions and potatoes becomes a political issue; while the government intervenes when prices are high, farmers are left to throw them on roads when prices fall (Photo 9.6). Yet, there has been no plan to stabilize prices of crops despite a plethora of government agencies working in agriculture.

Photo 9.6

A consequence of wild fluctuations.

Source: Sharma (2016).

Price fluctuations could be solved by creating buffer stocks, which in turn need storage facilities. Second, a demand assessment should be done for all agricultural products and farmers should be advised which crops to plant. Price support, which at present is skewed in favour of rice, wheat and sugarcane, should either be abolished or extended to all crops. Subsidies on fertilizers, power and irrigation for these crops amount to more than ₹10,000/ha, which skews the production curve. Third, farmers need to diversify their crops. A 1960s-style policy response to control the price of pulses will not work, but will be anti-farmer. Instead, export controls and stocking limits should be abolished and efficient storage facilities should be created across states.

If you were a bureaucrat in the agriculture ministry, how would you reform the system for price stabilization?

Sources for this Case Study:

Gulati, Ashok, and Shweta Saini. 2015. "From Plate to Plough: No Finger on the Pulses." *Financial Express*, 23 October.

Sharma, Devinder. 2016. "When Stock Markets Crash, Finance Minister Is on His Toes; and When Onion/Tomato Prices Crash ...." Ground Reality (Blog), May. Available at: http://devinder-sharma.blogspot.in/2016/05/when-stock-markets-crash-finance.html (Accessed on 17 April 2017).

The MSP has not been effectively implemented. Roy and Joshi (2015) cite NSSO data to show that only 6 per cent and mainly large farmers for wheat and rice utilize the MSP while the vast majority does not even know about it. A Planning Commission report (2007) says that the prices received by farmers are often below the MSP in large parts of India. Ramesh Chand (2012) has analyzed the price of paddy received by farmers in Uttar Pradesh and West Bengal from 1995–96 to 1999–2000. He shows that the average farm harvest price (FHP) in West Bengal received by farmers has remained lower than the MSP in all the years, with the gap widening in recent years. In Uttar Pradesh, wheat farmers received a price higher than the MSP in only two out of 13 years—the years the private sector was in the wheat market in a big way—while for the rest of the years, the selling price has been lower than the MSP.

He further shows that in the case of arhar in Maharashtra, the benefit of price increases has been captured by middlemen without any benefit to farmers. The price spread between the FHP of arhar (whole grain) in Maharashtra and the WSP of arhar dal (split and polished grain) in the Mumbai market increased from 25 per cent to more than 70 per cent between 2000 and 2009, showing that in 10 years, the middlemen margin recorded a three-fold increase in the state. In the same period, the price received by producers for arhar increased by less than 5 per cent per year, whereas wholesale and retail prices increased by more than 10 per cent per year. Furthermore, he also shows that the change in MSP of arhar announced by the Central government, relative to the change in the WSP at the beginning of the last decade, was more than 50 per cent of the WSP of arhar dal in the Mumbai market. The level of support declined steadily to one-third by 2009–10. Thus, an increase in the MSP of arhar, even though notional, did not keep pace with the increase in market price in this period.

The distortions in the present market system cause declining competitiveness, while the increases in prices at the consumer level of crops are not passed on to farmers. The poor spend more than 50 per cent of their income buying food for mere subsistence, while the government-procured grain is either spoilt or finds its way into the hands of corrupt officials, middlemen and grain traders.

Reforming Agricultural Price Policy

The many distortions in agricultural markets point to a system crying for reform. Till now, the price guarantee offered by the MSP has worked only in selected states and markets. Price guarantees also lead to price distortions. New mechanisms thus have to be devised to protect farmers from the prices crashing. It is time that instead of focusing on support prices, the government focuses on demand. Working on scientific demand forecasts, the total area under each crop must be worked out and farmers are advised about which crops to plant. Such a system would prevent overproduction and help stabilize prices in the market. There is also a need to open agricultural markets to the private sector. In recent years, some direct marketing initiatives have taken place which have helped farmers. Some of these initiatives are described here.

DIRECT MARKETING INITIATIVES

To promote direct sales to consumers, farmers' markets have been started in the form of Apni Mandis in Punjab, Rythu Bazaars in Andhra Pradesh, Uzhavar Santhai in Tamil Nadu, and Shetkari Bazaar in Maharashtra.

Gate Sales

When farmers sell agricultural produce directly to consumers, it is called farm gate sales. Farmers either sell directly by putting up a stall on the highway near their farm or establish contacts with bulk consumers such as restaurants, caterers and independent retailers to supply directly to them. Gate sales are a common type of marketing among farmers who have access to direct markets, are located on highways, or have the transportation and means to supply directly to their consumers.

Rural Primary Markets

There are many regular and periodical markets in rural and interior areas known as haats, shandies, painths and fairs. Farmers bring their produce there on fixed days of the week and sell it to consumers. However, these markets lack facilities and hygiene, and are highly congested, in deep contrast to agricultural markets in developed countries (Photo 9.7). There is much to be done to increase the marketing efficiency of these markets so that farmers get remunerative prices. These markets are usually managed by panchayats and municipalities who collect ground rent and fees but the funds are not used for their betterment or for developing infrastructure.

Apni Mandi Initiative in Punjab

The Apni Mandi was started by the Punjab Mandi Board on the lines of the 'Saturday Market' in the UK and the USA. It offers farmers and growers a place in towns of Punjab and Chandigarh to sell their produce directly to consumers. It was an effort to eliminate middlemen so that

Photo 9.7
An agricultural market in Dijon, France.

Source: Photograph by Dinesh Kumar.

both the growers and consumers benefit: the former by way of better prices while the latter get fresh produce at low prices. Apni Mandi was first established in 1987 at Mohali (Punjab) and after its success, it was introduced in 27 towns in the state. The number of farmers that participated in these mandis was 10,278 in 1988 which increased to 353,610 in the year 2010. The approximate sale of produce in these mandis was for ₹29,624,761 in the year 1988, which increased to ₹629,347,474 in 2010. A study of Apni Mandis of Ludhiana by Sukhmani and Goyal (2014) showed that the initiative had been a success but many retailers and middlemen also participated in them, and there was no way of identifying registered and non-registered farmers. The markets also suffered from lack of facilities and infrastructure despite farmers paying huge ground rents and fees (Photo 9.8).

PHOTO 9.8

Agricultural markets in India lack even the basic facilities. Picture taken at an Apni Mandi in Punjab.

Source: Photograph by Dinesh Kumar.

Contract Farming

When farmers enter into an agreement with a company to grow their produce as per its requirements and supply all of it to the company, it is called contract farming. The buyer specifies the quality, quantity and price, and the farmer delivers products to the buyer's premises. Food companies such as Pepsi, Nestlé and KFC enter into long-term contracts with them for supply of food items. The companies help farmers by providing them high-yield seed varieties, knowhow and other inputs and are assured of supplies for their business. Contract farming is used for many agricultural products.

Efforts are being made to link agricultural markets to provide easy access to farmers. These portals are described in Chapter 10. The biggest of these initiatives is the creation of NAM.

National Agricultural Market

The Economic Survey and Budget for 2015 called for bold actions such setting up a national common agricultural market. It severely criticized the operations of the APMCs on the grounds that their key positions were occupied by politically influential persons. Realizing that the APMC works to the detriment of the farmer, the Central government decided to integrate 585 wholesale markets across India and allocated ₹200 crore for three years to set up an online NAM, as reported in *The Hindu BusinessLine* (2015). It is hoped that unifying markets both at state and the national level would provide better price to farmers, improve the supply chain, reduce wastages and create a unified national market through an e-platform.

It is hoped that since agriculture markets are highly fragmented, NAM, with an online trading portal, would open up markets by linking farmers and consumers. Farmers can offer their produce to buyers in any part of the country through the e-platform. The Small Farmers' Agribusiness Consortium (SFAC) was designated as the lead agency for developing the NAM e-platform. Integrating wholesale markets across India and linking them online would also help farmers realize better prices.

The government launched the NAM on 14 April 2016. Initially, 21 mandis in eight states were integrated. *Chana*, castor seed, paddy, wheat, maize, onion, mustard and tamarind were to be traded in these mandis. The NAM is a nationwide electronic trading portal comprising a network of mandis and market yards. It envisions one licence state-wide, a single-point levy and use of electronic auctions for price discovery. It removes institutional and legal barriers to free circulation of commodities. Farmers or traders can sell with the same freedom across states as within their own state. Since a fragmented and high-cost agricultural economy prevents economies of scale and seamless movement of goods, NAM seeks to change this by lowering intermediation costs, wastage and ultimately prices for consumers. In NAM, the existing mandis provide the backend support for the electronic platform.

There are two major shortcomings of the NAM: fruits and vegetables have not been included in the NAM. Secondly, the country's two biggest mandis—Azadpur (Delhi) and Vasi (Mumbai)—have not agreed to come on board. By November 2016, only 250 regulated wholesale markets out of 585 such mandis were integrated with the NAM platform, reports *Financial Express* (2016). As a consequence, NAM has seen only tepid response. Haryana contributed a major portion of the turnover of NAM. Even among these NAM-linked mandis, electronic trade is limited to very few commodities.

Whether this scheme will help the farmers get better prices, however, remains to be seen. Mishra and Mukherjee (2015) write that setting up a trading portal alone is unlikely to bring substantial changes in a highly fragmented market. One major problem is that even if a farmer, using an online portal, is able to locate a buyer in a distant part of India, would it be possible to arrange transport and send the produce over large distances? Would the buyer be confident of getting the same grade and quality of produce that was shown on website? That is why, infrastructure such as transport, storage and grading is the backbone of agricultural marketing. There is a crying need to improve the facilities and systems for the NAM to succeed.

Cooperative marketing could well provide farmers with easy access to markets. This important activity is covered in the next section.

Cooperative Marketing

A cooperative marketing association is a voluntary organization established by its members to market farm products collectively. Small farmers, who do not have resources to market themselves, come together to benefit from a larger organization. Cooperative members are the owners and operators and are the direct beneficiaries of the earnings of the society. Cooperatives can help achieve economies of scale, hire talent and gain better bargaining power, which individual farmers cannot do. They also help in removing intermediaries.

Every state has a cooperative marketing society or marketing corporations run by the state governments. Some of these are:

- The Haryana State Cooperative Supply and Marketing Federation.
- Maharashtra State Agricultural Marketing Board.
- Gujarat Agro Industries Corporation Ltd.
- The Spices Trading Corporation Ltd.
- The A.P. State Trading Corporation.
- The Karnataka State Cooperative Marketing Federation Ltd.
- National Cooperative Consumers Federation of India Ltd.
- The North Karnataka Onion Growers Cooperative Society.
- West Bengal Essential Commodities Supply Corporation Ltd.
- M.P. State Agro Industries Development Corporation.
- Karnataka State Agricultural Produce Processing and Export Corporation.
- Madhya Pradesh State Cooperative Oil Seeds Growers Federation Ltd.
- The Andhra Pradesh Marketing Federation.
- Himachal Pradesh State Cooperative Marketing & Consumers Federation Ltd.
- The Kerala State Cooperative Rubber Marketing Federation Ltd.
- National Federation of Farmers' Procurement, Processing and Retailing Cooperatives of India Ltd (NACOF).
- Agricultural and Processed Food Products Export Development Authority (APEDA).

The main functions of cooperative marketing societies are as follows:

1. Marketing of agricultural produce of members.
2. Act as an agent for the supply of produce, provide transportation, safeguard the interests of members, get better prices for them, and save them from malpractices and excessive costs, and achieve economies of scale.
3. Provide credit facilities to members against their produce.
4. Build or provide scientific storage for agricultural produce.
5. Provide market information for better prices and also grading, processing and packing facilities.
6. Develop better bargaining power than the individual members.
7. Participate in exports of agricultural produce.
8. Arrange supplies of agricultural inputs for farmers, such as improved seeds, fertilizers, insecticides and pesticides.

Cooperatives work on the principle that people will get together and form organizations to help them achieve objectives that they individually cannot. They encourage voluntary and open membership, democratic control, economic participation of members and mutual benefit with limited interest on share capital. They can help in building common storage areas or other infrastructure, marketing agricultural produce and using collective power to get better prices, source raw materials and achieve economies of scale. They work on the principles of equality, equity and mutual self-help.

Cooperative marketing societies are of three types:

1. **Single Commodity Cooperative Marketing Societies:** Societies for marketing of only one agricultural commodity. Examples of such societies are Sugarcane Cooperative

Marketing Society, Cotton Cooperative Marketing Society and Oilseed Growers Cooperative Marketing Society.

2. **Multi-commodity Cooperative Marketing Societies:** Societies marketing a number of commodities produced by the members, such as foodgrains, oilseeds and cotton.
3. **Multi-purpose, Multi-commodity Cooperative Marketing Societies:** Societies that market a number of commodities and perform other functions as providing credit, arranging inputs and even providing domestic consumption goods.

Cooperative societies are active in Gujarat, Maharashtra, Andhra Pradesh and Tamil Nadu, where large quantities of foodgrains are marketed by them. Sugarcane, cotton and plantation crops are marketed by the cooperative societies in Maharashtra, Uttar Pradesh, Gujarat and Karnataka. In Gujarat, 84 per cent of milk is marketed through cooperatives. The performance of cooperatives in dairy and sugarcane sectors is very good. They have resulted in transforming the social and economic landscape of Gujarat and some other parts of the country. Dairy cooperatives present the most successful example of cooperative marketing.

However, the progress of cooperative marketing societies has not been very satisfactory in many parts of the country. They are dominated by politics and chairmen of these societies are appointed by politicians. Farmers feel that they are not able to get the best prices for their produce. The success of cooperative marketing is not universal across commodities, sectors and geographical regions. Most cooperatives are running in losses.

Cooperatives as a whole account for only 10 per cent of the total quantities of agricultural commodities marketed by the farmers. Singh and Pundir (2000) point out that there are many institutional, economic, social, political, organizational and managerial factors that affect the performance of cooperatives. When cooperatives are imposed by the government, they fail to get participation of members. It is only when cooperatives are established by the people themselves to solve common problems that they are likely to succeed. Acharya and Agarwal (2004) point out the reasons of slow progress of cooperative marketing:

1. Cooperative marketing societies are located in big cities or towns and have been unable to connect remote villages.
2. Farmers are indebted to local traders and enter into advance contracts with them for the sale of their crops.
3. Farmers are in immediate need of cash after the harvest and sell their produce to local traders before harvest.
4. Members lack confidence in cooperative organizations. There is lack of loyalty among members of cooperative societies as they fail to stick to the principles of democratic and cooperative functioning. Members feel betrayed by cooperatives if they are not able to influence decisions.
5. Cooperatives are not treated as business organizations and so they are inefficient and unprofitable. They lack professional management and working and are grossly undermanaged or mismanaged. Since many cooperatives are small, they are unable to attract the best people and compete with companies in marketing their produce.
6. The societies do not provide financial access or act as banks for the farmers. They also lack the means to raise resources from banks and capital markets.
7. Societies lack sufficient storage facilities. They, therefore, try to dispose of the produce soon after their arrival, which results in lower prices for the farmers.

8. Cooperatives suffer from excessive government control and political interference. They operate under the thumb of the government. Politicians or civil servants are nominated by the government to run these societies.
9. Cooperatives lack good leadership. A cooperative needs a dedicated leader, for instance, like Dr Kurien, who laid the foundation of Operation Flood in the country. But such people are rare.
10. Societies do not provide food or shelter to farmers at mandis and are ill-equipped to trade in mandis on behalf of farmers.

As a consequence of these limitations, many cooperative marketing organizations are not even financially viable and suffer from many shortcomings. If they cannot attract good managers and good leadership, they remain destined to serve limited interests. Outdated laws and excessive government control also limit their growth. Cooperatives could have a bright future in India if they had become member-owned autonomous organizations managed professionally and serving interests of the members.

Agricultural marketing is aided by commodity markets. Well-developed commodity trading platforms facilitate easy trade in such farmers' produce. It is explained in the next section.

Commodity Marketing

A commodity market is a market that trades in primary economic sector rather than manufactured products. It facilitates trading in various agricultural commodities such as spices, coffee, cocoa, sugar, soya beans and others. There are two types of trade: *spot market* means that commodities are bought and sold for immediate delivery, and in *derivatives market*, financial instruments based on commodities are traded.

Commodity futures are regulated under the Forward Contracts Regulations Act, 1952 by the Forward Markets Commission (FMC) set up in 1953. Commodity trading is done through regional exchanges and national commodity exchanges, such as the Multi Commodity Exchange (MCX), National Commodity and Derivatives Exchange (NCDEX), and National Multi Commodity Exchange of India Ltd (NMCE).

These markets help farmers by providing them price information, reducing the risk and enabling better returns. Transparency in prices helps them know about trade margins, improving the efficiency of marketing.

Spices Marketing

India is the largest producer of spices. The spices market in India consists of chilly, garlic, ginger, turmeric and coriander. The spices market in India is dominated by the unorganized sector.

Some large companies that are into spices marketing are MDH, ITC, Tata, Everest and Catch.

IMPROVING AGRICULTURAL MARKETING IN INDIA

The discussion in the preceding sections shows that agricultural marketing is in dire need of reforms (see Mini Case Study 9.4). Farmers suffer on all accounts, while supply chains are marked by inefficiencies due to unnecessary regulation. This section lists some reforms that can help agricultural markets in a big way.

Mini Case Study 9.4

Marketing Insight

Food marketing is regulated all over the world. In terms of silliness, Indian rules are not the only ones. This case, which illustrates the rules in USA, is about two girls, Zoey and Andria Green, who started a lemonade stand outside their home in Texas. After about an hour, local police came and shut the operation down.

The girls did not have a 'peddler's permit' which costs US$150, nor did they have a kitchen inspection by the state and a permit to sell anything that might spoil if stored at the wrong temperature. The authorities are meant "to act to prevent an immediate and serious threat to human life or health."

Sluggish job growth has encouraged more people to start home-based businesses. But regulating the sale of goods made in ordinary kitchens is a 'grey area'. States are passing 'cottage-food laws' allowing people to sell 'non-potentially hazardous' foods, such as baked goods and almost anything canned, from their homes.

Rules vary from state to state. Some states explicitly ban Internet sales, as products sold across state lines are subject to more stringent federal food laws. Lemonade, however, is not covered by Texas's cottage-food law, as it might get spoiled if it is not properly stored. But the girls learned a valuable lesson about commerce and regulation. They discovered that if they gave the lemonade away free, but put a box on the table for tips, they could still make money because the 'payments' thus became donations.

How can food marketing be liberated, given the fact that government must control its quality?

Source for this Case Study:

The Economist. 2015. "Is lemonade legal?" 11 July.

- **Linking farmers with markets:** Singh (2011) writes that linking small primary producers with markets is one of the major issues in improving livelihoods for millions of poor farming households. So far, the system has impoverished farmers, prevented modernization of agriculture and has led to huge food wastage. Mehta and Singh (2008) write that the Indian farmer suffers as he is not linked to the consumer, which has led to perpetuation of poverty, they write.
- **Improving infrastructure:** Poor transport, lack of infrastructure and marketing facilities ensure that farmers are unable to get good prices. The monopolistic systems encouraged by APMCs are also a hindrance. Isolated regional markets means that farmers cannot sell their produce where it is needed. As noted earlier, agents, wholesalers and processors enjoy significant clout in agricultural markets. Intermediaries at each stage earn sizeable margins for little value addition. One way of reducing the length of marketing channels is by limiting intermediaries through better connectivity consisting of roads, railway connections and lorries. This would remove geographical isolation and bring the farmer closer to the consumer. Better and accessible financial services, credit facilities helped by microfinance, will help the famer.
- **Storage facilities:** Modern systems of storage have still not been constructed in India; they are too expensive for individual farmers and government has not invested in them. Storage infrastructure such as warehouses and cold storages help save the harvested crops. Agricultural produce is still stored in jute bags. As a result, the produce cannot be stored for long. Many farmers resort to distress sale of their produce to clear the loans from moneylenders. They cannot even wait for government procurement. Nair (2015)

reports, "In collusion with unscrupulous local traders and commission agents, government agencies delay procurement of grains by, in some cases, as many as 50–60 days." This causes farmers to sell out to local traders at much lower prices. Storage facilities, even at the government-owned FCI, are lacking; produce is stored in the open, causing huge damage.

- **Direct sales:** Direct sales help bring the produce close to the customer. Some farmers are able to bring their produce at a highway and sell through makeshift stalls to passing vehicles. However, farmers' markets have not had a major impact on farm incomes as sales through this marketing channel are generally small, both in terms of number of the farmers participating and volumes of produce (see section on Direct Marketing).
- **Transportation:** Farmers face a double whammy to transport their produce: bad roads and lack of adequate transport. According to Planning Commission Report of the Working Group on Agricultural Marketing Infrastructure for the XII Five Year Plan 2012–17 (2011), transportation and handling facilities for perishable commodities are inadequate and poor. "Physical infrastructure in market yards is inadequate. Most of the rural primary markets (including livestock markets) have no infrastructure. Due to lack of proper handling facilities at the village level, about 7 per cent of foodgrains, 30 per cent of fruits and vegetables and 10 per cent of spices are lost before reaching the market," it says.
- **Access to finance:** The ability to hold on to stock depends on the financial condition of the farmer. Nair writes that most farmers are under debt; average debt per household is ₹47,000, while average income is ₹36,973 per annum. Nair (2015) writes, "While average income from 2002–03 to 2012–03 increased by 318 per cent, most worryingly, total debt per household increased by 273.5 per cent during the same period, proving that while income from sale of agricultural products increased due to a price advantage during the last one decade, it has not translated into a reduction in rural indebtedness." As a consequence, the farmer is always under pressure to sell stocks to meet his burden of debt.

  Farmers lack access to formal channels of finance in many parts of the country. Crops are not considered a financial asset against which farmers can take loans. Low-cost warehousing and negotiable receipts with an electronic registry for commodities can bring lenders closer to the farmers keen to pledge their crops.
- **Price information:** Farmers in remote villages lack the means to track prices in markets and are often at the mercy of agents. Even if they know the prices, they are unable to make use of the information, because harvesting and transporting of a crop cannot be done in a day.
- **Food processing facilities:** Food processing is a potential source for driving the rural economy as it helps farmers find a ready market for their produce. A well-developed food processing industry increases farm gate prices, reduces wastages and ensures value addition. It assists farmers in getting knowhow from factories and promotes crop diversification. However, unless government rationalizes food laws, sets up the mega food parks and encourages foreign investment, facilities for food production are unlikely to come up in a big way. Integrated facilities for procurement, processing, storage and transport complement the food processing industry. Private sector and foreign investments can play a role and for that the government must allow 100 per cent FDI in food processing, cold chain infrastructure and retail.

PHOTO 9.9

Grading and branding can improve value received for agricultural products.

Source: Photograph by Dinesh Kumar.

- **Free trade and an open market:** There is an urgent need to open up the agricultural sector by encouraging free trade and an open market. Government intervention creates distortions, cartelization and inaccessibility (see Mini Case Study 9.5). Moreover, even the most efficient farm will fail to produce profits if the harvest cannot be sold at the best possible price in a timely manner. That is why, only free trade will promote investment in better quality, crop diversification and packaging.

Importance of Trust

Most agricultural contracts are verbal and are based on trust. Masuku (2009) finds that trustworthiness and reputation of wholesale traders significantly affects the proportion of produce sold through them. This is not surprising since institutions such as contracts and enforcement mechanisms are less developed or absent. The development of relational contracts (shaped in a given social system) between supply chain participants is an appropriate strategy for agricultural marketing where formal contracts are non-existent. Relational contracts characterized by trust and cooperation are self-enforcing, which makes third-party enforcement mechanisms less needed. Marketing cooperatives, therefore, should work on building trust, improving price information networks and establish well-defined contracts that govern exchanges, grades and standards.

Mini Case Study 9.5

How Subsidies Distort Markets

The government foots the bill of about ₹175,000 crore as agricultural subsidies. Subsidies in agriculture distort markets, create inefficiencies, produce glut in some crops while shortages in others. They also represent a paradox: Despite the huge annual expenditure, why is the farm sector under so much distress? Clearly, subsidies are not as beneficial as they are made out by politicians to voters.

An ICRIER analysis, 'Supporting Indian farms the smart way', shows that subsidies are worsening matters across the country, and not just for the farmers. In the case of fertilizer subsidies, which account for over 40 per cent of the total agriculture subsidy, a large chunk actually goes to inefficient local producers. Mostly, larger farmers get the bulk of subsidies. Water and electricity subsidies add up to 4.8 per cent of the agricultural GDP or around 55 per cent of all farm subsidies. Subsidy spending is 9 per cent of agricultural GDP, which is three times of the investment in the sector. Perhaps if expenditure on subsidies was reduced, more investments would flow in the sector.

The study points out that for every million rupees spent on agriculture R&D, the number of poor would fall by 251. Subsidies spent does not achieve this figure. It is also estimated that every rupee spent on agriculture R&D increases agriculture growth by ₹7.68, whereas every rupee spent through subsidy raise agriculture GDP by a mere 35 paise.

Some of the consequences of high subsidies are given here:

- **High subsidy bill:** Less amount left for agricultural investment and R&D.
- **Free Electricity:** Depletion of groundwater, growing unsuitable crops in water-scarce regions.
- **Fertilizer subsidy:** Overuse of fertilizers, groundwater poisoning.
- **Interest subsidy:** High indebtedness.
- **MSP:** Glut in some crops, low crop areas for crops such as pulses.

Worse, subsidies create a negative impact. An example of this was the controversy over holding IPL matches in Maharashtra due to severe drought. Maintaining IPL pitches and grounds require 6 million litres of water, which seemed criminal considering that the state was going through a severe drought. However, 6 million litres of water would have produced just 3 tonnes of sugar, which is a minuscule figure considering that the state produces about 10 million tonnes of sugar annually. But because of free water, Maharashtra's farmers continue to plant sugarcane, a crop that is mainly responsible for the water crisis. Maharashtra is not alone—the ICRIER study mentions that nearly 80 per cent of groundwater reservoirs in Punjab and 60 per cent in Haryana are overexploited, a direct result of the irrigation and power subsidy.

Subsidies in fertilizers have resulted in excessive use of urea, resulting in a huge imbalance in usage and a consequent reduction in fertility of the soil. Tragically, successive governments have continued to push subsidies over investment and farmers merely react to market conditions. Ashok Gulati of ICRIER is a strong supporter of investment-based model rather than subsidies, given the fact that investments are far more powerful in boosting agricultural growth than subsidies. A report by Hoda and Terway (2015) shows how agricultural investments can be made more efficient.

What role do subsidies play in agriculture? Should they be abolished?

Sources for this Case Study:

Financial Express. 2016. "Subsidies vs Agriculture." 20 April.

Hoda, Anwarul and Prerna Terway. 2015. *Supporting Indian Farms the Smart Way: Rationalising Subsidies and Investments for Faster, Inclusive and Sustainable Growth.* ICRIER Working Paper 302, June.

SUMMARY

Producing food and its marketing is the backbone of any country, but in India it has remained neglected. Agricultural marketing has several roles, from supplying agricultural goods to consumers to establishing supply chains, assessing demand and providing incentives and knowhow for better productivity. The agricultural value chain starts from production and leads to harvesting and cleaning, transport, storage, grading, wholesale, direct marketing and waste management. Lacking infrastructure, agricultural value chains are skewed against farmers. Farmers therefore prefer to sell out to pre-harvest contractors, giving up their opportunity for value addition.

Agricultural marketing infrastructure has been the victim of monopoly, politics and lethargy. That is why, farmers depend on middlemen or arhatiyas and traders in primary markets. They do not have storage facilities, manpower for direct sales, transportation, access to finance and price information. They mostly sell to pre-harvest contractors to recover their investments in the field.

Agricultural marketing is dominated by government agencies. While this may have served a food-scarce economy, today it is preventing modernization and limits private investment. Procurement is done by FCI for major foodgrains, markets are controlled by APMCs, while the ECA prevents building of large storage facilities. The APMC Act, in particular, has resulted in establishing monopolies of agents who form cartels, charging high fees from farmers, and the high costs and margins are passed on to consumers. The market committees are controlled by politicians, who do no value addition but spend farmers' money on themselves. Some steps towards reforms have been taken but these are not enough.

Food marketing is controlled by FSSAI, which has been created for laying down standards for food articles, but adulteration has increased under its watch and outdated rules stymie imports. A plethora of government agencies and cooperatives (indirectly controlled by the government through nominee directors) add to problems in the agricultural marketing system. Indian agriculture thus suffers from too many agents, high fees, low productivity, volatile prices and farmer suicides.

Agricultural prices are also controlled through regulatory measures, market institutions and agricultural price policy. The government procures grains directly from the farmers at an MSP, which is decided by the Central government on the recommendations of the CACP. It has been successful to some extent but it distorts markets. There is an urgent need to improve infrastructure, storage, transportation and finance facilities and opportunities for direct marketing. Reports say that due to lack of proper handling facilities at the village level, about 7 per cent of foodgrains, 30 per cent of fruits and vegetables and 10 per cent of spices are lost before reaching the market.

Some direct marketing facilities, such a rural markets and contract farming are popular in certain areas. The government has also started the NAM with the hope of unifying markets. However, without investments in storage facilities, transportation, access to finance, food processing facilities and price information, marketing of agricultural products in the country will remain at the primitive stage that they are today.

CONCLUSION

Agricultural marketing suffers from huge inefficiencies such as a disconnect between the prices received by producers and the prices paid by consumers, fragmented and long marketing channels, poor infrastructure and policy distortions. Government regulations have stifled agricultural marketing and have prevented large-scale investments by the private sector. Agriculture is still regulated by outdated laws and the government is still using policy tools of the 1960s to regulate agricultural marketing. Urgent reforms are needed in agricultural marketing to achieve such goals and address the inadequacies now prevailing in markets.

Though some steps have been taken to improve agricultural infrastructure such as setting up of the NAM, there is a need to liberalize food marketing and free it from distortions and the shackles of excessive laws and subsidies. The ineffectiveness of current policy is evident from the fact that even after providing ₹175,000 crore as agricultural subsidies, farm distress in India has increased over the years. The money spent on subsidies is three times the amount spent on investments in agriculture, leading to slow capital formation and creating imbalances among crop supplies.

There is a crying need to modernize agricultural supply chains and to encourage investments in the area. A greater participation of the private sector would greatly enhance the efficiency of supply chains and build modern storage and transportation facilities that are so urgently required to modernize a crucial sector of the economy.

KEY TERMS

AGMARKNET: Agricultural Marketing Research and Information Network.

Agricultural value chain: A 'value chain' in agriculture defines the set of activities that bring a basic agricultural product from production in the field to final consumption, and value is added to the product at each stage.

APMC: Agricultural Produce Marketing Committee.

CACP: Commission for Agricultural Costs and Prices.

CCI: Cotton Corporation of India.

Cooperative marketing: A cooperative marketing association is a voluntary business organization established by its members to market farm products collectively for direct benefit to the members.

Contract farming: When farmers enter into an agreement with a company to supply produce to it, it is called contract farming.

FCI: Food Corporation of India.

JCI: Jute Corporation of India.

MSP: Minimum support price.

NACOF: National Federation of Farmers' Procurement, Processing and Retailing Cooperatives of India Ltd.

NAFED: National Agricultural Cooperative Marketing Federation of India Limited.

NAM: National Agriculture Market.

PDS: Public Distribution System.

CONCEPT REVIEW QUESTIONS

1. Define agricultural marketing. What are the roles it plays in the economy?
2. Describe the agricultural value chain and explain how value is added at each stage.
3. What is the existing system of marketing of agricultural produce? What are its drawbacks?
4. Explain the reasons that make farmers depend on agents. How can the situation be improved?
5. In what ways does the government exercise control over agricultural marketing? What are its drawbacks?
6. Describe the objectives of the APMC Act. What have been the benefits and shortcomings of the Act?
7. What are the deficiencies of agricultural marketing system in India? How can they be overcome?
8. How is price of agricultural products controlled in Indian markets?
9. Describe the direct marketing initiatives for agricultural marketing. Why have such initiatives not impacted farmers much?
10. What is a cooperative marketing federation? How does it work? Name some important cooperative marketing federations.

CRITICAL THINKING QUESTIONS

1. What is agricultural marketing? How is agricultural marketing different from conventional marketing? Why does the concept of 4Ps not apply here? Can you suggest an alternative framework for agricultural marketing?
2. The chapter shows a plethora of government and cooperative agencies working in the area of agricultural marketing. Yet, the plight of small or contractual farmers remains dismal. Why is this so? What steps can you suggest for improving the condition of the growers of food?
3. Should agricultural marketing be privatized? Can the problems of the sector be solved by getting rid of APMC and allowing private players to set up supply chains? If after 60 years of independence, we are still struggling for efficiency, should the system be scrapped altogether?
4. "The National Agriculture Market can be the reform promised by the Digital India initiative to bring succour to 56 million farmers and 1.2 billion consumers." Critically analyze the statement and comment whether NAM can reform the system of agricultural marketing in India.

PROJECTS AND ASSIGNMENTS

1. Visit a direct marketing vegetables market in your city. Talk to the vendors. Find out how farmers feel about the market. What do you conclude from your exercise?
2. See the websites of cooperative marketing federations. Analyze their figures to see whether they have been effective in meeting their objectives.

3. Take a trip to a nearby village. Talk to the farmers about how they sell their produce. Prepare a report on the system and also problems faced by them.
4. Have a discussion in your class about traditional marketing versus agricultural marketing. Can the same principles be applied to rural marketing? What are the points of similarity and difference?

WEB RESOURCES

Commission for Agricultural Costs and Prices (CACP) website: http://cacp.dacnet.nic.in
HAFED website: http://www.hafed.gov.in/
See a slideshow of food storage in the country: "Food stocks go waste while India's stand blocks WTO trade deal." http://www.livemint.com/Multimedia/NnxmmzazpjHLnZ8WeIg0ZN/Food-stocks-go-waste-while-India-fusses-about-food-security.html

REFERENCES

Acharya, S.S., and N.L. Agarwal. 2004. *Agricultural Marketing in India*. 4th Edition; New Delhi: Oxford and IBH Publishing.

Chand, Ramesh. 2012. "Development Policies and Agricultural Markets." *Economic & Political Weekly* 47 (52), 29 December: 53–63.

The Economist. 2015. "Farming in India: In a Time Warp." 25 June.

Financial Express. 2011. "Per Capita Availability of Pulses in India Going Down." 4 September.

———. 2016. "Digital India: Few Takers for Game-changer Initiative in Agriculture Sector." 6 November.

Himanshu. 2015. "Agricultural Price Policy's Failures." *Mint*, 17 March.

The Hindu. 2015. "Govt Allocates ₹200 Crore for National Agriculture Market." 2 July.

The Hindu BusinessLine. 2015. "Setting up National Agriculture Market, a Clear Warning for APMCs." 4 March.

———. 2016. "Curbing Food Wastage in a Hungry World." 30 October.

Indian Express. 2015. "Time to Reform Food Corruption of India." 26 January.

Jha, Shikha, P.V. Srinivasan and A. Ganesh Kumar. 2010. "Achieving Food Security in a Cost Effective Way: Implications of Domestic Deregulation and Liberalised Trade in India." In *Liberalising Foodgrains Markets, Experiences, Impact and Lessons from South Asia*, edited by A. Ganesh Kumar, Devesh Roy and Ashok Gulati, 47–89. New Delhi: Oxford University Press.

Masuku, M.B. 2009. "The Role of Trust in Contract Enforcement: An Analysis of Smallholder Farmers and Sugar Millers in Swaziland." Edited by Kirsten, J.F., Dorward, A.R., Poulton, C., and Vink, N. In *Institutional Economics Perspectives on African Agricultural Development*, 185–99. Washington DC, WA: International Food Policy Research Institute.

Mehta, Pradeep S., and V.V. Singh. 2008. "Freeing Farmers from Intermediaries." *The Hindu BusinessLine*, 16 April.

Mint. 2014. "India's Agricultural Yield Suffers from Low Productivity." 9 September. Available at: http://www.livemint.com/Opinion/nw9JKiPrDPpqCuWfmoibPN/Indias-agricultural-yield-suffers-from-low-productivity.html

Mishra, M., and S. Mukherjee. 2015. "Agri Market Chews the Cud over Rigid APMC Rules." *Business Standard*, 14 July.

Nair, K.P.P. 2015. "The Debt Story Less Told." *The Hindu BusinessLine*, 12 February.

NDTV Profit. 2014. "Why Abolition of APMC is a Good Idea." 18 June. Available at: http://profit.ndtv.com/news/economy/article-why-abolition-of-apmc-is-a-good-idea-532601 (Accessed on 17 April 2017).

Planning Commission. 2007. *Tenth Five Year Plan 2002–07—Agriculture*. Available at: http://planningcommission.gov.in/plans/planrel/fiveyr/10th/volume2/v2_ch5_1.pdf (Accessed on 17 April 2017).

Planning Commission, Agriculture Division, India. 2011. *Report of the Working Group On Agricultural Marketing Infrastructure, Secondary Agriculture and Policy Required for Internal and External Trade for the XII Five Year Plan 2012-17*. December. Available at: http://planningcommission.gov.in/aboutus/committee/wrkgrp12/agri/weg_rep_market.pdf (Accessed on 17 April 2017).

Raghavan, T.C.A. Sharad. 2014. "India's Agricultural Yield Suffers from Low Productivity." *Mint*, 9 September.

Roy, Devesh, and P.K. Joshi. 2015. "Raising the Pulse Profit." *Financial Express*, 13 July.

Sidhu, R.S., M.S. Sidhu and J.M. Singh. 2011. "Marketing Efficiency of Green Peas under Different Supply Chains in Punjab." *Agricultural Economics Research Review* 24 (July–December): 267–73.

Singh, Kartar, and R.S. Pundir. 2000. "Co-operatives and Rural Development in India." Research Paper 17, Institute of Rural management Anand (IRMA), August.

Singh, Sukhpal, and Naresh Singla. 2011. "Fresh Food Supermarkets in India: An Analysis of their Inclusiveness and Impact on Primary Producers." *Millennial Asia* 2 (1): 65–91.

Sukhmani, and P. Goyal. 2014. "Role of Punjab Mandi Board in Apni Mandis: A Study of Ludhiana City." *Indian Journal of Economics and Development* 10 (1a): 60–64.

The Tribune. 2015. "Punjab Mandi Board Pays for its Chief's King-size Life." 23 June.

Tuteja, Usha, and Subhash Chandra. 2012. "Impact of Emerging Marketing Channels in Agricultural Marketing—Benefits to Producer–Seller and Marketing Costs and Margins of Agricultural Commodities in Haryana." Research Study No. 2012/01, Agricultural Economics Research Centre, University of Delhi.

Woldie, Getachew A., and E.A. Nuppenau. 2011. "A Contribution to Transaction Costs: Evidence from Banana Markets in Ethiopia." *Agribusiness* 27 (4), 493–508.

Closing Case
Jain Irrigation Systems: An Integrated Agricultural Marketing Approach

JISL is a leading agribusiness company based in Jalgaon, Maharashtra, which has a big presence in drip irrigation systems and PVC pipes. "Our objective is to increase farmer incomes, strengthen agricultural viability and create a sustainable society," says its website. Since irrigation systems depend on farm incomes, the company took it upon itself to help farmers as well. It therefore set up a food processing business, wherein it buys agricultural produce from them for its food processing facility. In this way, it is helping farmers not only in getting modern irrigation tools, better agricultural inputs and practices, but also in selling their produce.

Haanaes et al. (2013) write that as Jain Irrigation had no expertise as an agricultural wholesaler and was venturing into a new area, it could have shareholder anger. But the move paid off: from 2006 to 2010, the company's CAGR of 40 per cent and EBITDA margins of 18 per cent were both well over industry averages. Today, 20 per cent of revenues now come from its agricultural wholesale business.

JISL has pioneered the first manufacturing unit for micro-irrigation in the country. Micro-irrigation systems help use water effectively and enhance the productivity of seeds, fertilizer and other inputs. It is now the world's second-largest micro-irrigation company, after Israel's Netafim. The company makes a number of products for irrigation and piping and buys back the farmers' produce to make dehydrated fruit puree and juice concentrates. Its business extends to plastic piping systems, plastic sheets, green houses, bio-fertilizers, solar products and food processing. Its website says that it is the second largest producer of drip irrigation equipment in the world, and the largest in tissue culture production of banana and pomegranate and mango processing.

It has won UNESCO's Water Conserver Award and the International Finance Corporation honour for its inclusive, sustainable business model. It is now a transnational company and is working with small farmers in association with the Melinda and Bill Gates Foundation and Coca-Cola for developing a business model for small farmers. After a devastating earthquake in Haiti in 2010, the Haiti Hope Project was launched bringing together a coalition of private and public sector partners. As part of the project, JISL developed a technology for mango production which resulted in Coca-Cola's Odwalla Haiti Hope Mango Lime-Aid. By donating 100 per cent of the profits from the sale of designated Haiti Hope beverages, the project helped Haiti's recovery and created opportunity for 25,000 mango farmers. It is also replicating its business model in Ethiopia, Kenya, Malawi, Swaziland and Uganda.

Its unique business model consists of:

- Transformation of farmers from subsistence crops to commercial alternatives.
- Providing the latest technology to farmers.
- Extension of its value chain from seed to soil to food processing to non-banking financial support.
- Balancing the use of natural resources on the principles of sustainable agriculture.

Instead of cost-plus pricing that leaves farmers to raise finances, JISL focused on reducing the delivered cost of farm solutions. It uses global best farm practices that help marginal farmers to farm crops and process them for sale in global markets. It buys the produce from the farmers and processes it in its own food-processing facility. This introduced income predictability for the farmers, saving them from distress prices due to overproduction. The company has also undertaken a number of initiatives to conserve, reduce, recycle and harvest water. It educates farmers in remote areas, giving them guidance on making farming more profitable and teaching techniques for conserving water, labour, fertilizer and power.

A diagram showing the marketing approach of the company is presented in Figure 9.4. It shows that the company achieves its objectives in the following ways:

- **Agricultural production enhancement:** The company provides drip irrigation, piping systems and agricultural knowhow to increase the productivity and yields of the farmers.
- **Building capacity:** By investing in R&D and providing high quality seeds, tissue cultured plants and bio-fertilizers, it helps build capacity of even the small farmers.
- **Marketing agricultural produce:** Farmers need not have anxiety about selling their produce as the company has a buyback arrangements with them, using the produce in its food-processing facility.
- **Adding value:** The company adds value to the produce by processing it and selling or exporting the food products.

FIGURE 9.4

The business model of JISL helps reduce the delivered cost of irrigation systems.

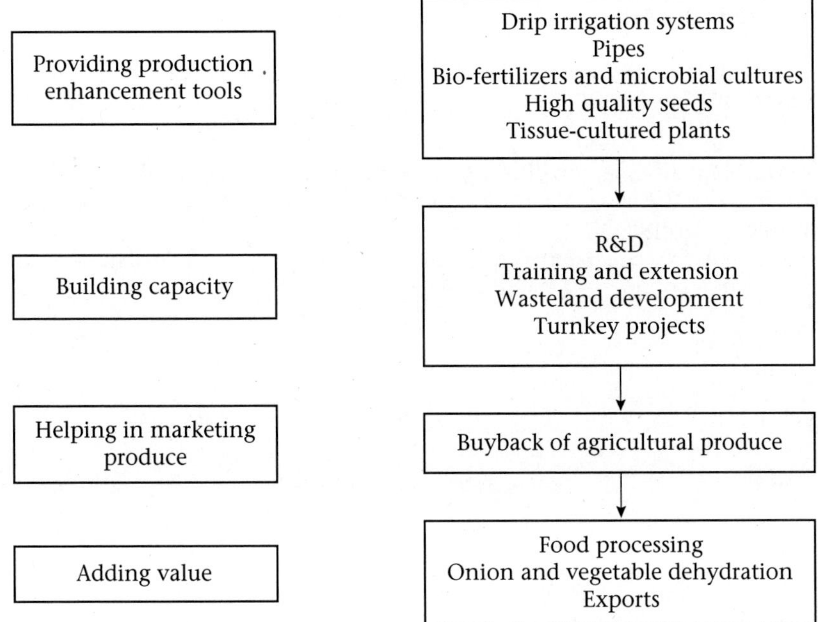

The business model of the company is shown in Figure 9.4.

The company set up a non-banking financial company to fund the subsidy provided by governments to farmers for the purchase of micro-irrigation systems and entered into tie-ups with banks for financing micro-irrigation purchases. However, since government payments are usually late, JISL must have bridging facilities and spend extra on working capital.

The company has completed several overseas acquisitions, including Israel's NaanDan, the world's fifth largest micro-irrigation company. It also bought Thomas Machines, a Swiss specialist in drip irrigation lines. It has plans to enter new markets, particularly in Africa, the Middle East and the US.

Farmers who could earlier not make two ends meet from small holdings have increased incomes through drip irrigation and diversifying crops. By better agricultural practices, the quality of the farm product has drastically improved, resulting in better prices. Playing a lead role in the state-sponsored micro-irrigation scheme in Tamil Nadu, Andhra Pradesh, Gujarat and Maharashtra, JISL is engaged in contract farming for onion and vegetables, banana, mango, papaya and tomato puree with over 10,000 farmers.

Questions for Discussion:

1. List the elements of the strategy undertaken by JISL. Describe how they were helpful both to the company and the community.
2. Why do you think did JISL start its integrated approach to rural marketing? What were the drivers for the change?

3. What benefits resulted to the company and farmers as a result of the change in approach?
4. Would JISL qualify to being a social enterprise (see Chapter 4)? Why?

Sources for this Case Study:

Web Resources

Haiti Hope Project website: http://www.coca-colacompany.com/stories/coca-cola-in-haiti
JISL website: http://www.jains.com/

Other Sources

Haanaes, Knut, David Michael, Jeremy Jürgens and Subramanian Rangan. 2013. "Making Sustainability Profitable" *Harvard Business Review*, March. Available at: https://hbr.org/2013/03/making-sustainability-profitable (Accessed on 17 April 2017).

JISL Annual Report 2013–14. Available at: http://jainpipe.com/Company/financial/PDF/14/shareholders%20information.pdf (Accessed on 17 April 2017).

10

CHAPTER

Internet and Communication Technologies in Rural Marketing

LEARNING OBJECTIVES

Modern Internet and communication technologies (ICT) promise to reach the most remote villages. They have the potential to bring products and services to remote areas, empowering them and connecting them to the development process. After reading this chapter, you will be able to:

- Understand the role of ICTs in rural areas: connectivity, content and enhancing capability.
- Analyze how ICTs are reducing distance in rural markets in a variety of ways.
- Learn about the innovative and crucial ways in which ICT impacts rural markets.
- Understand the problems in implementation of rural information and trading e-platforms.
- Extrapolate how ICT technologies can be modified for rural marketing.

Opening Case Taobao Villages in China

For years, Indian villages have been ignored by the government. If only a way can be found to add value to the village produce and to sell the goods, many jobs can be created for rural folk and transform villages. What is needed is infrastructure, marketing and financial linkages to enable rural entrepreneurs to start small-scale industries, writes Aiyar (2015). This in turn helps them become consumers and afford goods that they otherwise wouldn't. This case study describes the transformative power of ICT and how it can help in bringing remote villagers into the marketing mainstream.

A lesson could be learnt from China, where e-commerce is helping rural businesses to flourish through Taobao villages. Pioneered by e-commerce giant, Alibaba, Taobao has created 280,000 rural jobs in 2014. The Chinese government has stepped in, by giving grants to 55 poor counties to develop local industries. A Taobao village is defined as a cluster of rural entrepreneurs where at least 10 per cent of village households engage in e-commerce or at least 100 online shops have been opened by villagers, with total annual e-commerce transaction volume of at least RMB 10 million, about US$1.5 million.

The number of Taobao villages has been increasing: from 20 at the end of 2013 to 211 villages at the end of 2014. This shows that e-commerce can indeed improve rural participation. According to a report from AliResearch, the research arm of the Alibaba Group, there are now 780 Taobao villages, located in 17 different provinces. Most of them are situated in Zhejiang, Guangdong and Jiangsu and the majority of the villages are along the coast, with 176 of them in impoverished regions. These villages leverage cheap rural labour and local knowledge to produce goods, but the major challenge is distribution and logistics. This is overcome by clustering rural units, which creates incentives for transporters to provide services to villages.

Taobao villages have reversed the fortunes of many rural people, enabling many to become producers. It encourages villagers to organize themselves into groups and start selling their produce, such as handicrafts, clothes, weaves, value added agricultural products and gift items online (Figure 10.2). If the cluster is located next to factories, the village is able to supply manufactured goods as well.

One village in Guangdong has also opened a 'Taobao university' which teaches the concepts of e-commerce. Local governments are supporting villages with free wireless Internet, tax credits and even free storage space. A professional school to teach Taobao selling has also started, teaching computer skills to master customer service. The villages have helped empower the local people, reversing the trend of migration to cities and aiding in rural development. The government has helped. Party leaders have realized that e-commerce is one of the pillars of the local economy and must be encouraged under Beijing's initiative to modernize the economy. The local authorities have decided to exempt online businesses from paying rent and have provided them with a shared warehouse and a canteen.

The formation of an e-commerce cluster is shown in Figure 10.1. The first column shows the steps of cluster formation. Initially, the marketing portal provides an easy way to sell village products. Some entrepreneurs are attracted, who start small scale industries and become pioneers. Since initial orders may be slow in coming, the entrepreneurs have to show persistence, improving their quality as they go along. Soon, other families in the village get

FIGURE 10.1

Formation of an e-commerce village cluster.

Cluster Formation	**Govt. Support**	**Related Industries**
Marketing portal (Alibaba) ↓ Pioneer—village entrepreneur ↓ Other families get attracted ↓ Product differentiation ↓ Related industries (RM suppliers, technical support, etc.)	Infrastructure Electricity, roads, etc. Warehousing Internet Information Cheap loans	Financial services Logistics services IT services Marketing services Training and support

FIGURE 10.2
The Taobao site.

Source: https://world.taobao.com/ (Accessed on 10 January 2017).

attracted and start making similar products. They must invest in product differentiation otherwise prices will be forced down. As more families enter, the cluster attracts the interest of raw material suppliers, technical support services and so on.

The cluster formation requires government support. Instead of the usual rent seeking mentality of governments, they must develop a helping mentality and pitch in to provide common infrastructure and ensure access to Internet. This is given in the second column. Related industries soon establish their offices in the villages once they see volumes picking up.

The Taobao concept has helped the economic development of rural areas in addition to increase the income of the village people. The success of online sales has boosted other businesses such as delivery, logistics and service companies. Not only can the villagers sell their products but they also have access to goods that they can buy from outside. Further, Taobao plays an important role in sourcing products that can be exported across the world through Alibaba.

The initiative shows the transformative power of e-commerce: it can connect people in the remotest regions and turn them into entrepreneurs. For instance, one village, Dongfeng, has become a centre for low-cost furniture production consisting of a cluster of some 1,000 households. Using cheap local timber and labour, they were able to develop their capabilities. Now, the Dongfeng region has 40 logistics companies providing transport. CNBC describes another village, Beishan, which once just produced bread, but now has a company with annual sales of US$8 million worth of camping gear and sleeping bags.

Can India learn from the Taobao success? India's villages also represent populations that are cut off from the rest of the country. The people in these villages are unemployed or underemployed. However, the Indian IT revolution has been limited to urban areas. Though e-commerce sites are penetrating rural areas and small towns, it has not been able to induce the kind of transformation that is being seen in China. There are no doubt initiatives such as Fabindia and Jaipur Rugs, which use local knowledge and skills and help market locally produced goods in India and abroad, but the large scale transformation of villages into producer clusters is missing. The government promotes rural industries through its KVIC, which runs a network of *Khadi Bhandar* shops. However, it has not helped large scale rural transformation despite subsidies and reservation of various products for small scale industries. The trouble with most government-run rural marketing ventures is that they are run by bureaucrats and politicians, who have milked these organizations for personal perks and benefits.

Taobao villages show that e-commerce has the potential of turning a large section of neglected population into producers, solving problems of underemployment at the same time. However, the role of government and municipal corporations also becomes important: they have to give up their rent seeking mentality and build enabling infrastructure, helping villages to develop products. Some services have to be given free so that entrepreneurs are not loaded with costs at the inception stage. Can our government rise up to the challenge?

While reading this chapter, try to answer the following questions:

1. Can IT interventions result in large scale change in India?
2. What are infrastructure and government policy required to encourage such use of technology in India?
3. What is the difference between Taobao villages and initiatives such as e-choupal and e-seva?
4. How can ICT help in rural marketing? What are the problems it faces?

Sources for this Case Study:

Web Resources

Watch: Inside a Taobao village by CNBC: http://www.cnbc.com/2014/09/17/inside-a-taobao-village.html

Taobao changing fortunes of Hangzhou villages by Channel NewsAsia: http://www.channelnewsasia.com/news/business/taobao-changing-fortunes-of-hangzhou-villages/3101498.html

Other Sources

Aiyar, S. 2015. "China's Taobao Villages Show E-commerce Can Transform Rural India." *The Times of India*, 25 October.

The Economist. 2014. "Cash Cow, Taobao." 24 May.

The Guardian. 2014. "Alibaba Delivers Benefits of a New Digital Economy to Remotest China." 25 August. Available at: http://www.theguardian.com/technology/2014/aug/25/china-taobao-ecommerce-alibaba-rural-china (Accessed on 27 April 2017).

INTRODUCTION

We have seen in the earlier chapters that much of rural India is cut off from the winds of modernization and development. Villages remain pictures of neglect despite efforts of the government and other organizations. Urban-oriented government policy and media does little service to India's villages. Government intervention in agriculture by way of subsidies and restrictions end up squeezing none else but farmers and consumers. Suspicion of modern methods result in very little change in the way business in villages is done. Agriculture and all aspects related to its value chains thus remain poorly developed.

A game changer in this scenario could well be ICT. Such technologies have opened ways of connecting villages, providing them with crucial information regarding their livelihoods, engaging them, empowering them through e-governance and even improving rural livelihoods. All these open up new avenues of rural marketing.

Till now, only a few companies have used ICT in a big way in villages. Some of these initiatives, such as ITC's e-choupal, Amul's supply chain integration and HUL's Kan Khajura Tesan have been covered in this book. Other companies use new technologies for gains in efficiencies in logistics and distribution. Others hope that as smartphone penetration increases in villages, they will get easy access to rural markets.

It is, however, quite obvious that only companies that come up with innovative approaches will succeed. An urban approach to hooking customers through apps and services may not quite work. While smartphones do help in providing access to goods and services, physical delivery of these to remote villages will continue to be a challenge. This chapter describes how ICTs can be used in rural marketing and that such efforts will succeed only when they are coupled with physical supply chain modernization.

ICT ESSENTIALS

Rural areas have been neglected over the years and generally lag behind urban areas in terms of infrastructure and services. In India, rural isolation and deprivation negatively impacts growth and has created tensions in society.

ICTs can overcome many of these problems and remove the infrastructural constraints that have plagued villages since long. They can help people in rural areas to connect with the local, regional and national economy and to access markets, provide banking/financial services and employment opportunities. These technologies serve as an awareness creation instrument. They serve as a channel of delivery of government services, thus bridging the digital divide between urban and rural areas. ICTs have three essentials in rural areas, which can be remembered by the 3Cs: connectivity, content and capacity building (Figure 10.3).

FIGURE 10.3
The three Cs of ICT in rural areas.

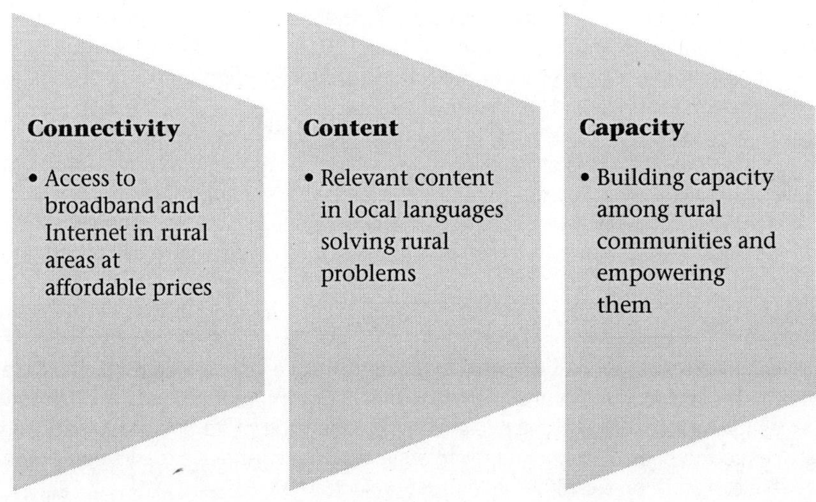

Connectivity

The first necessity of ICT is to connect millions of people by providing them basic telephony. Getting phone connections prior to liberalization posed a big problem and villages remained cut-off. Fortunately, they are leapfrogging into a new era: people can now buy mobile phones where even landlines were not available. The telecommunications revolution unleashed by a liberal policy environment in India has helped in the rapid growth of rural teledensity. The smartphone has become cheaper and popular and is connecting people in villages. As mobile services expand, traders and farmers will have better access to markets and the outside world.

Universal telecommunications access is now seen as a necessary condition for bringing about improved development and increase in socio-economic status of rural folk. Mobile phones and related services thus need to be available and affordable and operators are making efforts to do both.

Several companies are working towards providing connectivity. Reliance Jio has made data services cheaper for deep penetration; projects like the Google Loon (see Mini Case Study 10.1) are trying to make connectivity easier. Rural connectivity holds key to rural development through providing locally relevant information, engaging and empowering local communities, providing methods to improve health, education, promoting trade and e-commerce and supporting good governance.

Mini Case Study 10.1

Google's Project Loon: Connecting Rural Areas through Balloons

IT giants are keen on connecting rural India to the Internet. Facebook tried to offer free access to selected websites and apps through Free Basics, but failed. Google is trying to give connectivity to rural India through its Project Loon, which consists of high-altitude balloons that beam Wi-Fi down to remote areas. The goal of the project is to deliver Internet access to every corner of the world.

Project Loon balloons navigate stratospheric winds and communicate with ground-based antennas of a service provider to offer connectivity to the ground. The aim is to bring Internet access to the 2 out of 3 people in the world who aren't connected. In June 2014, Project Loon successfully beamed the Internet into the classrooms of a small town in rural Brazil for the first time. The technology has also been tried in Sri Lanka, Australia and Indonesia.

The technology is easy, affordable and replicable. Google launches these balloons with automated cranes and can now launch dozens of balloons a day, which can stay aloft for over a hundred days and are recyclable. A mission control centre monitors the balloons, guiding them into places to maximize Internet coverage. They can deliver widespread economic and social benefits by bringing Internet access to people who do not have it. Many of these people live in rural areas where cell towers or other infrastructure is not available. Google Loon thus provides a means for expanding Internet coverage considerably to the remotest and poorest areas on earth (Figure 10.4). The project does not fall into the trap of net neutrality as the Facebook free basics did.

Google hopes to earn ad revenue wherever it provides this service. It also expects cellular providers to rent access to the balloons to expand their networks. Since Internet markets in developed countries are more or less saturated, Google is looking at huge expansion of its business apart from providing Internet services to the poor. Facebook is trying a similar project and is experimenting with solar-powered drones so it can start its own airborne Internet project.

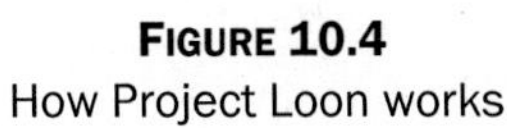

FIGURE 10.4
How Project Loon works.

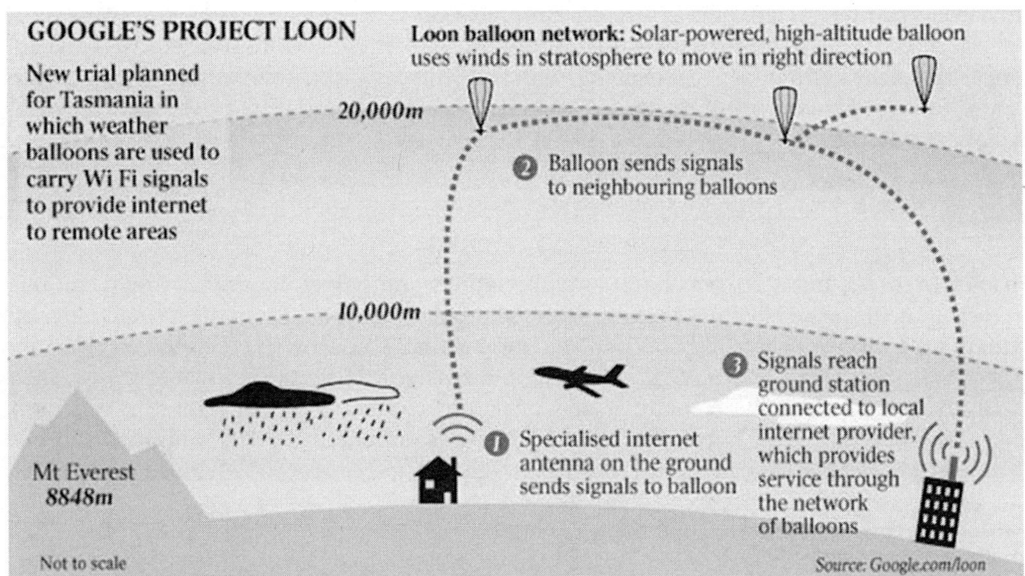

Source: google.com/loon (Accessed on 10 January 2017).

In trials, the balloons have provided high-speed connections to people in isolated parts of the world. *Indian Express* (2016) reports that in India, Google is working with the government to bring Project Loon to India and it has approved testing of the project. Google may initially partner with BSNL for testing this technology. The technology, used for 4G services, has the potential to replace mobile towers as it can directly transmit signals on 4G mobile phones.

The balloons float at a height of 20 km above earth surface and each balloon provides connectivity to a ground area about 40 km in diameter using a wireless communications technology. They use solar panel and wind to power the electronic equipment in them.

Can you think of other innovative ways of providing connectivity to villages?

Sources for this Case Study:

Web Resources

Check out Google's behind-the-scenes video for a closer look at the project at: https://www.google.com/loon/how/

"Google's Magic Internet Balloons Bringing Wi-Fi to India." Available at CNET: http://www.cnet.com/news/googles-magic-internet-balloons-bringing-wi-fi-to-india/

"Project Loon." Available at *MIT Technology Review*: https://www.technologyreview.com/s/534986/project-loon/

Other Sources

The Guardian. 2016. "Project Loon: Google Balloon that Beams Down Internet Reaches Sri Lanka." 16 February. Available at: https://www.theguardian.com/technology/2016/feb/16/project-loon-google-balloon-that-beams-down-internet-reaches-sri-lanka (Accessed on 27 April 2017).

Indian Express. 2016. "Govt to allow Google, Microsoft Pilots to Expand Internet Reach." 31 January.

Content

Smartphones can be useful only when relevant and usable content is available to rural people, which they can access and make use of. Though many portals and apps are available (see Appendix), many of them provide static and outdated content. Moreover, content has to be in local languages. Often it is translated, which results in bizarre outcomes. Content access has also to be provided through shared PCO type public access points to serve those who do not have a smartphone.

Capacity

Capacity building helps in developing rural markets. Initiatives to improve education and enhancing incomes are essential because without them, there would only be a small percentage of rural population who would benefit from connectivity. These are the literate people who can afford smartphones or laptops. IT schemes should therefore necessarily include things such as education and income enhancement. Merely providing connectivity and content is not enough. Google Internet Saathi (see Mini Case Study 10.2) is an example of capacity building in this field.

Mini Case Study 10.2

Google's Internet Saathi

Google tries to improve the Internet capacity in villages and has launched a scheme 'Internet Saathi' to engage rural women and enabling them to provide Internet services to villages. In association with Tata Trust, Google provides a bicycle and mobile or tablet devices to women who are trained by these companies to become Internet Saathi or master trainers. These Internet Saathis reach out to people in the village helping them with web-based information apart from training other women in the village to make them e-literate.

Apart from aiding women to gain access information and services, it also empowers women socially and economically, according to a report in *Business Standard* (2016). Google India pays them ₹1,000 a month for a period of six months. But the women can also charge from the villagers to whom they provide the services. In this way, they become the agents of change in rural India.

The project has been rolled out in nine states. About one lakh women in rural India have already benefited from this Internet literacy drive under the Internet Saathi initiative, according to *India Today* (2016).

Launched in July 2015, Internet Saathi operates in nine states: Rajasthan, Gujarat, Jharkhand, Andhra Pradesh, Madhya Pradesh, West Bengal, Assam, Uttar Pradesh and Tripura. The Internet Saathi initiative is a part of Google's Helping Women Get Online campaign which is aimed to generate awareness about the benefits of Internet usage among women in rural India.

Do such initiatives help? Can you think of other such projects meant to raise capacity in rural areas?

Sources for this Case Study:

Web Resource

Watch the Internet Saathi video at: https://www.youtube.com/watch?v=iYVx15KEEEs

Other Sources

Business Standard. 2016. "Women Help Google to Spread Internet Use in Villages." 9 June.

India Today. 2016. "1 Lakh Women Benefited from Internet Saathi Initiative: Google." 18 May.

The first step is to recognize telecom and broadband connectivity as a basic necessity and to develop an ecosystem for broadband to ensure its availability. Low cost content services help in the spread. Experience from other countries is helpful: for example, in Singapore, the Ministry of Communication and Information (MCI) is responsible for the telecoms, media and technology industries. The MCI oversees the activities of two statutory bodies: the Infocomm Development Authority (IDA) of Singapore and the Media Development Authority (MDA). The IDA is responsible for the development, promotion and regulation of the info-communications industry, which includes the telecoms and IT sectors. The MDA is responsible for the regulation of broadcast content. India could consider such a model for the adoption of broadband and content development.

ICT IN RURAL MARKETS

ICTs are technologies that interlink information technology devices with communication technologies. They are being used in many ways that were unimagined before and can be used to collect, store and share information between people using multiple devices. ICTs have great potential in rural areas, where they can address the immediate problems facing people. Their use offers new solutions to longstanding problems and can make a difference to people's lives. ICTs have contributed to improve communications in villages and have helped a number of entrepreneurs and small businessmen to increase incomes. Micro and Small Enterprises (MSEs) have benefitted from ICTs. Many organizations have expanded their network by using innovative methods of offering services to remote areas. Banks, for instance, provide services through banking correspondents with handheld devices in remote areas where branches do not exist.

Cairncross (1997) writes in his book, *The Death of Distance*, that technology is changing society like never before, shrinking distances that are now measured in communications speed and effecting change in employment, entertainment, gambling, shopping, demographics, government and market competition. One area that distances are still formidable is rural. Technology helps reduce distance as described in Mini Case Study 10.3, which shows how medical care is delivered to rural areas using technological innovations.

Mini Case Study 10.3

Using Technology in Rural Health Care

The Bill and Melinda Gates Foundation supports a programme that uses mobile phones to deliver advice and reminders to pregnant women in Ghana. The foundation and Grand Challenges Canada, a non-profit organization, gave US$32 million in grants for the development of mobile tools to help health care workers diagnose various ailments in rural Ghana. In Mexico, patients can phone Medicall Home, a telehealth service. If a patient needs care, Medicall Home can help to arrange a doctor's visit. But about two-thirds of patients' concerns can be addressed over the phone by a doctor. These programmes are expanding. Medicall Home is rolling out its service in Colombia and Peru as well.

Technology does not just allow diagnosis at a distance; it allows surgery at a distance, too. In 2001, doctors in New York used robotic instruments under remote control to remove the gall bladder of a woman in Strasbourg. Robots allow doctors to be more precise, making incisions more neatly than human hands can. The remarkable thing about this technology is that doctors can help patients in remote locations which may otherwise not have medical facilities.

Other technologies are also being developed. Chronic conditions are managed from Montefiore Medical Centre in New York by a team of 'care coordinators' who examine streams of data from health records and devices in patients' homes, such as the Health Buddy. Developed by Bosch, Health Buddy asks patients questions about their symptoms each day. Symptoms like a sudden weight gain in a patient with congestive heart failure or blood sugar increase in a diabetic patient are monitored and the patient is contacted or a nurse is alerted. Such measures have resulted in reducing trips to the hospital by diabetics by almost 30 per cent, leading to reduced costs by 12 per cent. Emergency alert devices for the elderly have helped in saving lives.

Patients learn to monitor themselves at home with gadgets bought online. This has created a growing market for self-monitoring gadgets. Philips, GE and others are investing in developing home health gadgets and widening markets. Soon, gadgets that measure critical health parameters are expected to become as common as a thermometer. In a study of 6000 patients in 2011, it was found that in Britain telehealth technology resulted in drop in admissions to the emergency room by 20 per cent and mortality by 45 per cent.

Reforms in medicine because of technology are slowly taking shape. In India, the health ministry has proposed a new three-and-a-half-year degree that lets graduates deliver basic primary care in rural areas. A pilot programme of rural health care workers found that the workers were correctly able to diagnose basic ailments and prescribe appropriate drugs. In America, the roles of nurse practitioners and physician assistants have expanded. The number of 'diagnostic medical sonographers' with two years of training is expected to jump in the near future, according to the Bureau of Labour Statistics. Such workers, with appropriate technology, can well provide health care in villages where none exists.

Can medical workers and technology deliver medical services effectively without doctors in rural areas?

Source for this Case Study:

The Economist. 2012. "The Future of Medicine." 2 June.

In this section we describe how ICTs are reducing distance in rural markets in a variety of ways. As Hofman (2016) puts it, "Inclusion, efficiency, innovation—these are the main ways in which digital technologies support development." The Taobao villages described in the Opening Case and delivery of medical care along with other examples cited in this book show how the Internet promotes inclusion, efficiency and innovation—and all of this in less than a decade.

Two-way communication helps in aiding people to understand needs and opportunities jointly. More than that, ICT is a means of empowerment and financial inclusion and could well provide a platform for trading of agricultural goods. Technologies help rural folk to get information, negotiate and buy and sell, which in turn helps them to participate as producers and not merely as consumers (see Mini Case Study 10.4). Clearly, ICTs have to move beyond delivering information to collecting better quality data for understanding consumers. ICTs can be used in rural markets in a variety of ways, which are given here and shown in Figure 10.5. Each of these ways contributes in some way to the three objectives: *innovation* to serve *inclusion* and *efficiency*.

1. Communication and media
2. Financial inclusion
3. Agricultural information and trading

4. Logistics and distribution
5. Digital payments
6. 3D printing
7. E-commerce
8. E-governance
9. Empowerment of local communities
10. Data analytics
11. Customer engagement
12. Crowdfunding for rural micro-businesses.

Communication and Media

Farmers in India are squeezed on both fronts—production and marketing. On the production front the farmer faces risks relating to weather, fake inputs and lack of timely knowledge about farm management practices. In marketing, the farmer faces lack of transparency

FIGURE 10.5
ICT in rural markets.

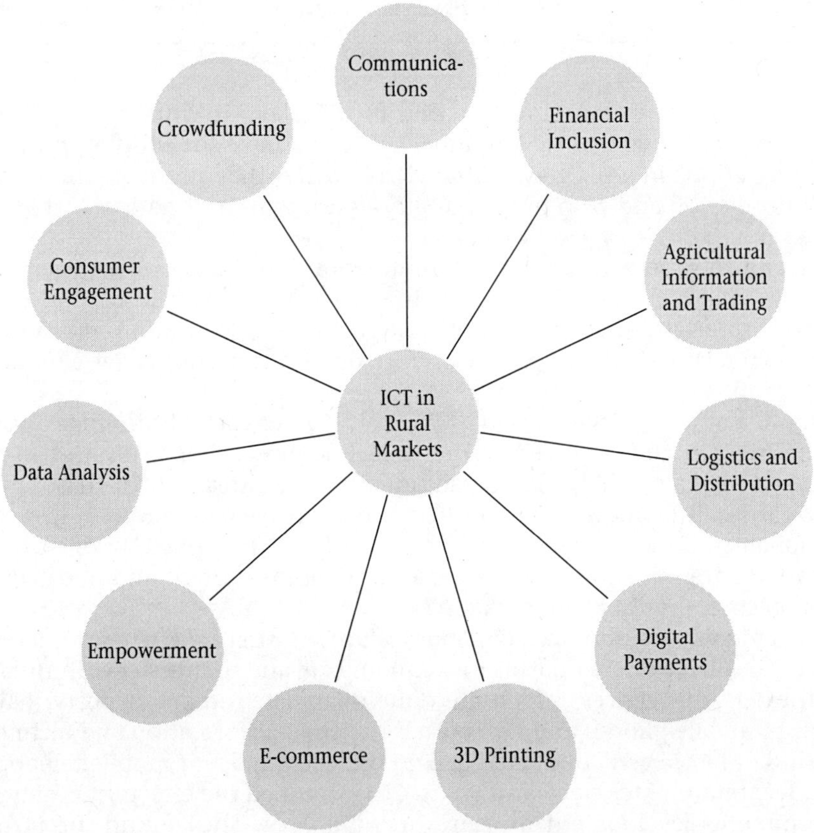

Mini Case Study 10.4

IT in Rural Markets: Dabur and HUL

FMCG companies have redoubled efforts to tap into rural India. Dabur India and HUL have both highlighted what they are doing to better their rural sales.

HUL's Project Shakti received a technology boost in 2012: about 40,000 Shakti Ammas were equipped with a basic smartphone. These smartphones had specifically designed software that enabled them to take and bill orders, manage inventory and receive updates on promotional schemes run by the company. This improved their efficiency.

Dabur India participates in fairs and melas around the harvest seasons when purchasing power is high. It also conducted school health camps to boost its toothpaste and chyawanprash portfolio. Dabur's rural sales force used mobile phones to report sales. Phones were equipped with maps showing the demographics and market potential of each locality. Handheld devices are used for sales and to generate data, which is then used to understand buying patterns and customize selling strategies. IT has also been used to provide information to and generate feedback from doctors on Dabur's formulations and products.

In what other ways can IT be used to simply business operations in rural areas?

Source for this Case Study:
The Hindu BusinessLine. 2013. "Dabur India, Hindustan Unilever's Tech Route to Rural Markets." 14 July.

on market information. Communication and media plays an important role in providing information on both these fronts. A number of studies have shown that information helps rural marketing efforts in a big way. Mittal (2012) writes that a farmer who receives quality up to date information and who has the ability to use that information is able to lessen the effect of risks in farming to a great extent.

Farmers require a variety of agricultural information, from usage of fertilizer, crop diseases, preventive and curative measures, modern irrigation methods, information on water conservation, HYV seeds and their usage, pre- and post-harvest education, market information, knowledge about fake agricultural products, crop rotation education, advice on fruits and vegetables, and so on.

According to a survey of the NSSO (2005), only 40 per cent of farming households have access to information about modern farming technologies. This is an area in which communication and media can help. Since traditional or mainstream media has limited reach in villages and carries little information of direct use to village communities, it is up to ICTs to provide actionable information to the farmers. Modern ICT can help bridge the information gap and can enhance the knowledge of farmers, providing current and updated information on various aspects of farming and marketing.

Smartphones have revolutionized communications in rural areas wherever telecom services are available. They have offered means to communicate and to interact with rural consumers. Agricultural extension services, which are quite dilapidated in the country, have benefited from the use of mobile phones and web portals to deliver information and technology.

Several studies have been conducted to find out the impact of mobile telephony on rural prosperity. Beuermann, McKelvey and Vakis (2012) studied the effects of mobile phone coverage on economic development measures in rural Peru. They found the introduction of mobile phones impacted a range of well-being measures. Health showed a real increase of 23.7 per cent, transport 19.2 per cent real increase and mobile phone expenditures increase of 231 per cent. These effects together imply the existence of a significant unmet demand for mobile services and positive effects associated with the provision of such services. Sizeable reductions in poverty were also found following mobile coverage introduction: about 8 per cent for overall poverty and 5 per cent for extreme poverty. The study showed that mobile coverage improved household well-being across villages—household real consumption increased by almost 11 per cent. Overall increases in all sub-components of expenditures have taken place, including investments in health services and transport. A surprising finding was that mobile coverage not only benefited people who owned a cellphone but also benefited non-owners. Such evidence suggests positive spill over effects flowing from owners to those who did not own a smartphone.

De Silva et al. (2011) study of the influence of mobile phone adoption at the BoP population in six Asian countries found that mobile phones helped in generating better social and business networks, leading to faster spread of knowledge and technology. Muto and Yamano's (2009) study on Ugandan maize and banana farmers also showed that the adoption of mobile telephony and its use in agricultural activities has led to a reduction in poverty.

Several portals and services have been initiated by the government and private companies. A list of portals containing advice and information on agriculture is given in appendix at the end of this chapter.

Some of the initiatives taken in the field of better communication with farmers through helplines and SMS are described here.

- **Agro-met advisories:** A system has been developed by India Meteorological Department and Ministry of Agriculture to provide weather-based agro-met advisories to the farming community through free SMS. To avail this service, farmers register their names on the toll-free number 1800-180-1717 along with their mobile numbers and the crops they grow. Once registered, farmers get an SMS for their specific crops every week on day-to-day agricultural operations as well as on weather.
- **Bayer helpline:** In 2014, Bayer launched a national helpline for farmers. Farmers can place a toll free call on Bayer's national helpline number 1800-200-6321. Calls are answered by local agricultural experts from four call centres located in Maharashtra, Punjab, Gujarat and Madhya Pradesh, according to its website.
- **eSagu:** eSagu is an IT-based personalized agro-advisory system which delivers personalized, farm-specific agro-expert advice to farmers. The advice is provided once a week from sowing to harvesting to farm productivity and quality. It uses database, Internet and digital photography to aid agricultural extension services. The agricultural scientist delivers expert advice by getting the crop status in the form of digital photographs and other information. The system is devised by IIIT, Hyderabad and Media Lab Asia.
- **Farmers' portal:** Farmers' portal has been started by the government to create a one stop shop for meeting all informational needs relating to agriculture, animal husbandry and fisheries. The portal features a map and the farmer can click on his state to get information on specific subjects around his village/block/district or state. This information is delivered in the form of text, SMS, email and audio/video in the local language.
- **Kisan Call Centre:** The government has established the Kisan Call Centre (KCC) through a toll free number 1800-180-1551, where they register themselves on the Kisan Knowledge Management System (KKMS). Kisan Call Centre agents known as Farm Tele

Advisors are graduates or above in Agriculture or allied sciences and are trained in communication skills in local languages (http://mkisan.gov.in/aboutkcc.aspx).

- **Kisan Sanchar:** IFFCO has launched IFFCO Kisan Sanchar Limited together with Bharti Airtel and Star Global Resources Ltd. The venture aims to provide income generating business opportunities and offer telecom services to farmers through cooperative societies. Kisan Sanchar delivers free of cost knowledge content developed by Krishi Vigyan Kendras and agricultural universities through Value Added Service (VAS), according to the IFFCO website. Kisan Sanchar is an interactive platform for scientists, agricultural experts and agricultural institutions for sharing their technology and knowledge with registered farmers.
- **Reuters Market Light (RML):** RML provides Agri Decision Support Solutions for farmers by creating services and tools for them. RMLdirect delivers agricultural information through SMS as well as the myRML App. It has also developed products such as FarmNutri, DigiMandi and the RML FARMER MAX which can transform the farmer's business through technology. RML's service works across all telecom service providers and mobile phone handsets. These messages, which are sent on a pre-paid subscription basis, are about crop prices in nearby markets, agricultural news relating to the crop or input prices, advices to improve yields and weather forecasts.
- **Agricultural Marketing Research and Information Network (AGMARKNET):** Launched by the Department of Agriculture and Cooperation, the scheme aims to link important agricultural markets in India and the State Agriculture Marketing Boards/Directorates for exchange of market information. The objective of the scheme is to facilitate collection and dissemination of information for better price realization. The portal covers market, price, infrastructure and promotion-related information.

Helplines and SMS help farmers to get timely information, which so far was not available to them. However, ICT in rural areas can only achieve interaction and communication. Schmidt (2011) writes that very often technology faces the barriers of translation and illiteracy. Some of the reasons why it is not spreading among the farmers as it should are:

1. **Lost in translation:** Much of the information is lost in translation to local languages. Faulty translation often results in limited utility of the phone—one phone with a Bengali interface used a translation for 'select an option' that means 'vote in an election' in Bengali.
2. **Illiteracy:** Eric Schmidt, before stepping down as CEO, revealed that Google's strategic initiatives involve mobile, including making smartphones accessible to the poor. He cites an ethnographic study by a student of how village farmers in Bangladesh have integrated mobile phones into their lives and work. He found that it is not smartphones they need, but devices that make sense to people who are partially literate in Bengali and less literate in English. For instance, instead of using the phones to store numbers, they used notebooks to write down phone numbers because they couldn't understand the phone's address book.
3. **Lack of physical infrastructure:** Though mobile phone infrastructure does have positive spillover effects on markets, it cannot replace investments in other infrastructure. Mobile phones cannot be a short-cut for poverty reduction tool for poor rural households. Sustainable development depends on physical infrastructure, such as power, roads and electricity along with ICT intervention.
4. **Lack of market access:** Farmers in India lack market access and have to go through agents and mandis, as explained in the earlier chapters. In this scenario, communication

can only help in a limited way. Most farmers, for instance, are unable to take advantage of the price information on portals as they lack storage and grading facilities and sell to pre-harvest agents under whom they are in debt.

5. **Digital divide:** Communication technologies sometimes fail because of the digital divide, that is, the huge gap between those who have access to computers and the Internet and those who do not. This has prevented the percolation of benefits to the poor. The main beneficiaries of the ICT revolution have been population segments in areas with a developed infrastructure, much to the exclusion of the poor.

It is clear that though ICT can help providing information to farmers, investments in infrastructure and supply chains are essential. Rural markets will only work efficiently if the farmer has access to information and a way to use the information.

Financial Inclusion

Financial inclusion means delivery of financial services at affordable costs to disadvantaged and low income segments of the society, or those who cannot access these services because of distance and availability. Gupta (2011) writes that RBI has taken steps to ease use of technology for banking operations in rural areas. Technology can play an important role in spreading banking services, particularly in the rural and unbanked areas. Technologies are available today that can drive financial inclusion. IT brings front-end operations to doorsteps of people and reduces transaction costs. Financial inclusion is aided by making small ticket retail transactions cheaper, easier and faster. Some of the steps taken by banks for financial inclusion are:

- **Automated teller machines (ATMs):** ATMs offer banking services even where branches do not exist. But they have been restricted to the urban areas because operating ATMs in remote areas, sometimes without electricity or transaction volumes, is not feasible.
- **Branchless banking:** The RBI has permitted banks to use intermediaries as BFs or BCs in rural areas for providing financial and banking services where branches do not exist. The BCs allow rural people to operate their bank accounts using hand-held devices. Some companies offering such services are Oxigen and Paytm, A Little World and Fino (see Mini Case Study 10.8). Many other companies such as Vodafone, Idea Cellular, Airtel, ITC, HUL, Reliance Jio and others operate electronic wallets or have expressed interest to become BCs. They have large distribution channels and pan-India presence, which will help them penetrate rural areas. The postal department too plans to install micro-ATMs and use its network of about 1.55 lakh post offices to provide financial services to villages. BFs identify borrowers, process loan applications and create awareness about bank products. They also promote SHGs and encourage savings among these groups.
- **Core banking solutions (CBS):** CBS enables customers to operate their accounts and avail of banking services from any branch of a bank. CBS offers customer convenience through Anywhere, Anytime Banking and also generates and manages information effectively.
- **General credit card (GCC):** RBI has asked banks to provide a credit card like facility in rural areas based on the assessment of income and cash.

- **Micro-ATMs:** Micro-ATM is a device that is used by BCs to deliver basic banking services. The platform enables branchless banking in villages. BCs use micro-ATMs to conduct instant transactions. These are used in remote villages with a population of just 2,000 for banking transactions.
- **No frills accounts:** The RBI and the government have been pushing banks for opening 'no-frills' accounts, without minimum balance requirements and charges.
- **Simpler norms:** Since rural households may not have identity documents, the KYC procedure for opening accounts have been simplified.

Despite these interventions, the viability of the BC model remains a challenge. For instance, a majority of no-frill accounts opened by BCs and under the Prime Minister's Jan Dhan Yojana remained non-operational till the government's demonetization move in 2016. There was a hope that social benefits would be transferred to these accounts under the UIDAI but this has not happened so far.

Agricultural Trading

One area in which farmers can benefit from ICT is agricultural trading. If market information was easily available, farmers could, theoretically at least, sell when they are likely to get high prices. Mobile phones can provide such information cheaply and easily, which could also assist farmers in identifying potential buyers over large geographic areas. Studies have found that price dispersion is reduced through better communication. Improved communication between farmers and traders could result in better quality output. Apart from telephone- and SMS-based information systems, trading portals could also put buyers and sellers in direct touch.

Price dispersion: Where information is limited or costly, as in developing countries, agents are able to exploit both producers and consumers alike. Information technologies can improve market performance by providing crucial information when and where it is needed. Several studies have found that information about agriculture and market conditions, disseminated through mobile phones, greatly helps in reducing price dispersion and is helpful both to farmers and consumers.

Jensen (2007) studied the impact of mobile phones on the market for fresh fish in Kerala. Using micro-level survey data, he showed that the adoption of mobile phones by fishermen and wholesalers was associated with a dramatic reduction in price dispersion, the complete elimination of waste and near-perfect adherence to the Law of One Price. Both consumer and producer welfare increased.

Aker's (2010) study of grain markets in Niger showed similar results. The introduction of mobile phones was found to be associated with a 10 to 16 per cent reduction in price dispersion across markets. He also provides evidence of a network effect, that is, mobile phones have a stronger effect on price dispersion once a critical mass of market pairs has mobile phone coverage.

Both studies find that price dispersion has been significantly reduced to near perfect adherence to the law of one price after mobile phone coverage.

ICTs can thus help poorly functioning markets work better and thereby increase incomes and/or lower consumer prices. In fact, it has become increasingly common to find farmers, fishermen and other producers throughout the developing world using mobile phones, text messages, pagers and the Internet for getting market information and for selling their goods.

Agricultural portals: Market information is provided through agricultural portals as well. Several agricultural portals have been started by private companies and the government bodies. We have covered ITC's e-choupal in this book and Nagarjuna Fertilizer's initiative Ikisan is described in Mini Case Study 10.5. Apart from these, the government provides information through various portals as well. The government has also launched an electronic platform for trading of agricultural goods, the National Agriculture Market.

e-NAM: The government launched the NAM in 2016 as a pan-India unified electronic trading portal. It networks the existing APMC mandis to create a national market for agricultural

Mini Case Study 10.5

Ikisan

Ikisan is an agricultural portal that provides content on crops, crop management techniques, fertilizers, pesticides and a host of other agriculture related material. Latest updates on related markets, products and weather forecasts are also available.

Ikisan is a division of Nagarjuna Fertilizers and Chemicals Ltd (NFCL), Hyderabad. It was initiated in 1999. NFCL has significant presence in the Indian agro-input sector encompassing crop nutrients, crop protection chemicals, micro-irrigation, agricultural research and development and biotechnology. The Nagarjuna group is involved in various initiatives such as market development programmes, farmer training programmes, Krishi Vigyan Kendra and providing Farm Management Services. The services provided by Ikisan cover:

- Information about crops, markets, prices, weather, agriculture news.
- Knowledge of crop management, pest management, water management, soil management, implements, agro-machinery.
- Solutions for problems such as pests and nutrition.
- Information on insurance, credit and other allied services.
- Facilitation of trading in inputs and output.
- Software services and IT enabled solutions for agriculture.

Some of the key customers/partners of the project include Electronics Corporation of India Ltd, State Agricultural Marketing Boards, Central Research Institute for Dryland Agriculture, Tamil Nadu, Centre for Development of Advanced Computing, Motorola Mobility, and so on.

An agribusiness management programme has been developed by Ikisan and XLRI, Jamshedpur. Ikisan provides the domain expertise while XLRI provides pedagogy. This programme is a combination of virtual learning and campus-based module at XLRI.

Ikisan provides software services such as Field Manager, Vyapar, Mandi, Quick Solutions Systems, Management Time Table, Agri Information System and Agrecommerz. It has also introduced Weather Based Crop Insurance, with Automatic Weather Stations.

Do farmers benefit from portals like the Ikisan and others described in this chapter? Why are farmers still suffering despite a plethora of information on these portals?

Sources for this Case Study:

Web Resources

Ikisan website: http://www.ikisan.com/index.html

Watch the Ikisan video at: https://www.youtube.com/watch?v=HhYNwbHX1g4

FIGURE 10.6
Working model of NAM.

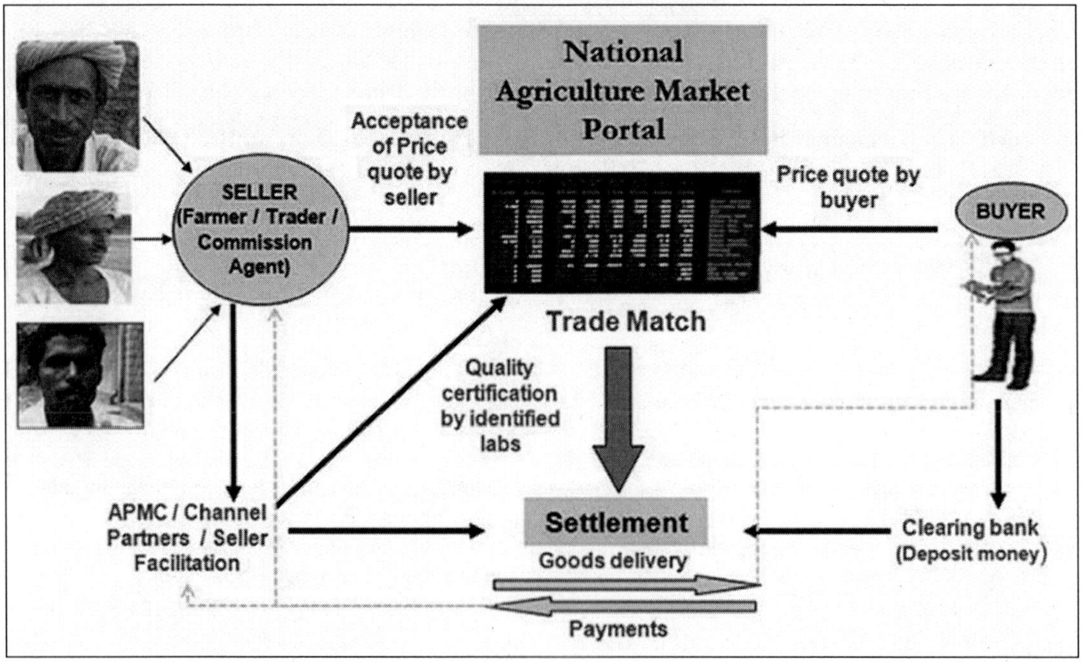

Source: http://sfacindia.com/Nam.aspx (Accessed on 27 April 2017).

commodities. The NAM portal provides a single window service for APMC related information, such as commodity arrivals and prices and trade offers with a provision to respond to them. However, agricultural produce flow continues through mandis (Figure 10.6).

It has long been felt that the APMC system, which under which states are divided into several market areas, leads to fragmentation of markets. The APMC also imposes its own fees. This hinders free flow of agricultural goods from one market area to another even within one state. Multiple handling and multiple mandi charges add to escalating prices for consumers. An electronic portal theoretically would address these problems by creating a unified market at state and national level.

However, whether these initiatives are actually helping the farmer remains doubtful. An electronic trading portal can work only when some of the bottlenecks are removed, such as:

- **Grading system:** Online trading of agricultural products can only work when there is a grading and certifying system in place so that the buyer knows exactly what quality of goods is being purchased. In the absence of a grading system, buyers will be unwilling to place orders before checking the produce physically.
- **APMC monopoly:** The trading portal does not lead to reduction in various levies imposed by states and mandi taxes and therefore has been of limited utility so far. The states have to amend their APMC Acts by bringing in a provision for electronic trading. Besides, states must provide a single licence to those who trade through NAM in a local mandi. Though

the e-NAM has been a first step, electronic trading of agricultural goods can only succeed when the APMC is integrated and when the APMC mandi monopoly is broken.

- **Easy deliveries:** Like e-commerce, trading portals work when buyers know of firm delivery schedules. Lack of transport and bad roads in villages means that firm delivery dates cannot be guaranteed. Assuming that a farmer is able to find a buyer online, can he promise that goods will reach at the committed dates?
- **Storage facilities:** If the farmer cannot store his produce at a safe place, he will be under pressure to sell it to the nearest agent because agricultural goods are perishable and attract rodents. Moreover, as the farmer is usually under debt by the harvest time, he is unable to leverage information in real life.
- **Payment gateways:** Online trading also assumes existence of bank accounts and payment gateways. In the absence of a banking network in remote villages, online trading platforms can achieve little.

Logistics and Distribution

Over the years, there have been huge investments in supply chains. Sophisticated technology exists to track goods right from raw material procurement to customer use and feedback, writes Kumar (2012). One company that has successfully done this in India is Amul (see Mini Case Study 10.6). This section describes the technologies that have been deployed by companies in this field.

- **Technology in logistics:** Automatic Identification (Auto ID) technology tracks products automatically and directly enters data in the computer system without an operating a keyboard. Auto ID is used for tracking containers, packages, products, cartons and even a truck carrying goods. Auto ID helps to achieve accuracy, cost saving, speed and convenience. Such technologies (see Mini Case Study 10.7) include bar coding, radio frequency identification (RFID), magnetic strip, voice recognition, Quick Response, Efficient Consumer Response, and Collaborative Planning, Forecasting and Replenishment (CPFR).
- **Tracking technologies:** Tracking technologies can identify and track products on the move. E-tracking systems are used in courier, air and sea cargo. These technologies include Very Small Aperture Terminal (VSAT), which communicates through satellite communication. A dish antenna is fixed on the vehicle, which allows communication between driver, consignor and consignee in real time.
- **Delivery technology:** Drone delivery can help deliver products to the remotest villages. Trials are already being conducted to explore how drones can safely and effectively deliver medicines and vaccines to remote locations. In the US, Amazon Prime Air is a future service that will deliver packages up to five pounds in 30 minutes or less using small drones. Operators will have to obtain government and defence approvals in India before drones can be used for product deliveries in India.

Geographical or Global Positioning System (GPS) is used to trace vehicles with the help of Geo Stationary Satellites. The data from these helps locate the latitude and longitude of a vehicle to an accuracy of one meter. Geographical Information System (GIS) uses data relating to locations from databases and integrates different databases into a detailed, clear visualization with respect to a location.

Web Based Tracking is used to track consignments. Automated Guided Vehicle System is an automated materials handling system that makes a use of a magnetic or optical guidance system. Information Directed System (IDS) consists of a central computer that controls material handling equipment. ERP is integrated software that encompasses all business operations. It is used in Supply Chain Management systems and has a focus on optimizing order fulfilment and movement of goods through logistics systems. The major ERPs in use are SAP, Baan and Oracle.

However, companies face tremendous challenges in deploying technology for low resource settings such as villages. Investments in the mentioned systems are hardly justified in the face of low volumes. Companies face the following problems when they build supply chains to villages:

- **Investments not justified:** High investments in supply chains cannot be justified because volumes in villages are low.
- **Lack of physical infrastructure:** Even if technology is deployed, supplying goods over bad roads and inadequate transport remains a major challenge.
- **Small dealers:** Since dealers are small operators, they are unwilling to invest in technology. They use manual systems for inventory control and supply.

Mini Case Study 10.6

Amul's IT Push Chain

Amul uses portal technology to connect its suppliers and even links information about their animals on its system. Using ICT, it connects farmers and their animals with the supply chains and goes right up to retailers. Collecting and checking milk and payments to farmers are automated. Amul has followed digitization with the objective of helping farmers. As described by Dr V Kurien, former chairman of the GCMMF, who is credited for revolutionizing the cooperative movement:

> Computers were not created to solve the problems of poverty, hence it is futile to expect that the world will be a better place if we all had access to computers and the Internet. But information is power and it stands to reason that if this power is shared equitably, all will benefit.

Following this principle, Amul uses ERP to cover operations such as market planning, advertising and promotion, stock control, sales and accounting and quality control management. All zonal and regional offices and member dairies are also connected.

One can argue that connecting farmers and helping them is not strictly part of marketing. But that is how rural marketing is different from mainstream marketing. It has to involve and empower the customers, without which they will hardly have the purchasing power required to buy the products and brands on offer. This case study shows that the scope of rural marketing goes much beyond merely supplying goods and services to villages. It consists of empowering rural people, building or reinforcing institutions and developing markets. This is the approach taken by this book.

Earlier, records of milk collected were kept manually. Farmers were given passbooks in which milk and payment transactions were recorded. Now the whole supply chain has been automated as explained in Figure 10.7.

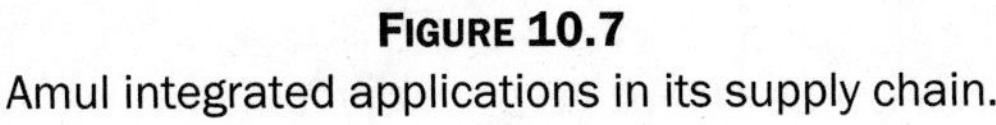

FIGURE 10.7
Amul integrated applications in its supply chain.

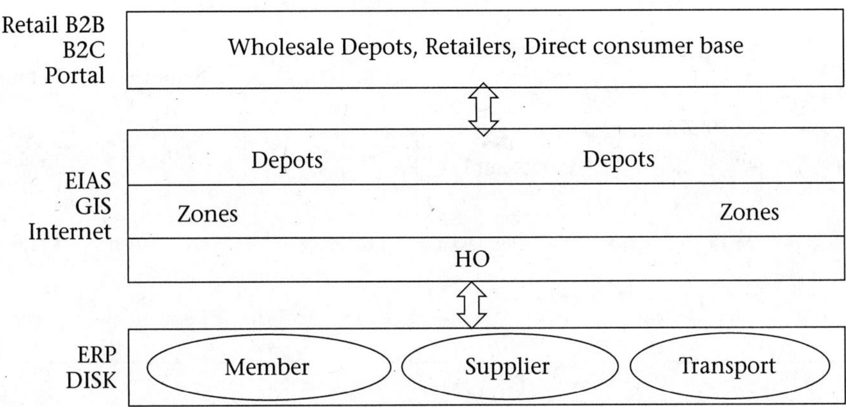

Source: https://www.slideshare.net/AkashTyagi8/amul-supplychain-futureinitiatives (Accessed on 27 April 2017).

Amul's digitization of supply chains has the following elements:

AMCUs: The Automatic Milk Collection Units (AMCUs) has been installed at village societies to capture member information, fat content, volume collected and amount payable. With the help of IT, farmers receive their payments in minutes. Farmers drop their plastic ID card into a box, which is then read by a computer attached to the weighing machine. The milk is emptied into a can kept on the weighing scale, where a 5 ml sample is tested for fat content on an electronic milk tester. Amount due is automatically calculated and either the payment is made or credited into the farmers' accounts.

EIAS: One important aspect in milk production is demand. Excess production would go waste, while low production would result in shortages and black market. Amul connects farmers to retailers and thus is able to get a good idea about demand and how much to supply through the Enterprise-wide Integrated Application System (EIAS). Implemented by Tata Consultancy Services, it covers operations such as market planning, advertising and promotion, distribution network planning, stock control, sales and accounting, budgetary control, quality control management and service management. Amul has connected all its zonal offices, regional offices and members dairies through VSATs for seamless exchange of information as shown in Figure 10.8.

GIS: Stocks at different levels of the supply chain are tracked through GIS. It tracks depot and distributor locations and their product-wise sales data and data of its farmer-members, including animal census data. This has enabled Amul to track information regarding milk production and productivity of animals, region-wise in Gujarat, ultimately leading to better forecasting of milk production. The system is also used to monitor veterinary health and controlling the outbreak of diseases.

DISK: The Dairy Information System Kiosk (DISK) is a database on the history of cattle owned by the farmers, containing details such as their medical history, reproductive cycle and history of diseases. Farmers can have access to information related to milk production, including best practices in breeding and rearing cattle. Implemented by IIM Ahmedabad, the system is used to forecast milk collection and monitor the produce from individual farmers.

FIGURE 10.8

The EIAS at Amul is able to integrate all functions of milk production and distribution right up to retail.

Farmers	Village Cooperative Societies	Member unions	GCMHFL	Distribution	Retailers
2.2 million numbers	10,675 Cooperative societies	12 units 10,000 cmpl	700 EMP	3000	500,000
Production of Milk	Milk Collection	Milk Processing	Marketing	Distribution	Retailing
AMCUS, DISK	3000 Screens	1000 Screens +12 VSAT	555 Screens + 7 VSAT	2500 Screens	Retail Portal

EIAS

Source: https://www.slideshare.net/AkashTyagi8/amul-supplychain-futureinitiatives (Accessed on 27 April 2017).

Online initiatives: Amul's online gifting service is capable of servicing consumers in more than 125 cities. Distributors can place their orders on the website, amulb2b.com, especially meant for accepting orders from stockists. Amul sells products via e-commerce and through a number of grocery sites, which has helped it to tap overseas markets.

Bridging digital divide: While the above describes the IT implementation in Amul, the success of the initiatives could only be achieved with local participation. For example, the Banas dairy is located in an underdeveloped region of district Banaskantha in Gujarat, not covered by modern communication media. It implemented a project in the rural area called 'Chiraag Banas Internet Sewa' in Gujarati. This project provides Internet access through information kiosks to the people in their language. This is a village-level effort at bridging the digital divide by providing information kiosks at the village cooperative level.

Distribution initiatives: To integrate distributors in the planning process, the company has a Self Leadership Development Programme (SLDP). Four distribution highways for the ambient, chilled, frozen and fresh products have been created. GCMMF has further enhanced its Virtual Private Network (VPN) by connecting all its sales offices, member unions, milk plants, milk chilling centres and warehouses on a common communication backbone to strengthen and automate the supply chain operations.

How can companies use technology in villages like the case described here?

Source for this Case Study:

Web Resource

Amul website: http://www.amul.com/m/about-us

Mobile-based Payments

Mobile-based payment is defined as the initiation and confirmation of the payment through mobile phones. Micro-payments through mobiles can make use of cash redundant. Business establishments, including small vendors and grocery traders, can accept payments by using their mobile number and Mobile Money Identifier (MMID) at the shop (see Mini Case Study 10.8).

Mini Case Study 10.7

VillageReach: Mobile Supply Chain Management Tool

Stock-outs and supply chain disruptions pose real challenges in low-resource communities. Rural marketing can learn much from public health systems, where technology has been deployed and supply chains developed to save lives through last mile distribution. According to a WHO report, 'last mile health delivery' in emerging countries is plagued with a lack of timely information and logistical challenges. To ensure availability of vaccines, health workers must keep tabs on their inventory and pass along information when supplies are getting low; procurement officials in the government need to know how much to order; and then delivery trucks, motorbikes, or cars need to make a timely delivery. The information chain often breaks down, resulting in stock-outs. For example, in Mozambique, there were stock-outs about 35 per cent of the time: that is, any woman going to a clinic to get her child vaccinated had a one-in-three chance of finding empty shelves and in the remotest areas this probability was much higher.

VillageReach is an organization with headquarters in Seattle and works in the area of health care in remote rural areas in the developing countries. Its mission is to "save lives and improve health by increasing access to quality health care for the most underserved communities."

The organization realized that accurate and timely data was a critical component in addressing last mile supply chain challenges. A high-quality logistics was developed, called OpenLMIS, with funding from the Rockefeller Foundation, the Bill & Melinda Gates Foundation, USAID, PEPFAR and PATH. OpenLMIS is an enterprise-level software platform that is freely available for any low or middle income country to manage its medical distribution. It has the following components:

- **Dedicated Logistics System (DLS):** DLS introduces efficiencies in Mozambique's vaccine supply chain resulting in significant increases in fully vaccinated children, dramatic reduction in stock-outs and reduced costs. The DLS is an example of a new approach to supply chain system design that is now being adopted by other countries.
- **OpenLMIS:** A logistics management information system (LMIS), built to manage medical commodity supply chains. The OpenLMIS initiative is a logistics management system for low-income countries. OpenLMIS is currently deployed in Tanzania, Zambia, Mozambique and Benin.
- **ODK Scan:** Developed in partnership with the University of Washington, it is an Android app that utilizes computer algorithms and the phone's built-in camera to automatically digitize data from paper forms. It enables a more efficient paper-to-digital process, which can significantly improve communications at the last mile of the health system.

OpenLMIS is an essential part of a comprehensive vaccine supply chain in Mozambique. It also includes a streamlined distribution process, dedicated logisticians and the supply of digital tools such as tablets to connect to the last mile local clinic to manufacturers. These system changes have dramatically improved the way medical supply chains work in Mozambique, leading to reduction in vaccine stock-out levels from an average of 35 per cent to under 5 per cent, for a population of more than 8.8 million. It has also been deployed in Tanzania, Zambia, Benin, Cote d'Ivoire and Zanzibar.

Open-source software was designed to strengthen logistics management using mobile technology. Users report stock levels, receipts and orders through SMS, a Java-enabled app; Android phones or tablets or the web. Monthly consumption, lead times and order fill rates are calculated based on this data. The system provides real-time and accurate information. It is expected that as more applications are developed, the body of open source technology in remote logistics will continue to grow.

Can companies learn from medical supply chains to use technology and develop similar distribution systems for consumer goods?

Sources for this Case Study:
An Introduction to OpenLMIS: https://www.youtube.com/watch?v=nWkXhnauweA
VillageReach website: http://www.villagereach.org/
WHO website: http://www.who.int/ehealth/resources/compendium_ehealth2013_6.pdf

Mini Case Study 10.8

Mobile Payments

In 2007, the leading mobile operator in Kenya, Safaricom, part of the Vodafone Group, launched a mobile money transfer service, m-pesa. 'Pesa' is the Swahili word for money and the 'M' is for mobile. The service has grown rapidly since launch and is currently used by over 8 million subscribers.

M-pesa is an SMS-based system that enables users to deposit, send and withdraw funds using their mobile phone. Customers need not to have a bank account and can transact at any of the country's retail agents. Registration and deposits are free and most other transactions are priced on a low tariff structure. Transactions are typically small. The service was developed by the Vodafone partly funded by the UK Department for International Development. The current arrangement between Safaricom and Vodafone Group is a revenue share model where Safaricom controls the on-the-ground operation of the product and Vodafone Group manages the delivery. M-pesa is now available in India as well.

Several other companies have started mobile wallets, such as Citrus Pay, FreeCharge, MobiKwik, mobile wallets, mRupee, Oxigen, Paytm and Idea Money. Banks too have their mobile money apps such as HDFC Bank's PayZapp and ICICI Bank's Mobile Money.

FINO PayTech, a financial solutions company, offers domestic remittances, rural lending and insurance and savings accounts under its payments bank umbrella. The company wants to set up bank branches across small towns and develop a network of around 50 BCs per branch to take banking to the far interiors of the country. It has established a network of more than 38,000 self-employed bandhus, or BCs. FINO provides them with technology and pays them a fee to offer banks' front-end operations such as opening accounts and providing insurance and remittances for rural customers. They also perform the due diligence in services such as lending money. On average, the bandhus earn ₹2,000 to ₹3,000 per month. Micro-payments have low margins and hence the business requires deep penetration. The BCs should be motivated by the goal of financial inclusion.

FINO PayTech has been in the business of rural payments for 10 years. This company has grown through a feet-on-street model. It has 400 points for remittances and bill payments named Fino Mart across the nation, which will be converted into bank branches. It also has 8,000 agents under Jan Dhan doing enrolments and already handles ₹7,000–8,000 crores in cash annually, with revenue of ₹300 crore in 2015–16. It does around 80 to 85 million transactions through its platform every year.

FINO PayTech supplements digital technology with physical infrastructure and has got a payments bank licence. It is trying the DigiCal or the PhysiTal model, which uses the country's demographics and creating a physical infrastructure that would be connected through digital technology. The other payment platforms are Paytm, India Post, Vodafone-m-Pesa and Airtel Money.

Can payments banks lead to widespread financial inclusion? How?

Sources for this Case Study:
Web Resources
FINO Paytech website: http://www.finopaytech.com/index.php
"Leaders of Tomorrow 2012: FINO PayTech." Available at: http://economictimes.indiatimes.com/et-now/corporate/leaders-of-tomorrow-2012-fino-paytech/videoshow/17899158.cms

Other Sources
Business Standard. 2016. "BPCL Acquires 21% Stake in Fino Paytech." 20 July.
The Economic Times. 2016. "Fino PayTech: A David among Payments Bank Goliaths." 6 July.

Mobile payments are a boon to villagers who otherwise store their savings in cash. They enable customers to make even small payments, which are linked to electronic wallets or savings accounts. People in rural areas can expand their markets and customer base and even buy goods online. Penetration of mobile payments may well result in reducing dependence by farmers on agents.

Mobile payments have been slow to take off in the country, but with the government move on demonetization, it is expected that a large number of non-users will acquire the habit of mobile wallets. A number of companies including established banks are offering mobile wallets in the country now.

3D Printing

3D printing or additive manufacturing is a process by which any three-dimensional object of any shape can be made or 'printed' just like a document on paper printers. This is achieved by an additive process whereby layers of materials are added through a 3D printer. The technology has found varied uses and benefits ranging from prototyping to making products at remote locations. 3D printers can make consumer goods and spare parts, enabling people to 'print' common household items rather than purchasing them from the market.

The technology can transform rural marketing, for example, by printing products on 3D printers set up by companies at common hubs that can serve villages. Birtchnell and Hoyle (2014) explain that the unique features of 3D printing make it "a useful tool for resource-constrained communities to draw on and this is demonstrable in the diverse array of projects." Agriculture machinery spare parts, health care products, items of daily use can be distributed directly to villages, reducing logistics costs. Companies such as Stratasys and Optomec already have partnerships in India and other companies are also making investments in India. Major players active in India 3D printing market are Altem Technologies, Imaginarium, Brahma 3, KCbots and JGroup Robotics.

Rajvanshi (2014) writes that 3D printing technologies and desktop manufacturing have an ability to transform the rural landscape by providing products even at remote locations (see Mini Case Study 10.9). It is quite possible that this will give rise to small scale manufacturing units in rural areas producing goods under license from large companies. It is expected that 3D machines will become cheap in the future and find wide applications in rural areas. Companies can get over their distribution problems through this technology.

Mini Case Study 10.9

Using 3D Technology in Emerging Markets

3D technology is already being used develop innovative products. A team of students from the University of Wisconsin–Madison has used 3D printing to create blades for a wind turbine which could be used to power cell towers in rural India. Named 'WiscWind', it is a wind turbine which can be installed on any existing tower, which can then generate energy to power itself. This device can be used to replace diesel generators in India and provide with renewable energy to power cell towers.

3D printing is already being used in rural areas in the developing world. iLab Haiti has brought 3D printers to rural Haiti to produce things most needed in local communities, such as umbilical cord clamps. However, such initiatives are relatively expensive and voluntary organizations that provide these facilities must be continually supported by rich donors. Dotz (2015) explains that 3D printers are small-scale manufacturing facilities in a box: with minimal resources, they enable rapid on-demand production. Products are made when needed, leading to decreased transportation, storage and customs costs. The pilot project in Haiti proved that the technology could be implemented locally in villages. The team identified high-demand medical supplies and broken equipment which could be fabricated through 3D fabrication. Sixteen 3D printable objects were identified and 3DPforHealth launched a 3D printing lab. Local people were trained in design using the Makerbot Rep 1 printers. An umbilical cord clamp prototype was designed and tested for sanitation, longevity and use on humans. The trials were a success. Local people were trained in 3D printing design.

The technology has found a new application—in humanitarian aid. When natural disasters strike, logistics are difficult and remain inefficient. 3D printing can bring much-needed products to disaster zones. For example, 3D printing has been used to mend pipes after the Nepal earthquake and the technology could radically change the speed and cost of delivering aid in affected areas. An organization, Field Ready flies in 3D printers to remote areas and makes humanitarian supplies right on the ground. Field Ready is now a programme that designs solutions that are shared with other resource-constrained environments, bypassing infrastructure and distribution limitations globally. *The Guardian* (2015) writes that 3D printing can bring much-needed products to disaster zones.

Birtchnell and Hoyle (2014) write that Dreambox Emergence set up a 3D printer centre in Guatemala, to print rulers for classrooms, valves and wrenches, water filters and eyewear. The company seeks "to mitigate inadequate supply chain failures, empowering emerging communities to innovate new products, develop sustainable business platforms and achieve organic growth by providing local production opportunities," says its website. Dreambox provides printers and production tools to stimulate community involvement in marginalized markets and produces items where they are needed most. Such interventions in rural areas can help use technology effectively to provide goods in remote areas in a big way.

Can rural hubs with 3D printers become the distribution technology of the future in rural India?

Sources for this Case Study:

Web Resources

Fieldready website: http://www.fieldready.org/

ILAB Haiti website: https://about.me/ilabhaiti

See the Dreambox Emergence overview at: http://www.fieldready.org/

See the WiscWind's Business Team Presentation at: http://www.wiscwind.org/

Wiscwind website: http://www.wiscwind.org/

Other Sources
Birtchnell, T. and W. Hoyle. 2014. *3D Printing for Development in the Global South: The 3D4D Challenge*. Basingstoke, UK: Palgrave-McMillan.

The Guardian. 2015. "When Disaster Strikes, It's Time to Fly in the 3D Printers." https://www.theguardian.com/global-development/2015/dec/30/disaster-emergency-3d-printing-humanitarian-relief-nepal-earthquake (Accessed on 17 April 2017).

E-commerce

E-commerce, or making commercial transactions electronically on the Internet, helps rural marketing in two ways: getting goods to remote markets and selling village produced goods to large urban markets. Large e-commerce firms such as Amazon, eBay and SnapDeal already carry a large number of goods sourced from small towns and villages. They are also building distribution hubs in towns.

SnapDeal has tied up with the National Institute of Electronics & Information Technology, Ministry of Communications and Information Technology, to train small and medium businesses on digital marketing. The company works with manufacturers to help them produce goods acceptable to the Indian market on the basis of intelligence gathered through data analytics, reports *Business Standard* (2016). It helps plan production cycles on the basis of predictive demand forecasts and customize products for specific consumer segments.

ShopClues hosts traditional crafts of Indian minorities with IndiMarket. It carries Rajasthani furnishings, Lucknowi chikan work, dokra craft and many others in its attempt to promote the 'Make in India' vision. IndiMarket has a large variety of items including fashion, footwear, home and kitchen, sports and other categories from different states of the country. ShopClues works with government bodies and associations of SMEs and indigenous artisans and promote rural entrepreneurship. It trains artisans and has ties with NIFT, National Institute of Design and Indian Institute of Packaging. Artisans sell under the USTAAD banner and offer a large collection of authentic ethnic products.

To succeed, e-commerce firms will have to invest in supply chains to villages. They also have to keep costs down, because serving rural markets is usually very expensive. However, a two-way supply of information and goods can only be good for developing rural markets.

E-governance

E-governance or electronic governance is the application of ICT for delivering government services to citizens. It is of great importance in rural areas since these areas have remained cut-off from the development process for decades. It consists of exchange of information, integration of various government records and services and communication between government and citizens. Through e-governance, government services are made available to citizens in a convenient, efficient and transparent manner. As rural people get better access to government schemes and services, they can be empowered as consumers as well.

According to its website, the government has formulated guiding principles for reforming services through technology are:

- **Form simplification and field reduction:** Forms to be made simple and user friendly.

- **Online applications and tracking:** Online applications and tracking of their status to be provided.
- **Online repositories:** Use of online repositories, for example, for certificates, educational degrees, identity documents and so on. so that citizens are not required to submit these documents in physical form.
- **Integration of services and platforms:** Integration of services and platforms, e.g., Aadhaar platform of UIDAI, payment gateway, Mobile Seva platform, sharing of data through open Application Programming Interfaces (API) and middleware such as National State Service Delivery Gateway to facilitate integrated and interoperable service delivery to citizens and businesses.

The government has set up the National Institute of Smart Governance (http://nisg.org/vision-mission) to assist in e-governance. It also offers a diploma on the subject with Sikkim Manipal University. Some of the initiatives to improve rural governance are given here.

E-Panchayat

The Ministry of Panchayati Raj has undertaken e-Panchayat Project to introduce and strengthen e-governance in the country. E-Panchayat is an initiative for the rural sector providing software solutions for automation of Gram Panchayat functions. It offers services such as birth and death registrations, issuance of certificates, statistics, house tax, issue of licenses, fee collection and so on. The ePanchayat Enterprise Suite has been planned with 10 core common applications and GIS layer module, which includes Local Government Directory, Area Profiler to gather socio-economic details, Plan Plus for decentralized and participatory planning, PriaSoft, a Panchayat Accounting software, ActionSoft for monitoring government works implementation, a National Asset Directory, Service Plus to facilitate service delivery, social audit and a National Panchayat Portal. Through e-Panchayat, rural India will be given access to the basic services and government interaction. E-governance, online resources and digital literacy can be achieved along with easy delivery of services through this initiative.

eSeva

The eSeva portals of state governments provide information on government schemes, citizen services such as Aadhaar and RTI, disaster management, bill payments, form downloads and much else. It was initiated with an aim of providing one-stop service by state governments. ESeva is a transparent service which brings government closer to the people. eForms, eFiling and ePayments are being provided by some states on their eSeva sites. However, the project still has to be fine-tuned as all states have not implemented eSeva and services are erratic in some areas.

Bhoomi

Bhoomi is the project of online delivery and management of land records in Karnataka. It provides transparency in land records management with citizen services and takes discretion away from civil servants at operating levels. The Revenue Department in Karnataka, with the technical assistance from National Informatics Centre (NIC), Bangalore, has built the BHOOMI system to provide services throughout the state. Already 20 million records of land ownership of 6.7 million farmers in the state have been computerized, according to its website.

As more government services are made available to rural consumers, it will lead to betterment of their lives. This will bring them into the development process and increase their quality of life.

Empowerment of Local Communities

Community empowerment refers to the process of enabling communities to increase control over their lives. Village communities refer to people in village clusters who share common interests, concerns or identities. ICTs have the promise of connecting remote villages and delivering services that have long been unavailable to them. These technologies can also bring about development of villages while empowering rural people. Communication technologies can deliver up-to-date information on practically all matters of importance to them. Banking and entertainment can also be delivered through these new technologies, which empowers the people.

Empowerment consists of (a) learning, recognizing the skills, knowledge and expertise that people contribute, (b) equality, or challenging discrimination and oppressive practices within communities, (c) participation, facilitating democratic involvement by people in the issues which affect their lives based, (d) cooperation, or working together to identify and implement action, encouraging networking and connections between communities and organizations and (e) social justice, enabling people to claim their human rights, meet their needs and have greater control over the decision-making processes which affect their lives

ICT introduces transparency, accountability and administrative efficiency of rural institutions and improves the efficiency and responsiveness of rural service delivery. It can also facilitate interaction between rural citizens and the government.

Since ICTs facilitate the flow of information and knowledge, it is a critical tool to tackle development issues leading to social transformation. It has the potential to improve living standards of people in remote areas through better access to markets, health and education. Government services can be delivered to villages to strengthen rural livelihood opportunities. ICT helps in providing support to local governance as well. Rural communities can seek their rights, entitlements and various schemes and extension services. Demand-driven information and communication services can be provided and thus reduce the opportunity costs of rural folk. ICT can plug the gaps between the people and the government. Some of the initiatives for empowerment are described here.

Information Village

The Information Villages project was started in 1998 in Pondicherry by the M.S. Swaminathan Research Foundation. The project links 10 villages near Pondicherry into an information network connected to the Internet with the goal to develop community ownership and collective action around new technologies, keeping with a 'pro-poor, pro-nature, pro-women' approach to development. The project uses a hub-and-spoke model, with a central information centre (hub) connected to knowledge centres in the surrounding villages (spokes). Volunteers, at least half of them women, are selected by the community to run the knowledge centres in the villages. The project won the Stockholm Challenge award for extending the benefits of information technology to rural villages.

E-choupal

E-choupal is an initiative of ITC Limited, which has built village Internet kiosks in villages. Farmers can access information related to weather, market price, risk management, information on scientific farm practices, farm prices and so on. They can also sell their produce and buy their requirements through e-choupal.

NGOs

Several NGOs operate in villages with varying reach. TARAhaat is an initiative of an NGO Development Alternatives (DA) and its rural marketing arm Technology and Action for Rural Advancement (TARA). TARAhaat, which works on a franchise model, provides access to villages such as commodity prices, health facilities, land records, local development programmes, business opportunities, jobs, matrimonials and so on. Users can shop for farm inputs such as seeds, machinery, spare parts and household items, now becoming popular in rural markets, such as bicycles, scooters and refrigerators. However, TARAhaat has met with limited success. Another NGO, Drishtee sustainable communities operates in UP, Bihar and Assam. Its website says that they are active in 6000 villages and provide vocational skills, rural BPO, government services, health, insurance, e-commerce, microfinance and so on. It helps rural communities by encouraging entrepreneurs to manufacture apparels and other goods.

Such e-initiatives help in governance and rural development. ICT has a great role to play in rural health care and education, which in turn help development of rural markets.

Consumer Engagement

Customer engagement is the process of building, nurturing and managing relationships with customers. We have already explained in Chapter 5 that traditional questionnaire base research does not quite work with villagers. Companies have to use alternate methods such as ethnographic research or engage consumers through SHGs. A way to supplement physical engagement with consumers is through apps and social media sites. Conducting product trials, seeking suggestions from customers, obtaining feedback—these tasks can be done by deploying ICT.

However, technology cannot replace physical intervention. Villagers must find a reason to engage with companies or to download the app. It is up to companies to build apps that actually solve some rural problems so that people are motivated to engage with companies, giving their suggestions or feedback. Many companies and the government have developed apps that provide information in agriculture and marketing. The government apps can be downloaded from the mKisan website while others can be downloaded from the android play store.

- **AgriMarket:** AgriMarket mobile app can be used to get the market price of crops in the markets within 50 km of the device's location.

- **Bhuvan Hailstorm:** A mobile app to capture crop loss due to hailstorm. This mobile app helps to photograph a field with latitude and longitude, with with sowing date and date of likely harvest.
- **Crop Insurance:** Crop Insurance mobile app can be used to calculate insurance premium for notified crops based on area, coverage amount and loan amount. It can also be used to get details of normal sum insured, extended sum insured, premium details and subsidy information of any notified crop in any notified area.
- **Farm-o-pedia:** Developed by CDAC, Mumbai, the application is a multilingual Android application targeted for rural Gujarat. The app is useful to get information on crops, weather and so on.
- **Kisan Suvidha:** An omnibus mobile app developed to help farmers by providing relevant information to them quickly.
- **Krishi Ville:** An Android based mobile application which provides information to farmers related to their agricultural activities.
- **Mandi Trades:** Lists government crop price updates, provides information for farmers in remote villages developed by Jayalaxmi Agro Tech.
- **mKisan:** This app enables farmers to obtain advisories and information by experts and government officials at different levels.
- **mPower Social:** Offers simple veterinary advice for cattle owners.
- **Pashu Poshan:** NDDB has developed an android-based software that can be used on phones as well as tablets, for managing animals.
- **Pusa Krishi:** An app by ICAR–IARI, it promotes Agribusiness Ventures through technology development and commercialization.
- **RainbowAgri: C**onnects local buyers and sellers.
- **Shetkari Masik:** The Android app for Shetkari magazine.
- **SmartAgri:** An app that communicates with underground sensors to deliver easy-to-understand data, such as soil moisture and mineral levels, to farmers' mobile devices.

It is seen from the list that most apps being developed for rural areas concern agricultural information and advice. These apps have to find ways of becoming sustainable. Though they provide valuable information, companies have to think further and devise innovative ways to engage their potential customers in rural areas. Like apps in urban areas, they have to help remote villages to find transport, entertainment, or consumables. Only then will such interventions succeed in the long run.

Data Analytics

Technology helps by deploying big data analysis. Big data and analytics refer to tools and methodologies to analyze data that is being generated by digital processes and social media exchanges at all times. As more rural areas get telecom and data services, people will use these services for searches and communication. This will generate data that, through analytics, will give insights into rural consumer behaviour like never before.

Analysis of big data means analyzing very large datasets from different sources and the tools and procedures used to manipulate and analyze them. So far few companies have used data analytics in rural marketing, but penetration of ICTs will generate data which companies can use to decipher consumer needs and behaviour. Computer algorithms are able to detect patterns, trends and correlations in diverse data and have predictive capability. Improved real-time connectivity helps in data-driven efficiency in transport, logistics, marketing and agriculture. This can contribute to the economic and social development of rural areas. For this, companies will have to invest in data collecting, storage, processing and analysis from diverse rural areas.

As more people in rural areas use the Internet or phones, a huge amount of data will be generated every day. Using GIS, customer engagement can be better designed. Initiatives taken by telecom companies are helping in expanding Internet spread. Google is expanding Internet in villages through its Loon project and through its Saathi project in India.

Crowdfunding

Crowdfunding, or P2P lending in the rural context means the process of raising money through contributions of a large number of people for starting a small business. In rural areas these businesses could be for instance, buying a buffalo or starting a small grocery store. Anyone can participate by making a small donation. Some sites facilitate loans and small contributions can be made to complete the loan required, which is returned with a nominal interest, which can then be re-invested again in another rural entrepreneur. As the Kiva website explains, "In rural India, there are countless individuals [who] have no financial options. Every day they struggle to make ends meet, with only a small amount of money standing between them and a sustainable future." A loan helps them become producers and become self-dependent. Companies selling expensive goods such as deep freezers, generators and refrigerators can participate in rural areas through crowdfunding. However, under RBI guidelines, loans made to such organizations repay lenders at least 3 years after a loan is made.

Though there are a number of crowdfunding platforms giving loans to urban dwellers, Kiva and Rang De platforms are focused on rural lending.

- **Kiva:** Kiva partners with organizations that reach remote, underserved communities. Its goal is to give loans that are tailored to help borrowers change their lives. In this way, it is different from microlending. Kiva gives loans that can support excluded and vulnerable groups such as widowed women and physically challenged individuals, improve drinking water and sanitation and promote solar and renewable sources of energy. Kiva is an international non-profit organization based in San Francisco, connecting people through lending. All the loans made through Kiva go to funding loans, as it covers costs through donations and grants.
- **Rang De:** Rangde.org is an Internet-based peer-to-peer microlending platform that facilitates micro, low-cost loans to rural entrepreneurs across India. Over 93 per cent of borrowers have been women. This not-for-profit crowdfunding portal has attracted more than 10,000 investors and disbursed more than 52,000 loans for people who are usually overlooked by banks and financial institutions. It works through field partners in several states of India. Loans are given at interest rates between 4.5 per cent to 10 per cent per year for collateral free loans. Rang De gets a nominal cut of 2 per cent on all the loans repaid by borrowers. Led by Smita Ram and N.K. Ram, an Ashoka fellow, Rang De is supported by Tata Trust.

While these and other initiatives help people in rural areas, there are others that have not done well. There are many problems of implementation, which are discussed next.

PROBLEMS IN IMPLEMENTATION

While ICTs have the potential to change much in rural areas, companies will have to overcome their traditional approaches and think of completely new ways of doing business. That's because the usual approach will work only in limited ways in rural areas.

The availability of basic public goods through IT interventions enhances market development in remote areas. Several rural marketing IT initiatives have in fact, contributed to rural development in many areas of India. Since government policy has more or less failed in rural areas, the idea that 'making markets work for the poor' has led to the private sector building institutions to support markets and consequently, development. Improving market access for farmers, managing market related risks and reducing them, develops markets for consumer goods also. An ICT developer is likely to face the following problems in making solutions for rural markets.

Infrastructure

Issues such as unavailability of electricity, lack of equipment, high level of illiteracy, lack of broadband services, user acceptance and local content have to be addressed before the full potential of ICTs role in rural development can be tapped. Further, ICT can only help in providing connectivity; unless backed by investments in roads, transport, storage and grading facilities, farmers have little option but to sell their produce at whatever rates they can get at the local mandis. Even when information about market rates is available, agents may exploit the situation by delaying their offers since they know that farmers have no facilities to store their goods. Hence, investment in ICT infrastructure is not enough and must be matched by investments in all other facilities.

APMC Monopoly

We have described the effects of APMC monopoly of Indian agricultural markets in Chapter 8. The laws restrict movement of goods and impose mandi fees. This is a major hindrance in online trading of raw agricultural produce. Unless laws are changed, ICT interventions will only provide information and be of limited use to the farmer, who wants help in selling his goods.

Apps and Websites

Many websites and apps meant for rural areas merely provide information. This has limited use and that prevents them from becoming popular. For instance, providing market information to farmers is fine, but if he is indebted and has to sell to the local agent, information on an app or website would be pretty much useless. For example, Indiagriline.com of EID Parry was set up as an agriculture portal but is now defunct; many others get little traction.

Urban Bias

A major problem in application of IT in rural areas is that the apps and the content are written or designed by people who have no idea about rural life. They are urban-trained, urban-exposed engineers who have not lived in rural areas. Villages for them are usually idyllic holiday places if not dirty, mosquito-infested and lacking basic facilities. That is the reason that many ICT systems and apps have an urban bias. An app for finding a restaurant or meal delivery, for instance, may work in a city but is useless to rural folk. Some companies have tried to get over their urban bias by translating content in local languages but if the content does not relate to rural life in some way, it will not get the patronage in villages.

Understanding the Customer

While engineers come up with clever apps, their lack of marketing orientation stands in the way of getting a large base of customers. All ICT intervention has to be developed in close collaboration with the local people, but many technology companies lack these skills. Further, to be acceptable, any ICT intervention has to solve at least one rural problem, but this requires a deep understanding of the areas and the people. It calls for different approaches in market research (see Chapter 5). Thus companies have to commit their highly trained manpower in rural areas for longer times to understand the customers there.

Lack of Manpower

Rural areas lack trained managers, doctors and engineers, nor are they willing to spend long periods of time in villages. This creates a severe shortcoming for companies. Some companies get over this by working with local people and provide training to them which enables them to provide products or service. But for a long term intervention, companies have to deploy trained people.

Marketing + Technology Skills

Companies usually have people who know everything about technology but nothing about rural customers or people who work in rural areas but are not tech-inclined. For rural marketing, companies have to develop a cadre of marketing + technology people who can recognize rural problems and find ways of solving them through technology.

SUMMARY

Despite huge efforts of the government and other organizations, much of rural India remains cut off from winds of modernization and development. ICT could well be a game changer in this scenario. ICTs can overcome many infrastructural constraints that have plagued villages since long. They can help connect rural areas with the local, regional and national economy and to access markets, banking/financial services and employment opportunities.

ICTs have three essential components in rural areas: connectivity, content and capacity building (3Cs). Connectivity increases tele-density and gives access of the outside world to remote villagers. Relevant and specific content increases utility of smartphones in rural areas. Capacity building is essential because without it, there would be only a small percentage of rural population who would benefit from connectivity.

The three main ways in which digital technologies support rural marketing are inclusion, efficiency and innovation. To meet these objectives, ICTs can be used in rural markets in eight ways: (a) communication and media, (b) financial inclusion, (c) agricultural information and trading, (d) logistics and distribution, (e) 3D printing, (f) empowerment of local communities, (g) data analytics and (h) customer engagement.

The chapter discusses 12 ways by which ICTs can be used in rural markets. Communication and media plays an important role in providing information two fronts: production and marketing. Several studies have found that mobile telephony has resulted in increase in rural prosperity in a variety of countries. It thus becomes an important tool in rural marketing. IT helps in financial inclusion by bringing frontend banking operations to doorsteps of people and reduces transaction costs. The use of micro-ATMs, branchless banking using handheld devices, employing banking correspondents, credit cards and mobile-based payments have helped in financial inclusion. Agricultural trading is greatly helped if farmers get market information easily through ICTs. Mobile phones can provide such information cheaply and easily, which could also assist farmers in identifying potential buyers over large geographic areas. Trading portals help farmers to trade electronically over large areas.

Logistics and distribution is helped by sophisticated technologies for tracking, information processing and identification. However, companies face problems of lack of infrastructure and small orders/fewer traders, which makes investment in technology impossible. Digital payments help remote villagers to make and receive payments through mobile phones. E-commerce helps in two ways: by bringing outside products to the villages and helping the villagers to sell their own products. ICT also helps in e-governance, or providing government services to rural areas. 3D printing is a disruptive technology that helps make any three-dimensional object of any shape in remote areas. It is already in use in many parts of the world to make objects in areas where they cannot be delivered easily. Rural governance is improved through technology by making people aware about rural schemes, rural institutions and rural service delivery. Initiatives such as e-Panchayat, eSeva, bhoomi and e-Choupal are using technology that helps in e-governance. Consumer engagement is facilitated through apps and social media sites. ICTs help in conducting product trials, seeking suggestions from rural customers and obtaining feedback.

Finally, as more people in villages use Internet and smartphones, they leave behind data trails that can be analyzed through data analytics. Computer algorithms are able to detect patterns, trends and correlations in diverse data and have predictive capability. Improved real-time connectivity helps in data-driven efficiency in transport, logistics, agriculture and logistics.

However, to use ICTs effectively, certain problems have to be removed. For instance, without physical infrastructure, farmers will be unable to use ICTs effectively. Moreover, the APMC monopoly, which prevents trading of agricultural goods over different mandis, must end. Such laws stymie electronic trading in agricultural markets.

CONCLUSION

ICTs have the potential to transform rural India. Indeed, many private, voluntary, multinational and government organizations have started initiatives to serve rural markets in a variety of ways. India has also got to learn from initiatives taken elsewhere in the world in logic-defying ways, some of which are covered in this chapter. However, the promise of ICT linked rural marketing can only be realized if the government and its various bodies gives up its stranglehold on rural markets. Government monopolies and outdated rules—some of them going back to pre-independence times—prevent ICTs in supply chains and agricultural marketing. Though government and its departments have started a plethora of websites and apps, they are of limited use if they contain static and outdated information. Moreover, this information is quite useless to the farmer because there is a long way to go before the hold of agents or *arhatiyas* is broken. Nor does the farmer have storage capabilities to hold and sell his stock when prices rise. So the trading portals will have limited value.

It may also be said in the conclusion that companies venturing into this area must change their mind-sets completely. Software engineers and marketing managers in urban areas simply cannot develop ICTs specific to rural areas. They have to live and work in rural areas to understand the local population. Only then will they be able to develop relevant ICT applications that solve rural problems.

KEY TERMS

3D Printing: A process by which any three-dimensional object of any shape can be made in remote areas. It is also called additive manufacturing.

Branchless banking: Providing financial and banking services where branches do not exist, allowing rural people to operate their bank accounts using handheld devices.

Community empowerment: The process of enabling communities to increase control over their lives.

Crowdfunding: Crowdfunding or P2P lending in the rural context means the process of raising money through contributions from a large number of people for starting a small business.

Customer engagement: The process of building, nurturing and managing relationships with customers.

Data analytics: Tools and methodologies to analyze data that is being generated by digital processes and social media exchanges at all times.

E-commerce: Making commercial transactions conducted electronically on the Internet.

E-governance: Electronic governance is the application of ICT for delivering government services to citizens. It consists of exchange of information, integration of various government records and services and communication between government and citizens.

eNAM: The government launched the NAM as a pan-India unified electronic trading portal, networking the existing APMC mandis to create a national market for agricultural commodities.

E-Panchayat: An initiative for the rural sector providing software solutions for automation of Gram Panchayat functions.

eSeva: The eSeva portals of state governments provide information on government schemes, citizen services such as Aadhaar and RTI, disaster management, bill payments, form downloads and much else.

Financial inclusion: The delivery of financial services at affordable costs to disadvantaged and low income segments of the society, or those who cannot access these services because of distance and availability.

Mobile-based payment: The initiation and confirmation of the payment through mobile phones.

CONCEPT REVIEW QUESTIONS

1. Why is it said that ICT is a game changer in rural marketing? In which areas is it useful?
2. What are the 3Cs of ICT in rural marketing? How can they help ICT penetration and use?
3. In which areas can communication and media help in making lives easier for rural customers? How?
4. Explain financial inclusion. How can rural customers avail of banking services? What are the steps taken for better financial inclusion?
5. How can ICT help in agricultural trading? Explain the working of eNAM.
6. Describe the new technologies being used in logistics. How can they be used in rural areas?
7. ICTs are often said to be helpful in empowering rural communities. How is it done?
8. What is data analytics? Comment on the use of data analytics in the context of rural marketing.
9. Describe the problems likely to be faced while implementing ICT projects in rural areas. How can they be overcome?
10. What is consumer engagement? In what ways can ICTs help in engaging rural engagement?

CRITICAL THINKING QUESTIONS

1. ICTs can deliver diverse solutions to rural areas. However, farmers in many areas still face a number of problems in using them properly, except for basic telephony. Why is this so? What can be done to rectify the situation?
2. Does ICT really help in reducing distances to rural areas, as predicted? If so, how can rural areas really be brought into the mainstream?
3. Despite huge amount of information available on government and non-government rural sites, why are farmers still in distress across states? Where do these initiatives lack? How can they really help rural empowerment?
4. Can 3D printing be used in India's rural areas to deliver products? How can the high cost of printers be offset? What are the common things that can be made by this technology in rural areas?

PROJECTS AND ASSIGNMENTS

1. Visit some of the portals and look up some apps listed in this chapter. Assess how useful would they be in assisting the farmer or the rural customer. Which ones contain current information and which ones have not been updated? Which of the apps really help the farmer in making decisions?

2. Visit agricultural trading portals. Find out the volume of goods traded on these portals. Assess whether these portals are successful in their stated objectives.
3. Visit some remote villages and find out how people are using ICTs in their daily lives. Make a presentation and show in the class. Also suggest ways that the use of ICTs can be increased.
4. Talk to some marketing managers and find out what new technologies they are using in rural marketing. Which technologies can they further use and how?

WEB RESOURCES

Bayer website: http://www.cropscience.bayer.in/en/Sustainable-Crop-Solutions/National-Helpline-for-Farmers.aspx
eNam portal: http://www.enam.gov.in/NAM/home/about_nam.html
eSagu website: http://agriculture.iiit.ac.in/esagu2012/overview.php
Farmers' portal website: http://farmer.gov.in
Fieldready website: http://www.fieldready.org
IFFCO Kisan website: http://www.iffcokisan.com/home/about
IndiaMeteorologicalDepartmentwebsite:http://imdagrimet.gov.in/farmer/FarmerRegistrationFrontpage/index.php
Kisan Sanchar website: https://www.kisansanchar.com/
mKisan website: http://mkisan.gov.in/downloadmobileapps.aspx
NIC website: http://www.nic.in/projects/e-panchayat
The Ministry of Panchayati Raj undertaken e-Panchayat Project Online website: http://panchayatonline.gov.in/viewPESHome.do
Reuters Market Light website: http://www.rmlglobal.com/wordpress/

REFERENCES

Aker, J. 2010. "Information from Markets Near and Far: Mobile Phones and Agricultural Markets in Niger." *American Economic Journal: Applied Economics* 2 (3): 46–59.

Beuermann, Diether W., Christopher McKelvey and Renos Vakis. 2012. "Mobile Phones and Economic Development in Rural Peru." *The Journal of Development Studies* 48 (11), 1617–28.

Birtchnell, T. and W. Hoyle. 2014. *3D Printing for Development in the Global South: The 3D4D Challenge*. Basingstoke, UK: Palgrave–McMillan.

Business Standard. 2016. "E-commerce Firms Ride Make in India to Reach Rural Markets." 17 April.

Cairncross, Frances. 1997. *The Death of Distance: How the Communications Revolution Will Change Our Lives*. Boston, MA: Harvard Business School Press.

De Silva, Harsha, Dimuthu Ratnadiwakara and Ayesha Zainudeen. 2011. "Social Influence in Mobile Phone Adoption: Evidence from the Bottom of the Pyramid in Emerging Asia." *Information Technologies & International Development* 7 (3), 1–18.

Dotz, A. Dara. 2015. "A Pilot of 3D Printing of Medical Devices in Haiti." In *Technologies for Development: What is Essential?* Edited by Silvia Hostettler, Eileen Hazboun and Jean-Claude Bolay. Switzerland: Springer International Publishing: 33–44.

Gupta, S.K. 2011. "Financial Inclusion—IT as Enabler." *Reserve Bank of India Occasional Papers* 32 (2): 129–48.

Hofman, Bert. 2016. "The Taobao Villages as an Instrument for Poverty Reduction and Shared Prosperity." The World Bank, 29 October. Available at: http://www.worldbank.org/en/news/

speech/2016/10/29/the-taobao-villages-as-an-instrument-for-poverty-reduction-and-shared-prosperity (Accessed on 27 April 2017).

Jensen, R. 2007. "The Digital Provide: Information (Technology), Market Performance, and Welfare in the South Indian Fisheries Sector." *Quarterly Journal of Economics* 122 (3): 879–924.

Kumar, Dinesh. 2012. *Marketing Channels*. New Delhi: Oxford University Press.

Mittal, S. 2012. "Modern ICT for Agricultural Development and Risk Management in Smallholder Agriculture in India." Socioeconomics Working Paper 3, International Maize and Wheat Improvement Center (CIMMYT), Mexico, D.F.

Muto, M. and T. Yamano. 2009. "The Impact of Mobile Phone Coverage Expansion on Market Participation: Panel Data Evidence from Uganda." *World Development* 37 (12), 1887–96.

NSSO (National Sample Survey Office). 2005. *Situation Assessment Survey of Farmers: Access to Modern Technology for Farming*, NSS report 499. Ministry of Statistics and Program Implementation, New Delhi.

Rajvanshi, Anil K. 2014. *Romance of Innovation: A Human Interest Story of R&D in Rural Setting*. Phaltan, Maharashtra: Nimbkar Agricultural Research Institute (NARI). Available at: http://www.nariphaltan.org/roi.pdf (Accessed on 17 April 2017).

Schmidt, Eric. 2011. "Preparing for the Big Mobile Revolution." HBR Agenda item, *Harvard Business Review*, April.

The Guardian. When Disaster Strikes, It's Time to Fly in the 3D Printers. https://www.theguardian.com/global-development/2015/dec/30/disaster-emergency-3d-printing-humanitarian-relief-nepal-earthquake (Accessed on 27 April 2017).

Closing Case
Grameenphone

Mobile phones are a means to empower the poor in developing countries. However, with basic telephony limited, the poor have suffered years of remaining cut off from the development process. Mobiles help these countries leapfrog to a connected world. This case study describes the innovative way that mobiles were introduced in rural Bangladesh.

Bangladesh, like other developing countries, has a very poor telephone service since its independence. Potential telecom users had to wait 4–6 years to get telephone connection. The service quality of the BTTB (the only telephone service provider) was poor and the call completion rate remained under 50 per cent. There was no telephone connection in rural areas.

Mobile phones helped the country leapfrog to a modern technology that not only created a new business opportunity for the poor, but also provided access to information, market, health and other services in the remote rural areas of Bangladesh. Placing cell phones in the hands of the women from the poorest households in remote villages was a major innovation, which no telecom operator had dared to do. It is remarkable that, in 1997, when the cell phone was a novelty, Grameen Telecom successfully initiated its use for empowering the rural poor.

The internationally acclaimed VPP was launched in 1997 jointly by Grameen Bank, Grameenphone and Grameen Telecom. Grameen Bank played a crucial role to the programme, which has now spread to more than 50,000 villages, in 61 out of 64 districts of the

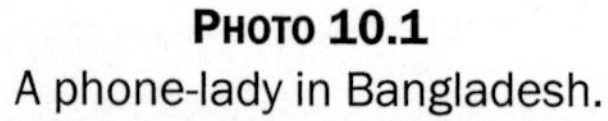

Photo 10.1
A phone-lady in Bangladesh.

Source: http://www.grameen-info.org/village-phones-2/ (Accessed on 5 June 2017).

country. The uniqueness and importance of the programme has been expressed in the Nobel Peace Prize acceptance speech by Dr Yunus:

> We gave loans from GB to the poor women to buy mobile phones to sell phone services in the villages. We saw the synergy between microcredit and ICT.... Telephone ladies quickly learned the art of telephone business and it has become the quickest way to get out of poverty and to earn social respectability.

The Grameen Bank and Grameenphone created a partnership model to provide microcredit to rural women, enabling them to buy mobile phone sets as well as discounted airtime to run retailing of mobile phone services in their villages. Through this, the villagers could access information about employment, market prices and government programmes and make calls as well, to keep in touch with friends and relatives. The VPP model not only empowered the poor women; it also empowered the village people over middlemen by providing them with timely and relevant information about market prices.

This model has created a social business called VPP programme where the village phone operators earn profits by renting out their phone to make calls and get information. Most of the phone ladies were housewives and not part of the traditional labour force but worked as daily wagers when they could find jobs. The mobile phone gave them a means to earn while bringing a technology to the village and helping out their fellow villagers get a coveted service.

The system worked as follows: Grameen Bank loans US$200 to women borrowers to buy a mobile handset from Grameen Telecom. The women, who are existing Grameen Bank borrowers, are selected as Village Phone Operators (VPOs) in rural villages because they are trusted Grameen Bank borrowers with good repayment record. Grameenphone supports the programme by providing airtime at discounted price. Grameen Telecom buys bulk airtime from Grameenphone at 50 per cent of the regular prices which are then passed on to the VPOs. Grameen Telecom also trains the operators and provides technical services to help the women borrowers run the phone business smoothly. They rent the phones with airtime to the neighbours in the adjoining areas in the village for a fee where no such facilities existed before. The VPP model is a shared business model where mobile phone services reach end customers through an intermediate device provider. Instead of each user owning a mobile handset, a group of them shares one. By removing the barrier of owning a mobile phone set, the ICT service becomes cheaper and affordable for the rural poor. The four parties in the project are:

- **Grameen Bank:** Grameen Bank selects VPOs on the basis of their past credit records. It provides loans to VPOs for the start-up cost, i.e., to buy mobile phone sets. It also ensures that VPOs repay their loan instalments regularly. Grameen Bank staff members are permanently located in villages and meet with borrowers at regular intervals to ensure that borrowers avoid moral hazards such as unwillingness to repay their loans.
- **Grameen Telecom:** Grameen Telecom supplies handsets, trains VPOs on how to operate mobile phones, repairs handsets and handles all service-related issues. It bears marketing and advertising costs of the VPP programme and prepares monthly bills for the airtime charges for each village phone.
- **Grameenphone:** Grameenphone provides telecom network infrastructure and sells airtime in bulk, with a 50 per cent discount to Grameen Telecom. Grameenphone incurs costs related to communication infrastructure, technical support, provision of airtime, government licensing and regulatory compliance, government financial and taxation liaison.
- **VPOs:** The VPO are selected from the large pool of Grameen Bank borrowers. In order to be eligible to become a VPO, these borrowers must meet the following requirements—they must be members of the Grameen Bank's microcredit programme with a good track record and be willing to invest in a phone.

Grameenphones's technology, Grameen Telecom's management support and Grameen Bank's microcredit, brand image and database of villagers, have been the critical success factors for the VPP model. Another important reason for its success is that call tariffs are kept low.

Village phones have also brought independence to rural women. The VPP model allowed them to have increased role in family decision making such as whether they would adopt family planning to limit their number of children. Mobile phones reduce information asymmetry, which gives undue advantage to the rich and lack of which results in disadvantage to the poor, part of what is called 'poverty premium'. The VPP programme increases the phone ladies' authority in their household and control over family resources. Village phones are also used as a tool for networking and information exchange.

The VPP initiative has made tremendous social and economic impact in the rural areas of Bangladesh. It received 'GSMA in the Community Award' in 2000, 'Commonwealth Innovation Award' in 2003 and 'Petersburg Prize' awarded by the Gateway Foundation in 2005. The profit for VPO is the difference between the end customer tariff and operator's tariff. This profit enables the women to meet not only basic need such as food, shelter and health care but also earn respect as earning members of the family.

Questions for Discussion:

1. Comment on the business model of Grameenphone. Can this model be replicated?
2. Can appliance goods companies deploy the same model, say of providing community washing machines or deep freeze machines in villages?
3. Would you describe Grameenphone as a social business? Give your reasons.
4. The success of rural marketing often depends on forming collaborations with other businesses. Do you know of some businesses who have built models through collaboration?

Sources for this Case Study:

Web Resource

Watch "Microcredit from Grameen Bank in Bangladesh: Phone ladies": https://www.youtube.com/watch?v=4VZ9i8NrcsY

Other Source

Grameen Bank website: http://www.grameen-info.org/village-phones-2/ (Accessed on 27 April 2017).

APPENDIX: INDIAN AGRICULTURAL WEBSITES

There are a host of websites offering information for farmers. This appendix lists some of them.

Agricoop.nic.in: The site of Department of Agriculture, Cooperation and Farmers Welfare displays information about government schemes.

Agriexchange.apeda.gov.in: A trade portal for farmers, suppliers and vendors.

Agriwatch: Information about commodities by Indian Agribusiness Systems Pvt. Ltd.

Apeda.gov.in: The site of Agricultural and Processed Food Products Export Development Authority (APEDA).

Assamagribusiness.nic.in: A comprehensive portal by Assam Small Farmers Agri-Business Consortium.

Ccafs.cgiar.org: CGIAR Research Programme on Climate Change, Agriculture and Food Security offers information about climate-smart agricultural practices. It is developed through a collaboration between the Consultative Group on International Agricultural Research (CGIAR) and the Earth System Science Partnership.

cmfri.org.in: Portal of Central Marine Fisheries Research Institute provides information about fisheries

Commerce.nic.in: Information about commodity exports and imports from the Ministry of Commerce.

Commodityindia.com: Comprehensive commodity information with a trading advisory.

FarmNest.com: An open, free platform to enable free sharing of agricultural information among everyone interested in Indian agriculture and farming.

Fciweb.nic.in: Food Corporation of India provides information on storage, food security, price stabilization and distribution of foodgrains through PDS.

Fert.nic.in: The website Department of fertilizers, Govt. of India, gives information on different aspects of fertilizers.

Fredisurti.com: This site offers garden consultancy and distributes vegetable and flower seeds.

Iffcolive.com: An information sharing initiative by IFFCO, which is one of the biggest agricultural cooperatives in the world.

Indiaagristat.com: A source for Indian agriculture statistics.

Indiacoffee.org: The site of the Coffee Board, Government of India.

Indiancommodities.com: Information on cotton, rice, wheat, oilseeds, pulses, spices, coffee and tea.

Indiantradeportal.in: Provides information on exports.

Isapindia.org: The Indian Society of Agribusiness Professional (ISAP) is a network of agriculture and allied sector professionals in India and developing countries.

Kissankerala.net: A multi-modal agricultural information system for Kerala.

Krishi.net: Agriculture B2B portal.

Indianspices.com: Information and links between the Indian exporters and importers of spices.

Mofpi.nic.in: Ministry of Food Processing Industries (MoFPI) provides information about modern technology and food processing industry.

Nationalfertilizers.com: NFL provides information about fertilizer use and availability.

Nhb.gov.in: Information about products and market information about fruit and vegetables.

Nhrdf.org: NHRDF guides farmers and exporters for improving the productivity and quality of vegetables and horticultural produce.

Rural.nic.in: This site provides information from the Ministry of Rural Development.

Teaboard.gov.in: Information on schemes about tea development.

11
CHAPTER

Management of Sales Force in Rural Marketing

LEARNING OBJECTIVES

Management of rural sales force calls for a complete change of thinking and approach by companies. Urban approaches do not work; companies have to attract, motivate and retail salespeople who are 'intrapreneurs'. After reading this chapter you will be able to:

- Understand the work of the rural salesperson and the line, staff and advisory functions of rural sales.
- Analyze the problems that arise in sales management in rural areas.
- Learn why a paradigm shift in thinking is required for rural sales.
- Understand the rural sales organization and the need for identifying rural clusters.
- Learn about recruitment, compensation, personality and skills, attitude and training in rural sales.
- Analyze the Human Resources (HR) issues in rural marketing and why the HR function must be reinvented.

Opening Case
Training Dealers: Coca-Cola Parivartan

Selling in rural India involves much more than the usual task of selling most people think of. It consists of finding willing workers and building their capability, apart from organizing BTL activities, demos, offering services and maintaining relationships with opinion leaders. This case study describes the efforts of Coca-Cola in finding and training village women and retailers to distribute its products.

Coca-Cola trains rural retailers through Parivartan, a programme that aims to enhance retailer capability. An initiative by Coca-Cola University, it provides skills, tools and techniques to the rural and urban retailers in India for enabling them to make their business more profitable and sustainable, says its website. The training is delivered in classrooms and

Photo 11.1
The Coca-Cola Splash Bar.

Source: http://www.productventures.com/coca-cola/ (Accessed on 27 April 2017).

through Coca-Cola University on Wheels, which consists of customized buses that have a seating area, presentation zone, audio-visual equipment and trainers. The buses travel to the villages reaching small retailers, who are trained on four key areas in regional languages: Shop Management, Stock Management, Customer Management and Financial Management. The company provides rural retailers with large, bright red solar-powered coolers sporting the company logo. It has trained over 260,000 retailers, making it one of the largest corporate rural initiatives.

The second stage of the programme is Advanced Parivartan, based on feedback from retailers. It includes modern methods of retailing such as acceptance of credit cards and using computers, customer engagement and sustainability including recycling. The programme has reached out to 200,000 retailers in more than 4,500 cities across India.

Women running the kiosks have turned them into community centres called splash bars (Photo 11.1). The concept consists of delivering products in the most affordable format and packaging, while also providing entrepreneurship opportunities to rural women, according to the Coca-Cola website. Now, there are more than 2,000 women serving Coca-Cola through such outlets.

Coca-Cola also has its '5by20' initiative, which imparts training to women entrepreneurs in areas such as business skills training, and provides access to financial services and support networks. It is active in more than 200 countries worldwide, providing millions of women opportunities to build their businesses and support their families. The 5by20 initiative focuses on women in six segments of Coca-Cola's value chain: producers, suppliers, distributors, retailers, recyclers and artisans. By doing so, it helps millions of women who own or operate a small business in Coca-Cola's value chain to face challenges to achieve business success. Coca-Cola collaborates with partners to provide women access to three essential economic enablers:

- **Business skills training:** Programmes include accounting, inventory management, human resources training and business planning exercises for the retail sector. Many programmes also integrate gender sensitivity training with course content.

- **Loans, financial services and assets:** A global partnership with the International Finance Corporation (IFC) provides financing and business skills training to small and medium-sized businesses that are owned or operated by women entrepreneurs across the value chain.
- **Peer networks and mentoring:** Women are typically grouped together with their peers and brought together to meet on a regular basis to share experiences and lessons learnt in running their businesses.

The programme is implemented in partnership with Coca-Cola's bottling partners; government organizations such as USAID, UK DFID and TESDA; and civil society organizations, including Mercy Corps, Bill & Melinda Gates Foundation, TechnoServe, ASTA, Hapinoy Sari-Sari Store and international organizations such as UN Women.

Through 5by20, the company addresses the common barriers women face when trying to succeed in the marketplace. Its website says that it hopes to help the economic empowerment of five million women entrepreneurs across our global value chain by 2020. Between 2010 and 2015, the 5by20TM initiative helped enable more than 1.2 million female entrepreneurs across the Coca-Cola global value chain. In 2015, more than 372,000 women participated in 5by20 programmes. Programmes have been implemented in a total of 60 countries around the world.

A programme extension, Parivartan E&D, was started for small-time roadside eateries or dhabas. This programme focuses on the critical success factors, namely, hygiene, customer satisfaction, branding and customer experience for such businesses. At the same time, it reinforces the company's association by placing Visi Coolers and Coca-Cola products at the eateries.

An externally validated study of 5by20 participants in South Africa saw an average of 44 per cent growth in business sales, while women farmers in Kenya saw their average incomes increase by 140 per cent over the course of a four-year programme, reports Zarya (2016).

While reading this chapter, try to answer the following questions:

1. What are the aspects of rural sales management?
2. What is the role of companies, distributors and salesmen in training people and selling products in rural areas?
3. How are HR aspects related to rural sales? How does HR need to change in this regard?
4. How will you recruit, retain and motivate semi-literate people to conduct sales in rural areas?

Sources for this Case Study:

Web Resource

Coca-Cola India website: http://www.coca-colaindia.com/university-wheels-coca-cola-parivartan-program/

Other Sources

Jenkins, Beth, Kara Valikai and Piya Baptista. 2013. *The Coca-Cola Company's 5by20 Initiative: Empowering Women Entrepreneurs across the Value Chain.* Cambridge, MA: The CSR Initiative at the Harvard Kennedy School and Business Fights Poverty. Available at: https://www.hks.harvard.edu/m-rcbg/CSRI/CSRI_BusinessFightsPoverty_5by20Report_September2013.pdf (Accessed on 18 April 2017).

Zarya, Valentina. 2016. "How Coke Is Changing the World." *Fortune*, 22 August. Available at: http://fortune.com/2016/08/22/coke-change-world/ (Accessed on 27 April 2017).

INTRODUCTION

It should be apparent to readers of this book that rural marketing is quite different from urban marketing. Owing to that, there should be a paradigm shift in thinking with regard to rural marketing. Naturally, sales management too has to be seen from a completely different perspective. The rural salesperson does not have the job of mere selling alone, as would be normally assumed, but has to be more of a superman, handling a multiplicity of tasks. This is because companies cannot afford to have separate departments handling different things in rural areas as they can in urban or high-density areas.

HR managers face the unenviable task of finding and retaining such supermen, who can perform the several tasks that must be performed in rural markets. A salesperson has to perform the task of advisor, trainer, service provider, market researcher, promoter and relationship manager. The salesman must do all this apart from the sales functions of selling and collecting orders and payments, keeping sales accounts, logistics, conduct promotions and activities, maintain inventories and depots and dealer relations. It is somewhat similar to the method of operation of small manufacturers who cannot afford large overheads, and this is perhaps why they are much more effective in rural areas than the bigger brands.

Very often the low volumes of orders generated are not enough to sustain keeping full-time salespeople. Companies thus look for part-time workers who can represent the company while also pursuing their other activities. Repairmen, teachers, housewives, retailers, small-time vendors and the like can well assist the company in sales while they have other jobs. This is no doubt cost effective, but companies lack the managerial skills to deal with such independent-minded people, who may also be illiterate or semi-literate.

It is easy to see that such people also need a high degree of autonomy. HR and recruiting managers have to develop the expertise of finding people, who are not available on any database, and then learning how to work with them. Companies will have to design the sales organization and a management system that recognizes these realities. This chapter looks at the problems and challenges of rural sales management and how these can be overcome.

PROBLEMS OF SALES MANAGEMENT IN RURAL AREAS

Rumblings about the role of HR in organizations have been heard since a long time. Cappelli (2015) writes, many leaders feel that HR managers focus too much on 'administrivia' and lack business knowledge, vision and strategic insight. While this is true in urban markets, the problem becomes compounded in rural markets: most HR managers have no idea about market conditions in rural areas, and lack the ability to find people and to administer them, given their urban orientation and training.

Managing people in rural areas is a challenging though the least explored area. However, since most companies wish to establish their rural presence, managers have to learn to manage a rural sales force. They have to learn to deal with problems that arise in dealing with people whose needs and motivations are quite different from people in urban areas.

A number of studies describe the problems faced by rural microfinance institutions (MFIs), which are also problems faced by all other companies venturing into rural marketing. They have long struggled with HR issues. A study by Jha and Singh (2015) of HR issues faced by MFIs found that organizations face problems of high labour turnover, low participation of women in employment, over burden of work, informal hiring, low compensation and lack of training and development facilities. Lombe et al. (2012) found that marginalized women, when they become part of an SHG felt empowered and acquired new energy to face their poor situation in society (see Mini Case Study 11.1).

Selvaraj (2012) writes that most of the essentials of HR functions in MFIs are being carried out on an ad hoc basis. Due to lack of standard people policies in the microfinance sector, companies have to follow practices and solve problems as they arise. HR managers in rural areas proceed without manpower planning, and therefore must deal with high employee turnover, lack of second line leadership, lower remuneration and other facilities to employees, lack of a system of rewards and recognition and inadequate organizational system for capacity building. There are also conflicts of orientation and values—companies face difficulties in combining professionalism with a laid back rural lifestyle.

A report on managerial and operational problems of MFIs by IRMA (2006) shows that getting or attracting professionals to augment the HR is a major challenge of the MFIs. A survey report of HR challenges in social enterprises by Intellecap (2012) also found that recruiting qualified staff was the biggest challenge. Not only is there a dearth of qualified professionals who can work as agents, but hiring them is also usually unaffordable. Even if the MFIs are able to attract some professionals or get the existing staff trained, there is the problem of high turnover of staff. Many MFIs have found it frustrating to lose the professionals and trained staff especially after making serious efforts to recruit and train them.

We can sum up the problems of human resources in rural areas as follows:

1. **Availability:** Recruiting qualified staff is the biggest human resource challenge because educated people usually prefer to migrate to urban areas. There is usually a shortage of willing and qualified people to work in rural areas.
2. **Socially committed:** Since rural marketing often has a social objective, companies seek people who wish to serve the company's social mission. They want sincere and committed people but finding such people is often difficult.
3. **High attrition:** Hiring full time on-roll people in rural areas is expensive, so companies often hire part-time workers on commission basis. Such people may not continue for long with the company. They look for alternate employment especially during the off season when earnings are reduced.
4. **Financial viability:** Volume of business in rural areas is not large enough to sustain salaries. So hiring full-time workers is not financially viable.
5. **Low participation of women:** Most of the microfinance clients are women, so are members of the SHGs with which companies must work. Yet, companies have few women in their sales force.
6. **Over burden of work:** Rural salespeople must do a variety of tasks apart from selling, as explained in this chapter. Moreover, travelling and staying facilities are also not as good as in urban areas. This results in over burden of work of the rural workers.
7. **Informal hiring:** Much of the hiring in villages is informal. Company managers often lack the skills to work with a large number of informal workers who are not full-time employees.
8. **Low compensation:** Compensation is often used as a retaining tool by HR managers. However, in rural areas high salaries are not viable. This creates a hurdle in retaining talent.
9. **Lack of training and development:** A rural sales force has to be trained but most companies lack training and development facilities in rural areas.

10. **Promotion and career paths:** Another hurdle is that there are less promotion opportunities for rural salespeople. This again results in high attrition.
11. **Lack of professionalism:** Reconciling a professional sales approach with rural life-styles is another problem faced by companies. Time-bound targets, for example, often do not work as transport and other facilities are unreliable.
12. **Long gestation:** We have seen that rural sales depend on building relationships and moulding opinions. It is thus a long process with a long gestation period. Many companies will find this situation quite unprofitable.

Doing business in rural areas thus comes with its own set of problems. Educated people leave villages to work in urban areas, so organizations struggle with finding and attracting educated, willing and committed salespeople. Companies need good communicators and relationship builders with a commitment to stay for the long term. Voluntary organizations initiating social causes get over this problem by working with people with very high commitment levels. For companies to create such a committed workforce in rural areas, a paradigm shift in approach is required, which has been described in the next section.

A PARADIGM SHIFT TO SERVE RURAL MARKETS

We have seen that the business environment in rural India is completely different from the the urban environment that businesses are accustomed to. The usual tools and techniques of human resource management are unlikely to find success here. Managing people in such areas calls for a paradigm shift both in thinking and approach. Managers trained in managing educated people will have to change their entrenched habits and procedures, since in rural areas they have to work with a completely different set of people who do not have the requirements or motivations of city-bred people working in office conditions. The methods and rigidities of human resource procedures have to be discarded, which is often quite difficult for organizations.

The foremost requirement in rural sales management is changing the company's own thinking and approach. Whereas the business model in urban areas is to meet sales targets and make profits, in rural areas long term sustainability can be achieved only by establishing a social business. We have seen in a large number of cases that companies that have modified their urban-oriented approach have found acceptability in rural areas. This calls for a complete change in the nature and approach of doing business.

That is to say, the very orientation of the top management and the HR function must change—from an administrative role to a more proactive one in establishing the company in rural minds. Employees who are committed to rural sales and willing to give their best are at the heart of organizational success. That is why managing and developing people becomes a crucial element in rural marketing. It is time for HR managers to make a transition from mere 'personnel' to actual Human Resource Management as it should be.

The change in thinking should be reflected in the company's approach and requires skills of managers that are rarely taught in business schools. We have identified four pillars of rural sales management that take into account the paradigm shift in a company's business model (Figure 11.1). These are explained as follows:

- **Putting villagers' interests before profits:** Numerous cases cited in this book show that companies that have succeeded in rural areas are the ones who have put people's interests above profits. The huge investments in IT made by ITC or the tremendous

FIGURE 11.1

The approach to rural sales management calls for a paradigm shift in thinking and approach.

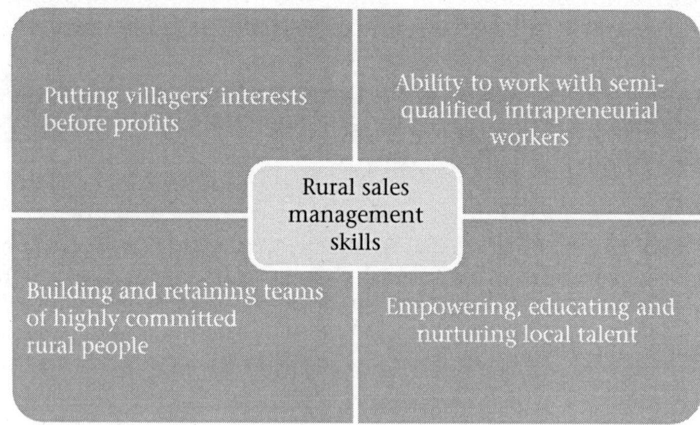

effort in training local people to become HUL's agents in villages have combined villagers' interests with long-term profitability. The approach of companies has to change towards keeping local interests above other objectives.

- **Ability to work with semi-qualified, intrapreneurial partners:** Since hiring full-time salesmen in rural areas may not be economically feasible because of low volumes, companies have to learn to work with a very large number of part-time, independent-minded workers who work with little or no supervision. Such people may have little or no educational qualifications, so training them becomes essential. The company has to give up control to some extent while working with such people. Even dealers in villages have to be trained in business methods (see Opening Case on Coca-Cola).
- **Building and retaining teams of highly committed rural people:** Interventions in public health in villages have shown that sales, accounts, supplies and logistics are all managed by highly committed people. The task therefore is to find and nurture such people. They may work on commission basis but their interest will only be sustained if the company provides some social security benefits or support in times of lean sales. This is something quite new for most companies to understand and implement.
- **Empowering, educating and nurturing local talent:** Going beyond commercial interests, companies have to be committed to training, hand holding and support at all times. They have to institute programmes to listen to them and solve their problems. Extension activities in communities help in raising stature of the local representative (Photo 11.2).

Cappelli (2015) has put forth five steps through which the HR function can change, which we have modified for rural marketing:

1. **Set the agenda:** Top management has to set the agenda for rural marketing so that it is an integral part of every department. HR managers have to be re-trained in rural areas and must demonstrate that they can identify and deliver on issues that matter to the business.

PHOTO 11.2
A PR group organized by a hospital in rural Haryana. The group is preparing a song to educate people about health and family planning issues.

Source: Photograph by Dinesh Kumar.

2. **Focus on rural issues:** HR should be able to discover rural issues and recruit committed salespeople who can solve local problems, which in turn will help sales and meeting company objectives. That is, HR has to play a much more proactive function than simple administration.
3. **Acquire business knowledge:** HR managers must acquire knowledge about the business—analytics, needs and motivations of rural folk. For example, knowhow about how and where to recruit rural workers is beyond the knowledge of many HR managers, so they require training for such tasks. The sales and the HR managers must be on the same page as far as achieving rural penetration is concerned.
4. **Highlight financial benefits:** HR must demonstrate financial benefits arising out of managing the rural sales force. In that sense, it has to be integrated with the sales function.
5. **Think long term:** Rural interventions yield results in the long term. HR managers must devise methods to measure long-term impact rather than evaluating sales performances on short-term target achievement measures.

This shows a paradigm shift in managerial thinking. Functional silos in companies of sales, service, delivery and training have to be broken and one integrated approach has to be developed. Technology helps to integrate these functions so that both managers and field workers can access and use information for efficient functioning of marketing supply chains. An understanding of the integral nature of work helps in resolving sales management issues and challenges that arise in rural areas.

RESOLVING RURAL SALES MANAGEMENT ISSUES

To achieve the paradigm shift described in the previous section, firms have to overcome several challenges in their approach and working, which are described as follows:

- **Managers must be trained in rural areas:** For successful rural marketing initiatives, managers must have a rural orientation. Rural sales can hardly be managed by urban salespeople who visit small towns and villages occasionally. Managers often have to live in villages for extended periods to understand the local conditions and requirements. They have to understand rural salespeople and the conditions in which they work (see next section). A physical presence of company managers also enhances the status of the local workers and serves as a motivating tool. Serving villages from nearby towns will not only result in disconnect with markets but also create supply chain bottlenecks.
- **Recruiting people:** We have seen that for rural sales, companies often look for people who are 'intrapreneurs,' or grass root entrepreneurs. Successful strategies like Tata Sky hiring local repairmen, HUL training women as *Shakti Ammas*, ITC's *Sanchalaks* for its e-choupals, Essilor's rural push or Novartis Arogya Parivar (see Closing Case) call for hiring and training local but committed workers. Recruiting such people is difficult and requires direct dealing with SHGs in villages and panchayats. Non-availability of educated and trained staff means that companies must develop skills among local workers.
- **Train and encourage women employees:** An important finding in studies about the rural workforce shows that employment of women in MFIs is very low even though most of their customers are women. This problem is faced by medicine and consumer goods companies too. Though women suffer from social and cultural limitations, companies must find ways of incorporate more women into their rural workforce. Nurturing and working with SHGs (see Mini Case Study 11.1) helps in reaching out to women, but to do so company managers also need to be women so that they are able to connect properly with rural workers.
- **Salaries:** A way has to be found to keep people from moving away, which calls for innovative compensation structures. Gradual enhancement of responsibilities and remuneration will help in retaining local salespeople. Compensation schemes must include insurance and social security for contractual workers. Companies have to offer innovative compensation packages so that interest of salespeople is sustained, while at the same time keeping an eye on financial viability. Cost reductions can be achieved by adopting local means; for instance, sending goods in a local bus or on a motorcycle helps reduce logistics cost.
- **Break up silos:** Companies need to break up departmental silos for rural marketing. None of the departments can function in isolation of each other because for the consumer the company is one. If, for instance, a company is unable to send its engineer to service one machine in a village, or fails to refund even a single customer, the entire village will be lost to future marketing efforts.

Mini Case Study 11.1

Self-help Groups (SHGs)

To recruit workers and to help spread a positive word in villages, companies often have to work through SHGs. SHGs are usually formed by voluntary groups of mostly 10–20 women who come together to initially start an internal savings and credit scheme. Individual members can take out a loan from the group's total savings collected which is returned in instalments. Peer pressure ensures that loans are returned. After some time, the SHG opens a bank account for safe deposit of money and to obtain bank credit.

Most SHGs are initiated by NGOs, companies such as Bandhan or the Grameen Bank, or a government body. An outside agency helps it become a catalyst in bringing together village women. It also becomes instrumental in obtaining access to a nearby bank where the group savings can be parked. Later, the groups are guided to find ways of increasing their standards of living, providing education, linking up with government programmes and to become producer groups. This helps the villagers to gain access to consumer goods as well.

SHGs are also instrumental in providing education and regular training in skills development, book-keeping, children's health and nutrition, and ultimately help to accomplish women empowerment. They signify a break with the dominant cultural norms regarding the role of women in society. Sometimes women report that even leaving the house to attend an SHG meeting in itself is a brave act, going against stringent cultural norms of rural families.

Some of the success stories of SHGs are that of SEWA, Jaipur Rugs, Lijjat Papad and Grameen Bank among others. According to its website, SEWA is an organization of poor, self-employed women workers, registered as a trade union in 1972. These are women who earn a living through their own labour or small businesses. They are the unprotected labour force of our country, and do not obtain regular salaried employment with welfare benefits like workers in the organized sector. Ela Bhatt became a trendsetter of sorts, when she founded a trade union of poor, unorganized self-employed women who work as vendors, hawkers, head-loaders and labourers. SEWA today has diversified to organic farming projects, recycled paper products, ICT skill-training centres for rural self-employed women and Gyan Vigyan resource centres for telemedicine and tele-agriculture queries of women, thereby changing lives of women in a big way. 'The main objective to organize women's own union was to make workers and producers owners and managers of their own trade, they improve their bargaining power through collective strength and bridge linkages with the mainstream market,' says the SEWA Annual Report for 2015.

Shri Mahila Griha Udyog Lijjat Papad is a women's organization manufacturing various products from Lijjat Papad, Appalam, Masala, Gehu Atta, Chapati, SASA Detergent Powder, SASA Detergent Cake (*Tikia*) and SASA Liquid Detergent.

JRF was founded in 2004 by Nand Kishore Chaudhary under the Rajasthan Public Trust Act. JRF reaches out to remote rural areas and establishes bonds with the village communities, enabling them to start weaving not just rugs but also improve their own lives. It exports rugs and carpets to the US and Britain among other countries. It works with weavers in villages in Rajasthan, Gujarat, Bihar, Uttar Pradesh and Jharkhand, offering them the option of making carpets as an attractive means of livelihood. It identifies BPL communities and employs unskilled, uneducated rural women, training them, giving them raw materials and buys back their produce.

Dr Muhammad Yunus of Bangladesh won the Nobel Prize for his work on microcredit and organizing SHGs. The Grameen Bank, which he founded, gave a new impetus to the philosophy of organizing the poorest of the poor into SHGs. His focus was on the savings and nurturing abilities of women.

The SHGs work primarily on the principle of empowering women. The concept has been adopted in India too and was introduced by NABARD in 1985. The objective was socio-economic-cultural betterment of rural women through 'self-actualization and self-initiative'. Microfinance SHGs promote lending finance and financial inclusion; they eliminate the need for collateral, and more important, they do away with exploitation by moneylenders.

SHGs today play a vital and effective role in removing poverty in rural India. Many rural people, especially women, engage in savings and credit and other SHG activities, such as income generation, natural resource management, literacy, childcare and nutrition and so on.

The authors visited the Swan River Integrated Watershed Management Project in Una, Himachal Pradesh, in which women were organized into SHGs and created their own thrift groups. The HP state forest department is the nodal agency for this project. The Swan Women Federation is a registered organization since March 2014, though it has been operational since 2009. These women form the largest rural collective of women in Himachal Pradesh. The federation was formed with the belief that women play a key role in transforming communities in sustainable ways.

PHOTO 11.3

A meeting of an SHG at a village in district Una, Himachal Pradesh.

Source: Photograph by Dinesh Kumar.

The women have been mentored to form SHGs to undertake a gamut of activities, all related to rural empowerment, with women as key agents. At present, there are about 450 SHGs, covering 50 panchayats of district Una, working with a formal organizational set-up. Each SHG, comprising 10 to

15 members, has three elected group leaders—president, secretary and treasurer. We talked to one such group and found that each member contributed ₹100 each for 2 months. The amount thus collected was used for inter-loaning by members for family needs. The money was loaned at 2 per cent interest. Later, a saving bank account was opened to put this money. Micro-loans are given out from this account to members in need. We were told that there has never been any incident of defaulting of paying back the loan or of monthly membership fees. Now they are selling spices and village produce to nearby towns.

Companies have to either start SHGs from a scratch or work with existing ones for better penetration in rural markets. Project Shakti (see Chapter 6) is one such example of how companies can work with SHGs to identify women and to provide credit to start a small distribution business. The rural women educate their neighbours and fellow villagers about basic hygiene and sell HUL products as well. The company worked through SHGs and local communities to identify such women. To work with SHGs, companies must have a presence in the villages, and identify and train women who are willing to work as distributors and salespersons.

Such groups have trained members who can serve as distributors. They can serve as nodal agencies for distribution to villages, and women can even take up the task of selling products, as in the case of Project Shakti, thereby enhancing their incomes.

Do companies have the capability to work with SHGs across the country?

Sources for this Case Study:

Web Resources

Jaipur Rugs website: http://www.jaipurrugsco.com/

SEWA website: www.sewa.org

Shri Mahila Griha Udyog website: http://www.lijjat.com/

- **Attrition:** While compensation schemes and social benefits can help in reducing attrition, HR policies too have to be changed to address this problem. Social recognition and increase in stature can serve as motivators, and companies need to devise schemes that enhance the local workers' prestige. Regular communication and commitment to social principles will often help achieve this. Many professionals use MFIs as launching pad for furthering their career. At times even remoteness and backwardness of the area of operation have resulted in high staff turnover. These must be addressed by the HR or sales managers.
- **Training:** Regular on-the-job training, skill development and exposure to best practices is required in rural areas. HR managers must go beyond their brief and help to increase the business of the agent and thereby increase their commissions. Further, performance evaluation has to be oriented not only towards business generated, but also towards groundwork such as demonstrations and relationship-building activities. HR managers also need to develop local trainers over time so that the cost of sending trainers from cities can be avoided.

Urban sales are divided into various distinct functions. Mostly, sales, service, promotion, and HR are distinct entities. Such a system works when volumes are very large and the expenses on each function are justified. But in rural areas this system does not work. It is the rural salesman who must do all the functions required in the village. It is therefore important to understand the mindset of the rural salesperson, which is described in the next section.

FIGURE 11.2
The various functions performed by a rural salesperson.

Functions Performed by a Rural Salesperson		
Line functions: Sales, payments, orders, material control, service, stakeholder relationships, promotions	Staff functions: Warehouse and supply, depot assistance, training	Advisory functions: Market research, forecasts, product and usage feedback, market information

THE RURAL SALESPERSON

In this section, we try to understand the rural salesperson. As mentioned earlier, the rural salesperson is a multifaceted figure. He performs various functions that are not strictly part of sales. Understanding the rural salesperson and his role has direct impact on the type of people that a company should recruit, as well as on the training and administration methods. These functions are shown in Figure 11.2 and have been described in this section.

Rural sales functions can be classified into three categories: line, staff and advisory. *Line functions* are those that help directly in sales, while *staff functions* consist of functions that assist in sales indirectly. Apart from these, since the salesman visits villages directly, he is the main person who has first-hand knowledge of rural markets and the rural consumer. He is a repository of information that the company can use, so he fulfils an *advisory role* both for the company as well as to the customer. These functions are described as follows:

Line Functions

Line functions are those that help directly in achieving sales. In rural markets, sales is achieved not merely by meeting customers and convincing them as in the case of urban markets, but by doing a host of other activities. The salesman must provide service as well as maintain relations with dealers and opinion leaders. He must be an information provider and trainer, manage promotions and payments, and be a change agent, introducing new products to villages. These functions are described as follows and summarized in Figure 11.3.

- **Sales and service:** Sales is helped in rural areas through dealers and opinion leaders. Regular visits are required for this. However, the sales and service functions, which are usually separated, have to be performed by the same person. Some companies use local repairmen and agents, as in the case of Tata Sky (see Mini Case Study 4.3), and relations have to be maintained with these people too. The salesman also collects payments where banking channels do not exist.

FIGURE 11.3

The rural salesperson must carry out a host of activities to accomplish sales.

- **Relationship manager:** Since the rural salesman is the only person from the company who visits villages regularly, he must meet all the people who matter—dealers, opinion leaders, consumers, publicity agents and so on. He must maintain relations with all of them.
- **Information provider and trainer:** The rural salesman is the main person who provides information to dealers and consumers. Many times he has to train them as well and provide demonstrations. If companies do not have rural outreach programmes, as in the case of Coca-Cola (see Opening Case), the salesman has to educate dealers about modern retailing, storing and accounting practices.
- **Promotion manager:** Village retailers are too small scale to worry about promotions and often fail to pass on company promotional schemes to consumers. The salesman ensures proper storage and display of goods and promotion materials, and also that schemes and offers are passed on (see Photo 11.4).
- **Payment and credit manager:** Rural salesmen perform another role, that of keeping track of payments and credit offered to local dealers. Often these dealers are small, so that means keeping track of a number of small retailers and wholesalers in the area.
- **Change agent:** A salesperson introduces new products in villages and influences the lifestyles of people. He tries to change consumption habits. In this sense, he brings change to rural lifestyles and acts as a change agent.

Photo 11.4

A salesman ensures visibility of goods and sticks posters in village shops apart from sales.

Source: Photograph by Dinesh Kumar.

Staff Functions

Staff functions help indirectly in rural sales. These are ensuring supplies to dealers, keeping track of warehousing and inventories, depot assistance and training and logistics. In urban areas, specialists are hired for each of these functions, but in rural areas the salesperson has to do it all. These functions are described as follows:

- **Warehouse and inventories:** To keep the rural dealers and retailers well supplied, the salesman has to work in close coordination with the depot of the company in the nearby town or city. Or, he must coordinate with the city wholesaler to ensure regular supplies to the village. He must keep track of inventories at different points in the supply chain.
- **Depot assistance:** Rural salesmen also provide depot assistance to the depot manager or C&F agent in maintaining stocks, accounts, transport, and so on. If goods are small, as in the case of medicines or spare parts, the salesman himself carries them from the depot/

PHOTO 11.5

Salesmen must visit small village shops such as these, collect orders and deliver goods and must conduct a host of staff functions.

Source: Photograph by Dinesh Kumar.

wholesaler and delivers them to the village retailer. Very often salesmen are attached to company depots for reporting and for ensuring supplies where they are needed.

- **Training:** If the product is new to the village, the salesman must show how it is used. This calls for training and showing demos to customers, dealers and retailers.
- **Logistics supervisor:** Getting goods to villages is difficult, and since there are many uncertainties, dealers often do not know when goods would be arriving. The rural salesman often has to arrange for transportation or ensure that the wholesaler comes to collect goods from the depot on his weekly round to the city (see Photo 11.5).
- **Retailer support:** One important staff function for the rural salesperson is that of providing knowhow and support to retailers. While some companies such as Dabur and Coca-Cola have dealer training programmes, for others it is just the salesperson who has to do this. Retailers are educated on modern display and retail methods, business skills, access to loans and financial services, use of technology, networking and sales support. Since sending a trainer from a city is quite expensive, the salesperson himself provides this support after initially learning it from the trainers.

Advisory Functions

Since the salesman visits villages regularly, he has direct knowledge of the people, customs and usage of products. He is therefore a repository of information about rural markets. At the same time, he is the representative of the company he works for. Thus, he is in a position to play advisory roles both to the company as well as to the dealers. The advisory functions are summed up as follows:

- **Market researcher:** We have mentioned in Chapter 5 that ethnographic research is most useful in rural areas. The rural salesman, by the nature of his work, can observe people as they live and can gain insights into rural habits. He becomes a de facto researcher who can provide valuable information to the company.
- **Sales forecasts:** The salesman is in touch with market conditions and has a complete knowledge about how products are moving off the retailers' shelves. He can assess the demand based on his knowledge. He can thus help in sales forecasts of the company in the area.
- **Product and usage feedback:** One of the most valuable insights that a salesman can provide to the company is about how people are buying and using the products. He can suggest product modifications based on this through which the company can improve its rural offerings.
- **Market information:** The rural salesman has complete information about the rural marketing environment. These are important inputs through which a company can modify its activities.
- **Competitor activity:** Companies have no idea about knowing competitor activity in rural areas. The salesman, however, knows the products and promotional schemes offered by them because he is in the field. Companies can thus get valuable information about competitors from their own salesmen.

The village salesperson does these and other valuable activities. It is up to the companies to manage their rural sales force well to get make its best use. The next section describes how rural sales force must be managed.

Kapur et al. (2014) say that companies have to do many tasks in rural markets, which are as follows:

- **Build relationships with channel partners:** One important skill that the rural salesman should have is to build relationships with customers, dealers and influencers. This task is quite different than that of an urban salesman, where the selling is likely to be more transactional. Rural salesmen must develop skills to locate and communicate with partners, retain them and keep them motivated. For example, Coca-Cola builds relationships by increasing its partners' skills through its Parivartan programme (see Opening Case).
- **Personal Bonds and Mutual Trust:** We have mentioned earlier in the book that the purchase decision among rural residents is based on word-of-mouth recommendations, personal bonds and mutual trust. The local salesperson must have capabilities to build such bonds and trust.
- **Engaging influencers:** Rural salesmen must have the ability to identify and gain the trust of influencers in a village. Teachers, doctors and health care professionals and panchayat leaders can become very helpful in spreading marketing messages. The rural salesman must have the skills to build strong and lasting relations with influencers.
- **Retaining customers:** Another skill that rural salesmen should have is to retain customers by providing reliable and cost-effective after-sales service. In urban areas, for instance, sales is done by a set of people while service is entrusted to a different set of people. This is not possible in rural areas, service outlets can only be made in a nearby town or city. Further, because rural markets rely on strong word-of-mouth

recommendations, if a customer faces a difficulty with a product after the sales, failure of servicing it will result in the reputation of the salesman being spoiled.

Having understood the roles and responsibilities of the rural salesman, we can now consider how such people must be managed and what should be the approach of the company. For this, companies have to modify their sales organizations; a hierarchal structure in unlikely to work for rural areas. Instead, a simple, flat structure should be aimed at.

RURAL SALES ORGANIZATION

The primary activities of sales force management in the rural context consist of having a sales organization geared to serve villages, accompanied by the HR functions of recruitment, compensation, training, supervision, evaluation and career growth. Unfortunately, most companies use the centralized HR located in their head office to manage rural activities. This does not quite work. Rural sales management requires a completely different approach, one that starts firmly from the villages. This section covers the design of the rural sales organization and the skills and orientation that must be developed in companies.

For companies that serve rural markets from their existing urban channels, the sales organization stops at the level of the city wholesaler and sometimes at the retailer in a town. From there, the dealers use their own sales force to supply goods to villages. The disadvantage in this structure is that goods are supplied only to villages that the wholesaler finds easy to cover, so penetration suffers. To have deep penetration in villages, a company must have a separate organization that can cater to village clusters through its salesmen.

A report by Bain and Company (Ledingham et al. 2013) says that achieving growth targets profitably requires a repeatable, high-return model for selling solutions. This calls for judicious investing in sales resources. A differentiated capability to deploy selling resources helps. The report found that companies which had built capabilities around market opportunities performed better than those that had not. It further says that overhauling sales models is greatly beneficial. Large, cumbersome sales organizations not only erode margins, but also miss the biggest opportunities.

It is therefore important that there are not too many layers of managers but the structure should have more salesmen. This can be achieved by designing a flat rural sales organization as far as possible.

One such structure is shown in Figure 11.4. In the figure, a company has sales managers for each district. Two of them have been shown. In each district, there is one rural sales hub which may consist of a depot. Under the depot there are several salesmen serving different rural clusters as identified by the company. There are no unnecessary levels of hierarchy.

The company can use two approaches in designing its sales organization: the *top-down* approach or the *bottom-up* approach.

- **Top-down approach:** A top-down approach consists of determining the sales volumes expected from each area, then establishing targets for each district and then going down to each village cluster. In this approach, the company sets the target for each district, which is broken down to the target of the sales depot. It then distributes the targets to salespeople to cover village clusters and to cover all areas.
- **Bottom-up approach:** A bottom-up approach works in the opposite direction. It consists of estimating sales potential in each village, then going up to village clusters to area to district, accumulating the figures as we go up. This approach depends on

sales estimates of salesmen of their clusters, which are accumulated for the rural hub and thereby for the whole district. In this way, one arrives at the organizational sales targets. This method is usually much more accurate than the top-down approach as it gets inputs from the ground.

FIGURE 11.4
An example of a rural sales organization.

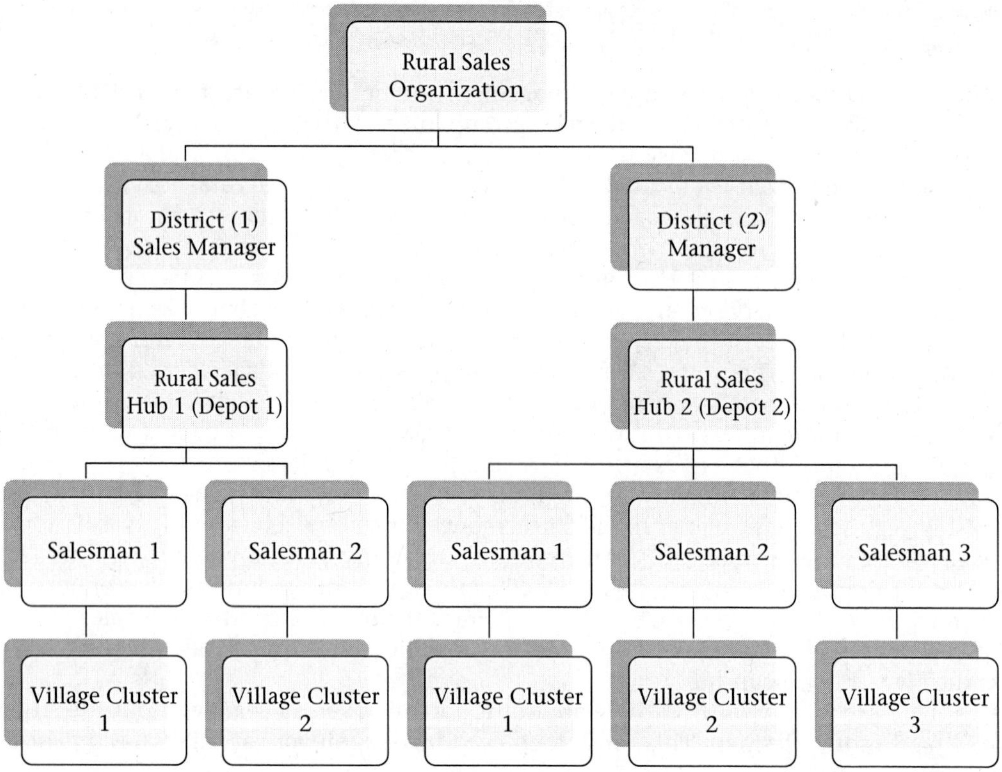

The important thing here is to identify village clusters so that companies can build depots that can easily serve these clusters. If volumes are not large, smaller sub-depots can be created that are easier for local salespeople to visit and restock. Each depot or sub-depot must serve a village cluster. It should be at a convenient location so that village distributors can easily visit and replenish stocks. Identifying clusters is discussed in the next section.

IDENTIFYING RURAL CLUSTERS

Sales management is aided if rural clusters are identified. Clusters consist of groups of villages that can be covered by a salesman or a sales office. They can either be manufacturing hubs, as in Taobao villages of China, or simply areas that are close together for designing a sales route plan.

Village clusters can be identified by various methods. In China, some 20 to 30 villages were grouped and called Town and Village Enterprises (TVEs). The TVEs manufacture goods for companies like Alibaba (see Chapter 9). For example, a food processing company will organize villages into TVEs, procure the raw material from the village and process it there. This eliminates transportation costs. The Chinese government encouraged these rural hubs in a big way. The result has been development of a large number of rural hubs in China.

In India, the basis of clustering can be proximity, only since there are few rural business hubs in the country. Clusters can be identified on the basis of geography, on the main agricultural crop and sometimes on the basis of livelihoods. Another way is to identify villages along the main roads, but this ignores those villages that are located deep in the hinterland. Such villages can serve as rural hubs from where a number of interior villages can be covered in one go. Villages along an irrigation source, like a canal, can also serve as rural hubs.

Sales Route Plan

One of the objectives of identifying clusters is to reduce travel time of salespeople while ensuring coverage of all villages. Ideally, clusters should be such that covering villages is facilitated while spending as little time in travelling as possible. Several methods have been suggested such as a circular route and a clover leaf route (Figure 11.5), which reduce travel time and cost of travelling for salespeople.

In the first method, the route plan is conceptualized in the form of a circle, with several villages lying on its circumference. A salesperson goes along the route and returns to his home. If distances are large and local dealers exist, the route is made of 22–25 days, which gives a rest of 5–8 days at home. The disadvantage is that each market gets covered only once a month. If distances are small or frequent coverage is required, then the circle consists of five stops, giving the salesperson two days at home. In this case, markets are covered once a week. The route can be modified by placing the salesman in the centre from where he/she can cover markets in the manner of spokes in a wheel. In this case, the prospect of night stay at the markets is eliminated.

FIGURE 11.5

Sales route plans: Circular and clover leaf.

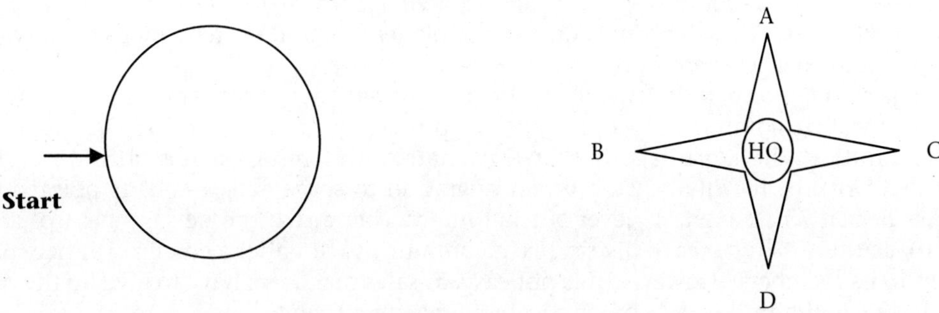

In the second method, the route is conceptualized as a clover leaf. The salesperson is placed in the centre. He or she makes a tour of five days along each leaf, A, B, C and D, and returns for two days' rest at home. In this method also, markets are covered once a month unless the clover leaves are designed for a weekly tour.

The method a company uses depends on its objectives, which can be: (1) minimizing travel time and cost, (2) giving adequate rest and family time to the salesperson, or (3) increasing frequency of coverage of markets.

REVAMPING HR AND SALES MANAGEMENT

It should be clear from the discussion in the previous sections that companies have to change their approach radically in order to serve rural markets. More so, the HR function, which has to break out of its traditional ways of operating and to get more in tune with villages. All functions, from recruitment to motivation, have to go through radical surgery.

Recruitment

While recruiting for rural marketing, companies are likely to face a number of challenges. For one, urban-trained HR managers tend to think in terms of tests and other hurdles over which candidates must jump to get recruited. They think in terms of minimum qualifications and efficiency parameters. However, these do not work in rural markets for the simple reason that qualified candidates are often not available. Second, the skills and qualifications of candidates are fluid, in the sense that a committed candidate with knowledge of local cultures may be more successful than a person who may have higher educational qualifications. Urban recruiting of salespeople is done through advertisements, consultants, or campus recruitment. HR managers habituated to these methods will almost certainly find that for rural recruitment these methods are of little use. Moreover, most rural people who acquire higher education do not want to live in villages and are hence difficult to find. Village recruitment is often done through village communities and SHGs.

Companies have to, therefore, tap into those people who have chosen to stay behind and serve their communities. They may not be qualified or even ideal for sales jobs. The challenge is to find and reach such people. Recruiting from towns and cities and sending people to work in villages is self-defeating, since the task is to get people who are willing to work in villages. Companies have to find local repairmen, teachers or the educated unemployed who can serve as their representatives. For example, a village ice cream vendor (Photo 11.6) could well be used to sell FMCG products during the off season, and thereby increase his earnings while providing deep penetration in villages.

Such a strategy was used effectively by Hindustan Latex (see Mini Case Study 11.2). However, finding committed people calls for physically going to the villages and talking to communities. The advantage is that this strategy will result in less attrition and more motivated workers. It will also stop urban migration to some extent and, as pointed out by Schumacher (1973), the whole level of rural life can be raised, the development of an agro-industrial culture, 'so that each district, each community, can offer a colourful variety of occupations to its members.' However, it is not easy, as sales managers have to give up the comfort of their offices and find people by physically identifying them.

PHOTO 11.6

A salesman of ice cream in a village presses his hooter to attract children.
Can companies work with such people for selling their products?

Source: Photograph by Dinesh Kumar.

Mini Case Study 11.2

Hindustan Latex: Spread of Family Planning Products in Villages

Hindustan Latex Family Planning Promotion Trust (HLFPPT) implemented a project aimed at strengthening the contraceptive social marketing in the rural areas of three states: Bihar, Jharkhand and Odisha. It included the marketing of Saheli, the world's first and only oral non-steroidal contraceptive pill with zero side effects. The pill was developed by Central Drugs Research Institute and was commercialized by Hindustan Latex in 1991. To increase the use of contraceptives in rural areas, it focused on accessibility, affordability and motivation.

A major innovation of the programme was that community based distribution was undertaken through unemployed youth in villages. Local non-conventional media was used to make people adopt modern spacing methods among the target population.

The project used rural distributors and village-level vendors by employing unemployed people from the local communities along with medical practitioners. In addition, the project used block-level service providers to initiate interpersonal communication on contraception and spacing methods.

To accomplish the mission, training of project managers, district project coordinators and other middle-level functionaries was undertaken. Communication was done through folk programmes (Daskathia, Pala, Nacha), video vans and street theatre. The video vans were used separately for males and females to get over social taboos. Such strategies were useful in reducing people's hesitation and also helped in improving the image of the grassroot level staff. The vendors were given special training to enhance community participation through a range of activities.

Singh et al. (2005) examined the effectiveness of contraceptive distribution system adopted by HLFPPT and its impact in enhancing contraceptive prevalence rates. It found that in each of the three states, people's participation in promotional activities of the project was quite satisfactory. There was a gradual increase in the number of couples purchasing the products available under the CBSM project.

The project has been a success in rural areas. Effective communication and promotional strategies, with trained and educated workers, could get over the cultural sensitivities of the population and maintain service delivery through a strong community based distribution network. Knowledge of Mala-D and Saheli pills was found to be almost universal. The brand name Saheli—a female friend—helped in the positioning of the product among communities. The results show that the use of contraception increased in all the districts. Exposure to the social marketing programme implemented by HLFPPT has been universal irrespective of the socio-economic background of the respondents. Participation of women in Mahila Mandal meetings was found to be preferred by women.

Hindustan Latex has now launched the contraceptive across various e-commerce portals for better availability, reports *The Hindu Business Line* (2013).

Comment on the effectiveness of this model. Can it be used in other industries? How?

Sources for this Case Study:

Web Resource

Hindustan Latex Ltd website: http://www.lifecarehll.com/

Other Source

Singh, S.K., H. Lhungdim and S. Niranjan. 2005. *Evaluation of Social Marketing of Contraceptives Undertaken by HLFPPT in Some Selected Districts of Bihar, Jharkhand and Orissa*. Mumbai: International Institute for Population Sciences.

The Hindu Business Line. 2013. "Saheli Oral Contraceptive Sales Go Online." 11 March.

Compensation

The next step is to devise compensation packages for rural areas. It is accepted today that a fixed salary structure does not motivate village workers in the long run. These workers must work without supervision and should be self-motivated. Commissions help to link compensation with output. However, a commission-only compensation structure ignores two things. First, that the earnings will not be stable and almost nil during the off-season. Salespersons will hence look for alternate employment when work is less and leave the company. Second, since commissions focus on quantity over quality, it may lead to pressure sales, which will harm the company in the long run.

Holmström (1999) had shown that a person's concern for a future career influences his or her incentives to put in effort for a job. That is, a person's productive performance is based on an 'implicit contract' that links today's performance to future wages. This shows that if a person does not see his future earnings rise, his performance will be good only for the short term. Hence, apart from present compensation plan, a company must chalk out a career plan for the rural salesperson.

A fixed salary is also therefore required, which may be in the form of a retainer so that stability is maintained. The compensation plan has to be such that the earnings have to be sizeable enough to keep alive the interest in sales and service. A performance review system that takes into account profitability must be established. The compensation plan should not be merely to achieve sales in the short run; what is important is that companies design compensation packages to promote behaviours that support long-term business goals: the system should be designed to achieve specific goals, such as rural market penetration, market share, giving demos to new customers and improving dealer performance. Giving social benefits after certain years of service, like a gratuity, may help retain salespeople for longer in rural areas.

Personality and Skills

It is normally believed that salesmen should have selling skills, communication skills and presentation skills. These are described in many books on sales management. However, rural sales management is a different cup of tea. Companies looking for textbook skills normally end up having difficulties in getting the right people, and then getting them to stay.

Attitude has a major role to play in sales. The company's training has to be geared towards inculcating the right approach and attitude. Rural marketing calls for some specific traits on the part of a salesman. These are described here.

1. **Willingness to work in the rural areas:** Only those who feel happy living and working in villages can become good rural salesmen. Since rural areas lack modern amenities compared to the urban areas, few urban dwellers are willing to relocate to rural centres. The answer is to find local people who fit into the village and do not have problems locating there.
2. **Cultural knowledge:** The rural salesman must be well acquainted with the local cultural aspects. A salesman who speaks the local dialect and gels with the local culture will be a greater asset than a town dweller visiting the village for sales. That is why companies prefer to employ local people to help them achieve market penetration in villages.
3. **Salesman attitude:** The rural salesman must have patience, because building relationships and rural sales calls for a lot of time. Urban customers may fix appointments and have limited time, but that strategy in rural areas falls flat. Sales is accomplished after a great deal of conversation. Rural customers are traditional and cautious in their approach.
4. **Ability to handle several product lines:** Rural salesmen usually handle all product lines of their companies. This means that their training has to be more broad-based than their urban counterparts.
5. **Creativity:** Rural selling also involves adaptability and creativity. Making the same sales presentation in different villages and expecting the same responses would not work. The salesman must adapt to situations as and when they arise.

6. **Developmental approach:** The approach of all rural selling has to be to solve local problems and helping people even when such activities are not related to the sale directly. A company that helps make rural lives simpler has a greater chance of establishing long-term loyalty than one that merely attempts to sell.

A change in attitude and improvement in skills is achieved by training, which is discussed in the next section. This becomes important since companies may have to hire candidates who are not perfectly ideal for the job, and require training in soft skills as well as selling skills.

Training

Skills improvement and attitude changes are achieved through constant training. There is thus need for strong in-house training facilities. A product that breaks down and cannot be fixed means that a promise is broken. Kapur et al. (2014) point out that in rural communities, a faulty product which is not repaired, may permanently lose an entire village for the company, since word of mouth carries so much weight. Companies rely on different strategies to deliver service: some companies train their salesmen, while others are building dedicated service infrastructures. To reduce costs, locals are hired to furnish no-frills support in their villages.

For its part, the company must provide a transparent career growth plan for its rural agents, which will result in their long-term commitment. The growth, supervision and evaluation system must be based on the developmental approach. In the long run, a social business is likely to succeed better than a mere commercial approach. That is why a person's commitment to stay with the company becomes important. After recruiting, companies must develop and nurture local talent, which is often less-than-perfect. Selling and communication skills, along with product knowledge are imparted through on-the-job training activities. Companies have to invest in skill building through workshops or courses for rural employees. This is sometimes done with partners like NGOs. Very often, written and verbal communication skills and office processes training must be imparted so that the salesperson can send reports as required by the head office. Dealers and retailers will also have to be trained along with salespeople. For them, accounting, merchandising and inventory management skills have to be imparted as in the case of Dabur (see Mini Case Study 11.3).

Retention Strategies

Training must cover retention strategies as well, since building a team to serve villages is very difficult. For this, a company must provide a positive work environment, flexibility of hours and encouraging employees to maximize their social impact in the village. Performance must be rewarded fairly and a promotion path specified. Opportunities for personal development must be created. As a person advances, retention becomes all the more important as other companies will always be looking out for trained rural personnel. Companies have to learn to work with highly independent-minded people who can change jobs frequently and may even quit without an alternate job in hand. Social security investments can go a long way in retaining rural people.

Mini Case Study 11.3

Dabur's Push for Rural Sales

Dabur, through its initiative called Astra, provides advanced sales training for retailers. Its sales and HR managers travel across the country to educate over 2,000 distribution channel partners. Sales and distribution is taught through the audio-visual medium and through role-plays staged by professional actors at their shops.

The programme was started to achieve sales growth through modern trade and institutions, using tried and tested methods. Dabur has a distribution reach of 25 lakh retail outlets across the country. About 75 per cent of the company's sales come from rural areas. The Astra training module is imparted in five vernacular languages: Bengali, Tamil, Telugu, Malayalam and Kannada. The company also expects rise in consumer spending in the rural areas and plans to spread the initiative in the rural market. Astra hopes to bring awareness among the distributors and standardize systems. Under Astra, Dabur has categorized its sales and distribution channels into finer segments, such as key grocers, mass grocers, chemist, wholesale, small outlet and modern trade. The programme addresses specific needs of each channel such as trade activation, promotion, brand/SKU focus, merchandising and managing channel conflict. It has also reduced attrition among stockists.

Can such training programmes help in better service to rural customers and in retaining them? If yes, how?

Source for this Case Study:
Business Standard. 2008. "Dabur Uses Astra to Boost Rural Sales." 4 July.

Motivation

The rural marketing task involves travelling over large distances, tackling difficult consumers and traders, and often involves working without facilities. In such a situation, motivating employees is a big challenge.

Intellecap (2012) says that the opportunity to take on leadership roles and a belief in the company's mission are the most common motivations for joining a social enterprise. Companies must therefore offer candidates greater opportunity to move up the ladder. There is ample opportunity for employees to move up as they work in rural sales, because so many sales activities have to be performed. Employees tend to be drawn towards the idea of combining a reasonable income with the satisfaction of achieving social impact.

Motivation is achieved by simple methods in rural areas. Director of Fruit Bageecha in Kotgarh (Himachal Pradesh), Anuradha Kanwar Budhraja, found that finding workers was a problem in rural areas, so the factory had to adjust to flexible working hours for its workers, most of whom are women. Since they have to travel over large distances in areas where public transport is almost non-existent, such simple measures go a long way in finding and retaining workers. These women had never ventured far from their homes, so a trip to a nearby fair (Photo 11.7) or a shopping trip to nearby Shimla was a great motivator for them. The factory organizes such trips regularly for its workers.

Location disadvantages are overcome by training workers to take on higher responsibilities. Most companies work with junior staff that is locally hired. Sending managers and trainers who periodically travel from bigger towns and cities is not only expensive but in many cases

Photo 11.7

Women at a stall in a fair at Thanedar in Himachal Pradesh.
Such outings are a great source of motivation.

Source: Fruit Bageecha (reprinted with permission).

irrelevant in villages. Companies would do well to train local people to take over supervisory and training responsibilities, which would be cost-efficient and motivate workers as well.

Career Planning

Companies tend to hire local workers to meet their immediate objectives of achieving sales or to have a presence in a village. They find workers too, but once a salesperson is effective, he or she may well leave to sell products of another company offering higher commissions. There is thus a need to retain talent that a company recruits.

A key to retaining talent is to have a career growth path for the workers. For instance, a saleswoman in a village cannot be expected to do just sales for the rest of her life. Unfortunately, companies usually do no career planning for their rural workers. Without seeing a clear growth path, motivation and retention efforts will fail. HR managers thus need to work out clear career-planning goals for their rural recruits. Since most of them are 'intrapreneurs' as described in the case of Aparajitas (see Mini Case Study 11.4), their career paths have to be innovatively planned. While some rural workers can be promoted to become trainers or depot coordinators along with their sales activities, others can be encouraged to set up shops in their villages.

Mini Case Study 11.4

Bata Rural Sales Program

The Bata Rural Sales Program (RSP) was developed with the non-profit organization Cooperative for Assistance and Relief Everywhere (CARE) supported by the UK government, in 2005. It gives women from rural communities the opportunity to become entrepreneurs and earn a living by selling affordable footwear manufactured from Bata-owned factories in Bangladesh. To make a viable business for the Aparajitas, as the sales agents are called, they earn around 10–15 per cent commission for each pair of footwear they sell. The most popular footwear to sell in villages are the company's flip-flops.

The programme gives the added benefit of providing affordable footwear in rural communities as opposed to locally made, low quality footwear that is available there. It helps people to protect their feet in the rough terrain.

To make the footwear affordable, Bata reduces its own cost. It employs cost-saving strategies such as integrating eco-design into the shoes. For instance, artificial and costly lighting is avoided during the day as its factories use natural light as far as possible. The factory has transparent roof at its production facilities where these shoes are made.

The rural women in Bangladesh are trained by CARE as part of a project on empowering women. Named 'Aparajita' (which means 'women who never accept defeat') these women are trained to sell products in their villages and others around them from door to door, bringing global products to villages (Figure 11.6). Other multinational and domestic companies have joined the venture since, from brands such as Bata, Unilever, Danone and Grameen to the most remote of villages. This has enabled expansion of products and market coverage: Aparajitas now sell soaps, shampoos and sanitary towels to mobile phone packages and shoes. The Rural Sales Program offers a sustainable source of income, lifting thousands of women out of poverty and offering them a dignified life.

FIGURE 11.6
Bata's Aparajita programme in Bangladesh.

Source: http://batalife.com/thinking-long-term/our-programmes/ (Accessed on 18 April 2017).

To start this venture, both Bata and CARE had to overcome great social hurdles. In its case study on UK government website ("An 'Avon lady' of Bangladesh" 2012), a RSP Joytara narrates her story and says that the main problem at first was social acceptance. People did not think a woman should do selling and they thought she was selling fake products, but now she has become accepted in the community. One success has been sanitary towels, for which female customers would not ever go to the market to buy, but Joytara has increased access to these sorts of products as the women can talk freely with her. In the process, she has gained financial independence. 'People used to shun us, they might give us food but they wouldn't lend us any money if we needed it. Now I lend money to others who are more needy, and I even advise people in the community,' she says.

Can the HR function of companies really gear up to develop such programmes? Are managers trained for this sort of sales management? What are the risks of this model?

Sources for this Case Study:

Web Resources

Bata website: http://batalife.com/thinking-long-term/our-programmes/

CARE website: http://www.care.org/

Other Source

"An 'Avon lady' of Bangladesh tells her story." 2012. A Case Study available at: https://www.gov.uk/government/case-studies/an-avon-lady-of-bangladesh-tells-her-story (Accessed on 27 April 2017).

REDEFINING HR

The discussion in this chapter would make it obvious that standard HR practices do not work while managing a rural sales force. Nor can it be left to sales managers only. Thus, a complete change in the approach and training of HR managers is needed. Most companies do not have adequate HR systems that are appropriate for rural areas. For one, HR managers need to move out of the comfort of their corporate offices, since no rural management can be done remotely. HR managers must get over their usual recruitment–evaluation–training models to a creative handling of the rural recruits. Companies will initially find it difficult to work with a workforce that is flexible and independent, but can certainly harness these qualities as they go along.

Human resource challenges in rural areas are multifaceted. HR managers will have to learn to live with SHGs and the people as described in several case studies in this chapter. They have to achieve the involvement of local people in the design and planning process while working with local groups and NGOs. Rural sales management requires cooperation between sales, HR, logistics, after-sales service as well with village communities and panchayats. In the final analysis, rural marketing calls for a redefining of many roles, a paradigm shift in thinking and a complete change in the way we manage organizations.

SUMMARY

Rural sales management is the coordination of people and resources to effectively sell and distribute in villages. It involves logistics and managing people to achieve a sustainable sales volume. However, because of low volumes, the rural salesperson has to handle a variety of tasks required to achieve sales in rural areas and must act as an advisor, trainer, service provider, market researcher and relationship manager. Getting such people is not easy, and companies are likely to face problems of high attrition, lack of training capacity, ineffective recruitment policies, low participation of women in employment, over burden of work, informal hiring, low compensation and lack of training and development facilities.

Rural sales management therefore requires a paradigm shift in approach, which consists of four pillars: (a) putting villagers' interests before profits, (b) ability to work with semi-qualified, intrapreneurial workers, (c) building and retaining teams of highly committed rural people and (d) empowering, educating and nurturing local talent. Functional silos of sales, service, delivery and training in companies have to be broken and one integrated approach has to be taken. That is why the rural salesperson has to be a multifaceted figure, to perform various functions that are not strictly part of sales—line, staff and advisory. Line functions are those that help directly in achieving sales, such as sales, service, building relationships, providing information, collecting payments and providing demos and training. Staff functions help indirectly in rural sales, such as ensuring supplies, keeping track of warehousing and inventories, depot assistance, training dealers and logistics. Finally, because the salesperson has direct knowledge of markets, the sales function includes advisory functions, which involves providing information both to the company as well as to the dealers.

Companies thus require to have a distinct rural sales force management structure, which has a distinct sales organization geared to villages, performing the HR functions of recruitment, compensation, training, supervision, evaluation and career growth.

A rural sales organization is designed through two approaches: the *top-down* approach or the *bottom-up* approach. A top-down approach in rural sales management consists of determining the sales volumes expected from each area, then establishing targets for each district and then breaking it up further for each village cluster. A bottom-up approach in rural sales management is one that consists of estimating sales potential in each village, then going up to village clusters to area to district, accumulating the figures as we go up for the district and then to the country. Both the approaches call for identifying village clusters, which are groups of villages that can be serviced by individual salespeople.

A rural sales organization must also accomplish the HR functions of recruitment, compensation, personality and skills development, building attitude and soft skills, retain and motivate salespeople and work on their career planning. For this, the HR function must be redefined and geared for rural sales force management.

CONCLUSION

Many companies treat rural markets just as an extension of the urban ones. They use the same methods and approaches that they have used for years. Such thinking results from the assumption that rural markets are full of opportunities and underserved customers who will happily buy whatever is offered to them. Time and again this assumption has been proved wrong. Selling low-priced sachets in small quantities calls for different selling skills, than selling goods in bulk to urban wholesalers.

Rural sales management calls for different HR and management skills and structures. Managers inured to methods that work in head offices of companies will be at a loss in villages. Thus, all tasks of recruitment, appraisals and retention require a deep rethink. Chambers (1983) rightly mentioned that outsiders are far removed from the rural reality. 'They are attracted to and trapped in urban "cores" which generate and communicate their own sort of knowledge while rural "peripheries" are isolated and neglected,' he wrote. Urban bred managers exhibit biases that prevent them from learning from rural people: *spatial*, meaning the physical distance; *person*, meaning that they tend towards those who are better off, men rather than women; *seasonal*, that is, they avoid bad times of travel; *professional*, meaning confined to the specialization of the visitor; and *diplomatic*, or not seeking out the poor for fear of giving offence.

All these biases have to be overcome if a strategy relevant to India's villages has to be worked out and implemented.

KEY TERMS

Advisory functions: Advisory functions include providing information both to the company as well as to the dealers.

Bottom-up approach: A bottom-up approach in rural sales management consists of estimating sales potential in each village, then going up to village clusters to area to district, accumulating the figures as we go up for the district and then country.

Intrapreneurs: Grassroot entrepreneurs who agree to represent the company along with their usual work.

Line functions: Line functions are those that help directly in achieving sales.

Microfinance institutions (MFIs): MFIs provide financial services and loans to low-income clients who traditionally lack access to traditional banking and related services.

Rural sales force management: Having a distinct sales organization geared to villages, accompanied by the HR functions of recruitment, compensation, training, supervision, evaluation and career growth.

Rural sales management: The coordination of people and resources to effectively sell and distribute in villages.

Self-help groups (SHGs): SHGs are voluntary groups of mostly 10–20 women who come together for a common purpose.

Staff functions: Staff functions are those that help indirectly in rural sales, including ensuring supplies, keeping track of warehousing and inventories, depot assistance, training and logistics.

Top-down approach: A top-down approach in rural sales management consists of determining the sales volumes expected from each area, then establishing targets for each district and then going down to each village cluster.

Village clusters: Groups of villages so that they can be serviced by individual salespeople.

CONCEPT REVIEW QUESTIONS

1. Describe the problems of sales management in rural areas. How can they be resolved?
2. The approach to rural sales management calls for a paradigm shift in thinking and approach. How can this paradigm change be accomplished?
3. How can rural sales management issues be resolved by companies? Which are the most important steps?

4. Explain and discuss the functions of a rural salesperson.
5. Discuss a rural sales organization. On what basis must it be structured?
6. What are top-down and bottom-up approaches in rural sales management? Explain with examples.
7. Describe methods of developing a rural sales route plan. How will you ensure that the objectives of market coverage and travel time reduction are achieved?
8. Discuss the HR functions and how they must be modified for rural areas. Why is it necessary to do so?
9. How would you fix the salary of a salesperson? What are the different methods of setting salaries and which do you think would be the most effective?
10. Describe the essential qualities a person must have to work as a rural salesperson.

CRITICAL THINKING QUESTIONS

1. Why is it necessary for companies to have a paradigm shift in their approach to rural management? What are its elements? Why cannot traditional marketing approaches be used in rural areas?
2. Do you agree with the statement that a rural salesperson has to be a superman? Why? How is the rural salesperson's task different from that of an urban salesperson?
3. Describe how rural sales should be organized in a company. Do you agree with the structure described in this chapter? Can you suggest a better organization structure for handling rural sales?
4. Why is it necessary to change the very approach to rural management? Why can traditional approaches work in rural areas?

PROJECTS AND ASSIGNMENTS

1. Study the rural sales organizations of some companies that you have access to. Draw their organization charts. What improvements can you suggest to them?
2. Visit some villages and meet with village salespersons. Find out their motivations and problems. Suggest ways of making their lives simpler.
3. Study an SHG in a village. Describe its working and comment on its success. Do you think that companies can find distributors or salespersons by working with such groups?
4. Meet a village salesman or a health worker and list down the functions that he or she performs. Do you agree that a salesperson performs duties that are beyond the strict nature of the job? How different is urban selling from rural selling?

REFERENCES

Cappelli, Peter. 2015. "Why We Love to Hate HR...and What HR Can Do about It." *Harvard Business Review* 93 (7–8): 54–61.

Chambers, R. 1983. *Rural Development: Putting the Last First.* Essex: Longmans.

Holmström, Bengt. 1999. "Managerial Incentive Problems: A Dynamic Perspective." *Review of Economic Studies* 66(1). doi: 10.1111/1467-937X.00083

Intellecap. 2012. *Understanding Human Resource Challenges in the Indian Social Enterprise Sector*. Available at: http://intellecap.com/sites/default/files/publications/intellecap_hr_report_web_0.pdf (Accessed on 18 April 2017).

IRMA. 2006. "Managerial and Operational Problems of Microfinance Institutions in India." Report of the workshop organized by MFMI Chair in Microfinance, 29–31 March 2005, Institute of Rural Management, Anand.

Jha, J.K., and, Manjari Singh. 2015. "Human Resources and Social Challenges Faced by Microfinance in India: A Framework." *Indian Journal of Industrial Relations* 50 (3): 494–505.

Kapur, Mamta, Sanjay Dawar and Vineet R. Ahuja. 2014. "Unlocking the Wealth in Rural Markets." *Harvard Business Review*, June. Available at: https://hbr.org/2014/06/unlocking-the-wealth-in-rural-markets (Accessed on 18 April 2017).

Ledingham, D, Mark Kovac, Michael Heric and François Montaville. 2013. "Is Complexity Killing Your Sales Model?" A Report by Bain and Co., 16 January. Available at: http://www.bain.com/publications/articles/is-complexity-killing-your-sales-model.aspx

Lombe, M., C. Newransky, K. Kayser and P.M. Raj. 2012. "Exploring Barriers to Inclusion of Widowed and Abandoned Women through Microcredit Self-help Groups: The Case of Rural South India." *Journal of Sociology and Social Welfare* 39 (2): 143–62.

Schumacher, E.F. 2010. *Small Is Beautiful: Economics as if People Mattered*. New York, NY: Harper Perenniel [Originally published by Blond & Briggs, London, 1973].

Selvaraj, S.N. 2012. "Challenging Tasks of Human Resource Department in Microfinance Institutions." *Arth Prabandh: A Journal of Economics and Management* 1 (5): 41–49.

Closing Case
Novartis Arogya Parivar

Health care in most Indian villages is primitive. Qualified doctors do not wish to work in villages, so medical care is left to the people and their own devices. People mostly depend on word-of-mouth recommendations from friends and neighbours, and the advice often means turning to traditional or herbal practitioners. A large segment of the business is held by registered medical practitioners (RMPs) who provide cheap and affordable health care for the village dwellers. The RMPs do not charge consultation but give out medicines for common ailments, sometimes for just one day as people can afford small quantities only. These medicines are procured from local sources and chemists in nearby towns. Prescriptions are not common as people do not see why they should pay for consultation. Common over the counter (OTC) medicines are stocked by the local grocer or kiryana shop. That is why you will not find a chemist's shop in most villages.

Swiss pharmaceuticals giant, Novartis, wanted to change that, and to provide quality medical care in villages. It had a difficult task ahead: how to make people aware of the diseases they could suffer from, building supply channels and how to find people who could do the job.

Using ethnographic research, Novartis first learned about health care consumption in villages. It found that urban-type health care could not work in villages because of issues of affordability and lack of doctors. To succeed, any programme had to work on the existing infrastructure, however rickety it might be.

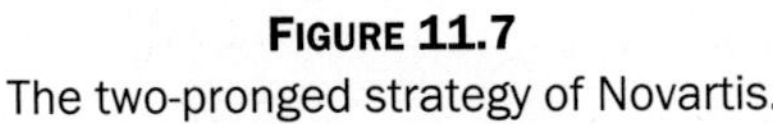

FIGURE 11.7
The two-pronged strategy of Novartis.

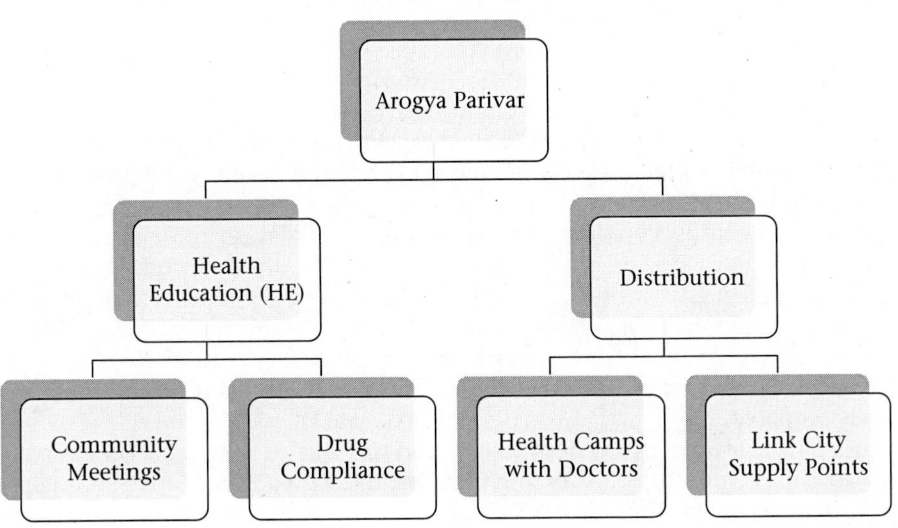

It launched its programme Arogya Parivar in 2007, to expand access to medicines, improved health infrastructure and community education in rural India. Only 35 per cent of rural population has access to essential medicines, while health-seeking behaviour and health expenditures are low in these communities. The problem is compounded by poor sanitation and lack of doctors in rural areas. Arogya Parivar uses a market-based approach for health care by offering education on diseases, treatment options and prevention as well as providing access to affordable medicines. It builds upon the existing network of doctors and health care providers to provide health care in villages.

Novartis decided to work on two fronts (Figure 11.7). On one front, it focuses on training local health educators and health supervisors, who teach their communities about health-related issues. Second, its sales supervisors ensure availability of the company's medicines. It conducts health camps in villages, bringing together the services of pharmacies, doctors and hospitals. The company has covered 33,000 villages, treating villagers and providing preventive care.

To make people aware of the need for proper health care, it decided to recruit women health educators (HEs) from the local population. There is a large number of unemployed youth in villages, who have completed some years of formal education but are unemployed. The HEs, mostly women, were people who had passed 10th standard and had some years of higher education. The most important quality looked for was energy and desire to communicate with people and to help them. The local women recruits were trained as travelling health educators, who visit two villages a day, on foot or by bike. They build lasting bonds with their neighbours because they address the most common health threats. The HEs did not have the task of selling, but merely educating villagers on health issues.

On the distribution side, Arogya Parivar built its network of doctor, chemists and stockists. Sales supervisors ensured that medicines were available through the trade chain. Doctors were under no compulsion to prescribe Novartis medicines, but were made available in case they wanted to include them in the cure.

Initially, the company publicized the programme through mobile vans. It fitted a Tata Tempo Traveller with an audio-visual projector and would carry a few HEs to conduct a programme for the community. This worked out too expensive. *Nukkad nataks* also were not found to be feasible because the actors could not travel as they had their own businesses to run. Finally, it was decided to send HEs to villages who would organize community meetings there. A story telling technique with pictures that HEs could easily carry was used. This worked out to be quite effective.

One problem was finding people to work in villages. The firm initially relied on contract sales organization that works in rural areas. However, this did not work well as the workers could not break out of their mindset of working as sales representatives to 'push' doctors to prescribe medicines. It then decided to work with Teamlease to recruit HEs. A mix of people were chosen, including some who had experience in pharmacy, while others who had experience in FMCG companies and in NGOs. This ensured that the team had a mix of knowledge, energy and compassion.

The recruits were trained in various diseases and to make people aware of services available, including doctors, camps, diagnostics and distribution. Instead of recommending drugs, they would refer patients to doctors. Arogya Parivar offers education on diseases, treatment options and prevention as well as increasing access to affordable medicines. It focuses on health issues affecting rural women and children, such as clean water and sanitation, undernourishment, iron deficiency, vaccinations and so on. Each educator covers a few villages every day, in an Arogya Parivar branded uniform, making them easily recognizable.

Locally recruited health educators raise awareness about diseases most prevalent in rural India and preventive health measures. They also refer sick people to doctors. Health supervisors interact with local pharmacies and collaborate with doctors to organize health camps where villagers can receive treatment and preventive care. The product portfolio consists of more than 100 medicines and 160 generic and over-the-counter products to treat conditions ranging from tuberculosis and diabetes to pain and cold relief. Products and services are tailored to meet the needs of rural population. Arogya Parivar broke even in 30 months and since 2007, sales have increased 25-fold.

Encouraged by Arogya Parivar's success in India, Novartis has expanded the concept to other emerging markets, including Kenya, Indonesia and Vietnam. Cung Song Khoe in Vietnam, launched in 2012, is a private–public partnership with the Services of Health at the province level, working with doctors at community health centres to expand access to health screening and treatment. Familia Nawiri in Kenya, also launched in 2012, works with locals, NGOs and outreach workers to address challenges of access and availability of medicines and doctors. Keluarga Sehat in Indonesia is also a private–public partnership, working with midwives from community health centres. It works to reduce maternal mortality rates caused by post-partum haemorrhage, as this is still a huge challenge in Indonesia.

The case study shows the importance of finding the right people in rural marketing, who have the right mix of knowledge and enthusiasm, backed by strong distribution. The programme is now profitable.

Questions for Discussions:

1. Comment on the sales management and recruitment strategy of Novartis. What kind of recruitment and training would it provide to its salesmen?
2. Describe the market-based approach of Novartis. What did it consist of?

3. Would you describe Novartis as a social enterprise? Or, did it start the project merely to increase market share?
4. What can other companies learn from this case? Can they replicate the model in FMCG goods or other categories?

Sources for this Case Study:

Web Resources

Business Call to Action Case Study: http://www.businesscalltoaction.org/case-studies/2013/10/novartis-commercial-innovation-for-improved-health/

INSEAD case study on Arogya Parivar: http://cases.insead.edu/arogya-parivar/

Novartis website: https://www.novartis.in/

Watch the Novartis Social Ventures Video: https://www.novartis.in/our-work/expanding-access-healthcare/novartis-social-ventures

12
CHAPTER

Future of Rural Marketing

LEARNING OBJECTIVES

Rural marketing cannot be ignored by companies but to be successful, they have to understand how the future looks like. Blindly going by numbers is unlikely to help; instead, they have to find solutions based on relevant technologies. This chapter covers the trends of rural marketing which give us an idea about how rural markets should be served in the future. After reading this chapter, you will be able to:

- Understand the leading and debilitating trends in rural markets.
- Analyze the social innovation process including disruptive, jugaad and frugal innovation.
- Learn about methods of measuring social objectives, such as Triple Bottom Line and Sustainable Scorecard.
- Understand the nature and operations of a social enterprise.
- Learn about new methods to identify rural markets, such as big data.

Opening Case
Danone: The Transforming of Business

We have seen in Chapter 4 that for rural marketing initiatives to succeed, a business must transform itself into a social business. This case study describes French multinational Danone's initiatives to address the low-income populations from emerging countries and how it transformed itself in the process into a social business. In many ways, this case study shows the future of rural marketing.

In the late 1990s, Danone realized that there were limits to the European understanding of 'social', which merely meant that it should treat its employees well. Business had a larger objective than to supply premium products to rich consumers in developed countries. Yunus

PHOTO 12.1
Danone Communities support nine social businesses.

Source: Danone.communities.

(2007), in his book, *Creating a World Without Poverty*, describes the thought process of Franck Riboud, the chairman and CEO of Group Danone:

> We don't want to sell our products only to the well-off people in those countries. We would like to find ways to help feed the poor. It is part of our company's historic commitment to being socially innovative and progressive, which dates back 35 years to the work of my father, Antoine Riboud.

It was this thinking that launched Grameen Danone Food Limited (GDFL), a joint venture between Danone and Grameen Group in Bangladesh, which is based on the model of social business. GDFL's first product was *shokti doi*, a tasty yogurt to meet the nutritional needs of children. The product was first distributed in rural areas by shokti ladies, who sold the product on commission basis.

Grameen Danone was launched in July 2006 with its mission to reduce poverty through a unique business model to supply daily healthy nutrition to the poor—a fortified yogurt at an affordable price under the brand name Shokti+. It started additional activities linked to social marketing, including educating consumers about their nutritional needs and health.

While other companies start projects or put their money in corporate social responsibility (CSR), Danone illustrates the future of rural marketing in which companies strive to fulfil social objectives and get transformed in the process. Starting from the early 2000s, the company has launched social business and BoP projects with the explicit intention of strategic renewal.

Grameen Danone has adjusted the company's entire value chain to its social mission and rural business environment. The company involves local communities in all parts of its value chain: it sources raw milk from small farmers, employs local residents in the factory and engages local women as sales ladies for door-to-door sales. In the absence of a cold chain, Grameen Danone emphasizes a quick turnaround of 48 hours from factory to consumer so that the product does not deteriorate. The company has a no-loss operation, with all profits to be reinvested for further expansion and improvement.

The organizational learning process is not limited to 'top down' dissemination of the leaders' intuitions, but also skills developed by field managers and employees spreading through the organization. Crossan, Lane and White (1999) explain the business model through 'the 4I's': Intuition, Interpretation, Integration and Institutionalization. This has played a significant role in the process of strategic renewal undertaken by the firm. The Danone case shows a number of disruptive innovations:

New approach to HR: New incentive systems were created. For example, executive bonuses were calculated on the basis managerial contribution of one-third economic, one-third managerial and one-third societal. Danone managers were encouraged to become 'intrapreneurs' in that they could act creatively and operate frugally. 'Social innovation labs' reunited the people in social business projects annually, along with other stakeholders. A social network, both internal and external, was built around 'danone.communities'. This helped building new individual skills which became collective and eventually organizational. The French concept of hyper efficiency was replaced with a more patient and modest behaviour. The HR policy includes skills acquired through working in BoP markets combined with long training that facilitates the paradigm shift.

Innovation: Radically new products were developed, such as nutrient-rich yogurt in Bangladesh and the 'pouch' in Senegal, which is a carton composed of local grain and milk that can be stored at room temperature. These are examples of an innovative and frugal methods adopted by the company. Innovative financing was implemented, such as employee savings and the danone.communities mutual fund, and investing guarantee schemes created by the French Development Agency.

Supply chain: The supply chain was tweaked to source milk and cereal from local sources. Distribution of products was done through a network of rickshaws and the 'shokti ladies' who sell products door-to-door. Rather than increasing the sophistication of products, it built on new skills in terms of improving last-mile delivery. It slowly developed the ability to develop disruptive business models with low capital intensity.

Production: The concept of micro-factory was developed, which used renewable energies such as 'bio-digesters'. Danone factories in Bangladesh are about one-hundredth the size of its factories in the Western world.

Market research: Unlearning their ways of thinking and acting, managers instead observed, listened and discovered the needs, expectations, habits and constraints of customers to design simpler and better offers for them. They knew very little about low-income consumers and learned to co-create with them and work with local communities.

That first social enterprise became the founding project of the danone.communities fund, Danone's incubator for social businesses. Today, nine social businesses are supported by danone.communities, together improving the daily life of over one million people around the world, according to its website.

Companies in rural marketing may well remember the words of Antoine Riboud, who had in 1994, said: "There will not be sustainable economic value creation if there is no personal development and human value creation at the same time."

While reading this chapter, try to answer the following questions:

1. Why is it necessary for companies to transform their objectives?
2. Why is innovation so important in rural markets?

3. What are the trends that are changing the face of rural markets?
4. What is the nature of a social enterprise? Is it the future of marketing?

Sources for this Case Study:

Web Resources

Danone.communities website: http://www.danone.com/en/

Watch the Danone Corporate movie at: http://www.danone.com/en/for-all/our-mission-in-action/our-film/

Watch "What is Danone Communities?" at: https://www.youtube.com/watch?v=pGTjDxsHZ_g

Other Sources

Crossan, M.M., H.W. Lane and R.E. 1999. White. "An Organizational Learning Framework: From Intuition to Institution." *The Academy of Management Review* 24(3), 522–537.

Faivre-Tavignot, Bénédicte. 2014. "The Danone Case, or How Social Innovation Can Help a Multinational Company Reinvent Itself." *Paris Tech Review*, 24 January. Available at: http://www.paristechreview.com/2014/01/24/danone-case-social-innovation/ (Accessed on 27 April 2017).

Humberg, Kerstin, and Boris Braun. 2014. "Social Business and Poverty Alleviation: Lessons from Grameen Danone and Grameen Veolia." In *Social Business: Theory, Practice, and Critical Perspectives*, edited by A. Grove and G.A. Berg: 201–23. Berlin: Springer–Verlag.

Yunus, Muhammad. 2007. "Creating A World Without Poverty: Social Business and the Future of Capitalism." New York, NY: PublicAffairs.

INTRODUCTION

Despite efforts by social organizations, rural intervention schemes of the government, corporate social responsibility spending by for-profit organizations, calculations of rural growth published in research papers and studies put out by reputed consultancies and planning agencies, rural poverty is not going away in a hurry.

This is a fact that companies venturing into rural marketing can ill-afford to ignore. According to the provisional findings of the SECC, reported by *The Hindu* (2015), in nearly 75 per cent off rural households, the main earning family member makes less than ₹5,000 per month. In just 8 per cent of households does the main earning member make more than ₹10,000 per month. With low purchasing power, companies wishing to sell products in rural areas face a serious challenge. Even so, writes Gupta (2012), "most corporations are mindlessly targeted at only selling things to rural people without looking at what they can buy from them."

True, there are pockets of prosperity, but the data for the whole of the country is hardly encouraging. That is why, rural marketing requires a complete shift in approach compared to what textbooks on traditional marketing teach.

Some companies try to get over their guilt by starting CSR projects or giving money to them. However, the future belongs to those companies that build social objectives right into their DNA. This chapter describes the major trends and the paradigm shifts that have taken place in marketing. Such interventions give us an indication about the future of rural marketing.

TRENDS IN RURAL MARKETING

Several trends in rural marketing have been observed. In this section, we describe the trends that may impact life in villages, and thereby companies' efforts in rural marketing. We have divided the trends into leading trends, which have a positive impact on rural consumption, and debilitating trends, which stymie efforts of change and modernization.

Increase in income and education are important factors that affect marketing. As rural folk become more aware, it is expected that they will start consuming modern products just like their urban counterparts. Aiding in this are the banking and MFIs, which are slowly spreading their area of influence. As ICTs penetrate villages and micro-payment systems proliferate, it is expected that more people would benefit by coming into the financial mainstream. Innovation and modernization, aided in part by social businesses and NGOs, would help transform the lives in villages.

However, we cannot ignore trends that debilitate rural India. These headwinds threaten to keep villages in a time warp of tradition, poverty and backwardness. Farm indebtedness and distress is increasing in Indian villages: a bad monsoon pushes back purchasing power across rural areas in the country. Global warming is expected to accentuate this. An imbalanced society, which deliberately excludes a large population and prevents penetration of technology stands in the way of modernization. Add to this primitive infrastructure, consisting of bad roads, warehousing and communications, and we have strong forces that block efforts of rural marketing. The efforts of government have historically been full of shortcomings, while private organizations and NGOs, though noble, have at best a limited impact. These leading and debilitating trends are summarized in Table 12.1.

Which trends become stronger than others will determine the future of rural marketing. There are two opposing views regarding the outcomes. In its report, *Bird of Gold*, McKinsey Global Institute (2007) shows that, given a growth rate of 7–8 per cent, incomes will triple by 2025, which will reduce poverty and help India's bird of gold take flight. Accenture, too, echoes this and writes in its report, *Masters of Rural Markets* (2010): "There is no question that India's rural markets are becoming a powerful economic engine." It gives five reasons for greater business confidence in rural India: (a) rural spending is now less dependent on farm income, (b) increase in the minimum support prices that farmers earn on produce sold to the government, (c) increase in government spending in rural areas, (d) improved access to finance and institutional credit and (e) government measures such as waiver of agricultural loans and the MGNREGS.

The SECC data from *The Hindu* (2015), on the other hand, points to a rather bleak scenario: despite more than six decades after independence, economic growth seems to have

TABLE 12.1

Leading and debilitating trends in rural India.

Leading Trends	Debilitating Trends
Increase in income, education	Farm indebtedness and distress
Government poverty alleviation schemes	Seasonal incomes, dependent on monsoons
Microfinance and financial innovation	Large number of farmer suicides
Penetration of ICTs	Imbalanced society, social exclusion
Innovation and modernization	Very slow rate of change
Companies and NGOs starting social businesses	Impact in limited areas, farm productivity declining, global warming makes intensity of monsoons uncertain
Increase in rural consumption	Primitive infrastructure

TABLE 12.2

Optimistic outcomes and SECC data point at two opposing scenarios.

Optimistic Outcomes	Reality Checks from SECC Data
Indian incomes will triple by 2025	In nearly 75 per cent off rural households, the main earning family member makes less than ₹5,000 per month
Rising incomes will reduce poverty and increase the size of the middle class, which will spread beyond the large cities	The vast majority—over 90%—of rural India, does not have salaried jobs. Over half of all rural households derive their household income mainly from casual and seasonal manual labour
India will become the fifth largest consumer market by 2025	Over half of rural India owns no land at all. Among households who do own land, 40 per cent is not irrigated. Just four per cent own any sort of mechanized agricultural equipment, and 10 per cent own any irrigation equipment. Fewer than four per cent have an agricultural credit card
Increasing education and literacy levels	Fewer than 10 per cent make it to higher secondary or above and just 3.41 per cent of households have a family member who is at least a graduate
Outcomes depend on economic growth of 7–8%; India's Bird of Gold may take flight by 2025	Substantial difference in the standard of living of Scheduled Castes and Scheduled Tribes and 'others'. Fewer than five per cent of SC and ST households have a main earner who makes more than ₹10,000 per month
The share of the wallet will shift from basic necessities to discretionary spending	With household incomes very low, shift to discretionary spending will occur in pockets

Sources: Left column: McKinsey Global Institute (2007); Right column: SECC data from *The Hindu* (2015).

bypassed India's villages. The data shows that the rural market comprises almost three-fourths of households in which the main earning member earns less than ₹5,000 per month, which means that a majority of households are either poor or very close to destitution. The optimistic outcomes are contrasted with SECC data in Table 12.2.

In the future, will India's bird of gold take flight or poverty and social exclusion continue to dog developmental efforts? Will rural India become the growth engine for consumer goods companies or will it remain the bleak landscape with pockets of prosperity?

The SECC data certainly points to the fact that the situation is not very bright. Rural markets seem attractive because of millions of underserved customers, but companies have to really tread carefully between the two opposite scenarios. They have to go beyond commercial objectives and try to improve rural lives to succeed in the long run. Many companies, whose case studies are covered in this book, have actually transformed some aspect of rural lives while also serving their business objectives. The opening case of Danone shows that companies can and do transform lives through four approaches:

- Introduce social innovation in products and processes by approaching rural marketing as a distinct discipline.

- Change the performance parameters of the business from the bottom line to the triple bottom line.
- Change the nature of business completely and become a social business.
- Develop relevant technology to solve local problems.

This approach not only transforms marketing but also lays the foundation of an economic system that does not focus on consumption but on sustainability. These are further helped by a change in economic models and reporting on environmental and sustainability that will impact on the how companies tackle rural marketing in the future. We thus discuss the future on the following five major trends:

- A change in economic thinking.
- Innovation in products and processes.
- Development of reporting methods for sustainability.
- Emergence of a new business model—the social enterprise.
- Application of new technologies such as big data.

TOWARDS A NEW ECONOMIC SYSTEM

A slow realization is dawning that companies cannot continue to operate in the unsustainable ways that they have in the past. There is also a rethinking about the model of capitalism that dominates world economies. It is increasingly being felt that while capitalism has contributed to increased wealth and better quality of life, it has also caused deep negative environmental and social impacts. Thus, the understanding that profit generation and maximization, while being legitimate objectives of companies, must also be accompanied by economic, social and environmental betterment. In other words, the world is heading to a more 'humane capitalism'. Companies realize that the 'business-as-usual' approach—one in which natural resources are exploited ruthlessly—is creating problems of pollution and sustainability across the globe. If such development goes unchecked, we are in for great social and environmental upheavals that may well destroy the planet.

The reorientation of business as a social enterprise is now recognized as essential for the future of business itself. Writing that the global economic system is under threat, Bower et al. (2011a) point out in their book, *Capitalism at Risk: Rethinking the Role of Business*, "Business must serve both as innovator and activist—developing corporate strategies that effect change at the community, national, and international levels." Reich (2016) writes in his book, *Saving Capitalism*, "We are lurching toward a capitalism so top-heavy it cannot be sustained."

Stiglitz (2002) had echoed this in his book *Globalization and Its Discontents*, "Globalization today is not working for many of the world's poor; it is not working for much of the environment; it is not working for the stability of the global economy." That is, we have a system today in which the rich are reaping the benefits of development, while vast numbers of poor live in traditional livelihoods bordering on poverty (Photo 12.2). It is also being felt that the limits of sustainability have been reached—the planet cannot sustain the runaway consumption that the economic system dictates. This can best be described as an unstable system. A positive future for the planet depends on a new paradigm that links business and development and promotes social, economic and environmental stability around the world.

Corporations thus have a broader role in society. Porter and Kramer (2002) write, "We are learning that the most effective way to address many of the world's most pressing problems is

Photo 12.2
Making jaggery in a village unmindful of globalization. A vast majority of rural people still rely on traditional livelihoods.

Source: Photograph by Dinesh Kumar.

to mobilize the corporate sector where both companies and society can benefit." It is time that companies understood that social and economic goals are integrally connected. Preserving the environment benefits not only the society but companies too, because reducing pollution and waste leads to a more productive use of resources. Boosting social and economic conditions in developing countries can create more productive locations for a company's operations as well as new markets for its products.

Bower et al. (2011b) argue that businesses must identify the issues that could disrupt the global market system in the coming decades: they look to modifying the market capitalism system in which business must lead as an innovator and as an activist, mobilizing resources to spread the innovations. All this will shape the future of marketing: it will depend on how companies fulfil their objectives of profits, sustainability and inclusive growth (see Mini Case Study 12.1). Indeed, many companies are doing so, as this book has shown.

THE FUTURE OF RURAL MARKETING

Many businesses in developing countries have realized that serving rural markets is not about simply selling products. They have expanded the nature of their businesses from mere commercial motives to social ones as well. The case studies that we have covered in this book prove that businesses succeed if they go beyond their mandate of making profits. The future

Mini Case Study 12.1

Philips: Philanthropy by Design

Many households in rural areas rely on *chulhas* (mud stove) for their cooking, burning wood or cow dung patties in them. This results is exposing families to health risks as they inhale smoke involuntarily.

To get over this very serious problem, Philips has developed a smokeless stove. In 2005, Philips held a workshop, 'A Sustainable Design Vision—Design for Sense & Simplicity' with the aim of envisioning products and services for helping the community. Some 80 design ideas emerged, which were filtered for their fit with the company's corporate strategy, social investment policy alignment, technological feasibility and MDGs set by the UN. Philips calls this approach *Philanthropy by Design*, meaning leveraging on design creativity to provide meaningful solutions for empowering some of the more fragile categories of society. It works both ways—it helps people living at very low income, but it is also very profitable for the company.

Under this programme, the company decided to develop a smokeless wood-burning stove, initially intended for rural and semi-urban India. The stove would be simple to use and maintain, locally produced and distributed, relatively cheap, easily made and able to significantly reduce indoor pollution. In doing so, the company hoped to solve the cause of respiratory illness that affects the large number of people who still cook indoors with biomass fuels. It is estimated that over 1.6 million people die each year as a result of this. India, in particular, is badly affected, accounting for 25 per cent of such fatalities.

A design team from Philips Design Pune turned the initial design idea into two, field-tested prototypes, a collaborative effort involving local NGOs, entrepreneurs, SHGs and a few families. It also tied up with Appropriate Rural Technology Institute (ARTI), an NGO, which had expertise in the smokeless cooking chulhas. The design team gathered deeper, more specific insights by carrying out research in several villages in Maharashtra. It emerged that the successful stove would have to accept different biomass fuels available in different seasons and locations and be able to accept different, non-standard cooking vessels.

Another aspect was the chimney, which helped in reducing pollution. Conventional chimneys, which were made from a single length of pipe, were difficult to transport. On the other hand, the 'Chulha' stove has a chimney assembled from several sections, which makes it easier to manufacture and transport. It can also be disassembled for easy cleaning.

The company then allowed local stakeholders to use the design for free, making it much easier to achieve widespread distribution of the stoves and help keep costs down. A complete support package was created which includes not only the details of the stove's physical design but also marketing information for entrepreneurs, communication materials for NGOs and installation instructions. A training programme is also being developed together with ARTI.

Philips, a company renowned worldwide for technical innovation, thus came up with a product made of clay and concrete. Using appropriate technology, the company tackled a huge problem using a minimum amount of resources.

There are two versions of the 'Chulha' smokeless stove; Sampoorna and Saral. The Sampoorna is an all-in-one unit intended for cooking/boiling with an integrated steamer for preparing rice, lentils, and so on. The Saral is a modular system which has a basic cooking block and allows the addition of other blocks such as extra pots, steaming or a 'hot box' for keeping food warm or for heating it up. Both stove types are made of concrete and are coated with local clay. It has been estimated that, compared to traditional cooking fires, the Sampoorna and Saral reduce indoor smoke pollution by up to 90 per cent.

Which other products help solve local problems?

Source for this Case Study:

Web Resource

Philips website: http://www.design.philips.com/about/design/designnews/newvaluebydesign/helping-400million_people_give_up_smoking.page rests on three paradigm shifts taking place in rural approaches: *innovation*, transformation of companies into *social enterprises* and *technological advancements* that bring rural consumers closer to companies.

This means that companies need to reinvent their business models and their very approach of doing business. Such companies stand a greater chance of success and long-term survival in rural areas. We have taken elements from the business models of these companies to figure out what the future looks like.

The companies, we find, followed the design thinking pattern: a solution-focused and action-oriented mindset towards creating a preferred future. Vaitheeswaran (2012) writes that to tackle the world's most wicked problems, we need a paradigm of *design thinking*, the open-minded, no-holds-barred approach that designers bring to their work, rather than the narrow, technical view of innovation traditionally taught at many business and engineering schools. Firms that think like designers, which means embracing experimentation via rapid prototyping and fast failure, stand to win huge new markets and profits. They invest in distribution and training of local resources, develop innovative products and processes, involve stakeholders and, above all, build a social purpose in their objectives.

The task is not easy, of course. Haanaes et al. (2013) write that straying from their core purpose could well attract the ire of shareholders who invest in companies for financial returns. They could well see a company's social investments as reducing their returns. Still, the thrust for transforming business has happened because of the following reasons:

1. To seek growth and market shares.
2. The growing need for sustainable business activities.
3. To reach a large, underserved market.
4. To develop good corporate citizenship and corporate image.

Growth and market shares: Because of saturated markets in the West and of saturated urban markets in developing countries, it is increasingly being recognized that growth will come from (a) emerging markets and (b) underserved markets within emerging countries. Radical changes in business models to serve the poor have helped the companies to achieve high growth rates and outperform their competitors. These companies report better revenues, growth rates and market shares than other companies in the category.

Sustainable business: Another reason for this huge change is the realization that companies must work sustainably and that the unchecked consumption of natural resources cannot continue unabated. Increasingly, there is pressure on companies to operate in a sustainable manner.

Serving larger markets: Radjou and Prabhu (2012) write that multinationals have realized the importance of enhancing their capabilities in emerging economies. Products developed in the West and imported to developing countries are too expensive to be sold in rural markets, so MNCs are stepping out of their comfort zones by investing in local R&D and factories to design and produce locally relevant products and services. Between 2003 and 2007, multinationals have invested some US$24 billion in more than 1,100 R&D centres in India and China. "This approach has clear advantages over importing and selling high-priced products and services developed and produced in the West," they write. The challenge for them is to move from serving urban customers to the much larger BoP population of urban and rural poor.

Good corporate citizenship: Pressure is also mounting on organizations to focus on good corporate citizenship. Such organizations pursue their objectives while building a social business. Kanter (2011) writes that firms have to think of themselves as social institutions than merely profit-making companies. This gives them a long-term perspective to invest in the human side of the organization.

These four driving forces have resulted in interventions like the invention of microfinance, information and problem-solving apps and impact-investing for difficult problems in rural markets. These ideas are becoming popular as private companies, NGOs and development agencies are increasingly applying BoP ideas to their initiatives. Eggers and Macmillan (2013), in their book, *The Solution Revolution*, explain how this is giving rise to the 'Solution Economy' in which individuals, businesses and, sometimes, governments work together to solve societal problems and also make a profit. The *solution revolution* can be seen as an interaction between three crucial factors: wavemakers, technology and innovative business models, as described in the following. All three have to operate simultaneously.

- **Wavemakers:** Wavemakers are firms and individuals that further social agendas by developing or funding compelling solutions. There are different types of wavemakers: investors, conveners and MNCs. For instance, investors such as Warren Buffet and the Bill & Melinda Gates Foundation who pledge large sums of money to social causes can be termed as wavemakers. Conveners are individuals and organizations that can assemble groups of people and leaders to solve societal problems—opinion leaders like the Honeybee Network are examples of conveners. MNCs that integrate social missions into their corporate missions while serving markets help a great deal in providing much needed rural solutions.
- **Disruptive technologies:** These are technologies that have the power to transform Indian villages. Some of these technologies are described later in this chapter.
- **Business models:** Business models have to incorporate public benefits. These help in solving societal problems by economic relationships, facilitating knowledge sharing and through technology. We have seen in this book that the most successful rural marketing interventions are those that have helped solve problems in some way, whether it is providing reading glasses for people in villages or helping rural people to start small distribution businesses of FMCG products. An example of business model innovation is described in Mini Case Study 12.2.

Mini Case Study 12.2

ARZU: Innovation in a Business Model

In 2003, Connie Duckworth visited Afghanistan as part of a US delegation to improve the lives of women there. She saw village women working on making trinkets and rugs. The industry relied on child labour. The rug trade was controlled by agents and they fetched up to US$8,000 in the US but little went back to workers. She got the idea of building a responsible, sustainable business that would employ only adults and treat them humanely. The enterprise was named Arzu, or hope.

Arzu learned how to buy wool, contract with dyers and create the most saleable rug patterns. The task also involved understanding the lives of the women, for which design thinking was used. For instance, it was observed that to improve pregnant women's access to medical care, the real problem was not shortage of doctors and clinics, but cultural norms that do not allow women to leave home without a female companion even if she was bleeding to death. Another problem was how to transport women to the nearby clinic. Arzu decided to tackle these problems head-on by including social objectives in its business model, which are described here.

Social contract: Families who wanted to work with Arzu had to enter into a 'social contract' negotiated with male heads of the household. If a family wants to weave for Arzu, they must agree to the following conditions:

- All children, including girls, must attend government school full-time.
- All adult women must be 'released' from family confines to attend Arzu's literacy classes.
- Women to be transported to a clinic when pregnant—families were often reluctant to let a woman go to a clinic for prenatal care or during labour, even if she was dying.

Education and medical care: Arzu created incentives for women to seek education and health care. It arranged vehicles and chaperones to transport pregnant women to and from clinics.

Recruiting workers: Recruiting weavers required an intensive, house-to-house outreach. Arzu representatives met with the tribal elders in every village to explain the concept and to get permission to work there. Women representatives explained to the women that they would be paid local market rate for weaving as a salary, with an additional 50 per cent of that rate as a bonus for the highest-quality work. Earlier, agents delayed payment for months until a rug had been completed and sold. Once some weavers had signed on and began receiving payments, word spread quickly, and many more families joined.

Marketing: The biggest challenge came from marketing and distributing the rugs in the US. The rug industry is highly fragmented and sales is accomplished through multiple channels. ARZU sold directly and through interior designers and commercial design firms markets. An architects' firm designed gifted modern patterns which the women could make.

Impact: ARZU is a small operation, but a socially meaningful one. It has a staff of 55 people in Afghanistan and works with about 500 weavers. About 30 per cent of the weavers are widows, who lost their husbands in the prolonged war in the country. They are desperately poor, having spent years in refugee camps in Pakistan. Its website says that Arzu weavers earn 68 per cent more than the average Afghan, 55 per cent own a house, 70 per cent own cell phones while all of them are literate in contrast to 90 per cent of rural Afghan women who are not. Twenty per cent of Arzu families have at least one child in university. In the area of women's health, it has eliminated childbirth deaths drastically in a country with one of the world's highest maternal death rates: it has not lost a single woman in childbirth.

Can you think of other organizations that have implemented similar business models?

Sources for this Case Study:

Web Resources

ARZU website: https://arzustudiohope.org/

Watch several Arzu videos at: https://www.youtube.com/user/ArzuStudioHope

Other Source

Duckworth, Connie. 2016. "Arzu's Founder on Shaping Culture through Social Enterprise." *Harvard Business Review*, September. Available at: https://hbr.org/2016/09/arzus-founder-on-shaping-culture-through-social-enterprise (Accessed on 27 April 2017).

FIGURE 12.1

The intersection of wavemakers, technologies and business models give rise to the solution economy.

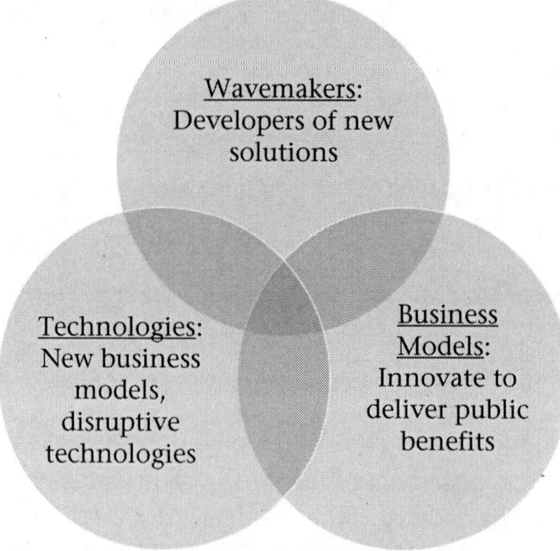

Source: Adapted from the book, *The Solution Revolution* by Eggers and Macmillan (2013).

To be successful, a solution must have a working technology, a wavemaker to spread the good word and a business model by which the idea can be commercialized (Figure 12.1). By doing this, companies are changing themselves to serve larger markets. Sabeti (2011) writes that there is a blurring in boundaries between for-profit and non-profit models and a different model is emerging, called 'for-benefit' corporations, "that generate earned income but give top priority to an explicit social mission." At heart of these models is social innovation.

INNOVATION

Innovations for rural areas are relatively rare. Gupta (2012) writes that, for example, cell phones are used around the world but an application to use the phone as switching device attached to a tube well was developed by a school dropout. No big company gave such a choice to rural consumers.

Social innovation refers to new ideas that work in meeting social goals. Phills et al. (2008) defines social innovation as a novel solution to a social problem that is more effective, efficient, sustainable or just than current solutions and for which the value created accrues primarily to society as a whole rather than companies. As described in the earlier sections, businesses have a commitment to both social purpose and earned profits. In Chapter 4, we have seen that the BoP ventures are expected to generate acceptable economic returns for themselves and societal returns for the local communities simultaneously. For this, they have to work with the community. Hart and Milstein (2003) write that companies such as Johnson & Johnson, Dow, DuPont, Coca-Cola and Procter & Gamble are beginning to take steps to understand how to leverage their skills and resources to meet the basic needs of the poor. Earlier, people did not matter to these companies, who were merely seen as consumers but the future of marketing depends on working with local communities.

This mutual working leads to development of technologies, products and services to meet the needs of rural people. Companies that can do so can thus unlock future markets of immense scale and scope. In this section, we describe several types of innovation that has changed rural lives: Agarwal (2016) has given nine approaches to product centric innovation that has worked in villages:

1. **Jugaad:** A creative and improvised way of solving problems in a resource constrained environment. Jugaad, which means 'making do', overcomes harsh environmental constraints by developing effective solutions using whatever is available. Examples of jugaad innovation are seen in using discarded water bottles as slippers, running a tube well motor on a scooter engine or using a water pump to run a vehicle. Though it has been acclaimed in a book by Radjou et al. (2012), it actually shows how poor people make do with whatever is available in remote, cut-off areas, ignored in the development process.
2. **Disruptive innovation:** The term was popularized by Christensen (1997) in his book, *The Innovator's Dilemma*. The theory explains the phenomenon by which innovators disrupt markets with good enough products: existing markets are transformed by introducing simplicity, convenience, accessibility and affordability instead of complicated products. It means developing simple, cheap, small and easy-to-use products that cater to the needs of underserved markets. Initially, a disruptive innovation is formed in a niche market, but eventually the new product or idea completely redefines the industry. Disruptive innovations are not breakthrough technologies but innovations that make products and services more accessible and affordable to a larger population.
3. **Frugal innovation:** Frugal innovation involves developing good enough affordable products that suffice the needs of resource-constrained consumers. It is a bottom-up approach to innovation. The characteristics of frugal innovation are affordability, availability, accessibility, usability and customer awareness.
4. **Frugal engineering:** Frugal engineering is the process of reducing the complexity and cost of a good and its production. It refers to introducing cost-effective products quickly in a resource-constrained environment. The principles of frugal engineering are robustness, portable, de-featuring, leapfrogging technology, mega scale production and service ecosystem.
5. **Reverse innovation:** Reverse engineering is the process of taking apart an object, extracting knowledge or design information from it in order to duplicate and reproduce it. The process often involves disassembling a device or product, analyzing its

components and workings in detail and duplicating it. Reverse engineering is used to duplicate imported products in emerging markets or modifying them to make cheaper products.

6. **Gandhian innovation:** Gandhian innovation refers to the process of using science and technology for the benefit of all (see Mini Case Study 12.3). Prahalad and Mashelkar (2010) write that innovation consists of two ends: at one end, companies can disrupt business models by using existing capabilities but at a lower cost. At the other, they create entirely new capabilities. Those in the middle modify capabilities. This classification leads to three types of Gandhian innovation: (a) disrupting business models, (b) modifying organizational capabilities and (c) creating or sourcing new capabilities.
7. **Grassroots innovation:** Grassroots inventions are generated by people in villages to solve their own problems, which are neither recognized by institutions nor can be solved in R&D labs.
8. **Indigenous innovation:** This is a process in which established products are improved through R&D in developing countries. Products imported from the West—like machines used in medical diagnosis—tend to be very expensive for developing countries. The companies therefore establish R&D in host countries to modify them to become more suitable to work in harsh environments.

It is easy to see such innovations in villages because people devise ways to solve their own problems in the absence of resources. We describe some examples of jugaad, frugal, grassroots and disruptive innovation in the next section. These are of particular importance in rural marketing, as they help in developing products that are of immediate importance in villages.

Jugaad

Radjou et al. (2012) describe that jugaad consists of human ingenuity as people try to solve their problems with whatever materials they have at hand. It is now being used by MNCs who are using the same principles to drive innovation in a resource-strapped world. It is actually a makeshift or 'bandage' solution and is not really innovation in the real sense of the word. It thrives in environments which are harsh, politically and economically unstable, bureaucratic and with poor infrastructure and inadequate access to finance and skilled human resources. Jugaad means adapting available materials to develop much needed products in villages. For example, we found electricity connections in villages that were wrapped around with a discarded plastic bottle for protection because factory made connectors were not available.

The term 'jugaad' was initially used to describe a vehicle developed and used by villagers in north India. The vehicle was a boon in village areas where public transport was lacking. Called 'Maruta', it consisted of a cart which was propelled by an irrigation pump. Marutas were used to transport people and agricultural produce because the problem of village transport was acute. Such innovation is seen in villages, with tractor engines propelling bus chassis, scooter engines powering threshing machines and motorcycle engines propelling tractor carts. Such vehicles are used for sending children to school and solve the problem of mobility in villages since local bus services are often not available. Another example of jugaad is from Africa, where villagers used discarded plastic water bottles to make slippers by attaching a rope on the flattened plastic (Photo 12.3).

PHOTO 12.3

Jugaad innovations: Slippers made out of discarded plastic bottles (Left) and a Maruta (Right).

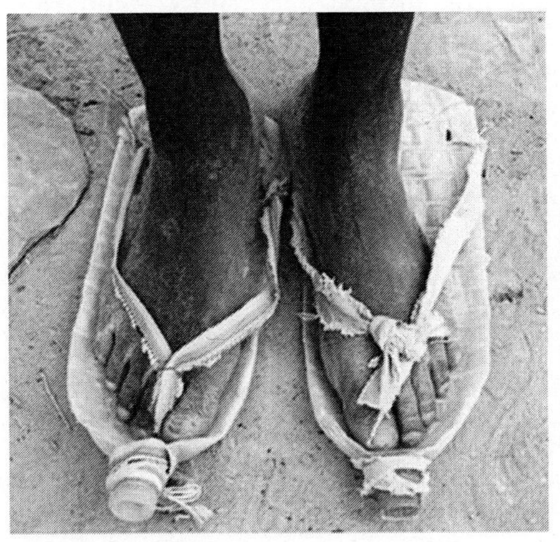

Source: pinterest.com and tumblr.com

Jugaad innovation features simplicity as it works with locally available materials. The six principles of jugaad are:

1. **Opportunity in adversity:** Adversity produces resilience and creativity.
2. **Do more with less:** Jugaad uses whatever material is available. It is frugal innovation and optimizes use of scarce resources.
3. **Think and act flexibly:** Jugaad calls for flexible thinking, which is not just outside the box but consists of creating a new box.
4. **Keep it simple:** Jugaad looks for solutions simple enough to have broad applicability and accessibility.
5. **Solve a problem:** Jugaad innovation is especially useful as it is inclusive and serves the purpose of underserved, marginal customers by creating affordable solutions.

Frugal Innovation

Frugal innovation is directly seen in rural areas. Radjou and Prabhu (2015) in their book, *Frugal Innovation* write that 'frugal engineering', a term invented by Carlos Ghosn, former CEO of Renault–Nissan, describe the ability to innovate quickly and at low cost under severe resource constraints. Frugal innovation reduces not just the financial cost of doing business but also its environmental cost. Frugal innovation comes from six components:

1. **Engage and iterate:** The company builds a market-focused, agile R&D model, starting off with 'good enough' solutions based on customer involvement.
2. **Flexible assets and supply chains:** Companies experiment with new materials, manufacturing tools and supply chain techniques to improve distribution and procurement. Technologies such as 3D printers, micro-factories and supply chain analytics are used to create flexible systems.

3. **Sustainable solutions:** Environmental sustainability is usually treated as an optional CSR addition but frugal innovation demands that it become an essential strategy. Companies invest in recycling and reusing solutions. Sustainability has to be built right into the R&D phase and has to be promoted as cool and aspiration-oriented.
4. **Shape customer behaviour:** In addition to changing their own goals and structures, companies also actively engage with their customers. This is done through social comparison, social learning and storytelling, which help to motivate and empower customers.
5. **Co-create value with prosumers:** Consumers in villages are transformed into prosumers, who are producers as well as consumers of the company's products. Companies must pursue a strategy of development, marketing and branding with prosumers.
6. **Innovative collaborations:** Companies partner with suppliers, competitors, government, NGOs and customers to serve rural people.

These principles can be brought about only by bold leadership, setting of inspirational goals, choosing measurable targets, reinventing business models and cultural change management. An example of frugal innovation is shown in Photo 12.4—a water heater that does not require electricity. Villagers use crop residues, twigs and dried grass to get warm water during winters.

Another example of frugal innovation is MittiCool (see Mini Case Study 12.3), a low cost, biodegradable refrigerator made out of clay, which can be made with limited capital with locally available material.

PHOTO 12.4

Frugal innovation in villages: Water heaters that do not work on electricity and use crop residues as fuel.

Source: Photograph by Dinesh Kumar.

Mini Case Study 12.3

Frugal and Grassroots Innovations

Frugal innovations actually solve some problems faced by villagers. Traditional research done in labs is simply not able to recognize or understand these problems or develop solutions to them. That is why, companies have to work in close connection with grassroots inventors to find products that have immediate relevance in rural markets. We give here some products, which are not only simple but also help to solve local problems, changing rural lives to a great extent.

- **Eco-friendly cow dung pot for nursery:** To replace conventional plastic bags that are used to plant saplings.
- **Cow dung collection and dispensing device:** Instead of collecting it manually, the device helps in collecting dung without touching.
- **Bicycle sprayer:** A mechanical innovation, it is an attachment which uses the circular motions of the cycle to move the piston of a spray pump which generates pressure to spray pesticides.
- **Motorcycle-driven ploughing machine:** Using the chassis and power of an Enfield Bullet motorcycle in front, the innovator retrofitted an attachment with two wheels at the rear with a tool bar to fit various implements that help in ploughing, weeding and sowing seeds.
- **Bicycle weeder:** For farmers who cannot afford bullock or tractor, this device, made of bicycle components, helps in weeding farms.
- **MittiCool refrigerator:** A fridge that does not require electricity and keeps food fresh. MittiCool is made of clay and works on the principle of evaporation of water (see Photo 12.5a). A clay cooker has also been developed.

Photo 12.5
The MittiCool refrigerator.

Source: Mitticool.in (Accessed on 27 April 2017).

Photo 12.6
Earthen utensils produced by MittiCool.

Source: Photograph by Dinesh Kumar.

- **Low-cost wind mill:** A windmill to generate electricity, which was developed by GIAN in association with Alstom Foundation, France. Alstom Foundation provided financial support for installation of 50 wind mills in the first phase.
- **Head load reducing device:** Rural women walk tens of miles every day with heavy load on their head which causes stress, discomfort and eventually head and neck injuries. The product is an ergonomically designed device fixed on top of the head which transfers the weight carried on the head to the shoulders.

Government and institutions have failed to notice or solve local, everyday problems like the ones discussed here. For instance, women transplanting rice stand for long hours in water and those plucking tea leaves maintain an ergonomically poor posture for hours. Such occupations have considerable scope to be made less burdensome, but nobody notices these real problems that people face. Such problems have been solved with simple innovations like Santi, a motorcycle-based plough, and the mechanization of the Asu process, used to make the intricate weave of Pochampally sarees. Many more simple innovations have been assisted by GIAN.

Such innovation goes much beyond urban approach to innovation, which is limited to apps and IT applications. Many IT portals and apps developed for farmers, for instance, provide information but are useless for them as they cannot access markets. What is most commendable in grassroots innovations is that they are not only relevant but happen without government or any other support. Schemes like the MNREGA provide livelihoods but do not build creative capabilities. Innovation funding usually is limited to companies and individuals in urban areas.

Photo 12.7
A device that reduces stress of carrying water.

Source: www.gian.org (Accessed on 27 April 2017).

Can you find out other common problems faced by villagers? Can you discover other grassroots innovations that have helped change life in rural India?

Sources for this Case Study:
Web Resources
GIAN website: http://www.gian.org/
Mitticool website: http://www.mitticool.in
SRISTI website: http://www.sristi.org/cms/

Sometimes such inventions end up being catalysts for other products. Christensen et al. (2006) describe *catalytic innovation* as support for organizations that are approaching social sector problems in a fundamentally new way. Catalytic innovations have five qualities:

1. They create systemic social change through scaling and replication.
2. They meet a need that is either overserved because the existing solution is too complex, or not served at all.
3. They offer products and services that are simpler and therefore less costly than existing alternatives, but users consider them to be good enough.
4. They generate resources, such as donations, grants, volunteer manpower or intellectual capital in ways that are initially unattractive to existing companies.
5. They are often ignored and disparaged by existing players for whom the business model is unprofitable or otherwise unattractive.

Grassroots Innovations

Innovations described in the previous section can also be called *grassroots innovations,* which are community-led solutions for sustainability. Some organizations that are assisting grassroots innovations in India are Society for Research and Initiatives for Sustainable Technologies and Institutions (SRISTI), the National Innovation Foundation (NIF), which is an autonomous institution of the Department of Science and Technology, Gujarat Grassroots Innovation Augmentation Network (GIAN), which has been instrumental in a large number of innovations in the rural sector, and the Honeybee Network (see Mini Case Study 12.4).

Mini Case Study 12.4

Honey Bee Network

Grassroots innovations usually recognize a local problem that is not recognized by the established R&D structure. These innovations also go unnoticed as they are a source of amusement for urban dwellers. Can they be discovered, documented, patented if possible and spread to other villages where similar problems exist?

Honey Bee Network does exactly that. It is a network of organizations that work on rural innovation. Author of *Grassroots Innovation*, Anil Gupta (2016) started one of the world's largest movements in the 1980s to identify, document and reward 'grassroots' innovators. These were people without a scientific or technical education but who used ingenious solutions to their problems. Many of these innovators are discovered through *shodh yatras* or missions of discovery, or a one-week walk through a district in different parts of the country. This method becomes a catalyst for further innovation. Gupta focuses on the importance of *samvedana* (empathy) and *srijansheelta* (creativity) in driving meaningful innovation. Gupta is an agricultural scientist and, during his research in India and Bangladesh, he found that many farmers had found smart ways to tackle pests and other problems. These solutions are practical and effective, but formal agriculture research does not recognize them. He notes that 90 per cent of the village innovations are sustainable and frugal inventions. They use second-hand parts and are far ahead in reuse and recycling than Western countries.

The Honey Bee website says that more than 70 technologies have been commercialized, 700 patents have been filed and 10,000 innovations are being used in villages. It is now present in more than 75 countries. It not only discovers village level innovations, but acknowledges the knowledge provider in order to protect his or her IPR and ensures that proceeds accruing from the use of innovations or traditional knowledge go back to the knowledge holders.

Its *Honey Bee* newsletter is published in seven Indian languages and English. It documents innovations and is spread among needy people in villages. Over the years, it has documented more than 100,000 ideas, innovations and traditional knowledge practices.

Can local innovations spread through such networks? Do other networks exist? How can you help the village innovators?

Source for this Case Study:

Gupta, Anil K. 2016. *Grassroots Innovation: Minds on the Margin are not Marginal Minds*. New Delhi: Penguin Random House India.

Disruptive Innovation

Many of the inventions mentioned in this chapter could well be termed disruptive, as they change traditional ways of doing tasks at farms or in village homes. Christensen et al. (2015) describe disruptive innovations as new products, services and processes that challenge industry incumbents by offering simpler, good enough alternatives to an underserved group of customers. They write that disruptive innovations start in two types of markets. Low-end footholds exist because companies try to sell to most profitable customers, paying less attention to poorer customers, creating an opportunity for a disrupter focused on providing low-end customers with a 'good enough' product. The second foothold is one in which disrupters create a market where none existed, or try to turn non-consumers into consumers.

Eggers and Macmillan (2013) list several ways that organizations can change their approach for innovation:

- **Change the lens:** Big problems can be solved by changing the approach and a new way of looking at problems opens up possibilities of new ways of doing things and new solutions.
- **Target the gaps:** Companies need to discover gaps and develop new markets by meeting neglected needs and market gaps.
- **Rethink constraints:** Resource constraints should not narrow the vision of solutions; social organizations focus on an end goal and consider how outside resources can support that goal (see Mini Case Study 12.5).
- **Embrace lightweight solutions:** Organizations have to sacrifice old methods, models and traditional jobs. For instance, we saw how Bata used natural lighting in its factories to reduce prices of its products in BoP markets.
- **Buy differently:** Companies can save large sums of money by sourcing differently and cheaply.
- **Measure what matters:** By instituting right metrics, companies know what they must measure and institute methods to introduce those metrics in their reporting. This has given rise to techniques such as the triple bottom line and the sustainable scorecard for social business, which are described in the next section.

Mini Case Study 12.5

Agricultural Innovations and Venture Capital

Apart from grassroots innovations, several companies and start-ups are selling innovative products, giving a boost to rural marketing and supply chains. In a country where agricultural based innovation is rare, such activity shows that entrepreneurs are looking at village problems now, reports *The Economic Times* (2016). Venture capital is now boosting start-ups in agricultural technology. A few innovations that have started in the field areas are described here:

Solar powered cold storage: Farmers of perishable produce face a common problem that whatever produce they cannot sell goes to waste. Cold storages are few and distant. An invention that could help farmers is a solar powered cold storage. These units can be used to store perishable commodities for a few days, helping the farmer to stock up his harvest without the need to sell his produce at throwaway prices. Such a system could also help reduce the massive wastage of fruit, flowers and vegetables that Indian agriculture has to bear with. The solar powered cold storage is made by EcoZen Solutions and it offers a quarterly lease to customers. It hopes that farmers will use the product and eventually buy it. The company, which was among world's top 30 business ideas at Stanford's E-bootcamp and winner of Technology and Sustainable Development at Eureka, IIT Bombay, also has solar powered irrigation solutions.

Bioengineering: Automation and bioengineering can help in reducing labour in farming as well as in farm inputs. Satish KS, cofounder of Flybird Farm Innovations has developed an automatic, low-cost irrigation controller called Siri which reduces water losses and labour costs and increases crop yields. Since 2014, Siri has been installed in more than 65 farms in Karnataka and Andhra Pradesh. Satish is now working on making the product wireless. Flybird has raised more than ₹1 crore in equity and grant-funding and plans to develop a wireless irrigation system as well.

Food processing: Food processing can add value to farm produce and also helps in finding an outlet for perishable goods. YCook has developed a unique process that allows fresh produce to retain its natural freshness, colour, texture, flavour and nutrients for 12 months without any preservatives or additives or even refrigeration. It operates in the category of minimally processed vegetables, sweet corn, lentils and fruits. YCook is a start-up that not only sells organic, ready-to-cook processed foods, but also trains farmers to grow and handle post-harvest processing. The company works with over 1,000 farmers from Andhra Pradesh, Karnataka, Telangana and other states. Farmers tend to be suspicious of city-bred youngsters claiming to solve their problems and this is one hurdle that an innovation has to cross.

Automated sprayers: Automated airblast sprayers, used in cleaning certain crops, are sold by Machines Information Technology Resources Agriculture (MITRA). It provides orchard and vineyard sprayers and dry chemical dispensing units. It is the pioneer in India in Airblast spraying technology and is the only Indian branded player in the segment. The products represent major savings, as sprayers from abroad require more horsepower and are costly. MITRA sprayers are about 30–50 per cent cheaper than foreign ones and use less energy. They also allow the farmer to keep chemical sprays at a minimum, which helps in export of the produce.

Natural pesticides: Barrix Agro Sciences has developed non-chemicals based alternatives for pesticides which do not harm the environment. The pesticides are pheromone-based traps for flies, sticky sheets and chromatic traps. It also sells plant growth supporters that help save up to ₹20,000 per acre of land for farmers. Barrix has sold its products to more than two lakh farmers in India and exports to Mauritius, Tanzania and Sri Lanka as well. It is the winner of power of ideas 2012 by *The Economic Times*.

Farm data collection: Aarav Unmanned Systems, Airwood Aerostructures and Drona Aviation have developed products that use drones to collect farm-related data. A camera-like system is attached to the drones to record information in real time. It helps in 3D mapping and image processing, precision agriculture, geographical mapping and survey, research, thermal inspection and disaster/event management. Aarav plans to introduce a Hexacopter, which can be used for multiple purposes from precision agriculture to topographic surveying and inspection.

These innovations are not all. Young entrepreneurs see rural problems and try to solve them. Thus, innovations are being tried all over the country. Interest has been shown by venture capital as well, even though much of their funding goes to consumer technology in urban India. It is hoped that some venture capital filters into agro-tech, too.

What role can venture capital play in agro-tech? How can such start-ups obtain venture funding for their ideas?

Sources for this Case Study:
Web Resources
Aarav Unmanned Systems website: http://www.aus.co.in/
Barrix Agro Sciences website: http://www.barrix.in/
Ecozen Solutions website: http://www.ecozensolutions.com/
Flybird Farm Innovations website: http://www.flybirdinnovations.com/
MITRA website: http://mitraweb.in/
YCook website: http://www.ycook.in/

Other Source
The Economic Times. 2016. "How the Startup Boom is Helping Farmers and Forcing Investors to Pay Attention to Agriculture." 24 June.

TRIPLE BOTTOM LINE

The move to becoming social businesses has spawned new thinking in measuring the outcomes of business. The Triple Bottom Line (TBL) is an accounting framework that incorporates three dimensions of performance: social, environmental and financial. It differs from traditional reporting as it includes ecological and social measures that are often difficult to measure.

Along with profits, companies are inspired to measure their impact on social aspects also through TBL. This accounting framework goes beyond the traditional measures of profits and economic returns to include environmental and social dimensions. First coined in 1994 by John Elkington, it says that companies should be measuring three different outcomes. One is profit, the first 'bottom line'. The second is the company's 'people account', measuring the social responsibility of an organization in its operations and the impact it makes on people's lives. The third is the company's 'planet' account, measuring how environmentally responsible it has been (Elkington 1994).

The triple bottom line changes the focus of business almost completely. It consists of 3 Ps: *profit, people* and *planet*. It aims to measure the financial, social and environmental performance of the corporation over a period of time. It is a governance concept in which companies provide quantitative and qualitative descriptions of their financial, environmental and social performance over one year.

Interest in TBL accounting has been growing. Many businesses, non-profit organizations and even governments have adopted the TBL framework to evaluate their performance.

Behind the TBL is the principle that companies will measure things that they are required to report. Elkington (1997) calls it sustainability auditing, which will make businesses transparent. Companies focused on revenues like to go on cost-cutting sprees, often ignoring the hidden social and environmental costs. But this is changing because of public pressure. The Fairtrade movement, which adds its brand to products that have been produced and traded in an environmentally and socially fair way, also added to this awareness. From small beginnings, the movement has picked up steam in recent years. Nevertheless, the Fairtrade movement is still only small, focused essentially on coffee, tea, bananas and cotton, but may well spread to other crops.

TBL reporting is becoming common in the developed world and some developing countries, too. Suttipun (2012) studied the TBL reporting by Thai listed companies and shows

TABLE 12.3
Economic, environmental and social measures in TBL.

Economic Measures	Environmental Measures	Social Measures
Sales and profits	Recovery of greenhouse gas emissions	Employment provided
Growth	Reducing carbon footprint	Impact on education, public health, hygiene, etc.
Market share	Waste management	Impact on stakeholders
Contribution to GDP	Electricity and fuel consumption	Safety, security and quality of life

that the development of regulations has increased the disclosure of social and environmental information. Mandatory TBL reporting is likely to be introduced by countries globally in the future, as sustainability issues gain importance.

Measuring TBL

The first step in measuring and quantifying social and environmental impacts is to know what to measure. Environmental performance refers to the quantity of resources that a firm uses in its operations and the reduction of waste, pollution and its carbon footprint. It incorporates air and water quality, energy consumption, natural resources, solid and toxic waste and land use/land cover. Social variables refer to social dimensions of a community or region. They include measurements of education, equity and access to social resources, health and well-being, quality of life and social capital. The measures listed in Table 12.3 present a small snippet of potential variables measured in TBL. Such reporting may well become mandatory in the near future.

When companies start reporting on these measures, their activities will necessarily include their social and environmental activities (see Mini Case Study 12.6). The TBL, thus, gives an impetus to rural marketing initiatives that include social objectives. However, measuring performance against these measures is not an easy task.

One problem with the TBL is that the three separate accounts cannot easily be added up. It is difficult to measure the planet and people accounts in the same terms as profits, that is, in terms of cash. The full cost of dumping wastes, for example, is immeasurable in monetary terms, as is the cost of displacing communities to make dams or the cost of child labour.

THE SUSTAINABLE BALANCED SCORECARD

Another approach to measure organizational sustainability is to include social and environmental issues in the existing Balanced Scorecard (BSC) framework to produce a Sustainable Balanced Scorecard (SBSC) that integrates the TBL and BSC frameworks.

The BSC is commonly used in strategic planning and management to align business activities to the vision and strategy of the organization, improve internal and external communications and monitor organization performance against strategic goals. Given by Kaplan and

Mini Case Study 12.6

ITC's TBL Reporting

Though many companies in India include reporting on CSR in their annual reports, ITC is one of the companies that includes environmental and social impacts in its annual reports. "The Triple Bottom Line commitment of the Company to simultaneously build economic, social and environmental capital has spurred innovation to orchestrate a symphony of efforts that address some of the most challenging societal issues including widespread poverty and environmental degradation," says its annual report for 2016. It says that these efforts have led to the creation of sustainable livelihoods for around six million people, many of whom represent the most disadvantaged in society. The following are extracted from its annual report for 2016:

Environmental excellence: To reduce its carbon footprint, the company has adopted a low carbon growth strategy which includes afforestation efforts, increasing use of renewable energy and a quest to maximize natural resource efficiencies. ITC is the only company of comparable dimensions in the world to be carbon positive for 11 years, water positive for 14 years and solid waste recycling positive for 9 years. Its luxury hotels are Leadership in Energy and Environmental Design (LEED) Platinum Certified and the energy usage in its total energy consumption is 47.3 per cent.

Reporting on sustainability initiatives: For the past 12 years, ITC has published Sustainability Reports that show its performance across the three dimensions of the TBL.

The Report and Accounts 2016 of the company provides a review of its TBL performance.

Responsible sourcing: Recognizing that poverty in rural India gets accentuated by inadequate access to knowledge, information, price discovery, quality agricultural inputs and markets, ITC has built models for farmer empowerment. These interventions support sustainable agriculture, enhance productivity and contribute to livelihood creation. Its globally acknowledged e-choupal has transformed rural communities into economic organizations by leveraging information technology to provide real-time information on weather, market prices and agricultural best practices. It also provides customized extension services and training through 'Choupal Pradarshan Khets'. The e-choupal system has enabled efficient sourcing and raised rural incomes. The company promotes environmentally sustainable farm practices such as zero tilling, micro-irrigation and watershed development. Customized extension services, knowledge of silvicultural practices, and biodiversity enhancement enrich farmers' capacity while augmenting natural capital.

Environment, health and safety: The company has been recycling over 98 per cent of solid waste generated by its units for the past nine years. For 2015–16, over 99 per cent was recycled. It has undertaken several water conservation and harvesting initiatives. ITC is a pioneer in the green buildings movement, which commenced with the establishment of the ITC Green Centre at Gurgaon in 2004.

Social sector: The two most important stakeholders of ITC are:

- Rural communities with whom its agribusinesses have forged long and enduring partnerships through crop development and procurement activities.
- Communities residing in close proximity to its production units, situated in urban and semi-rural locations.

To help and empower these stakeholders, ITC has started programmes in social forestry, education, watershed development, animal husbandry, women's economic empowerment, sanitation and waste management.

Which other companies report of their impact on local communities?

Sources for this Case Study:

ITC Annual Report 2015–16.

ITC website: www.itcportal.com

TABLE 12.4
The six measures of a SBSC.

Financial measures: As published in annual reports: profitability, growth, financial ratios	**Internal processes:** Productivity, production, inventory management, etc.	**Customers:** Market share, new customers, loyalty, rejection rates
Learning and development: New products, R&D, training	**Social performance:** Community actions, village problems solved, involvement of people	**Environmental performance:** Energy and resources used per unit, emission control, carbon footprint, effect on downstream communities

Norton (1996), it translates a company's vision and strategy into a set of performance measures consisting of financial measures, customer knowledge, internal business processes and learning and growth.

Figge et al. (2002) give ways of including sustainability in the BSC to develop the SBSC. The SBSC includes economic, environmental and social perspectives in a company's strategic management system and provides a method of measuring it. The SBSC embeds the TBL and the BSC framework; for example, water use and energy efficiency fall within internal processes, while developing renewable, recyclable resources is a financial measure.

Hubbard (2009) gives four areas in the environment and social areas that can be added to the existing framework of BSC. In the environment section, material or resources used per unit and emissions are included as a measure of the efficient use of resources. In the social performance area, a broad view of stakeholders is included, such as employees, suppliers and community.

Table 12.4 shows the measures of an SBSC. The six measures are illustrated with examples covering different stakeholder perspectives. Companies can add additional measures, depending on their operations. The SBSC gives a dashboard for companies to measure social and environmental impacts; however, to be successful, they have to install systems to collect data on community relationships and social actions and highlight them in their annual reports.

Both the TBL and SBSC frameworks give methods to quantify impacts of a company's operations. Whether these methods are used in developing countries depends on either the companies themselves or may well be introduced in the future by legislation. However, it cannot be denied that reporting on nature, society and well-being is an idea whose time has come and will be used widely in the future (an example of such reporting is given in Mini Case Study 12.7).

SOCIAL ENTERPRISE

Finally, we discuss transformation of commercial businesses into social businesses. Social enterprises are businesses that trade to tackle social problems, improve communities, people's life chances or the environment. They make their money from selling goods and services in the open market, but they reinvest their profits back into the business or the local community.

Sabeti (2011) describes the emergence of 'for-benefit' organization. Such organizations have two characteristics: a commitment to a social purpose and a reliance on earned profits. They

Mini Case Study 12.7

Measuring Environmental Benefits

While economic measures are well-developed and environmental measures can also be incorporated, social benefits are by far the hardest to measure. An example the calculation of social benefits of growing *arhar* over paddy has been shown in Table 12.5.

TABLE 12.5
Social benefits of arhar compared with paddy.

(₹/hectare)

	Fertilizer Subsidy (S)	Groundwater Subsidy (S)	Nitrogen Benefit (N)	Greenhouse Emissions (G)	Total Social Cost (S-N+G)
Tur	2878	1500	3883	0	495
Paddy	6897	5000	0	1838	13735
Net benefits	4019	3500	3883	1838	13240

Source: Subramanian (2016).

The table shows the social benefit of planting arhar over paddy: it will see a reduction of fertilizer usage and thereby subsidy and also the use of less water, calculated by difference in groundwater subsidy, and will replenish the soil with nitrogen, unlike paddy, which depletes the soil. Thus, per hectare social benefit of arhar over paddy is calculated as ₹13,240.

Calculate social benefits of the activities of any company. Calculate the social benefits of your own actions. Make a presentation to your class.

Source for this Case Study:

Subramanian, Arvind. 2016. "The Arhar Solution to Pollution." *Indian Express*, 9 November. Available at: http://indianexpress.com/article/opinion/columns/delhi-pollution-arhar-pulses-demand-supply-gap-burning-of-paddy-4364802/ (Accessed on 18 April 2017).

are emerging as a whole new sector of the economy—one powerful enough to change the course of capitalism. Bornstein (2007) in his book, *How to Change the World*, writes that social entrepreneurs advance systematic change, changing behaviour patterns and perceptions. The book shows how this change can be brought about. Martin and Osberg (2015) define social entrepreneurship as direct action aimed at transforming, rather than incrementally improving an existing system called 'equilibrium shifting'. Social entrepreneurs are able to bridge the need to earn profits with efforts to provide services to citizens, and the creative combination of elements from both poles enables them to build innovative models. Yunus et al. (2015) describe the social business model that is emerging and demonstrate how radically it differs from traditional low-cost business models.

- **Customer exclusivity:** Unlike low-cost models, social business models are exclusive. Companies determine the target beneficiaries and the product or service is offered to no one else. The target may also be narrowly defined, such as poor consumers older than 60 (Essilor) or poor families with a child aged 6 to 24 months (Danone). Companies usually work with NGOs and local communities to identify such persons.

- **High-quality products and services:** In contrast to producers who sell low quality, low-cost goods to poor consumers, in a social business model, the offer can remain unchanged if the economics allow. This is what Aravind and Nirmal Hridalaya offered (see Chapter 1). The only difference was in the choice of room and fewer choices for other services. Social businesses do not lower their costs by redesigning products or manufacturing processes but instead change the economics of sales and distribution.
- **Carefully designed solutions:** A social business often offers products and services as a solution to a problem that customers have. E-wallets, for example, were created for micro-payments, which solved many problems of unbanked customers. Thinking in terms of solutions can help companies with the challenge of costs.

Social enterprises should have the following ideals weaved into their missions:

- **Social and/or environmental mission:** The primary aim of all social enterprises must be social or environmental. The organization's social mission must be explicit in its governing documents and that social enterprises should be able to explain and justify the value of the social change they aim to bring about.
- **Trade:** Social enterprises are businesses. Hence, they must generate more than 50 per cent of their income through trade. This separates them from NGOs that rely on donations.
- **Reinvest profits:** Though social enterprises make profits, more than half of the profits should be reinvested to further its social or environmental mission.
- **Autonomous:** An important condition is autonomy. Social enterprises must be autonomous organizations that are independent of the state or commercial interests.
- **Ownership and control:** The majority of shareholders should be oriented towards the social mission. An asset-lock is introduced to ensure that a social enterprise operates in the wider interests of society and is not at risk of sale.
- **Accountability and transparency:** Social enterprises are accountable to their members—consumers, staff or community members.

Technology is by far the biggest catalyst in this endeavour. The Internet has helped spawn technologies that promise to provide solutions to age-old problems. These include mobile devices and apps that have been designed for life-saving services and social media platforms that help people to connect and create online communities to tackle social issues, opening up collaboration, crowdsourcing and engaging directly with government agencies. Data mining and analytics can be used to know about consumers and their habits. Cloud computing allows large numbers of people to collaborate and work together and helps people launch new initiatives and resources quickly and cheaply.

Using Big Data

Big data is a technology that may change the face of rural marketing. As smartphones become cheaper and popular in rural areas, consumers will leave data trails about their online activities. Analyzing such data will give companies insights into consumer behaviour. Goyal et al. (2012) explain how data analysis can be used to identify micro-markets. They write that companies have to slice and dice geography into hundreds of micro-markets and identify areas that are underexploited or find the pockets of prosperity, and then deploy their sales force to the greatest effect. The process involves combining and analyzing huge amounts of data on villages, customers and competitors to identify communities, for which solutions are developed.

The first step in pursuing a micro-market strategy is to create an 'opportunity map' of potential areas. The map uses internal and external data sets from a number of sources. Data analytics is used to build a picture of the future opportunity. After the map is made, the company examines why markets vary across areas and looks at drivers of consumer behaviour. Growth opportunities can thus be spotted. Getting data for villages will be a shortcoming, but as data gathering techniques improve, companies can collect data sets from government and other agencies. Sales and marketing teams have to work together with data analysts to identify and create solutions for each micro-market. The micro-market in this case can mean a village or village cluster, or homogenous groups within a village.

Once micro-markets are identified, the company devises solutions for them, and also creates sales 'plays' for each. This includes identifying salespeople, opinion leaders, local communities and other partners than can help implement the strategy in each village. Products are also tested with different price points and service bundles to see which would work best. The maps will also help the company in making sales route plans so that salespeople do not have to travel far from their homes. The salespeople should be trained on how to use the opportunity map to approach the villages.

Micro-markets are identified through five steps:

1. By defining the optimal micro-market size.
2. By determining the growth potential for each.
3. By gauging the market share in each.
4. By understanding the causes of variation in market share.
5. By prioritizing markets to focus on.

SUMMARY

Rural marketing is affected by both macro and micro-trends. There are some leading trends such as economic growth and national economic indices but, at the same time, farm indebtedness and farmer suicides point to a rather grim rural landscape. But one thing is clear: capitalism as we know it must change and take into account its effects on the poor, if the instability arising from social inequalities is to be avoided. Our study of companies in this book shows that those who reinvent their business models and their approach of doing business stand a greater chance of success and long-term survival in rural areas. They have to unleash a solution revolution, which is an interaction between three crucial factors: wavemakers, technology and innovative business models. All three have to operate simultaneously.

At the heart of the new business models is innovation. Social innovation refers to new ideas that work in meeting social goals. This includes techniques such as jugaad, disruptive, frugal and grassroots innovation, also called Gandhian revolution. Each of these leads to developing relevant products and processes to serve consumers in the most remote areas.

New methods of measuring the social and environmental impact of the activities of firms have to be implemented: the TBL and SBSC have been suggested. These measures are likely to be used widely in the future.

Companies have to give up their sole pursuit of profit and transform themselves into social enterprises, businesses that trade to tackle social problems, improve communities, people's life chances or the environment.

We expect rural markets to be transformed by big data analysis, which is using and analyzing large data sets from diverse sources to dice and sieve through rural data to decipher markets and consumer behaviour.

CONCLUSION

The earlier approach of business was focused on profits and shareholder returns, as made famous by Milton Friedman in *Capitalism and Freedom* (1962):

> There is one and only one social responsibility of business—to use its resources and engage in activities designed to increase its profits so long as it stays within the rules of the game, which is to say, engages in open and free competition without deception or fraud.

However, it is increasingly becoming clear that companies must solve the problems of society in which they operate. This is truer in rural markets. Companies will be more acceptable in rural areas if they serve some social objectives. Indeed, companies that have incorporated social objectives in their missions have been more successful in rural marketing.

The future thus depends on companies transforming themselves to serve rural consumers in some way. Ironically, it is going back Gandhian economics:

> Recall the face of the poorest and the weakest man whom you may have seen, and ask yourself, if the step you contemplate is going to be of any use to him. Will he gain anything by it? Will it restore him to a control over his own life and destiny? In other words, will it lead to swaraj for the hungry and spiritually starving millions?

This is exactly what companies described in this book have done. This, in a very important way, sums up the essence of BoP marketing.

KEY TERMS

Balanced scorecard (BSC): A strategic planning and management tool to align business activities to the vision and strategy of the organization, improve internal and external communications and monitor organization performance against strategic goals.

Big data: The process of combining and analyzing huge amount of data on villages, customers and competitors to identify communities on various parameters or behaviour.

Design thinking: An open-minded, no-holds-barred approach that designers bring to their work, rather than the narrow, technical view of innovation, to solve rural India's persistent problems.

Disruptive innovation: The phenomenon by which innovators disrupt markets with good enough products: existing markets are transformed by introducing simplicity, convenience, accessibility and affordability instead of complicated products.

For-benefit corporation: A firm that generates earned income but gives top priority to an explicit social mission.

Frugal innovation: The process of reducing the complexity and cost of a good and its production.

Gandhian innovation: The process of using science and technology for the benefit of all.

Grassroots innovation: Ecologically and socially accepted products and services, consisting of inventions generated by people in villages to solve their own problems.

Indigenous innovation: The process in which established products are improved through R&D in developing countries.

Jugaad: A creative and improvised way of solving problems in a resource-constrained environment.

Reverse innovation: The process of taking apart an object, extracting knowledge or design information from it, in order to duplicate and reproduce it.

Social enterprise: Social enterprises are businesses that trade to tackle social problems, improve communities, people's life chances or the environment.

Social innovation: A novel solution to a social problem that is more effective, efficient, sustainable or just than existing solutions, and for which the value created accrues primarily to society as a whole rather than companies.

Solution economy: Consisting of individuals, businesses and sometimes governments who work together to solve societal problems; the solution revolution can be seen as an interaction between three crucial factors: wavemakers, technology and innovative business models.

Sustainable balanced scorecard (SBSC): The SBSC includes economic, environmental and social perspectives in a company's strategic management system and provides a method of measuring it.

Triple bottom line (TBL): An accounting framework that incorporates three dimensions of performance: social, environmental and financial.

CONCEPT REVIEW QUESTIONS

1. Describe the trends that you think will impact the future of rural marketing, both positively and negatively. Which are the most important?
2. How have companies transformed themselves for rural realities? Give examples to support your view.
3. What are the paradigm shifts that are taking place that impacts the future of rural marketing? Describe each of them briefly.
4. Which three things are essential for rural solutions to spread widely among people?
5. Describe the types of innovations that have worked in villages.
6. What is frugal innovation? Describe its components. Support your answer with examples of frugal innovation.
7. Explain the concept of social innovation. How will it impact rural initiatives?
8. Describe jugaad and grassroots innovation and explain by giving examples.
9. Describe the new methods of reporting that will help rural marketing efforts. Do you think such methods should be made compulsory?
10. What is big data? How will it help in rural marketing?

CRITICAL THINKING QUESTIONS

1. While reports talk of a great 'rural opportunity', the SECC data and economic/social indicators point to a rather distressing scenario. Why is this so? Which do you think is a more realistic scenario? Why?
2. Several views have been expressed against the current trend of globalization that it does not work sustainably or for the poor. Do you agree? Give reasons for your answer. Should the economic system be changed? If so, how?
3. Why is a paradigm change required for rural marketing? Why can't principles of traditional marketing be used in rural areas? How should marketing change?
4. While some companies are doing well in rural areas simply by supplying goods, others have worked out elaborate social methods. Give examples and analyze whether making social models were necessary. Could the companies have maintained a good growth rate had they simply supplied goods from nearby towns to rural markets?

Projects and Assignments

1. Study some annual reports of large companies. Assess how many are using the Triple Bottom Line reporting. Give your opinion whether such reporting methods are successful or not.
2. Visit a remote village and study its socio-economic condition. Would you agree with the views expressed by consultancies that rural market is an opportunity waiting to be tapped or would you go more by the SECC data presented in this chapter? What advice would you give to a company that is venturing into rural areas?
3. Study the leading and debilitating trends in rural markets presented in this chapter. Discuss with friends and decide which ones are more powerful than others. Then make a shortlist and decide which ones are likely to prevail in the future.
4. Discuss the pros and cons of economic systems such as capitalism and socialism. Discover their shortcomings as far as their impact on rural markets is concerned. Is a new system necessary? If so, how should the new system be devised?

WEB RESOURCES

Honeybee Network website: http://www.sristi.org/hbnew/aboutus.php
Mahatma Gandhi quotation. Available at: http://www.mkgandhi.org/gquots1.htm
Watch a BBC World video of National Innovation Foundation at: https://www.youtube.com/watch?v=s137JlAakaQ
Watch a presentation by Professor Anil Gupta at: https://www.youtube.com/watch?v=1lqIPuJ-21A

REFERENCES

Accenture. 2014. "From Touchpoints to Trustpoints: Winning over India's Aspiring Rural Consumers." Available at: https://www.accenture.com/in-en/_acnmedia/597E512993C24B218EBF43F999278A50.ashx (Accessed on 18 April 2017).

Agarwal, Nivedita. 2016. *Innovation Landscape in Developed and Developing Markets: A Conceptual and Empirical Study on Technology Convergence and Low Cost Innovations*. Bamberg: University of Bamberg Press.

Bornstein, David. 2007. *How to Change the World: Social Entrepreneurs and the Power of New Ideas.* New Yourk, NY: Oxford University Press.

Bower, Joseph L., Herman B. Leonard and Lynn S. Paine. 2011a. *Capitalism at Risk: Rethinking the Role of Business.* Boston, MA: Harvard Business Review Press.

———. 2011b. "Global Capitalism at Risk: What Are You Doing About It?" *Harvard Business Review,* September. Available at: https://hbr.org/2011/09/global-capitalism-at-risk-what-are-you-doing-about-it (Accessed on 18 April 2017).

Christensen, Clayton M. 1997. *The Innovator's Dilemma: When New Technologies Cause Great Firms to Fail.* Boston, MA: Harvard Business School Press.

Christensen, Clayton M., Heiner Baumann, Rudy Ruggles and Thomas M. Sadtler. 2006. "Disruptive Innovation for Social Change." *Harvard Business Review,* December. Available at: https://hbr.org/2006/12/disruptive-innovation-for-social-change (Accessed on 27 April 2017).

Christensen, Clayton M., Michael E. Raynor and Rory McDonald. 2015. "What Is Disruptive Innovation?" *Harvard Business Review,* December. Available at: https://hbr.org/2015/12/what-is-disruptive-innovation (Accessed on 27 April 2017).

Eggers, William D., and Paul Macmillan. 2013. *The Solution Revolution: How Business, Government, and Social Enterprises Are Teaming Up to Solve Society's Toughest Problems.* Boston, MA: Harvard Business Review Press.

Elkington, John. 1994. "Towards the Sustainable Corporation: Win-Win-Win Business Strategies for Sustainable Development." *California Management Review* 36 (2).

———. 1997. *Cannibals with Forks: the Triple Bottom Line of 21st Century Business.* Oxford, UK: Capstone.

Figge, F., T. Hahn, S. Schaltegger and M. Wagner. 2002. "The Sustainability Balanced Scorecard—Linking Sustainability Management to Business Strategy." *Business Strategy and the Environment* 11 (5), 269–284.

Friedman, Milton. 1962. *Capitalism and Freedom.* Chicago, IL: University of Chicago Press.

Goyal, Manish, Maryanne Q. Hancock and Homayoun Hatami. 2012. "Selling into Micromarkets." *Harvard Business Review,* July–August. Available at: https://hbr.org/2012/07/selling-into-micro-markets (Accessed on 27 April 2017).

Gupta, A.K. 2012. "Innovations for the Poor by the Poor." *International Journal of Technological Learning, Innovation and Development* 5 (1/2): 28–39.

Haanaes, Knut, David Michael, Jeremy Jürgens and Subramanian Rangan. 2013. "Making Sustainability Profitable." *Harvard Business Review,* March. Available at: https://hbr.org/2013/03/making-sustainability-profitable (Accessed on 27 April 2017).

Hart, Stuart L., and Mark B. Milstein. 2003. "Creating Sustainable Value." *Academy of Management Executive* 17 (2): 56–67.

Hubbard, Graham. 2009. "Measuring Organizational Performance: Beyond the Triple Bottom Line." *Business Strategy and the Environment* 18 (3): 177–191.

Kanter, Moss Rosabeth. 2011. "How Great Companies Think Differently." Harvard Business Review, November. Available at: https://hbr.org/2011/11/how-great-companies-think-differently (Accessed on 18 April 2017).

Kaplan, Robert S., and David P. Norton. 996. *The Balanced Scorecard: Translating Strategy into Action.* Boston, MA: Harvard Business School Press.

Martin, Roger L. and Sally R. Osberg. 2015. *Getting Beyond Better—How Social Entrepreneurship Works.* Boston, MA: Harvard Business Review Press.

McKinsey Global Institute Report. 2007. *The 'Bird of Gold': The Rise of India's Consumer Market,* May. Available at: http://www.mckinsey.com/global-themes/asia-pacific/the-bird-of-gold (Accessed on 18 April 2017).

Phills, J.A., K. Deiglmeier and D.T. Miller. 2008. "Rediscovering Social Innovation." *Stanford Social Innovation Review* 6 (4): 34–43.

Porter, Michael E., and Mark R. Kramer. 1999. "Philanthropy's New Agenda: Creating Value." *Harvard Business Review*, November–December. Available at: https://hbr.org/1999/11/philanthropys-new-agenda-creating-value (Accessed on 27 April 2017).

Prahalad, C.K., and R.A. Mashelkar. 2010. "Innovation's Holy Grail." *Harvard Business Review*, July–August. Available at: https://hbr.org/2010/07/innovations-holy-grail (Accessed on 27 April 2017).

Radjou, Navi, and Jaideep Prabhu. 2015. *Frugal Innovation: How to Do Better with Less*. London, UK: Profile Books.

———. 2012. "Mobilizing for Growth in Emerging Markets." *MIT Sloan Management Review*, Spring.

Radjou, Navi, Jaideep Prabhu and Simone Ahuja. 2012. *Jugaad Innovation: A Frugal and Flexible Approach to Innovation for the 21st Century*. New Delhi: Random House India.

Reich, Robert B. 2016. *Saving Capitalism: For the Many, Not the Few*. London, UK: Icon Books.

Sabeti, Heerad. 2011. "The-For Benefit Enterprise." *Harvard Business Review*, November. Available at: https://hbr.org/2011/11/the-for-benefit-enterprise (27 April 2017).

Stiglitz, Joseph. 2002. *Globalization and Its Discontents*. New Delhi: Penguin Books.

Suttipun, Muttanachai. 2012. "Triple Bottom Line Reporting in Annual Reports: A Case Study of Companies Listed on the Stock Exchange of Thailand." *Asian Journal of Finance & Accounting* 4 (1): 69–92.

The Hindu. 2015. "8 Reality Checks from the SECC." 3 July. Available at: http://www.thehindu.com/data/socio-economic-and-caste-censuss-data-on-standard-of-living-of-rural-households/article7383259.ece (Accessed on 18 April 2017).

Vaitheeswaran, Vijay V. 2012. *Need, Speed, and Greed: How the New Rules of Innovation Can Transform Businesses, Nations to Greatness, and Tame the World's Most Wicked Problems*. New York: Harper Business.

Yunus, M., Frédéric Dalsace, David Ménascé and Bénédicte Faivre-Tavignot. 2015. "Reaching the Rich World's Poorest Consumers." *Harvard Business Review*, March. Available at: https://hbr.org/2015/03/reaching-the-rich-worlds-poorest-consumers (Accessed on 27 April 2017).

Closing Case
Usha International's Silai Schools

Usha International Ltd is part of the Siddharth Shriram group which owns the brand, USHA. The brand has become a household name in India. A review revealed that although the company's products were available in small towns with sub-dealers and retail, the company's direct distribution network was limited to only 25 per cent of the towns with population of more than one lakh. The company realized it was not tapping into its biggest market, the rural consumer. The company makes household and kitchen appliances, fans, engine pump sets and electric pumpsets. The sewing machine continues to be the largest selling item of the company.

The company realized that it did not have enough rural coverage and wanted a method to reach rural women. It devised two strategies: hire enough representatives to cover new markets and start a movement of stitching schools in villages. It could thus cover new rural markets that had sprung up in rural areas which also involve rural women it its best-selling product.

PHOTO 12.8

Kaviben, who is from the Rebari community and lives in Kotay village in Bhuj district of Gujarat, with her sewing machine.

Source: http://www.ushasilaischool.com/ (Accessed on 27 April 2017).

It launched a pilot and a small team was constituted to spend three months in the Gorakhpur region in Uttar Pradesh to understand markets and geographies, with the aim to visit all the towns which had a population below one lakh. The team collected market intelligence, estimated market potential and brand share and studied the primary distribution network. The research showed that 95 per cent of consumers prefer to purchase from small towns, instead of travelling long distances to larger towns. It also found that rural consumers were aware of most brands and wanted quality products at reasonable prices. As a consequence, the company realized that it was necessary to have an authorized representation in the small-town markets.

A rural initiative was launched in Uttar Pradesh in April 2013, called 'Project Sampark', to reach out to consumers in 648,000 villages and 7,500 small towns. The idea was to ensure brand presence and product availability at the last mile.

Project Sampark helped the company reach out to over 400,000 households by 2013. It has subsequently conducted over 2,000 rural haats and reached 10 lakh rural customers. The company appointed a team of 'rural business officers' to do an in-depth study of the rural markets and set up a network of more than 3,600 authorized retail dealers (ARDs) stocking all USHA products. This helped reach the brand in remote markets.

Within one year of the project's inception, the company attained a leading position in eastern Uttar Pradesh in terms of sales growth. ARDs actively promote USHA's products by strategically tying up with other companies and undertaking development activities such as haats, melas and working with SHGs. ARDs are appointed in every small town and are trained in product features so that they can recommend the right product to consumers. They act as a one-stop shop where consumers find all product lines displayed.

This resulted in sales of USHA products increased by almost 40 per cent in rural markets. Rural India continues to remain the focus for the company, which aims to cover all 7,500 towns. The rural business team has also identified another set of 800 places in rural India, which have the potential and are the business hubs for many villages and rural consumers. The company plans to expand its rural retail format 'Usha Joy Stores' in rural pockets and Tier-IV towns with population of less than 50,000, reports *Business Standard* (2016).

To reach village women, it adopted a unique initiative, that is, to partner with NGOs to set up Silai Schools in some of the country's most remote and rural corners. Under the model, women are given a sewing machine and are imparted with sewing skills as well as training in maintenance and repair of sewing machines. NGO partners facilitate and support USHA to identify, set up and motivate village women to join Silai Schools.

Usha provides expertise and help to former Silai School learners to become teachers themselves in their community. Once trained, the women use their skills to earn their livelihood and become financially independent. They generate income by stitching clothes and also setting up their own Usha Silai Schools. They charge a fee from new learners, do job-work in the community and also earn from repair of sewing machines.

The Silai Schools have helped village women tailors operating out of their homes become confident and economically liberated. In Dewas district, 15,000 women have been liberated from scavenging and 50 women are being rehabilitated through tailoring with financial support of UNDP and technical support of Usha International Ltd. (UIL). Across India, HIV-positive women, transgender and the disabled are being rehabilitated through Usha Silai Schools. Till the end of 2014, there were 5,542 Silai Schools in the country, with Rajasthan leading with 519, followed by West Bengal (467), Uttar Pradesh (446) and Madhya Pradesh (403). Based on the UIL syllabus, the trained teachers teach others for a fee that varies from ₹30 to ₹300 a month. The Silai Schools have raised the self-esteem of women within their own family and in the community. Many women who did not have any say in their family are today key decision-makers.

Questions for discussion:

1. Comment on the future of rural marketing in the light of this case study.
2. Is the way forward converting into social business? Is there an alternative?
3. What are the benefits to companies of empowering rural consumers?
4. Is Gandhian economics the way forward?

Sources for this Case Study:

Web Resources

Usha website: http://www.usha.com/about-us

Usha Silai School website: http://www.ushasilaischool.com/

Watch the Silai school overview at: https://www.youtube.com/watch?v=ZO1SgYbgUvE

Watch videos of Usha Silai School and its impact at: http://www.ushasilaischool.com/

Other Sources

Business Standard. 2016. "Usha International to Launch Rural Retail Format in UP." 25 May.

The Hindu. 2015. "Progressing, Stitch by Stitch." 5 April.

The Hindu BusinessLine. 2015. Usha International Bets Big on 'Brand-conscious' Rural Consumers." 1 April. Available at: http://www.thehindubusinessline.com/industry-and-economy/usha-international-bets-big-on-brandconscious-rural-consumers/article7057169.ece (Accessed on 27 April 2017).

INDEX